The Handbook of Work and Health Psychology
Second Edition

The Handbook of Work and Health Psychology

Second Edition

Edited by

Marc J. Schabracq
University of Amsterdam, The Netherlands

Jacques A.M. Winnubst
University of Utrecht, The Netherlands

Cary L. Cooper
University of Manchester Institute of Science and Technology, UK

JOHN WILEY & SONS, LTD

Other Wiley Editorial Offices

John Wiley & Sons Inc., 111 River Street, Hoboken, NJ 07030, USA

Jossey-Bass, 989 Market Street, San Francisco, CA 94103-1741, USA

Wiley-VCH Verlag GmbH, Boschstr. 12, D-69469 Weinheim, Germany

John Wiley & Sons Australia Ltd, 33 Park Road, Milton, Queensland 4064, Australia

John Wiley & Sons (Asia) Pte Ltd, 2 Clementi Loop #02-01, Jin Xing Distripark, Singapore 129809

John Wiley & Sons Canada Ltd, 22 Worcester Road, Etobicoke, Ontario, Canada M9W 1L1

British Library Cataloguing in Publication Data

A catalogue record for this book is available from the British Library

ISBN 0–471–89276–9

Typeset in 10/12pt Times by TechBooks, New Delhi, India
Printed and bound in Great Britain by Antony Rowe Ltd, Chippenham, Wiltshire
This book is printed on acid-free paper responsibly manufactured from sustainable forestry,
in which at least two trees are planted for each one used for paper production.

Contents

Part III: Specific Issues in Work and Health Psychology

Part IV: Preventive and Curative Interventions

About the Editors

Marc J. Schabracq works at the Department of Work and Organisational Psychology, University of Amsterdam, Roeterstraat15, 1018 WB, Amsterdam, The Netherlands. He is also an organisational consultant (email: schabracq@humanfactor.nl).

Jacques A.M. Winnubst is Professor of Medical Psychology at University of Utrecht, Stratenum, P.O. Box 80.036, 3508 TA, Utrecht, The Netherlands.

Cary L. Cooper C.B.E. is Professor of Organisational Psychology and Health and Deputy Vice Dean at the Manchester School of Management, UMIST, P.O. Box 88, Manchester, M60 1QD, UK.

List of Contributors

Ronald J. Burke, *Faculty of Administrative Studies, York University, 4700 Keele Street, North York, Ontario, Canada M3J 1P3*

Bram P. Buunk, *Psychologisch Inst. Heymans, University of Groningen, Grote Kruisstraat 2/1, 9712 TS Groningen, The Netherlands*

Neil Conway, *School of Management and Organizational Psychology, Birkbeck College, Malet Street, London WC1E 7HX, UK*

Cary L. Cooper, *Manchester School of Management, UMIST, PO Box 88, Manchester M60 1QD, UK*

Tom Cox, *Institute of Work, Health and Organisations, University of Nottingham, University Park, Nottingham NG7 2RD, UK*

Marjolein de Best-Waldhober, *Department of Psychology, University of Amsterdam, Roeterstraat 15, 1018 WB Amsterdam, The Netherlands*

Carsten K.W. De Dreu, *Department of Psychology, University of Amsterdam, Roeterstraat 15, 1018 WB Amsterdam, The Netherlands*

Evangelia Demerouti, *Social and Organizational Psychology, Utrecht University, PO Box 80.140, 3508 TC Utrecht, The Netherlands*

Carla L. Dunahoo, *St Francis Hospital, Mental Health Clinic, 241 North Road, Poughkeepsie, NY 12601, USA*

Ben (C) Fletcher, *Business School, University of Hertfordshire, Mangrove Road, Hatfield, Hertfordshire SG13 8QF, UK*

Pamela A. Geller, *Department of Clinical & Health Psychology MCP Hahnemann University, 245 North 15th Street, MS 515 Philadelphia, PA 19102, USA*

Sabine A.E. Geurts, *Department of Work and Organizational Psychology, University of Nijmegen, 6500 HE Nijmegen, The Netherlands*

Seigfried Greif, *University of Osnabrück, Neuer Graben / Schloss, 49069 Osnabrück, Germany*

Amanda Griffiths, *Institute of Work, Health and Organisations (I-WHO), University of Nottingham, William Lee Buildings 8, Science and Technology Park, Nottingham NG7 2RQ, UK*

David E. Guest, *The Management Centre, King's College London, Franklin-Wilkins Building, 150 Stamford Street, London SE1 9NN, UK*

Andrew Guppy, *Department of Psychology, Middlesex University, Queensway, Enfield, Middlesex EN3 4SF, UK*

Kai-Christoph Hamborg, *University of Osnabrück, Neuer Graben / Schloss, 49069 Osnabrück, Germany*

Stevan E. Hobfoll, *Applied Psychology Centre, Kent State University, PO Box 5190, Kent, Ohio P2-0001, USA*

Fiona Jones, *School of Psychology, University of Leeds, Leeds LS2 9JT, UK*

Rolf J. Kleber, *Department of Clinical Psychology, Utrecht University, Postbox 80.140, 3508 TC Utrecht, The Netherlands*

Michiel A.J. Kompier, *Department of Work and Organizational Psychology, University of Nijmegen, 6500 HE Nijmegen, The Netherlands*

John Marsden, *Institute of Psychiatry, King's College London, Department of Psychology, De Crespigny Park, Denmark Hill, London SE5 8AF, UK*

Joan L. Meyer, *Vakgroep Arbeids & Organisatiepsychologie, University of Amsterdam, Roeterstraat 15, 1018 WB Amsterdam, The Netherlands*

Lawrence R. Murphy, *NIOSH Division of Biomedical and Behavioral Science, 4676 Columbia Parkway, Cincinatti, Ohio 45226, USA*

Paul B. Paulus, *Graduate School of Business, University of Texas at Arlington, PO Box 19313, Arlington, TX 76019-0313, USA*

James Campbell Quick, *Graduate School of Business, University of Texas at Arlington, PO Box 19313, Arlington, TX 76019-0313, USA*

Raymond Randall, *Institute of Work, Health and Organisations, University of Nottingham, University Park, Nottingham NG7 2RD, UK*

Kathleen D. Ryan, *The Orion Partnership, 4414 184th Ave Se, Bellevue, Issaquah, WA 98027, USA*

Marc. J. Schabracq, *Department of Work and Organisational Psychology, University of Amsterdam, Roeterstraat 15, 1018 WB Amsterdam, The Netherlands*

Wilmar B. Schaufeli, *Vakgroep, RUU, Heidelberglaan 13, 3584 CS Utrecht, The Netherlands*

Norbert K. Semmer, *Universität Bern, Institut für Psychologie, Unitobler Muesmattstrasse 45, CH-3000 Bern 9, Switzerland*

Arie Shirom, *Faculty of Management, Tel Aviv University, POB 39010, Tel Aviv, Israel 69978*

Töres. Theorell, *IPM, Karolinska Institutet, Box 230, 171 77 Stockholm, Sweden*

Peter G. van der Velden, *Institute of Psychotrauma, PO Box 266, 5300 AG Zaltbommel, The Netherlands*

D. van Dierendonck, *Department of Psychology, University of Amsterdam, Roeterstraat 15, 1018 WB Amsterdam, The Netherlands*

James L. Whittington, *University of Dallas, 1845 E. Northgate Drive, Irving, TX 75062-4799, USA*

Jacques A.M. Winnubst, *Stratenum, University of Utrecht, PO Box 80.036, 3508 TA Utrecht, The Netherlands*

Preface

With the ever-increasing demands of workloads and deadlines, with massive technological change, with the internationalization of work and the changing nature of the family (i.e. two-earner couples), the workplace itself has become a health issue.

Unhealthy work organizations can create enormous human as well as financial costs. The collective cost of stress to US companies for absenteeism, reduced productivity, compensation claims, health insurance and direct medical expenses has been estimated at $150 billion per year (Murphy & Cooper, 2000). Figures from the Confederation of British Industry (the major employers' organization in the UK) calculate that millions of working days are lost annually through sickness, at a cost to the economy of £11 billion, of which it is estimated that 40% or over £4 billion is stress-related.

In addition to the direct costs of sickness absence, labour turnover and the like, there are also indirect costs. The most obvious is "presenteeism"; that is, the costs to organizations of people turning up to work who are so distressed by their jobs or some aspect of their organizational environment or climate that they contribute little, if anything, to the product or service they are employed to produce.

The increasing interdependence of work and health has been recognized in almost all industrialized societies. Studs Terkel, the social anthropologist, in his acclaimed book *Working*, after interviewing hundreds of American workers from shop floor to top floor, concluded that "work, is by its very nature, about violence—to the spirit as well as to the body. It is about ulcers as well as accidents, about shouting matches as well as fistfights, about nervous breakdown as well as kicking the dog around. It is above all (or beneath all), about daily humiliations. To survive the day is triumph enough for the walking wounded amongst the great many of us" (Terkel, 1977, p. 1). Theorell and his Swedish colleagues (Alfredsson et al., 1982) have demonstrated in case-controlled studies in Sweden that increased risk of heart attacks was associated with work and occupations characterized by hectic work and low control over the degree of variety and work pace. Cooper and his colleagues in the UK have found in numerous studies (Cooper, 2001) that work stressors are responsible for a myriad of ill health effects of employees at all levels in an organization and in many difficult jobs, organizations and industries.

All of this work and much more has led increasingly to the development of a new interdisciplinary field: work and health psychology. Although these two areas have different origins and have developed out of different traditions, large elements of each now find themselves in this same conceptual and empirical arena. This book is part of that development, an effort to begin to place the foundation stones of this new interdisciplinary field and map the current state of the art and future territory of this important growing discipline.

All of the chapters are written by leading scholars in their field and help to identify not only the problems but also some possible solutions to creating healthier work organizations.

It is hoped that senior executives, occupational physicians and human resource managers will take into account some of these ideas in creating move "livable work cultures", as Kornhauser (1965) said of the American workforce as long ago as 1965:

> Mental health is not so much a freedom from specific frustrations as it is an overall balanced relationship to the world, which permits a person to maintain a realistic, positive belief in himself and his purposeful activities. Insofar as his entire job and life situation facilitate and support such feelings of adequacy, inner security and meaningfulness of his existence, it can be presumed that his mental health will tend to be good. What is important in a negative way is not any single characteristic of his situation, but everything that deprives the person of purpose and zest, that leaves him with negative feelings about himself, with anxieties, tensions, a sense of lostness, emptiness and futility.

Cary L. Cooper
Marc J. Schabracq
Jacques A.M. Winnubst

REFERENCES

Alfredsson, R., Karasek, T., Theorell, J., Schwartz, J. and Pieper, C. (1982). Job psychosocial factors and coronary heart disease. In *Psychosocial Problems Before and After MI: Advanced Cardiology*, vol. 29. Basel: Karger.

Cooper, C.L. (2001). *Managerial, Occupational and Organizational Stress Research*. Hampshire: Ashgate Publishers.

Cooper, C.L., Dewe, P. & O'Driscoll, M. (2001). *Organizational Stress*. London: Sage.

Kornhauser, A. (1965). *The Mental Health of the Industrial Worker*. New York: John Wiley & Sons.

Murphy, L. & Cooper, C.L. (2000). *Healthy and Productive Work*. London: Taylor & Francis.

Terkel, S. (1977). *Working*. Harmondsworth: Penguin.

CHAPTER 1

Introduction

Marc J. Schabracq
University of Amsterdam, The Netherlands
Cary L. Cooper
UMIST, Manchester, UK
and
Jacques A.M. Winnubst
Utrecht University, The Netherlands

1.1 A REVISED EDITION

Since 1996, the year of the publication of the first edition of this book, the world has gone through a turbulent development. Apart from the sheer increase in the number of people living on the planet, global communication, transport and trade have increased at an unprecedented rate. At the same time, technological developments have accelerated everywhere, also in a way we have never witnessed before. The separate national economies of the world, stemming from completely different cultures, are becoming more interdependent, while global competition has become much more intense and complex. We are all confronted by the challenge of feeling at home in a rapidly changing, multicultural place, where we have to cope with the influences of vaguely known powers from all over the world. Some of these influences are far from friendly, as witnessed by the attacks on the World Trade Center and the Pentagon in September 2001.

In a sense, the world has become smaller. This is not only a matter of space, but also of time. Our economies have become more of a 24-hours-a-day affair. Moreover, as a consequence of logistically oriented approaches such as just-in-time management combined with more client-oriented forms of flexibility of production, organisations experience more explicitly a growing shortage of time. As a result of all this, our organisations and our work are in a state of continuous flux and reorganisation. The only prediction we can make about this process now is that, for the time being, the number and pace of changes in our organisations are most likely to go on increasing. Though the global economy shows a much slower growth now, this probably will not soften the competition, but only reinforce the necessity of clever organisational adaptations.

All this certainly has had a crucial impact on the area of well-being and health at the workplace. During the past five years, the problems in that area have become more urgent

The Handbook of Work and Health Psychology. Edited by M.J. Schabracq, J.A.M. Winnubst and C.L. Cooper.
© 2003 John Wiley & Sons, Ltd.

and prominent. In Section 1.2, we go into that issue in more detail. At the same time, however, we have acquired more experience in dealing with these problems.

So here we are in a changed world, proud and happy with this revised edition of the *Handbook*. The *Handbook* has changed too. It has been updated with the latest research findings by people who make this discipline. Some authors have left us; new ones make their entry. However, the major change is probably that we have reserved more space for the applications and solutions that work and health psychology has to offer. In this way, we hope to improve the applicability of work and health psychology itself.

In Section 1.3, we present a short outline of the book. However, we first pay attention to the interest in work and health psychology, which, since the publication of the first edition of this *Handbook* in 1996, has grown considerably.

1.2 THE INCREASING INTEREST IN WORK AND HEALTH PSYCHOLOGY

Since 1996, well-being and health in our work have become more and more prominent issues. In particular, the problems around stress, fatigue and burnout have received a lot of attention. This is not a new development. After all, the previous edition of this *Handbook* was instigated also by the growing concern about these matters. It is neither an unexpected nor illogical development. Especially not, if we realise that a stress process is the result of having to do something which we do not want or are unable to do (Chapter 2). Here, we go into the following reasons for the still increasing public and scientific interest in the field:

- the undesired effects of problems with occupational health and well-being, both at the individual and organisational level;
- the greater prominence of some sources of problems;
- the ageing of the workforce;
- the growing knowledge about these matters and new legislation;
- the influence of human resource management.

1.2.1 Undesired Effects

First of all, the undesired effects of problems in the field of work and health psychology have become more manifest, and probably also more frequent. For instance, work stress and its consequences—in our opinion the main problems in the field—have received much more attention lately, and for good reasons. Stress reactions may disturb the adaptation to the environment in a very serious way, both at a personal and an organisational level. As such, these reactions have all kinds of undesirable and also very expensive consequences.

Individual Effects of Stress

For individual employees, we distinguish the following negative consequences of work stress (Schabracq et al., 2000). Stress tends to lead to diminished creativity and stagnation of personal development. As such, it negatively affects work motivation, pleasure and well-being. Moreover, it diminishes the quality of social relations, resulting in conflicts and isolation. As a result, overall individual effectiveness can be greatly diminished. Ultimately, stress can lead to all kinds of psychological and physical complaints and illnesses, which may contribute to a premature death.

Effects of Stress for Organisations

At the level of organisations, stress can lead to a number of effects that each can jeopardise the position and survival of any organisation (Schabracq et al., 2000). The following effects, among others, are of importance here. First, stress can result in low production quality and quantity, as well as all kinds of production errors and disturbances. This, for instance, may take the form of overlooking possible solutions and missing crucial business opportunities and chances. Also, stress can lead to internal conflicts, ineffective cooperation, disturbed internal relationships and an unpleasant working climate. This may not be an internal affair only: failing communication with and loss of clients and suppliers, as well as problems with other companies and the government, are very real pitfalls too. Another harmful consequence, which is becoming more and more urgent, is high turnover of well-qualified and scarce employees. All this can damage the corporate image and lead to negative public relations, making it hard to recruit new employees. Lastly there is the issue of the high costs of sick leave and work disability, as well as of hiring and breaking in temporary replacements, who do not perform optimally at once. Though, traditionally, most attention has been focused on the last issue, we believe that the other issues together can have a much more serious impact on organisations.

1.2.2   The Greater Prominence of Some Sources of Problems

The next point is that certain factors causing problems in health and well-being in organisations have become much more prominent during recent decades (Schabracq et al., 2000). We mention the following examples.

First, there is the increased amount and accelerated rate of change in our organisations. Examples are repetitious reorganisations, mergers, introduction of new technologies and new ways of organising work (see Chapters 3 and 29). Another issue is the automation of much skilled work, which deprives people of their skill use and leaves them with altered tasks, often of an impoverished nature (Gaillard, 1996). Then, there is the shift from physical to mental work tasks, which tend to cause more stress. Also, the shortage of well-educated people in many sectors results in shortage of employees and task overload. At the same time, there is a definite increase in deadlines and instances of acute peak task load. This is due to the emphasis on flexibility of production and being client-oriented on the one hand, and just-in-time management and other logistically oriented approaches, focusing on prevention of storage and slack, on the other. Moreover, reduction of middle-management and working in autonomous task teams have led to more responsibilities at lower organisational levels for employees who are not trained in coping with such responsibilities (involving decisions about production and expensive machinery, with major financial consequences in the event of errors or forgetfulness). This may lead to delaying important decisions and tasks, resulting in unmanageable piles of decisions. Lastly, there is an increase in role conflicts and role ambiguity, due to working in projects and matrix structures, and to discrepancies between official policy and daily practice.

1.2.3   Ageing of the Workforce

The impact of the factors mentioned above is made more severe by the ongoing ageing of the working population in the Western world. This applies particularly to the necessity to adapt continuously to all kind of changes. This is considered to be more difficult for senior personnel, especially when these changes are ill-considered and forced upon them. This is not to say that senior employees cannot make important contributions here. On the contrary, some of them actually have developed a kind of wisdom from which any organisation in a turbulent environment may profit greatly (see Chapters 16 and 17). However, senior employees develop in different ways and not all problems can be solved by wisdom.

1.2.4   Growing Knowledge and New Legislation

During the past few years, knowledge about occupational health and well-being stemming from all kinds of research has been disseminated rapidly throughout society. On the one hand, this is a matter of knowing about the severe consequences—financial and otherwise. On the other hand, there is a growing insight into the nature of the factors behind these phenomena. A good example of the latter is the growing understanding that task underload—mainly stemming from work that offers too few challenges—may act as an important source of trouble, especially when it comes in big quantities (e.g. Karasek & Theorell, 1990). Also, there is now much more knowledge about interventions (see for example Cartwright & Cooper, 1997; Kompier & Cooper, 2000; Kompier et al., 1996; Schabracq et al., 2001), though this knowledge is still less widespread than we would like to see.

The costs and other problems related to occupational health have induced governments to make laws and to enforce policies to protect their working population. This legislation has led, especially in the UK, to lawsuits and jurisprudence about compensation claims.

As a result, phenomena such as stress and burnout have received a lot of media coverage. Consequentially, these phenomena now are part of the mental maps of the average citizen of the EU, Japan and North America. Occupational health and well-being have even become something with which money can be made. Unions have discovered stress, or "work pressure", as a commodity which can be traded for somewhat higher wages. Also, a lot of studies are conducted to explore the risks in this area. Moreover, many specialised courses, training programmes and all kinds of other interventions are now available.

1.2.5   Human Resource Management

The last reason for the increased interest in occupational health and well-being to be mentioned here is found in the rising popularity of ideas about human resource management (HRM) and human resource development (HRD). HRM and HRD consider the employees as the most important asset of an organisation, the so-called human capital. From this perspective, unnecessarily exposing employees to risks to their health and well-being is only a foolish way of de-investing and destruction of this "capital". Something similar applies when the concept of "employability" is the point of departure: here too, unneeded health risks are to be avoided, as these are detrimental to employability.

1.3 OUTLINE

In this last section, we give a short outline of the remainder of the book.

Part I looks at the notions underlying work and health psychology. In Chapter 2, Schabracq examines the concepts of well-being and health in normal, everyday work and organisations, as well as the motivation behind such work. In the next chapter, he discusses the concept of organisational culture and the impact of change on it. Shirom then surveys the effects of stress on health in Chapter 4, while Semmer pays attention to the role played by individual differences when it comes to stress and health in Chapter 5. In the remainder of this part, Jones and Fletcher look at job control (Chapter 6), Guest and Conway examine the psychological contract (Chapter 7), and Theorell discusses flexibility (Chapter 8).

Part II, consisting of two chapters, examines some issues of research and diagnosis. In Chapter 9, Griffiths and Schabracq discuss some of the dilemmas they encounter doing research and publishing in the field of work and health psychology. In Chapter 10, Cox, Griffiths and Randall describe their methodology for assessing psychosocial hazards in organisations.

Part III deals with some specific issues that play a part in work and health psychology. Hamborg and Greif survey the impact of computer technology (Chapter 11). The next three chapters centre around some dilemmas women face at work. In Chapter 12, Hobfoll, Geller and Dunahoo deal with the specifics of the more communal orientation of women's coping. In Chapter 13, Burke examines experiences of stress and health among managerial and professional women. In Chapter 14, Geurts and Demerouti discuss the work/non-work interface, an issue that also plays a crucial role for women at work. The problems posed by alcohol and drug misuse are surveyed by Guppy and Marsden in Chapter 15. Schabracq then pays attention to the specific issues of the second career half (Chapter 16), as well as the specific policies and strategies that are available here (Chapter 17). In Chapter 18, Kleber and van der Velden examine acute stress in the work situation, while Schaufeli and Buunk survey the literature about burnout in Chapter 19.

Part IV is about interventions of a preventive as well as a curative nature. First, Kompier surveys interventions in the area of job design to improve well-being and health in Chapter 20. Meyer discusses the contributions of the learning organisation in this respect in Chapter 21. Whittington, Paulus and Quick do the same for management development in Chapter 22. In Chapter 23, De Dreu, van Dierendonck and De Best-Waldhober survey the contributions of solving conflicts. In Chapter 24, Ryan discusses creating shared commitment as a general technique to improve well-being and health. Murphy reviews the state of the art of stress management programmes in Chapter 25, while Fletcher describes his FIT approach to work stress and health in Chapter 26. Meyer, in Chapter 27, then goes into coaching and counselling, while Schabracq in Chapter 28 gives an overview of what an organisation can do about its employees' well-being and health.

Lastly, in the Epilogue (Chapter 29) the editors look at some possible future developments in the field of work and health development.

REFERENCES

Cartwright, S. & Cooper, C.L. (1997) *Managing Workplace Stress*. Thousand Oaks, CA: Sage.

Gaillard, A.W.K. (1996). *Stress, produktiviteit en gezondheid [Stress, Productivity and Health]* Amsterdam: Uitgeverij Nieuwezijds.

Karasek, R.A. & Theorell, T. (1990) *Healthy Work. Stress, Productivity and the Reconstruction of Working Life*. New York: Basic Books.

Kompier, M.A.J., Gründemann, R.W.M., Vink, P. & Smulders, P.G.W. (1996) *Aan de slag [Get Going]*. Alphen aan de Rijn: Samsom Bedrijfsinformatie.

Kompier, M.A.J. & Cooper, C.L. (1999) *Preventing Stress, Improving Productivity: European Case Studies in the Workplace*. London: Routledge.

Schabracq, M.J., Maassen Van den Brink, H., Groot, W., Janssen, P. & Houkes, I. (2000). *De prijs van stress [The Price of Stress]*. Maarsen: Elsevier.

Schabracq, M.J., Cooper, C.L., Travers, C. & van Maanen, D. (2001). *Occupational Health Psychology*. Leicester: British Psychological Society.

PART I

Understanding Work and Health Psychology: Theory and Concepts

CHAPTER 2

Everyday Well-Being and Stress in Work and Organisations

Marc J. Schabracq
Utrech University, The Netherlands

2.1 INTRODUCTION

As the primary object of work and health psychology consists of occupational health and well-being in their own right, this chapter goes into the dynamics of everyday working life and its relation to well-being.

The first part of the chapter focuses on everyday working life and the concept of integrity. This concept refers to the habitual organisation of the interaction between person and environment, which is conducive to good task performance, well-being and motivation, as well as to personal development and integration in the social environment. Appropriate integrity furthermore gives us a feeling of reality and normality. As integrity is not an intra-personal concept, the perspective here is essentially a cultural–anthropological one. Attention is paid to the repetitive nature of everyday working life and the discipline of attention inherent in it. The parallel with animal territories and the role of social representations, which connect us to the rest of the social world, are explored.

In the next section, the focus is on the motivational dynamics of integrity. This is about why we start working at all, why we go on, what makes it fun, the outcomes for other life realms and the necessary conditions to be able to work at all. As such, the perspective here is more of a psychological nature.

The last section goes into the breakdown of integrity. Stress is described as an important signal that something has gone wrong with integrity, a signal that can be used as a fruitful starting point for personal as well as organisational development.

2.2 EVERYDAY WORKING LIFE

In this section, we show how overwhelmingly repetitive our everyday life actually is. By continuously acting in a familiar way and not paying attention to other options, we create

The Handbook of Work and Health Psychology. Edited by M.J. Schabracq, J.A.M. Winnubst and C.L. Cooper.
© 2003 John Wiley & Sons, Ltd.

and maintain our own small niche in the world, our own treadmill. This niche has an obvious resemblance to an animal territory and has similar outcomes as well. This niche is tied in with the rest of the social world with the help of social representations, cognitive structures of meanings, images and rules that we share with other people.

2.2.1 Repetition

The role of repetition in everyday (working) life, and its impact on well-being has not been studied extensively in psychology. This may be the case because the idea of repetition does not appeal to us. Leading a life of continuous repetition sounds to most of us more like a punishment, the sad fate of slaves and prisoners, than the normal way of living. After all, aren't we free and creative, can't we choose what we want? We just love excitement and think that we lead challenging lives. However, maybe we just don't notice the repetition in our lives because is it so omnipresent, so common and normal. Isn't the fish the last one to detect the water?

So let us take a closer look at a normal working day. Each day, we rise at the same time, probably with the help of an alarm clock. Next to us, either somebody is lying who is highly familiar to us, or there is nobody there and in either case we are not surprised. What follows is a series of highly familiar routines, by which we expose ourselves actively to all kinds of highly familiar sensory input on all channels. So, there are the typical smells of our bed, maybe our partner, our home, our urine, our usual toothpaste and soap, our aftershave or make-up. There are also the pleasant tastes of our breakfast, consisting of the more or less fixed items we prefer, our coffee or tea, and so on. When we look around, we see very familiar surroundings. We see a familiar face in the mirror and, if there are other people around, they also look and sound very familiar. If there is nobody else, we can put on the TV or radio, which happens to broadcast very familiar programmes brought to us by familiar people. We will not go into the modalities of touch, temperature, kinaesthetics and hearing, but we all know that these too are far from strange to us. Then, it is "time" to go to work, usually by a familiar route and by our usual means of transportation.

Now we've got the hang of it, we realise that our work, its environment, the people there, the more or less fixed hours, punctuated by our usual coffee, tea and lunch breaks, are not so exotic either, and neither is the lunch itself. The same applies to the rest of our day. Finally, we return to our beds again. Maybe we indulge in some sexual activity, but then—after having set our alarm clock!—we are overtaken by sleep, at least when everything is going well, and lose consciousness again. We call this a day.

Striving toward stability by continually repeating ourselves obviously has a high priority for us and takes a lot of effort and energy, also in our working life. Seen from a more distant point of view, we choose a place to work, subject it—as much as possible—to our taste and preferences, and adapt ourselves to it. We develop fixed lines of conduct there and fixed ways to divide our attention, and then we repeat these over and over, with a calm kind of fanaticism. In spite of our individual differences in this respect, we all greatly limit the variety of our daily work life, at least compared to the endless possibilities of variation that—at least in principle—are open to us. All in all, when we look honestly at a normal working day, we can only be surprised about the immense quantity of repetition we bring about. Think of all those emotional processes, familiar thoughts, feelings, smells and other sensations that we evoke time after time, by our normal projects, our normal ways of acting and everyday conversations.

What are the consequences of all this repetition? What does it afford us? The following quotation by Schutz (1970, p. 63) gives a good impression of what this is about:

> The experiences are apprehended, distinguished, brought into relief, marked out from one another; the experiences which were constituted as phases within the flow of duration now become objects of attention as constituted experiences.

We learn to use our feelings as clues to where, or how far, we are, and whether we are still on the right track. Apparently, we learn to recognise or install some markers in the activities. These act as signposts and milestones that tell us where we are and what turn we have to take now. In this way, we structure these activities, we punctuate them and invest them with a growing sense of reality. So, the repetition of the experiences enables us to distinguish different activities and projects and locate ourselves in these different activities.

This punctuation enables us—after ample practice—to activate automatically the right mental contents. Generally speaking, we find ourselves in a focused state of consciousness: we are busy, with a certain intensity and effort, bodily as well as mentally, focusing exclusively on our activity of the moment, without unnecessary role switches. The activity dominates what we think. It also steers our memory, in the sense that relevant information is automatically retrieved. We experience all of this as living in the here and now, temporally forgetting about the rest of the world. However, this only happens if our activities are sufficiently challenging and engrossing to get and keep us involved (Goffman, 1963). At the same time, this challenge should not be too great, in the sense that the activity should not be too difficult or too much.

Living in the here and now means also that we experience what we are doing as the only reality possible at this moment. James (1890/1950) describes this state of mind as one of faith (we come back to this in Section 2.3.3). Though we abstain in this way from all other possible realities at that moment, most of the time, we do not experience this as a restriction. Still, as life happens only once and is of a limited length, every reality that we abstain from is a lost possibility forever: by behaving as we do, we develop our talents in a certain direction, while necessarily aborting further developments in all other directions.

In the process, each activity or project becomes more and more an independent *Gestalt*. Repetition also helps us to feel at home in a project and helps to remind us that we are our normal selves. Apparently, we are constantly busy rebuilding and re-enacting our surrounding reality. Being ourselves is obviously a lot of work. The result, however, is a nice comfort zone, consisting of some well-trodden paths of repetition, spiralling through our lives. As a result, we can see ourselves as able and competent. Moreover, we also think of ourselves as the originators or authors of our activities and their results. We know we can do it, because we have done it before, many times. We have developed skills.

2.2.2 Discipline of Attention

The repetition inherent in normal functioning can also be described as a form of self-discipline: we see to it that we attend only to what matters to us, over and over, while ignoring the rest. For example, in the elevator or in the canteen, we hardly pay attention to employees whom we don't know personally, even when their faces look familiar. By keeping to these "rules of irrelevance" (Goffman, 1972), we prevent losing ourselves needlessly in new situations and further contact with people we don't know. This is, in such a situation, the normal conduct and, most of the time, we don't even notice it as such. The existence of these rules only becomes obvious when they are violated. Being stared at or being caught out studying a stranger's face can give us unpleasant feelings of startle and uneasiness (Goffman, 1963; Schabracq, 1991).

By this discipline of attention, we enable ourselves to live in the present repeating situation as if it were the only possible reality. We do so by actively sheltering ourselves from all possible other situations; that is, by not paying any special attention to any other potential situation and by showing that we do so. In this way, we actively prevent ourselves from experiencing unexpected events and provide our everyday reality with clear "borders". We seldom pass these borders, though we don't experience them as such most of the time, simply because we don't pay attention to them. They are the result of habit, our usual ways of acting and perceiving.

However, we share these borders with the other people in our environment: this is not a personal thing, but a matter of our common culture. Our culture helps us in this way to limit our personal reality. At the same time, it enables us to stay in the familiar situations that are conducive to reaching our goals, such as completing a work task. In other words, acting in this way keeps our mind free for work and other issues we find relevant.

Confining ourselves in this way to one situation that is instrumental to accomplishing important goals and ignoring all other potential situations can be seen as a shared, culturally determined form of problem solving or coping. It is a common way of acting that enables us to attain our goals without experiencing any stress, even without realising that stress was an option at all. This is just how we do these things. All in all, this is a valuable and important outcome of this form of discipline of our attention.

Besides "borders", reality can show "holes" too. To prevent our performance from being disturbed, we sometimes ignore or overlook issues that other people in our position would notice immediately. This is called "denial", a way to suppress experiences somewhat or completely, which we can apply in a well-directed and well-closed way (Breznitz, 1983). Here too, we do so because this allows us to keep our attention on our immediate goals. In the case of drastic forms of denial—resulting in "big holes"—we automatically tend to fill the resulting emptiness with something less threatening, disturbing or disagreeable (Dorpat, 1985).

Essentially, this discipline we exercise over our attention is an important way to keep ourselves in our recurrent activities, though we are hardly aware of the fact that we do it in such a way.

2.2.3 Social Representations and Organisational Culture

An important feature of our "stability by repetition" approach is that we learn to use representations of this self-chosen and partly self-designed environment. These representations encompass, among other things, standard procedures to deal with this environment. These representations are neither individual by nature, nor of our own making: they are a product of culture. We only may make them our own by reinventing them. Moscovici (1984) speaks of "social representations", a slight alteration of Durkheim's (1925) "collective representations", the alteration being that social representations are not completely unchangeable.

Social representations can be described as collective schemas shared by all members of a (sub)culture (Moscovici, 1984; Schabracq, 1991, 1992). As such, they are experiential and linguistic structures, which encompass meanings, images and templates of objects, events and processes, as well as procedural knowledge for dealing with these. This makes social representations intentional as well as action-oriented. Together they form the system with which we approach and think about our world and ourselves. As all members of the (sub)culture recognise, denominate and use these social representations, they also comprise the medium for communication with them. In this way, social representations are the cognitive building blocks of our common reality.

In the case of a work environment, the common social representations amount to what is called an organisational culture. Such a culture represents and determines what actually exists in the organisation, what is of value there, as well as what is good or bad. It also is about how things are done, which forms everything gets, how power is divided, and—not to forget—what people say, think and feel about all this (see Chapter 3 for a more elaborate description).

Why are social representations relevant here? Essentially, because they tie up the individual reality to the greater organisational reality. In this way, there can be communication and shared signification (see Section 2.3.1). Moreover, access to the social representations of the organisation implies also access to the organisational treasury of proven solutions to the kind of problems that the organisation has encountered and solved up to now.

2.2.4 Territory

Our self-chosen and partly self-designed environment with its standardised conduct strongly resembles what in ethology, the science of animal behaviour, is called a territory. Generally speaking, a territory is a certain space that an animal takes care of (Kaufman, 1971). Within such a space, an animal selects and builds a place to sleep. It develops fixed behavioural sequences, in which its skills are optimally attuned to the characteristics of its environment. By repeatedly going the same routes, it literally develops paths. It also assembles knowledge about different kinds of food supplies and places where it can drink or hide.

As a result, an appropriate territory has a crucial survival value, as it enables the animal to obtain food, shelter, some safety and options for procreation. If necessary—and possible—animals defend their territories. This is accompanied by the activation of an emotional process with displays of threat, aggression and defence (Emlen, 1958; Rowell, 1972). Serious infractions and (partial) loss of territory lead to serious stress and ultimately, sometimes, to death.

This all sounds familiar. Don't we, human beings, try to develop our own relatively stable niche to live and work in too? An important difference between these human niches and most animal territories is that humans, differently from many animal species, can make free use of a huge, relatively safe, communal space and all kinds of means of transportation. Also, humans may have more variable and differently located partial territories (Ashcraft & Scheflen, 1976), such as houses, workplaces and hotel rooms. Of course, language and processes of signification are more important also among humans. Though all this allows human beings more flexibility in this respect, infractions on and losses of (parts of) territory may evoke quite similar stress reactions in humans and other mammals, certainly at a physiological level (Eibl-Eibesfeldt, 1970).

2.3 INTEGRITY

In this section, we go into the concept of integrity. Essentially, integrity is about the way we organise our dealings with our self-chosen and self-designed environment. As such, integrity gives us control over our own functioning and our environment. Though integrity may remind us of what usually are described as ego processes, it is not meant as a psychological or intra-personal concept. Of course, integrity is about us, but it is also about our environment, including the persons present there: it is about the more or less fixed ways in which we behave in this environment and interact with other people there. Integrity helps us to accomplish good task performance, well-being and motivation, as well as personal development and integration in the social environment. Appropriate integrity furthermore enables us to experience both ourselves and our world as real and normal.

2.3.1 The Concept of Integrity

Acting, thinking and feeling in familiar ways implies abandoning other possible ways of functioning, a huge reduction of options resulting in a radical simplification of our lives (James, 1890/1950). By turning our world into a sequence of familiar and cyclical stretches of functioning (Schabracq, 1991), we willingly limit the scope of our life drastically. This is only normal: everybody does it or at least tries to do so, and—at least in our society—this conforms to every value in the book. We call it learning, and by this we more or less install our own niche, our own human territory. This allows us to develop skills to deal with our everyday life. Such skills soon become an automatism, leaving our consciousness free for what we find important at each moment (Schabracq, 1991).

Limiting our life in such a way is a form of self-structuring. We start out doing things in a certain way and then keep on doing them in the same way. It is like making a path by constantly stepping in our own footsteps. In such a way, we structure the way in which we are dealing with our environment, a way that can also be followed by other persons. This leads ultimately to a whole system. Such a system consists of social representations, interpersonal relations, resources and equipment. It allows us to design and to shape our environment, to behave in a meaningful way and to control, to a certain degree, our environment and personal functioning, as well as its outcomes, though admittedly within a relatively small world. In this way we behave completely along the lines of the German proverb: "in limitation, the master shows himself". Following Meijman (oral communication, also in Ouwerkerk et al., 1994), we call this system "integrity of functioning", or for short: "integrity". Integrity is used here first in its meaning of an intact whole. The reason to elaborate here on integrity lies in the fact that when integrity prevails we are free of stress complaints. In the following, we have a closer look at what integrity means and implies. Doing so, we lean here and there rather heavily on Goffman (1974) and Schutz (1970).

While acting in integrity, each activity at hand has a beginning, an end and an internal structure of separate acts, each of which has to be performed successively. Beginning an activity implies that we have to sever ourselves from our previous involvement. Our general orientation is goal-directed. Essentially, we aim at reaching the end state, but in practice, we are primarily focused on finishing each separate act at hand. At the end, we re-incorporate ourselves again in the rest of the world; that is, we lose ourselves in another activity or event. The beginning and the end, as well as the transition points in the internal structure, function as markers. These help us to locate ourselves in the stream of acts comprising each activity.

The transition points are also of use in communicating to others what we are doing. As such, the transition points may be somewhat highlighted or dramatised (see, for instance, Birdwhistell, 1972; Scheflen, 1973). Put in more general terms: by integrity, we integrate ourselves into the surrounding inter-subjective world of communication and social action. We do so in an experiential way, as well as a spatial and temporal way. We experience ourselves as present there and we adapt to the time perspective prevailing there. We share this world with all others who are present there. What we are doing, our activity, is comprehensible to them, while what they are doing is comprehensible to us, at least in principle. Essentially, all working acts are a form of communication between all concerned.

Acting in integrity means also that we are willing to do what we are doing, and, also, that this does not go against our convictions and values. As such, we are at that moment mentally undivided (Haberman, 1994; Laborde, 1987). The part of us that is acting is, for the time being, in total control. As such, this being undivided, congruent or one-pointed is a sign of well-being and mental health, sought after by all kinds of psychotherapeutic approaches such as *Gestalt* therapy (Perls et al., 1951) and NLP (Laborde, 1987) or even religious practices (e.g. Goleman, 1988; Haberman, 1994).

A mostly unwanted consequence of fully developing a sub-persona that is in total control is that we may also develop a kind of inverse sub-persona, acting from the opposite values, as a kind of side-product of the original sub-persona. The inverse sub-persona normally lives a completely latent life. Its existence is only hinted at when the sub-persona who is in control is confronted by somebody else, who shows characteristics of the inverse sub-persona. Then it leads often to instant dislike and rejection. For instance, when we see ourselves primarily as responsible for everything, we tend to dislike careless people who show no responsibility at all. However, this inverse sub-persona, called the "shadow side" (Jung, 1970) or "allergy" (Ofman, 1995), can make its appearance and become dominant when integrity breaks down, for instance in the second stage of a stress process, as discussed later in this chapter (see also Schabracq et al., 2000).

The fact that we do not go against our own convictions or values is essentially a moral issue: integrity has strong moral connotations, completely conforming to the usual meaning of the term. Work, for instance, provides us with an opportunity to act in a morally sound way, perform activities that are morally valued and live a respectable life. Moreover, we can do our work as well as possible, which may earn us respect and recognition from other people. In the Jewish-Christian tradition, this ethical side of work is heavily emphasised: work as penance for the primal sin and good works as a means to get a place in heaven (see Achterhuis, 1984; Arendt, 1958; Schabracq & Boerlijst, 1992). In short, the devil finds work for idle hands and there is nobility in labour.

The moral aspects of integrity follow from its use of social representations, which are part of the surrounding culture. After all, culture is also about how things should be done (see also Chapter 3) and is, in that way, always a matter of morality and ethics. As a matter of fact, we can use social representations actively to build up and defend our integrity. We apply meanings to describe, rectify, justify, celebrate, modulate or negate our actions. We choose a certain line of action with a valued meaning or actively attach meanings to what we do and make, and we communicate these meanings. Sometimes, we have to convince others of their authenticity. This may involve some negotiating. Sometimes also we have to adjust the meanings that we had in mind. We call this signification.

In signification, we make use of the prevailing social representations, modelled by our relevant others. In doing so, we strive for internal consistency; that is, we prefer meanings that do not lead to conflicting thoughts or actions. This process tends to evolve into an integrated, consistent system of meanings, the cognitive side of our integrity. Such a system serves our goals in life, is open for further evolution and, at the same time, is attuned to the prevailing meanings of our relevant others. As such, it contributes to our self-esteem and the respect that we get from others.

The forms integrity takes vary: there are, for example, substantial variations among individuals in the degree to which they strive toward fixed situations and procedures. Some need a completely structured environment. Others need more freedom and challenges. However, in each case, the outcome of integrity may be an environment that fits our specific configuration of abilities and needs. As such, adequate integrity refers to the stable, meaningful and morally sound organisation of our functioning in our environment. It enables us to control that functioning as well as its environment. It also makes it possible to maintain rewarding and productive relationships with other people and to integrate ourselves in the social structure there. In this way, integrity allows us to do a good job. This encompasses being effective and efficient, being motivated and having pleasure, as well as being creative and developing ourselves. This all is conducive to our well-being and health.

In the light of all these positive outcomes, it comes as no surprise that we tend to hold on to our integrity. If it is threatened, we defend it fiercely, if necessary and possible, just as animals defend their territory. This is often called—rather derogatorily—"resistance against change".

Though the concept of integrity obviously is related to concepts such as "identity", "self", "ego" and "personality", there is one important difference. Differently from these terms, integrity essentially is not at all an exclusively intra-psychical concept and not even an exclusively psychological concept. Integrity explicitly refers to the interaction of individual human beings and their individual environments. Without such an environment, integrity is a completely empty concept. The following words of Perls et al. (1951, p. 73) are a good illustration of this idea:

> *You* and your *environment* are not independent entities, but *together* you constitute a functioning, mutually influencing, total system.

Though integrity is not the most common concept, it has a respectable history in this area. It was used in similar ways by Rümke (1939), Lecky (1945), Cofer & Appley (1964) and Fromm (1955), while Erikson (1968) reserved it for the last life phase: integrity as the crown on the development of identity.

2.3.2   The Figure–Ground Configuration in Integrity

When integrity prevails, acting appears to go by itself. At any moment, there is a very precise division of attention, guided by a certain hierarchy of what is more and less important, the so-called "hierarchy of relevances" (Schutz, 1970). When the task proceeds, this hierarchy changes in a stringent, but implicit and more or less automatic, way. The task "binds" our attention, without any apparent effort or force from our side. In *Gestalt* psychological terms, this means that the specific task at hand acts as "figure", and its immediate environment as "ground" (e.g. Rubin, 1921, in Köhler, 1947). In the words of Perls et al. (1951, p. 56):

> If both attention and excitement are present and working together, the object of attention becomes more and more a unified, bright, sharp figure against a more and more empty, unnoticed, uninteresting ground.

As "figures", the relevant task elements come to the fore from their immediate surroundings, the "task grounds". The task becomes a *Gestalt* with its own identity and acquires a somewhat greater "reality value" than the ground. To enable the figure to function as such, the ground ideally should not attract too much attention. At the same time, the rest of the world, the wider surroundings of the task, tends to disappear from our awareness altogether. Once such a division of attention is realised, it enables us to keep our attention on what is most important within the frame of the task. As such, this division is highly instrumental and functional. The reason that we go into this is that figure and ground can each be interfered with in their own separate ways, both resulting in the disturbance of overall integrity.

A task can function as a figure in so far as it is involving and challenging enough; that is to say, when it affords us enough, when it has sufficient "affordance" (Gibson, 1979). This means that it has to appeal to us emotionally, trigger our feelings, fantasies and imagery, and activate our behaviour (James, 1890/1950, vol. II, p. 300; Frijda, 1986). In short, this is about motivation (to which we return later in this chapter). If this motivation is insufficient, the task loses its figure quality. It then cannot effectively suppress other activities that interfere with it and, as a result, the available processing capacity becomes too small for good performance (Shallice, 1978).

The phenomenon of "ground" in itself is not elaborately specified in the *Gestalt* psychological literature. An appropriate ground just should not attract too much attention. However, research has shown that grounds are scanned from time to time on irregular and unexpected features (Lindsey & Norman, 1977). Also we may assume that a task ground is, generally speaking, very well known and familiar to us, because of the repetition inherent in work. It is this familiarity that enables us to monitor it at an automatic level for changes and events that might need our conscious attention. In this way, we keep our conscious attention free for the task at hand. As a result, the task ground is not only familiar to us, but we also experience it as our own, even as a part of ourselves, or better: as a part of our integrity, just like the task itself.

2.3.3   Reality and Normality

Most of us usually do not experience reality as something to be afraid of. On the contrary, to most of us reality is a comfortable place, something essentially predictable, which holds no big surprises. To say the least, this is a strange way to think about a world full of ugly wars, earthquakes, illnesses, drunken drivers and so on. It is so strange that it makes us think that we are talking about two kinds of reality here. This is actually the case. The experienced predictability indicates that this reality does not refer to the chaos out there, which makes out our factual environment, but more to our fixed ways of dealing with this chaos. It is our set of habitual ways of doing things in our familiar niches, with their familiar steps and limited horizons, which is so familiar to us. So, we create our own reality. James' often cited passage from his *Principles of Psychology* illustrates this nicely:

> The real world as it is given at this moment is the sum total of all its beings and events now. But can we think of such a sum? Can we realize for an instant what a cross-section of all existence at a definite point of time would be? While I talk and the flies buzz, a sea

gull catches a fish at the mouth of the Amazon, a tree falls in the Adirondack wilderness, a man sneezes in Germany, a horse dies in Tartary, and twins are born in France. What does that mean? Does the contemporaneity of these events with each other and with a million more as disjointed as they form a rational bond between them, and unite them into anything that means for us a world? Yet just such a collateral comtemporaneity, and nothing else, is the *real* order of the world. It is an order with which we have nothing to do but to get away from it as fast as possible. As I said, we break it: we break it into histories, and we break it into arts, and we break it into sciences; and then we begin to feel at home. We make ten thousand separate serial orders of it. On any one of these, we may react as if the rest did not exist. (James, 1890/1950, vol. II, footnote, p. 635)

This is what integrity is about. As long as integrity prevails, we know what to expect. By integrity, we install continuity and consistency. We make ourselves familiar with ourselves and our environment. We do so by repeating ourselves and consistently applying the same meanings. As a result, we experience our own feelings and sensations resulting from this repetitious interaction as familiar, a seemingly continuous background to our functioning. Such a self-made background we trust as a solid reality. Yet—as we saw in Section 2.2.1— this usually involves a lot of work.

For instance, by allowing our attention to be determined by familiar working tasks, we synchronise our functioning time after time with the task structure, as well as with the organisation and its further environment (Schutz, 1970). In the reality resulting from this task performance, we know what to do, what to think and what to feel. As long as everything goes well, we submit ourselves to the situational rules without a thought and, more or less automatically, get into the corresponding state of consciousness as well. Behaving in the right way, we "slide" from one situation into the next: our attention is systematically not directed to places where, from a task perspective, there is nothing to attend to. So, reality becomes something like a journey through a landscape of realistic looking stage scenes. It is as if a competent and attentive magician seems to go out of his way to make sure that our attention is diverted to the intended direction every time it is about to be focused on something that is incompatible with task performance (Schabracq, 1987). Of course, we ourselves are the magicians here. The most important point, however, is that this actually works: most of us feel that we inhabit a solid reality. As a result, we can experience ourselves also as real persons: we exist as persons and because we are continuously more or less the same, we experience ourselves and our environment as quite normal.

By working, we also make the surroundings shaped by our activities more real and normal, for ourselves as well as for others. In this way, we contribute to the reality of the organisation within which we perform our tasks. Think of what would remain of it if we collectively decided to stop working there. Of course, the buildings, equipment and other props still would be around, but that would be all. It would certainly not be an organisation any more. To a smaller degree, something similar even applies to the society at large of which the organisation is a part. The disappearance of the organisation would also imply a loss for the society. Enough of such losses and the whole society would be gone. In this way, work provides the possibility of inhabiting a familiar and shared reality during an important fraction of our time.

As became clear from the description of reality as a journey through a landscape of stage scenes, reality is essentially living an illusion, though a self-chosen and—partly—self-constructed one. But then again, as we stated before, it appears to do the trick. Still, popping out of reality is not such an unusual experience:

> We have all experienced the instant amnesias that occur when we get too far on some tangent so we "lose the thread of thought" or "forget what we were going to do". Without the bridging associative connections, consciousness would break down into a series of discrete states with as little continuity as is apparent in our dream life. (Erickson et al., 1976, p. 299)

We usually experience this many times a day, for instance when we wake up, when we are startled by something, when we cannot concentrate and, essentially—if we at least would pay attention to it—each time we blink our eyes:

> I imagine, sometimes, that if a film could be made of one's life, every other frame would be death. It goes so fast we're not aware of it. Destruction and resurrection in alternate beats of being, but speed makes it seem continuous. But you see, kid, with ordinary consciousness you can't even begin to know what's happening. (Bellow, 1982, p. 295)

Still, to most us, these phenomena do not represent a serious problem. We feel we are, more or less, witness to the whole world, as if we are actually living in the kind of reality that James described at the beginning of this section.

Feelings that everything is unreal do occur, however. When people actually complain about such things, this is usually seen as a serious psychiatric symptom, called depersonalisation or derealisation. However, in a less spectacular way, loss of reality lies at the base of—or is at least a normal accompaniment to—all work stress phenomena, though this seldom is worded in this way. This happens when we have to perform a certain task which we are not able or willing to perform, for example because something from the outside is interfering with what we are doing. This is of course also a matter of disturbed integrity. In the last section of this chapter we return to this issue.

So reality and normality, of ourselves and our environment, appear to be a matter of continuously re-enacting them and anchoring them by giving them familiar meanings that we share with the other people around (social re-presentations; Moscovici, 1984). In this way, we attune and connect our private reality to the more general, inter-subjective one of the surrounding society. Reality and normality are among the most important outcomes of integrity.

However, as integrity is not permanent, reality is not either. It can be disturbed and brought down altogether in the same way as integrity can be. This does not mean that reality does not exist, as often is stated. It only means that it is not always there. When it is there, it is the result of a lot of our own hard work. As such, it is dependent on the same factors that keep integrity in the air. In the next section we go into these factors.

2.4 MOTIVATION

What are the factors behind the everyday reality inherent in integrity? What makes us start working and what keeps us going? To answer these questions, we turn to the psychological literature on motivation.

Successively, we go into the following issues:

- What makes us start working at all?
- Which factors inherent in work make us go on with work, even when the work in itself is not so rewarding?

- Which factors inherent in work make work fun?
- Which other factors make our work worthwhile to us, in the sense that these have positive outcomes for our other life domains?
- Which other factors underlie the figure–ground configuration of successful task performance or, in short, a functional work situation?

Beforehand, we want to point out that these factors are not a matter of either–or. For every working person, several of these factors are active at the same time. Moreover, these factors may show a considerable overlap.

2.4.1 Starting

Why do we begin to work at all? First of all, because work is so overwhelmingly present that most of us hardly see any alternative. This is an illustration of the principle that, if certain things take the form they do, this effectively prevents other forms from appearing (Bourdieu, 1989, pp. 86–7). Working is a basic and very present element of our society. The division of labour and the role of money make it so. We render services or make products and get some money in return. Working is also a part of leading a normal life, a part of our *Normalbiografie*, as it is called in German, at least of a male one. As such, most of our upbringing and education focus on preparing us for some kind of work. To live in our societies, you need money. If you are not born—or married—rich and you want to make an honest living, working is the way. This has a lot to do with the ethical considerations described before. By working, you make money and it gives you a respectable position and role in society. As such, working is for many of us a logical and self-evident line of conduct. The main question is not so much whether we are going to work at all, as which line of work it is going to be.

2.4.2 Continuing

Of course, work can be fun, and we come back to that later. But then again, much work is not so funny at all, at least not all the time. This leads to the next question: what makes us go on when work is not so pleasant? What follows is a list of such mechanisms.

The first motivational factor in the continuation of work to be mentioned here is probably the most basic one. It refers to the idea that we have a biologically determined need for a certain level of activity and activation. We need such a level in order to develop ourselves and to stay healthy (Hebb, 1966). Living too long at a too high or too low level of activation can be both unpleasant and unhealthy. Because everyday work is so repetitive and familiar to us, we know exactly what it does to us. As such, it is an activity that we can dose very precisely. This makes it suitable to play an important part in fulfilling this need for a certain level of activity and activation. Radical changes in our work would threaten this factor.

Another factor is the well-known fact that over-learned behaviour gets its own motivational characteristics, something along the lines of "habit becomes drive" (Woodworth and Schlosberg, 1954). In this way, a certain pattern of behaviour may become a "motive" (or "motif") in both of its meanings. On the one hand, there is the meaning of "driving force", such as in the motive for a murder; on the other, we have the meaning of "well-specified, recurrent pattern or figure", such as in a musical composition or a novel, or on wallpaper. As much work tends to be repetitive—though the length of the cycle may vary—this principle may be of great importance in the continuation of work. Of course, radical changes in our work would threaten this factor too.

The next factor comes from *Gestalt* psychology (see, for example, Köhler, 1947). The term *Gestalt* itself, a well-specified pattern in perception, experience or behaviour, comes close to the concept of "motive" for that matter. The factor meant here is the principle of closure. Though originally more a perceptual phenomenon—for instance, a line drawn with the help of a pair of compasses that almost constitutes a circle is seen by us as a circle anyhow, only with one part "missing"—this idea was also applied to working tasks. This can take the form of the so-called Zeigarnik effect, the tendency to finish unfinished tasks, just for the sake of finishing it, also when this serves no external purposes anymore. This phenomenon was studied in the 1920s by Zeigarnik (1927) and Ovsiankina (1928). Many working tasks can also be described as well-specified behavioural patterns, repetitive *Gestalten* that, once instigated, "strive for" closure.

Another, probably closely related, factor is described in the early French literature about suggestion. It is called the "law of unconscious goal-directed activity". This law states that, once a goal-directed idea, called a suggestion, has taken hold of us, its execution in behavioural form, including the selection and use of the right means, is automatically processed at an unconscious level (Baudouin, 1924). So, once we have really chosen to do something, the supervision over its execution and continuation becomes more or less automatic, as they are transferred to mechanisms outside of our immediate awareness. In the everyday practice of work, this may mean that we may just go on as long as the end state is not accomplished.

Another related and very basic factor stems from the limitations of our mental and motor capacities. These limitations imply that various behavioural patterns have to use the same mental and motor systems. As a result, we cannot execute these patterns at the same time without serious mutual interference. However, such interference is prevented by the operation of a hierarchical organisation of these patterns. The "dominant" pattern inhibits automatically the activation of all other patterns that are incompatible with it. Moreover, in as much as this inhibition is successful, attempts to activate sub-dominant behavioural patterns only result in increased arousal, and, by that, in increased activation and invigoration of the dominant pattern (Shallice, 1978). This mechanism, known as reciprocal inhibition, is a well-established fact, both in brain physiology and in behavioural therapy. It probably plays an important role in the perseverance of familiar work tasks.

In the early French literature about suggestion psychology, a similar mechanism is de-scribed as the "law of inverted effort". This law states that once an idea has evoked a suggestion, all attempts of the person in question to oppose that suggestion—to the degree that that suggestion controls us—will only make this suggestion stronger (Baudouin, 1924). This law is used mainly to explain phenomena such as addictions, fear of heights and the attraction that a hole in the ice holds for an untrained skater. However, it also can be applied to the continuation of unpleasant work, once the idea of doing it—the suggestion—is firmly installed in the worker's mind. So, very pleasant weather with all its options of attractive outdoor leisure activities actually may induce us to work harder in our dreary, indoor office. Amsel (1992) also describes a comparable principle. By manipulating the environment of his subject animals—rats, of course—they were left with only one behavioural sequence to get a certain reward. When this sequence did not immediately result in the expected reward, the rats persevered with more energy in that same sequence. Amsel's explanation was that the emotional arousal activated by the frustration of expectations, by a kind of reciprocal inhibition, reinforced the only possible sequence.

One point is crucial for all these forms of reciprocal inhibition described above: they are only effective as long as the dominant response remains dominant. However, all responses tend to lose their dominance sooner or later. Other response tendencies become stronger. For example, we get hungry or thirsty, or we have to go to the toilet. Also, we become tired and have to get some rest. All kinds of biological cycles, each with its own duration, play a part here (Luce, 1972). At an experiential level, this usually manifests itself more as a feeling of no longer wanting to do the activity at hand than of altogether being unable to (see Meijman, 1991, who discusses this matter in the context of fatigue). Obviously, such cyclical biological processes are of influence on all motivational factors discussed in this section. The same applies, of course, to other factors such as our state of health and fitness.

A last factor we want to mention here is the mechanism of denial, which we described before as a special instance of discipline of attention. We may keep ourselves going by denying unpleasant sides of our work. We may ignore these in order to get the job done. For instance, we may deny all the pleasant options we give up, the loss of freedom or even the downright coercion and emotional blackmail by our manager. This even may be part of the implicit—or even explicit—socialisation in that organisation. However, this is not a healthy way of working. As such, it may be a characteristic coping mechanism of the second stage of stress (see Section 2.4), though it is also common in the first stage of stress. In the first stage especially, it is often masked by another mechanism, which resembles the mechanism that Anna Freud (1964) described as "identification with the aggressor" (Bolen, 1989). In order to prevent feelings of alienation and emptiness—normal accompaniments of massive denial—we overly identify with the rules and goals laid out by our superiors and organisation. We learn to see the world through our superiors' eyes and to think along their logic. This usually is, more or less, an automatic process. As a result, our sacrifices appear to be normal to us. Ultimately, however, it may lead to the bleak and joyless existence of the second stage of stress (Schabracq et al., 2000).

All the mechanisms described above also play a role in the well-known centring effect of familiar working tasks. As work becomes the dominant behavioural pattern, inhibiting all other possibilities, it can positively influence our peace of mind by keeping away interfering, unpleasant ideas originating from other life domains. Essentially, this is the mechanism of compulsive neurosis: endlessly washing our hands in order not to feel anxiety. This mechanism probably also plays a part in "workaholism" as well as in occupational therapy. Another side of this phenomenon is that work may become a welcome refuge, when the rest of our life is not going so well, for example when we are confronted with a very ill or dying family member at home.

2.4.3 Inherent Rewarding Factors

As stated before, work can be fun too. We now go into some mechanisms inherent in work that may account for those pleasurable sides.

As we have seen in Section 2.3, a task ideally binds our attention without any effort or force from our side: it gets us involved. This happens for instance when it challenges us in the right way. This means that the challenge inherent in the work is neither too low nor too high.

The challenge is too low when the task is boring, in the sense of being too easy, too monotonous and too meaningless (for example Hackman & Oldham, 1980), or when it does not offer enough activity to keep us busy. Such a task does not provide sufficient meaning to justify our presence at the work site, especially when we realise that it is keeping us away from more meaningful and rewarding activities. We may experience concentration problems and feelings of irritation and boredom, diminishing the ability to perform the task even further. As we must perform the task anyhow, we have to force ourselves to attend to it. Such forced attention soon becomes very tiring and we can sustain it only for a very limited period of time (Schabracq, 1991). Then we become drowsy, lose control over our own performance, and find ourselves unable to go on.

The challenge also can be too high. This is the case when the task is too difficult or simply too big for us, or—put differently—when the task demands too much from us. In this case too, we face a loss of control and the task loses its figure quality. Chaos sets in and ultimately this also leads to task breakdown.

What the right level of challenge is depends, of course, on our individual preferences and abilities. However, in a way, it is always a kind of "middle zone" (see Chapter 3). Though we return to this later, we now already want to state that the challenge inherent in the task is not only dependent on the intrinsic task characteristics. Completely extrinsic factors, such as money, can play a role here too.

One way to make a working task challenging in a pleasurable way is trying to do it as well as possible. This is a well-known and apparently autonomous tendency. In *Gestalt* psychology, it is described as the principle of "pith" (in German *Prägnanz*; see Köhler, 1947), that is a tendency to strive for a "good" and "pithy" *Gestalt*. In terms of activities, this then becomes doing things in the best possible way. In the context of body movements, Buitendijk (1948) describes this principle as striving for optimal movements, in terms of both energy conservation and aesthetics. He also states that such a way of performing in itself gives us pleasure: it feels good to do something in such a way. In a comparable context, Karl Bühler, in 1924, used the term "functional pleasure" (in German '*Funktionslust*'). So, striving for and succeeding in a good performance can be rewarding and pleasurable in themselves. As such, succeeding in doing things well has to be regarded as an important motivating characteristic of working tasks. Put more strongly, work can be a stage for performing well and demonstrating our aptitude and skills.

Csikszentmihalyi (1988) describes a slightly different but obviously similar mechanism as "flow", a pleasant, flush-like feeling of being centred that stems from losing ourselves completely in a perfect performance of a difficult task for which we are highly trained. Flow stems from the complete "fusion" of the task and the person performing it. At such a moment of flow, we "are" our task. It presupposes an optimal balance between task difficulty and the performer's competence. Examples are a perfect performance in sports (the perfect race, jump, throw, dive or whatever) or the performing arts (a perfect show in theatre, ballet, music etc.). Once we have mastered the task too well, however, we lose the experience of flow. So being addicted to flow implies that we have to heighten our standards continuously. This means that we learn a lot. It also may mean that we may find ourselves in a blind alley one day.

In cases of hard physical labour, another mechanism may play a role. Such kinds of hard work can lead to states characterised by high levels of catecholamines—adrenalin and noradrenalin—and even endorphins—morphine-like substances produced by our own bodies—in the bloodstream. Such a state is, at least by some of us, highly valued: we feel good; there is a general feeling of control; and intrusions of unwanted thoughts are reduced to a minimum. However, this may not be an especially healthy mechanism. Such work can even turn into a form of addiction. It may then be at the expense of our reserves, also because it makes it difficult to unwind, which interferes with our sleep and recuperation.

Simpler tasks may have rewarding features too. As executing these tasks does not demand our full mental capacity, it leaves us with some reserve, which we may use to do something else, something that we like to do and that does not interfere with our task.

We can use this reserve capacity, for example, to chat and joke with colleagues. In some simple jobs, such as working at an assembly belt, this often is experienced as the most pleasant side of the work. It may even be one of the main reasons to do it (Krijnen, 1993).

If a job leaves us with some mental reserve capacity, another option consists of surrendering ourselves to reflection and daydreaming, which can be very pleasurable to some of us. A special variant is practising an explicitly meditative form of working, aiming at the voluntary transcendence of the everyday experience of work. In this way, simple work can get a completely new meaning. It even may become an unexpected means to experience deeply felt bliss and sensations of "seeing it all". Such a way of working used to be, and in some places still is, a familiar part of monastery life (Arendt, 1958). Recently, a similar practice was taught by the Baghwan sect.

A closely related possibility for executing simple tasks consists of treating them as rituals and to use them to nourish our peace of mind. Though rituals of course have religious connotations, they also can be described as simple behavioural sequences that have to be performed as well as possible and that have no other purpose than evoking a pleasant, centred state of mind (Schipper, 1988). If this still may sound somewhat too exotic, it may be remembered that many of us can get a good feeling from simple activities such as gardening, needlework, simple repair work around the house, cleaning up or doing the dishes. Such work tasks are especially expedient to recover from taxing mental tasks, as well as to survive times of crisis and chaos, when goals have become obscured or absent. As such, these activities may become a kind of temporary comfort zone.

Lastly, there are the kinds of tasks that demand some vigilance, but involve little activity most of the time. Examples are the jobs of night porters, underground train drivers (on fully automated trains), shepherds, night watches and bridge attendants. The beautiful thing about this kind of job is that, besides the freedom inherent in them, they allow you to do other things such as reading, studying or some handicraft. They can also be used to recover from more taxing tasks.

All the factors described above may play a role in making work fun, but probably the most important one—that is, if we are lucky—is that we often love what we are doing at work. We tend to select work with which we have affinity. This affinity can have very diverse causes and reasons. We may choose a line of work because we have a special aptitude, interest or even fascination for it. Already at a very tender age, most of us have specific ideas about what we want to do when we grow up and some of us actually choose that line of work. Then there are the influences of our families, their hopes for us, the scripts that they install in us (Berne, 1966). In addition, there are the influences of other relevant persons such as friends, teachers or just people in the neighbourhood. Sometimes our attention is caught by a historical person, who acts for us as a role model. Some of us are steered in our occupational choice by deeply felt values. An exhaustive list of such reasons is impossible. What counts, is that many of us may have or develop a deeply felt special interest in our occupation and profession.

The organisation plays an important role here too. Organisations select their employees. Ideally, they hire only those who fit in generally, are thought to be able to do the present job and hold some promise for a successful further career within the organisation. Once employees are hired, they start to become socialised: they grow into their work and the organisation. When this socialisation is unsuccessful or when they turn out not to be able to do the job well, people don't feel at home there and generally don't like what they are doing. As a result, the chances are that they may leave by themselves or be sent away. The ones staying behind may grow further into the organisation. The job and the membership of the organisation become part of them: they tend to identify themselves with their work and organisation (Schneider, 1987).

All in all, the result may be that our work becomes a part of ourselves, and also that we are particularly interested in what we do, or even love what we do. Moreover, we tend to become good at what we do. So we may become proud of our profession or craft, our services and products. This is about prestige, respect, control, well-being and self-esteem, about who and what we are and want to be. These, of course, are very strong motivating factors. In short, we are again talking about integrity here.

2.4.4 Other Motivating Factors

Apart from factors inherent in the work, there are other factors that make our work worth while. Here, we are talking about factors that have a positive influence on the rest of our life and as such can be interpreted as rewards or reinforcing factors of our work.

Being paid for our work is often experienced as the most salient motivating factor. This is indeed an important one, though, by the way, not all work is paid. Still, pay usually allows us to make a living, be autonomous and experience a certain freedom: to become our own man or woman. If our work is paid very well, it even may allow us a luxurious lifestyle and a high position in society.

Pay is not the only issue here. If the quality of the results of our work—the services we render, the products we manufacture—are highly valued in society, these too may provide us high status and prestige. All of these may be strong "extrinsic" reinforcements to our work. As such, these can even make tasks that are not challenging in themselves challenging enough to fully bind our attention after all. In addition, these factors may be of great influence on our integrity in the non-work domains and the way we arrange our whole life. Generally speaking, these factors have a relatively high visibility, and everybody knows about them. That is why we only mention them here in passing.

One other thing about pay is that it can also function as a statement about the evaluation of our work, compared to that of others. In this context, a raise or a bonus can also have a more intrinsically rewarding character, regardless of whether it is big or relatively small.

Another, less visible, outcome of work is that it helps to structure our life in a temporal way. First, by working, we create free time, a "real" weekend and holidays. By working fixed hours then, we create a more or less regular life, with fixed times for eating and sleeping as well. By working normal working hours, say from 9 to 5—which is becoming increasingly rare for that matter—we moreover synchronise our life with the rest of society. In practice, this may mean that we are able to see our children, watch TV, join clubs and visit friends and family members, go to theatres and church, and so on. Work then acts as a "time giver" (in German *Zeitgeber*), an event acting as a marker that helps to set our clock. Though this may be not the most salient outcome of work at first sight, it certainly is something that we often miss dearly when we retire or lose our job. Our time is no longer punctuated. It just creeps on and it appears as if there are no real occasions to do anything special anymore.

2.4.5 Other Factors Underlying a Functional Work Situation

Some other factors (Schabracq et al., 2001) also influence the task as well as its immediate environment. The right level of these factors is necessary to keep the figure–ground configuration functional, i.e. to allow the task to bind our attention as if by itself. Similarly to the challenge inherent in the task, only the middle zone of these factors allows for a functional figure–ground configuration of work and work situation. Here too, "too much" or "too little" of such a factor affects the functionality of the work and the work situation in a negative way. This can be seen as an illustration of a very old and widespread ethical concept, namely "the narrow path of virtue" or "the golden mean". This is a central concept in the Nicomachean Ethics of Aristotle (1941) and Christian philosophy, as well as in classical Chinese philosophy.

We only point out these factors here briefly. In Chapter 3, we return to these in more detail. The first factor is orderliness. On the one hand, our work can become so chaotic that we cannot manage it any more, for instance as a result of a drastic, but ill-conceived job redesign. On the other hand, a task can be so overly orderly that it does not bind our attention enough. An example is the task of driving a car over an endless monotonous road. As for the department or organisation, chaos as well as too much emphasis on order and orderliness go at the expense of our task involvement also.

The other factors meant here are social embedding, safety and compatibility of the own values and goals with the organisational ones. For all three, there exists a middle zone that offers optimal conditions to task involvement, while the extremes, too little and too much, lead to task breakdown. This applies to the work task itself as well as its environment (see Chapter 3).

A fifth bipolar factor, of a somewhat different nature, is the degree to which work makes out an autonomous life realm. Too much implies that the work realm suppresses or interferes with the other life realms. Other life realms are for example our inner life, our home situation, our circle of friends and the public realm. Too much emphasis on working diminishes the positive outcomes of these other domains. As these outcomes are of influence on our general quality of functioning and well-being, their diminishment may affect the quality of our work negatively also. Too little means here that a preoccupation with another life realm interferes with our work. Both too little and too much represent a form of imbalance that may lead to trouble with good task performance (see Chapters 13 and 14).

2.4.6 Conclusion

All motivational factors described up to now help us to develop and maintain our integrity and its outcomes such as control, well-being and a sense of reality. We bring this about by the repetition of tasks and discipline of attention within the tasks, as well as by acts of signification, and the continuity stemming from all that. Work also helps to keep up our integrity in our other life domains. It does so by providing means (money, position, status and prestige) and some temporal structure, which enable us to maintain integrity there too, again by repetition, discipline of attention and acts of signification. In this respect, work may be one of the main providers of continuity and the sense of reality stemming from it.

This part of work happens to be reflected in the etymology of the word "reality"—and all comparable words in the Roman languages such as *réalité, realita, realidad* etc.—which stems from the adjective *realis* of the Latin substantive *res*, which means, among other things, "business". However, it becomes even clearer in the Dutch and German words *werkelijkheid* and *Wirklichkeit*, both meaning reality, where the stems *werk* and *wirk* correspond to the English "work". So, *werkelijkheid* is said to be derived from being busy with worldly good works (Van Dale, 1991).

Work is one of the important fundaments of reality; our relations with each other form another. To work and to love, *arbeiten und lieben*, as Freud stated, probably are the most important human activities indeed when it comes to manufacturing reality. Their common characteristic is that they give us anchors: they both provide some continuity and stability by providing us with a structure within which we can repeat ourselves. Another important influence here, which also provides anchors, consists of the results of all that work and those relations, the physical structures we erect and inhabit and all the gear and tools that we produce. These too are important providers of stimuli that we use to condition our own repetitious behaviour and discipline of attention. Lastly, there are the rules that can be derived from all that repetition and their underlying suppositions, as well as the stories that highlight them. Together this all makes out our culture, the reality that we share with each other. In Chapter 3 we return to these issues.

One last remark we want to make here is that all the factors described above presuppose a more or less stable status quo, which in its turn demands a more or less stable environment. Changes in the status quo and the environment would upset our integrity. A new orientation and adaptation would then become necessary. This usually makes the division of attention inherent in the work more problematic. As such, change is the main threat—and challenge, for that matter—to integrity. Something comparable may occur when we are no longer able and/or willing to attend to our work optimally because of some event. In the next section we go into that issue.

2.5 WHAT IS STRESS?

What is work stress? How is it activated? What effects and what stages can be distinguished?

In this chapter, work stress is considered to be a response to a loss or lack of control over our work performance. This leads to the following definition:

> Stress evolves when we must do something that we are not able and/or willing to do.

In a work context, this is related to the appropriateness of the work and its environment; that is, the degree to which they allow us to attend to the work and be involved in the work. In everyday practice, this appropriateness is a kind of middle zone. The next chapter gives an elaborate description of this middle zone in the case of the work environment—or in other words, the organisational culture. In general, it can be stated that a work environment that makes it too hard to keep our attention to the work leads to stress. The middle zone of the work itself can be described as an appropriate degree of challenge (Schabracq et al., 2001).

Work that becomes too challenging demands more knowledge, skills and abilities than we can mobilise. It becomes impossible to deal with the task in a systematic and orderly way. Chaos takes over, our involvement vanishes and task performance breaks down. As we lose control over our task performance, having to perform the task anyhow then becomes a serious stress source. This activates a primordial response pattern, which is only appropriate in situations that quickly demand intensive bodily activity, for examples in situations of life or death. In situations of a different kind, it can activate a lengthy vicious cycle, which affects our effectiveness, motivation and creativity. It can also isolate us and violate our well-being and health.

On the other hand, work that offers too little challenge to keep us involved (Goffman, 1963), while we must do it anyhow, demands from us that we force ourselves to stay involved. This soon becomes very tiring and we can go on in this way only for a limited time. Our attention wanders. We become bored and drowsy, and sometimes somewhat irritated. The work becomes less and less manageable, and this too can give rise to stress, though of a different quality than the kind of stress discussed above (as described later in this section, this essentially corresponds to the kind of stress of the second stage of a stress process).

2.5.1 The General Adaptation Syndrome

Stress is an old animal reaction pattern to adapt ourselves to life-threatening circumstances that we cannot manage with our normal behaviour patterns. Selye (1956) speaks of the "general adaptation process" and distinguishes three stages in it. The fact that we share this pattern with other animals implies that it is not attuned to the subtleties of our everyday life and work. The following three subsections describe a possible human variant of this pattern, focusing on a work context.

Stage 1

Our everyday life tends to be so repetitive and familiar that we perceive each interference or infraction almost immediately. When we assess such events as unwanted or even threatening, we then can consider what we can do about it (Lazarus, 1966). When there is nothing to be done about it immediately, we enter stage 1 of the general adaptation syndrome or stress process.

The disturbance binds our attention, keeps it focused and sharpens our senses. We tend to stop doing whatever we were doing and to confine ourselves more or less automatically to everything which is of importance within our favourite approach to this kind of problem, the one that suits us best and at which we are most adroit. Often, this approach becomes somewhat enlarged and exaggerated. This makes out our personal "pitfall" (Ofman, 1995). Such forms of exaggeration are not well attuned any more to the situational demands, often are irritating to others and imply a loss of creativity. Though these surely are stress reactions, we ourselves often do not experience them as such. We tend to find them normal and sometimes even familiar and pleasant reactions. It is important to recognise a pitfall as such: an exaggeration of a valuable characteristic. This makes it easier to relate to people who show these characteristics. Designating what irritates us as too much of something valuable is a powerful means to make that less irritating: "Of course, you only want . . . , but . . . ".

Preoccupied by a stress source, minding something else becomes a tiresome and fruitless undertaking. When this happens at our work, we usually are no longer able to keep our attention on our work tasks. This implies that we lose control over our activities. As our consciousness functions in a serial way—essentially it can process only one thing at a time—these activities make out our life at that moment. So, in a sense, we lose control over our life. This triggers a primordial emotional response pattern: we act as if we are in danger and our survival is at stake. Reserve energy is released to forcefully confront or avoid a potential life-threatening event. There are three of these response patterns, the so-called f-responses: either we become angry and are suddenly prepared to fight, or we get scared and are prepared to flee, or we freeze as we startle.

The logic behind fighting and fleeing is simple: there is a danger and we want to take it out or avoid it. The accompanying physiological changes enable our body to display the additional efforts needed for sudden, forceful activity. Freezing often comes before the two other f-responses. Here too, there is a quick mobilisation of the body for great activity, but by delaying action we give ourselves the freedom to collect more information to allow ourselves to reach a better decision. As such, freezing is, seen from an evolutionary perspective, the more advanced response. In the animal kingdom, fighting and fleeing can result in high costs. Fighting can lead to becoming wounded or even to death, while fleeing implies that the animal surrenders its own territory, which until then has provided sufficient food, protection and shelter.

Though the fight response is mostly suppressed, which usually leads to some physical tension, some stress reactions of stage 1 of the stress process are derivatives of the fight response. Examples are the feelings of anger and irritation, and accompanying behaviour such as threatening and openly accusing others, violent verbal reactions and biting sarcasm. Another familiar example at the workplace is a heightened sense of territory. This expresses itself in striving for control over our environment, seeing something as an infraction at an earlier stage than usual and unexpectedly violent defensive reactions (Bernstein & Craft Rozen, 1989). This applies to everything we experience as our own, so also to our rights, privileges and claims. This inflated need for control is expressed in being easily diverted and irritated, for instance by other people's talking, laughing, smoking or restlessness. Other manifestations are being overly irritated by traces of other people's presence. Examples are a coat on a chair, dirty coffee cups and ashtrays, clutter and stains. These are all taken as signs that our territory is violated and defiled. Though being angry actually may feel good, it obviously is at the expense of functioning flexibly in a work context.

Stress reactions stemming from the flight response are mostly suppressed as well, which also leads to physical tension. Though derivatives of the flight response occur also, they usually are less clearly recognisable. Examples are non-verbal behavioural elements such as gaze direction (looking at where we want to go, at somebody from whom we expect protection or at our watch, as well as quickly alternating gaze directions). Other examples are all kinds of intention movements such as shuffling, posture changes, placing our hand on our upper legs or chair arms, changing our bodily inclination and orientation.

Another, somewhat neglected, aspect of flight is that we flee to some destination, a place where we expect protection, help and consolation, from each other or from someone more powerful than us. However, this demands some extra activity from the fleeing party. This is about presenting ourselves as desirable, displaying flattery, admiration and veneration, complaining, gossiping and making furtive accusations, as well as non-verbal reactions such as much smiling and nodding. This enables some of us to maintain ourselves in an otherwise uncontrollable environment. Such conduct demands much attention and can interfere with our actual work. Some people however are so good at this that they experience no stress at all. They even enjoy it and prosper in environments where this is the main game. There, they also are valued for this. This happens for instance in environments where power and status are more important than products, and orderliness and the way people relate draw the most attention.

A characteristic of the f-responses is that they give evidence of much energy. Which f-response occurs and how intense it is depends of course on the events and person in question. There are great individual differences in this respect (Chapter 5). This is about the nature of the response, the easiness and quickness with which it is evoked, the events that evoke it, its extensiveness and the time that it remains active. Some people find especially the fight response pleasurable, also at their work. Well-proven methods to evoke it are doing many things at the same time, taking up each challenge and pushing everybody aside when it is about action ("Where is the fire?"). In the stress literature, these people are called "type A" persons. In some organisations, such employees are highly valued and are glad to set good examples to each other.

As said before, the f-responses are global emotional response patterns, mostly suited to deal with certain life-threatening events. However, in our work, our life seldom is threatened really. Usually, it is much more a matter of being unable or not willing to keep our attention on our work, while we still have to do so. Most of the time, this makes the f-responses at our work only cumbersome: sitting hollow-eyed and startled behind our desks does not help. The same applies to biting or kicking the boss, or fleeing from the office building. So we have to suppress these responses. This demands extra attention and effort, while our activation does not diminish, and that in a difficult or even threatening situation. This makes it more difficult to handle the situation well. Moreover, we often find it difficult to calm down and to sleep well. In addition, the normal maintenance and recovery of the body occur at a lower level.

Sometimes, stage 1 is skipped more or less in a work context. In such cases, we do not experience this stage at all. This occurs when it is obvious from the start that the work has little to offer to bind our attention. Many people then are inclined to go along, especially when their new colleagues do not appear to be overly concerned about this. Trying to make a change here might be taken as moaning. Obviously, this is how it is, at least as long as we cannot find another job. Such work then soon leads to a kind of adaptation resembling stage 2 of the stress process.

Stage 2

Stage 2 is about dealing with threatening or interfering circumstances that we cannot change in a significant way. We pay as little as possible attention to these circumstances and their effects. They become "normal" to us. The work is still cumbersome, but we go along. We work as much as possible around the problems and deny what is going on. Still, our overall effectiveness, motivation and creativity decrease.

As an effect, we limit ourselves to a smaller world, in which not much happens. We pay as little as possible attention to the people and events that might agitate or threaten us. All this is at the expense of our creativity and our possibilities to learn. Options to do something new mostly pass unnoticed and when we do notice them, we do not make any use of them:

we pass many opportunities. Our feelings become shallower also. Sometimes, there is still a flare of irritation, or another unexpected intense feeling—grief for instance—but most of the time, we do not feel much. Gradually, the positive, motivating feelings, including those for others, disappear. By this, the forms of learning based on reward and need satisfaction disappear also. Pleasure is gone. The same applies to our motivation to do our work as well as possible. What remains are vague feelings of alienation or depression.

The diminishing interest in other people often leads to avoidance of social contacts. Forced to interact with others, we tend to behave more impersonally and rudely than we usually do. Essentially, this is a primitive form of self-defence: because we cannot deal with others appropriately, we keep them at a distance in this way. All this can lead to conflicts, with members of the organisation, but also with outsiders such as customers. This may lead to more stress. It also interferes with our relationships—as far as they still exist—and this makes that their outcomes wither away as well. This is foremost a matter of emotional support and outcomes of our informal power position in the organisation (getting and giving help, information, means and people; see Chapter 3). As it is, the avoidance of social interaction appears to be more a male than a female reaction. Taylor et al. (2000) show that women tend to cope with stress in the opposite way, namely by interacting more (in Weusten, 2000). As such, women tend to be more successful in coping with stress than men.

Another part of the responses in stage 2 is that we display now and then a strange kind of personality change. We behave in a way we always have suppressed, opposite to how we always wanted to be and have presented ourselves, a behavioural style that has always irritated us in other persons also. In terms of Jung (1970), this is about our "shadow side", in terms of Ofman (1995) about our "allergy". A playful joker can become a rigid dogmatic, or somebody who suddenly wants a safe and conventional life. Another example is the woman who always has made a point of helping and pleasing other people, who now suddenly transforms into a sadistic and unscrupulous shrew, or into somebody who suddenly finds rules more important than people. A final example is a real performer, who changes into a hesitant coward or an ineffective melancholic.

A last point to be made about stage 2 is that hormones play a role here too, especially those of the adrenal cortex. We still live on spare energy. Maintenance and recovery of our body still have low priority. Moreover, our immunity gradually is going to function less appropriately and we become more susceptible to all kinds of illnesses and afflictions.

Stage 3

Stage 3 is the stage of the breakdown. We are no longer able to focus our attention in such a way that we can still go on working at some level. Our performance breaks down. There are several scenarios here.

The most favourable scenario is that we chuck our work in time: we cannot bring our-selves to work around the difficulties any more. Often, we already have become distant, impersonal or rude in dealing with other people. Attention is not to be disciplined any more. We feel very tired and do not want to go on. We realise that we have given everything we have got and have received very little in exchange. As far as there are feelings, they are about indignation and resentment, to our manager and our organisation, as well as relief that it is all over now. Two things we know for sure: we will never let things go this far again, and for the time being they will not see us again at our work. I speak here of burnout, though this term is used in rather diverse ways (see also Chapter 19).

Another scenario is that a serious disease or affliction overtakes us. This may be a matter of weakened immunity, which can lead to an increased chance of all kinds of infections and cancers. As stress also leads to an increased cholesterol level in our blood vessels, it may also lead to afflictions such as heart and brain infarcts. Moreover, stress also may lead to high blood pressure and consequently to a brain haemorrhage or stroke (see Chapter 4, for a much more detailed overview). Another possible outcome consists of the kind of functional illnesses that effectively prevent us from doing our work. Examples are ME (fatigue syndrome) and RSI (repetitive strain injury).

Also, we run a higher risk of having an accident. Different causes can play a part here. Stress can be at the expense of our motor suppleness, with all inherent consequences. It can also affect the division of our attention, so that we overlook certain dangers. Moreover, stress may induce some people to take greater risks, while the increased use of medicines and alcohol by some people does not help to prevent accidents either.

Lastly, recovery—both from illnesses and accidents—usually will be relatively slow, because of the bad shape we are in at this stage.

A third scenario is that we simply cannot go on anymore. Complete exhaustion takes over and working is out of the question. Recovery usually takes a very long time then. In Japan, the phenomenon of *kiroshi* exists, sudden death caused by excessive overtime (and stress, and a totally unbalanced life etc.).

2.5.2   Stress as a Self-Enhancing Process

The emotions, the division of attention and the excitement accompanying stress at the work-place make it harder to deal with our work appropriately. Stress reactions usually are seen as inappropriate or abnormal. They can interfere with the normal way of affairs and evoke disapproval, irritation and avoidance among colleagues. This can make it more difficult to keep our attention on our work. In addition, stress reactions do not tend to take away the stress causes. Lastly, we try to suppress these reactions as much as possible, which implies an additional attack on our available mental resources. All in all, stress reactions only make it more difficult to keep our attention on our work. Apparently, stress reactions are not only effects of stress, but can also be causes of stress: stress processes tend to enhance themselves.

All this does not make one happy. However, we should realise that here the most unrestrained forms of a stress process have been discussed. Then again, stress is not an incurable illness that has to run its course. Stress is a choice.

2.6   STRESS PROBLEMS AS SIGNALS

As long as integrity prevails, we are able and willing to do the work that we have to do. However, things may happen that interfere with our integrity. These may be factors in our working tasks, in our work environment and in ourselves. As a result, it becomes difficult or even impossible to do our work. This may be a matter of not being able to attend to our work, of not willing to attend to it, or both. If we still have to do our work, this implies that we lose control over our own functioning. This may be the start of a stress process.

Stress begins at the moment that we must do something that we are not able and/or willing to do. This implies a serious loss of control, which our mammalian brain interprets as a threat to our existence. It responds by activating a biological process that we share with all other vertebrates. This, however, is only appropriate in situations that quickly demand intensive bodily action. Seen from a biological perspective, this is primarily about life and death situations. In situations of a different kind, such as at our work site, this process is less appropriate and can activate a lengthy vicious cycle. This negatively affects our effectiveness, motivation and creativity, isolates us and violates our well-being and health.

Though stress has gradually become something like a modern manifestation of evil in general, it may have a positive value too. At the level of our own life, we can interpret being troubled by stress problems as a signal that we apparently have to do something that we are not able and/or do not want to do. Some form of (self-) examination and some study of the environment may then help us to find out what exactly is going on and what we can do about it. What matters here is that we can use our own complaints as a signal that we have to change something, either in our environment or in ourselves. In this way, recognition of stress reactions can offer us an entrance to personal development and growth. This process fits in well with emotional functioning in general as described by Frijda (1986, p. 229):

> like and dislike, pleasantness and unpleasantness . . . are expressions of match and mis-match with sensitivities and set-points, embedded in behavior systems. They are, in principle, useful signals, for learning what situations to seek or avoid in the future and, more directly, for beginning or pursuing a given course of action, for terminating action or changing tacks.

The same idea of stress as a signal can be applied to an organisational context as well. Here too, such complaints can have an important signalling function. Work stress for instance is evoked foremost when employees find it impossible to keep their attention to their work sufficiently, because they are unable and/or unwilling to do so. So, many stress complaints at a clearly described spot in the organisation make clear that it is difficult there, or even down-right impossible, to focus attention on the work at hand in a self-evident way. Apparently, something is the matter there, and probably something that has more undesired effects than just the individual stress complaints. As such, it may indicate that the present adaptation of the organisation to the environment is troublesome. When we speak of a clearly described spot, we can think for instance of a certain department, job, group of jobs or a certain floor.

In Schabracq et al. (2001), where we introduced the idea of stress as a signal, we talk in this context about the human mine canary. This is a little bird in a cage, which coal miners used to take with them into the mine to detect firedamp, a highly explosive gas mixture. To this end, the cage was put on the floor of a mine gallery. As firedamp is heavier than air, its presence would deprive the bird of oxygen and it would suffocate. When the bird fell off its perch, this was the signal to leave the mine as fast as possible (and its happy whistling an encouragement to light up a cigarette). This is not meant to be plea to hire an employee who is extra sensitive to stress. However, it is an admonition to pay attention when somebody goes down and to find out what is going on.

So mapping stress complaints with the help of interviews and surveys can be used as a technique to trace bottlenecks, other systemic errors in the organisation and possible solutions and improvements. In this way, we make it possible to learn something about the systemic causes and other coinciding problems as well. This then may enable us to solve not only the individual complaints, but also to make structural improvements at the level of these causes. This opens up possibilities for a better adaptation to the outside world in general also.

The general objective of such interventions is to enable the employees involved to keep their attention on the work in a self-evident and pleasurable way. In realising this objective, the most important guidelines are challenging the organisation and its employees to strive in their work for:

- more creativity, as well as more personal and professional development of those involved;
- better relationships and a better social climate;
- more work pleasure and higher motivation;
- greater effectiveness and better production quality.

REFERENCES

Achterhuis, H. (1984) *Arbeid, een eigenaardig medicijn* [*Labour, A Peculiar Medicine*]. Baarn: Ambo.

Amsel, A. (1992) *Frustration Theory*. Cambridge: Cambridge University Press.

Arendt, H. (1958) *The Human Condition*. Chicago, IL: University of Chicago Press.

Aristotle (1941) *The Basic Works of Aristotle*. New York: Random House.

Ashcraft, N. & Scheflen, A.E. (1976) *People Space*. Garden City, NY: Anchor Press/Doubleday.

Baudouin, C. (1924) *Psychologie de la suggestion et de l'autosuggestion* [*Psychology of Suggestion and Autosuggestion*], 4th edn. Neuchâtel: Editions Delachaux & Niestlé.

Bellow, S. (1982) *The Dean's December*. New York: Pocket Books.

Berne, E. (1966) *Principles of Group Treatment*. Oxford: Oxford University Press.

Bernstein, A.J. & Craft Rozen, S. (1989) *Dinosaur Brains*. New York: Ballantine.

Birdwhistell, J. (1972) *Kinesics and Context*. Harmondsworth: Penguin.

Bolen, J.S. (1989) *Gods in Everyman*. San Francisco, CA: Harper & Row.

Bourdieu, P. (1989) *Opstellen over smaak, habitus en het veldbegrip*. [*Essays about Taste, "Habitus" and the Concept of Field*]. Amsterdam: Van Gennep.

Breznitz, S. (1983) The seven kinds of denial. In S. Breznitz (ed.) *The Denial of Stress*. New York: International Universities Press, pp. 257–80.

Bühler, K. (1924) *Die geistige Entwicklung des Kindes* [*The Spiritual Development of the Child*], 4th edn. Jena: G. Fischer.

Buitendijk, F.J.J. (1948) *Algemene theorie der menselijke houding en beweging* [*General Theory of Human Posture and Movement*]. Utrecht: Het Spectrum.

Burns, E. (1973) *Theatricality*. New York: Harper & Row.

Cofer, C.N. & Appley, M.H. (1964) *Motivation: Theory and Research*. New York: Wiley.

Csikszentmihalyi, M. (1988) Introduction. In M. Csikszentmihalyi and I.S. Csikszentmihalyi (eds) *Optimal Experiences*. Cambridge: Cambridge University Press.

Van Dale (1991) *Etymologisch woordenboek der Nederlandse taal*. [*Etymological Dictionary of the Dutch Language*]. Den Haag: M. Nijhoff.

Dorpat, T.L. (1985) *Denial and Defence in the Therapeutic Situation*. New York: Aronson.

Durkheim, E. (1925) *Les formes elementaires de la vie religieuse*. (*The Elementary Forms of Religious Life*), 2nd edn. Paris: F. Alcan.

Eibl-Eibesfeldt, I. (1970) *Ethology, The Biology of Behavior*. New York: Holt, Rinehart & Winston.

Emlen, J.T., Jr (1958) Defended area? A critique of occasion, territory concept and of conventional thinking. *Ibis*, **99**, 352.

Erickson, M.H., Rossi, E.J. & Rossi, S.I. (1976) *Hypnotic Realities*. London, John Wiley & Sons.

Erikson, E. (1968). *Youth, Identity and Crisis*. New York: Norton.

Freud, A. (1964) *Das Ich und die Abwehrmechanismen* [*The Ego and the Defence Mechanisms*]. München: Kindler & Schiermeyer Verlag.

Fromm, E. (1955) *The Sane Society*. New York: Rinehart.

Frijda, N.H. (1986) *The Emotions*. Cambridge: Cambridge University Press.

Gibson, J.J. (1979) *The Ecological Approach to Visual Perception*. Boston, MA: Houghton Mifflin.

Goffman, E. (1963) *Behavior in Public Places*. Glencoe, IL: Prentice Hall.

Goffman, E. (1972) *Encounters*. Harmondsworth: Penguin.

Goffman, E. (1974) *Frame Analysis*. New York: Harper & Row.

Goleman, D. (1988) *The Meditative Mind*. Los Angeles, CA: J.P. Tarcher.

Haberman, J. (1994) *The God I Believe in*. New York: Free Press.

Hackman, J.R. & Oldham, G.R. (1980) *Work Redesign*. Reading, MA: Addison-Wesley.

Hebb, D.O. (1966) *A Textbook of Psychology*. Philadelphia, PA: Saunders.

James, W. (1890/1950) *The Principles of Psychology*, vols I & II. New York: Dover.

Jung, C.G (1970) *Civilization in Transition*. Princeton, NJ: Princeton University Press.

Karasek, R.A. & Theorell, T. (1990) *Healthy Work. Stress, Productivity and the Reconstruction of Working Life*. New York: Basic Books.

Kaufman, J.H. (1971) Is territoriality definable? In A.H. Esser (ed.) *Behavior and Environment*. New York: Plenum Press, pp. 36–40.

Köhler, W. (1947) *Gestalt Psychology*. New York: New American Library.

Kompier, M.A.J. & Cooper, C.L. (eds) (1999) *Preventing Stress, Improving Productivity. European Sudies in the Workplace*. London: Routledge.

Kompier, M.A.J., Gründemann, R.W.M., Vink, P. & Smulders, P.G.W. (1996) *Aan de slag [Get Going]*. Alphen aan de Rijn: Samsom Bedrijfsinformatie.

Krijnen, M.A. (1993) *Onderzoek WAO-Instroom 1991, AH-Operations* [*Study Influx Disablement Insurance Act 1991, AH-Operations*]. Amsterdam: University of Amsterdam.

Laborde, G.Z. (1987) *Influencing with Integrity*. Palo Alto, CA: Syntony.

Lazarus, R.A. (1966) *Psychological Stress and the Coping Process*. New York: McGraw-Hill.

Lecky, P. (1945) *Self-Consistency: A Theory of Personality*. New York: Island Press.

Luce, G. (1972) Biological rhythms. In R.E. Ornstein (ed.) *The Nature of Human Consciousness*. San Francisco, CA: W.H. Freeman, pp. 421–44.

Lindsey, P.H. & Norman, D.A. (1977). *Human Information Processing*. London: Academic Press.

Meijman, T.F. (1991) *Over vermoeidheid [About fatigue]*, dissertation, University of Amsterdam.

Moscovici, S. (1984) The phenomenon of social representation. In R.M. Farr & S. Moscovici (eds) *Social Representations*. Cambridge: Cambridge University Press, pp. 3–69.

Ofman, D.D. (1995) *Bezieling en kwaliteit in organisaties*. [*Inspiration and Quality in Organisations*]. Cothen: Servire.

Ouwerkerk, R. van; Meijman, T. & Mulder, B. (1994) *Arbeidspsychologie en taakanalyse* [*Work Psychology and Task Analysis*]. Utrecht: Lemma.

Ovsiankina, M. (1928) Die Wiederaufnahme von unterbrochenen Handlungen [Resuming interrupted Acts]. *Psychologische Forschungen* [*Psychological Studies*], **11**, 302–89.

Perls, F., Goodman, R.F. & Hefferline, P. (1951) *Gestalt Therapy*. New York: Delta Books.

Rowell, T. (1972) *Social Behaviour of Monkeys*. Harmondsworth: Penguin.

Rümke, H.C. (1939) *Levenstijdperken van de man* [*Life Stages of Man*]. Amsterdam: De Arbeiderspers.

Schabracq, M.J. (1987) *Betrokkenheid en onderlinge gelijkheid in sociale interacties* [*Involvement and Mutual Similarity in Social Interaction*], dissertation, University of Amsterdam.

Schabracq, M.J. (1991) *De inrichting van de werkelijkheid. Over de relatie tussen situaties en personen* [*The Design of Reality. About the Relation between Situations and Persons*]. Meppel: Boom.

Schabracq, M.J. (1992) Sociale representaties en sociale psychologie [Social Representations and Social Psychology]. *Psychologie en maatschappij* [*Psychology and Society*], **16**, 123–32.

Schabracq, M.J. & Boerlijst, G. (1992) Oudere medewerkers [Elderly Employees]. In J.A.M. Winnubst & M.J. Schabracq (eds) *Handboek "Arbeid en Gezondheid"-Psychologie. Hoofdthema's* [*Handbook Work and Health Psychology: Main Themes*] Utrecht: Lemma, pp. 92–105.

Schabracq, M.J., Maassen Van den Brink, H., Groot, W., Janssen, P. & Houkes, I. (2000). *De prijs van stress* [*The Price of Stress*]. Maarsen: Elsevier.

Schabracq, M.J., Cooper, C.L., Travers, C. & van Maanen, D. (2001) *Occupational Health Psychology: The Challenge of Workplace Stress*. Leicester: British Psychological Society.

Scheflen, A.E. (1973) *Communicational Structure*. Bloomington, IN: Indiana University Press.

Schipper, K. (1988) *Tao: de levende religie* [*Tao: The Living Religion*]. Amsterdam: Meulenhoff.

Schneider, B. (1987) The people make the place. *Personnel Psychology*, **40**, 437–53.

Schutz, A. (1970) *On Phenomenology and Social Relations*. Chicago, IL: University of Chicago Press.

Selye, H. (1956) *The Stress of Life*. New York: McGraw-Hill.

Shallice, T. (1978) The dominant action system: an information-processing approach to consciousness. In K.S. Pope and J.L. Singer (eds) *The Stream of Consciousness*. New York: Plenum Press.

Taylor, S.E., Cousino Klein, L., Lewis, B.P., Gruenewald, T.L, Gurung, R.A.R & Updegraff, J.A. (2000) Biobehavioral responses to stress in females: tend-and-befriend, not fight-or-flight. *Psychological Review*, **107**, 3, 411–29.

Weusten, S. (2000). Koesteren en kleppen [*Fostering and jabbering*]. *Psychologie Magazine*, **19** (12), 22–3.

Woodworth, R.S. & Schlosberg, H. (1954) *Experimental Psychology*, rev. edn. New York: Holt.

Zeigarnik, B. (1927) Über das Behalten von erledigten und unerledigten Handlungen [About the conservation of completed and uncompleted acts]. *Psychologische Forschungen* [*Psychological Studies*], **9**, 1–85.

CHAPTER 3

Organisational Culture, Stress and Change

Marc J. Schabracq

University of Amsterdam, The Netherlands

3.1 INTRODUCTION

In this chapter, we look at the relations between organisational culture and stress. Also, we have a look at the impact of change and what might be done about this. We start by describing a number of characteristics and functions of organisational cultures, the most important function probably being providing standardised solutions to the recurring problems of the organisation. We go into some imperfections of organisational cultures, which usually lead to stress problems of individual employees. We discuss how change affects organisational cultures and introduce the concept of functionality of working tasks and their environment. Functionality is here considered as the degree to which the organisation allows the employees to divide their attention in such a way that they can perform their tasks appropriately.

Four processes or variables underlying functionality are described. These are orderliness, social embedding, compatibility of convictions and values, and safety. Generally speaking, only the middle ranges of these variables allow for functionality. Too much or too little of each of them interferes with functionality, and may lead to stress reactions in individual employees. For each of these four variables, we give examples of what too much or too little looks like. In the discussion, we briefly examine the effects of change on each of these four variables. We also discuss what can be done to counteract the undesired effects of change, per variable and in a more general way.

3.2 WHAT IS ORGANISATIONAL CULTURE?

It is very hard, if not impossible, to define organisational culture in a single sentence. Instead of trying to come up with a brilliant one-sentence definition, we here follow Parsons' ideas about the problems each organisational culture has to solve in order to survive.

The Handbook of Work and Health Psychology. Edited by M.J. Schabracq, J.A.M. Winnubst and C.L. Cooper.

3.2.1 Parsons' Functions

These problems and their corresponding functions have been grouped by Parsons into four categories (Parsons, 1960; Smit, 1997):

- goal attainment
- adaptation
- integration
- latency and pattern maintenance.

We take a brief look at each of these functions here, while the next section can be seen as an elaboration of the latency function.

Goal Attainment

An organisation has a reason for being there: it is there to accomplish something or to manufacture certain products. In business terms, it must have a mission. Essentially, it must provide something that the environment needs or at least wants to have. This gives the organisation its purpose, and also its general form and direction. This involves an orientation on the future, sometimes in the form of a "vision", a picture of an ideal future to be realised in a well-specified number of years. In short, an organisation must have goals or there is no organisation. It also means that its activities are essentially goal-directed.

Adaptation

An organisation can only exist in an environment. Apart from formally logical reasons, it needs its environment for its survival. The environment provides raw materials, employees and everything else it needs, while it buys its products and sees to its overall needs of safety etc. Very important also, the environment must provide the money to go on, grow, pay expenses and make a profit. So, an organisation has to adapt to that environment, that is to say to its resources, its contingencies, its weaknesses and the changes in it, or it will not survive.

Integration

A third set of problems centres around the internal structure, the division of roles and the cooperation between different persons and departments. This essentially is the problem of becoming one organism, a whole that has more to offer that the sum of its separate parts. An organisation that does not create synergy and does not deliver a surplus value in this respect usually has no reason to exist at all.

Latency and Pattern Maintenance

The last problem is how to integrate the former three sets of problems in such a way that all occurring problems are actually met and solved, without having to invent the wheel each time anew. As most of the latency problems stem from permanent causes, these problems tend to present themselves as being recurrent and repetitious. Consequently, they can be solved each time in a similar way. This leads to another essential characteristic of organisational cultures: an organisational culture provides recurrent solutions to recurrent problems. We continuously re-enact, re-construct, re-cognise, re-present and re-cite the forms and meanings of culture, and abstain from other possibilities (Moscovici, 1984). We even re-create ourselves. This continuous repetition is similar to the endless repetition in our own individual lives, described in Chapter 2. Much of this repetitious character stays out of our awareness. We just do it, do not pay attention to other possibilities and ignore that we do not pay attention. In this way, a latent structure of repetitive forms comes into being, by which, we create stability and continuity, as well as normality and reality. If this integration is insufficiently realised, the organisation falls apart.

3.2.2 Latency and Pattern Maintenance

Flaws and Lacunas

Failures or weak points in solving each group of problems lead to problems for the overall organisation, but also for individual employees. For instance, changes in the environment can make an organisational culture clearly dysfunctional and obsolete. The same applies to problems in the area of goal attainment, the attuning of parts, and the creation of stability and continuity. When these problems are not solved, each of them can seriously undermine the effectiveness of the organisation. As such, they may lead to individual stress complaints. The frequent occurrence of stress problems may be a signal that one or more of these functions are not fulfilled sufficiently (see Chapter 2). Though these problems stem from all four kinds of problems, all of them ultimately can be described as latency problems. Here, we examine some of these flaws of organisational culture.

A major flaw of organisational culture may consist of incompatible sets of rules, seemingly based on a contradiction between the axioms underlying the organisational culture. As a result, the organisational culture shows inconsistencies, which undermine its reality and create difficulties for the employees. A familiar instance of such an incompatibility is seen in the contradiction between the "official" culture, the so-called "espoused theory" and the actual culture, the "theory in use" (Schon, 1983). The first often advertises all kinds of morally and ethically correct views and approaches, while the second appears to be much more down to earth and certainly less ethically correct. An example is a hospital that states that it exists to give its patients the best possible care, but actually tries to keep its beds filled at the lowest possible cost per bed. The value conflicts that this may cause form one of the causes of severe stress and burnout problems, especially in organisations that attract highly ethically driven personnel such as schools, hospitals and churches (Cherniss, 1995; Maslach & Leiter, 1997). Though it is open to discussion whether this is really a matter of conflicting axioms, as the "theory in use" actually can be seen as the only "true" culture around, this is often not obvious to all members.

Though solving problems more or less automatically is a basic characteristic of organisational cultures, which has great positive outcomes, it also has a less desirable consequence. Once we have stumbled upon a feasible solution, we usually take it up in our repertory and do not question it any more. In this way, we often settle for "just good enough" solutions. These solutions do the trick, though they are often far from optimal. However, they do not create a major constraint in the organisation (Goldratt, 1990), as long as other factors are much more critical in this respect. The same principle also plays a role in biological evolution. Calvin (1992) gives the following example of such a "just good enough" solution. Ducks are relatively slow when it comes to gathering food in the water. In order to stay afloat, they have little glands under their wings, which keep their wings oily, making them water-repellent. Cormorants, being proficient fishers, are much more efficient in collecting sufficient food in a very short period of time. As there is no need for them to grow oil glands under their wings to prevent them from sinking, they just sit for hours with their wings spread to dry them. Until they get hungry and dive into the water again. Turning again to organisational culture, good enough solutions can become a source of trouble in times when change is necessary.

Other flaws stem from the fact that each organisational culture, as a treasury of standard solutions for standard problems, also has its unproductive standard explanations, solutions and blind spots (Argyris, 1983). These have their own rhetoric, which makes them sound as if we are talking about the effects of a law of nature, which are "really" too simple to explain. The blind spots involve certain problems, as well as certain options and solutions, which go against prevailing rules or assumptions. In general, they resemble the forms of denial mentioned in Chapter 2, in the sense that people from outside the organisation usually do not find it difficult to spot immediately what is denied or overlooked. In Schabracq et al. (2001), a number of examples are given.

These unproductive standard explanations, solutions and blind spots especially come to the fore when something goes wrong for which the organisational culture does not have an adaptive approach. These then are used to deny that things have gone wrong at all. Their general logic is something like: "There is no problem because there cannot be a problem. No, it is only a matter of . . . , and we should just . . . ". These reactions can aggravate problems of individual employees who actually are bothered by these problems. As such, these reactions may lead to stress, also because they put these employees in an impossible situation, without logic and reality value. These unproductive standard explanations, solutions and blind spots are also used when the organisational culture is threatened by an imposed change. We come back to this later in this section.

Another flaw in the effectiveness of organisational culture stems from the fact that the culture determines also what we don't do in our organisation, and also what we should not say, think and feel about it (Ryan & Oestreicher, 1988). The culture determines in this way, at least to a certain degree, what is impossible, unthinkable and unspeakable within the organisation (Schabracq et al., 2001, give some examples). As a result, we cannot apply or follow certain solutions, approaches and policies. This may also be the case when these are clearly the best options, not only to "objective" outsiders, but also to members of the organisation who honestly are of the opinion that "the only thing is that this is just impossible in this organisation". Some options are even considered to be unthinkable. We are not supposed to put these into words—unless as a joke in bad taste—because they are incompatible with the organisational frame of reference. Lastly, there are the "unspeakables", options that we can talk about, but only with reliable and familiar colleagues, and certainly not with those who can make a difference on this issue. As we are talking about the consequences of deeply rooted suppositions, effectively doing something about impossibilities, unthinkables or unspeakables implies a serious change of the organisational culture.

Usually, these mechanisms only become manifest—or at least are felt to exist—if there is a serious problem in that area, but even then they prevent us from effectively dealing with that problem. As such, these mechanisms can keep these problems alive. Moreover, they also undermine the everyday reality and normality reality of the organisation, and may induce stress reactions in individual employees.

Resistance to Change

Though organisational cultures show a certain development and in that sense allow for some change, they essentially tend to minimise change. As a repertory of standard solutions to standard problems, it is only logical that an organisational culture aims at stability and continuity. This is also why an organisational culture is such an excellent provider of reality and normality to its members. However, this goes one step further: organisational cultures actively resist external pressure to change, even when it is about changes for the best, at least from an outside perspective. To understand this, we have to look at what happens in this respect at the level of the individual employees.

As employees, we have all invested a lot of effort in acquiring our present skills and their outcomes. These have become a part of us, and a self-evident one at that. As a result, we experience pressure to change these adaptations as infractions on our own identity and reality, certainly when these changes are forced on us from without. This may evoke stress reactions in us, involving all kinds of unpleasant emotions. Generally speaking, we prefer to prevent and avoid such a state of mind. Also—at the level of the content of the change—we know what we have, not what we are going to get. This response to having to give up our familiar ways of doing resembles the reactions of animals when their territory is invaded (see Chapter 2).

We are not alone in these feelings. We share them with many of our colleagues. It feels only logical to support each other on this one. This can make our resistance surprisingly effective and well coordinated. Our impossibles, unthinkables and unspeakables turn out to be effective tools to reach a common point of view about the impending changes. Our main weaponry here consists of the arsenal of already mentioned unproductive standard explanations, solutions and blind spots. As these are shared among members of all ranks of the organisation, we are convinced that these represent valid points of view. However, the people who have to implement a change usually have little understanding of these arguments or blind spots. To them, this all sounds stupid, if not completely disturbed. In their eyes, we—the employees—are acting like little children. The problem here is that seeing and treating us as little children or disturbed persons does not make it simpler to convince us. It only helps to get us into a conflict, with all the accompanying emotions, followed by our refusal of all communication. In such a way, the organisational culture is often successful in stalling the intended change or stopping it altogether.

What exactly will happen, of course, depends on the support we can organise. If that is insufficient, the change will be brought about anyhow, much to our dislike. We have lost, obviously betrayed by colleagues and bosses, whom we trusted. Such a course of events usually has serious and long-lasting effects on our well-being and health.

3.2.3 Change

It appears to be only natural for organisational cultures to fight change. However, seen from an adaptation perspective, this might be a deadly course. The point is that the occurrence of change in our environment has increased, and still is increasing, enormously and at an accelerating pace. This obviously is related to the globalisation of our economy and technology, and the enormously accelerated development of the latter in various areas. The other factors that usually determine the environment of our organisations—such as sociocultural and political–juridical developments—can only follow (Schabracq & Cooper, 2000; see also Chapter 29).

Many companies have only one option, namely adapting, as fast as they can. This means using the last technological developments and attuning to the demands that these develop-ments generate. It also implies other ways of working, producing and organising. To the employees, it means different contracts, permanent education and new ways of training and learning. Moreover, they are faced by all kinds of reorganisations, mergers, management buy-outs, outsourcing, and so on. Though this does not apply equally to all organisations to the same degree, it has become clear that employees everywhere are confronted more and more with changes they did not ask for.

These changes upset the existing latency functions of organisational cultures, their way of solving recurring problems in recurring ways. The once standardised problems change rapidly and we need new solutions. These new solutions then have to be integrated in a new form of pattern maintenance. Though the question is whether this kind of integration is possible at all, change has become the normal state of affairs in many organisations. We might state that this is an anomaly or even a perversion of our culture, but that statement is not very helpful when it comes to adapting to these changes.

As these are also exactly the kinds of changes that evoke stress reactions, in the next section we look at what causes stress in organisations. So, we describe four factors—already mentioned in Chapter 2—of which the middle zones allow us to share the relatively stress-free reality of a functional organisational culture. Later on, we briefly examine the effects of change on these factors.

3.3 FUNCTIONALITY

In Chapter 2, we described that not being able and/or willing to attend to tasks that we still have to perform leads to stress problems. Acting in integrity becomes difficult or im-possible. The reality inherent in the working task tends to dissolve. We lose some control over our own functioning and environment, and this may start up a stress process. This combination—of having to do something and not being able and/or willing to do it—is determined for a large part by the working task itself and its environment; that is, the department and the organisation. As such, organisational culture is a crucial determinant of working stress. The degree to which the organisational culture allows us to divide our attention in such a way that we are able and willing to do our work properly we call the functionality of that organisational culture. A culture that allows for optimal task perfor-mance we call highly functional; a culture that makes task performance impossible highly dysfunctional.

In this section, we examine four variables that influence the latency and pattern main-tenance functions of organisational culture. These four variables affect both the working task itself and its environment. As such, they are important determinants of the culture's functionality. As these variables impact our division of attention, they determine the at-tention that we are able and willing to pay to our working task, and—by that—our risk of stress reactions. The middle range of all these variables is conducive to functionality (see Chapter 2 for an elaboration of this principle of the middle zone). "Too much" or "too little" of each of these implies a lower functionality. What exactly is too much or too little varies, of course, for each individual. Though we do not go into individual differences in this section, such differences play an important role. What is too much or too little for some people may be exactly right for others (see Chapter 5).

These four variables have been derived from Salomon Asch (1971), who formulated them as criteria for the reality of hypnotic trance, with the distinct purpose to prove that such a trance essentially is a very common phenomenon. We agree with Asch, but we also think that in his rejection of hypnotic trance, he touched upon four variables that more or less underlie every functional reality. This is about the following variables:

- orderliness
- social embedding
- compatibility of values and goals
- safety.

In this chapter, we only describe processes within the organisation and do not consider the spill-over between work and the other life realms, which also can be of influence on the experienced functionality and reality of working life. We just want to emphasise here how all-important a well-balanced life is—that is, a life in which our work doesn't chew up all our time and attention. This is not only to be nice. This is also about the importance of the positive outcomes of sufficient attention for these other life realms. These outcomes, such as loving and being loved, taking care and being taken care of, are of paramount importance to the functionality of our work, especially when it comes to coping with change. The same applies to the outcomes of spending enough time in physical activity, amusement and good sleep, as well as to all kinds of personal social and public relationships. And last but not least, it is also important to keep up our general knowledge and to find some sense and meaning in it all (see, for example, Covey, 1989). For descriptions of the interface of work and non-work, we refer to Chapters 13 and 14.

3.4 ORDERLINESS

As orderliness affects the task itself and its environment somewhat differently, both are treated seperatedly in this section.

3.4.1 Orderliness of Task Environments

Essentially, orderliness of our task environment is about the way we fabricate and use the material forms of the places where we work. This involves their architecture and interior design, as well as the furniture, machinery and other equipment. All of these should allow us good physical work conditions, in the sense of lighting, sound, temperature, comfortable seating, effort in using the equipment, air quality and so on. Ideally, this amounts to a fully functional task environment, free of irrelevant elements that demand attention—by any of our sensory channels—and, as such, might interfere with task performance. The relation between the physical environment and our habitual behaviour is, by the way, of a highly dialectical nature, in the sense that the way in which we design our environment determines how we behave and vice versa.

In order to be functional and not to attract needless attention, a task environment has to be "in order". This means that it is also relatively constant and unchanging. This enables us to familiarise ourselves with it quickly. Primarily, it is important that everything we need for this task, including provisions to undo disturbances in the task performance, is familiar to us. Then, we know what to do, what can go wrong and what to do in such a case. We also know where to look for each item. Preferably, all equipment is accessible and present in the right place, ideally, in a way that meets the priorities inherent in the task.

When something breaks down, it should be repaired or replaced. As a result, all equipment is in a working state. In addition, it is well-maintained and clean. This implies that we actively have to re-institute the order of the work environment repetitiously. From day to day, it has to be "reconstructed" and tidied, time after time, which in itself is a lot of work.

In addition, orderliness is often accentuated somewhat by emphasising and marking distinctions and relations (Ashcraft & Scheflen, 1976; Kaplan & Kaplan, 1982). An example is placing objects together that belong together, for instance based on a common function. Moreover, we can give them a common background, colour and label, enclose them by some sort of frame that functions as a visual border and provide them with a marker such as a label that indicates their function. Other possible markers are special forms such as lines, thresholds, arrows and pictograms, openings such as doors and gates, special materials, written texts, special lettering and so on. With their help, we can highlight certain borders, the passing of which implies a relevant transition, as well as points that sometimes need our special attention.

This kind of orderliness helps to keep our environment easy to scan and survey, by providing us with clear criteria and "set-points" of what is normal (Frijda, 1986). This facilitates the automatic intermittent scanning of the task environment for possible intrusions, disturbances and threats, because these stand out more in this way. This is probably also one of the reasons why tidying and cleaning can have such a pleasant centring effect.

Such a stylised display of orderliness suggests that this is all a matter of a well-considered purpose, the outcome of a plan that takes care of everything: apparently, everything goes as it is meant to go, for things are not supposed to be in this kind of order by themselves. It suggests a form of control, which seems to exclude surprises. Many organisations even go further and have designed everything in their own specific company style, with their own logo on all kinds of objects, to make sure that nobody forgets which club is running things here. The message is clear: everything goes as it is meant to go. This may provide a pleasant feeling of control and safety.

As an orderly work environment draws no special attention, it appears to make itself invisible. In this way, it makes it possible for us to "blindly" proceed with our tasks. It facilitates the exercise of our own discipline of attention (see Chapter 2). Its repetitious maintenance and reconstruction may cost us some effort, but it provides us with a normal, continuous and real background for our working task, which also adds to the reality of that task. Though some orderliness is needed in every working environment, it is logical to assume that difficult and complex tasks, as well as tasks with many unpredictable elements, profit most from an orderly and stable environment, because they demand our undivided attention.

Too Little Orderliness of the Work Environment

Too little orderliness of the work environment means that an organisation or a department turns into a collection of stress sources. All kinds of issues fight for our attention, which makes it more difficult to attend to our actual task. Things around us go wrong, are changed, still do not work and are changed again. We witness how some colleagues are handling things badly and step in or at least are tempted to do so. We often have to deal also with our colleagues' stress symptoms and their violent emotions, which are often quite contagious (Hatfield et al., 1994; Kiritz & Moos, 1981; Meerloo, 1972; Schabracq, 1987, 1991). Also, we are exposed to ambiguous and inconsistent cues that may put us on the wrong track. Some people just love this kind of chaos and thrive on it. To others, the work environment becomes fragmented and degenerates into a succession of daily hassles (Kanner et al., 1981).

Examples can be found in stock exchanges, some dealer rooms and in some television studios. It also occurs in times of (successive) reorganisations and mergers. In such a case, the old rules are no longer applicable, while new ones still have to be developed, and there are all kinds of rumours about changes of jobs and departments, early retirements and lay-offs. This is a collective process that can evoke violent and highly contagious emotions.

Too Much Orderliness in the Work Environment

Too much orderliness in the work environment means that orderliness in the organisation or department demands so much attention that it turns into a goal in itself, which is achieved at the expense of actual task performance. Working then may become a source of alienation and stress. This is a common phenomenon in bureaucracies with their strict hierarchies and lines of communication. Examples are some ministries and armies in peacetime.

In an overly orderly organisation, we do not take many risks, afraid as we are to make a bad impression. As long as we play along, the organisation takes care of us. So, we stick to the conventions, disapproving ostentatiously of deviations. We just go through the moves, but still want everything to go our way. As the climate is often highly political, we develop a good eye for rank, status symbols, up and down movement, and their possibilities and dangers. The language is far from concrete and is full of hints and innuendo, the language use of a permanent conspiracy, dripping with suspicion and distrust of outsiders.

Too much orderliness also leads to hiding of emotions, denial of problems and conflicts stemming from annoying occasions from the past. Many colleagues feel bored and alienated. They complain about stress and high work pressure, though they usually have few results to show for it. Because deviant moods and activation states are contagious (Schabracq, 1991), this may have a serious paralysing effect. Actually, such a way of working is typical of the second stage of a stress process (Schabracq et al., 2000; see also Chapter 2), where tunnel vision and denial keep us going in a small and bleak world without much feeling.

3.4.2 Orderliness of Tasks

Until now, we have talked about the orderliness of task environments. Tasks themselves should also show the right degree of orderliness in order to be performed well. This means that tasks should not be too chaotic or overly regulated. This area has received much attention in the literature of work and health psychology elsewhere under the denominator of task characteristics (e.g. Hackman & Oldham, 1980; Ouwerkerk et al., 1994; see also Chapters 6 and 20), which is why we look at it here only briefly.

In Chapter 2, we have seen that a working task's capacity to draw and bind our attention, such that we can optimally perform it, can be brought about by extrinsic factors, such as money or status, as well as by factors more inherent in the task itself. Here, it is about factors of the second kind. So tasks should be of the right:

- size, that is not too big or too small
- difficulty, that is not too difficult or too easy
- pace, that is not too fast or too slow
- length, that is not too long-cycled or too short-cycled
- variety, that is not too varied or too monotonous
- autonomy, that is not too much or too little autonomy
- consequences, that is not too great or too small consequences.

The orderliness of a task is also determined by the clarity of its identity. We have to know what is expected of us. This clarity involves knowledge and timely feedback about:

- the expected outcomes of the task
- the way in which the outcomes are realised
- priorities
- the succession of sub-tasks
- a time path
- criteria for performances and quality
- caveats and pitfalls
- responsibilities
- sanctions.

Another issue here is internal consistency of responsibilities and sub-tasks. This means the different responsibilities should be compatible and should not lead to role conflict.

A last issue is the liability of the task to interruptions, which of course should not be too high.

Too Little Orderliness of Tasks

Too little orderliness of a task makes it hard if not impossible to keep our attention focused on it. Chaos is the result. If we then still have to finish our task, stress reactions become a serious risk. This may be a matter of tasks that are too big, difficult, fast, long-cycled, varied, autonomous, consequential and unclear. It may also be a matter of tasks that are characterised by inconsistent responsibilities or too many interruptions, and that too easily lead to all other kind of error, failure and impasse.

Too little task orderliness may be a matter of an organisational environment that is turbulent, quickly changing or competitive, and that continuously demands action at once. Something similar may happen in an organisation without sufficient structure, for instance in a starting or a quickly growing organisation. Another instance is an organisation with high sick leave, high turnover or many quickly changing temporary employees, where the regular employees are mostly busy breaking in temporary replacements. Lastly, all kinds of changes of our task can lead to a lack of orderliness. This can be a matter of, for example, a reorganisation, a merger, a new computer program, new machinery, or a poor job redesign project.

Too Much Orderliness of Tasks

When orderliness becomes a goal in itself, the way the task is performed can become much more important than its results and outcomes. The task then turns into painstakingly sticking to time-consuming formal procedures, checks and double checks, a ritual way of working, capitalising on following conventions, without paying attention to or even disdaining outcomes and results. The task itself may even become empty and devoid of meaning. To actually get something done is nearly impossible: too many rules, too much hierarchy, too many people who have to approve first, too long communication lines. This may make it hard, if not impossible, to keep our attention focused on the task. All this occurs frequently in big bureaucratic organisations, such as ministries and other public and semi-public organisations, but also in big companies and other organisations with a rigid hierarchy, such as (para)military organisations and some churches.

Too much orderliness of tasks, however, is not the exclusive privilege of bureaucracies. The same task characteristic occurs everywhere where people have to perform tasks that are too small, too easy, too slow, too short-cycled, too monotonous, too inconsequential and have too little autonomy, over and over, every day of the week. Such tasks are often of a fragmented nature and very limited difficulty. Essentially, these are tasks with insufficient meaning to keep our attention on their execution by itself. This makes them into possible stress sources. Examples are assembly tasks at a conveyor belt and working at a counter or call centre.

Moreover, some tasks are so overly regulated and controlled that there is no freedom at all to influence anything. Everything—pauses, the sequence of partial tasks, work pace, etc.—is fixed. This occurs for example at counters or call centres, as well as when our work hooks us up to a machine or assembly line that we cannot influence. Such work often is strictly supervised, with or without the help of electronic devices.

Often, these tasks also have to be performed at a high pace. Having to do much meaningless work at a high pace is known as the "high strain" condition, which is infamous for its serious harmful effects on our health and may contribute to an early death (Karasek & Theorell, 1990).

3.5   SOCIAL EMBEDDING

Because it is difficult to make a consequent and clear distinction between the social character of the task and its social embedding in the work environment, these two here are not discussed separately.

Stress researchers traditionally have studied the effects of social relationships on stress phenomena in organisations under the denominator of "social support" (e.g. House, 1981). They have convincingly documented direct curative effects of social support on stress phenomena in a great number of studies (Winnubst & Schabracq, 1996). Appropriate social support has positive effects on stress prevention, the recovery from stress-related complaints and reintegration after a traumatic event or a period of sick leave. However, we use a different angle here. From our more anthropological point of departure, we see social support as an outcome of a social network, which in its turn results from being embedded in the organisation as a whole.

In general, an organisation consists of social relationships. Social relationships are seen here as the relatively stable ways in which people relate to each other. The forms relationships take are based on more or less standardised cultural formats and scenarios, as well as on their own history. Within a relationship we know more or less what to do and what to attend to, as well as what we may expect from the other in this respect. As such, relationships are an important factor in bringing repetitiveness and stability into our lives. There are of course different kinds of relationships, varying, among other things, in psychological distance (Hall, 1963).

Within the organisation where we work, there are people with whom we seldom or never relate. We just work in the same organisation. We may or may not know each other by face. In elevators or in a hall, we may or may not greet each other. Still, these relationships have important outcomes for us. We come back to this later in this section. First, we turn to the relationships with the people in the organisation with whom we relate regularly and frequently.

In general, work is a logical place to meet other people and to enter into more distinct relationships with them. The relationships with the people with whom we interact regularly in the organisation form our social network. A good network is big enough and extends over different organisational levels and departments. It consists mostly of persons we more or less trust and like. It makes business as usual pleasurable and manageable. As the contacts in most relationships are often highly repetitive in character, they give us room for a familiar repertoire of activity specific to that particular relationship. We know what to do to make the contacts into pleasurable events. Such a network takes time. It has to be developed and taken care of in an active way. The contacts within these relationships have to be repeated over and over. Such relationships need history. Though this may sound boring, we actively seek these relationships and generally like being present in them. However, there are of course great individual differences in preference for the number and kind of relationships.

An important outcome of a social network in an organisation is the opportunity for pleasant and meaningful contacts. Working together also means sharing experiences, both good and bad. Moreover, because we are in the same line of work, the chances are good that we have similar interests and hobbies, and even that we are of a likeminded nature. These are all well-known conditions for getting along well. So, we develop personal preferences and some relationships grow out into social and even personal ones (Hall, 1963). We find protectors, as well as favourite subordinates, colleagues and people elsewhere, with whom it is pleasurable to interact. No wonder that, when we lose or quit our job, the loss of these relationships and their outcomes is often felt to be the most unpleasant consequence. The need for such relationships also turns out to be one of the primary reasons to take on a job again at a later age (Krijnen, 1993).

The pleasant contacts inherent in such relationships can result in emotional support and a general sense of belonging. As such, they can help to reduce tension and stress. This is brought about by entering the different kind of reality of just socialising, a kind of time-out from the sometimes hard-nosed reality of work. This probably is also a matter of emotional contagion (Schabracq, 1991), in this case of being "infected" by others' pleasant mood and liveliness, a phenomenon that Montaigne described as long ago as the sixteenth century (Montaigne, 1580/1981).

Independent of the pleasurable contacts, belonging to a team or group can be rewarding in itself. Doing things together and being part of a greater social system, being part of a "we", can be gratifying in itself. The fact that the others are there as well and do their work too appears to suggest that there is some meaning and logic in our presence and activities at the work site as well. Moreover, the other people present at the work site are usually familiar to us. Unfamiliar persons habitually are introduced, in such a way that their presence becomes understandable and normal to us (Goffman, 1971, 1972): "This is John, from sales, he will join us today because . . .".

Another outcome of a good network is that it enables us to get and give strategic information, warnings, advice, factual help, protection and feedback about our own performance and position. It acts as an early warning system when something is up. It allows us to team up with other employees and to form alliances to fight our battles. As such, a social network is important for our control over our position, environment and future. This is about our own informal power position in the organisation and its politics. This power position and its outcomes probably are of paramount importance in the above-mentioned positive effects of social support on stress complaints.

As said before, being embedded in the relationships of the organisation as a whole can also have important outcomes for us. A very important one is that it provides us with the kind of consistent continuity that enables us to experience our presence in the organisation as normal and real. Similarly to what was described in the previous section on orderliness, this is a matter of continuous repetition, in this case of "normal" patterns of behaviour, and of keeping up a normal appearance to show that nothing special is going on. So, everybody displays the expected everyday conduct and appearances implicitly prescribed by the organisation. For instance, in most organisations, one is not supposed to display intense emotions.

Most of the time, this involves a kind of conduct and appearance that is considered to be normal in the external environment of the organisation as well. Still, these may show a certain styling, specific to the particular organisation. In this way, we show how well socialised we are. We demonstrate we belong there: we are true members, who can be trusted not to do anything irresponsible or unexpected. We actually can use the word "we". By the style of our behaviour and appearance, we habitually display also our place and function in the organisational culture, as well as the kind of relationship we have with each other (Vrugt and Schabracq, 1991). This style involves our body language, linguistic usage, clothing, hairdo and the use of accessories such as glasses, bags and jewellery. Though all this is based on tacit rules and is seldom the object of deliberate attention, a transgression (wrong conduct, wrong clothes, wrong shoes) usually is obvious at once to all parties. By enacting this prescribed conduct, we continuously supply each other, in a completely self-evident way, with the right cues to allow each other, and ourselves, to act in an obvious and logical way (Schabracq, 1991).

When something goes wrong, in the production process or in the social realm, we dispose of a repertoire of ways to repair the normal state of affairs. For instance, we may act in a way that shows that everything is under control anyhow, for instance by a smile and a funny face when we are slipping. Other examples are reassuring each other verbally that nothing has happened really, or by explaining to each other that these things happen, are nobody's fault, but do not undermine the reality of our projects. For a goldmine of other examples we refer to Goffman (1971, 1972).

As such, our relationships provide us with a continuous, highly redundant, but also implicit series of relational propositions about what is expected of us and what we can expect from others (Watzlawick et al., 1968). It is so redundant and omnipresent that it suggests a solid reality, where everything is under control and nasty surprises are excluded. Harré (1979) even speaks of "social musak" ("musak" being the music in elevators and supermarkets that is supposed to soothe us into feeling at ease).

Another outcome of being embedded in the social relationships of an organisation is that it can serve as a stage for us. Being embedded in an organisation implies that we can use our work to show off highly valued work-related qualities, such as professional skill, diligence, collegiality, persistence, sense of humour, courage and creativity. We can even go one step further: we can use the organisation as a theatre to be good in general.

The terms "stage" and "theatre" are not accidental here. An organisation usually offers more distance and privacy than a family, a bigger audience, as well as more off-stage opportunities and time for preparation. We can use our work in this way to develop and demonstrate a beautiful "public" character of a more general kind. Many organisations are ideally fit for such "self-expression". Here, we can play out our good and lofty characters, ostentatiously driven by the highest of values, while the risk that our less noble sides are exposed is much lower than at home.

Consequentially, we demonstrate shamelessly our great needs for perfection, helping others, doing the perfect project, being creative, knowing everything, making it all possible, coming up with the latest developments, being the perfect boss and creating a wonderful atmosphere. All in all, some of us are able to project a very favourable image of ourselves, well-suited to be commemorated during official speeches. Though this works best within the organisational reality, it also may have offshoots in wider circles. At least, it is good exercise stuff.

3.5.1 Too Little Social Embedding

Too little social embedding implies that we have to live in our work without some or all of the outcomes of that embedding—such as pleasurable contacts, belonging to a group, a comfortable, informal power position, a solid social reality and a stage to perform on. Without these outcomes, many people find it hard to keep their attention on their working task, especially when that task is not very interesting in itself or doesn't have other outcomes that they highly value. Some people, moreover, experience being separated from people they know well, and the anonymity resulting from it, as unpleasant. As mentioned before, social contact at work is to many people the main reason to come to work every day.

The sudden partial or complete loss of this embedding can be very painful and often is experienced as a real life event, that is, a matter that unsettles our fixed ways of doing things and paying attention and demands a new adaptation from us. As such, a loss in this area may act as a serious stress source in its own right. This may be a matter of our own departure from our department or organisation as well as the disappearance of other people. Such a loss of social embedding may evoke feelings of grief and alienation, just as in the case of the loss of a loved one. Insufficient social embedding and losses in this area may have very diverse causes, which each can be described as a stress source. We give the following examples.

A lack of feedback and appreciation can be a simple but frequently occurring cause. This may be a matter of a manager with poor social skills or one who is too busy with other things. It may also be a consequence of the habit of only giving feedback about things that go wrong.

Role transitions, such as entry in a new organisation or change of jobs, can be a cause too. These often imply saying goodbye to certain social relationships inherent in the old position, at a moment when the new ones are still not so distinct (for example, Allen & Van der Vliert, 1984).

The decay of social networks is another cause. This often happens to elderly employees when their colleagues, superiors and regular clients successively disappear from the organisation. An additional problem to many of them is that they find it difficult to find replacements (Schlüter & Schabracq, 1994). When an organisation fires many employees, those who stay behind experience similar problems. In addition, however, this may lead to feelings of unpleasantness, guilt and alienation, in combination with a loss of trust in the organisation, the so-called survivors' sickness (Kets de Vries & Balazs, 1997).

Lastly, there may be all kind of barriers that prevent us from establishing appropriate social relationships. These may be physical, such as noise or the protection against noise, which makes it impossible to have a conversation, or an isolated work site. These barriers may also be of a more psychological or social nature. For instance, there are the barriers between the different levels of an organisation—resulting for example in being "lonely at the top"—or between different departments or divisions. A more radical cause may lie in a general climate of distrust and conflicts.

3.5.2 Too Much or Undesired Social Embedding

Our social embedding can cause all kinds of undesired effects, such as territorial infringements, undesired intimacies and conflicts. As these primarily affect our sense of safety, we deal with these in the section about that specific issue. Here, we limit ourselves to some other examples. The mechanism each time is that the social embedding demands too much conscious attention from us. This is done at the expense of the attention to perform our real working task properly.

A good example of too much and undesired social embedding is lack of privacy, such as may occur in an open-plan office. Apart from being annoying and distracting in its own right, this may also lead to self-consciousness and even anxiety about failure. Essentially, lack of privacy is an issue in every work environment that exposes us too defencelessly to the supervision of our executives, or their electronic devices, and the perception of others in general.

Another example occurs in organisations where everybody habitually talks about their own emotional and most personal affairs. This may easily interfere with an appropriate division of attention needed for work.

Another instance is having to work continuously in different and changing teams or projects, with different managers and diverse people, with divergent priorities and competencies. This is what regularly occurs in a matrix organisation. When we work for a multinational organisation, this may also be a matter of working in different locations in different countries, with people from diverse cultural and linguistic backgrounds. Getting sufficiently acquainted and becoming more familiar with each other then becomes a necessary but time-consuming project, which may interfere with the actual working tasks. A seemingly simpler variant of this in a relatively stable work environment is getting a new manager.

The final example stems from the kind of unbalanced social exchange resulting from being a "star", that is getting much more attention than we give. As a result, everyday reality becomes bigger than life, while we only are able to cope with a normal size life. When we ourselves believe in our star status, we are in trouble. This may happen to everyone who is "media material", but also to some persons at the top of our organisations.

3.6 COMPATIBILITY OF CONVICTIONS AND VALUES

Organisational cultures provide rules. These rules in their turn provide repetition and, by that, normality and reality. In addition, rules steer our attention, to prevent us from losing ourselves in activities that, seen from the organisational perspective, are irrelevant. These rules may be based on the ideas of the original founders, the typical ideas that are prevalent in the specific branch, the ideas and goals of the present management, and so on.

However, we also have our own rules, which do the same for us, but then on a more individual basis. These rules stem from our upbringing, our education and the other influences from our background culture. From all of these, we make our own selection.

All these rules, the organisational ones as well as our own, follow from axioms about what reality is and should be. These axioms are often hard to verbalise. So in order to say anything at all about this matter, we take our refuge in derivatives of these axioms, namely convictions and values, which can be verbalised. Convictions here are regarded primarily as statements about how things are and how they come about. Values, on the other hand, are general and generic ideas about how things should be. However, this is not, and is not meant to be, a very hard distinction. Both convictions and values are used here in their quality as kinds of representations of sets of a great number of rules. In their verbalised forms, they can act as guidelines for our actions.

Generally speaking, both the organisational convictions and values and our own stem from the same pool of social representations prevailing in the surrounding culture of our society. As long as the personal and organisational convictions and values coincide, which usually is the case, they jointly determine and shape the forms of our repetitive behaviour in our everyday work and relationships. Though this may bring along its own problems—we return to that in Section 3.6.2—this is not the primary reason to talk about convictions and values here.

This primary reason is that, in some cases, the organisational convictions and values and our personal ones may differ too much, in spite of the fact that they originate from the same pool. This is mostly a matter of differences in the priorities of the relevance and importance of specific convictions and values. Still, these differences can be so great that they may amount to contradictions at the level of everyday behaviour. This, of course, interferes with the optimal division of attention to act in a self-evident way, to say the least. Rather simple examples here are the problems of a teetotal bartender and a vegetarian butcher. Though these examples are about incompatibility centring around the task, the task environment can generate similar problems. When our teetotaller and our vegetarian were only doing the bookkeeping in these same organisations, they might have a problem also, though maybe a less serious one. A better example here is somebody doing a completely innocent job for an abject political regime. Though there are differences between the two types of incompatibility, mostly of degree, they are not very significant. That is why we do not describe them separately.

However, this is not all. The fact that both the organisational convictions and values and our own ones stem from the same pool of social representations prevailing in the surrounding culture of our society has one other important implication. It means namely that we share in our society a lot of deeply rooted ideas about what reality is and should be. This is not to say that there are no differences of opinion about a lot of things. Still, our everyday life would be impossible if we didn't take a lot of common assumptions for granted. So, we know and agree about what places such as houses, shops, bars, police stations, offices, schools and churches are for. We mostly understand and respect social relationships such as marriage and friendship. We habitually make use of the rule systems that regulate traffic, everyday conversations, work and all kinds of other transactions, and we tend to be quite successful at that.

Apparently, we all willingly subscribe to the principles and assumptions underlying the rules that regulate all this. If something goes wrong with this, we usually explain our position by articulating these principles ("I came from the right", "I was here first", "That's my wife", etc.) and most of us are very adept at this. Essentially, these are ethical principles. By explicating these, we show that we tacitly assume that they apply to everyone and also that everyone agrees about them. Most of the time, we get an answer, phrased in terms from the same kind of ethical stock, which proves us to be right in those assumptions.

The crucial point here is that all these ethical principles amount to an ethical system that is surprisingly effective in regulating our mutual relations, at least when we would stick to it. If, for example, everybody actually lived according to the seven Christian main virtues and kept away from the seven deadly sins, our mutual relations would be practically without conflicts. At the same time, the available resources would be divided more equally, with less adverse ecological effects (see for an elaboration Schabracq, 1991). This is not meant to be an orthodox Christian credo. The same probably can be said about other ethical systems, coupled to other religions.

In a sense, we know all about this. At least, we have learned to trust such an ethical system. When we relate to other people, we expect them to behave according to the common rules that the general system supplies for the situations in which we meet them. For example, we usually don't expect to be robbed or stabbed when we enter a shop. When we are raised well, we have something like basic trust and faith in the reality of this ethical system. However— and this is crucial—when somebody else acts in a way that we feel to be completely inconsistent with the overall system, the relevance of the whole system appears to vanish. As a result, we do not know what to expect and are unable to go on with what we are doing. In essence, this is what incompatibility of convictions and values is about: we fall out of the overall system that is supposed to regulate all our mutual relationships in a known and safe way. To proceed, we have to take it one step at a time, being alert as to what might happen. This obviously interferes with the division of attention needed for normal task performance.

Concerning our own convictions and values as employees, the most important ones here are those by which we want to shape our everyday activities and relationships and from which we derive our goals for the future. Essentially, we are talking here about our "free will", our faculty to choose and set our own goals (Schabracq, 1991). Using our free will, we can shape, at least to some extent, our own repetitive activities. We may live a spiralling life of very familiar daily cycles, but we still have some influence on the nature of these cycles.

Another point here is that, most of the time, we do not experience our convictions, values and goals as such. Usually, we are only aware of their existence when something happens that makes it difficult or impossible to use them as guidelines. This may happen as a result of changes in the organisation or our working tasks.

To give some idea of the possible problems resulting from incompatibilities of organisational convictions and our own, we mention a number of issues which may give rise to such incompatibilities. This leads to the following list of (not mutually exclusive) examples (for a similar, more extended list, see Schabracq et al., 2001):

- How the organisation relates to its environment.
- What the organisation is about, its reason for being there, its goals.
- What the constituent parts of the organisation are and how these relate.
- What "really" exists and what "does not exist" in the organisation. This has of course all kinds of implications for what we are and are not able and allowed to do, think and say.
- What is good and what is bad in the organisation. This is about the virtues and sins in the organisation, and their relative importance and priority.
- How power is divided and exercised in the organisation.
- How the organisation sees and treats its employees, and the relevant categories of employees and criteria here.
- How the members of the organisation are expected to relate to each other.
- The commitment, effort and productivity that is expected and demanded, and the acceptability of work stress and burnout.

Generally speaking, a good fit of personal and organisational convictions and values on the above issues is an important factor when it comes to functionality of a work environment. A good fit allows us to deal with our work in a self-evident way, without putting question marks at everything that happens and everything we do.

From our individual perspective, a good fit means also that we can achieve our personal goals to a sufficient degree by our work. Only if this is the case can the working task appropriately captivate our attention, and only then do our task and work environment remain functional. However, accomplishing a perfect fit is a complicated matter, which is seldom fully actualised.

A similar but more global kind of compatibility, that between person and environment in general, the so-called P-E fit, is the central concept in the Michigan stress model (see for example French et al., 1982; Kahn & Byosiere, 1992). This model was very popular for some time, but due to conceptual problems and measurement issues it has now lost its central place (see for example Winnubst et al., 1996).

As pointed out in Chapter 2, the compatibility of personal and organisational convictions and values usually comes about rather organically, also in the area of the realisation of personal goals. Organisations and potential employees select each other. The employees who stay in the organisation become socialised by the organisation. They come to learn about and accept the organisational convictions and values. In the longer run, the acceptation turns into identification and the organisational convictions and values become their own. The people who do not fit in often leave by themselves or are dismissed (Schneider, 1987), though this, of course, does not exclude individual problems.

3.6.1   Too Little Compatibility of Convictions and Values

It has become clear that too little compatibility between our own and the organisational convictions and values leads to poor functionality of both tasks and task environments. The same applies to work in or by which we cannot sufficiently realise our personal goals in this respect. In essence, there are several kinds of problem here.

First, there are the persons for whom it is difficult, for all kinds of reasons, to find such compatibility anywhere. This applies for instance to some people from a different national culture. However, similar problems arise for everybody who differs too much in convictions and values, or has "non-realistic" goals. From the perspective of the organisation, many of them disappear from view. Some of them, however, adapt themselves to a certain degree and stay in the organisation, under far from optimal circumstances.

In the latter case, they come to coincide with the people of the second group of employees, who work in organisations because they see no other way to make a living. They stay, without many illusions about realising other personal goals in this way. In a sense, this group habitually lives more or less in the second stage of a stress process. This stage is characterised by denial, a bleak and small life without much feeling (see Chapter 2). Essentially, this is the same group that performs all kinds of tasks with little meaning, which was described earlier, in Section 3.4.2, in connection with too much task orderliness.

Thirdly, there are problems resulting from some kind of change, either of the organisation or of the person. Both kinds of change may result in an incompatibility of convictions and values, which interferes with the functionality of tasks and task environments. Employees may embrace new convictions and values, for instance as a result of psychotherapy or by becoming a member of a radical sect or political party. Organisations can change too, for example as the result of a merger or on purpose by some form of planned culture change. When such a planned cultural change involves emphasising values such as flexibility and being market-directed, traditional values such as technical perfection and professional freedom may lose their dominant role. However, these latter values may have been to us the very reason to join that organisation. We are then left with work that is stripped of much of its challenge and meaning. These kinds of problems are especially relevant to elderly employees (see Chapters 16 and 17).

A final issue of incompatible convictions and values to be mentioned here is usually more problematic to younger employees, namely the problems that may arise when the organisation is ambiguous about its own convictions and values. This mostly is a matter of depicting an image of its own convictions and values that is much nicer—the "espoused theory"—than the convictions and values that determine the actual everyday reality—the "theory in use" (Schon, 1983). When newcomers innocently identify with the nicer image, they are bound for trouble (see Section 3.2.2).

3.6.2   Too Much Compatibility of Values and Goals

A too uninhibited coincidence of values or a too narrow focus on the achievement of goals can negatively affect the functionality of the work environment as well, because it can lead to various forms of overload and a lack of recuperation. This often goes together also with the disturbance of the balance between work and further life.

When we embrace organisational values and goals too intensely, we lose our borders and cannot say no any more against what we see as our calling. As a result, we keep on going until we are completely exhausted. The first form of imbalance is regarded as an important factor behind burnout (see Chapter 19). Examples are to be found in the caregiving business and social sector. An important causal factor is the role of values such as self-sacrifice in professions that involve saving or helping people. Another is the discrepancy between espoused theory and theory in use, mentioned before, in organisations where such professionals are employed. A final one is being unwilling or unable to learn about personal limits. The impersonal, sometimes even antisocial, behaviour of burnout can be seen as an awkward form of self-protection against this imbalance.

Another trap here is losing oneself too much in other character roles. This is about wanting to be a real perfectionist, innovator, expert, leader, and so on. Each of these callings may have too high a price. These stories are very similar to the now almost classical one about giving more than we get. After all, helping and saving people is just another nice character role and, the same causal factors may play a part in all character roles.

3.7 SAFETY

In order to be functional and not to attract unnecessary attention, we have to experience our working task and its environment as safe. This is more or less the same for all kinds of reality. When a reality becomes too unsafe, we snap out of it. This applies equally to hypnosis, dreaming, being lost in a novel or a movie, working and so on. It applies equally to our work. Apart from the task itself, this is also about our physical surroundings, such as the building, the equipment and furniture, and our social environment. This implies, for example, trusting our colleagues, managers and subordinates, as work becomes much more complicated when we know for sure that they are out to get us.

Though safety is comparable to the previous three variables, because too much emphasis on safety and too little safety both disturb the division of attention needed for good job performance, there are also significant differences. In a sense, safety is an outcome of the other three, which are also of a more structural nature. Realising the right amount of orderliness, social embedding and compatibility of convictions and values is probably the best way to evoke a feeling of safety. Where proper orderliness results in the right physical conditions and a repetitive and familiar reality, which is easy to survey, appropriate social relationships lead to pleasurable contacts, feelings of belonging and control, as well as to Harré's social musak. Lastly, appropriate compatibility of the organisational convictions and values and our own suggests that everything happens in accordance with the overall ethical system that makes our society a place to live in without fear for our fellow man. So all three suggest that everything is under control and going according to plan, nasty surprises being out of the picture. In short, they suggest that everything is safe.

But what does safe mean here? Does it mean being invulnerable to any threat? That would hardly be realistic. Vulnerability is one of our essential characteristics. We all know for instance that we will grow older, that all of our functions must come to an end and that we will die.

These thoughts are similar to what we encountered in Chapter 2, about reality. There, it turned out that our feeling of reality was mainly about the way we deal with our environment, namely by limiting ourselves to a very small part of all possible options. Here, something similar applies. Safety refers only to what counts in the situation at hand and its possible consequences in the near future. So feeling safe here only means that it is—probably—harmless to lose ourselves in the stretch of reality at hand, as long as we have no indication of the opposite. This may be our work, our thoughts, a conversation or whatever. Safety acts as a green light to enter that reality and to go on with it. Safety also implies that we do not have to go into the mechanics of what we are doing or about to do. We just do it or let it happen. In this way, the feeling of safety keeps us going in certain directions and keeps us away from other ones. It acts as a kind of compass in the maze of our life.

A drawback may be that this "safety compass" keeps us too much in our own comfort zones, and keeps us away from new experiences, because they do not feel safe enough. However, exploring the world outside our comfort zones might broaden our horizon and further our development. It could take us out of our daily rut (Knope, 1998; McGraw, 1999) and would help us to overcome "just good enough" solutions.

Both reality and safety are essentially feeling states. As such, they are of a rather subtle kind, in the sense that we hardly notice them, until they are no longer there. However, the results of the disappearance of each are different. When reality vanishes, this leads to other vague feelings such as alienation, depersonalisation, derealisation or what Goffman (1974) calls a "negative experience", the sensation that something is absent or missing. Safety on the other hand is replaced by more distinct and immediately noticeable feelings such as apprehension, fear and anxiety. As such, safety has—compared to reality—a more definite signal value to us. As long as we feel that things are safe, we can go on with what we are doing. The disappearance of this feeling usually makes us stop, in order to find out what exactly is going on and whether we can and should do something about it. This, by the way, is often accompanied by the loss of the reality of what originally was going on. Obviously, the concepts of reality and safety are closely related—though not identical—while both concepts are also closely related to the concepts of trust and faith. For instance, when our trust and faith have been violated in the past by some traumatic event, this may interfere with our present feelings of safety and reality.

As the disappearance of safety signals that we feel something is not right, it is related to what we have said about the signal function of stress in Section 2.6.

3.7.1 Too Little Safety

Feeling unsafe interferes with the division of attention needed for losing ourselves in our work carelessly. We here discuss a number of causes. Each of these may act as a source of stress.

Traumatic experiences, especially at our work site, are an important cause of feeling unsafe there (see Chapter 18). These are events that threaten our life or imply another gross violation of our personal integrity. Examples are accidents, hold-ups and client aggression. Such events help us to remember that we are less safe than we thought we were and may completely unsettle our trust in the safety of our work environment for a long time. Events that are harmless in themselves, but remind us of the traumatic event, may then evoke violent stress reactions also.

Less dramatic, but still unpleasant events also can undermine our feeling of safety, especially when these occur repetitiously. Examples are conflicts (see Chapter 23), discourteous treatment and intimidation by clients or the general public, unwanted intimacies and other confrontations with malevolent or unreliable colleagues and bosses. This can also be a matter of painful experiences in the past, which have never been settled in a satisfying way. Examples are being a survivor of a slimming down operation (also mentioned in Section 3.5.1), being passed (repeatedly) for a due promotion, loss of rights and privileges, broken promises and all kinds of offences and humiliations by colleagues or managers.

When this is a lengthy phenomenon—and it often is—the resulting stress reactions are usually those of the second stage of stress (see chapter 2).

Lastly, uncertainty and rumours about the future of our job and organisation can unsettle our feelings of safety as well. Taking into account the growing amount of radical changes and their accelerated pace, this is becoming an increasingly important factor. Lifetime employment, for example, is becoming a gradually waning phenomenon, though this is obscured for the moment by the scarcity of well-educated personnel. This may evoke all kinds of disaster scenarios, also about the fate of other people, inside or outside the organisation, for whom we feel responsible.

3.7.2   Too Much Safety

Paying disproportionately much attention to procedures that result in more safety may go at the expense of the attention to our task performance. This may adversely affect the functionality of both the working task and its environment. It can also lead to ignoring some of the safety prescriptions, because following these prescriptions is experienced to be "too much work". This, of course, can be very dangerous.

Another, more treacherous, point is that an overly safeguarded environment and overly regulated task performance can make us feel too safe. This may have two kinds of undesired outcomes. First, it may work as a sedative. It lulls us into a state in which we are no longer alert enough to deal appropriately with dangerous eventualities that may always happen. Good examples are traffic situations that are so overly regulated that they take away our wakefulness completely. Secondly, just like most sedatives, too much safety also turns out to be addictive. To many of us, such a state appears to be so attractive that we do not want to leave it any more. Instead, we prefer to forget that this feeling of being completely safe may not last forever. This makes that we do not want to take new initiatives and do not care any longer about further development. However, when we lose contact with other developments and do not develop skills for other jobs, the effect may be that we gradually sentence ourselves to life-long imprisonment in our present job.

As a result, we are stuck there, also when it is no longer rewarding to us at all, and no longer safe, for that matter. As it then becomes difficult to keep up the right division of attention for job performance, this may lead to stress reactions of the second stage of a stress process. This primarily is a problem of elderly personnel. There are a number of variants when it comes to causes, which can also occur in different combinations. Clinging to the present job, though it is not rewarding or safe any more, is the constant factor. For a more elaborate description, see Chapter 16. Many of these mechanisms occur especially—though not exclusively—in organisational cultures that avoid competition, conflict, feedback about inappropriate task performance and open communication in general.

3.8   DISCUSSION

In this chapter, we went into the relation between organisational culture and stress. Organisational culture appears to be primarily a collective coping mechanism, focused on solving the recurring problems of the organisation in recurring ways. When the problem solving does not lead to its desired outcomes, this may result in individual stress problems. These stress problems tend to result mainly from issues of what Parsons called the latency or pattern maintenance function of cultures, i.e. solving the recurring problems of the organisation with the help of a latent structure of repetitive procedures. This is only logical, because here all the problems evoked by the other three functions of culture come together. Here the old drawing board is no longer the playing field, but this is the real thing: the human factor gets involved and needs a manageable reality.

One of the major problems of organisations is dealing with change. We have seen that organisational cultures tend to resist change. However, in a quickly changing environment as ours, this may be suicidal. So, in order to get clues about how an organisational culture might cope with change in a more productive way, we looked at the processes by which an organisational culture provides conditions for creating its inter-subjective reality. These are precisely also the processes that underlie the latency or pattern maintenance function. Here, we attempt to explore how change affects each of these processes, and what—at first sight—can be done about this to prevent, neutralise or diminish the possible negative effects of change in each of these processes.

Though we only touched superficially on the importance of a good balance between work and the other life realms, it is clear that here lies an important resource when it comes to dealing with change. Being well-rooted in these other life realms supplies us with outcomes such as emotional stability, health, good physical condition, a broad horizon and even a certain form of wisdom. All of these are important assets when it comes to coping with change.

The effects of change on orderliness are diverse. Essentially, change disrupts orderliness. Our adaptation to change, however, may result in too much orderliness, of the kind that is characteristic of the second stage of a stress process (see Chapter 2). A good approach here is to give the employees in question enough influence to control the way their working environment is redesigned. As far as possible, this applies also to their tasks. Moreover, it is important that they keep a record of everything that goes wrong and the possible solutions and improvements that they see. This then can be discussed later and lead to actual improvements. A final option is to teach managers and employees how they can implement changes in a standard, unchanging way (see Chapter 29 for a somewhat more elaborate description). The idea is that, if change can be turned into a standardised process, we know what to look for, while we also can have more influence on it. This may eliminate or at least soften the disruptive effects of change.

Change can disrupt existing relationships and lead to too little as well as too much social embedding. However, social relationships can always play an important role in dealing appropriately with change. Making optimal use of this possibility is a matter of dedicating sufficient time, information and attention to this issue (Doeglas & Schabracq, 1992). The main option here is to teach everybody about the importance of relationships in general and, more specifically, of appropriate social networks and how to develop, maintain and use these. Of course, it is also important—though easily overlooked—to actually give everybody sufficient time and opportunities to develop such networks. A rather simple training course in social skills, focusing on establishing and maintaining good social and personal relationships, and dealing with some issues of assertiveness as well, can be very helpful here.

Change can easily lead to all kinds of incompatibilities between personal and organisational convictions and values. The main method to prevent this is participation by everybody involved in the design of the change at their own level of the organisation, within the context of their own team or department. Also, when change is considered, it is probably wise to be conservative. Change only for the sake of change should be avoided. Moreover, when we have decided to change something, this should be done in ways that disrupt the existing organisational culture as little as possible, preferably in ways that make use of the existing characteristics of the culture.

Lastly, we have seen that change can disrupt the feeling of safety that is inherent in a good working task and work environment. The main approach here is to use this datum and to look more closely at our own feelings in this respect. If loss of safety has a signal function, why shouldn't we use it in a more deliberate and well-considered way? It might help us to find out about things that can be improved, which otherwise would go unnoticed. On the other hand, we also may learn to be less easily fooled by the feelings of safety provided by a well-cushioned job. We have to learn that a job essentially is only a temporary affair. This implies that we have to get or make time to keep ourselves up to date in our own profession. At the same time, we also should keep up with what is ahead of us, professionally as well as in the sense of career opportunities and limitations.

In the approaches sketched above, there is an all-important role for the contribution of the individual employees. We think that it has to be like this. There is simply no alternative. The world has become too complicated and it changes too fast for anyone to be able to steer such processes successfully in a top-down way. And why not? The employees after all are the ones who have the greatest interest in keeping their own work manageable and functional. Moreover, they are the experts here.

What more can we do to improve our aptitude in dealing with change?

First, we should create the right conditions. This is mainly about the right attitude of everybody involved. This is also about mutual trust of employees and management, and about faith in the possibility of a promising future. Among other things, this means that everything that has gone wrong in this respect in the past should be settled in a way that is satisfying to all parties concerned. This is far from easy. An excellent manual in this respect, which gives all kinds of guidelines, is Ryan & Oestreicher (1988).

Another option is teaching managers to focus more than they do now on the effectiveness, motivation and development of their employees, as well as on the implementation of change. When this is not feasible or sufficient—and often it isn't—installing special employees who are responsible for these issues in a department, so-called co-managers or social controllers, may be a better option (see Chapter 28).

Another answer is that we should learn, better and faster than we used to. But how? Cultures are not known for their excellent learning abilities. There are several options here.

First, we might study organisations that are quite good at coping with change, and these exist. We might go over and have a look there. We might also turn to the existing literature on learning organisations (for example Bertrams, 1999; Mintzberg et al., 1998; Nonaka & Takeuchi, 1997; Senge, 1990; see also Chapter 21). One of the important things that can be learned is that recording new approaches and communicating about them within the organisation, for instance by intranet, can be very effective. Another one is that it is useful to develop scenarios for several possible futures (De Geus, 1997). These enable us to think through in advance how we can approach the opportunities and difficulties inherent in each of these optional futures.

Another option is studying organisations that went down due to changes in their environment. What exactly went wrong? What things could they have done better? What can we learn from that?

Still another option—a very obvious one, though seldom practised—is studying the history of our own organisation. How did we deal with change in the past? What were our strong and weak points? What are probably still our most obvious pitfalls? What can we do about these and what can we do better in general?

Studying history in general from this perspective is also an option, though this probably is less suited for an organisation than for somebody who can do this from a scholarly or scientific position. From a scholarly and scientific point of view, it might also be very enlightening to look for parallels in other disciplines, such as cultural anthropology or biology, or at first sight much less likely candidates such as military science (Vinke & Schabracq, 2000). In classical Chinese thought, it was, for example, quite common to study the behaviour of animals, such as rats in their natural habitat (and not in some stupid experimental set-up), to learn about dealing with difficult situations.

All in all, organisations have to learn to survive and to flourish—in short, to exist—in a changing world, and that will involve a lot of change in organisational cultures. We hope to have pointed out some of the issues, as well as some possible directions.

REFERENCES

Allen, V.L. & Vliert, E. van de (1984) *Role Transitions*. New York: Plenum Press.

Argyris, C. (1983) *Strategy, Change and Defensive Routines*. Boston, MA: Pitman.

Asch, S.E. (1971) The doctrine of suggestion. In L.L. Barker & R.J. Kibler (eds) *Speech Communication Behavior*. Englewood Cliffs, NJ: Prentice Hall, pp. 255–66.

Ashcraft, N. & Scheflen, A.E. (1976) *People Space*. Garden City, NY: Anchor Press/Doubleday.

Bertrams, J. (1999) *De kennisdelende organisatie [The Knowledge-Sharing Organisation]*. Schiedam: Scriptum.

Calvin, W.H. (1992). *De cerebrale symfonie [The Cerebral Symphony]*. Amsterdam: B. Bakker.

Cherniss, C. (1995) *Beyond Burnout*. New York: Routledge.

Covey, S.R. (1989) *The Seven Habits of Highly Effective People*. New York: Simon & Schuster.

Doeglas, J.D.A. & Schabracq, M.J. (1992) Transitiemanagement [Transition management]. *Gedrag en Organisatie [Behaviour and Organisation]*, **5**, 448–66.

French, J.R.P., Jr, Caplan, R.D. & Harrison, R.V. (1982) *The Mechanisms of Job Stress and Strain*. London: John Wiley & Sons.

Frijda, N.H. (1986) *The Emotions*. Cambridge: Cambridge University Press.

Geus, A. de (1997) *The Living Company*. New York: Longview.

Goffman, E. (1971) *Relations in Public*. New York: Harper & Row.

Goffman, E. (1972) *Interaction Ritual*. Harmondsworth: Penguin.

Goffman, E. (1974) *Frame Analysis*. New York: Harper & Row.

Goldratt, E. (1990) *What Is This Thing Called Theory of Constraints and How Should it be Implemented?* Croton on Hudson, NY: North River Press.

Hackman, J.R. & Oldham, G.R. (1980) *Work Redesign*. Reading, MA: Addison-Wesley.

Hall, E.T. (1963) *The Silent Language*. Garden City, NY: Anchor Press/Doubleday.

Harré, R. (1979) *Social Being*. Oxford: Blackwell.

Hatfield, E., Cacioppo J.T. & Rapson, R.L. (1994) *Emotional Contagion*. Paris: Cambridge University Press.

House, J.S. (1981) *Work, Stress and Social Support*. Reading, MA: Addison-Wesley.

Kahn, R.L. & Byosiere, P. (1992) Stress in organizations. In M.D. Dunnette & L.M. Haugh (eds) *Handbook of Industrial and Organizational Psychology*, 2nd edn, vol. 3. Palo Alto, CA: Consulting Psychologists Press, pp. 571–650.

Kanner, A.D., Coyne, J.C., Schaefer, C. & Lazarus, R.S. (1981) Comparison of two modes of stress management: daily hassles and uplifts versus major life events. *Journal of Behavioral Medicine*, **4**, 1–39.

Kaplan, S. & Kaplan, R. (1982) *Cognition and Environment*. New York: Praeger.

Karasek, R.A. & Theorell, T. (1990) *Healthy Work. Stress, Productivity and the Reconstruction of Working Life*. New York: Basic Books.

Kets de Vries, M.F.R. & Balazs, K. (1997) The downside of downsizing. *Human Relations*, **50**, 11–50.

Kiritz, S. & Moos, R.H. (1981) Physiological effects of social environments. In A. Furnham and M. Argyle (eds) *The Psychology of Social Situations*. Oxford: Pergamon Press, pp. 136–58.

Knope, M. (1998) *The creatiespiraal* [*The Creation Spiral*]. Nijmegen: KIC.

Krijnen, M.A. (1993) *Onderzoek WAO-Instroom 1991, AH-Operations*. [*Study Influx Disablement Insurance Act 1991, AH-Operations*]. Amsterdam: University of Amsterdam.

Maslach, C. & Leiter, M.P. (1997) *The Truth about Burnout*. San Francisco, CA: Jossey-Bass.

McGraw, P.C. (1999). *Leer te leven* [*Learn to Live*]. Utrecht: Het Spectrum.

Meerloo, J.A.M. (1972) *De taal van het zwijgen* [*The Language of Being Silent*]. Wassenaar: Servire.

Mintzberg, H., Ahlstrand, B. & Lampel, J. (1998) *Strategy Safari*. London: Prentice Hall.

Montaigne, M. (1580/1981) *Essays*. Harmondsworth: Penguin.

Moscovici, S. (1984) The phenomenon of social representation. In R.M. Farr and S. Moscovici (eds) *Social Representations*. Cambridge: Cambridge University Press, pp. 3–69.

Nonaka, I. & Takeuchi, H (1997) *The Knowledge-Creating Company*. Oxford: Oxford University Press.

Ouwerkerk, R. van, Meijman, T. and Mulder, B. (1994) *Arbeidspsychologie en taakanalyse* [*Work Psychology and Task Analysis*]. Utrecht: Lemma.

Parsons, T. (1960) *Structure and Process in Modern Societies*. Glencoe, IL: Free Press.

Ryan, K.D. & Oestreich, D.K. (1988) *Driving Fear out of the Workplace*. San Francisco, CA: Jossey-Bass.

Schabracq, M.J. (1987) *Betrokkenheid en onderlinge gelijkheid in sociale interacties* [*Involvement and Mutual Similarity in Social Interactions*], dissertation, University of Amsterdam.

Schabracq, M.J. (1991) *De inrichting van de werkelijkheid. Over de relatie tussen situaties en personen* [*The Design of Reality. About the Relation between Situations and Persons*]. Meppel: Boom.

Schabracq, M.J. & Cooper, C.L. (2000) The changing nature of work and stress. *Journal of Management Psychology*, **15**, 227–41.

Schabracq, M.J., 'Maassen van den Brink, H., Groot, W., Janssen, P. & Hgoukes, I. (2000) *De prijs van stress* [*The Price of Stress*]. Maarsen: Elsevier.

Schabracq, M.J., Cooper, C.L., Travers, C. & van Maanen, D. (2001) *Occupational Health Psychology: The Challenge of Workplace Stress*. Leicester: British Psychological Association.

Schlüter, C.J.M. and Schabracq, M.J. (1994) *Ouder worden in organisaties* [*Growing Older in Organizations*]. Deventer: Kluwer.

Schneider, B. (1987) The people make the place. *Personnel Psychology*, **40**, 437–53.

Schon, D. (1983) *The Reflective Practitioner*. New York: Basic Books.

Senge, P. (1990) *The Fifth Discipline*. New York: Doubleday.

Smit, I. (1997) *Patterns of coping*, dissertation, Utrecht University.

Vinke, R. & Schabracq, M.J. (2000) De binnenkant van cultuur [The inner side of culture]. *Gids voor Personeelsmanagement* [*Guide to Human Resource Management*], **79**(1), 14–17.

Vrugt, A.J. & Schabracq, M.J. (1991) *Vanzelfsprekend gedrag. Opstellen over nonverbale communicatie* [*Behaviour that Goes without Saying. Essays on Nonverbal Communication*]. Amsterdam: Boom.

Watzlawick, P., Beavin, J.H & Jackson, D.D. (1968) *Pragmatics of Human Communication*. London: Faber & Faber.

Winnubst, J.A.M. & Schabracq, M.J. (1996) Social support, stress and organizations: toward optimal matching. In M.J. Schabracq, J.A.M. Winnubst & C.L. Cooper (eds) *Handbook of Work and Health Psychology*. Chichester: John Wiley & Sons, pp. 87–102.

Winnubst, J.A.M., De Jong, R.D. & Schabracq, M.J. (1996). The diagnosis of role strains at work. In M.J. Schabracq, J.A.M. Winnubst & C.L. Cooper (eds) *Handbook of Work and Health Psychology*. Chichester: John Wiley & Sons, pp. 105–25.

CHAPTER 4

The Effects of Work Stress on Health

Arie Shirom
Tel Aviv University, Israel

4.1   THE OBJECTIVES AND SCOPE OF THE REVIEW

Researchers may disagree on the conceptual definition of work-related stress (Beehr, 1995; Cooper, 1998). There is basic agreement, however, that stress may be implicated in cardiovascular disease risk factors, specifically physiological ones like elevated cholesterol and blood pressure levels, and in certain maladaptive behavioral responses (Kahn & Byosiere, 1992). Recent evidence supporting these relationships is reviewed here. However, a thorough review of all types of stress that may affect maladaptive health responses is beyond the scope of this chapter. I focus on empirical studies of work-related stress, with emphasis on its etiological role in each of the maladaptive health responses selected for this review.

The chapter begins by describing a general theoretical perspective, within which this review on effects of stress on maladaptive health responses is embedded. The section that follows discusses the effects of work-related stress on three risk factors for cardiovascular disease: elevated levels of blood pressure, blood lipids and uric acid. Later, I discuss the effects of work-related stress on behavioral responses, namely absenteeism, smoking behavior, sleep disturbances and caffeine use. The concluding section discusses the limitations of this review and highlights promising avenues for future research in this field.

Several considerations guided the choice of the maladaptive health responses covered here. First, since this review focuses on empirical studies, a body of such studies should exist. Second, preference was given to maladaptive responses already covered in part by meta-analytic reviews. Third, an explicit attempt was made to avoid duplication with other chapters of this volume, including chapters that specifically cover the maladaptive health responses of psychological distress, drug abuse and alcoholism. The broad scope of this review necessarily limits the depth of the presentation. Readers should note that the range of the literature covered probably reflects the author's personal viewpoints on several key issues.

The Handbook of Work and Health Psychology. Edited by M.J. Schabracq, J.A.M. Winnubst and C.L. Cooper.
© 2003 John Wiley & Sons, Ltd.

4.2 A GENERAL FRAMEWORK FOR THE STUDY OF THE HEALTH CONSEQUENCES OF STRESS AT WORK

The theoretical model guiding this chapter is represented in Figure 4.1. Within the model, an individual's state of health is viewed as determined by multiple factors, including heredity, environment, early background and socioeconomic influences. This theoretical model draws on earlier conceptualizations (Kinicki & McKee, 1996; Moos & Schaefer, 1993; Quick et al., 1997, pp. 65–89). Among the multiple causal chains leading to maladaptive health responses is the effect of work-related stress. This effect is depicted as moderated by individuals' coping resources and constitutional built-up factors. To simplify the presentation of the main effects, the arrows indicating moderating effects were omitted from Figure 4.1. In this chapter, I focus on this chain of effects, primarily since the two panels in question

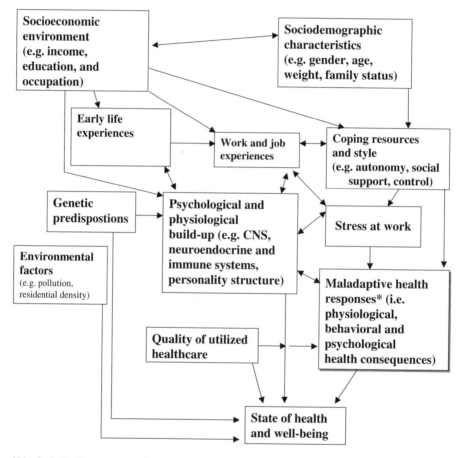

* Maladaptive health responses constitute the focal set of outcome variables for this review. Behavioral health consequences include smoking, sleep disturbances and substance abuse. Psychological health consequences include alienation, burnout and depressive symptoms. Physiological health consequences include elevated levels of risk factors of conoary heart disease like hypertension.

Figure 4.1 A general framework for the study of the health consequences of stress at work

represent proximal influence processes rather than distal (e.g., when stress is used to predict cardiovascular morbidity and mortality; Kristensen, 1996). Stress is posited in Figure 4.1 as precipitating the development of maladaptive health responses, like when it is implicated in prompting non-smokers to start smoking, or in raising a person's blood pressure from normal to borderline. Evidence supporting this postulated path of influence is reviewed below. The following is a brief discussion of the theoretical model presented in Figure 4.1. It is introduced by a description of the conceptual approach followed toward the definitions of stress and maladaptive health responses.

Two major conceptual approaches have guided the study of work-related stress. The first conceptualizes stress as a state that occurs when employees perceive a demand addressed to them as taxing, exceeding or otherwise threatening their adaptive resources (Lazarus, 1999). Such a demand arouses the central nervous system and—depending upon the characteristics of the stress, the physiological and psychological susceptibility of the person, and his or her coping resources—may engender a maladaptive health response (Kristensen, 1996). This approach therefore emphasizes people being active in selecting among alternative coping options. The second major approach conceptualizes stress in terms of individuals' exposure to stressful events, whether minor ones like being reprimanded or critical work events like being demoted (Eden, 1982; Lazarus, 1999, pp. 49–52, 144–9). To the extent that these two approaches have been systematically compared in terms of their influence on a maladaptive health response, the results of the relevant studies will be specifically reviewed.

Most of the research on work stress and health relates stress to the ultimate criterion that appears in Figure 4.1: state of health and well-being (for reviews of this vast area of research, see Danna & Griffin, 1999; Ganster & Schaubroeck, 1991; Landy et al., 1994; Mackay & Cooper, 1987; Semmer, 1996). By health and well-being, I refer to psychological and physical health and well-being, including states of health defined by indicators such as physical symptomatology and epidemiological rates of physical and mental illnesses and diseases. By maladaptive health responses, I refer to a subclass of what has been labeled strain in the Michigan model, namely any deviation from the normal state of responses of the person (e.g. French et al., 1982, p. 5). This definition of strain included psychological strain, such as job satisfaction and anxiety, physiological strain like high blood pressure, and behavioral symptoms of strain such as excessive smoking and consumption of alcohol. Continuing high levels of strains were postulated to affect morbidity and mortality levels (French et al., 1982). In this review, I refer only to the latter two types of strain, and I therefore adopted the term maladaptive health responses to refer to them.

The model guiding the review, as presented in Figure 4.1, provides an overall view of the nomological network of stress and maladaptive health responses relationships. There are several reasons for introducing the model in this chapter. First, as argued by several researchers (Kasl, 1996; Marmot, 1993; Syme, 1988), studies of the relationships among stress and maladaptive health responses need to maintain a broad conceptual perspective of the etiology of these responses. Specific etiological factors leading from the work environment to health responses are embedded in a complex matrix of additional psychosocial influences. There are several classes of variables that are included in Figure 4.1, but are not discussed or reviewed here because of space limitations. The potential usefulness of each of those panels needs to be considered by future researchers. Salient examples are socioeconomic indicators, stable individual differences in skills and abilities, and work role and work environment characteristics that represent individuals' exposures to earlier work and job experiences. Second, Figure 4.1 depicts several bi-directional arrows. These double-headed arrows represent interactions or non-recursive processes between panels of variables. To illustrate, the bi-directional arrow between the panel of stress at work and the panel of psychological and physiological build-up factors represents reciprocal feedback loops that can occur, as when stress affects the immune system (Herbert & Cohen, 1993; O'Leary, 1990; Rabin, 1999). Again, given the confines of this review, it was not possible to discuss each double-headed arrow in detail.

To illustrate, I shall briefly explore the meaning of adding to the effects of stress on maladaptive responses, the chain of effects on which I focus, yet another focus: socioeconomic disadvantage. This additional set of variables, socioeconomic disadvantage, complements the one chosen in this review. That is, it illustrates the meaning of providing a larger context of potential antecedent variables, having direct and indirect influences on maladaptive health responses. Decades of research have shown that socioeconomic status is a significant predictor of stress, strain and state of health (e.g. Kawachi & Kennedy, 1999; Wilkinson, 1996). For example, mothers with young children who experience low income and economic stress are particularly susceptible to depressive symptomatology (Kawachi & Kennedy, 1999). Socioeconomic status differences are found for rates of morbidity and mortality from almost every disease and health condition (Adler et al., 1994). Components of socioeconomic status, income, education and occupation shape individuals' early life experiences, including early-age health habits like diet and exercise, and significantly influence their work experiences, including access to coping resources such as social support at work (Danna & Griffin, 1999).

Researchers often have posited a strong relationship among perceived stress, an individual's coping resources and coping mechanism, and the etiology of stress-related maladaptive health responses (Lazarus, 1999). How an individual handles stress plays an important role in determining the health outcomes of the individual's encounter with stress. Coping may be loosely defined as things we think and actions we take to ameliorate or remove the negative aspects of stressful situations, including indirect coping like avoidance. Some of the maladaptive health responses considered here may be categorized as coping tactics, like smoking and absenteeism. The ability to cope with stress is represented in Figure 4.1 by the panel of work-related coping resources. These resources interact with individuals' subjective appraisal to determine their experienced stress. If a situation is not appraised as taxing or exceeding one's coping resources, it is not likely to be experienced as stress. Personality factors like hardiness represent additional coping resources. For space reasons, this chapter does not cover the issue of effective coping mechanisms that may prevent psychosocial and physiological disequilibria that may in turn lead to stress-related illnesses.

Adaptive and maladaptive responses to stress represent a complex set of an organism's reactions intended to re-establish psychosocial and physiological equilibriums. Here, I focus on certain maladaptive health responses. The effects of stress may appear in any combination of the physiological, behavioral, cognitive and emotional domains of strain, and in any combination of the maladaptive health responses considered here. To illustrate, smoking behavior and caffeine consumption often co-occur. The synergic relationships among the panels of Figure 4.1 indicate that there is not any consistent maladaptive health response applicable to most people in all work situations. This basic premise of inter-individual variability in stress response is related to the direct and indirect effects of coping resources and coping effectiveness considered above, and in addition to other individual difference variables depicted in other panels of Figure 4.1. To sum up the presentation of the theoretical model displayed in Figure 4.1, note that there are qualitative differences, along several dimensions, among the set of maladaptive health responses considered in this chapter. Absenteeism illustrates the point: in contrast to the other behavioral outcomes, which are considered problematic to the health of those engaging in them excessively, absenteeism, while detrimental to the organization, is not necessarily deleterious to the health of the employees who are absent from work. Some common problems in the research on these outcomes are discussed in the concluding section.

4.3 EFFECTS OF WORK STRESS ON PHYSIOLOGICAL RISK FACTORS

In this section, I shall consider the effects of work stress on certain physiological risk factors for cardiovascular disease. These risk factors represent but a subset of possible physiological strains that may be impacted by work-related stress. For example, the effects of stress may include alterations in neuroendocrine factors, the autonomic nervous system and immune functions.

4.3.1 Blood Pressure

Blood pressure and other biological parameters such as catecholamines continuously fluctuate in response to changes in the external or internal environment, to facilitate the adaptation of individuals to their environments (James & Brown, 1997). The maximal pressure of the pulse of blood expelled by the heart's left ventricle during contraction into the aorta is labeled systolic blood pressure, while the minimal pressure, exerted when the heart is at rest just before the next heartbeat, is labeled diastolic blood pressure. Arterial blood pressure may change substantially within seconds, in response to the physiological state and environmental conditions of the individual. The systolic and diastolic blood pressures most commonly used in epidemiological studies are taken when the subject is seated. As elaborated by Fried (1988), blood pressure may change in response to a variety of environmental artifacts, including measurer–subject interaction effects (like opposite gender measurer) and time of day. Therefore, researchers tend to use non-invasive ambulatory monitors that can measure blood pressure response many times during daily life while the subjects go about their normal activities (Pickering, 1993).

The etiology of elevated blood pressure among the elderly remains unknown, but it is well accepted that multiple factors are responsible for this risk factor, the most prevalent one in this age group in economically advanced countries (Pickering, 1995; Schwartz et al., 1996). Acute diastolic blood pressure reactivity to various stresses has been prospectively linked to increased incidence of cardiovascular disorders, including coronary heart disease, stroke and renal disease (Fredrikson & Matthews, 1990). The growing interest in the effects of work-related stress on blood pressure is explained by the consistent finding that blood pressure measured at work is higher than all other measures of blood pressure taken during the day, independent of the time of day (James & Brown, 1997).

Personality factors interact with activity in affecting blood pressure. Meta-analytic evidence indicates that individuals whose behavior is characterized by impatience, chronic time urgency, enhanced competitiveness, aggressive drive, and inclination toward hostility (Type A personality; see Booth-Kewley & Friedman, 1987) show a greater diastolic pressure increase to daily activities relative to non-Type A individuals (Lyness, 1993). However, these differences were found to be rather small (Lyness, 1993). Type As were found to have especially greater and significant increases in blood pressure in situations characterized as having (a) positive or negative feedback evaluation, (b) socially aversive elements such as verbal harassment and criticism, and (c) elements inherent in playing video games (Lyness, 1993). Anger experience was found in a meta-analysis to correlate with elevated blood pressure, but the relationship was small (average effect size below 0.10) and highly variable (Suls et al., 1995).

Blood pressure has repeatedly been found to be especially high during periods of increased work demands (James et al., 1996). Chronic exposure to job-related demands may be associated with increased physical activity and changes in posture. These changes in activity level may in turn give rise to elevated levels of blood pressure. Yet another possible path leading from chronic stress to high blood pressure may involve one's feelings of autonomy and control. This is one of the findings of a series of studies that used both job-control and job-demands appraisals to predict ambulatory blood pressure in a sample of working adults followed longitudinally. In these studies, the combination of low control (low decision latitude) and high demand (high workload) predicted elevated levels of blood pressure both at work and while at home and during sleep (for a review, see Schwartz et al., 1996). This consistent finding has focused researchers' attention on the pivotal role of perceived job control as a powerful moderator of the effects of work-related stress on elevated blood pressure levels. Subsequent attempts to replicate this finding on samples of working men and women provided mixed support, sometimes confirming the expected interaction (e.g. Fox et al., 1993) and sometimes failing to do so (e.g. Fletcher & Jones, 1993; Kamarck et al., 1998; Weidner et al., 1997). The carefully conducted study of the effects of task (job) strain on ambulatory blood pressure (Kamarck et al., 1998) did report a main effect of decisional control: situations rated in this study as high on control were associated with lower levels of diastolic blood pressure activity, suggesting that control may protect against acute sympathetic activation.

Main effects of chronic stress on elevated levels of blood pressure are still being investigated, but the evidence for their existence is inconclusive (Schwartz et al., 1996). Counterintuitive results like a negative relationship of job demands and blood pressure (e.g. Fletcher & Jones, 1993), no relationship (e.g. Fox et al., 1993; Steffy & Jones, 1988), or an expected positive association but only for Type As (Ivancevich et al., 1982) are reported in the literature. There is considerably more support for the hypothesis that short-term stress, like critical job events (Eden, 1982), is implicated in elevated blood pressure levels (Schwartz et al., 1996).

4.3.2   Blood Lipids

Elevated concentrations of blood lipids, including cholesterol and triglycerides, have been shown to be associated with increased risk of coronary heart disease (Brindley et al., 1993; Niaura et al., 1992). Levels of serum lipids, in turn, have been shown to be influenced by several factors, including heredity, gender, body mass, dietary intake of fat, physical activity and cigarette smoking (Rosenman, 1993; NIH Consensus Conference, 1993). It has been noted, however, that all the above factors combined account for only a small fraction of the variability of serum lipids. This has prompted a continuous research effort aimed at exploring the possible role of psychosocial stress. Dimsdale & Herd (1982) and Niaura et al. (1992), in their qualitative reviews of the literature on this subject, concluded that there was some evidence, albeit inconsistent, implicating objective or perceived stress as a source of elevated blood concentrations of lipids, particularly those lipid fractions that are most atherogenic. Niaura et al. (1992) and Stoney & West (1997) have suggested several physiological and behavioral mechanisms to account for these relationships.

The relationship between cholesterol and coronary heart disease (CHD) is graded and continuous (Niaura et al., 1992). To illustrate, in the Framingham Heart Study, for every 1% reduction in serum cholesterol, CHD risk was reduced by 4%, controlling for other risk factors, such as age, obesity and blood pressure (NIH Consensus Conference, 1993). This dose–response relationship suggests that an individual's continuous exposure to psychosocial stress may be implicated in the etiology of CHD via the elevated levels of serum lipids. Studies of specific types of chronic stress, including occupational instability and job insecurity, have shown that these stresses were implicated in elevations of total cholesterol (Mattiasson et al., 1990; Siegrist et al., 1988). These studies reported that the elevated concentrations of cholesterol persisted as long as the stress was present, often for one or two years (Mattiasson et al., 1990; Siegrist et al., 1988). Using a quasi-retrospective design, Shirom et al. (1997) found that among female manufacturing employees, overload predicted subsequent elevation of total cholesterol, after controlling for age, obesity, emotional reactivity, fatigue and emotional burnout. Still, with the exception of such studies as noted above, past research has been concerned with episodic, or event-based, stress (Dimsdale & Herd, 1982; Melamed, 1994; Niaura et al., 1992). Event-based and ongoing, chronic exposure-based conceptualizations of stress derive from differing theoretical approaches (Derogatis & Coons, 1993) and have often been found to be differently related to physiological risk factors in coronary heart disease (Kahn & Byosiere, 1992), including elevated serum lipids (Kasl, 1984).

Stoney et al. (1999b) have examined the effects of stress on the elevation of lipid concentration among middle-aged men and women. They compared the effects of low versus high occupational stress and acute laboratory stress on an extensive battery of lipid and lipoprotein measures. Most lipid parameters were found to significantly increase during the chronic and acute stress exposures. In their research report, Stoney et al. (1999b) provided a summary of an unpublished meta-analytic study of the literature on stress and blood lipid concentrations. A total of 101 studies were included in this meta-analysis, and each study was separately analyzed according to whether the stress was chronic (lasted more than 30 days), episodic (demands addressed during a period of 1 to 30 days) or acute (lasting no more than 24 hours). Acute and episodic stress relationships with lipids were both found to have positive effect sizes on several lipids' parameters. In comparison, chronic stress and total cholesterol associations resulted in a small positive effects size, but none of the other lipid parameters provided a significant effect size with chronic stress. Stoney et al. (1999b) concluded that the evidence for a connection between acute and episodic stress on the one hand and lipid reactivity on the other is generally more consistent than the evidence for a connection between chronic stress and lipid reactivity. It should be noted, however, that these meta-analytic results might stem in part from the arbitrariness of the stress classification criteria and from the small number of studies available on chronic stress and lipid parameters.

In another study, of 100 men and women whose lipid reactivity to stress was assessed during acute and chronic stress, Stoney et al. (1999a) reported that these stresses induced significant and transient atherogenic-lipid elevations that were not due to changes in diet, exercise, level of activity, sleep patterns or plasma volume shifts. That is, the elevations in lipids were found present even after statistically controlling for the above possible confounders.

4.3.3   Uric Acid

Evidence that serum uric acid levels change in response to socially and psychologically stressful situations and achievement-related behaviors was available to researchers beginning in the early 1970s (Mueller & French, 1974; Mueller et al., 1970). With few exceptions (e.g. Najem et al., 1997; Zorbas et al., 1996), behavioral science researchers have left this pattern of associations relatively unexplored. This is all the more striking in view of the epidemiological evidence implicating elevated levels of serum uric acid in the pathogenic processes leading to coronary arteriosclerosis (e.g. Lee et al., 1995) and coronary heart disease (e.g. Brand et al., 1985; Cappuccio et al., 1993; Frohlich, 1993). Elevated levels of serum uric acid carry increased risk of gouty arthritis or renal stones (Kelley & Palella, 1987) and may be toxic to central nervous system activity (Mueller et al., 1970).

Mueller et al. (1970) noted that the possible mechanisms that link stress with central nervous system activity and with body production of serum uric acid might include metabolic precursors of serum uric acid. Twin studies conducted in the UK and the USA (Jensen et al., 1965; Boyle et al., 1967) have indicated that environmental factors are considerably more important than genetic factors in explaining concentrations of serum uric acid. More specifically, it has been shown that exposure to objective stress, like a critical job event or a natural disaster, can produce arousal of the pituitary adrenal system and might cause elevated levels of serum uric acid (Eden, 1982; Lee et al., 1995; Trevisan et al., 1997).

Based on the above evidence, adverse work and environmental conditions that may prevail in a typical industry are likely to affect serum uric acid levels. Workers in a typical industry are likely to be simultaneously exposed to safety hazards, overcrowding, cognitive and physical demands, and environmental stressors. Evidence supports the contention that combined exposure to the above factors, expressed as the ergonomic stress level, was associated with higher levels of serum uric acid among male manufacturing employees (Shirom et al., 2000). In the same study, however, the measure of subjective stress used, environmental annoyance, was found to be negatively associated with serum uric acid levels, again only for male employees.

4.4   EFFECTS OF WORK STRESS ON BEHAVIORAL OUTCOMES

The behavioral outcomes considered in this section are characterized by multifactorial etiology, with stress at work being one of the potential culprits. The number of studies that have systematically examined the associations between work-related stress and behavioral outcomes was noted to be rather small in comparison with those that have investigated stress–health relationships (Beehr, 1995). This may be due in part to researchers' failure to find these associations, accompanied by the well-known reluctance of periodicals to publish research reporting null results. Another feature of the literature is the inconsistent results that concern stress relationships with the behavioral outcomes covered in this section. To illustrate this point, consider two large-scale national samples of employees in the USA.

The first, by French et al. (1982), failed to find significant correlations between work-related stress and smoking, drug use or caffeine ingestion on the job. The second, by Mangione and Quinn (1975), did report such associations.

The study of the behavioral outcomes of stress is further complicated because these outcomes frequently appear in pairs or triads, analogous to the comorbidity patterns of chronic illnesses. Different combinations of outcomes are the rule rather than the exception. A well-known example is the very close associations of stress, smoking and caffeine use (see the evidence cited below). Another example concerns the comorbidity of post-traumatic stress disorder (PTSD), alcoholism and drug abuse (Kofoed et al., 1993). This is a basic characteristic of several behavioral outcomes considered in this chapter. It has led to the construction of dual-diagnosis and triple-diagnosis schemes and to the development of comprehensive, multifaceted treatment approaches. The pattern of appearance of several outcomes in an individual may vary, depending on background characteristics and genetic and environmental factors.

4.4.1 Smoking Behavior

Cigarette smoking and the use of other tobacco products constitutes the single most devastating preventable cause of death in many market economies (Quick et al., 1997). A large body of epidemiological, clinical and pathological studies relates cigarette smoking to the development of cardiovascular heart disease and other chronic diseases, including emphysema, chronic bronchitis and non-fatal strokes. Moreover, a considerable body of research has demonstrated the adverse health consequences of passive smoking, the involuntary exposure of non-smokers to tobacco smoke from smokers in confined environments. This research has led many countries to regulate smoking in public places (Quick et al., 1997). As is the case with the other behavioral outcomes considered here, smoking behavior is multifactorial in its etiology, and there is evidence pointing to its genetic origins. Twin studies have demonstrated that genetic factors contribute to the initiation of smoking and influence the intensity of smoking cigarettes (number of cigarettes smoked per day; see Pomerleau & Kordia, 1999). A meta-analysis of the data from five studies, each involving more that 1000 twin pairs, found an estimated 60% of the propensity to smoke may be explained by genetic factors (Heath & Madden, 1995). Cigarette smokers are over-represented in many disadvantaged groups, including those with psychiatric and behavioral disorders (Parrott, 2000). Still, there is evidence that environmental and job-related stress may account for a significant proportion of the variance of smoking behavior. Consequently, interest in the pathway leading from stress, and stress at work, to smoking behavior is growing.

Stress and associated emotional responses, including anxiety and irritability, are attenuated by smoking. These effects have been shown to be short-lived (Parrott, 1995). Mood and affective state impairments tend to occur between cigarettes in a repetitive cycle. This cycle provides a clear rationale for the addictive use of cigarettes (Parrott, 1995). Smokers, therefore, obtain only short relief from adverse states of anxiety and irritability that follow the experience of stress. There is evidence from smoking abstaining studies that nicotine-withdrawal symptoms are worse under high environmental stress than under low environmental stress, while post-cigarette relief was also correspondingly greater (Parrott, 2000).

In empirical research, stress is often found to predict smoking behavior while interacting with other predictors, like lack of social support. In a review of the research on smoking behavior among nurses, Adriaanse et al. (1991) found that excessive smoking among both female and male nurses was explained by work stress, lack of social support, and unmet expectations that characterize nurses' professional socialization. Nurses' smoking is considered a public health problem since they often act as role models to patients and their families. In several studies, smokers who express high motivation to smoke have reported above-average stress that they had experienced before the smoking, rather than below-average stress after smoking (Parrott, 1995). Consequently, stress management and anxiety reduction programs at the workplace have the potential to influence motivation to smoke. Workplace-based smoking cessation programs do bring to the fore, however, the conflict between health and performance. Among aviators, as an example, smoking is a health hazard in the cockpit. Pilots who are required to abstain from smoking during and before flights may suffer cockpit performance decrements (Sommese & Patterson, 1995).

Yet another facet of the complex relationship between stress and cigarette smoking was described by Parrott (1999), who proposed that the evidence on this relationship might be reinterpreted to suggest that smoking actually causes stress. Parrott (1999) pointed out that regular smokers are more stressed than their non-smoking counterparts and that smokers experience an overall reduction in stress when they quit smoking. Another theory holds that smoking may redistribute stress by modulating moods (Piasecki & Baker, 2000).

Work organizations contribute to and may inhibit (or induce) smoking behavior by three basic processes documented in the research literature. First, work organizations may develop organizational norms with respect to smoking on the job, including the local official definition of permissible smoking and the mechanisms of its control established by management. Second, stressful working conditions, like sustained overload or machine-paced jobs characterized by lack of control, may induce heavy smoking as a coping strategy to alleviate the stressful job conditions. Third, work organizations may explicitly or implicitly encourage the development of occupationally based smoking subcultures. In a survey of 12 000 professional people in 14 occupational categories, Russek (1965) found significant differences in the prevalence of smoking in high-stress occupations as compared with low-stress occupations.

4.4.2 Caffeine Ingestion

Caffeine is the most widely consumed pharmacologically active substance in the world. The evidence on its possible implications for human health, that is, whether it has chronic physiological effects on habitual consumers, is as yet inconclusive (Benowitz, 1990). It has long been suspected that repeated exposure to caffeine may produce tolerance to its physiological effects (James, 1994). The consumption of caffeine is known to improve physical performance and endurance during prolonged activity at sub-maximal intensity (Nehling & Debry, 1994). Caffeine's physiological effects are linked to the antagonism of adenosine receptors and to the increased production of plasma catecholamines (Nehling & Debry, 1994).

The study of the relationship between work-related stress and caffeine ingestion is confounded by the high correlation between coffee consumption and smoking (Conway et al., 1981). A meta-analysis of six epidemiological studies (Swanson et al., 1994) has shown that about 86% of smokers consumed coffee while only 77% of the non-smokers did so. Three major mechanisms have been suggested to account for this close association between caffeine intake and smoking: (a) conditioning effect, (b) reciprocal interaction; that is, caffeine intake increases arousal while nicotine intake decreases it, and (c) the possibility of a third variable affecting both. Stress, and particularly work-related stress, is a possible third variable influencing both caffeine and nicotine intake (Swanson et al., 1994).

Caffeine consumption is often regarded as reinforcing and augmenting the psychological and physiological effects of stress (France & Ditto, 1992; Lane et al., 1990). This synergetic relationship has been explained as due to the effects of both on the elevation of blood catecholamines (Lane et al., 1990). Experimental laboratory studies have found that as opposed to a placebo drink, consumption of high levels of caffeine interacts with stress in worsening the effects of stress on psychological and physiological strain (France & Ditto, 1992; Lane & Williams, 1987).

4.4.3 Sleep Disturbances

The modern era of sleep research began in the 1950s with the discovery that sleep is a highly active state rather than a passive condition of non-response. The most prevalent type of sleep disturbance, insomnia, may occur in a transient short-term or a chronic form. Stress is probably the most frequent cause of transient insomnia (Gillin & Byerley, 1990). Chronic insomnia usually results from an underlying medical or psychiatric disorder. Between one-third and two-thirds of patients with chronic insomnia have a recognizable psychiatric illness (Gillin & Byerley, 1990).

One of the explanations suggested for the effects of stress on sleep disturbances is through the changes in the cerebral system at different levels and changes in the biochemical body functions that disturb the 24-hour rhythms (Gillin & Byerley, 1990). Some evidence suggests that personality characteristics, such as Type A or hostility, moderate the above linkages. Stress and sleep disturbances may reciprocally influence each other: stress may promote transient insomnia, which in turn causes stress and increases risk for episodes of depression and anxiety (Partinen, 1994).

Chronic stress associated with jobs that are monotonous, are paced by machines and require vigilance—jobs frequently found in continuous-process manufacturing—may lead to sleep disturbances, causing decrements in performance (Krueger, 1989). Some evidence indicates that work-related stress, circadian rhythms and reduced performance are synergetic (Krueger, 1989). The adverse effects of sleep loss, interacting with overload and a high level of arousal, on certain important aspects of job performance have been documented in several studies of sleep deprivation among junior hospital doctors (Spurgeon & Harrington, 1989).

The study by Mattiasson et al. (1990) provides intriguing evidence linking chronic job stress, sleep disturbances and increases in plasma cholesterol. In this study, 715 male shipyard employees exposed to the stress of unemployment were systematically compared with 261 controls before and after the economic instability stress was made apparent. The findings: sleep disturbances were positively correlated with increases in total cholesterol among the shipyard employees exposed to job insecurity, but not among the controls. This is a naturalistic field study in which the actual lay-offs did not occur until about a year after some employees received notices that they would lose their jobs. Thus, the stress studied was real and severe—spanning a year of uncertainty about the lay-offs—and could be considered chronic.

4.4.4   Absenteeism

Absence behavior may be viewed as an employee-coping behavior that reflects the interaction of perceived job demands and control with self-assessed health and family conditions The dominant model in the absence literature states that employees use absenteeism as a mechanism to withdraw from aversive situations at work (Hulin, 1991). Therefore, one would expect a positive correlation between the experience of work stress and the level of absenteeism.

Absenteeism has several major dimensions, including duration, spells and reasons for being absent. A European sample showed that about 60% of the hours lost to absenteeism were lost because of illness (Ilgen, 1990). To the extent that work-related stress was implicated in these illnesses, there should be some relationship between stress on the job and that part of absenteeism classified as sick days. The literature on absenteeism covered primarily blue-collar employees, and few studies have reviewed stress systematically (McKee et al., 1992). Jackson & Schuler's (1985) meta-analysis of the consequences of role stress reported an average correlation between role ambiguity and absence of 0.09, and between role conflict and absence of −0.01. Later studies also supported this correlation (Hendrix et al., 1991; Kristensen, 1991; Steel & Rentsch, 1995). Yet, the observed relations between these work stressors and absenteeism have been weak and inconsistent. As several meta-analytic studies of the literature on absenteeism show, stress is but one of many variables accounting for these phenomena, so we should not expect work-related stress and absenteeism to be strongly correlated (Beehr, 1995).

The absenteeism literature suggests that the relationship between work-related stress and absenteeism may be mediated by employee-specific characteristics. Among them, the literature refers to the propensity to use avoidance coping in response to stress at work, and to being emotionally exhausted or physically fatigued (Saxton et al., 1991). To illustrate, Kristensen's (1991) study of several thousand Danish slaughterhouse employees over a year showed that those who reported high job stress had significantly higher absence rates and that perceived health was closely associated with sickness absenteeism.

Several studies support the conclusion that relationships between stress and absenteeism may be occupationally determined (Baba & Harris, 1989). To illustrate, work-related stress among managers tends to be associated with the spells of absenteeism, but not with days lost due to sickness absences, while the opposite holds with regard to shop-floor employees (Cooper & Bramwell, 1992). Occupational specificity of the stresses predisposing employees to become absent has been regarded as a major explanation of the meager amount of absence variance explained by work-related stress across many studies (Baba & Harris, 1989). Several studies have found that among blue-collar employees who work on jobs considered stressful—those that possess a combination of the characteristics of assembly-line jobs, a very short cycle of operations and a piece-rate wage system—job stress is a strong predictor of unexcused absence. (For a recent review of these studies, see McKee et al., 1992. Note that this study does not support the conclusion.)

The literature on stress and absenteeism provides a convincing example of a limitation noted in the introduction. The reference is to the failure of most research studies on the relationships between stress and behavioral outcomes to cover systematically in their design stresses in several life domains, including work, family and leisure. It was noted that in absenteeism research, non-work stress contributed more than work-related stress to the prediction of absence, lending support to the view that absence may be influenced by non-work behavior more than work-related behavior (Baba & Harris, 1989). A recent meta-analysis of this area found a relatively weak relationship between the chronic stresses of role ambiguity, role conflict and role overload and absenteeism (Fried et al., 2001). The relation between role ambiguity and absenteeism was significantly higher when the data were collected from organizational records, and job satisfaction was found to mediate the relationship between overall stress and absenteeism (Fried et al., 2001).

4.5 SUMMARY AND CONCLUSIONS

In this concluding section, I discuss some of the theoretical and methodological issues that characterize the literature that has been reviewed in this chapter, point out some of the limitations of the review process implemented, and suggest promising avenues for research on stress and maladaptive health responses.

4.5.1 Major Conclusions

The maladaptive health responses covered by this chapter were all characterized as having multifactor etiology. For each of the responses considered here, stress at work is but one of the possible culprits. For the great majority of the studies cited in this review, a different combination of predictors (including stress at work) in explaining each of the maladaptive health responses is the rule. Therefore, and also because of other limitations of the research covered noted below, only very tentative and inductive conclusions may be offered. With these caveats in mind, a major conclusion of this review is that stress at work accounts for a significant proportion of the variance of most of the maladaptive health responses that I focused on. For some of the physiological risk factors, such as hypertension, the additional impact of exposure to high levels of stress at work may mean that individuals move from the relatively benign category of borderline to that of inflicted with hypertension and in need of medications.

4.5.2 Theoretical Issues in the Field Reviewed

A major theoretical postulate of this chapter has been that stress at work influences maladaptive health responses. Whenever possible, support for this underlying assumption was provided in the review of each specific maladaptive health response. However, the relationships between stress and maladaptive health responses may be reciprocally related or the direction of influence may flow from the health response, such as sleep disturbance, to stress appraisal. Some support for the interdependence assumption was proposed for the relationship of cigarette smoking and stress. Given the cross-sectional nature of most of the research reviewed above, however, possible reciprocal relationships among stress and maladaptive responses or possible recursive relationships among the health responses considered and stress were not systematically examined. For much the same reason—that is, the predominance of retrospective and cross-sectional research designs in the area reviewed—the question of how changes in the level of work-related stress affect changes in the level of the health responses cannot be answered in a definite way.

An additional theoretical path of influence may flow through a third variable. That is, the empirical link between stress at work and maladaptive health response might be spurious, arising from the relationship of both stress and maladaptive response to a third variable, such as a certain personality trait that may be genetically determined. For example, negative affectivity, or a person's predisposition to experience negative mood states such as depressive symptomatology, anger, guilt and fearfulness, may affect both stress appraisals and maladaptive health responses (Watson & Clark, 1984). Negative affectivity may lead to stress since it is reflected in individuals being extremely vigilant in scanning their environment for stimuli that may threaten their well-being (Watson et al., 1988). Negative affectivity may be associated with reduced physical activity, obesity and elevated blood pressure (Burke et al., 1993). Certain coping resources may buffer the effects of environmental stressors on stress appraisals and may also positively influence certain maladaptive health responses. The quality and quantity of a person's social relationships at work, with emphasis on social support, have been shown to affect stress at work (Ganster et al., 1986; Viswesvaran et al., 1999; Winnubst & Schabracq, 1996). Focusing for the purpose of illustrating the main effects of social support on the maladaptive health response of elevated levels of blood pressure, a recent meta-analysis (based on 21 correlational studies) revealed a significant mean effect size ($r = 0.08$), suggesting a small but reliable positive effect of social support on blood pressure (Uchino et al., 1996).

4.5.3 Methodological Issues in the Field Reviewed

A methodological limitation of the research literature covered in the review concerns the two approaches toward the conceptualization of stress referred to earlier, the one that focuses on chronic stress and the one that emphasizes critical or minor job events. These two approaches to stress measurement have seldom been combined in a single study designed to predict an outcome considered here (cf. Frese & Zapf, 1988). The same generalization is relevant to the combined use, in the same study, of family-related and work-related stress to predict either of the above outcomes. Most of the studies referred to in this chapter were based on a cross-sectional design and employees' self-reports on their stress appraisals (cf. Frese & Zapf, 1988). In most of the research that concerned behavioral outcomes of work-related stress, the joint moderating or mediating roles of predisposing personality variables, like Type A or hardiness, and situational variables like social support and control, have hardly been investigated. Seldom have antecedent variables, like objectively measured job stress, been included in the research designs of the studies reviewed here. Finally, the research covered by this chapter has employed divergent methodologies. Because of these limitations, a frequently encountered conclusion in this chapter is that the evidence for work-related stress being a precursor of a maladaptive health response is inconclusive.

4.5.4 Limitations of the Current Review

Some limitations of the current review are common to any narrative review of a phenomenon. I have made an effort to cover, for each of the maladaptive health responses discussed, meta-analytic studies that included stress as a predictor. When such meta-analytic studies were not available, the most recent narrative reviews and empirical studies were consulted.

Earlier attempts to review and synthesize the pertinent literature were incorporated throughout this review. For each of the stress linkages with a maladaptive health response that was not quantitatively summarized by a meta-analytic review, explicit attention was given to inconsistencies in the findings of the relevant studies. I could not resolve these inconsistencies by reference to magnitude of effect or systematic differences in study methods. Resolving such inconsistencies constitutes a major challenge for future meta-analytic investigations of the pertinent stress–maladaptive health response associations.

4.5.5 Suggestions for Future Research

Six major theoretical perspectives guide most of the research currently being carried out in the field of stress, strain and health. The first four, elaborated in a recent volume (Cooper, 1998), are the person–environment fit, the demand–control–support model, the effort–reward imbalance perspective, and the social ecological approach. In addition, the model of role stress is still being extensively used (Kahn & Byosiere, 1992), and the Conservation of Resources (COR) theory, constructed and applied by Hobfoll and his colleagues (for a recent review, see Hobfoll, 1998), is increasingly being applied to explain stress–strain linkages. Several prior reviews of the area of stress and health have attempted to organize the empirical research under any combination of these theoretical perspectives (e.g. Ganster & Schaubroeck, 1991; Schwartz et al., 1996). This classification system for empirical studies has not been adopted here primarily because of the paucity of relevant studies for most of the maladaptive health responses covered.

The theoretical perspectives on stress–health relationships differ in their conceptualization of stress, strain and health, and place different emphasis on some of the antecedent mediating and moderating variables depicted in Figure 4.1. One of the more promising avenues for research in this area is to systematically compare the predictive validity of these theoretical perspectives with regard to maladaptive health responses. In a recent study, Bosma et al. (1998) compared the predictive validity of the effort–reward-imbalance perspective and the demand–control–support model with respect to coronary heart disease. Bosma et al. (1998), in a study of men and women (6895 and 3413, respectively) working in British government offices, found that low job control and high-cost/low-gain work conditions independently influenced the development of heart disease. This research exemplifies the advantages of combining several theoretical perspectives, in a longitudinal design, to predict maladaptive health responses.

Each of the maladaptive health responses may be conceptualized along several dimensions, including its level, variability or consistency, forms of appearance, temporal intensity, and trajectory. Each of these possible dimensions could be independently affected by stress. To illustrate, Fried and his associates (2001) reported that in past research, stress at work was hardly found to be linked with length of absences, but was consistently found to be weakly associated with frequency of absences. Future research on each of the maladaptive health responses covered in this review may consider including in the study design several important dimensions of the response investigated.

Another promising avenue for research concerns the interactive effects of stress and socioeconomic disadvantage in predicting maladaptive health responses. Most epidemiological studies that assess the effects of work-related stress on physiological risk factors for cardiovascular disease, including the maladaptive health responses of elevated levels of uric acid, blood lipids and blood pressure considered here, statistically control for the effects of the subjects' age, sex, race-ethnicity, obesity, smoking behavior, and a family history of hypertension or hyperlipidemia. Such a model assumes that stress influences the maladaptive health response under consideration independently of the confounders that were controlled for. Often, this assumption is unwarranted. It is well known that stress affects obesity and smoking behavior as well as diet. In addition, it is plausible that some of the antecedent variables tapping socioeconomic disadvantage, discussed earlier in this chapter, interact with stress to influence some of the maladaptive health responses. In future research, researchers should consider adopting theoretical models that allow for moderating or mediating influences of the above confounders on the relationships between stress and the maladaptive health response under consideration.

REFERENCES

Adler, N.E., Boyce, T., Chesney, M.A., Cohen, S., Folkman, S., Kahn, R.L. & Syme, S.L. (1994). Socioeconomic status and health: the challenge of the gradient. *American Psychologist*, **49**, 15–24.

Adriaanse, H., Van Reek, J., Zandbelt, L. & Evers, G. (1991). Nurses' smoking worldwide. A review of 73 surveys of nurses' tobacco consumption in 21 countries in the period 1959–1988. *International Journal of Nursing Studies*, **28**, 361–75.

Baba, V.V. & Harris, M.J. (1989). Stress and absence: a cross-cultural perspective. *Research in Personnel and Human Resource Management*, **1**, 317–37.

Beehr, T.A. (1995). *Psychological Stress in the Workplace*. London: Routledge.

Benowitz, N.L. (1990). Clinical pharmacology of caffeine. *Annual Review of Medicine*, **41**, 277–88.

Booth-Kewley, S. & Friedman, H.S. (1987). Psychological predictors of heart disease: a quantitative review. *Psychological Bulletin*, **101**, 343–62.

Bosma, H., Peter, R., Siegrist, J. & Marmot, M. (1998). Two alternative job stress models and the risk of coronary heart disease. *American Journal of Public Health*, **88**, 68–74.

Boyle, J.A., Greig, W.R., Jasani, M.K., Duncan, A., Diver, M. & Buchanan, W.W. (1967). Relative roles of genetic and environmental factors in the control of serum uric acid levels in normouricaemic subjects. *Annals of Rheumatic Diseases*, **26**, 234–8.

Brand, F.N., McGee, D.L. & Kannel, W.B. (1985). Hyperuricemia as a risk factor of coronary heart disease: the Framingham Study. *American Journal of Epidemiology*, **121**, 11–18.

Brindley, D.N., McCann, B.S., Niaura, R., Stoney, C.M. & Suarez, E.C. (1993). Stress and lipoprotein metabolism: modulators and mechanisms. *Metabolism*, **42**, 3–15.

Burke, M.J., Brief, A.P. & George, J.M. (1993). The role of negative affectivity in understanding relations between self-reports of stressors and strains: a comment on the applied psychology literature. *Journal of Applied Psychology*, **78**, 402–12.

Cappuccio, F.P., Strazzullo, P., Farinaro, E. & Trevisan, M. (1993). Uric acid metabolism and tubular sodium handling: results from a population-based study. *Journal of the American Medical Association*, **270**, 354–9.

Conway, T.L., Vickers, R. R., Ward, H.W. & Rahe, R.H. (1981). Occupational stress and variation in cigarette, coffee and alcohol consumption. *Journal of Health and Social Behavior*, **22**, 155–65.

Cooper, C.L. (ed.). (1998). *Theories of Organizational Stress*. New York: Oxford University Press.

Cooper, C.L. & Bramwell, R.S. (1992). Predictive validity of the strain component of the occupational stress indicator. *Stress Medicine*, **8**, 57–60.

Danna, K. & Griffin, R.W. (1999). Health and well-being in the workplace: a review and synthesis of the literature. *Journal of Management*, **25**, 357–84.

Derogatis, L.R. & Coons, M.L. (1993). Self-report measures of stress. In L. Goldberger & S. Breznitz (eds) *Handbook of Stress*, 2nd edn. New York: Free Press, pp. 200–34.

Dimsdale, J.E. & Herd, J.A. (1982). Variability of plasma lipids in response to emotional arousal. *Psychosomatic Medicine*, **44**, 413–27.

Eden, D. (1982). Critical job events, acute stress, and strain: a multiple interrupted time series. *Organizational Behavior and Human Performance*, **30**, 312–29.

Fletcher, B.C. & Jones, F. (1993). A refutation of Karasek's demand-discretion model of occupational stress with a range of dependent measures. *Journal of Organizational Behavior*, **14**, 319–30.

Fox, M.L., Dwyer, D.J. & Ganster, D.C. (1993). Effects of stressful job demands and control on physiological and attitudinal outcomes in a hospital setting. *Academy of Management Journal*, **36**, 289–318.

France, C. & Ditto, B. (1992). Cardiovascular responses to the combination of caffeine and mental arithmetic, cold pressure, and static exercise stressors. *Psychophysiology*, **29**, 272–82.

Fredrikson, M. & Matthews, K.A. (1990). Cardiovascular responses to behavioral stress and hypertension: a meta-analytic review. *Annals of Behavioral Medicine*, **12**, 30–9.

French, J.R.P., Caplan, R.D. & Van Harrison, R. (1982). *The Mechanisms of Job Stress and Strain*. New York: John Wiley & Sons.

Frese, M. & Zapf, M. (1988). Methodological issues in the study of work stress: objective vs subjective measurement of work stress and the question of longitudinal studies. In C.L. Cooper & R. Payne (eds) *Causes, Coping and Consequences of Stress at Work*. Chichester: John Wiley & Sons, pp. 375–411.

Fried, Y. (1988). The future of physiological assessment in work situations. In C.L. Cooper & S.V. Kasl (eds). *Causes, Coping and Consequences of Stress at Work*. Chichester: John Wiley & Sons, pp. 343–75.

Fried, Y., Shirom, A., Cooper, C., Ager, J. & Stepanski, K. (2001). *Does stress affect absenteeism? A meta-analysis*. Submitted.

Frohlich, E.D. (1993). Uric acid: a risk factor for coronary heart disease. *Journal of the American Medical Association*, **270** (3), 378–9.

Ganster, D.C. & Schaubroeck, J. (1991). Work stress and employee health. *Journal of Management*, **17**, 235–71.

Ganster, D.C., Fusilier, M.R. & Mayes, B.T. (1986). The role of social support in the experience of stress at work. *Journal of Applied Psychology*, **71**, 102–10.

Gillin, J.C. & Byerley, W.F. (1990). The diagnosis and management of insomnia. *New England Journal of Medicine*, **322**, 239–48.

Heath, A.C. & Madden, P.G. (1995). Genetic influences on smoking behavior. In J. R. Turner, L. R. Cardon, & J. K. Hewitt (eds) *Behavior Genetic Approaches in Behavioral Medicine*. New York: Plenum Press, pp. 37–48.

Hendrix, W.H., Steel, R.P., Leap, T.L. & Summers, T.P. (1991). Development of a stress-related health promotion model: antecedents and organizational effectiveness utcomes. *Journal of Social Behavior and Personality*, **6** (7), 141–62.

Herbert, T.B. & Cohen, S. (1993). Stress and immunity in humans: a meta-analytic review. *Psychosomatic Medicine*, **55**, 364–79.

Hobfoll, S.E. (1998). *Stress, Culture, and Community*. New York: Plenum Press.

Hulin, C.L. (1991). Adaptation, persistence, and commitment in organizations. In M.D. Dunnette & L.M. Hough (eds) *Handbook of Industrial and Organizational Psychology*, 2nd edn., vol. 2. Palo Alto, CA: Consulting Psychologists Press, pp. 445–507.

Ilgen, D.R. (1990). Health issues at work. *American Psychologist*, **45**, 273–83.

Ivancevich, J.M., Matteson, M.T. & Preston, C. (1982). Occupational stress, Type A behavior, and physical well being. *Academy of Management Journal*, **25**, 373–91.

Jackson, S.E. & Schuler, R.S. (1985). A meta-analysis and conceptual critique of research on role ambiguity and role conflict in work settings. *Organizational Behavior and Human Decision Processes*, **36**, 16–78.

James, G.D. & Brown, D.E. (1997). The biological stress response and lifestyle: catecholamines and blood pressure. *Annual Review of Anthropology*, **26**, 313–53.

James, G.D., Broege, P.A. & Schlussel, Y.R. (1996). Assessing cardiovascular risk and stress-related blood pressure variability in young women employed in wage jobs. *American Journal of Human Biology*, **8**, 743–9.

James, J.E. (1994). Psychophysiological effects of habitual caffeine consumption. *International Journal of Behavioral Medicine*, **1**, 247–63.

Jensen, J., Blankenhorn, D.H., Chin, H.P., Sturgeon, P. & Ware, A.G. (1965). Serum lipids and serum uric acid in human twins. *Journal of Lipid Research*, **6**, 193–205.

Kahn, R.L. & Byosiere, P. (1992). Stress in organizations. In M.D. Dunnette & L.M. Hough (eds) *Handbook of Industrial and Organizational Psychology*, 2nd edn, vol. 3. Palo Alto, CA: Consulting Psychologists Press, pp. 571–651.

Kamarck, T.W., Shiffman, S.M., Smithline, L., Goodie, J.L., Paty, J.A., Gnys, M. & Jong J.Y.K. (1998). Effects of task strain, social conflict, and emotional activation on ambulatory cardiovascular activity: daily consequences of recurring stress in a multiethnic adult sample. *Health Psychology*, **17**, 17–29.

Karasek, R.A. & Theorell, T. (1990). *Healthy Work*. New York: Basic Books.

Kasl, S.V. (1984). Stress and health. *Annual Review of Public Health*, **5**, 319–41.

Kasl, S.V. (1996). The influence of the work environment on cardiovascular health: a historical conceptual and methodological perspective. *Journal of Occupational Health Psychology*, **1**, 42–56.

Kawachi, I. & Kennedy, B.P. (1999). Income inequality and health: pathways and mechanisms. *Health Services Research*, **34**, 215–27.

Kelley, W.N. & Palella, T.D. (1987). Gout and other disorders of purine metabolism. In E. Braunwald, K.J. Isselbacher, R.G. Petersdorf et al. (eds) *Harrison's Principles of Internal Medicine*, 11th edn. New York: McGraw-Hill, pp. 1623–32.

Kinicki, A.J. & McKee, F.M. (1996). Annual review, 1991–1995: occupational health. *Journal of Vocational Behavior*, **49**, 190–220.

Kofoed, L., Friedman, M.J. & Peck, P. (1993). Alcoholism and drug abuse in patients with PTSD. *Psychiatry*, **64**, 151–71.

Kristensen, T.S. (1991). Sickness absence and work strain among Danish slaughterhouse workers: an analysis of absence from work regarded as coping behaviour. *Social Science and Medicine*, **32**, 15–27.

Kristensen, T.S. (1996). Job stress and cardiovascular disease: a theoretical and critical review. *Journal of Occupational Health Psychology*, **1**, 246–60.

Krueger, G.P. (1989). Sustained work, fatigue, sleep loss and performance: a review of the issues. *Work and Stress*, **3**, 129–41.

Landy, F., Quick, J.C. & Kasl, S. (1994). Work, stress, and well-being. *International Journal of Stress Management*, **1**, 33–73.

Lane, J.D. and Williams, R.B. (1987). Cardiovascular effects of caffeine and stress in regular coffee drinkers. *Psychophysiology*, **24**, 157–64.

Lane, J.D., Adcock, A., Williams, R.B. & Kuhn, C.M. (1990). Caffeine effects on cardiovascular and neuroendocrine responses to acute psychological stress and their relationship to level of habitual caffeine consumption. *Psychosomatic Medicine*, **52**, 320–36.

Lazarus, R.S. (1999). *Stress and Emotion: A New Synthesis*. New York: Springer-Verlag.

Lee, J., Sparrow, D., Vokonas, P.S., Landsberg, L. & Weiss, S.T. (1995). Uric acid and coronary heart disease risk: evidence for a role of uric acid in the obesity–insulin resistance syndrome. *American Journal of Epidemiology*, **142** (3), 288–94.

Lyness, S.A. (1993). Predictors of differences between Type A and B individuals in heart rate and blood pressure reactivity. *Psychological Bulletin*, **114**, 266–95.

Mackay, C.J. & Cooper, C.L. (1987). Occupational stress and health: some current issues. *International Review of Industrial and Organizational Psychology*, **1**, 167–99.

Mangione, T.W. & Quinn, R.P. (1975). Job satisfaction, counterproductive behavior, and drug use at work. *Journal of Applied Psychology*, **60**, 114–16.

Marmot, M. (1993). Work and other factors influencing health. In L. Levi & F. LaFarla (eds) *Healthier Work Environment*. Copenhagen: World Health Organization, pp. 236–46.

Mattiasson, I., Lindgarden, F., Nilsson, J.A. & Theorell, T. (1990). Threat of unemployment and cardiovascular risk factors: longitudinal study of quality of sleep and serum cholesterol concentrations in men threatened with redundancy. *British Medical Journal*, **301**, 461–6.

McKee, G.H., Markham, S.E. & Scott, D.K. (1992). Job stress and employee withdrawal from work. In J. C. Quick, L.R. Murphy & J.J. Hurrell, Jr (eds) *Stress and Well-Being at Work*. Washington, DC: American Psychological Association, pp. 153–64.

Melamed, S. (1994). Life stress, emotional reactivity and their relation to plasma lipids in employed women. *Stress Medicine*, **10**, 167–75.

Moos, R.H. & Schaefer, J.A. (1993). Coping resources and processes: current concepts and measures. In L. Goldberger & S. Breznitz (eds) *Handbook of Stress: Theoretical and Clinical Aspects*, 2nd edn. New York: Free Press, pp. 234–58).

Mueller, E.F. & French, J.R.P. (1974). Uric acid and achievement. *Journal of Personality and Social Psychology*, **30**, 336–40.

Mueller, E.F., Kasl, S.V., Brooks, G.W. & Cobb, S. (1970). Psychosocial correlates of serum urate levels. *Psychological Bulletin*, **73**, 238–57.

Najem, G.R., Seebode, J.J., Samedy, A.J., Feuerman, M. & Freidman, L. (1997). Stressful events and the risk of symptomatic kidney stones. *International Journal of Epidemiology*, **26**, 1017–23.

Nehlig, A. & Debry, G. (1994). Caffeine and sport activity: a review. *International Journal of Sports Medicine*, **15**, 215–23.

Niaura, R., Stoney, C.M. & Herbert, P.N. (1992). Lipids in psychological research: the last decade. *Biological Psychology*, **34**, 1–34.

NIH Consensus Conference (1993). Triglycerides, high density lipoprotein, and coronary disease. *Journal of the American Medical Association*, **269**, 505–10.

O'Leary, A. (1990). Stress, emotion, and human immune function. *Psychological Bulletin*, **108**, 363–82.

Parrott, A.C. (1995). Stress modulation over the day in cigarette smokers. *Addiction*, **20**, 233–44.

Parrott, A.C. (1999). Does cigarette smoking cause stress? *American Psychologist*, **54**, 817–20.

Parrott, A.C. (2000). Cigarette smoking does cause stress. *American Psychologist*, **55**, 1159–60.

Partinen, M. (1994). Sleep disorders and stress. *Journal of Psychosomatic Research*, **38**, 89–91.

Piasecki, T.M. & Baker, T.B. (2000). Does smoking amortize negative affect? *American Psycologist*, **55**, 1156–8.

Pickering, T.G. (1993). Appliactions of ambulatory blood pressure monitoring in behavioral medicine. *Annals of Behavioral Medicine*, **15**, 26–32.

Pickering, T.G. (1995). Hypertension. In A. J. Goreczny (ed.) *Handbook of Health Rehabilitation Psychology*. New York: Plenum Press, pp. 219–43.

Pomerleau, D.F. & Kordia, S.L.R. (1999). Introduction to the featured section: genetic research on smoking. *Health Psychology*, **18**, 3–6.

Quick, J.D., Horn, R.S. & Quick, J.C. (1986). Health consequences of stress. *Journal of Organizational Behavior Management*, **8**, 19–31.

Quick, J.C., Quick, J.D., Nelson, D.L. & Hurrell, J.J. (1997). *Preventive Stress Management in Organizations*. Washington, DC: American Psychological Association.

Rabin, B.S. (1999). *Stress, Immune Function, and Health*. New York: John Wiley & Sons.

Rosenman, R.H. (1993). Psychological influences on the variability of plasma cholesterol. *Homeostasis in Health and Disease*, **34**, 129–36.

Rosenman, R.H. (1997). Neurogenic and behavioral influences on plasma lipids. In M. Hillbrand & R. T. Spitz (eds) *Lipids, Health and Behavior*. Washington, DC: American Psychological Association, pp. 15–47.

Russek, H. (1965). Stress, tobacco, and coronary heart disease in North American professional groups. *Journal of the American Medical Association*, **192**, 189–94.

Saxton, M.J., Phillips, J.S. & Blakeney, R.N. (1991). Antecedents and consequences of emotional exhaustion in the airline reservations service center. *Human Relations*, **44**, 583–95.

Schwartz, J.E., Pickering, T.G. & Landsbergis, P.A. (1996). Work-related stress and blood pressure: current theoretical models and considerations from a behavioral medicine perspective. *Journal of Occupational Health Psychology*, **1**, 287–310.

Semmer, N. (1996). Individual differences, work stress and health. In M.J. Schabracq, J.A.M. Winnubst & C.L. Cooper (eds) *Handbook of Work and Health Psychology*. Chichester: John Wiley & Sons, pp. 52–86.

Shirom, A., Westman, M., Shamai, O. & Carel, R.S. (1997). Effects of work overload and burnout on cholesterol and triglycerides levels: the moderating effects of emotional reactivity among male and female employees. *Journal of Occupational Health Psychology*, **2** (4), 275–88.

Shirom, A., Melamed, S. & Nir-Dotan, M. (2000). The relationships among objective and subjective environmental stress levels and serum uric acid: the moderating effects of perceived control. *Journal of Occupational Health Psychology*, **5**, 374–86.

Siegrist, J., Matschinger, H., Cremer, P. & Seidel, D. (1988). Atherogenic risk in men suffering from occupational stress. *Atherosclerosis*, **69**, 211–18.

Sommese, T. & Patterson, J.C. (1995). Acute effects of cigarette smoking withdrawal: a review of the literature. *Aviation, Space and Environmental Medicine*, **66**, 164–7.

Spurgeon, A. & Harrington, J.M. (1989). Work performance and health of junior hospital doctors: a review of the literature. *Work and Stress*, **3**, 117–28.

Steel, R.P. & Rentsch, J.R. (1995). Influence of cumulation strategies on the long-range prediction of absenteeism. *Academy of Management Journal*, **38** (6), 1616–34.

Steffy, B. D. & Jones, J. W. (1988). Workplace stress and indicators of coronary-disease risk. *Academy of Management Journal*, **31**, 686–98.

Stoney, C.M. & West, S. (1997). Lipids, personality, and stress: mechanisms and modulators. In M. Hillbrand & R.T. Spitz (eds) *Lipids and Human Behavior*. Washington, DC: American Psychological Association, pp. 47–66.

Stoney, C.M., Bausserman, L., Niaura, R., Marcus, B. & Flynn, M. (1999a). Lipid reactivity to stress: II. Biological and behavioral influences. *Health Psychology*, **18**, 251–61.

Stoney, C.M., Niaura, R., Bausserman, L. & Matacin, M. (1999b). Lipid reactivity to stress: I. Comparison of chronic and acute stress responses in middle-aged airline pilots. *Health Psychology*, **18**, 241–50.

Suls, J., Wan, C. K. & Costa, P. T., Jr (1995). Relationship of trait anger to resting blood pressure: a meta-analysis. *Health Psychology*, **14**, 444–56.

Swanson, J.A., Lee, J.W. & Hopp, J.W. (1994). Caffeine and nicotine: a review of their joint use and possible interaction effects in tobacco withdrawal. *Addictive Behaviors*, **19**, 229–56.

Syme, S.L. (1988). Social epidemiology and the work environment. *International Journal of Health Services*, **18**, 635–45.

Theorell, T. (1998). Job characteristics in a theoretical and practical health context. In C. L. Cooper (ed.) *Theories of Organizational Stress*. New York: Oxford University Press, pp. 205–20.

Trevisan, M., O'Leary, E., Farinaro, E., Jossa, F., Galasso, R., Clentano, E., Scottoni, A., Fusco, G. & Panico, S. (1997). Short- and long-term association between uric acid and a natural disaster. *Psychosomatic Medicine*, **59**, 109–13.

Uchino, B.N., Cacioppo, J.T. & Kiecolt-Glaser, J.K. (1996). The relationship between social support and physiological processes: a review with emphasis on underlying mechanisms and implications for health. *Psychological Bulletin*, **119**, 488–531.

Viswesvaran, C., Sanchez, J.I. & Fisher, J. (1999). The role of social support in the process of work stress: a meta-analysis. *Journal of Vocational Behavior*, **54**, 314–34.

Watson, D. & Clark, L.A. (1984). Negative affectivity: the disposition to experience aversive emotional states. *Psychological Bulletin*, **96**, 465–90.

Watson, D., Clark, L.A. & Carey, G. (1988). Positive and negative affectivity and their relation to anxiety and depressive disorders. *Journal of Abnormal Psychology*, **97**, 346–53.

Weidner, G., Boughal, T., Connor, S. L., Pieper, C. & Mendell, N.R. (1997). Relationship of job strain to standard coronary risk factors and psychological characteristics in women and men of the family heart study. *Health Psychology*, **16**, 239–47.

Wilkinson, R.G. (1996). *Unhealty Societies: The Afflictions of Inequality*. London: Routledge.

Winnubst, J.A.M. & Schabracq, M.J. (1996). Social support, stress, and organization: toward optimal matching. In M.J. Schabracq, J.A.M. Winnbust & C.L. Cooper (eds) *Handbook of Work and Health Psychology*. Chichester: John Wiley & Sons, pp. 87–103.

Zorbas, Y.G., Yaroshenko, Y.N. & Federenko, Y.F. (1996). Serum urate and cholesterol levels in endurance trained volunteers during acute and rigorous bed test conditions. *Panminerva Medicine*, **38**, 223–8.

CHAPTER 5

Individual Differences, Work Stress and Health

Norbert K. Semmer
University of Bern, Switzerland

5.1 INTRODUCTION

Despite many problems of individual studies, links between work stress and health—physical as well as psychological—are now quite well established (Adler & Matthews, 1994; Cooper, 1998; Kahn & Byosiere, 1992; Karasek & Theorell, 1990; Keita & Sauter, 1992; Marmot et al., 1999; Sonnentag & Frese, in press; Theorell & Karasek, 1996). And a growing number of longitudinal studies now support the contention that work stress is, indeed, a causal factor in this process (Theorell & Karasek, 1996; Marmot et al., 1999; Siegrist, 1996; Sonnentag & Frese, in press). The relationships found are typically not very strong, with correlations between 0.20 and 0.30, and seldom higher. However, given the complex aetiology of physical morbidity and psychological symptoms, it would be strange if measures of stress at work could really explain more than about 10% of the variance (Semmer et al., 1996). In addition, the interpretation in terms of explained variance may be quite misleading and seriously underestimate the real impact of these factors, especially given the distributions of many of the variables involved, which limit the maximum correlation. As soon as one translates correlations into relative risks (Rosenthal, 1984) these turn out to be substantially higher for those exposed to highly stressful conditions (Frese, 1985; Marmot et al., 1999).

Thus, in the study by Frese (1985), the risk of severe psychosomatic impairments is three times as high in the high than the low stressor group (15 vs. 5%), where stressors are measured by ratings of trained observers. The correlation coefficient is r = 0.19. Marmot et al. (1999) report a two- to sixfold elevated risk for coronary heart disease (CHD) associated with effort–reward imbalance. There are many examples like these, and associations like these should not be taken lightly.

On the other hand, there can be no doubt that associations of this type do not hold for everyone in the same way (Spector, 2002). People differ in the probability of *encounting stressors*, depending on their social environment but also on their own behaviour, as some stressors may be self-created, for instance, conflicts with others provoked by low social skills or antagonistic behaviour. People differ in their *appraisal* of stressors, as when people low in self-esteem regard failure as "self-diagnostic" and thus more stressful (Brockner, 1988). And people differ in their way of coping with stress, thus terminating (or, at least, alleviating) stress if coping attempts are successful and the costs of coping low, but aggravating and prolonging it if coping is not successful and/or the costs of coping are high (as an example of successful but "costly" coping consider the example of somebody coping with work overload by working overtime, which in turn leads to fatigue and thus undermines his or her capacity to work efficiently or leads to problems with the family etc.—cf. Schönpflug & Battmann, 1988).

However, one important warning seems necessary: in current stress research there is a tendency to emphasize individual differences to the point where stress is being re-duced to nothing but a problem of idiosyncratic appraisals and coping styles, rendering such concepts as "environmentally induced stress" useless, as Lazarus & Folkman (1986, p. 75) assert (see also Perrewé & Zellars, 1999). This view tends to equate "interpretation" with "confined to the individual", and "environment" with "physical environment", and to neglect that the social environment is a powerful reality, where people in the same culture share "rules of appraisal" (Averill, 1986) and ways of dealing with the world (cf. Semmer, 1992; see Hobfoll, 2001; Kahn & Byosiere, 1992, for a similar argument, and cf. the analysis of Cooper & Payne, 1992, of cultural differences in stress appraisal and coping). Thus, it should be kept in mind that not all individual differences found are only differences between individuals, but often differences between the (sub)cultures they belong to! As this chapter deals with individual differences, and thus tends to sup-port the tendency to lose sight of this fact, it is emphasized here and should be kept in mind.

This chapter deals with the question of what makes "stressors" "stressful", concentrating on goals people have. It then discusses individual differences in resources, such as what will be called "resourceful belief systems", and, finally, it deals with individual differences in coping. The chapter does not represent an exhaustive review of the literature. Rather, it tries to tie together various "literatures" under common themes. Furthermore, I do not emphasize the differences between various concepts, important as they are. Rather, I try to integrate along the "greater lines". This inevitably leads to oversimplifications. Yet, I am convinced that all too often we tend to dwell on differences and difficulties, and sometimes it seems worth while to see if there is some forest emerging behind all the different trees.

Stress is used as a rather general term in this chapter, denoting a state of tension that is experienced as aversive. Stress, therefore, involves negative emotional states such as anxiety, frustration, anger, guilt, and the like (Lazarus, 1999). This is, I believe, in essence what most stress researchers adopt as a working definition of stress, even though the concrete wording of their definitions vary considerably. Stressors are characteristics of the environment that tend to elicit such emotional states in a given population (cf. Semmer, 1992).

Note that this is a probabilistic concept of stressors. It does not require that each and every individual will experience stress *vis-à-vis* a stressor—an argument which is often raised against an environmentally oriented concept of stressors (e.g. Lazarus & Folkman, 1986). All it requires is that in a given population certain characteristics tend to be interpreted as stressors, on the basis of shared meaning, or "social representations" (Farr & Moscovici, 1984) in a given culture (cf. Kahn & Byosiere, 1992; Semmer, 1992).

5.2   WHAT MAKES STRESSORS STRESSFUL? THE ROLE OF GOALS AND ASPIRATIONS IN THE STRESS PROCESS

Basically, stress has to do with appraisals of threat and/or loss (Lazarus & Folkman, 1984). Challenge, which is mentioned as the third category belonging to stressful appraisals, is not considered as stressful *per se*, as it involves positive appraisals and emotions, and the reappraisal of a threatening demand as challenge actually has the potential of terminating the state of stress (cf. the concept of hardiness, as discussed below).[1]

This implies that stress has to do with the—anticipated or experienced—thwarting of goals (this term is used in a very broad sense here, referring to all kinds of desired states at different levels of abstraction—cf. Carver & Scheier, 1990; Cropanzano et al., 1993; Schönpflug, 1985).

As Cropanzano et al. (1993) point out, personality may be described as a hierarchy of goals, ranging from very general dispositions (such as approach positive or avoid negative states) over values, self-identities, personal projects, to task goals. Emmons (1989) presents a similar hierarchical approach (see also Emmons, 1996).

Values are rather abstract guiding principles, such as achievement, comfort, power, good relations to others, justice, or maintaining a positive self-image. Self-identities are roles one identifies with, such as "citizen", "parent", "spouse", "executive", "lathe operator", etc. Personal projects is a term introduced by Little (1983). As used by Cropanzano et al. (1993), it is a summary term encompassing a variety of similar terms such as "personal strivings"(Emmons, 1989), "current concerns" (Klinger, 1987), life tasks (Cantor & Langston, 1989), which have in common that they "are all explicitly goal-directed and situated in a hierarchy just below relatively abstract self-identities and just above more specific action plans" (Cropanzano et al., 1993, p. 289). They may include such things as "trying to build or maintain a good relationship with colleagues", "trying to always beat the deadlines", "avoiding being made responsible for things outside one's control" etc.

The lower levels often are not at the centre of these conceptions, which are oriented towards motivation and personality in a more general sense. For work psychology, however, it is quite important to consider lower levels as well.

Thus, Semmer and colleagues (Semmer, 1984; see also Frese & Zapf, 1994; Semmer et al., 1995) have presented a concept of work related stress, that includes "barriers to task fulfilment", which follow from such aspects as having to work with poor tools or materials, encountering frequent interruptions, having unclear or conflicting tasks, and the like. Assuming that the task is accepted by the person, all these aspects are considered stressful because they endanger the fulfilment of task-related goals. And, indeed, such aspects have been found to be experienced as stressful and to be correlated with psychosomatic symptoms (e.g. Semmer et al., 1996; Zapf, 1989; see Greiner et al., 1997; Leitner, 1993, for a related concept and similar results). In a similar vein, Keenan & Newton (1984) studied the role of frustration—obstacles to successfully doing one's work—and found that it was related to emotional reactions, especially emotions of anger and hostility (see also O'Connor et al., 1984; Peters & O'Connor, 1980; Spector & Jex, 1998).

---

[1] Of course, the appraisal of challenge may be ambivalent, oscillating between the concentration on the potential gains and the reflection of the potential dangers. To the extent that the dangers are salient, there is appraisal of threat, and thus, stress.

5.2.1   Stress and Commitment to Goals

If the reasoning is correct that stress has to do with thwarted goals, then people with high goals should experience more stress under the same threat to these goals—all other things being equal. Although there is surprisingly little systematic research directly on this issue, there are several lines of research that yield insights on these questions.

In the area of *job satisfaction*, which is used as an indicator of stress in many studies, there is interesting research by Roberson (1989, 1990, Roberson et al., 1990). They identified work-related goals by way of the Work Concerns Inventory. Many goal dimensions, such as probability of success, the proportion of positive/negative goals, commitment to the goals, and a clear time frame for goal attainment, were related to job satisfaction. Rice et al. (1991) have shown that affective responses were more pronounced for job facets judged to be of high importance, an effect that has also been noted by Locke & Latham (1990) and that is in line with analogous research outside of the domain of work, such as that of Emmons (1986, 1989; see also Bandura, 1989).

Another line of research supporting the consideration of goals is that on *person–environment fit* (Edwards et al., 1998). This research tradition assumes that it is the discrepancy between what people want (P) and what they get (E) that determines the stress they experience. While results are ambiguous—in that in many cases one of the components alone determines most of the variance, often a positive discrepancy (too much) has a different impact from a negative one (Edwards, 1998; cf. Warr's, 1987, "vitamin model" of stress), and, especially, often aspiration level must not be accepted as a valid indicator of values and needs without qualifications (see below)—they do suggest that in many cases the discrepancy does, indeed, explain variance over and above main effects of either P or E.

P-E fit research is not concerned with the question of where the specific aspiration levels come from, and therefore is also silent with regard to their exact meaning or their nature as stable characteristics of people. Other lines of research are concerned with this issue, and this research deals with the question of whether certain motive structures make people more vulnerable to stress.

Among this is research by McClelland and others about the implications of *motives*, especially the power motive, for stress (e.g. McClelland, 1987; McClelland & Jemmott, 1980; McClelland et al., 1980). Basically, these findings indicate that people with a high, but inhibited, power motive are likely to report more physical illness and to show lower immune function when experiencing "power stress", that is, stressful life events the content of which has to do with power. In contrast, people high on the need for affiliation, especially when combined with low inhibition (so called "relaxed affiliative syndrome"; McClelland, 1987, p. 366), tend to show better health and superior immune function. The impact of n_{Pow} goes, however, beyond stressors that are related to the power theme. People high in n_{Pow} also show the strongest association between *affiliative* stress (losing a loved one) and illness, thus implying that this group is simply particularly prone to react strongly to *all* kinds of stressful events (Jemmott, 1987; see also Furnham, 1992). Likewise, the expected specific relationship between n_{Aff} and sensitivity to affiliative stress has not been well established. Jemmott (1987) therefore concludes more cautiously that people high in inhibited n_{Pow} may be at a higher health risk in general and react more strongly to all kinds of stressors, while people high in n_{Aff} may be at a lower health risk in general, especially if they are low in inhibition. Conceivably, people high in n_{Pow}, who tend, by definition, to interpret ambiguous stimuli in terms of the power theme, will tend to define stressors in terms of this theme and react strongly to anything that reduces their influence and control (see, however, Langan-Fox et al., 1997, who did not find associations between n_{Pow}, stress, and coping).

There has been less research on the need for achievement and its relationship to stress. There is some evidence that people high in n_{Ach} tend to be rather healthy in general (Veroff, 1982). However, Roger and colleagues (e.g. Birks & Roger, 2000) have suggested that n_{Ach} may be separated into a "toxic" (TA) and a "non-toxic" (NTA) component. The first "is characterized by impatience, a hostile need to win at all costs, and anger if that goal is thwarted" (Birks & Roger, 2000, p. 1095); the latter is characterized by items such as "I play to win but if I lose I don't hold a grudge". They report data suggesting that TA is a risk factor for males, while NTA is a protective factor for females.

What is especially interesting in the present context is the similarity of the inhibited power motive to the Type A behavior pattern. This pattern is typically characterized by a variety of symptoms such as high ambition, competetiveness, hostility and aggressiveness, high need for control etc. (cf. Adler & Matthews, 1994). Hostility, anger, and anger expression seem to be key components of the pattern (Adler & Matthews, 1994; Dembroski & Costa, 1988; Siegman, 1994a—see below), and the "toxic" need for achievement seems to reflect this.

With regard to goals, it is especially the high need for control attributed to Type A people that is of interest. Type As show a tendency to maintain control under all conditions (even conditions where control cannot be attained), and they react strongly—both behaviourally and in terms of cardiovascular reactivity—to threats to control (Contrada & Krantz, 1988; Edwards, 1991; Glass, 1977). Siegrist and associates have shown that in addition to job-related measures (high quantitative demands, working in a job which does not match one's training level—or "status inconsistency"—and job insecurity), and medical variables (systolic blood pressure and LDL-cholesterol), a high need for control was associated with an elevated risk for cardiovascular disease both in cross-sectional and in longitudinal studies (Marmot et al., 1999; Siegrist, 1996, 1998). Thus, the threat to a highly valued attribute (in this case, control) contributes to the experience of stress and, in the long run, disease. In addition to the more generic goals of keeping control, there is also evidence that, compared to Type Bs, Type As tend to set task goals for themselves which are too high with regard to their capabilities; this leads to a higher percentage of failures to reach the goal which, in turn, leads to dissatisfaction and distress (Ward & Eisler, 1987).

A similar case can be made with regard to *role conflict*. It has been shown repeatedly that role conflict is experienced as stressful and that it is associated with symptoms of impaired well-being (Kahn & Byosiere, 1992). By definition, role conflict involves conflicting goals, either within the work role or between the work role and other roles, such as the parent role.

This becomes especially apparent when looking at *multiple roles* of women, especially the combination of work and family roles. The bulk of the evidence indicates that multiple roles do not, in general, have detrimental, and often have positive, effects on women's well-being (Barnett & Hyde, 2001; Gutek et al., 1988; Kandel et al., 1985; Moen, 1997; Repetti et al., 1989; Ross & Mirowsky, 1995). Again, goals seem to play an important role, since positive effects of labour force participation seem to depend, at least in part, on women's positive attitude towards, and thus acceptance of, this working role (Repetti et al., 1989). At the same time, there are also indications that participation in the workforce makes women (who still carry the bulk of the duties involving home and children) more vulnerable with regard to parental stress (Cleary & Mechanic, 1983; Emmons et al., 1991; Frankenhaeuser, 1991a; Simon, 1992). While the picture is much less clear with regard to marital stress, there are indications that the impact of marital stress on well-being may be reduced for working women (Cleary & Mechanic, 1983; Kandel et al., 1985). It is tempting to speculate that marital stressors are much more easily compensated or "put into place" by work experiences, whereas the obligations towards children who, after all, are dependent on their parents, does not allow such a more philosophical attitude towards problems connected with them. The study by Simon (1992) shows that this is likely to depend on the identification with the parental role. Women in this study showed higher symptoms of distress. Also, they were more strongly committed to their parental role. Controlling for parental stress rendered the coefficient for gender insignificant, and for both men and women there was a stronger relationship between parental stress and distress when commitment to the parental role was high.

Thus, it seems that high commitment to goals may increase vulnerability. This is shown, for instance, in work by Brockner et al. (1992). Their results show that "people reacted particularly negatively when they were highly committed to the institution beforehand, but felt that they had been treated unfairly in some recent encounter with the institution" (Brockner et al., 1993, p. 237).

A final field of investigation related to this line of reasoning are gender differences in reactions to stressful situations. Thus, Frankenhaeuser (1991b) reports that hormonal reactions of women to a number of stressors tend to be less pronounced that those of men. Frankenhaeuser and her co-workers then tested the hypothesis that this cannot be explained by genetic differences (at least not exclusively) but has to do with *gender roles*. In a series of studies it is shown that women entering traditionally male occupations show reactions similar to men in response to achievement-related stress situations, and that women react as strongly as men when confronted with stressors connected with the traditional female role (parental stress). This is much in line with the analyses carried out by Kessler & McLeod (1984), which show that women are more strongly affected by stressors experienced by *other* people in their social network ("network stress"). And finally, it is important to note that both Frankenhaeuser (1991a) and Kessler & McRae (1981) report that gender differences in response to certain classes of stressors are diminishing, which is attributed to an increasing similarity in male and female work roles. (That this is not accompanied by a comparable breakdown in the division of labour with regard to family and household—see Eckenrode & Gore, 1990; Frankenhaeuser, 1991a, b—is, of course, likely to increase the risk of conflicts between working role, and family role, which, in turn, may work against the potentially positive effects of labour force participation.)

So, the conclusion from these considerations is that one of the most important differences in vulnerability to stressful experiences should be sought in people's goals—be they connected with specific tasks, concrete projects, more or less permanent roles, or even more global identities. Hobfoll's (1989, 2001) conceptionalization of stress as an experienced or anticipated net loss of resources also emphasizes this aspect, as does the approach of Schönpflug (1985).

5.2.2 Reducing Goals (or Goal Commitment) as a Way of Reducing Stress

It follows from this that an efficient way of dealing with stress might be to alter one's goals. And, indeed, one of the recommendations given by Jackson (1984) for preventing burnout is to foster realistic expectations of what can and cannot be achieved. Schönpflug and colleagues (Schönpflug, 1985; Krenauer & Schönflug, 1980) have shown experimentally that the reduction of goals can alleviate stress. Avoiding unrealistically high goals and expectations also lies at the heart of Ellis' "rational-emotive therapy" with its emphasis on correcting "irrational beliefs" such as being liked by everybody (Ellis & Bernard, 1985), as well as of Wanous' concept of "realistic job preview" (Wanous, 1992). Perez & Reicherts (1992a) propose a coping category which they call "evaluation-oriented" and which contains the change of intention or goals, and Siegrist, who emphasizes an exaggerated need for control as a risk factor, incorporates its reduction in stress management courses (Aust et al., 1997).

Yet, reducing one's aspirations seems to be a double-edged sword (Hobfoll, 2001). It may be helpful and recommendable in many cases, but it may have high costs in others. Thus, the analyses of Edwards & Van Harrison (1993) with regard to P-E fit show that in some cases, indeed, it is perfect fit between what people want and what they get which is associated with least strain. There are cases, however, where "fit" at low levels is different from "fit" at high levels: distress symptoms were higher for people who wanted (P) and had (E) little complexity than for those who aspired high complexity and had it. Aspiring to only a little complexity might indicate a problem. In the same vein, Menaghan & Merves (1984) report that restriction of expectations as a coping strategy was associated with higher symptoms of distress. Similarly, "control rejection", that is, a preference for being told what to do, not taking responsibility etc. does not protect against the impact of stressors (Frese, 1992), but rather is associated with a number of indicators of well-being, such as depression, psychosomatic complaints, job satisfaction, self-esteem and self-efficacy, always in the direction of more control rejection being related to lower well-being (Frese et al., 1994).

All this is reminiscent of a concept of job satisfaction proposed by Bruggemann (1974; see Büssing, 1992; Büssing et al., 1999). She distinguishes different forms of job satisfaction, one of which is based on a reduction in aspirations as a result of initial job dissatisfaction. Bruggemann calls this "resigned job satisfaction", and studies of our group show that this type of "satisfaction" tends to go with lower values in well-being, higher turnover intentions and reduced goal-setting activities.

Thus, it seems that aspirations and expectations cannot be reduced *ad lib*. Rather, such reductions may in many cases be indicators of "a failed person–work interaction", as Büssing (1992, p. 254) concludes for the case of "resigned job satisfaction" (see also Semmer & Schallberger, 1996).

5.2.3 Balanced Commitment versus Resentful Adaptation

Evidently, the reduction of aspiration levels can be either beneficial or problematic. What would distinguish the two?

In the problematic case, it seems that the reduction does not really succeed. The original standards are not really given up; rather, a "double standard" is established: one that one would desire, and another that one feels forced to settle for. Items from the "resignation" aspect of job satisfaction show this quite clearly, including wordings such as "My job is not ideal but, after all, it could be worse" or "In my position, one can really not expect too much". This is a sort of defensive adaptation, aiming at avoiding further disappointment, rather than a positive reappraisal of the situation. I will call this "resentful adaptation" further on. This applies also to Frese's control rejection: "If I reject responsibility, I cannot be blamed". Hallsten (1993) speaks of a "strenuous non-commitment" in such a case (see also Schönpflug, 1985). And it should be noted here that the concept of hardiness (Kobasa, 1988; see also Orr & Westman, 1990) includes commitment, and thus regards loss of commitment as problematic. Also, the commitment scale of the Jenkins Activity Survey, a common measure of Type A behaviour, does not predict CHD (Booth-Kewley & Friedman, 1987).

In the positive case, aspirations are recognized as being unrealistically high and can be replaced with standards that still are considered worth pursuing. As Hallsten (1993) puts it, an "absorbing commitment" makes one vulnerable because failures are not taken as inevitable drawbacks but rather as indicators of a general personal failure; they are considered "self-diagnostic" (Brockner, 1988). In contrast, a positive reappraisal leads, in Hallsten's concept, to a "balanced commitment", with failures leading to "circumscribed frustration" rather than being self-diagnostic. This reasoning is in line with the results of Scheier et al. (1986), who find that optimists can deal better with single defeats, just because they are taken as *single* defeats and not as indicators of a global failure (cf. also the globality component in the concept of attributional style by Seligman and associates (e.g. Buchanan & Seligman, 1995).

All this points to the consideration that standards, aspirations and expectations cannot be taken for granted without considering the frame of reference people have. And this, in turn, points to the necessity to consider individual processes of adaptation in relation to reality, and not only as an intrapsychic problem, a tendency often found in stress research, where things tend to be regarded as idiosyncratic as soon as interpretations are involved (e.g. Vossel, 1987), ignoring the fact that interpretations are themselves shaped by one's culture (cf. Averill's, 1986, "rules of appraisal"). The reality I refer to is, for the most part, *social* reality (Semmer, 1992; see Hobfoll, 2001, for a similar point): people cannot easily chose to ignore standards set by society at large, or by their more proximal reference group. As Harter (1993) argues for the case of the relation of self-esteem to certain goals such as scholastic achievement, social acceptance and the like, such standards are upheld by many people in the mainstream culture, "making it difficult for those feeling inadequate to discount their importance" (p. 93). She adds that this applies only to those who choose to remain within the cultural mainstream. However, leaving this mainstream is in itself associated with high costs so that, at least until one is settled in a subculture, it is like the choice between Scylla and Charybdis (and, of course, the new subculture will impose new standards upon the individual the violation of which is punished, thus creating new sources of stress which may, at least in part, replace the "old" ones encountered in mainstream culture). In a similar vein, giving up the goal of having work that is interesting may be difficult in an environment where interesting work is highly valued, resulting in the "resentful" lowering of aspirations I have referred to. Furthermore, sometimes it is part of one's role obligations to set high standards! A manager, for instance, will be expected to have ambitious goals for him- or herself as well as for his or her team. Reducing them would certainly be associated with quite high costs (Semmer & Schallberger, 1996), and "reappraisal of more basic aspects of the self and the environment are more likely to backfire against the individual—resulting in a sense of insecurity and despair—than they are to have stress-moderating effects" (Hobfoll, 1989, p. 520).

All this also points to some difficulties with the concept of "stress-resistant" people, a concern that is sometimes raised in the context of selection procedures (Cascio, 1987). Of course, if such a "stress resistance" stems from high resources, there is nothing wrong with it. However, in so far as high standards make one vulnerable to stress, the danger must be considered that people achieve "stress resistance" by lowering standards, avoiding stress by trying not to be bothered too much by the problems that come up. Cobb alerted us to this dilemma in 1973 when he stated that persons with a high sense of responsibility were at special risk in occupations with high responsibility for people, but that it is exactly this type of persons that is needed in these positions.

5.2.4 Summary

To sum up, one important aspect of different reactions to potentially stressful circumstances is the goals that people pursue, ranging from low-level task goals, to strivings for a certain role identity, to very general desires, e.g. for a positive self-image. Stress occurs to the extent that goals are thwarted. At the same time, while different goals induce individual differences, these goals are typically not simply idiosyncratic. Rather, they are embedded in one's culture—ranging from subcultures like families, neighbourhoods, people working at the same place, people holding the same occupation, or members of the same club, to states and countries, and even broader cultural contexts, such as cultures emphasizing individualism versus collectivism (see Hofstede, 1991, and the analysis of differential reactions to stressors based on these cultural differences by Cooper & Payne, 1992). Reducing standards may in some cases be a viable strategy, as in cases where people have unrealistically high goals. This strategy is, however, in many cases not feasible, because in many cases it is prohibitive to distance oneself from these standards for ethical (parent role) or social (norms defined by one's (sub)culture) reasons, or because these goals are integral to self-integrity (Hobfoll, 2001). The most protective way of dealing with this is what Hallsten (1993) calls "balanced commitment", which implies being committed but also being able to put things (especially unavoidable failures) into perspective so that they do not become "self-diagnostic" but lead to "circumscribed frustration" (Roger et al., 1993).

Of course, the nature and ambitiousness of goals is not the only aspect contributing to individual differences in stress and health. Rather, response and appraisal tendencies, as well as individual differences in resources, are major factors of influence. These latter will be taken up next.

5.3 VULNERABLE VERSUS RESILIENT PERSONS

5.3.1 Beliefs about the World and One's Relationship to it

Hardly anyone doubts that characteristics of the person strongly influence whether events and circumstances are perceived as stressful, how people cope with them, how they deal with failures in coping, etc. (e.g. Cohen & Edwards, 1989; Cooper & Payne, 1991; Costa et al., 1996). The aspects to be discussed in this section are not specific coping styles but rather more general characteristics which often are thought to co-determine the more proximal coping behaviours. As the heading indicates, these characteristics typically involve beliefs about the world and one's relationship with it, especially one's possibilities to deal with it.

Candidates for this kind of variables range from very broad ones such as hardiness (e.g. Kobasa, 1988) or sense of coherence (Antonovsky, 1991, 1993) to more specific ones such as explanatory style (Peterson & Seligman, 1984), locus of control (Rotter, 1966), self-efficacy (Bandura, 1989, 1992), optimism (Scheier & Carver, 1992, 1999), and self-esteem (Brockner, 1988; Mossholder et al., 1981; see also Hobfoll, 2001, Jerusalem & Schwarzer, 1992; Lazarus & Folkman, 1984). Finally, although it involves more than beliefs, hostility is a central concept here (cf. Siegman, 1994a).

Popular Concepts

Hardiness is conceived of as being composed of the three components commitment, challenge and control (Kobasa, 1988; Maddi, 1997; Orr & Westman, 1990): "*Commitment* is the ability to believe in the truth, importance, and interest value of who one is and what one is doing; and thereby, the tendency to involve oneself fully in the many situations of life ... *Control* refers to the tendency to believe and act as if one can influence the course of events ... *Challenge* is based on the belief that change, rather than stability, is the normative mode of life." (Kobasa, 1988, p. 101).

From this concept it follows that people high on hardiness should better be able to deal with stressful aspects of life. Research shows that quite often, main effects of hardiness on physical and psychological health are found (Bartone, 2000; Cohen & Edwards, 1989; Contrada, 1989; Greene & Nowack, 1995; King et al., 1998; Maddi, 1999; Okun et al., 1988; Orr & Westman, 1990). Both stress appraisal and coping seem to be mediators of this relationship (Florian et al., 1995), as implied by the concept. Evidence on moderator effects is mixed (Cohen & Edwards (1989; Orr & Westman, 1990; see also Steptoe, 1991), with some studies finding interactions (e.g. Maddi, 1999), and others not (e.g. Greene & Nowack, 1995).

The measurement of hardiness has been of concern for many authors (Funk, 1992; Ouelette, 1993; Maddi, 1997). It was originally measured by several existing scales (Ouelette, 1993). Since then, several hardiness scales have been produced, most notably the Personal Views Survey (Maddi, 1997), and the related Dispositional Resilience Scale (Bartone, 2000), and the Cognitive Hardiness Scale (Greene & Nowack, 1995), which avoids the highly negative formulations of the original "alienation" scales. Possibly, at least in part, due to these negative formulations, the confound between hardiness and neuroticism (or negative affectivity) is a serious problem for this concept. Controlling for neuroticism sometimes eliminates the effects of hardiness (Allred & Smith, 1989; Williams et al., 1992; see also Funk, 1992; Orr & Westman, 1990). Results by Kravetz et al. (1993), suggest, however, that hardiness scales may be important indicators for a "health proneness" factor which is strongly related to, but not identical with, a "negative affectivity" (NA) factor. Also, Sinclair & Tetrick (2000) found that hardiness was confounded with, yet distinct from, neuroticism; the overlap was due to the negatively worded items. Controlling for NA, the positively worded items were related to academic problems, anxiety, and depression, and with regard to the negatively worded items the three-way interaction between the components was significant in predicting anxiety and depression. The authors suggest that positive items reflect stress resilience, whereas negative items (which are largely redundant with neuroticism) reflect stress sensitivity. This notion is somewhat similar to that of Kravetz et al. (1993).

Sense of coherence (SOC) is also quite a broad construct. Its three main features are that the environment is perceived as structured, predictable, and explicable, and thus as *comprehensible*, that one perceives oneself to have the resources necessary to deal with one's environment, thus perceiving *manageability*, and that the demands posed by one's environment are interpreted as challenges which are worthy to be taken up, leading to the perception of *meaningfulness* (Antonovsky, 1991). The overlap with hardiness is obvious (Antonovsky, 1993; Geyer, 1997; Maddi, 1997), and in the analyses of Kravetz et al. (1993) both load on the same factor of health proneness.

Research on SOC shows relationships with a number of indicators of well-being and health (Antonovsky, 1993; Feldt, 1997; Johansson-Hanse & Engström, 1999; Söderfeldt et al., 2000). Main effects are predominant, but interactions with working conditions also are sometimes found (e.g. Feldt, 1997; Johansson-Hanse & Engström, 1999; Söderfeldt et al., 2000). Effects of SOC have also been demonstrated longitudinally. Thus, Feldt et al. (2000) found that that some of the effects of adverse working conditions on well-being over time are mediated by SOC. Suominen et al. (2001) demonstrated that SOC predicts subjective health ratings over four years, controlling for initial health status.

As for hardiness, rather strong relationships with anxiety (Antonovsky, 1993), depression (Geyer, 1997), and other indicators of well-being (Ryland & Greenfeld, 1991; Udris & Rimann, 2000) have raised doubts about its distinctiveness from neuroticism, or negative affectivity (see Geyer, 1997). This is supported by the finding by Kravetz et al. (1993) that their model could be improved substantially by allowing SOC to load on both the "health proneness" and the "negative affect" factors. Thus, although effects of SOC have been demonstrated, its status as a distinct construct is somewhat doubtful.

Locus of Control is one of the variables that has very often been shown to be related to well-being (Cvetanovski & Jex, 1994; Spector, 2002). (Remember also that many measures of hardiness include locus of control.) It is the only variable where even the very cautious review by Cohen & Edwards (1989) concludes that it is likely to act as a buffer between stress and health (see also Kahn & Byosiere, 1992), which is confirmed in a recent study by May et al. (1997). Locus of control may also be a moderator of the interaction proposed by Karasek (Karasek & Theorell, 1990). Thus, Parkes (1991) finds the proposed interaction between demands and control only for those high in external locus of control. Her findings refer to both cross-sectional and longitudinal data. Nevertheless, in general the evidence for moderator effects is less conclusive in longitudinal studies (Sonnentag & Frese, in press).

Like locus of control, *self-efficacy* has very consistently been shown to be related to well-being (Bandura, 1992). In its generalized form (Jerusalem & Schwarzer, 1992) it seems quite indistinguishable from *self-esteem*, at least from those parts of self-esteem that are related to one's perceived competences (Judge & Bono, 2001). Self-efficacy and self-esteem seem especially important for dealing with negative feedback and failure in terms of distress as well as persistence (Bandura, 1989; Brockner, 1988; Jerusalem & Schwarzer, 1992, Kernis et al., 1989a). A number of studies indicate that it is not simply the level of self-esteem that is important but also its stability. High but labile self-esteem is associated with more hostility and anger (Greenier et al., 1995; Kernis et al., 1989b). That self-esteem is related to well-being is rather trivial, as it can legitimately be regarded as an indicator of well-being (Judge et al., 2000; Schaubroeck & Ganster, 1991; Wofford & Daly, 1997). Interactions are therefore more interesting, since it is plausible to assume that self-esteem might buffer the influence of stressors. Cohen & Edward (1989) are very sceptical about this, although some more recent studies sometimes do show such interactions (Ganster & Schaubroeck, 1991; Jex & Elaqua, 1999; Pierce et al., 1993). Similarly, a number of studies have found self-efficacy to buffer the effects of stressors (Jex & Bliese, 1999; Jex et al., 2001; May et al., 1997; van Yperen & Snijders, 2000) or of resources like control (Jimmieson, 2000).

Schaubroeck et al. (2000) report such interactive effects for individual self-efficacy in the US but for collective self-efficacy in Hong Kong. It also seems noteworthy that some recent findings suggest that the interaction between demands and control as specified in the Karasek model (Karasek & Theorell, 1990) might be valid only for people high in self-efficacy or related personal resources (Jimmieson, 2000; Schaubroeck & Merritt, 1997; Schaubroeck et al., 2001).

Optimism is distinct from control-related concepts because it does not require that the course of events is influenced by one's own actions (even though it may instigate active attempts to exert influence). Rather, it includes the belief that things are likely to turn out reasonably well anyway (thus being related to a belief in a basically benign world). It has been shown to influence stress appraisals, well-being (both physical and psychological) and coping strategies (Carver & Scheier, 1992, 1999). Optimists tend to employ more problem-solving strategies under controllable conditions, and more reinterpretation and acceptance under less controllable conditions. Pessimists, in contrast, tend to use more denial-oriented strategies. Of special importance is the finding, already mentioned above, that optimists tend to accept failures better, which relates to the "circumscribed" frustration as described by Hallsten (1993) and is indicative of the capability of putting things into perspective.

Finally, *explanatory style* (Buchanan & Seligman, 1995; Peterson & Seligman, 1984) contains elements of optimism/pessimism as well as control, in that it implies the belief that negative events are due to internal, stable and global causes. Internality concerns the aspect of locus (but note that the internal attribution of negative events here implies negative consequences, whereas internality in general is associated with positive consequences); stability is quite similar to pessimism in that it implies the conviction that things are going to stay that way, and globality concerns the question of whether a failure has circumscribed reasons or is indicative of one's lack of capabilities in general (cf. the notion of negative feedback being interpreted as more "self-diagnostic"; Brockner, 1988). Explanatory style has been shown to be related to psychological well-being, especially depression (Peterson & Seligman, 1984) but also to physical health (Buchanan, 1995; Peterson et al., 1988) and to immune functioning (Kamen-Siegel et al., 1991).

Hostility is regarded as the major "toxic" component of the Type A behaviour pattern (Adler & Matthews, 1994; Ganster et al., 1991; Siegman, 1994a). The accumulated evidence suggests that "hostility is associated with and predictive of ill health, CHD, and all-cause mortality" (Miller et al., 1996; see also Williams, 1996). Recent studies show it to be associated with vascular resistance during interpersonal stress (Davis et al., 2000), stronger neuroendocrine, cardiovascular and emotional responses to interpersonal harassment (Suarez et al., 1998), coronary artery calcification (Iribarren et al., 2000), and higher peak blood pressure at work in people in low prestige jobs (Flory et al., 1998). Hostility shows an inverse relationship with socioeconomic status, and might be one of the factors that mediate the relationship between SES and mortality (Flory et al., 1998; Kubzansky et al., 1999; Siegler, 1994).

Conceptually, one can distinguish between (i) a cognitive component, involving hostile beliefs and attitudes about others (cynicism, mistrust, hostile attributions of others' undesired behaviours), (ii) an emotional component, involving anger, and (iii) a behavioural component, involving physical or verbal assault (Buss & Perry, 1992). Given the cultural constraints on physical assault, the latter typically contains the expression of hostility and anger through verbal or nonverbal and paraverbal means (Barefoot, 1992; Siegman, 1994b). Many of the findings cited above are based on the (MMPI-derived) Cook–Medley Ho Scale

(Cook & Medley, 1954), which is heterogeneous but predominantly seems to measure the cognitive component of cynicism, distrust and hostile attributions (Barefoot, 1992).

The *expression* of anger and hostility has received special attention, as it shows the clearest association with CHD (Miller et al., 1996). This expressive component seems to be revealed best in overt behaviour. Thus, the potential for hostility derived from the Structured Interview measure of Type A or related measures, which code not only for hostile content but emphasize expressive style, quite consistently emerge as predictors of cardiovascular reactivity, CAD or CHD. A hostile expressive style is characterized by such behaviours as talking in a loud and explosive voice, having a short response latency, interrupting the interviewer, classifying questions as pointless, and showing a demeaning attitude towards the interviewer. Results based on self-report measures typically are somewhat weaker (Barefoot, 1992; Helmers et al., 1994; Siegman, 1994b). Many of these contain both the expressive component, often labelled as "antagonistic hostility" (Dembroski & Costa, 1987) and contained, for instance, in the State–Trait Anger Expression Inventory (STAXI; Spielberger et al., 1995) and in the Buss–Durkee Hostility Inventory (BDHI; Buss & Durkee, 1957), where it typically yields one of two factors, and the experiencing component (often called "neurotic" hostility; Dembroski & Costa, 1987), which is more characterized by the *experience* of anger and is contained in the other factor of the BDHI, and in the Trait Anger as measured by the STAXI. The Ho Scale loads on both components, but higher on neurotic than antagonistic hostility (Siegman, 1994a).

There has been quite some debate on the role of anger-in versus anger-out as predictors of CHD, with some authors (e.g. Steptoe, 1996) regarding anger-in, and others (e.g. Siegman, 1994b) anger-out as the important component. Recent evidence seems to be more supportive for anger-out as a predictor of CHD (Miller et al., 1996). Anger-out has also been predictive of stroke in participants with a history of ischaemic heart disease (Everson et al., 1999) and of early morning elevations in cortisol among people with high job strain (Steptoe et al., 2000).

Note, however, that the implication is not that components of hostility other than anger-out are irrelevant. They are weaker predictors only with regard to CHD, but they are good predictors of mortality from all causes (Miller et al., 1996). Anger-in may be especially important for the development of cancer (Siegman, 1994b), and being low in anger expression may be involved in the development of high blood pressure (Steptoe, 2001). Nevertheless, the expression of anger may be especially important not only because the feedback of one's own behavior may "feed" the anger, but also because it may imply offences to others, leading to prolonged aversive interactions and the undermining of social relationships (Flory et al., 1998; Siegman, 1994b). The real issue, however, is likely to be the way in which the anger is expressed (see "Expressing emotions", p. 105).

Convergences

Judging from one perspective, the different concepts and the findings related to them are rather confusing. There is some overlap between different concepts; it is quite unclear how many different constructs are involved. Some authors work only with a single construct, such as hardiness or SOC, ignoring overlap with other concepts or being satisfied if it can be shown that their construct explains variance over and above NA. Those who compare several constructs sometimes find two distinct but highly related factors (e.g. Kravetz et al., 1993; Sinclair & Tetrick, 2000), sometimes one very general construct (e.g. Judge & Bono,

2001; Judge et al., 2000), sometimes a hierarchical structure with one very general construct at the top but lower-order factors as well (Bernard et al., 1996). Certainly, more studies are needed that investigate the communalities and differences involved, and these studies should not only work on the level of instruments but also on the level of items, since different construct names may well imply similarity in items.

From another perspective, however, the picture is not so gloomy. There do seem to be some common elements that appear in different studies—including investigations of positive effects of traumatic events (Updegraff & Taylor, 2001)—and although their exact relationship is rather unclear, their basic importance is not. So, if one looks at the "great lines", one might come to a conclusion like the following:

People who are resilient

- tend to interpret their environment basically as benign, that is, they expect things to go well (optimism) and people to not intend harm (trust, agreeableness). All this does not apply unconditionally—which would be a sign of naïvety—but it is the "default" interpretation as long as there are no reasons to believe otherwise.
- tend to accept setbacks and failures (and, thus, stressful experiences) as normal, not necessarily indicative of their own incompetence nor indicative of a basically hostile world. Negative experiences are, therefore, put into perspective, interpreted as part of a larger picture, as having meaning beyond the present situation, for instance, as aversive but necessary and legitimate experiences on one's way to a larger, more overarching goal, as corresponding to the will of God, etc. Optimistic attributional style is relevant here, as it implies negative experiences to be not indicative of a global negative picture (globality), of a general failure which will go on (stability) and of one's general incompetence (internality). Sense of coherence is also relevant here, especially with regard to the dimensions of comprehensibility and meaningfulness, as is the hardiness dimension of commitment which includes "an overall sense of purpose" (Antonovsky, 1991; Kobasa, 1988; Thompson, 1981).
- tend to see life as something that can be influenced and acted upon (internal locus of control), and to see themselves as capable of doing so (self-efficacy, manageability dimension of sense of coherence, competence elements of self-esteem). Related to this is the tendency to see stressful events as a challenge (challenge dimension of hardiness; challenge aspect of the meaningfulness dimension of sense of coherence).
- All this implies also that people who are resilient do show emotional stability and do not have a tendency to experience negative emotions (of all kinds—neuroticism, NA).

The Impact of Resourceful Belief Systems at Various Stages of Stressful Transactions

Theoretically, the concepts mentioned should influence coping strategies, which would imply, as pointed out by Cohen & Edwards (1989), that they should act as moderators in the relationship between stress and outcome variables. Such findings are obtained quite often (see above) but not nearly as consistently as one would expect theoretically.

One reason for this is certainly to be found in methodological difficulties, because moderated regression procedures tend to yield very conservative estimates of interaction effects (Cohen & Edwards, 1989).

A further reason for this might be that the resourceful belief system pictured here has an influence at a much earlier point; that is, it changes the stress appraisal in the first place (Spector, 2002). And, indeed, there are at least some indications that events are appraised as less stressful, for instance, by people high in self-efficacy (Jerusalem & Schwarzer, 1992), self-esteem (Brockner, 1988), locus of control (Jackson, 1989; Payne, 1988) and hardiness (Orr & Westman, 1990). On the other hand, Scheier et al. (1986) find no evidence that pessimists appraise events as more stressful.

However, the study by Scheier et al. (1986) illustrates one of the problems involved in this kind of research with regard to the question of whether or not measures of resourcefulness influence stress appraisal. Using the Ways of Coping instrument (Lazarus & Folkman, 1984), people are asked to describe how they dealt with "the most stressful situation they have encountered in the last two months" (Scheier et al., 1986, p. 1258). By definition, such a measurement limits the variance in the appraisal of the situation as stressful, and it does not allow conclusions if the same event is, indeed, appraised as more or less stressful, depending on one's belief system.

This question can only be investigated if a broad range of events is investigated, which do not have to be appraised as particularly stressful to be eligible, or if events (or dimensions of chronically stressful conditions) are predefined by investigators, as in life-event research or—and this is more germane to our topic—in the area of job stress. Here, the question of individual differences being responsible for the appraisal of the same "stressors" in different ways is being hotly debated, the personality variable discussed most often being NA (Watson et al., 1987). Some investigators claim that much, if not most, of the variance in associations between stressors and strain is due to NA (e.g. Brief et al., 1988; Burke et al., 1993). This has, however, not gone unrefuted (e.g. Chen & Spector, 1991; Spector et al., 2000). Analyses with different indicators of job stressors (e.g. self-report and ratings by trained observers) in our research have consistently shown that correlations between stressors and symptoms are, indeed, inflated by method variance but that substantive associations remain when this is controlled (Semmer & Zapf, 1989; Semmer et al., 1996; Zapf, 1989). Nevertheless, although the relationship between NA and stressors does not necessarily invalidate the association between stressors and strain, it may, at least partly, reflect an appraisal process that leads to higher stress appraisals of the same situation by people high in NA. To the extent that this is true, and to the extent that the resourceful belief systems discussed here are themselves associated with NA, these findings make it likely and plausible that these belief systems operate already on the appraisal phase, thus making moderating effects less likely.

A further possibility is an operation at even earlier stages. People high in NA are more likely to be in high-stress jobs (Spector et al., 1995), people high in self-esteem are more likely to end up in jobs they like (Brockner, 1988), as are people with an internal locus of control (Furnham, 1992). Thus, there may be a tendency for people low in resources to end up in more stressful situations or to even "create" stressors to a greater degree—something that is especially likely for social stressors (Spector et al., 2000). Again, this would work against a moderating effect of resources.

Is it Only Negative Affectivity?

While these mechanisms may, at least in part, explain why moderating effects are not found as consistently as one would expect theoretically, there is another question which is important here: Why is it that resources in the sense of the belief systems discussed here are so often found to be directly related to symptoms, regardless of levels of stressors? After all, this might be interpreted to imply that people low in resources simply score higher on indicators of mental health, and all the mediating and moderating hypotheses surrounding these concepts are needless.

One obvious possibility is that that all these measures are really indicators of NA (Watson et al., 1987—see above), or neuroticism (Dembroski & Costa, 1987). Indeed, the measures discussed here are often found to correlate with one another; some are even part of a larger construct, as discussed above (see, for instance, Bernard et al., 1996; Judge & Bono, 2001; Kravetz et al., 1993; Wofford & Daly, 1997). In many cases controlling for NA significantly reduces associations between belief systems and symptoms (e.g. Orr & Westman, 1990; Schaubroeck & Ganster, 1991; Sinclair & Tetrick, 2000; Smith et al., 1989). Indeed, it would be quite strange if belief systems that have to do with an environment that is meaningful, basically benign, and influenceable, and with a self-concept that involves the capability to actually influence this environment in accordance with one's goals, should not show strong relationships with such a broad construct as NA. Also, the aetiology being proposed for constructs like hardiness, locus of control, sense of coherence, or self-esteem involves experiences of mastery, of failure that can be dealt with and thus stays circumscribed, etc. (cf. Antonovsky, 1991; Bandura, 1986; Brockner, 1988), and, of course, these are conditions that one would also assume to influence NA. And, indeed, chronic stress conditions are found to influence changes in NA over time (Spector et al., 2000). In line with the arguments presented above, more research on the exact type of relationship between belief systems and NA is certainly needed. The most plausible relationship at this time, it seems to me, would be a model that assumes a very high-level construct of health (or disease) proneness (e.g. Bernard et al., 1996; Judge & Bono, 2001; Wofford & Daly, 1997) but would follow a hierarchical approach, with subconstructs that contain a more belief-oriented factor (as, for instance, in Kravetz et al., 1993: hardiness and locus of control) on the one hand and a more affectively oriented factor (e.g. neuroticism, NA, anger, anxiety, depression) on the other. The latter might be separated, at least at a lower level, into positive and negative affect. Interestingly, this would not be too far from concepts in research on subjective well-being, where the basic distinction seems to be similarly between more cognitive (satisfaction) and affective aspects (Diener et al., 1999). Further down, finer and finer distinctions can be made.

Note, however, that attributing an important role to neuroticism, or NA, in concepts of a disease (or health) prone personality does not imply that associations between stressors at work and well-being and health can be reduced to reflecting NA. Rather, NA (or broader constructs that encompass it, as well as more specific concepts that constitute it) would, as all measures of health and well-being, be seen as a factor that may influence the experience and perception of, as well as the reactions to, stress factors, but at the same time may be influenced by these factors (Spector et al., 2000).

In this context, the role of NA in physical health should briefly be mentioned. Studies on resourceful belief systems have often found such associations. In contrast, many authors concluded that the relationship between NA and physical health does not appear to be very strong, except where the association is strongly mediated by health-related behaviour (Costa & McCrae, 1987). There is some evidence casting doubt on this conclusion (e.g. Booth-Kewley & Friedman, 1987; Matthews, 1988; Somervell et al., 1989), leading Adler & Matthews (1994) to conclude that it may be premature to write off an association between

NA and physical health. Indeed, a recent review (Rozanski et al., 1999), concludes that both anxiety and depression—typical indicators of NA—predict CAD, and that these effects cannot be reduced to the influence of health behaviour.

Beliefs and Reality

One final word of caution seems in order: no matter how they are conceived of in detail, the conclusion might seem plausible that resourceful belief systems as depicted here will always be positive, helping to interpret things in a positive way, dealing with them in an efficient way, etc. While this is true in general, it should be pointed out that there must be a minimum amount of correspondence between one's beliefs and reality. Positive illusions seem to be healthy, but only if they are moderate, that is, not completely illusory (Taylor & Brown, 1988), and if they are amenable to clear feedback (Colvin & Block, 1994). High self-esteem may induce poor strategies such as overconfidence in seemingly plausible, but premature, solutions to a problem where further information should be sought (Weiss & Knight, 1980); too high hopes may lead to equally high disappointment, as shown by Frese & Mohr (1987) with regard to unemployed people, and the belief in a benign world, if fostered too strongly, may lead to a threatening challenge to one's total world view by single experiences to the contrary (Brown & Harris, 1978; Wortman & Silver, 1992). An optimistic outlook, a positive evaluation of one's own competencies, and a view of the world as controllable are healthy, but "Illusions destroyed are worse than realistic pessimism" (Frese, 1992, p. 82).

5.3.2   Other Resources

The discussion has, so far, concentrated on beliefs about the world and one's relationship to it. There are, in addition, many other resources that influence one's tendency to experience stress and one's capacity to deal with it (Hobfoll, 1989; Lazarus & Folkman, 1984; Schönpflug & Battmann, 1988). Among them are physical health status, energy level, social support and social status (Fletcher, 1991).

Especially important in the present context is that *experience* and *training* are related to vulnerability to stress (e.g. Fiedler, 1995; Perrez et al., 1992), which has obvious implications for the importance of adequate vocational training.

Another aspect which is discussed quite a bit in health psychology but, so far, has not been taken up sufficiently in industrial and organizational stress research, is that social support is not a something which simply "is there". Being a resource that requires interaction, the amount and quality of support one gets is likely to depend not only on those who supply it but also on those who receive it (cf. Buunk, 1990; Nadler, 1990; Peeters, 1994; Silver et al., 1990). Thus, *eliciting support* may require quite some social, especially self-presentational skills, because highlighting one's distress and complaining about it may make others feel uncomfortable and induce them to avoid contact. What helps to induce people to give support is to show not only that one is distressed but also that one is actively doing something about it and, therefore, not to be blamed (cf. Silver et al., 1990). Paradoxically, this implies that getting help may require resources which those who are most in need may be least likely to possess, implying "that those in greatest need of social support may be least likely to get it" (Silver et al., 1990, p. 398). Furthermore, seeking or accepting social support may imply a threat to self-esteem: Seeking help conveys a lot of information, one of them being that one is "helpless", not able to adequately deal with a problem by oneself, appearing vulnerable. This has been shown to pose a threat to self-esteem (Nadler, 1990; Peeters, 1994). Interestingly, this is one of the areas where something that normally is a positive resource may prove detrimental, namely, self-esteem. There is evidence that people high in self-esteem are especially sensitive to this threat, which may induce them not to seek help when they need it (Nadler, 1990).

Rosenbaum (1990) has suggested the concept of *learned resourcefulness*. Its theoretical status is somewhat difficult to determine, because it mixes aspects of beliefs ("a general belief in one's ability to self-regulate internal events", p. 15), and the use of specific coping strategies, namely both problem-solving and planning (e.g. "When I am faced with a number of things to do, I usually plan my work") and strategies of emotion-control (e.g. "When I feel down, I try to act cheerful so that my mood will change"). Being high in learned resourcefulness has been found to be beneficial in a number of studies, most of which are, however, not work related.

A variable that has recently been investigated with regard to stress and appears promising is the distinction of *action versus state orientation*, where action orientation is conceived of as "the ability to facilitate the enactment of context-adequate intentions" (Kuhl, 1994, p. 14), whereas state orientation is characterized by the inability to "protect" oneself from competing intentions and intrusions of thoughts (and behaviours) that hinder the implementation of an intention (preoccupation), as well as by a general inability to take steps towards implementation of an intention (hesitation). While there are distinct advantages of state orientation as well (Beckmann, 1994), state orientation in general seems to be related to reactivity to stress, to nervousness, and to disruptive self-regulatory and emotional thoughts (Kanfer et al., 1994; Klinger & Murphy, 1994). State orientation is associated with stronger reactions to failure, and state-oriented people ruminate more about their failures and develop more self-doubt (Walschburger, 1994), yet are less able to give up unrealistic goals after failure (Wiedemann et al., 1994). In sum, action orientation may facilitate active, problem-oriented coping modes but also the acceptance of failure and the reduction of too high aspirations, whereas state-oriented people tend to show more passive coping modes, combined with rumination about their failures. What makes this variable especially interesting is not that it is "yet another" belief (or belief system) but that it is concerned with the link between intentions and actions. Thus, it may help explain how the belief systems discussed above may be translated into coping strategies.

Finally, a concept that deserves more attention is *cognitive failure* as conceptionalized by Broadbent et al. (1982). It measures poor attentional control, a tendency towards "absent-mindedness" (e.g. reading something but not taking it in, forgetting why one went from one part of the house to another, starting one thing but continuing with another, confusing left and right, throwing away something one wanted to keep while keeping what was to be thrown away etc.), and it seems to be quite a stable trait (although it also does, of course, show fluctuations according to changing situations; cf. Reason, 1988). It is easily conceivable that such a tendency should lead to errors and should be increased under states of stress where it may be vital to adequately distribute one's attention. Broadbent et al. (1982) therefore conclude that it increases vulnerability to stress. And, indeed, several studies find that the Cognitive Failure Questionnaire (CFQ) correlates with psychiatric symptoms for groups with high, but not with low, levels of stress (Reason, 1988). Cognitive failure has been shown to act as a moderator of the effects of simplified jobs and mental health, with those who have very simple jobs and perceive them as not using their skills showing poorer mental health, but only if they are high in cognitive failure (Clegg & Wall, 1990), a finding which is particularly intriguing because it replicates a similar finding of an earlier study (Clegg et al., 1987). This variable also deserves further investigation, and there may be some interesting relations to state orientation, as this is also related to cognitive failure (Kanfer et al., 1994) and poor attentional control (Klinger & Murphy, 1994).

5.4 RESPONSE TENDENCIES AND COPING

Coping is one of the most important concepts in research on stress. It refers to all attempts (regardless of their success) to manage a stressful transaction, to make it less stressful (Lazarus & Folkman, 1984). These attempts are based on an appraisal of the situation (primary appraisal) and one's possibilities to deal with it (secondary appraisal) and are, therefore, specific to the characteristics of the situation (e.g. a controllable situation tends to elicit more active coping strategies than an uncontrollable one). Nevertheless, it has become increasingly clear that people also have person-specific tendencies to use certain coping strategies (Carver et al., 1989; Ferring & Filipp, 1994; McCrae & Costa, 1986; Miller, 1990). In addition, stable individual differences in coping do not require that certain people will always employ strategy A and others strategy B. There may also be differences on a "meta-level" in that some people are habitually more flexible in their strategies. Thus, Scheier et al. (1986) have shown that optimists are more likely to accept uncontrollable situations and more likely to use active coping strategies in controllable situations than are pessimists. In other words, optimists show a tendency towards coping strategies that are adequate for the situation (Carver & Scheier, 1999)! Similar results are reported by Perrez & Reicherts (1992b) and by Reicherts et al. (1992), who found that depressives tend to be more rigid, and to adjust their coping strategies less in the course of events. Overall, however, people seem to take situational variables into account and adjust their ways of coping to them (Reicherts & Pihet, 2000).

5.4.1 Classifications of Coping

There are many classifications of coping, the most basic one being the dichotomy between problem-focused versus emotion-focused coping, as suggested by Lazarus and his group (Lazarus & Folkman, 1984). Others expand this by adding a category like "appraisal-focused" coping (Billings & Moos, 1984; Pearlin & Schooler, 1978, have a similar dimension which they call "perception-focused").

A somewhat different approach concentrates on the tendency to seek or avoid information concerning the stressful aspects of the situation. This is most clearly expressed in the coping styles called "monitoring" and "blunting" by Miller (1990). Somewhat similarly, Cronkite & Moos (1984) distinguish between "approach and avoidance".

There are many expansions and blends of these approaches. Thus, Endler & Parker (1990) distinguish between problem-focused, emotion-focused and avoidance coping. Carver et al. (1989) have four (second-order) factors which involve active coping, denial and disengagement, acceptance, and a combination of seeking social support and concentration on as well as venting of emotions. McCrae & Costa (1986) distinguish only two main factors which they call "mature" versus "neurotic" coping. A similar dichotomy is suggested by Koeske et al. (1993), who distinguish between "control coping" and "avoidance coping".

Finally, Thoits (1986) proposes a two-by-two matrix involving problem-focused versus emotion-focused coping in one dimension and behavioural versus cognitive strategies in the second one. A similar distinction is made by Steptoe (1991), who further adds the possibility of an approach versus avoidance strategy in each of the four cells.

This short (and not exhaustive) enumeration shows that there is by no means consensus over the number and kind of the dimensions to be employed. This problem is further aggravated by the fact that the same labels do not necessarily imply the same concept.

Thus, items like "consuming alcohol", "eating", "smoking" are sometimes part of an avoidance or denial factor (e.g. Endler & Parker, 1990; Carver et al., 1989; Koeske et al., 1993), but sometimes they belong to an emotion-focused factor (e.g. Billings & Moos, 1984; Latak, 1986); this is especially interesting as Endler & Parker also have an emotion factor, and Latak also has an avoidance factor. "Distraction" is part of "cognitive problem-focused coping" in Thoits' classification but belongs to denial and disengagement in the analysis of Carver et al. (1989). These examples could easily be continued.

In light of this confusion it is surprising that nevertheless there are some tendencies where research is converging. Thus, in general (and with many exceptions), the tendency to employ problem-focused coping (including problem-focused cognitive coping, as defined by Steptoe; that is, a positive reinterpretation) is associated with better mental (and sometimes physical) health while emotion-focused coping tends to show the opposite relationship (Aldwin & Revenson, 1987; Billings & Moos, 1984; Carver et al., 1989; Koeske et al., 1993; Latak, 1986; McCrae & Costa, 1986; Scheier & Carver, 1992). This applies also to self-rated coping efficiency, which is higher in the study by McCrae & Costa (1986) for what they call "mature" coping and lower for what they label "neurotic" coping. Problem-focused coping has also been found to moderate the relationship between control and demands according to the Karasek model (Karasek & Theorell, 1990), in that people who show "active coping" profit from control under conditions of high stress (De Rijk et al., 1998). Avoidance-oriented coping is often found to be beneficial in the short run but detrimental in the long run (Suls & Fletcher, 1985). Also, not surprisingly, avoidance is more beneficial if the problem is uncontrollable whereas approach is more instrumental when something can be done about the situation (Miller, 1990). Finally, Miller (1990) finds that a discrepancy between one's preferred style and aspects of the situation (e.g. being a monitor but not getting enough information, and being a "blunter" but getting a lot of information) may be more detrimental in many situations than coping style *per se*.

5.4.2   The Difficult Role of "Emotion-Focused Coping"

Instrumental and Detrimental Aspects of Emotion-Focused Coping

One of the aspects of this research that are somewhat difficult to interpret is the often-reported finding that "emotional coping" tends to be associated with poorer mental health and poorer outcomes (Edwards, 1998). The reason why this is puzzling is that many authors postulate that emotional coping should not be detrimental *per se*. Rather, highly stressful experiences may require some management of one's intensive emotions before one is able to deal with the problem in a more active and direct way, thus making strategies like symptom management, denial, avoidance, etc. potentially instrumental in regaining the resources needed for active, problem-oriented coping (Lazarus, 1999; Lazarus & Folkman, 1984; Reicherts & Perrez, 1992).

When used alone, or as the dominant mode of coping, however, it does make sense theoretically that the problem at hand is not altered, and emotional coping should, therefore, not be very helpful, unless the problem is uncontrollable to a large extent. It is, therefore, not surprising that these forms of coping tend to correlate with personality traits such as neuroticism (e.g. Carver et al., 1989; Frese, 1986; McCrae & Costa, 1986), in some cases with hostility (Dembroski & Costa, 1987), or with aspects of resourceful belief systems such as optimism, internal locus of control, self-esteem or hardiness (Carver et al., 1989), while problem-oriented forms of coping (including cognitive ones like positive reappraisal) tends to show the opposite pattern of associations.

As long, however, as we do not have more studies on the combination of different coping modes and their change over time, it will be quite difficult to detect positive effects of emotional coping. However, apart from studies that follow patients through various phases of an illness, there is surprisingly little research on the instrumentality of emotional coping for (re) gaining the resources needed to deal with the problem effectively

Some support for this reasoning can be found in a study by Koeske et al. (1993), who conclude that "avoidance coping" tends to be detrimental only when it is used alone, but may even be beneficial if used in conjunction with "control coping". It is also interesting to note that the concept of learned resourcefulness mentioned above (Rosenbaum, 1990) contains items on the effective regulation of emotions. Also, Billlings & Moos (1984) have two scales on emotion-focused coping which seem especially interesting. One is called "affective regulation", and it contains items such as "got away from things for a while", "told myself things that helped me to feel better", "exercised more to reduce tension", "got busy with other things to keep my mind off the problems". This scale has some connotation of using palliative strategies in the instrumental way discussed here. Theoretically, therefore, it should be more beneficial than the other emotion-focused scale, which is called "emotional discharge" and contains items like "took it out on other people" or "tried to reduce tension by drinking more". And, indeed, the "affective regulation" scale correlates positively with self-confidence and negatively (albeit significantly only for women) with depression severity, while the "emotional discharge" scale correlates positively with depression and physical symptoms, and negatively with self-confidence.

An especially interesting approach to this problem is presented by Reicherts and colleagues (Perrez & Reicherts, 1992a; Reicherts & Perrez, 1992; Reicherts & Pihet, 2000). They formulate a "behaviour rules approach" which specifies which coping strategies should work best under what conditions. Thus, in line with many others, they postulate that under conditions of greater controllability there should be more active and less avoidance coping. With regard to self-directed coping, and this is more new to the field, they "prescribe" more palliative coping under high stressfulness (high negative valence) and more re-evaluation of standards when the probability of re-occurrence of the situation is judged to be high. Using a computer-assisted self-observation system where subjects record events in a pocket computer and are then guided through a number of questions concerning their appraisal of the situation, their coping behaviour, etc., they were able to show that conforming to these rules is associated with greater coping effectiveness (measured as reports about to what extent the problem was solved and to what extent people coped in a way they would like to cope). Also, depressives and schizophrenics conform less to these rules. Especially interesting in the present context is the finding that conformity to the rules regarding "self-directed coping", i.e. palliation and re-evaluation, is related to indicators of psychological health.

In taking into account the "fit" between characteristics of the situation and the coping strategies used, and by allowing analyses of how appraisals of and coping with a situation may change over time, this seems an especially interesting approach which can be expected to greatly enhance our understanding of coping effectiveness and of the role of individual differences in coping processes. Further research along this line seems, therefore, especially important (for a similar approach, focusing on stress and social interactions at work, see Buunk, 1990; Peeters, 1994).

Coping or Distress Intensity?

Emotion-Focused Coping as "Inability to Cope"

There is an additional problem, however, with the conceptualization and, especially, the operationalization of "emotion-focused" coping. For a number of items typically contained in scales with this label it is doubtful whether they actually measure coping, that is, an attempt to deal with the problem at hand.

Consider a few examples. Carver et al. (1989) report a scale they call "focus on and venting of emotions", with items such as "I get upset and let my emotions out", or "I get upset, and am really aware of it". This scale correlates with anxiety. Aldwin & Revenson (1987) report an emotion-focused scale that taps "self-blame" and is positively related to symptoms and negatively related to perceived coping efficiency. McCrae & Costa (1986) also have a self-blame scale and also report items such as "thought about the problem over and over without reaching a decison". Both are related to neuroticism (see also Costa et al., 1996). Endler & Parker (1990) report an "emotion-oriented subcale" containing, again, self-blame but also items like "I became very tense". The scale correlates with several scales indicative of NA, such as anxiety, depression and neuroticism. Frese (1986) reports a "brooding" scale (e.g. "I think about it for some days"), which correlates with psychosomatic complaints. Nowack (1989) reports a scale on "intrusive negative thoughts" (e.g. "blame and criticize myself"), which correlates with distress.

There are many more examples of this, but the point should be clear: if one defines coping as cognitions and behaviours designed to deal with the stressful transaction (Cox & Ferguson, 1991, p. 19) or as "efforts to manage specific external and/or internal demands (Lazarus & Folkman, 1984, p. 141), in other words, as an *attempt to do something about the stressful situation*—be that changing of the situation or changing one's feelings about it—then it is doubtful whether what is being measured here can really be called *coping*. Rather, items like these seem to measure how strongly one feels distressed (e.g. "I become very tense") and the inability to concentrate on anything other than the distressing thoughts (brooding, blaming). Nothing in these items indicates that one is *trying to regulate one's emotions*; rather, they seem to measure the inability to do so!

Not surprisingly, there are scales which intend to measure the *impact* of events and which contain items that are quite overlapping, for instance, by measuring "intrusion", that is, the tendency to ruminate about stressful events and, in doing so, to keep experiencing the feelings associated with them (Horowitz et al., 1979; Ferring & Filipp, 1994). In a similar vein, Keenan & Newton (1984) describe "emotional reactions" to frustration in organizations, consisting of items such as "I sometimes feel quite frustrated over things that happen at work" or "On occasion I have found it difficult to keep my temper at work".

In other words, the suspicion arises that scales like these, rather than being measures of coping styles, really come close to being measures of emotional reactivity in response to potentially stressful events or circumstances—or, to put it differently, measures of experienced stress as far as they ask about circumscribed historical events and measures of the tendency to experience stress in the case of generalized "coping" styles. If neuroticism is regarded as "a chronic condition of irritability and distress-proneness which is relatively independent of objective conditions" (Costa & McCrae, 1987, p. 302), then "coping" measures of this type may well be regarded as "distress-proneness" *vis-à-vis* potentially stressful conditions.

Indeed, one can easily imagine that this tendency grows stronger and stronger as a result of stressful experiences, undermining resources (such as resourceful belief systems) and leading into a spiral where the "threshold" for reacting with distress is successively lowered, so that finally situations previously considered "normal" by the person in question (and still considered normal by most other people) now are sufficient to elicit stress reactions.

Our research group (Semmer et al., 2001) has compared the effects of a "classical" emotion-oriented coping measure (CISS) (Endler & Parker, 1990; see Endler, 1998) with an item from the instrument by Reicherts (1999) that measures successful palliative coping ("normally, I succeed to calm down"). This items is positively associated with "Positive Attitude towards Life" (Grob et al., 1991), and it predicts it in some longitudinal analyses. At the same time, it correlates negatively with "emotional coping" as measured by the CISS, which, in turn, is negatively associated with Positive Attitude towards Life, as one would expect. Such results support the position advocated here; further research along these lines certainly seems necessary and promising.

A similar position has been advocated by Stanton and colleagues (Stanton & Franz, 1999; Stanton et al., 2000). They have developed a scale that measures approach-oriented aspect of emotional coping, namely "emotional processing" and "emotional expression". At least for women, emotional approach coping seems to be beneficial, whereas for men, associations with rumination were found. However, coping through emotional expression was found to be associated with higher life satisfaction in both sexes, and a receptive context seems to render emotional approach coping adaptive for men as well. Certainly more work on the adaptiveness of emotional processing and expression is needed as it is related to gender, context, and its dependence on the joint use of different strategies (for instance, in one of the studies by Stanton et al. the joint use of emotional processing and emotional expression turned out to be maladaptive). However, the concept of "coping through emotional approach" certainly is a major breakthrough that deserves attention in future research.

Expressing Emotions: Coping or Intensifying of Distress?

Although this is conceptually more difficult, a similar point can be made with regard to "venting" of emotions, that is, showing them, taking them out on other people etc. Items like these often go together with the "reactivity" items discussed above; sometimes items capture both in one formulation (e.g. Carver et al., 1989). In many cases, the expression of an emotion tends to make the emotion stronger (Baumeister et al., 1994; Schwenkmezger & Hank, 1996; Siegman 1994b). It feeds back into the experience of the emotion; it keeps the attention on the emotion and on the circumstances that elicited it, and thus keeps "nourishing" the emotional experience. In addition, in many cases it elicits negative or avoidance reactions in others.

Thus, the expression of anger may antagonize others and undermine their willingness to give social support (Weber, 1993); "dysphoric interactions" may elicit negative reactions (Strack & Coyne, 1983), and distress in general may lead to feelings of helplessness, rejection, and unwillingness to give social support, at least as long as the "victim" does not "behave like a 'good' victim", that is, show signs of efforts to deal effectively with his or her situation (Silver et al., 1990).

That the expression of emotions keeps them alive is, of course, a somewhat controversial statement (and, as we shall see shortly, it is not true unconditionally). Especially in the case of anger and its association with CHD it has often been found that *not* expressing one's anger (anger-in) might be risky, especially for hypertension, although the evidence now seems to be pointing more to an effect of anger-out (see above).

However, surprisingly little research deals with the crucial question of whether the (non) expression of anger is effective in ending one's state of anger. As Baumeister et al. (1994) state, "the decisive issue is whether the person stays angry or not" (p. 108). And this may not depend simply on expressing anger or not. One's anger may dissipate when one thinks about different things, or one may ruminate and thus stay angry (Roger & Jamieson, 1998). Expressing it may give relief, or it may keep the focus on the emotion and the circumstances that caused it (note that in the study of Engebretson et al., 1989, expressing their anger was only *relatively* more effective for people high in anger-out, but in absolute terms they showed higher blood pressure during and after the provoking situation than those high in anger-in). Results by Weber (1993) show that both strategies have helpful and hindering aspects, the most crucial variable being what Weber terms "antagonism". Expression of anger can be constructive (e.g. explaining one's feelings to a partner) or antagonistic (offending, blaming the partner). Indeed, the rather simple manipulation of instructing people to describe anger-arousing events in a loud and rapid voice results in stronger elevations of blood pressure and heart rate than asking them to describe them in a low and soft voice (Siegman, 1994b). Likewise, not expressing the anger may be antagonistic if associated with ruminating, self-pity, dreaming about revenge etc. ("silent seething"; Baumeister et al., 1994; see also Roger & Jamieson, 1998) but it may be non-antagonistic by putting things into perspective, trying to see them from a humorous side, trying to understand the other's perspective, etc. The non-antagonistic mode will tend to end the state of anger while the antagonistic one will tend to sustain or even increase it. Similar results were found by Davidson and colleagues (e.g. Davidson et al., 2000), who also reported a successful intervention aiming at the constructive expression of anger (Davidson et al., 1999).

This reasoning is also supported by the work of Pennebaker and colleagues on the health effects of talking or writing about traumatic experience (e.g., Smyth & Pennebaker, 1999). They conclude that the positive effects are attained only if the experience is translated into a coherent narrative that has meaning. Increased used of terms implying causality or insight is associated with gaining from sharing the experience. Using very few negative emotion words (repression) hinders this constructive process, but so does overuse of negative emotion words, which may indicate "a recursive loop of complaining without attaining closure" (Smyth & Pennebaker, 1999, p. 81). Thus, the real question may not necessarily be whether people express their emotions or not, but whether not expressing them results in unprocessed, and recurring, negative emotions or in getting over things, and whether expressing negative emotions creates a positive feedback loop or a constructive process of coming to terms with one's emotions. These distinctions have to be taken up in measures of emotional coping in order to gain insight in its effectiveness.

5.4.3 Summary

Thus, in general, people who have the tendency to cope by dealing actively with the problem tend to be better off. However, where the situation is taken into account, it becomes clear that palliative modes of coping may be beneficial (i) in highly stressful situations where palliation may be instrumental in building up the resources needed for other forms of coping, and (ii) in situations that cannot be controlled. The latter also call for a re-evaluation of one's goals. Such coping strategies do seem to have a habitual component, as does the tendency to adjust one's strategy to the characteristics of the situation and its changes over time.

These strategies, in turn, depend, at least in part, on personality characteristics such as hostility and, especially, neuroticism, and they also depend on resourceful belief systems and other resources as discussed above.

5.5 FINAL COMMENTS

While there are many qualifications and differentiations to this, the picture seems to be emerging of a person who is low on neuroticism and antagonism, has coping resources such as resourceful belief systems, a good training, and the social skills to elicit social support, as well as the tendency to use active, problem-oriented coping strategies wherever possible, but also the capability to realistically (and not resentfully) adjust to reality where it cannot be altered, and the capability of dealing with one's negative emotions in a constructive way.

Two final comments are in order with regard to this picture:

1. It becomes increasingly clear that resilient people have a certain way of dealing with *reality*. Coping actively under all circumstances, nourishing illusions over one's capabilities that are far from reality, or having a naive optimism are not characteristics of this effectiveness. While individual differences with regard to coping with, and suffering from, the stressors of working life, and life in general, are pervasive, they should not seduce us to reduce everything to idiosyncratic, exclusively subjective, phenomena (Hobfoll, 2001; Semmer, 1992).

2. While, in many cases, it is not the objective situation *per se* but the way people deal with it that decides about outcomes, it should be kept in mind that resiliency itself is, albeit only partly, a product of such circumstances. If one examines the effects of stress on (physical or psychological) health on the one hand and on the development of resiliency versus vulnerability on the other, the parallels are striking. Apart from overwhelming, traumatic single experiences, it is *chronically stressful conditions* that overtax people's resources, which impairs their health and well-being—and it is the same conditions that undermine their coping resources. The same applies to a lack of challenge, because the experience of mastering difficult situations also seems necessary for the development of both well-being and coping resources. Thus, a vicious circle may develop in which the most damaging long-term effect of stress may be its capacity to undermine the very

resources needed to deal with it effectively. This often leads to the perception of the person being "the cause" of the problems, because he or she seems unable to deal with problems that other people do deal with effectively. This supports an attribution error—for laypeople and scientists alike—that induces people to overemphasize individual differences and to underemphasize reality and not to see the vicious circle in which one is reinforcing the other. The picture even worsens when some of these cumulative effects refer to characteristics of the person which, by themselves, tend to irritate others (e.g. excessive complaints; Silver et al., 1990) or even antagonize them (e.g. aggressive behaviour, lack of dependability in cooperative work, etc.). In such a case, the person does, indeed, create new stressors for him- or herself as well as for others, and it becomes very difficult for others to see how much this "actor" is also a "victim" of stressful life circumstances during his or her life.

REFERENCES

Adler, N. & Matthews, K. (1994). Health psychology: why do some people get sick and some stay well? *Annual Review of Psychology*, **45**, 229–59.

Aldwin, C.M. & Revenson, G.A. (1987). Does coping help? A reexamination of the relation between coping and mental health. *Journal of Personality and Social Psychology*, **53**, 337–48.

Allred, K.D. & Smith, T.W. (1989). The hardy personality: cognitive and physiological responses to evaluative threat. *Journal of Personality and Social Psychology*, **56**, 257–66.

Antonovsky, A. (1991). The structural sources of salutogenic strengths. In C.L. Cooper & R. Payne (eds) *Personality and Stress: Individual Differences in the Stress Process* (pp. 67–104). Chichester: John Wiley & Sons, pp. 67–104.

Antonovsky, A. (1993). The structure and properties of the Sense of Coherence Scale. *Social Science and Medicine*, **36**, 725–33.

Aust, B., Peter, R. & Siegrist, J. (1997). Stress management in bus drivers: a pilot study based on the model of effort-reward imbalance. *International Journal of Stress Management*, **4**, 297–305.

Averill, J.R. (1986). The acquisition of emotions during adulthood. In R. Harré (eds) *The Social Construction of Emotions*. Oxford: Basil Blackwell, pp. 98–118.

Bandura, A. (1986). *Social Foundations of Thought and Action: A Social Cognitive Theory*. Englewood Cliffs, NJ: Prentice Hall.

Bandura, A. (1989). Self-regulation of motivation and action through internal standards and goal systems. In L.A. Pervin (ed.) *Goal Concepts in Personality and Social Psychology*. Hillsdale, NJ: Lawrence Erlbaum, pp. 19–85.

Bandura, A. (1992). Exercise of personal agency through the self-efficacy mechanism. In R. Schwarzer (ed.) *Self-Efficacy: Thought Control of Action*. Washington, DC: Hemisphere, pp. 3–38

Barefoot, J.C. (1992). Developments in the measurement of hostility. In H.S. Friedman (ed.) *Hostility, Coping and Health*. Washington, DC: APA, pp. 13–31.

Barnett, R.C. & Hyde, J.S. (2001). Women, men, work, and family: an expansionist theory. *American Psychologist*, **56**, 781–796.

Bartone, P.T. (2000). Hardiness as a resilience factor for United States forces in the Gulf War. In J.M. Violanti, D. Paton & C. Dunning (eds) *Posttraumatic Stress Intervention: Challenges, Issues, and Perspectives*. Springfield, IL: Charles C. Thomas.

Baumeister, R.F., Heatherton, T.F. & Tice, D.M. (1994). *Losing Control. How and Why People Fail at Self-Regulation*. San Diego, CA: Academic Press.

Beckmann, J. (1994). Volitional correlates of action versus state orientation. In J. Kuhl & J. Beckmann (eds) *Volition and personality: Action Versus State Orientation* (pp. 155–166). Seattle, WA: Hogrefe & Huber, pp. 155–66.

Bernard, L.C., Hutchison, S., Lavin, A. & Pennington, P. (1996). Ego-strength, hardiness, self-esteem, self-efficacy, optimism, and maladjustment: health-related personality constructs and the "Big Five" model of personality. *Assessment*, **3**, 115–31.

Billings, A.G. & Moos, R.H. (1984). Coping, stress, and social resources among adults with unipolar depression. *Journal of Personality and Social Psychology*, **46**, 877–91.

Birks, Y. & Roger, D. (2000). Identifying components of type-A behaviour: "toxic" and "non-toxic" achieving. *Personality and Individual Differences*, **28**, 1093–105.

Booth-Kewley, S. & Friedman, H.S. (1987). Psychological predictors of heart disease: a quantitative review. *Psychological Bulletin*, **101**, 343–62.

Brief, A.P., Burke, M.J., George, J.M., Robinson, B. & Webster, J. (1988). Should negative affectivity remain an unmeasured variable in the study of job stress. *Journal of Applied Psychology*, **73**, 193–8.

Broadbent, D.E., Cooper, P.F., FitzGerald, P. & Parkes, K.R. (1982). The Cognitive Failures Questionnaire (CFQ) and its correlates. *British Journal of Clinical Psychology*, **21**, 1–16.

Brockner, J. (1988). *Self-Esteem at Work*. Lexington, MA: Lexington Books.

Brockner, J., Tyler, T.R. & Cooper-Schneider, R. (1992). The influence of prior commitment to an institution on reactions to perceived unfairness: the higher they are, the harder they fall. *Administrative Science Quarterly*, **37**, 241–61.

Brockner, J., Wiesenfeld, B.A. & Raskas, D.F. (1993). Self-esteem and expectancy-value discrepancy. The effects of believing that you can (or can't) get what you want. In R.F. Baumeister (ed.) *Self-Esteem: The Puzzle of Low Self-Regard*. New York: Plenum Press, pp. 219–40.

Brown, G.W. & Harris, R. (1978). *Social Origins of Depression: A Study of Psychiatric Disorder in Women*. New York: Free Press.

Bruggemann, A. (1974). Zur Unterscheidung verschiedener Formen von "Arbeitszufriedenheit" [The distinction of different forms of job satisfaction]. *Arbeit und Leistung*, **28**, 281–4.

Buchanan, G.M. (1995). Explanatory style and coronary heart disease. In G.M. Buchanan & M.E.P. Seligman (eds) *Explanatory Style*. Hillsdale, NJ: Lawrence Erlbaum.

Buchanan, G.M. & Seligman, M.E.P. (1995). *Explanatory style*. Hillsdale, NJ: Erlbaum

Burke, M.J., Brief, A.P. & George, J.M. (1993). The role of negative affectivity in understanding relations between self-reports of stressors and strains: a comment on the applied psychology literature. *Journal of Applied Psychology*, **78**, 402–12.

Buss, A.H. & Durkee, A. (1957). An inventory for assessing different kinds of hostility. *Journal of Consulting Psychology*, **21**, 343–9.

Buss, A.H. & Perry, M. (1992). The aggression questionnaire. *Journal of Personality and Social Psychology*, **63**, 452–9.

Büssing, A. (1992). A dynamic view of job satisfaction in psychiatric nurses in Germany. *Work and Stress*, **6**, 239–59.

Büssing, A., Bissels, T., Fuchs, V. & Perrar, K.-M. (1999). A dynamic model of work satisfaction: qualitative approaches. *Human Relations*, **52**, 999–1028.

Buunk, A.P. (1990). Affiliation and helping interactions within organizations: a critical analysis of the role of social support with regard to occupational stress. In W. Stroebe & M. Hewstone (eds) *European Review of Social Psychology*, vol. 1. Chichester: John Wiley & Sons, pp. 293–322.

Cantor, N. & Langston, C.A. (1989). Ups and downs of life tasks in a life transition. In L.A. Pervin (ed.) *Goal Concepts in Personality and Social Psychology*. Hillsdale, NJ: Lawrence Erlbaum, pp. 127–67.

Carver, C.S. & Scheier, M.F. (1990). Principles of self-regulation: action and emotion. In E.T. Higgins & R.M. Sorrentino (eds) *Handbook of Motivation and Cognition*, vol. 2. New York: Guilford, pp. 3–52.

Carver, C.S. & Scheier, M.F. (1992). Confidence, doubt, and coping with anxiety. In D.G. Forgays, T. Sosnowski & K. Wrzesniewski (eds) *Anxiety: Recent Developments in Cognitive, Psychophysiological, and Health Research*, Series in health psychology and behavioral medicine. Washington, DC: Hemisphere, pp. 13–22.

Carver, C.S. & Scheier, M.F. (1999). Optimism. In C.R. Snyder (ed.) *Coping: The Psychology of What Works*. New York: Oxford University Press, pp. 182–204.

Carver, C.S., Scheier, M.F. & Weintraub, J.K. (1989). Assessing coping strategies: a theoretically based approach. *Journal of Personality and Social Psychology*, **56**, 267–83.

Cascio, W. F. (1987). *Applied Psychology in Personnel Management*, 3rd edn. Englewood Cliffs, NJ: Prentice Hall.

Chen, P.Y. & Spector, P.E. (1991). Negative affectivity as the underlying cause of correlations between stressors and strains. *Journal of Applied Psychology*, **76**, 398–407.

Cleary, P.D. & Mechanic, D. (1983). Sex differences in psychological distress among married people. *Journal of Health and Social Behavior*, **24**, 111–21.

Clegg, C. & Wall, T. (1990). The relationship between simplified jobs and mental health: a replication study. *Journal of Occupational Psychology*, **63**, 289–96.

Clegg, C.W., Wall, T.D. & Kemp, N.J. (1987). Women on the assembly-line: a comparison of main and interactive explanations of job satisfaction, absence and mental health. *Journal of Occupational Psychology*, **60**, 271–87.

Cobb, S. (1973). Role-responsibility: the differentiation of a concept. *Occupational Mental Health*, **3**, 10–14.

Cohen, S. & Edwards, J.R. (1989). Personality characteristics as moderators of the relationship between stress and disorder. In R.W.J. Neufeld (ed.) *Advances in the Investigation of Psychological Stress*. New York: John Wiley & Sons, pp. 235–83.

Colvin, C.R. & Block, J. (1994). Do positive illusions foster mental health? An examination of the Taylor and Brown formulation. *Psychological Bulletin*, **116**, 3–20.

Contrada, R.J. (1989). Type A behavior, personality hardiness, and cardiovascular responses to stress. *Journal of Personality and Social Psychology*, **57**, 895–903.

Contrada, R.J. & Krantz, D.S. (1988). Stress, reactivity, and type A behavior: current status and future directions. *Annals of Behavioral Medicine*, **10**, 64–70.

Cook, W.W. & Medley, D.M. (1954). Proposed hostility and pharasaic-virtue scales for the MMPI. *Journal of Applied Psychology*, **38**, 414–18.

Cooper, C.L. (ed.) (1998). *Theories of Organizational Stress*. Oxford: Oxford University Press.

Cooper, C.L. & Payne, R. (eds) (1991). *Personality and Stress: Individual Differences in the Stress Process*. Chichester: John Wiley & Sons.

Cooper, C.L. & Payne, R.L. (1992). International perspectives on research into work, well-being and stress management. In J. Campbell Quick, L.R. Murphy & J.J. Hurrell, Jr (eds) *Stress and Well-Being at Work. Assessments and Interventions for Occupational Mental Health*. Washington, DC: American Psychological Association, pp. 348–68.

Costa, P. T. & McCrae, R.R. (1987). Neuroticism, somatic complaints, and disease: is the bark worse than the bite? *Journal of Personality*, **55**, 299–316.

Costa, P.T., Somerfield, M.R. & McCrae, R.R. (1996). Personality and coping: a reconceptualization. In M. Zeidner & N.S. Endler (eds) *Handbook of Coping: Theory, Research, Applications*. New York: John Wiley & Sons, pp. 44–61.

Cox, T. & Ferguson, E. (1991). Individual differences, stress and coping. In C.L. Cooper & R. Payne (eds) *Personality and Stress: Individual Differences in the Stress Process*. Chichester: John Wiley & Sons, pp. 7–30.

Cronkite, R.C. & Moos, R.H. (1984). The role of predisposing and moderating factors in the stress–illness relationship. *Journal of Health and Social Behavior*, **25**, 372–93.

Cropanzano, R., James, K. & Citera, M. (1993). A goal hierarchy model of personality, motivation, and leadership. *Research in Organizational Behavior*, **15**, 267–322.

Cvetanovski, J. & Jex, S.M. (1994). Locus of control of unemployed people and its relationship to psychological and physical well-being. *Work and Stress*, **8**, 60–7.

Davidson, K., MacGregor, M., Stuhr, J., Dixon, K. & MacLean, D. (2000). Constructive anger verbal behavior predicts blood pressure in a population-based sample. *Health Psychology*, **19**, 55–64.

Davidson, K., MacGregor, M., Stuhr, J. & Gidron, Y. (1999). Increasing constructive anger verbal behavior decreases resting blood pressure: a secondary analysis of a randomized controlled hostility intervention. *International Journal of Behavioral Medicine*, **6**, 268–78.

Davis, M.C., Matthews, K.A. & McGrath, C.E. (2000). Hostile attitudes predict vascular resistance during interpersonal stress in men and women. *Psychosomatic Medicine*, **62**(1), 17–25.

De Rijk, A.E., Le Blanc, P.M., Schaufeli, W.B. & de Jonge, J (1998). Active coping and need for control as moderators of the job demand–control model: effects on burnout. *Journal of Occupational and Organizational Psychology*, **71**, 1–18.

Dembroski, T.M. & Costa, P. (1987). Coronary prone behavior: components of the Type A pattern and hostility. *Journal of Personality*, **55**, 211–35.

Dembroski, T.M. & Costa, P.T. (1988). Assessment of coronary prone behavior: a current overview. *Annals of Behavioral Medicine*, **10**, 60–3.

Diener, E., Suh, E.M., Lucas, R.E. & Smith, H. (1999). Subjective well-being: three decades of progress. *Psychological Bulletin*, **125**, 276–302.

Eckenrode, J. & Gore, S. (1990). *Stress between Work and Family*. New York: Plenum Press.

Edwards, J.E. (1991). The measurement of Type A behavior pattern: an assessment of criterion-oriented validity, content validity, and construct validity. In C.L. Cooper & R. Payne (eds) *Personality and Stress: Individual Differences in the Stress Process*. Chichester: John Wiley & Sons, pp. 151–80.

Edwards, J.R. & van Harrison, R. (1993). Job demands and worker health: three-dimensional re-examination of the relationship between person–environment fit and strain. *Journal of Applied Psychology*, **78**, 628–48.

Edwards, J.R. (1998). A cybernetic theory of organizational stress. In C.L. Cooper (ed.) *Theories of Organizational Stress*. Oxford: Oxford University Press, pp. 122–52.

Edwards, J.R., Caplan, D. & van Harrison, R. (1998). Person–environment fit theory. In C.L. Cooper (ed.) *Theories of Organizational Stress*. Oxford: Oxford University Press, pp. 28–67.

Ellis, A. & Bernard, M.E. (1985). What is rational-emotive therapy (RET)? In A. Ellis & M.E. Bernard (eds) *Clinical Applications of Rational-Emotive Therapy*. New York: Plenum Press, pp. 1–30.

Emmons, C.-A., Biernat, M., Tiedje, L, B., Lang, E.L. & Wortman, C.B. (1991). Stress, support, and coping among women professionals with preschool children. In J. Eckenrode & S. Gore (eds) *Stress between Work and Family*. New York: Plenum Press, pp. 61–93.

Emmons, R.A. (1986). Personal striving: an approach to personality and subjective well-being. *Journal of Personality and Social Psychology*, **51**, 1058–68.

Emmons, R.A. (1989). The personal striving approach to personality. In L.A. Pervin (ed.) *Goal Concepts in Personality and Social Psychology*. Hillsdale, NJ: Lawrence Erlbaum, pp. 87–126.

Emmons, R.A. (1996). Striving and feeling: personal goals and subjective well-being. In J. Bargh & P. Gollwitzer (eds) *The Psychology of Action: Linking Motivation and Cognition to Behavior*. New York: Guilford, pp. 314–37.

Endler, N.S. (1998). Stress, anxiety and coping: the multidminesional interaction model. *Canadian Psychology*, **38**, 136–53.

Endler, N.S. & Parker, J.D.A. (1990). Multidimensional assessment of coping: a critical evaluation. *Journal of Personality and Social Psychology*, **58**, 844–54.

Engebretson, T.O., Matthews, K.A. & Scheier, M.F. (1989). Relations between anger expression and cardiovascular reactivity: reconciling inconsistent findings through a matching hypothesis. *Journal of Personality and Social Psychology*, **57**, 513–21.

Everson, S.A., Kaplan, G.A., Goldberg, D.E., Lakka, T.A., Sivenius, J. & Salonen, J.T. (1999). Anger expression and incident stroke: prospective evidence from the Kuopio Ischemic Heart Disease Study. *Stroke*, **30**, 523–8.

Farr, R.M. & Moscovici, S. (1984). *Social Representation*. Cambridge: Cambridge University Press.

Feldt, T. (1997). The role of sense of coherence in well-being at work: analysis of main and moderator effects. *Work and Stress*, **11**, 134–47.

Feldt, T., Kinnunen, U. & Mauno, S. (2000). A mediational model of sense of coherence in the work context: a one-year follow-up study. *Journal of Organizational Behavior*, **21**, 461–76.

Ferring, D. & Filipp, S.-H. (1994). Teststatistische Ueberprüfung der Impact of Event-Skala: Befunde zu Reliabilität und Stabilität [Statistical testing of the impact of event scale: reliability and stability]. *Diagnostica*, **40**, 344–62.

Fiedler, F. (1995). Cognitive resources and leadership performance. *Applied Psychology: An International Review*, **44**, 5–28.

Fletcher, B. (C) (1991). *Work, Stress, Disease and Life Expectancy*. Chichester: John Wiley & Sons.

Florian, V., Mikulincer, M. & Taubman, O. (1995). Does hardiness contribute to mental health during a stressful real-life situation? The roles of appraisal and coping. *Journal of Personality and Social Psychology*, **68**, 687–95.

Flory, J.D., Matthews, K. & Owens, J. F. (1998). A social information processing approach to dispositional hostility: relationships with negative mood and blood pressure elevations at work. *Journal of Social and Clinical Psychology*, **17**(4), 491–504.

Frankenhaeuser, M. (1991a). The psychophysiology of workload, stress, and health: comparison between the sexes. *Annals of Behavioral Medicine*, **13**, 197–204.

Frankenhaeuser, M. (1991b). The psychophysiology of sex differences as related to occupational status. In M. Frankenhaeuser, U. Lundberg & M. Chesney (eds) *Women, Work, and Health. Stress and Opportunities*. New York: Plenum Press, pp. 39–61.

Frese, M. (1985). Stress at work and psychosomatic complaints: a causal interpretation. *Journal of Applied Psychology*, **70**, 314–28.

Frese, M. (1986). Coping as a moderator and mediator between stress at work and psychosomatic complaints. In M.H. Appley & R. Trumbull (eds) *Dynamics of Stress*. New York: Plenum Press, pp. 183–206.

Frese, M. (1992). A plea for realistic pessimism: on objective reality, coping with stress, and psychological dysfunction. In L. Montada, S.-H. Filipp & M.J. Lerner (eds) *Life Crises and Experiences of Loss in Adulthood*. Hillsdale, NJ: Lawrence Erlbaum, pp. 81–94.

Frese, M. & Mohr, G. (1987). Prolonged unemployment and depression in older workers: a longitudinal study of intervening variables. *Social Science and Medicine*, **25**, 173–8.

Frese, M. & Zapf, D. (1994). Action as the core of work psychology; a German approach. In H.C. Triandis, M.D. Dunnette & L.M. Hough (eds) *Handbook of Industrial and Organizational Psychology*, vol. 4. Palo Alto, CA: Consulting Psychologists Press, pp. 271–340.

Frese, M., Erbe-Heinbokel, M., Grefe, J., Rybowiak, V. & Weike, A. (1994). "Mir ist es lieber, wenn ich genau gesagt bekomme, war ich tun muß": Probleme der Akzeptanz von Verantwortung und Handlungsspielraum in Ost und West ["I prefer to be told exactly what to do": Problems with accepting responsibility and control in East and West]. *Zeitschrift für Arbeits- und Organisationspsychologie*, **38**, 22–33.

Funk, S.C. (1992). Hardiness: a review of theory and research. *Health Psychology*, **11**, 335–45.

Furnham, A. (1992). *Personality at Work. The Role of Individual Differences in the Workplace*. London: Routledge.

Ganster, D.C. & Schaubroeck, J. (1991). Role stress and worker health: an extension of the plasticity hypothesis of self-esteem. *Journal of Social Behavior and Personality*, **6**, 349–60.

Ganster, D.C., Schaubroeck, J., Sime, W.E. & Mayes, B.T. (1991). The nomological validity of the Type A personality among employed adults. *Journal of Applied Psychology*, **76**, 143–68.

Geyer, S. (1997). Some conceptual considerations on the sense of coherence. *Social Science and Medicine*, **44**, 1771–80.

Glass, D.C. (1977). *Behavior Patterns, Stress, and Coronary Disease*. Hillsdale, NJ: Lawrence Erlbaum.

Greene, R.L. & Nowack, K.M. (1995). Hasseles, hardiness and absenteeism: results of a 3-year longitudinal study. *Work and Stress*, **9**, 448–62.

Greenier, K.D., Kernis, M.H. & Waschull, S.B. (1995). Not all high (or low) self-esteem people are the same: the importance of stability of self-esteem. In M.H. Kernis (ed.), *Efficacy, agency, and self-esteem*. New York: Plenum Press, pp. 51–72.

Greiner, B.A., Ragland, D.R., Krause, N.K., Syme, S.L. & Fisher, J.M. (1997). Objective measurement of occupational stress factors—an example with San Francisco urban transit operators. *Journal of Occupational Health Psychology*, **2**, 325–42.

Grob, A., Lühi, R., Kaiser, F.G., Flammer, A., Mackinnon, A. & Wearing, A. (1991). Berner Fragebogen zum Wolbefinden Judenglicher (BFW) [Berne Questionnaire on adolescents' subjective well-being]. *Diagnostica*, **37**, 66–75.

Gutek, B.A., Repetti, R.L. & Silver, D.L. (1988). Nonwork role and stress at work. In C.L. Cooper & R. Payne (eds) *Causes, Coping, and Consequences of Stress at Work*. Chichester: John Wiley & Sons, pp. 141–74.

Hallsten, L. (1993). Burning out: a framework. In W.B. Schaufeli, C. Maslach & T. Marek (eds) *Professional Burnout. Recent Developments in Theory and Research*. London: Taylor & Francis, pp. 95–113.

Harter, S. (1993). Causes and consequences of low self-esteem in children and adolescents. In R.F. Baumeister (ed.) *Self-Esteem: The Puzzle of Low Self-Regard*. New York: Plenum Press.

Helmers, K.F., Posluszny, D.M. & Krantz, D.S. (1994). Associations of hostility and coronary artery disease: a review of studies. In A.W. Siegman & T.W. Smith (eds) *Anger, Hostility, and the Heart*. Hillsdale, NJ: Lawrence Erlbaum, pp. 67–96.

Hobfoll, S.E. (1989). Conservation of resources: a new attempt at conceptualizing stress. *American Psychologist*, **44**, 513–24.

Hobfoll, S.E. (2001). The influence of culture, community, and the nested-self in the stress process: advancing conservation of resources theory. *Applied Psychology: An International Review*, **50**, 337–421.

Hofstede, G. (1991). *Cultures and Organizations: Software of the Mind.* New York: McGraw-Hill.

Horowitz, M.J., Wilner, N. & Alvarez, W. (1979). Impact of event scale: a measure of subjective stress. *Psychosomatic Medicine*, **41**, 209–18.

Iribarren, C., Sidney, S., Bild, D.E., Liu, K., Markovitz, J.H., Roseman, J.M. & Matthews, K. (2000). Association of hostility with coronary artery calcification in young adults: the CARDIA study. *Journal of the American Medical Association*, **283**(19), 2546–51.

Jackson, S.E. (1984). Organizational practices for preventing burnout. In A.S. Sethi & R.S. Schuler (eds) *Handbook of Organizational Stress Coping Strategies*. Cambridge, MA: Ballinger, pp. 89–111.

Jackson, S. E. (1989). Does job control control job stress? In S.L. Sauter, J.J. Hurrell, Jr. & C.L. Cooper (eds) *Job Control and Worker Health*. Chichester: John Wiley & Sons, pp. 25–53.

Jemmott, J.B. III (1987). Social motives and susceptibility to disease: stalking individual differences in health risks. *Journal of Personality*, **55**, 267–98.

Jerusalem, M. & Schwarzer, R. (1992). Self-efficacy as a resource factor in stress appraisal. In R. Schwarzer (ed.) *Self-Efficacy: Thought Control of Action*. Washington, DC: Hemisphere, pp. 195–213.

Jex, S.M. & Bliese, P.D. (1999). Efficacy beliefs as a moderator of the impact of work-related stressors: a multilevel study. *Journal of Applied Psychology*, **84**, 349–61.

Jex, S.M. & Elaqua, T.C. (1999). Self-esteem as a moderator: a comparison of global and organization-based measures. *Journal of Occupational and Organizational Psychology*, **72**, 71–81.

Jex, S.M., Bliese, P.D., Buzzell, S. & Primeau, J. (2001). The impact of self-efficacy on stressor–strain relations: coping style as an explanatory mechanism. *Journal of Applied Psychology*, **86**, 401–9.

Jimmieson, N.L. (2000). Employee reactions to behavioural control under conditions of stress: the moderating role of self-efficacy. *Work and Stress*, **14**, 262–80.

Johansson-Hanse, J. & Engström, T. (1999). Sense of coherence and ill health among the unemployed and re-employed after closure of an assembly plant. *Work and Stress*, **13**, 204–22.

Judge, T.A. & Bono, J.E. (2001). Relationship of core self-evaluations traits—self-esteem, generalized self efficacy, locus of control, and emotional stability—with job satisfaction and job performance: a metaanalysis. *Journal of Applied Psychology*, **86**, 80–92.

Judge, T.A., Bono, J.E. & Locke, E.A. (2000). Personality and job satisfaction: the mediating role of job characteristics. *Journal of Applied Psychology*, **85**, 237–49.

Kahn, R.L. & Byosiere, P. (1992). Stress in organizations. In M.D. Dunnette & L.M. Hough (eds) *Handbook of Industrial and Organizational Psychology*, vol. 3 Palo Alto, CA: Consulting Psychologists Press, pp. 571–650.

Kamen-Siegel L., Rodin, J., Seligman, M.E.P. & Dwyer, J. (1991). Explanatory style and cell-mediated immunity in elderly men and women. *Health Psychology*, **10**, 229–35.

Kandel, D.B., Davies, M. & Raveis, V.H. (1985). The stressfulness of daily social roles for women: marital, occupational, and household roles. *Journal of Health and Social Behavior*, **26**, 64–78.

Kanfer, R., Dugdale, B. & McDonald, B. (1994). Empirical findings on the action control scale in the context of complex skill acquisition. In J. Kuhl & J. Beckmann (eds) *Volition and Personality: Action versus State Orientation*. Seattle, WA: Hogrefe & Huber, pp. 61–77.

Karasek, R.A. & Theorell, T. (1990). *Healthy Work*. New York: Basic Books.

Keenan, A. & Newton, T.J. (1984). Frustration in organizations: relationships to role stress, climate, and psychological strain. *Journal of Occupational Psychology*, **57**, 57–65.

Keita, G.P. & Sauter, S.L. (eds) (1992). *Work and Well-Being*. Washington, DC: American Psychological Association.

Kernis, M.H., Brockner, J. & Frankel, B.S. (1989a). Self-esteem and reactions to failure: the mediating role of overgeneralization. *Journal of Personality and Social Psychology*, **57**, 707–14.

Kernis, M.H., Grannemann, B.D. & Barclay, L.C. (1989b). Stability and level of self-esteem as predictors of anger arousal and hostility. *Journal of Personality and Social Psychology*, **56**, 1013–22.

Kessler, R.D. & McLeod, J. (1984). Sex differences in vulnerability to undesirable events. *American Sociological Review*, **47**, 217–27.

Kessler, R.D. & McRae, J. (1981). Trends in the relationship between sex and psychological distress: 1957–1976. *American Sociological Review*, **46**, 443–52.

King, L.A., King, D.W., Fairbank, J.A., Keane, T.M. & Adams, G.A. (1998). Resilience-recovery factors in post-traumatic stress disorder among female and male Vietnam veterans: hardiness, postwar social support, and additional stressful life events. *Journal of Personality and Social Psychology*, **74**, 420–34.

Klinger, E. (1987). Current concerns and disengagement from incentives. In F. Halisch & J. Kuhl (eds) *Motivation, Intention, and Volition*. New York: Springer-Verlag, pp. 337–47.

Klinger, E. & Murphy, M.D. (1994). Action orientation and personality: some evidence on the construct validity of the Action Control Scale. In J. Kuhl & J. Beckmann (eds) *Volition and Personality: Action versus State Orientation*. Seattle, WA: Hogrefe & Huber, pp. 79–92.

Kobasa, S.C.Q. (1988). Conceptualization and measurement of personality in job stress research. In J.J. Hurrell, Jr, L.R. Murphy, S.L. Sauter & C.L. Cooper (eds) *Occupational Stress: Issues and Developments in Research*. New York: Taylor & Francis, pp. 100–9.

Koeske, G.F., Kirk, S.A. & Koeske, R.D. (1993). Coping with job stress: which strategies work best? *Journal of Occupational and Organizational Psychology*, **66**, 319–35.

Kravetz, S., Drory, Y. & Florian, V. (1993). Hardiness and sense of coherence and their relation to negative affect. *European Journal of Personality*, **7**, 233–44.

Krenauer, M. & Schönpflug, W. (1980). Regulation und Fehlregulation im Verhalten. III. Zielsetzung und Ursachenbeschreibung unter Belastung. [Regulation and misregulation of behavior. III. Goal setting and causal attribution under stress]. *Psychologische Beiträge*, **22**, 414–31.

Kubzansky, L.D., Kawachi, I. & Sparrow, D. (1999). Socioeconomic status, hostility, and risk factor clustering in the normative aging study: any help from the concept of allostatic load? *Annals of Behavioral Medicine*, **21**, 330–8.

Kuhl, J. (1994). A theory of action and state orientations. In J. Kuhl & J. Beckmann (eds) *Volition and Personality: Action versus State Orientation*. Seattle, WA: Hogrefe & Huber, pp.9–46.

Langan-Fox, J., Deery, T. & van Vliet, S. (1997). Power motivation, illness, coping strategies and psychological stress in police trainees. *Work and Stress*, **11**, 186–95.

Latak, J.C. (1986). Coping with job stress: measures and future directions for scale development. *Journal of Applied Psychology*, **71**, 377–85.

Lazarus, R.S. (1999). *Stress and Emotion*. London: Free Association Books.

Lazarus, R.S. & Folkman, S. (1984). *Stress, Appraisal, and Coping*. New York: Springer-Verlag.

Lazarus, R.S. & Folkman, S. (1986). Cognitive theories of stress and the issue of circularity. In M. Appley & R. Trumbull (eds) *Dynamics of Stress*. New York: Plenum Press, pp. 63–80.

Leitner, K. (1993). Auswirkungen von Arbeitsbedingungen auf die psychosoziale Gesundheit [Effects of working conditions on psychosocial health]. *Zeitschrift für Arbeitswissenschaft*, **47**, 98–107.

Little, B.R. (1983). Personal projects: a rationale and method for investigation. *Environment and Behavior*, **15**, 273–309.

Locke, E.A. & Latham, G.P. (1990). *A Theory of Goal Setting and Task Performance*. Englewood Cliffs, NJ: Prentice Hall.

Maddi, S.R. (1997). Personal Views Survey II: a measure of dispositional hardiness. In C.P. Zalaquett & R.J. Wood (eds) *Evaluating Stress: A Book of Resources*. Lanham, MD: Scarecrow Press, pp. 292–309.

Maddi, S.R. (1999). The personality construct of hardiness: I. Effects on experiencing, coping and strain. *Consulting Psychology Journal: Practice and Research*, **51**(2), 83–94.

Marmot, M., Siegrist, J., Theorell, T. & Feeney, A. (1999). Health and the psychosocial environment at work. In M. Marmot & R.G. Wilkinson (eds) *Social Determinants of Health*. Oxford: Oxford University Press, pp. 105–31.

Matthews, K.A. (1988). Coronary heart disease and Type A behaviors: update on and alternative to the Booth-Kewley and Friedman (1987) quantitative review. *Psychological Bulletin*, **104**, 373–80.

May, D.R., Schwoerer, C.E., Reed, K. & Potter, P. (1997). Employee reactions to ergonomic job design: the moderating effects of health locus of control and self-efficacy. *Journal of Occupational Health Psychology*, **2**, 11–24.

McClelland, D.C. (1987). *Human Motivation*. Cambridge: Cambridge University Press.

McClelland, D.C. & Jemmott, J.B. (1980). Power motivation, stress and physical illness. *Journal of Human Stress*, **6(4)**, 6–15.

McClelland, D.C., Floor, E., Davidson, R.J. & Saron, C. (1980). Stressed power motivation, sympathetic activation, immune function and physical illness. *Journal of Human Stress*, **6(2)**, 11–19.

McCrae, R.R. & Costa, P.T. (1986). Personality, coping, and coping effectiveness in an adult sample. *Journal of Personality*, **54**, 385–405.

Menaghan, E.G. & Merves, E.S. (1984). Coping with occupational problems: the limits of individual efforts. *Journal of Health and Social Behavior*, **25**, 406–23.

Miller, S.M. (1990). To see or not to see: cognitive informational styles in the coping process. In M. Rosenbaum (ed.) *Learned Resourcefulness: On Coping Skills, Self-Control, and Adaptive Behavior*. New York: Springer-Verlag, pp. 95–126.

Miller, T.Q., Smith, T.W., Turner, C.W., Guijarro, M.L. & Hallet, A.J. (1996). A meta-analytic review of research on hostility and physical health. *Psychological Bulletin*, **119**, 322–48.

Moen, P. (1997). Women's roles and resilience: trajectories of advantage or turning points? In J.H. Gotlib & B. Wheaton (eds) *Stress and Adversity over the Life Course*. Cambridge: Cambridge University Press, pp. 133–56.

Mossholder, K.W., Bedeian, A.G. & Armenakis, A.A. (1981). Role perceptions, satisfaction, and performance: moderating effects of self-esteem and organizational level. *Organizational Behavior and Human Performance*, **28**, 224–234.

Nadler, A. (1990). Help-seeking behavior as a coping resource. In M. Rosenbaum (ed.) *Learned Resourcefulness: On Coping Skills, Self-Control, and Adaptive Behavior*. New York: Springer-Verlag, pp. 127–62.

Nowack, K.M. (1989). Coping style, cognitive hardiness, and health status. *Journal of Behavioral Medicine*, **12**, 145–58.

O'Connor, E.J., Peters, L.H., Pooyan, A., Weekley, J., Frank, B. & Erenkrantz, B. (1984). Situational constraint effects on performance, affective reactions, and turnover: a field replication and extension. *Journal of Applied Psychology*, **64**, 663–72.

Okun, M.A., Zautra, A.J. & Robinson, S.E. (1988). Hardiness and health among women with rheumatoid arthritis. *Personality and Individual Differences*, **9**, 101–7.

Orr, E. & Westman, M. (1990). Does hardiness moderate stress, and how?: a review. In M. Rosenbaum (ed.) *Learned Resourcefulness: On Coping Skills, Self-Control, and Adaptive Behavior*. New York: Springer-Verlag, pp. 64–94.

Ouelette, S.C. (1993). Inquiries into hardiness. In L. Goldberger & S. Breznitz (eds) *Handbook of Stress: Theoretical and Clinical Aspects*, 2nd edn. New York: Free Press, pp. 77–100.

Parkes, K.S. (1991). Locus of control as moderator: an explanation for additive versus interactive findings in the demand-discretion model of work stress? *British Journal of Psychology*, **82**, 291–312.

Payne, R. (1988). Individual differences in the study of occupational stress. In C.L. Cooper & R. Payne (eds) *Causes, Coping, and Consequences of Stress at Work*. Chichester: John Wiley & Sons, pp. 2090–232.

Pearlin, L.I. & Schooler, C. (1978). The structure of coping. *Journal of Health and Social Behavior*, **22**, 337–56.

Peeters, M. (1994). Supportive interactions and stressful events at work: an event-recording approach, dissertation, University of Nijmegen, Faculty of Social Sciences.

Perrewé, P.L. & Zellars, K.L. (1999). An examination of attributions and emotions in the transactional approach to the organizational stress process. *Journal of Organizational Behavior*, **20**, 739–52.

Perrez, M. & Reicherts, M. (1992a). A situation-behavior approach to stress and coping. In M. Perrez & M. Reicherts (eds) *Stress, Coping, and Health*. Seattle, WA: Hogrefe & Huber, pp. 17–38.

Perrez, M. & Reicherts, M. (1992b). Depressed people coping with aversive situations. In M. Perrez & M. Reicherts (eds) *Stress, Coping, and Health*. Seattle, WA: Hogrefe & Huber, pp. 103–11.

Perrez, M., Bomio, D., Malacrida, R., Matathia, R. & Reicherts, M. (1992). Work stress in medical care units. In M. Perrez & M. Reicherts (eds) *Stress, Coping, and Health*. Seattle, WA: Hogrefe & Huber, pp. 147–59.

Peters, L.H. & O'Connor, E.J. (1980). Situational constraints and work outcomes: the influences of a frequently overlooked construct. *Academy of Management Review*, **5**, 391–7.

Peterson, C. & Seligman, M.E.P. (1984). Causal explanations as a risk for depression: theory and evidence. *Psychological Review*, **91**, 347–74.

Peterson, C., Seligman, M.E.P. & Vaillant, G.E. (1988). Pessimistic explanatory style is a risk factor for physical inllness: a thiry-five-year longitudinal study. *Journal of Personality and Social Psychology*, **55**, 23–7.

Pierce, J.L., Gardner, D.C., Dunham, R.B. & Cummings, L.L. (1993). Moderation by organization-based self-esteem on role condition–employee response relationships. *Academy of Management Journal*, **36**, 271–88.

Reason, J. (1988). Stress and cognitive failure. In S. Fisher & J. Reason (eds) *Handbook of Life Stress, Cognition and Health*. Chichester: John Wiley & Sons, pp. 405–21.

Reicherts, M. (1999). *Comment gérer le stress. Le concept des règles cognitivo-comportementales* [*Coping with Stress: The Behavior Rules Approach*]. Fribourg: Editions Universitaires.

Reicherts, M. & Perrez, M. (1992). Adequate coping behavior: the behavior rules approach. In M. Perrez & M. Reicherts (eds) *Stress, Coping, and Health*. Seattle, WA: Hogrefe & Huber, pp. 161–82.

Reicherts, M. & Pihet, S. (2000). Job newcomers coping with stressful situations: a micro-analysis of adequate coping and well-being. *Swiss Journal of Psychology*, **59**, 303–16.

Reicherts, M., Kaeslin, S., Scheurer, F., Fleischhauer, J. & Perrez, M. (1992). Depressed people coping with loss and failure. In M. Perrez & M. Reicherts, (eds) *Stress, Coping, and Health*. Seattle, WA: Hogrefe & Huber, pp. 113–23.

Repetti, R.L., Matthews, K.A. & Waldron, I. (1989). Employment and women's health: effects of paid employment on women's mental and physical health. *American Psychologist*, **44**, 1394–1401.

Rice, R.W., Gentile, D.A. & McFarlin, D.B. (1991). Facet importance and job satisfaction. *Journal of Applied Psychology*, **74**, 591–8.

Roberson, L. (1989). Assessing personal work goals in the organizational setting: development and evaluation of the Work Concerns Inventory. *Organizational Behavior and Human Decision Processes*, **44**, 345–67.

Roberson, L. (1990). Prediction of job satisfaction from the characteristics of personal work goals. *Journal of Organizational Behavior*, **11**, 29–41.

Roberson, L., Korsgaard, M.A. & Diddams, M. (1990). Goal characteristics and satisfaction: personal goals as mediators of situation effects on task satisfaction. *Journal of Applied Social Psychology*, **20**, 920–41.

Roger, D. & Jamieson, J. (1998). Individual differences in delayed heart-rate recovery following stress: the role of extraversion, neuroticism and emotional control. *Personality and Individual Differences*, **9**, 721–6.

Roger, D., Jarvis, G. & Najarian, B. (1993). Detachment and coping: the construction and validation of a new scale for measuring coping strategies. *Personality and Individual Differences*, **15**, 619–26.

Rosenbaum, M. (1990). The role of learned resourcefulness in the self-control of health behavior. In M. Rosenbaum (ed.) *Learned Resourcefulness: On Coping Skills, Self-Control, and Adaptive Behavior*. New York: Springer-Verlag, pp. 3–30.

Rosenthal, R. (1984). *Meta-Analytic Procedures for Social Research*. London: Sage.

Ross, C.E. & Mirowsky, J. (1995). Does employment affect health? *Journal of Health and Social Behavior*, **36**, 230–43.

Rotter, J.B. (1966). Generalized expectancies for internal versus external control of reinforcement. *Psychological Monographs: General and Applied*, **80**, 1 (whole no. 609).

Rozanski, A., Blumenthal, J.A. & Kaplan, J. (1999). Impact of psychological factors on the pathogenesis of cardiovascular disease and implications for therapy. *Circulation*, **99**, 2192–217.

Ryland, E. & Greenfeld, S. (1991). Work stress and well being: an investigation of Antonovsky's Sense of Coherence model. In P.L. Perrewé (ed.) *Handbook on Job Stress, Journal of Social Behavior and Personality* (special issue), **6**, 39–54.

Schaubroeck, J. & Ganster, D.C. (1991). Associations among stress-related individual differences. In C.L. Cooper & R. Payne (eds) *Personality and Stress: Individual Differences in the Stress Process*. Chichester: John Wiley & Sons, pp. 33–66.

Schaubroeck, J. & Merritt, D.E. (1997). Divergent effects of job control on coping with work stressors: the key role of self-efficacy. *Academy of Management Journal*, **40**, 738–54.

Schaubroeck, J. Jones, J.R. & Xie, J.L. (2001). Individual differences in utilizing control to cope with job demands: effects on susceptibility to infectious disease. *Journal of Applied Psychology*, **86**, 265–78.

Schaubroeck, J., Lam, S.S.K. & Xie, J.L. (2000). Collective efficacy versus self-efficacy in coping responses to stressors and control: a cross-cultural study. *Journal of Applied Psychology*, **85**, 512–25.

Scheier, M.F. & Carver, C.S. (1992). Effects of optimism on psychological and physical well-being: theoretical overview and empirical update. *Cognitive Therapy and Research*, **16**, 201–28.

Scheier, M.F. & Carver, C.S. (1999). Control theory: a useful conceptual framework for personality-social, clinical, and health psychology. In R.F. Baumeister (ed.) *The Self in Social Psychology. Key Readings in Social Psychology*. Philadelphia, PA: Psychology Press/Taylor & Francis, pp. 299–316.

Scheier, M.F., Weintraub, J.K. & Carver, C.S. (1986). Coping with stress: divergent strategies of optimists and pessimists. *Journal of Personality and Social Psychology*, **51**, 1257–64.

Schönpflug, W. (1985). Goal directed behavior as a source of stress: psychological origins and consequences of inefficiency. In M. Frese & J. Sabini (eds) *Goal Directed Behavior: The Concept of Action in Psychology*. Hillsdale, NJ: Lawrence Erlbaum, pp. 172–88.

Schönpflug, W. & Battmann, W. (1988). The costs and benefits of coping. In S. Fisher & J. Reason (eds) *Handbook of Life Stress, Cognition and Health*. Chichester: John Wiley & Sons, pp. 699–713.

Schwenkmezger, P. & Hank, P. (1996). Anger expression and blood pressure. In J.M.T. Brebner, E. Greenglass, P. Laungani & A.M. O'Roark (eds) *Stress and Emotion: Anxiety, Anger and Curiosity*, vol. 16. London: Taylor & Francis, pp. 241–59.

Semmer, N. (1984). *Stressbezogene Tätigkeitsanalyse. Psychologische Untersuchungen zur Analyse von Stress am Arbeitsplatz* [*Stress-Related Job Analysis. Psychological Analyses of Stress at Work*]. Weinheim: Beltz.

Semmer, N. (1992). One man's meat, another man's poison? Stressors and their cultural background. In M.V. Cranach, W. Doise & G. Mugny (eds) *Social Representations and the Social Bases of Knowledge*. Bern: Huber, pp. 153–8.

Semmer, N. & Schallberger, U. (1996). Selection, socialization, and mutual adaptation: resolving discrepancies between people and their work. *Applied Psychology: An International Review*, **45**, 263–88.

Semmer, N. & Zapf, D. (1989). Validity of various methods of measurement in job analysis. In K. Landau & W. Rohmert (eds) *Recent Developments in Job Analysis*. London: Taylor & Francis, pp. 67–78.

Semmer, N., Zapf, D. & Dunckel, H. (1995). Assessing stress at work: a framework and an instrument. In O. Svane and Ch. Johansen (eds) *Work and Health–Scientific Basis of Progress in the Working Environment*. Luxembourg: Office for Official Publications of the European Communities, pp. 105–13.

Semmer, N., Zapf, D. & Greif, S. (1996). "Shared job strain": a new approach for assessing the validity of job stress measurements. *Journal of Occupational and Organizational Psychology*, **69**, 293–310.

Semmer, N.K., Kaelin, W., Elfering, A. & Dauwalder, J.P. (2001). Work experience and quality of life in Switzerland: Work, stess, and personality development. Report to the Swiss National Science Foundation. Berne, Switzerland: University of Berne, Department of Psychology.

Siegler, I.C. (1994). Hostility and risk: demographic and lifestyle variables. In A.W. Siegman & T.W. Smith (eds) *Anger, Hostility, and the Heart*. Hillsdale, NJ: Lawrence Erlbaum, pp. 199–214.

Siegman, A.W. (1994a). From Type A to hostility to anger: reflections on the history of coronary-prone behavior. In A.W. Siegman & T.W. Smith, (eds) *Anger, Hostility, and the Heart*. Hillsdale, NJ: Lawrence Erlbaum, pp. 1–21.

Siegman, A.W. (1994b). Cardiovascular consequences of expressing and repressing anger. In A.W. Siegman & T.W. Smith (eds) *Anger, Hostility, and the Heart*. Hillsdale, NJ: Lawrence Erlbaum, pp. 173–97.

Siegrist, J. (1996). Adverse health effects of high-effort/low-reward conditions. *Journal of Occupational Health Psychology*, **1**, 27–41.

Siegrist, J. (1998). Adverse effects of effort–reward imbalance at work. In C.L. Cooper (ed.) *Theories of Organizational Stress*. Oxford: Oxford University Press, pp. 190–204.

Silver, R.C., Wortman, C.B. & Crofton, C. (1990). The role of coping in support provision: the self-presentational dilemma of victims of life crises. In B.R. Sarason, I.G. Sarason & G.R. Pierce (eds) *Social Support: An Interactional View*. New York: John Wiley & Sons, pp. 397–426.

Simon, R.S. (1992). Parental role strains, salience of parental identity and gender differences in psychological distress. *Journal of Health and Social Behavior*, **33**, 25–35.

Sinclair, R.R. & Tetrick, L.E. (2000). Implications of item wording for hardiness structure, relation with neuroticism, and stress buffering. *Journal of Research in Personality*, **34**, 1–25.

Smith, T.W., Pope, M.K., Rhodewalt, F. & Poulton, J.L. (1989). Optimism, neuroticism, coping, and symptom reports: an alternative interpretation of the Life Orientation Test. *Journal of Personality and Social Psychology*, **56**, 640–8.

Smyth, J.M. & Pennebaker, J.W. (1999). Sharing one's story: translating emotional experiences into words as a coping tool. In C.R. Snyder (ed.) *Coping: The Psychology of What Works*. New York: Oxford University Press, pp. 70–89.

Söderfeldt, M., Söderfeldt, B., Ohlson, C.-G., Theorell, T. & Jones, J. (2000). The impact of sense of coherence and high demand/low-control job environment on self-reported health, burnout and psychophysiological stress indicators. *Work and Stress*, **14**, 1–15.

Somervell, P.D., Kaplan, B.H., Heiss, G., Tyroler, H.A., Kleinbaum, D.G. & Obrist, P.A. (1989). Psychologic distress as a predictor of mortality. *American Journal of Epidemiology*, **130**, 1013–23.

Sonnentag, S. & Frese, M. (in press). Stress in organizations. In W.C. Borman, D.R. Ilgen & J.R. Kimoski (eds) *Comprehensive Handbook of Psychology*, vol. 12: *Industrial and Organizational Psychology*. New York: John Wiley & Sons.

Spector, P. E. (2002). Individual differences in health and well-being in organizations. In D.A. Hoffman & L.E. Tetrick (eds) *Individual and Organizational Health*. San Francisco, CA: Jossey-Bass.

Spector, P.E. & Jex, S.M. (1998). Development of four self-report measures of job stressors and strain: Interpersonal Conflict at Work Scale, Organizational Constraints Scale, Quantitative Workload Inventory, and Physical Symptoms Inventory. *Journal of Occupational Health Psychology*, **3**, 3256–367.

Spector, P.E., Jex, S.M. & Chen, P.Y. (1995). Personality traits as predictors of objective job characteristics. *Journal of Organizational Behavior*, **16**, 59–65.

Spector, P.E., Zapf, D., Chen, P.Y. & Frese, M. (2000). Why negative affectivity should not be controlled in job stress research: don't throw out the baby with the bath water. *Journal of Organizational Behavior*, **21**, 79–95.

Spielberger, C.D., Reheiser, E.C. & Sydeman, S.J. (1995). Measuring the experience, expression, and control of anger. In H. Kassinove (ed.) *Anger Disorders: Definitions, Diagnosis, and Treatment*. Washington, DC: Taylor & Francis, pp. 49–76.

Stanton, A.L. & Franz, R. (1999). Focusing on emotion: an adaptive coping strategy? In C.R. Snyder (ed.) *Coping: The Psychology of What Works*. New York: Oxford University Press, pp. 90–118.

Stanton, A.L., Kirk, S.B., Cameron, C.L. & Danoff-Burg, S. (2000). Coping through emotional approach: scale construction and validation. *Journal of Personality and Social Psychology*, **78**, 1150–69.

Steptoe, A. (1991). Psychological coping, individual differences and physiological stress responses. In C.L. Cooper & R. Payne (eds) *Personality and Stress: Individual Differences in the Stress Process*. Chichester: John Wiley & Sons, pp. 205–33.

Steptoe, A. (1996). Psychophysiological processes in the prevention of cardiovascular disease. In K. Orth-Gomér, K. & N. Schneiderman (eds) *Behavioral Medicine Approaches to Cardiovascular Disease Prevention*. Mahwah, NJ: Lawrence Erlbaum, pp. 135–48.

Steptoe, A. (2001). Psychophysiological bases of disease. In D.W. Johnston & M. Johnston (eds) *Health Psychology*, vol. 8: *Comprehensive Clinical Psychology*. Amsterdam: Elsevier, pp. 39–78.

Steptoe, A., Cropley, M., Griffith, J. & Kirschbaum, C. (2000). Job strain and anger expression predict early morning elevations in salivary cortisol. *Psychosomatic Medicine*, **62**, 286–92.

Strack, S. & Coyne, J.C. (1983). Social confirmation of dysphoria: shared and private reactions to depression. *Journal of Personality and Social Psychology*, **44**, 798–806.

Suarez, E.D., Kuhn, C.M., Schanberg, S.M., Williams, R.B. & Zimmermann, E.A. (1998). Neuro-endocrine, cardiovascular, and emotional responses of hostile men: the role of interpersonal challenge. *Psychosomatic Medicine*, **60**, 78–88.

Suls, J. & Fletcher, B. (1985). The relative efficacy of avoidant and non-avoidant coping strategies: a meta-analysis. *Health Psychology*, **4**, 247–88.

Suominen, S., Helenius, H., Blomberg, H., Uutela, A. & Koskenvuo, M. (2001). Sense of coherence as a predictor of subjective state of health: results of 4 years of follow-up of adults. *Journal of Psychosomatic Research*, **50**, 77–86.

Taylor, S.E. & Brown, J.D. (1988). Illusion and well-being: a social psychological perspective on mental health. *Psychological Bulletin*, **103**, 193–210.

Theorell, T. & Karasek, R.A. (1996). Current issues relating to psychosocial job strain and cardio-vascular disease research. *Journal of Occupational Health Psychology*, **1**, 9–26.

Thoits, P.A. (1986). Social support as coping assistance. *Journal of Consulting and Clinical Psychology*, **54**, 416–23.

Thompson, S.C. (1981). Will it hurt less if I can control it? A complex answer to a simple question. *Psychological Bulletin*, **90**, 89–101.

Udris, I. & Rimann, M. (2000). Das Kohärenzgefühl: Gesundheitsressource oder Gesundheit selbst? [Sense of coherence: health resource or health itself?]. In H. Wydler, P. Kolip & T. Abel (eds) *Salutogenese und Kohärenzgefühl*. Weinheim: Juventa, pp. 129–47.

Updegraff, J.A. & Taylor, S.E. (2001). From vulnerability to growth: positive and negative effects of stressful life events. In J.H. Harvey & E.D. Miller (eds) *Loss and Trauma: General and Close Relationship Perspectives*. New York: Brunner-Routledge, pp. 3–28.

Van Yperen, N.W. & Snijders, T.A. (2000). A multilevel analysis of the demands-control model: is stress at work determined by factors at the group level or the individual level? *Journal of Occupational Health Psychology*, **5**, 182–90.

Veroff, J.B. (1982). Assertive motivations: achievement vs. power. In D.G. Winter & A.J. Stewart (eds) *Motivation and Society*. San Francisco, CA: Jossey-Bass.

Vossel, G. (1987). Stress conceptions in live event research: towards a person-centred perspective. *European Journal of Personality*, **1**, 123–40.

Walschburger, P. (1994). Action control and excessive demand: effects of situational and personality factors on psychological and physiological functions during stressful transactions. In J. Kuhl & J. Beckmann (eds) *Volition and Personality: Action versus State Orientation*. Seattle, WA: Hogrefe & Huber, pp. 233–66.

Wanous, J.P. (1992). *Organizational Entry*, 2nd edn. Reading, MA: Addison-Wesley.

Ward, C.H. & Eisler, R.M. (1987). Type A behavior, achievement striving, and a dysfunctional self-evaluation system. *Journal of Personality and Social Psychology*, **53**, 318–26.

Warr, P.B. (1987). *Work, Unemployment and Mental Health*. Oxford: Oxford University Press.

Watson, D., Pennebaker, J.W. & Folger, R. (1987). Beyond negative affectivity: measuring stress and satisfaction in the work place. In J.M. Ivancevich & D.C. Ganster (eds) *Job Stress: From Theory to Suggestion*. New York: Haworth Press, pp. 141–57.

Weber, H. (1993). Ärgerausdruck, Ärgerbewältigung und subjektives Wohlbefinden [Expression of anger, coping with anger, and subjective well-being]. In V. Hodapp & P. Schwenkmezger (eds) *Ärger und Ärgerausdruck*. Bern: Huber, pp. 253–75.

Weiss, H.B. & Knight, P.A. (1980). The utility of humility: self-esteem, information search, and problem solving efficiency. *Organizational Behavior and Human Performance*, **25**, 216–23.

Wiedemann, A., Busjahn, A., Heinrich, B., Listing, J., Mueller, W. & Richter-Heinrich, E. (1994). State versus action orientation after failure: prevalence of coping strategies and related personality factors in two groups of hypertensives (with and without antihypertensive medication). In J. Kuhl & J. Beckmann (eds) *Volition and Personality: Action versus State Orientation*. Seattle, WA: Hogrefe & Huber, pp. 267–80.

Williams, P.G., Wiebe, D.J. & Smith, T.W. (1992). Coping processes as mediators of the relationship between hardiness and health. *Journal of Behavioral Medicine*, **15**, 237–55.

Williams, R.B. (1996). Coronary-prone behaviors, hostility, and cardiovascular health: implications for behavioral and pharmacological interventions. In K. Orth-Gomér & N. Schneiderman (eds)

Behavioral Medicine Approaches to Cardiovascular Disease Prevention. Mahwah, NJ: Lawrence Erlbaum, pp. 161–8.

Wofford, J.C. & Daly, P.S. (1997). A cognitive-affective approach to understanding individual differences in stress propensity and resultant strain. *Journal of Occupational Health Psychology*, **2**, 134–47.

Wortman, C.B. & Silver, R.C. (1992). Reconsidering assumptions about coping with loss: an overview of current research. In L. Montada, S.-H. Filipp & M.J. Lerner (eds) *Life Crises and Experiences of Loss in Adulthood*. Hillsdale, NJ: Lawrence Erlbaum, pp. 341–65.

Zapf, D. (1989). *Selbst- und Fremdbeobachtung in der psychologischen Arbeitsanalyse. Methodische Probleme bei der Erfassung von Streß am Arbeitsplatz* [*Observation and Self-Observation in Psychological Job Analysis: Methodological Problems in the Assessment of Stress at Work*]. Göttingen: Hogrefe.

CHAPTER 6

Job Control, Physical Health and Psychological Well-Being

Fiona Jones
University of Leeds, Leeds, UK
and
Ben (C) Fletcher
University of Hertfordshire, Hatfield, UK

The amount of control or autonomy an employee has over his or her own work is perhaps one of the most crucial aspect of working life and one which has been extensively researched. It is a key feature of major theoretical approaches to stress (e.g. Karasek, 1979; Payne, 1979; Warr, 1987), and, together with the related concepts of discretion and autonomy, is a central feature of job design theories (Hackman & Oldham, 1980; Wall et al., 1990a). Furthermore, the importance of job control and related concepts is recognised in the management literature, where it is generally seen as important for releasing employee potential and increasing performance. For example, Peters & Waterman's (1982) analysis of innovative companies intimately links autonomy with entrepreneurship. The related concept of "empowerment" is a central motivation for many organisational changes and total quality approaches. While control has been linked to a wide range of outcomes, including improving performance and motivation, this chapter focuses on the implications of the construct for health and well-being.

In the psychological literature, "control" can be viewed as both a characteristic of the environment and a characteristic of the individual. For example, machine-paced assembly work is intrinsically lacking in control; however, the employees themselves may nevertheless be viewed as being high in control, in terms of having high mastery or self-efficacy (Bandura, 1977). The individual may further be seen as having greater or lesser need for control (Burger & Cooper, 1979). Typically, models of stress and job design have treated "control" (and the similar concepts of "decision latitude", "discretion" and "autonomy") as characteristics attached to a particular work role or job task, and this approach is the focus of this chapter. However, the fact that individuals vary in terms of their preferences and perceptions of personal control has implications for these models. Hence individual differences are increasingly being incorporated into approaches to stress and job design.

The Handbook of Work and Health Psychology. Edited by M.J. Schabracq, J.A.M. Winnubst and C.L. Cooper.
© 2003 John Wiley & Sons, Ltd.

This chapter aims to introduce two key theoretical approaches to the topic of control in the workplace, the demand–control (or job strain) model (Karasek, 1979), and the job characteristics model (Hackman & Oldham, 1976). Both of these approaches were designed to provide practical guidance to practitioners and managers on the design of work. More recent theoretical developments focusing on more specific types of job control will also be discussed. The chapter provides a brief overview of the evidence relating to the damaging effects of low control for health and well-being. This includes consideration of the nature of the relationship between job control and health and the effects of individual differences on these relationships. The chapter discusses the implications of this research for job design interventions and the evidence concerning the effectiveness of such interventions. It finally considers job control in the context of new technology and new work designs.

The literature on job control and health is now vast and a number of comprehensive reviews of various aspects of this literature exist (Ganster & Fusilier, 1989; Kristenson, 1996; Schnall et al., 1994; Terry & Jimmieson, 1999; Van der Doef & Maes, 1998, 1999). This chapter therefore does not aim to duplicate such reviews, but rather to summarise recent key issues and trends in the research literature and their implications for managers and practitioners.

6.1 JOB STRESS AND WORK DESIGN THEORIES

6.1.1 The Demand–Control ("Job Strain") Model

While job control is an important feature of a number of approaches to occupational stress, the most well known approach, which has been responsible for most of the impetus of research in this area, is Karasek's demand–control model. This model is described in detail in Chapter 8. However, the key feature of the model is that both psychological and physical strain can be predicted from a combination of demands and control. The model has evolved over the years and, perhaps as a result, there is now a certain amount of uncertainty in its specification (Kasl, 1996). In particular, there is a lack of clarity concerning the exact nature of the hypothesised relationship between the two key variables in the model and strain outcomes. One hypothesis examined in many studies focuses on the negative impacts of jobs that are high in demand and low in control, suggesting that these two variables have an additive effect. A further hypothesis, mooted by Karasek (1979), is that the two variables have an interactive effect such that the combination of high demand and low control produces greater strain than the simple additive effect. This is often viewed as a central feature of the model (e.g. Terry & Jimmieson, 1999). However, the implications of the interactive model are clearly not the same as the additive model. If the effect is interactive (and demand is harmful primarily in conditions of low control) strain could, in practice, be reduced by increasing control without reducing workload (Karasek, 1979; Parkes, 1991). This strategy would be less effective in the case of additive effects.

Further lack of clarity exists concerning the actual nature of the interaction. Kasl (1996) points out that some researchers seem to regard decision latitude as buffering the effect of job demand, such that risk due to high demands will only be present at low levels of control. However, others regard the interaction as synergistic, i.e. both low demand and high control are associated with risk but the combination of the two increases the risk beyond the additive effect. These two approaches are usually not clearly distinguished. Kasl suggests that in many studies the data are presented in such a way that it is not even possible to interpret whether the effect is truly additive or interactive. It is often also the case that the variables are combined into a single "job strain" variable so that it is not possible to separate the effects of demand and control.

A further area of ambiguity which has been widely discussed in the literature is the operationalisation of the key variables (e.g. Ganster & Fusilier, 1989; Jones et al., 1998; Smith et al., 1997). In its original version, Karasek's model measured decision latitude, a construct which was rather wider than the popular meaning of control, by combining a measure of decision authority with a measure of skill discretion (Karasek, 1979). While decision authority assesses the extent to which people have freedom over how they do their work and have a say over what happens, skill discretion is concerned with the level of skill required and the non-repetitive nature of work. While the two concepts have been shown to be related, they are clearly distinct. Over the years a range of different measures of job control has been used; however, in recent years, a key development in the model has been the increased sophistication in the operationalisation of this variable. This will be discussed further below.

The model has been further developed to include social support (Johnson & Hall, 1988). This is sometimes referred to as the "iso-strain model". Here again two alternative hypotheses have been identified, the additive hypothesis and the interactive hypothesis, suggesting that support acts as a buffer (Van der Doef & Maes, 1999). Karasek & Theorell (1990) have further proposed the addition of job insecurity and physical demands to the model. However, these latter two variables are seldom included.

The job strain or iso-strain models have been tested using a variety of methods and levels of analysis. At one extreme, long-term epidemiological studies have followed individuals over years to predict coronary heart disease and other disease outcomes (Alterman et al., 1994). At the other extreme, researchers have used laboratory tasks varying in degree of demand and control to examine immediate changes in pulse or other physiological responses (Perrewe & Ganster, 1989). However, the most common approach is the cross-sectional study using self-report measures of demands and control to investigate the predictors of psychological well-being (also based on self-reports) or other symptoms (Dollard et al., 2000; Fletcher & Jones, 1993).

The model has been subject to considerable criticism (Ganster & Fusilier, 1989; Jones et al., 1998; Kristenson, 1996; Muntaner & O'Campo, 1993). For example, concerns have been expressed about the nature and subjectivity of measurement, the statistical tests used to test the interaction, the tendency for its core dimensions to be confounded with socioeconomic status and the lack of account it takes of both wider sociocultural issues and individual differences. It has also been criticised for its simplicity and lack of scope. Nevertheless, perhaps because of its clarity and simplicity, it has stimulated a vast amount of research into the effects of job control on health, in addition to research aiming to improve the model itself.

While Karasek's model is probably the most influential approach to job control and health, a substantial strand of work investigating psychological well-being and job satisfaction is based on the similar construct of autonomy contained in the motivation and job design literature, frequently in the context of the job characteristics model.

6.1.2   The Job Characteristics Model

In motivation and job design research, the notion of autonomy is implicit in the early work of Maslow (1970) and Herzberg et al., (1959). However, its key place in job design research is ensured by the job characteristics model (JCM) (Hackman & Oldham, 1976) and its accompanying measurement instrument, the job diagnostic survey (JDS) (Hackman & Oldham, 1980; Idasdak & Drasgow, 1987). This model suggests that there are five core job characteristics: skill variety, task identity, task significance, autonomy and feedback. The construct of "autonomy" is similar to Karasek's notion of decision authority and includes items concerned with freedom to decide how to do the job and opportunity to use your own discretion.

It is hypothesised that these dimensions (via the mediation of the critical psychological states of experienced meaningfulness, experienced responsibility and knowledge of results) predict work motivation, job satisfaction and work effectiveness. In calculating the overall motivating potential of a job, autonomy and feedback are particularly important and are each given equal weighting to the other three elements added together. It is hypothesised that the relationship between job characteristics and the above outcomes is moderated by the individual difference variable, "growth need strength". The model did not initially suggest relationships between the core job characteristics and health, but later researchers added mental health as an outcome variable (Wall et al., 1978, 1986).

The model has also been adapted to look at job enrichment at both an individual and a group level. For example, in semi-autonomous work groups or self-directed teams, the group may have increases in autonomy and other task characteristics, but the individuals' jobs may not be improved (Langred, 2000; Wall et al., 1986).

As with Karasek's model, there has been considerable criticism of the research investigating the JCM, particularly in relation to the strong bias towards the use of cross-sectional studies relying on self-reports alone (Roberts & Glick, 1981). The model is based on the premise that the direction of causation is such that job characteristics cause high or low satisfaction and also that self-reports of job characteristics are an accurate reflection of the objective characteristics of a job. As a result, it is assumed that improving the task to afford greater control will lead to people becoming more motivated as they perceive themselves to have more control. However, it is now widely recognised that there are some problems with this assumption and that self-reports may not always closely correspond to more objective ratings (Sanchez & Levine, 2000; Spector & Jex, 1991). Furthermore, perceptions of work characteristics may be quite easily manipulated (Adler et al., 1985) and the direction of causation may be reciprocal (Wong et al., 1998). The relationship may also be influenced by individual difference variables such as positive and negative affectivity (Munz et al., 1996). Nevertheless, despite these limitations, the model has been extremely influential and has been successful in predicting a number of outcomes, but most frequently it has been used to investigate the predictors of job satisfaction (Champoux, 1991; Loher et al., 1985). This research is considered further below.

6.1.3   Theoretical Developments and the Concept of Job Control

More recent theoretical developments in stress and job design have helped to clarify what is meant by "job control" and have improved the measurement of the construct by differentiating between various specific types of control. This idea is not new. Karasek himself, in the original paper introducing the model in 1979, suggested that future work should distinguish between different aspects of decision latitude. A number of researchers have since developed typologies. This is potentially useful both to improve the predictive power of the theories but also to provide clearer guidelines for practitioners.

Breaugh (1985), for example, suggested three specific facets of autonomy. *Work method autonomy* refers to the degree of discretion concerning the procedures and methods used in conducting the work. *Work scheduling autonomy* is the extent of control over scheduling, sequencing or timing of activities and *work criteria autonomy* describes the degree to which workers can determine the criteria for evaluating their performance.

More recently, Jackson et al. (1993) have developed measures of control over how to do the work (*method control*) and when the work is done (*timing control*), in addition to more specific demand concepts. These were originally developed in the context of advanced manufacturing technology but norms have subsequently been developed for a wider range of shop-floor and related jobs, including administrative and managerial posts (Wall et al., 1995). While these factors refer essentially to direct control over the task, Mullarkey et al. (1995) have also suggested a measure of *individual role breadth*, which encompasses influence over and involvement in decisions affecting broader aspects of work that impact upon the employee. Other types of control may also be important in particular contexts. So, for example, Wall et al. (1990b) consider *boundary control* (that is, control over secondary aspects of the task such as maintenance and servicing of machines) to be crucial in the context of advanced manufacturing technology. Similarly, Soderfeldt et al. (1996) suggest taking into account a wide range of aspects of control in a study of human service organisations. These include *administrative control*, *ideological control* and *control within and over a situation*.

These specific approaches to job control are now increasingly being utilised in the context of Karasek's model and have potential for extending the model (e.g. Sargent & Terry, 1998). There is, as yet, however, little research investigating either the differential effects of these variables on health or the effectiveness of interventions targeting specific types of control.

6.2   EFFECTS OF JOB CONTROL ON HEALTH AND WELL-BEING

In recent years, the concept of job control or decision latitude has increasingly been incorporated into many studies in the medical literature looking at a wide range of aspects of physical health. This is largely due to the success of Karasek's model in offering a simple framework enabling key work variables central to his theory of job strain to be measured using brief scales. Thus, it has been suggested that high demands and low control (i.e. job strain) are related to musculoskeletal disorders (e.g. neck pain) in sales people (Skov et al., 1996) and adverse outcome of pregnancy in clerical and commercial workers (Brandt & Nielsen, 1992). Job strain has also been shown to be associated with non-medical drug use (Storr et al., 1999). There is less evidence for associations in the few studies that have looked at cancer risk (Achat et al., 2000; Courtney et al., 1996; Van Loon et al., 2000). However, the bulk of the literature focuses on cardiovascular disease and the associated risk factors.

6.2.1   Cardiovascular Disease

Schnall et al. (1994) conducted an extensive review of the literature in relation to heart disease. They considered 36 studies published between 1981 and 1993 and concluded that most found a significant relationship between job strain and cardiovascular or all-cause mortality, or between job strain and risk factors for cardiovascular disease (CVD).

Epidemiological studies examining morbidity and mortality have used two main methods of classifying employees according to the job strain dimensions. A number of studies have tried to achieve a relatively objective measurement of the work stressors associated with particular jobs by using a methodology that classifies individuals on the job strain dimensions according to their job title (based on average ratings of job incumbents). Thus, for example, waiters might all be classified as having low-control, high-demand jobs. Using this occupation-level analysis, Alfredsson et al. (1982) found that hectic work combined with low control was associated with higher incidence of heart disease. Other studies have assessed job stressors using the more subjective method of asking individuals to rate their levels of demand and control. For example, Johnson et al. (1989) found the greatest risk was in high-demand, low-control isolated jobs.

Increasingly, studies have also focused on the relationship between job strain and the risk factors that are implicated in CVD such as high blood pressure (Brisson et al., 1999; Fletcher & Jones, 1993; Fox et al., 1993) or measures of adrenalin and cortisol (Fox et al., 1993; Pollard et al., 1996). For example, Fox et al. in their study of nurses found that the combination of high demands and low control predicted both blood pressure and cortisol levels. However, Fletcher & Jones (1993), in a sample from heterogeneous occupations, found no relationships between control and blood pressure, and where demands showed relationships, these were in the opposite direction to that predicted (i.e. those with lower demands had higher blood pressure). Such mixed findings seem typical of this area. For example, Schnall et al. (1994) in their review, found that in eight studies of casual blood pressure (measured in a clinic) only one found a significant association, but five out of nine found associations for ambulatory blood pressure (which is a more reliable measure).

In an attempt to shed light on the possible mechanisms whereby job strain may impact on health, there are a small number of experimental studies that have manipulated levels of job strain in the laboratory. These have examined the relationship of experimental tasks to short-term physiological indicators that are implicated in CVD development. These include heart rate levels and cortisol (Perrewe & Ganster, 1989; Steptoe et al., 1993). For example, Steptoe et al. found that middle-aged men showed greater changes in blood pressure when they could not control the pace at which they performed laboratory tasks involving problem solving and mirror drawing. However, pacing had little effect on cortisol, suggesting work pace has a specific effect on cardiovascular functioning.

A review by Van der Doef & Maes (1998) of the impact of job strain on health concluded that, across different populations, measurement methods and job designs, there is substantial support for the hypothesis that high-demand, low-control jobs lead to increased CVD. However, the focus of this review is on the combined effects of demands and control rather than their independent impacts. The earlier review of Schnall et al. agreed with the conclusion of Van der Doef & Maes, but where possible they also considered the separate effects. They concluded that while 17 out of 25 studies found significant associations between job decision latitude and outcome, only 8 out of 23 studies showed significant relationships between demand and outcome. A few studies have also found an effect for demands opposite to that predicted (Alterman et al., 1994; Hlatky et al., 1995; Steenland et al., 1997).

Overall, therefore, deriving a clear message from this literature is difficult. However, where demand and control are separated, the evidence seems to point to the importance of job control more strongly than demands. While evidence here is mounting, further work is needed (including more laboratory studies) to find out what specific aspects of control may be important. For example, is it control over pace of work that is important (i.e. control that enables the employee to modify demand) or does more general involvement in decisions about work have an impact? Furthermore, research evidence needs to clarify the nature of the relationship and the effects (if any) of individual differences (see below).

6.2.2   Psychological Well-Being

Many researchers have studied the effect of job control on psychological well-being, not only because psychological distress is important in its own right, but because it is assumed to be the vehicle whereby work stressors ultimately may lead to illness (both mental and physical). As a result there is a plethora of research indicating that low job control is associated with poor psychological well-being. This is typically measured in terms of scores on the General Health Questionnaire (Goldberg, 1978) or on more specific measures of anxiety, depression or job satisfaction. Although there are many exceptions, studies also generally support the relationship between a combination of low control and high demand with poor psychological well-being, with additive effects found more frequently than moderated effects (Van der Doef & Maes, 1999). However, the majority of studies are subject to serious methodological limitations. Typically, studies are cross-sectional and based on self-reports of both control and psychological well-being. Such methods have a number of well-established difficulties, not least the fact that they are open to the alternative explanation that being anxious or depressed may cause people to describe their jobs more negatively.

The fact that people who report low levels of demand and control also report high levels of distress at work is likely to be important for employers. However, the assumption that these associations are causal and further that they represent the first step towards damaged physical health and serious psychiatric illness is, as yet, not well tested. In particular, while many studies use validated self-report measures of psychiatric symptoms, there is surprisingly little research looking at the associations between job control and independently verified psychiatric illness. However, a few studies have looked at psychiatric illness using diagnostic interview schedules. These are often designed to be administered by non-clinicians and are used to classify individuals according to well-established psychiatric criteria (e.g. DSM-III). They are typically thorough and are likely to be both more objective and more valid than assessments based on brief self-report measures. A number of such studies have found associations between low control and psychiatric symptoms. For example, Muntaner et al. (1991) and Mausner-Dorsch & Eaton (2000) found that occupations associated with lower levels of control had higher levels of depression. Furthermore, Cropley et al. (1999), in a study of teachers, found that job strain was associated with neurotic disorder.

A sizeable literature also investigates the impact of autonomy on self-reported psychological well-being using the JCM (research which also typically suffers from the limitations discussed above). The most popular outcome considered, in this context, is job satisfaction. A meta-analysis of 28 studies of the relationship between job characteristics and job satisfaction found support for this relationship and found that of all the core job characteristics, autonomy had the strongest relationship with satisfaction (Loher et al., 1985). Other outcomes considered have included anxiety, depression and general mental health. An early meta-analysis by Spector (1986) looked at perceived control (most commonly based on the measures taken from the JDS) in relation to 19 outcome variables, including some health-related outcomes. This supported the relationship between autonomy and emotional distress (as well as absenteeism and physical symptoms). More recently Saavedra and Kwun (2000) have used the model to predict other affective states, including positive affect, and found that autonomy is particularly associated with enthusiasm, the implication being that not only will increasing autonomy relieve job dissatisfaction but it may also serve to "energise, reinforce and maintain work behaviour" (p. 147).

6.2.3   Health Behaviour

While the effect of job control on psychological well-being is considered to be one possible mechanism whereby job control may impact on health, an alternative mechanism is that job control may influence health by its effect on health behaviour. Thus, it would be hypothesised that having a low-control, high-demand job may lead to people perhaps smoking and drinking alcohol more, eating less healthily and exercising less. This hypothesis was confirmed by Weidner et al. (1997), who found that general health damaging behaviour (smoking, drinking alcohol, drinking coffee and failing to exercise) increased under conditions of low control, if demand was high. However, it seems that there may be different patterns of relationships depending on the health behaviour under consideration.

Smoking has been subject to the greatest amount of research but findings are nonetheless mixed. A number of studies have found that, after controlling for socioeconomic variables, men in high-strain jobs tend to smoke more (Green & Johnson, 1990; Hellerstedt & Jeffrey, 1997), yet others have failed to find this association (Alterman et al., 1994; Reed et al., 1989). Johannson et al. (1991) found that only demands and not control were associated with increased smoking. Hellerstedt & Jeffrey also found this to be the case in the women in their sample. In contrast, Alterman et al. only found that low levels of decision latitude had an impact on smoking. Similarly mixed findings exist in relation to alcohol use (Landsbergis et al., 1998).

A few studies have also looked at the effects of demands and control on exercise and diet. Johannson et al. (1991) found both demands and control were predictive of exercise, whereas Hellerstedt & Jeffrey (1997) found that decision latitude but not demand was related to exercise. However, job demands were related to increased fat intake in men and higher body mass index in women.

One prospective study by Landsbergis et al. (1998) looked at change in job characteristics and change in health behaviour in a sample of male employees in a variety of jobs. They found that an increase in decision latitude was associated with a decrease in smoking in men over a period of three years. However, change in job characteristics was not associated with any change in weight or alcohol consumption.

Overall, as can be seen, the pattern of results remains somewhat inconsistent. It is certainly not clear that high levels of demand and control are linked to uniformly worse health behaviours, and any impact of these variables on health behaviours may be modest (Landsbergis et al., 1998). Nevertheless, Landsbergis et al. suggest that increasing job decision latitude may help reduce smoking. More research is needed into the exact mechanisms whereby job strain impacts on health behaviour. However, one longitudinal study suggests that the mechanisms may not be straightforward (Payne et al., in press). This study found that people high in job strain tended to exercise less than those in low-strain jobs (though they did not intend to do any less) and that high job demands and low control were related to low self-efficacy for exercise (a predictor of actual exercise). However, once people had formed an intention to exercise, demands rather than control disrupted these intentions.

6.2.4   Impacts of Job Control on Home Life and Well-Being of Other Family Members

A considerable body of research suggests that the effects of work (including the types of activities people engage in at work and their resulting affective states) *spill over* into the home environment. For example, Rousseau (1978) asked individuals to rate aspects of work and non-work using the JDS and found positive relationships between home and work ratings. She also found relationships between work and non-work satisfaction. Karasek et al. (1987) also found that low job control was related to lower levels of social participation. This was particularly the case for women, for whom low levels of job control were associated with lower levels of participation in political and sporting activities. However, it is by no means clear that these spillover effects are caused by job characteristics rather than by other influences such as personal preferences for both low control and low activity. Furthermore, a more limited body of research supports an opposing hypothesis that employees may *compensate* for work stressors in their home environment and leisure pursuits (for a review see Kinman & Jones, 2001). This would suggest, for example, that someone with low control at work might be expected to exert greater control in the home environment.

In addition to the spillover and compensation processes affecting the employees themselves in their home environment, it has further been suggested that work stressors may affect marital partners, a process known as *crossover*. For example, a number of studies have found one person's work stressors to be associated with anxiety and depression in their spouse (e.g. Jones & Fletcher, 1993; Westman, 2001). This literature has seldom explicitly addressed the effects of job control. However, a longitudinal study by Stets (1995) specifically examines the effects of work autonomy in husbands and wives and finds that lack of autonomy not only leads to depression in the job holder, but can also lead people to compensate for the lack of control by controlling their spouse. This in turn is related to increased levels of depression in the spouse, suggesting a mechanism whereby job control at work may be implicated in the crossover of strain to partners.

6.2.5   Summary of Effects of Job Control

Overall, there is now mounting evidence for the importance of job control as a variable implicated in both increased coronary heart disease and reduced psychological well-being and it may even also impact on the well-being of marital partners. Nevertheless, there are many inconsistent studies that have failed to find effects and the mechanisms remain unclear. More particularly, however, there are conflicting findings in relation to the nature of the relationship. These are discussed in the following section.

6.3   THE NATURE OF THE RELATIONSHIP BETWEEN JOB CONTROL AND STRAINS

Research remains divided over the issue of whether job control acts as a buffer or not. Terry & Jimmieson (1999) extensively reviewed this literature and concluded that the majority of both cross-sectional and longitudinal studies found little support for the interaction in predicting employee adjustment (as measured by job satisfaction, for example). They conclude, perhaps surprisingly, that the strongest support for the interaction is based on studies using objective indicators of job features and/or strains (e.g. Dwyer & Ganster, 1991; Fox et al., 1993). Some support has also been found in studies using experimental methods (Perrewe & Ganster, 1989), suggesting that control may buffer the effects of the demands of specific work tasks. Research looking at cardiovascular outcomes has seldom directly tested the interaction effect, but where it does, Terry & Jimmieson conclude that the findings have generally not been significant.

Terry & Jimmieson discuss reasons for these inconsistencies. One suggestion is that the interaction only occurs for some outcomes, i.e. they argue that they may be specific to non-affective outcomes such as absenteeism (Dwyer and Ganster, 1991; Parkes, 1991) and some physiological measures (Fox et al., 1993). Another possibility is that it is highly dependent on the measure of control. This argument is put strongly by Wall et al. (1996), who suggested that Karasek's predicted interaction effect is seldom demonstrated because the decision latitude measure used lacks specificity. They compared a focused measure combining timing and method control with the conventional decision latitude measure in a study that aimed to predict psychological strain. They found a significant interaction effect with demand for the specific measure but not for the conventional measure. However, Terry & Jimmieson argue that many studies using focused measures of control are not consistent with Wall et al. (e.g. Carayon, 1993; Kushnir & Melamed, 1991).

The use of multidimensional measures assessing different aspects of control shows some promise in clarifying the nature of relationships. For example, Sargent & Terry (1998) suggest that specific types of control that are relevant to the task will buffer the effects of demands, whereas more peripheral forms of control will not.

It has also been suggested that the relationship between work stressors, including job control, is curvilinear, i.e. not only are low levels of job control harmful but very high levels may also be harmful (Warr, 1987). This poses some potential problems for the demand–control model because models which fail to take into account nonlinear relationships may show spurious interactive effects due to nonlinear effects of either of the variables comprising the interaction term (Lubinski & Humphreys, 1990). Few studies have examined curvilinear relationships, leaving open the possibility that where interactions were significant these may have been spurious. Warr (1991), in a study of over 1600 employed people, found significant nonlinear components and taking these into account in the final regressions found no evidence for an interactive effect in predicting job related anxiety, depression and job satisfaction.

Furthermore, a study by Fletcher & Jones (1993) examined the effects of demand and control in a heterogeneous sample of over 3000 men and women, and found, for men, that there was some evidence that the two variables interacted to predict job satisfaction and life satisfaction. However, this effect disappeared once the nonlinear relationships were taken into account, suggesting that it was indeed a spurious effect.

A further reason for the inconsistency in the findings in relation to the interactive effects, which is increasingly attracting attention, is that it may be highly dependent on individual differences. These are discussed below.

6.4   INDIVIDUAL DIFFERENCES AND THE IMPACT OF JOB CONTROL

6.4.1   Personality Variables

Karasek's model of job control was designed to provide a general model of work redesign and hence did not incorporate individual difference variables. However, a range of personality variables have been found to moderate the impact of demands and control on strain outcomes and are now thought to be one possible explanation for the ambiguous findings in relation to the model (Parkes, 1991). Over the past few years the focus on finding such variables has increased. Typically, personality variables examined are those most closely related to perceptions of personal control such as perceptions of Type A personality, locus of control and self-efficacy. There are two possible ways that personality can act as a moderator. It can either be a buffer or resistance factor, decreasing the impact of stressors or strains, or it can act as a vulnerability factor, increasing the impact. For example, Type A behaviour pattern, characterised by high achievement orientation, time urgency and hostility (Friedman & Rosenman, 1974), is seen as a vulnerability factor. Type A personalities have been shown to be more prone to psychological strain than Type Bs under high-demand working conditions with little control (Kushnir & Melamed, 1991).

Locus of control refers to whether an individual generally believes that the causes of events in their lives are substantially within their control (internal locus) or controlled by external factors (Rotter, 1966). This characteristic has been viewed as both a buffer and a vulnerability factor. For example, Parkes (1991), in a study of civil servants, found that external locus of control increased the vulnerability of driving examiners and student teachers to the psychological impacts of job strain. Thus, the interactive demand-discretion model predicted anxiety for subjects with external locus of control but not for those with internal locus. Daniels & Guppy (1994), however, suggest that having an internal locus of control buffers the effect of stressors on psychological well-being.

Belief that the individual has internal control may not always be coupled with confidence that the individual is able to take that control and succeed in taking a particular desired course of action. This kind of belief has been termed "self-efficacy" (Bandura, 1977) and has also been shown to moderate the impact of job strain. For example, Schaubroeck et al. (2000), in a study of American bank tellers, found that perceived job control moderated the impacts of job demands on psychological strain only for those who were high in self-efficacy. Where they had low self-efficacy, having high control exacerbated the effect of demands. Schaubroeck & Merritt (1997) further found that self-efficacy moderates the effect of job strain on blood pressure such that for individuals with high self-efficacy, job control mitigated the effects of job demands.

Related to the concept of self-efficacy is the dispositional trait of proactive personality. Characteristics of proactive people include being unconstrained by situational forces, effecting environmental change, showing initiative and taking action (Bateman & Crant,

1993). Parker & Sprigg (1999) found that this characteristic, like self-efficacy, moderated the effect of job strain. The effect was such that job demands caused psychological strain except in circumstances where employees had opportunities to reduce demand—that is, they had job control, and they had proactive personality, enabling them to take advantage of this opportunity. For passive employees (those lacking a proactive personality), job control did not mitigate the effects of demands, and for such employees interventions to increase control may have little impact.

Proactive people are likely to use coping strategies that involve taking control, such as analysing the problem and taking action. Such strategies have been characterised as active coping (de Rijk et al., 1998). The role of this type of coping in moderating job strain has been examined by de Rijk et al., who found that for nurses high on active coping, job control was a stress buffer, whereas for those low on active coping, it seemed to increase the effects of job demands on emotional exhaustion.

Overall, these studies suggest that only for individuals high in personality traits such as internal locus of control, self-efficacy and with proactive styles of personality and coping are the impacts of demands reduced by job control. For those low in such characteristics then enhancing control will have little benefit and may even make matters worse.

Most studies have considered the moderating effects of personality variables on psychological well-being or minor physical symptoms. There is less evidence in relation to coronary heart disease. However, Bosma et al. (1998) examined the impact of several personality variables in the relationship between job control and heart disease in the Whitehall II study of British civil servants. They suggest that psychological characteristics such as hostility, need for control, negative affectivity, angry coping and unassertive coping had little impact on the association. They acknowledge that they have not considered the effects of all possible psychological factors. For example, they excluded self-efficacy (a factor which Schaubroeck & Merritt (1997) suggest moderates the effects of stressors on blood pressure). Nevertheless, they argue that their study suggests that "increasing job control could, in principle, lower risk of heart disease for all employees" (p. 402).

Thus, it seems likely that different mechanisms are implicated depending on the outcome measure considered. One possibility discussed by Bosma et al. (1998) is that work stressors impact on bodily responses without conscious awareness of being under stress, hence personality styles are less important when physical well-being is the outcome. However, in the case of psychological well-being, the individual's personality may substantially influence appraisals and, ultimately, well-being. In terms of implications, interventions which focus on the individual's appraisals and coping (for example, by increasing self-efficacy or active coping) may be effective in reducing psychological distress among workers lacking in job control. However, based on current research evidence, this may be less likely to have an impact on physical outcomes such as heart disease.

Individual differences in work motivation and needs are seldom considered as moderators of the effect of job strain although de Rijk et al. (1998) found that need for control did not have any moderating effect. However, other kinds of needs and motivation may be important moderators. For example, Homer et al. (1990) used the model to predict women's risk of delivering preterm, low-birth-weight babies. They found that women working in jobs high in demand and low in control were more likely to deliver such babies than women in other jobs, but only where they did not want to remain working.

Unlike Karasek's model, the moderating effect of needs is built into the job characteristics model in the form of the variable growth need strength (GNS). This variable assesses the need for personal accomplishment and for learning and development. While there have been inconsistent findings (Roberts & Glick, 1981), meta-analyses support the importance of this variable (Loher et al., 1985; Spector, 1985). For example, Loher et al. (1985) found that the relationship between job characteristics and job satisfaction was stronger for those employees higher in GNS. More recently, Champoux (1991) looked in more detail at relationships and found different patterns of relationship dependent on level of GNS. Those with high levels responded positively to enriched jobs, as predicted; however, distinctly negative responses were found in individuals low in GNS.

More recent work by Landeweerd & Boumans (1994) looked at need for autonomy as a moderator (a variable which they consider to be close to GNS) in a study which used the JDS to predict both satisfaction and health in nurses. They found that perceived autonomy was related to job satisfaction and health complaints but not to absenteeism. When the moderating effect of preference for autonomy was added they found that more job autonomy leads to increased absenteeism in nurses with relatively little preference for autonomy. No significant relationship was found for those who have greater preference for autonomy.

Overall, therefore, notwithstanding the indications that high levels of control are generally associated with positive outcomes, individual differences do seem to be important, and for some people increasing autonomy may actually be related to negative outcomes.

6.4.2 Gender

Many early studies examining job control focused exclusively on men's work and health, and although studies have increasingly looked at gender differences, it remains unclear whether effects are the same for women. Schnall et al. (1994), in their review focusing on CVD, found that in eight out of eleven studies in which comparisons between men and women could be made effect sizes were similar for both men and women. While conflicting evidence still exists, a number of more recent studies have suggested that effects of demands and control may be somewhat lower for women than for men. For example, Weidner et al. (1997) found that having a high-demand/low-control job was unrelated to standard coronary risk factors in both sexes but that it was related to increased medical symptoms and health damaging behaviour in a sample of men but not women. Unlike Weidner et al., Wamala et al. (2000) found that even after controlling for standard risk factors, women in the lowest occupational class had a heart disease risk more than twice that of executive and professional women. However, while job control did contribute to this risk, they concluded that neither lack of job control nor the combination of low demand and high control made a substantial contribution. They argue that the impact of such factors is much less for women than for men, perhaps because, for women, job control may not "adequately capture all the negative aspects of their jobs". Furthermore, women may face multiple stressors, including a range of non-work stressors. This point is reinforced by Brisson et al. (1999), who found that a combination of family responsibilities and high-strain jobs had a greater effect on the blood pressure of white-collar women than exposure to either factor alone.

Similar patterns emerges for psychological well-being. Studies reviewed by Van der Doef & Maes (1999) also find less support for the effects of low control and high demands for psychological health for women. However, not all studies support this view. For example, Mausner-Dorsch & Eaton (2000) found that job strain was more strongly related to major depression in women.

Overall, when looking at redesigning work for women, employers may need to consider a wider range of influences on psychological well-being.

6.5   HAS JOB CONTROL RESEARCH HELPED GUIDE INTERVENTIONS AND JOB REDESIGNS?

A startling feature of Karasek's model is that despite the fact that it was explicitly designed to aid job redesign, as far as can be ascertained from the published literature, it has had minimal impact in this area. Instead, it has had huge impact in terms of enabling dimensions of work to be incorporated in medical and epidemiological studies investigating the effects of work on health. As a result we now have a large literature providing quite convincing evidence about the negative effects of job control for health, but little use of the model to guide job design.

One reason why this may be so is that the construct of control included in psychological theories tends not to be specific enough to guide interventions. For example, Reynolds (1997) argues that the concept of job control is "somewhat diffuse" and that within a single organisation different individuals will have different levels of control over different aspects of work, as well as different preferences. Reynolds further suggests that we do not have sufficiently well-developed methods for bringing about changes in organisations. These factors help explain her findings in a study comparing an organisational change intervention (increasing control) and a counselling scheme. Reynolds found that neither had any influence on people's perceptions of work stressors. However, the counselling intervention, but not organisational change, led to improvements in psychological well-being.

A further reason that the model may not be used to guide interventions in practice may be due to its emphasis on such limited aspects of work. It may be clear to employers that problems in a particular occupational group are related to a much wider range of variables (Jones et al., 1998).

Intervention studies that do aim to enrich jobs by increasing control have had mixed results. They also highlight difficulties with both implementing these kind of changes and assessing their effectiveness in the context of rapidly changing organisations (Landsbergis & Vivona-Vaughan, 1995; Maes et al., 1998). For example, Landsbergis & Vivona-Vaughan in the USA (1995) used an intervention based on a range of approaches, including Karasek's model, to reduce stress in a public service agency. Two matched pairs of departments were assigned to either a treatment or a waiting list control group. The intervention involved employees participating in problem solving committees. They identified stressors and developed action plans to reduce them and to encourage and assist management to implement changes. Priority stressors included such factors as uneven or repetitive workload and poor communication. At the end of one year there were mixed results in one department and negative or negligible impact in the other. It seems likely that the failure of the intervention can be attributed to the fact that it was only department wide while workers were also affected by a range of organisational changes. In this case these included a major agency reorganisation without any employee or union involvement. This produced frustration and disappointment. Both departments lost directors who had supported the changes and some planned changes were not completed. This study clearly demonstrates the wide range of impediments to this kind of organisational change.

It is possible, however, that although employers have not explicitly used the demand–control model, they have nevertheless taken on board the concept of control as a necessary part of job design. The frequent rhetoric of empowerment and the incorporation of control concepts in the management literature suggests that this might be the case. For example, Landsbergis et al. (1999) suggest that new working methods such as "lean production" incorporate total quality management approaches and multi-skilling, techniques which are described in texts as involving increased employee control. However, Karasek (2001) considers that such job enriching approaches are often also accompanied by tougher managerial control. While research is limited on the impact of these new methods of working, Landsbergis et al. (1999) reviewed 38 studies which look at the impact of a range of new work systems and conclude that there is little to suggest that they empower employees. They argue that job control typically remains low while pace of work increases—creating high-strain jobs in Karasek's terms. Overall, a recent report by Merllié & Paoli (2001), which draws on surveys spanning Europe over the period from 1990 to 2001, states that while work intensity has grown, work control has not increased significantly. More specifically, they suggest that increases in employee control from 1990 to 1995 were not sustained in the following five years. In fact, some groups, such as plant and machine operators and sales and service workers, report a decline in the control they have over work.

Evidence for interventions based on the JCM is similarly unimpressive. For example, Kelly (1992) reviewed longitudinal studies of 31 field experiments in job redesign, all of which changed one or more of the dimensions of the JCM (i.e. not necessarily autonomy). They found only limited support for the model, with job redesign leading to significant improvements in job satisfaction in only 17 out of 30 instances. However, where employees perceived an improvement in job content they were more likely to experience increased job satisfaction (though not necessarily motivation or performance). Others have also found inconsistent results in predicting other psychological well-being outcomes. For example, Wall et al. (1986) studied the introduction of semi-autonomous work groups in a longitudinal study and found that while there were increases in extrinsic satisfaction, there were no effects on mental health. Briner & Reynolds (1999) reviewed the evidence for job redesign interventions generally and concluded that there is limited evidence for their effectiveness, and effects are not uniformly positive. They attribute much of this failure to theoretical limitations.

It is both a strength and a limitation of models such as the demand-discretion model and the job characteristics model that they try to provide simple parsimonious models to fit all situations. By necessity they ignore job-specific factors (Jones et al., 1998) and they ignore contextual factors such as social class (Muntaner & O'Campo, 1993) or organisational factors (Cordery & Wall, 1985). Increasingly, there are calls for much more explicit theories to explain particular phenonoma (Briner & Reynolds, 1999) or to apply to particular occupational groups (Sparks & Cooper, 1999). It is becoming clear that simple parsimonious theories which try to explain a broad range of outcomes can only take us so far in indicating the likely impact of stressors. In the applied context, we need to know what particular specific stressors lead to specific outcomes in particular situations. Theoretical developments towards more specific job control constructs and measures are a helpful move in this direction.

6.6   JOB-SPECIFIC APPROACHES

6.6.1   Control in Advanced Manufacturing Technology

The introduction of new technology has had great impact on the design of work, an impact that is likely to increase in the future. The form that this will take has been much debated. A central element of concern is the implication of such changes for job control. While some have argued that job simplification, deskilling and reduction in control is inevitable, Wall et al. (1987) suggest that AMT technology may (at least in some circumstances) offer opportunities for improving the characteristics of workers' jobs, including the element of autonomy. Wall et al. speculate that the more advanced the technology, the greater the choice over the design of the operators' jobs.

Wall et al. have extended research into job control by developing an approach which is specific to work using advanced manufacturing technology (Wall et al., 1990a). They developed a framework that goes some way towards integrating findings from the JCM and Karasek's demand–control approach as well as utilising more specific measures of control. In addition, it clearly illustrates the value of developing specific models for particular types of work which take into account the work context, including the role of technological factors.

The approach taken by Wall et al. focuses on the importance not only of timing and method control but a third type of control which they refer to as boundary control. This is concerned with the extent to which the operator has responsibility for secondary activities that support the primary task of operating the machine. This would include such tasks as maintenance, modifying programmes and quality assurance. They suggest that these three types of control are differentially related to well-being and performance (Wall et al., 1990a). In this context, the crucial factor affecting performance is likely to be boundary control since this may enable the operator to intervene to correct operational problems, hence reducing downtime, the principal barrier to output. They suggest that "job strain results from the co-occurrence of high demands (high monitoring demand with both low timing and method control) with low boundary control" (p. 212). This effect will be accentuated in conditions of low social support.

One test of this approach provides some limited support for the model in relation to well-being (Wall et al., 1990b). This is a longitudinal study of a work redesign intervention involving operators of CNC machines. A change in job design involved operators being trained so that, instead of simplified jobs which involved loading, unloading and monitoring the machines and calling for specialists if required, they became multi-skilled operators responsible not only for the above basic tasks but also for some aspects of maintenance and programming. This change was associated with greater productivity, an increase in intrinsic job satisfaction and a decrease in perceived pressure. However, there was no improvement in general strain as measured by the General Health Questionnaire or in job-related strain. It may be that, as suggested by Wall & Clegg (1981), a longer time scale after a change may be required to demonstrate such changes.

Wall et al. also found that the effectiveness of this change was dependent on the specific type of technology involved. This has also been found in other contexts. For example, Wright & Cordery (1999) found that production uncertainty was an important variable in a study of production operators in a waste water treatment plant. They found that when there was little production uncertainty, those employees with low job control reported higher levels of job satisfaction than those with high job control. However, when production uncertainty was high, the situation was reversed. Similar findings were reported for intrinsic motivation and, in both cases, the least satisfied employees were those that were given high control through the introduction of self-managed teams, but who in fact found that there were few opportunities to exercise this control because production uncertainty was low. Their results demonstrate that job design interventions are more complex than just a consideration of demands and control, and that it is not necessarily beneficial to provide greater control if in reality there is little opportunity to exercise this latitude. It is perhaps unwise to raise employee expectations if fact there is little scope for any real benefit.

6.7 CONCLUSION

Overall, the models and approaches to job control and autonomy discussed in this chapter have had considerable impact in highlighting the importance of job control for psychological and physical well-being. As yet, unfortunately, they have had less impact on interventions. As suggested by Briner & Reynolds (1999), there is now a need to develop job-specific approaches. Such approaches need to identify the particular work characteristics (including different types of control) that are relevant in specific work environments and relate to more specific outcomes. We have seen that some progress is being made in developing measures and a model appropriate for advanced manufacturing technology. Progress is also being made in developing measures for other work groups. For example, Haynes et al. (1999) have produced measures for health services research.

Meanwhile, the work environment is changing fast with rapid technological advances giving opportunities for greater employee control, particularly in terms of control over timing and location of work and other flexible working practices. However, technology also creates opportunities for increasing monitoring and managerial control. Existing evidence suggests that careful choices need to be made in implementing new job designs if health and well-being (as well as performance) are not to be compromised. While models suggest the importance of control there are as yet few specific guidelines to help the manager. Models such as Karasek's model or the JCM may form a useful basis on which more specific models can be built which take into account the complicating factors operating in different contexts, including the nature of the technology and the characteristics and preferences of the employee group.

REFERENCES

Achat, H., Kawachi, I., Byrne, C., Hankinson, S. & Colditz, G. (2000). Lifestyle risk factors for cancer: the relationship with psychosocial work environment. *International Journal of Epidemiology*, **29**(5), 785–92

Adler, S., Skov, R. B. & Salvemini, N. J. (1985). Job characteristics and job satisfaction: when causes become consequences. *Organizational Behavior and Human Decision Processes*, **35**, 266–78.

Alfredsson, L., Karasek, R. & Theorell, T. (1982). Myocardial infarction risk and psychosocial work environment: an anlysis of the male Swedish working force. *Social Science and Medicine*, **16**, 463–7.

Alterman, T., Shekelle, R. B., Vernon, S. W. & Burau, K. D. (1994). Decision latitude, psychologic demand, job strain, and coronary heart disease in the Western Electric Study. *American Journal of Epidemiology*, **139**(6), 620–7.

Bandura, A. (1977). Self efficacy: towards a unifying theory of behavioral change. *Psychological Review*, **84**, 191–215.

Bateman, T. S. & Crant, J. M. (1993). The pro-active component of organizational behaviour: a measure and correlates. *Journal of Organizational Behavior*, **14**, 103–18.

Bosma, H., Stansfield, S. A. & Marmot, M. G. (1998). Job control, personal characteristics, and heart disease. *Journal of Occupational Health Psychology*, **3**(4), 402–9.

Brandt, L. P. A. & Nielsen, C. V. (1992). Job stress and adverse outcome of pregnancy: a causal link or recall bias? *American Journal of Epidemiology*, **135**(3), 302–11.

Breaugh, J. A. (1985). The measurement of work autonomy. *Human Relations*, **38**(6), 551–70.

Briner, R. & Reynolds, S. (1999). The costs, benefits, and limitations of organizational level stress interventions. *Journal of Organizational Behavior*, **20**(5), 647–64.

Brisson, C., Laflamme, N., Moisan, J., Milot, A., Masse, B. & Vezina, M. S. O. (1999). Effect of family responsibilities and job strain on ambulatory blood presure among white collar women. *Psychosomatic Medicine*, **61**(2), 205–13.

Burger, J. M. & Cooper, H. M. (1979). The desirability of control. *Motivation and Emotion*, **3**, 381–93.

Carayon, P. (1993). A longitudinal test of Karasek's job strain model among office workers. *Work and Stress*, **7**, 299–314.

Champoux, J. E. (1991). A multivariate test of the job characteristics theory of work motivation. *Journal of Organizational Behaviour*, **12**, 431–6.

Cordery, J. L. & Wall, T. D. (1985). Work design and supervisory practice: a model. *Human Relations*, **38**(5), 425–41.

Courtney, J. G., Longnecker, M. P. & Peters, R. K. (1996). Psychosocial aspects of work and the risk of colon cancer. *Epidemiology*, **7**(2), 175–81.

Cropley, M., Steptoe, A. & Joekes, K. (1999). Job strain and psychiatric morbidity. *Psychological Medicine*, **29**, 1411–16.

Daniels, K. & Guppy, A. (1994). Occupational stress, social support, job control and psychological well-being. *Human Relations*, **47**(12), 1523–41.

de Rijk, A. E., Le Blanc, P. M. & Schaufeli, W. B. (1998). Active coping and need for control as moderators of the job demand–control model: effects on burnout. *Journal of Occupational and Organizational Psychology*, **71**, 1–18.

Doef, M. Van der & Maes, S. (1998). The job demand–control (–support) model and physical outcomes: a review of the strain and buffer hypotheses. *Psychology and Health*, **13**, 909–36.

Doef, M. Van der & Maes, S. (1999). The job demand–control (–support) model and psychological well-being: a review of 20 years of empirical research. *Work and Stress*, **13**(2), 87–114.

Dollard, M. F., Winefield, H. R., Winefield, A. H. & de Jonge, J. (2000). Psychosocial job strain and productivity in human service workers: a test of the demand–control–support model. *Journal of Occupational and Organizational Psychology*, **73**(4), 501–10.

Dwyer, D. J. & Ganster, D. C. (1991). The effects of job demands and control on employee attendance and satisfaction. *Journal of Organizational Behaviour*, **12**, 595–608.

Fletcher, B. C. & Jones, F. (1993). A refutation of Karasek's demand-discretion model of occupational stress with a range of dependent measures. *Journal of Organizational Behaviour*, **14**, 319–30.

Fox, M. L., Dwyer, D. J. & Ganster, D. C. (1993). Effects of stressful job demands and control on physiological and attitudinal outcomes in a hospital setting. *Academy of Management Journal*, **36**, 289–318.

Friedman, M. & Rosenman, R. H. (1974). *Type A Behavior and Your Heart*. New York: Knopf.

Ganster, D. C. & Fusilier, M. R. (1989). Control in the workplace. In C. L. Cooper & I. Robertson (eds) *International Review of Industrial and Organizational Psychology*. Chichester: John Wiley & Sons.

Goldberg, D. (1978). *Manual of the General Health Questionnaire*. Windsor: NFER.

Green, K. L. & Johnson, J. V. (1990). The effects of psychosocial work organization on patterns of cigarette smoking. among male chemical plant employees. *American Journal of Public Health*, **80**(11), 1368–71.

Hackman, J. R. & Oldham, G. R. (1976). Motivation through the design of work: test of a theory. *Organizational Behavior and Human Performance*, **16**, 250–79.

Hackman, J. R. & Oldham, G. R. (1980). *Work Redesign*. London: Addison-Wesley.

Haynes, C. E., Wall, T. D., Bolden, R. I., Stride, C. & Rick, J. E. (1999). Measures of perceived work characteristics for health services research: test of a measurement model and normative data. *British Journal of Health Psychology*, **4**(3), 257–84.

Hellerstedt, W. L. & Jeffrey, R. W. (1997). The association of job strain and health behaviours in men and women. *International Journal of Epidemiology*, **26**(3), 575–83.

Herzberg, G., Mausner, B. & Snyderman, B. B. (1959). *The Motivation to Work*. Chichester: John Wiley & Sons.

Hlatky, M. A., Lam, L. C., Lee, K. L., Clapp-Channing, N. E., Williams, R. B., Pryor, D. B., Califf, R. M. & Mark, D. B. (1995). Job strain and the prevalence and outcome of coronary artery disease. *Circulation*, **92**(3), 327–33.

Homer, C. J., James, S. A. & Siegel, E. (1990). Work-related psychosocial stress and the risk of preterm, low birthweight delivery. *American Journal of Public Health*, **80**(2), 173–7.

Idasdak, J. R. & Drasgow, F. (1987). A revision of the Job Diagnostic Survey: elimination of a measurement artifact. *Journal of Applied Psychology*, **73**, 647–56.

Jackson, P. R., Wall, T. D., Martin, R. & Davids, K. (1993). New measures of job control, cognitive demand, and production responsibility. *Journal of Applied Psychology*, **78**, 753–62.

Johannson, G., Johnson, J. V. & Hall, E. M. (1991). Smoking and sedentary behavior as related to work organization. *Social Science and Medicine*, **32**(7), 837–46.

Johnson, J. V. & Hall, E. M. (1988). Job strain, work place social support and cardiovascular disease: a cross-sectional study of a random sample of the working population. *American Journal of Public Health*, **78**, 1336–42.

Johnson, J. V., Hall, E. M. & Theorell, T. (1989). Combined effects of job strain and social isolation on cardiovascular disease morbidity and mortality in a random sample of the Swedish male working population. *Scandinavian Journal of Work and Environmental Health*, **15**, 271–9.

Jones, F. & Fletcher, B. C. (1993). An empirical study of occupational stress transmission in working couples. *Human Relations*, **46**(7), 881.

Jones, F., Bright, J. E. H., Searle, B. & Cooper, L. (1998). Modelling occupational stress and health: the impact of the demand–control model on academic research and on workplace practice. *Stress Medicine*, **14**, 231.

Karasek, R. A. (1979). Job demands, job decision latitude and mental strain: implications for job design. *Administrative Science Quarterly*, **24**, 285–308.

Karasek, R. (2001). Towards a psychosocially healthy work environment: broader roles of psychologists and sociologists. In N. Schnedierman, M. A. Speers, J. M. Silva, H. Tomes & J. H. Gentry (eds) *Integrating Behavioural and Social Sciences with Public Health*. Washington, DC: American Psychological Association.

Karasek, R. A. & Theorell, T. (1990). *Healthy Work. Stress, Productivity and the Reconstruction of Working Life*. New York: Basic Books.

Karasek, R., Gardell, B. & Lindell, J. (1987). Work and non-work correlates of illness and behaviour in male and female Swedish white collar workers. *Journal of Occupational Behaviour*, **8**, 187–207.

Kasl, S. V. (1996). The influence of the work environment on cardiovascular health: a historical, conceptual, and methodological perspective. *Journal of Occupational Health Psychology*, **1**(1), 42–56.

Kelly, J. (1992). Does job re-design theory explain job re-design outcomes? *Human Relations*, **45**(8), 753–74.

Kinman, G. & Jones, F. (2001). The home–work interface. In F. Jones & J. Bright (eds) *Stress: Myth, Theory and Research*. London: Prentice Hall.

Kristensen, T. S. (1995) The demand–control–support model: methodological challenges for future research. *Stress Medicine*, **11**, 17–26.

Kristenson, T. S. (1996). Job stress and cardiovascular disease: a theoretical critical review. *Journal of Occupational Health Psychology*, **1**(3), 246–60.

Kushnir, T. & Melamed, S. (1991). Work load, perceived control and psychological distress in Type A/B industrial workers. *Journal of Organizational Behaviour*, **12**(2), 155–68.

Landeweerd, J. A. & Boumans, N. P. G. (1994). The effect of work dimensions and the need for autonomy on nurses' work satisfaction and health. *Journal of Occupational and Organizational Psychology*, **67**(3), 207–17.

Landsbergis, P. A. & Vivona-Vaughan, E. (1995). Evaluation of an occupational stress intervention in a public agency. *Journal of Organizational Behavior*, **16**(1), 29–48.

Landsbergis, P. A., Schnall, P. L., Deitz, D. K., Warren, K., Pickering, T. G. & Schwarz, J. E. (1998). Job strain and health behaviors: results of a prospective study. *American Journal of Health Promotion*, **12**(4), 237–45.

Landsbergis, P. A., Cahill, J. & Schnall, P. (1999). The impact of lean production and related new systems of work organization on worker health. *Journal of Occupational Health Psychology*, **4**(2), 108–30.

Langred, C. W. (2000). The paradox of self-management: individual and group autonomy in work teams. *Journal of Organizational Behavior*, **21**, 563–85.

Loher, B. T., Noe, R. A., Moeller, N. L. & Fitzgerald, M. P. (1985). A meta-analysis of the relation of job characteristics to job satisfaction. *Journal of Applied Psychology*, **70**(2), 280–9.

Loon, A. J. Van, Tijhuis, M., Surtees, P. G. & Ormel, J. (2000). Lifestyle risk factors for cancer: the relationship with psychosocial work environment. *International Journal of Epidemiology*. **29**(5), 785–92.

Lubinski, D. & Humphreys, L. G. (1990). Assessing spurious "moderator effects": illustrated substantively with the hypothesized ("synergistic") relation between spatial and mathematical ability. *Psychological Bulletin*, **107**(3), 385–93.

Maes, S., Verhoeven, C., Kittel, F. & Scholten, H. (1998). The effects of a Dutch work-site wellness-health program: the Brabantia Project. *American Journal of Public Health*, **88**, 1037–41.

Maslow, A. H. (1970). *Motivation and Personality*. New York: Harper.

Mausner-Dorsch, H. & Eaton, W. W. (2000). Psychosocial work environment and depression: epidemiologic assessment of the demand–control model. *American Journal of Public Health*, **90**(11), 1765–70.

Merllié, D. & Paoli, P. (2001). *Ten Years of Working Conditions in the European Union*. Dublin: European Foundation for the Improvement of Living and Working Conditions.

Mullarkey, S., Jackson, P. R. & Parker, S. K. (1995). Employee reactions to JIT manufacturing practices: a two-phase investigation. *International Journal of Operations and Production Management*, **15**(11), 62–79.

Muntaner, C. & O'Campo, P. J. (1993). A critical appraisal of the demand/control model of the psychosocial work environment: epistomological, social and class considerations. *Social Science and Medicine*, **36**(11), 1509–17.

Muntaner, C., Tien, A. Y., Eaton, W. W. & Garrison, R. (1991). Occupational characteristics and the occurrence of psychotic disorders. *Social Psychiatry and Psychiatric Epidemiology*, **26**(6), 273–80.

Munz, D. C., Huelsman, T. J., Konold, T. R. & McKinney, J. J. (1996). Are there methodological and substantive roles for affectivity in job diagnostic survey relationships? *Journal of Applied Psychology*, **81**(6), 795–805.

Parker, S. K. & Sprigg, C. A. (1999). Minimizing strain and maximizing learning: the role of job demands, job control and proactive personality. *Journal of Applied Psychology*, **84**(6), 925–39.

Parkes, K. R. (1991). Locus of control as a moderator: an explanation for additive versus interactive findings in the demand-discretion model of work stress? *British Journal of Psychology*, **82**, 291–312.

Payne, N., Jones, F. & Harris, P. (in press). The impact of working life on health behaviour: the effect of job strain on the cognitive predictors of exercise. *Journal of Occupational Health Psychology*.

Payne, R. L. (1979). Demands, supports, constraints and psychological health. In C. Mackay & T. Cox (eds) *Response to Stress: Occupational Aspects*. London: IPC.

Perrewe, P. L. & Ganster, D. C. (1989). The impact of job demands and behavioural control on experienced job stress. *Journal of Organizational Behaviour*, **10**, 213–29.

Peters, T. J. & Waterman, R. H., Jr (1982). *In Search of Excellence*. New York: HarperCollins.

Pollard, T., Ungpakorn, G., Harrison, G. A. & Parkes, K. R. (1996). Epinephrine and cortisol responses to work: a test of the models of Frankenhaueuser and Karasek. *Annals of Behavioral Medicine*, **18**(4), 229–37.

Reed, D. M., LaCroix, A. Z., Karasek, R. A., Miller, D. & MacLean, C. E. (1989). Occupational strain and the incidence of coronary heart disease. *American Journal of Epidemiology*, **129**, 495–502.

Reynolds, S. (1997). Psychological well-being at work: is prevention better than cure? *Journal of Psychosomatic Research*, **43**(1), 93–102.

Roberts, K. H. & Glick, W. (1981). The job characteristics approach to job design: a critical review. *Journal of Applied Psychology*, **66**(2), 193–217.

Rotter, J. B. (1966). Generalized expectancies for internal versus external control of reinforcement. *Psychological Monographs*, **91**, 482–97.

Rousseau, D. M. (1978). Relationship of work to non-work. *Journal of Applied Psychology*, **63**, 513–17.

Saavedra, R. & Kwun, S. K. (2000). Affective states in job characteristics theory. *Journal of Organizational Behavior*, **21**(5), 131–46.

Sanchez, J. I. & Levine, E. L. (2000). Accuracy or consequential validity: which is the better standard for job analysis data? *Journal of Organizational Behavior*, **21**, 809–18.

Sargent, L. D. & Terry, D. J. (1998). The effects of work control and job demands on employee adjustment and work performance. *Journal of Occupational and Organizational Psychology*, **71**(3), 219–36.

Schaubroeck, J. & Merritt, D. E. (1997). Divergent effects of job control on coping with work stressors. *Academy of Management Journal*, **40**, 738–54.

Schaubroeck, J., Lame, S. S. K. & Xie, J. L. (2000). Collective self-efficacy in coping responses to stressors and control: a cross-cultural study. *Journal of Applied Psychology*, **85**(4), 512–25.

Schnall, P. L., Landsbergis, P. A. & Baker, D. (1994). Job strain and cardiovascular health. *Annual Review of Public Health*, **15**, 381–411.

Skov, T., Borg, V. & Orhede, E. (1996). Psychosocial and physical risk factors for musculoskeletal disorders of the neck, shoulders, and lower back in salespeople. *Occupational and Environmental Medicine*, **53**(5), 351–6.

Smith, C., Tisak, J., Hahn, S. E. & Schmeider, R. A. (1997). The measurement of job control. *Journal of Organizational Behavior*, **18**, 225–37.

Soderfeldt, B., Soderfeldt, M., Muntaner, C., O'Campo, P., Warg, L. E. & Ohlson, C. G. (1996). Psychosocial work environment in human service organizations: a conceptual analysis and development of the demand–control model. *Social Science and Medicine*, **42**(9), 1217–26.

Sparks, K. & Cooper, C. L. (1999). Occupational differences in the work–strain relationship: towards the use of situation-specific models. *Journal of Occupational and Organisational Psychology*, **72**, 219–29.

Spector, P. (1985). Higher-order need strength as a moderator of the job scope–employee outcome relationship: a meta-analysis. *Journal of Occupational Psychology*, **58**, 119–27.

Spector, P. E. (1986). Perceived control by employees: a meta-analysis of studies concerning autonomy and participation at work. *Human Relations*, **39**(11), 1005–16.

Spector, P. E. & Jex, S. M. (1991). Relations of job characteristics from multiple data sources with employee affect, absence, turnover intentions, and health. *Journal of Applied Psychology*, **76**(1), 46–53.

Steenland, K., Johnson, J. & Nowlin, S. (1997). A follow-up study of job strain and heart disease among males in the NHANES1 population. *American Journal of Industrial Medicine*, **31**, 256–60.

Steptoe, A., Fieldman, G., Evans, O. & Perry, L. (1993). Control over work pace, job strain and cardiovascular responses in middle aged men. *Journal of Hypertension*, **11**, 751–9.

Stets, J. E. (1995). Job autonomy and control over one's spouse: a compensatory process. *Journal of Health and Social Behaviour*, **36**, 244–58.

Storr, C. J., Trinkoff, A. M. & Anthony, J. C. (1999). Job strain and non-medical drug use. *Drug and Alcohol Dependence*, **55**(1–2), 45–51.

Terry, D. J. & Jimmieson, N. L. (1999). Work control and employee well-being: a decade review. *International Review of Industrial and Organizational Psychology*, **14**, 95–148.

Wall, T. D. & Clegg, C. W. (1981). A longitudinal field study of group work redesign. *Journal of Occupational Behaviour*, **2**, 31–49.

Wall, T. D., Clegg, C. W. & Jackson, P. R. (1978). An evaluation of the job characteristics model. *Journal of Occupational Psychology*, **51**, 183–96.

Wall, T. D., Kemp, N. J., Jackson, R. P. & Clegg, C. W. (1986). Outcomes of automonous work groups: a long term field experiment. *Academy of Management Journal*, **29**, 280–304.

Wall, T. D., Clegg, C. W., Davies, R. T., Kemp, N. J. & Mueller, W. S. (1987). Advanced manufacturing technology and work simplification: an empirical study. *Journal of Occupational Psychology*, **8**, 233–50.

Wall, T. D., Corbett, J. M., Clegg, C. W., Jackson, P. R. & Martin, R. (1990a). Advanced manufacturing technology and work design: towards a theoretical framework. *Journal of Organizational Behavior*, **11**, 201–19.

Wall, T. D., Corbett, J. M., Martin, R., Clegg, C. W. & Jackson, P. (1990b). Advanced manufacturing technology, work design and performance: a change study. *Journal of Applied Psychology*, **75**, 691–7.

Wall, T. D., Jackson, P. R. & Mullarkey, S. (1995). Further evidence on some new measures of job control, cognitive demand and production responsibility. *Journal of Organisational Behavior*, **16**, 431–55.

Wall, T. D., Jackson, P. R., Mullarkey, S. & Parker, S. K. (1996). The demand–control model of job strain: a more specific test. *Journal of Occupational and Organisational Psychology*, **62**(2), 153–66.

Wamala, S. P., Mittleman, M. A., Horsten, M., Schenck-Gustafsson, K. & Orth-Gomer, K. (2000). Job stress and the occupational gradient in coronary heart disease risk in women. The Stockholm Female Coronary Risk Study. *Social Science and Medicine*, **51**, 481–9.

Warr, P. (1987). *Work, Unemployment and Mental Health*. Oxford: Oxford University Press.

Warr, P. B. (1991). Decision latitude, job demands and employee well-being. *Work and Stress*, **4**(4), 285–94.

Weidner, G., Boughal, T., Pieper, C., Connor, S. L. & Mendell, N. R. (1997). Relationship of job strain to standard coronary riusk factors and psychological characteristics in women and men of the Family Heart Study. *Health Psychology*, **3**, 239–47.

Westman, M. (2001). Stress and strain crossover. *Human Relations*, **54**(6), 557–91.

Wong, C. S., Hui, C. & Law, K. S. (1998). A longitudinal study of the job perception–job satisfaction relationship: a test of three alternative specifications. *Journal of Occupational and Organizational Psychology*, **71**, 127–46.

Wright, B. M. & Cordery, J. L. (1999). Production uncertainty as a contextual moderator of employee reactions to job design. *Journal of Applied Psychology*, **84**(3), 456–63.

CHAPTER 7

The Psychological Contract, Health and Well-Being

David E. Guest
King's College, London, UK
and
Neil Conway
Birkbeck College, London, UK

7.1 INTRODUCTION

This chapter examines the concept of the psychological contract and considers its relation to stress, health and well-being. Since there has been very little published work addressing this issue, the chapter differs somewhat from many others in this book. It starts by describing the nature of the psychological contract and explains why it has become a focus of research interest. It then outlines some of the core research on the psychological contract. Particular attention is paid to the notion of violation of the contract which begins to address the consequences for employee well-being of a breakdown of the psychological contract. The remainder of the paper presents a framework for studying the state of the psychological contract and presents data within this framework that explores the relationship between the psychological contract and aspects of health and well-being. Building on this, the need for a fuller research agenda is presented together with an evaluation of the benefits to the study of health and well-being at work of incorporating the psychological contract into the analysis.

7.2 WHAT IS THE PSYCHOLOGICAL CONTRACT?

The use of the term "the psychological contract" can be traced back to the 1960s and the writing of Argyris, Levinson and Kotter, among others. It was developed further in the 1970s by writers such as Schein, who had a particular interest in its application to the study of careers. Its recent rise to a position of greater prominence owes much to the research and writing of Rousseau (1995), who has set the concept in a contemporary context and encouraged international and comparative research (Rousseau & Schalk, 2000).

The Handbook of Work and Health Psychology. Edited by M.J. Schabracq, J.A.M. Winnubst and C.L. Cooper.
© 2003 John Wiley & Sons, Ltd.

Among the early writers, Kotter (1973) defines the psychological contract as "an implicit contract between an individual and his organization which specifies what each expects to give and receive from each other in their relationship". Schein (1980) similarly describes it as "a set of unwritten reciprocal expectations between an individual employee and the organization". In both cases there is a clear notion of exchange and an implied contract involving two parties. Rousseau has offered a different perspective, arguing that organizations cannot have a psychological contract and that it is inappropriate to anthropomorphize the organization. She therefore defines the psychological contract as "an individual's belief regarding the terms and conditions of a reciprocal exchange agreement between the focal person and another party. A psychological contract emerges when one party believes that a promise of future returns has been made, a contribution has been given and thus, an obligation has been created to provide future benefits" (Rousseau, 1989). While many contemporary American researchers have followed Rousseau's definition, it has proved less attractive in Europe, and the work of writers such as Herriot & Pemberton (1995) has maintained the view that the psychological contract is best seen as a two-way exchange which can be defined as "the perceptions of both parties to the employment relationship, organization and individual, of the obligations implied in the relationship. Psychological contracting is the process whereby these perceptions are arrived at". Since it can be argued that the psychological contract is a metaphor for an exchange between at least two parties and both parties have a legitimate interest in the exchange, we support the dominant tradition of viewing the psychological contract in terms of this exchange. We therefore define the psychological contract along very similar lines to Herriot & Pemberton as "The perceptions of both parties to the employment relationship, organization and individual, of the reciprocal promises and obligations implied in the relationship". The variations reflect a view that it is useful to distinguish between promises and obligations.

7.3   WHY THE INTEREST IN THE PSYCHOLOGICAL CONTRACT?

Acknowledging that the term has been used occasionally since the 1960s how can we explain its much wider use in the 1990s? One answer is that it has been presented more effectively in the academic community through the powerful analysis and research of Rousseau. Another is that it fits with a growing concern that the world of work has been changing. There is a popular view, albeit not strongly supported by empirical evidence, that the traditional psychological contract, which might be expressed for some workers as a fair day's work for a fair day's pay and for others as a career and employment security with an organization in return for loyalty and high-quality work, has broken down. It is not clear what has taken its place although there is much discussion of boundaryless careers, career self-management and flexible employment contracts. The key point is that those who entered employment expecting the traditional career promise may feel that this promise has been broken.

The inability to keep promises is associated with the increasing pace of change in organizations. A key feature of the psychological contract is the importance of implicit promises. For example, a manager may make a promise to a subordinate about promotion possibilities; but if that manager moves on and is replaced, or if reorganization takes place, then the implicit promise may not be kept. One implication of this analysis is that as implicit promises are increasingly broken, employees will reduce their commitment to the organization and display lower levels of motivation and extra-role or citizenship behaviour. In other words, the psychological contract matters to organizations. Despite the interest in contract "violation", relatively less attention has been paid to the consequences for individual well-being and there is little extant theory and research to draw on. In this chapter, we therefore present a conceptual framework and some empirical data on the association between the psychological contract and aspects of employee well-being that begin to fill this gap.

7.4   HOW HAS THE PSYCHOLOGICAL CONTRACT TYPICALLY BEEN STUDIED?

As we have already noted, much of the recent research has been spear-headed by Rousseau. In a series of papers, she and her colleagues have explored the content of the psychological contract, defined in terms of perceptions among workers of what they believe the organization is obliged to do for them and what they are obliged to do for the organization in return. Obligations of the organization might include regular pay, fair treatment by management, provision of equal opportunities for advancement, reasonable job security, interesting work and sufficient training to do the job effectively. Obligations on the part of the individual might include arriving at work on time, behaving honestly and helping out in a crisis. Obligations can be complemented by an identification of promises made by both sides. In these analyses there is some variation in the focus of study between obligations, expectations, commitments and promises.

There has been much conceptual ground-clearing about dimensions along which the psychological contract can be studied. One of the most widely used distinctions is between relational and transactional features of psychological contracts. The relational elements include the more implicit understandings about fair treatment, support for a promotion application, opportunities to get on key development programmes and so on. The transactional elements are more explicit and clear-cut and might include the timing of holidays, the basis for overtime payment and the criteria for achievement of performance targets. In practice, the border between relational and transactional, as between implicit and explicit, contracts can become blurred and perceived in different ways by the parties to the psychological contract. Much of this work is summarized in Rousseau (1995) although it continues to be developed to address a range of work-related issues. To take one example, McLean Parks et al. (1998) identify seven dimensions along which the psychological contracts of contingent workers might usefully be measured. They label these dimensions stability, scope, tangibility, focus, time frame, particularism, multiple agency and volition. There remains the challenge of finding reliable and valid ways to measure these dimensions. Given the variety of workers and organizational contexts, there is also, inevitably, variation in the content of the psychological contract. Attempts have been made to develop scales to capture the content but to date they have not been wholly successful when transferred from one context to another, probably in part because of the idiosyncratic nature of psychological contracts.

As implied, much of the research has been concerned to identify the content or the important dimensions of the psychological contract. Typically, this research has been based on the use of survey questionnaires. There are some exceptions to this. For example, Herriot et al. (1997) used the critical incident technique to identify the content of the psychological contract, and Rousseau & Anton (1991) employed a policy-capturing methodology to investigate more precisely the exchange underlying transactional and relational contracts. Much of this research has been atheoretical and it does not help us to understand how the psychological contract is related to antecedents or consequences. When mechanisms are proposed relating the psychological contract to attitudinal or behavioural outcomes, they usually draw on exchange theory (Blau, 1964); while offering a distinctive perspective on the exchange, they do not move beyond this well-established framework.

It is only with Rousseau's (1989) introduction of the concept of "violation" of the psychological contract that a distinctive link to outcomes becomes possible. Prior to that, the mechanism underpinning the psychological contract, while reflecting an exchange, was based on some concept of "matching" of employer and employee expectations. Where a match occurred, positive outcomes were anticipated. However this matching concept has been poorly theorized; for example, in the present context, the implications for well-being of a match based on low mutual expectations are very unclear. In contrast, the concept of violation, while limited in its negative implications, offers a convincing and testable link to attitudinal and behavioural outcomes. It also fits well with the growing concern about the breakdown of the traditional psychological contract. It is this concept of violation and the broader focus on the "state" of the psychological contract developed below that offer the best basis for linking the psychological contract to aspects of employee health and well-being.

We therefore explore both these concepts and their link to various outcomes in more detail.

7.5   VIOLATION OF THE PSYCHOLOGICAL CONTRACT

Psychological contract violation occurs "when one party in a relationship perceives another to have failed to fulfil promised obligation(s)" (Robinson & Rousseau, 1994, p. 247). Violations of psychological contracts, like perceptions of obligations, may be wholly subjective. In other words, an employee may perceive that an organization has violated an agreement, but an organization (or agent representing the organization) may not perceive any violation or even be aware that an underlying agreement exists. The perceived discrepancy between what was expected and what was received can also vary considerably. As Rousseau (1995, pp. 111–12) notes, "contract violation can run the gamut from subtle misperceptions to stark breaches of good faith. . . . Given the subjectivity of contract terms, a contract could hardly exist without some inadvertent violation".

A problem with this analysis is that "violation" is a strong and emotive word for a phenomenon that can be nothing more than "subtle misperception". Reflecting this concern, Morrison & Robinson (1997) argued that violation as defined above, reflecting as it does a cognitive comparison of what is received against what is expected, is better defined as contract breach. The term "violation" should be reserved for the occasions when the breach is serious enough to engender strong emotional and affective states. They present a model of escalating steps leading to psychological contract breach and then on to violation, opening up a fuller research agenda. For example, they propose that the step from breach to violation is moderated by a number of variables relating to various interpretation processes, such as why and how the breach occurred and the social contract governing the relationship. The distinction between breach and violation has been widely accepted and in the present context, it is plausible to hypothesize that breaches of the psychological contract are relatively minor and commonplace and will have little effect on well-being whereas violations, with their emotional reaction, may well have a negative effect on levels of stress and well-being.

Morrison & Robinson (1997) argue that when breaches escalate to violation, they have serious individual and organizational implications. First, they are likely to result in strong affective reactions, such as feelings of injustice and betrayal (Robinson et al., 1994) and consequent deleterious effects on satisfaction with the job and the organization (Robinson & Rousseau, 1994). Second, an employee's perception of a violation undermines the relationship through a resultant loss of trust, faith and fair dealing (Robinson, 1996; Rousseau, 1989). Third, violation affects an employee's beliefs regarding the reciprocal obligations in place between themselves and the organization (Robinson et al., 1994). Following a violation, the employee may feel less obligated to be committed (Robinson, 1995) and to perform extra-role behaviours (McLean Parks & Kidder, 1994), and in extreme cases may wish to exit the relationship altogether (Robinson & Rousseau, 1994).

Robinson & Rousseau (1994) argue that the effects of violation on attitudinal and behavioural outcomes go beyond those associated with inequity and unmet expectations. Beliefs in inequity need not involve broken promises, therefore inequity can theoretically be redressed by restoring the balance between contributions and inducements, whereas the damage caused by a violation, involving a broken promise, goes beyond inequity and produces concomitant beliefs in a loss of trust and feelings of betrayal (Robinson et al., 1994). Turning now to expectations, responses to violations are "likely to be more intense than in the case of unfulfilled expectations. The intensity of the reaction is attributable not only to unmet expectations of specific rewards and benefits, but also to more general beliefs about respect for persons, codes of conduct, and other patterns of behaviour associated with relationships" (Robinson & Rousseau, 1994). Further, violation may also deprive the employee of those inducements from work that are important sources of work satisfaction (Robinson & Rousseau, 1994). However, debates about the distinctions between breach and violation and between these and other closely related concepts such as equity are ongoing (Arnold, 1996; Conway, 1996; Guest, 1998), and there has been insufficient empirical investigations directly comparing the concepts.

Empirical investigations of the relationship between breach and outcomes are fairly recent, and relatively few studies have been conducted. Indeed, in most cases, it is not always clear whether what is being reported constitutes breach or violation. Most studies have technically measured breach but have discussed their results in terms of violation, thus making a not unreasonable assumption that high ratings of perceived breach is a reasonable proxy for violation. For the remainder of this review we shall adopt Morrison & Robinson's distinction between breach and violation. Breach and/or violation has been operationalized in several ways, underlining several researchers' observations that, as yet, there is no accepted measure of the psychological contract (Freese & Schalk, 1996; Guzzo et al., 1994). In the main, researchers (e.g. Robinson, 1995, 1996; Robinson & Morrison, 1995; Robinson & Rousseau, 1994) have measured breach by adapting a measure of perceived obligations by Rousseau (1990) and have asked participants to rate the extent to which they believe the organization has fulfilled the "promised obligations they owed you" (Robinson & Rousseau, 1994, p. 251). However, Guzzo et al. (1994) used two different sets of measures to assess the state of the psychological contract. The first measure assessed the extent to which employees saw their psychological contract as being fulfilled, focusing on the extent to which what was being provided by the organization differed from what they thought *should* be provided; the second measure was argued to be a more global indicator of the state of the psychological contract, using Eisenberger's et al. (1986) measure of Perceived Organizational Support.

These studies have found that perceived breach or violation of the psychological contract is associated with lower levels of employees' trust in the organization, satisfaction with organization and job, organizational commitment, intentions to remain, citizenship behaviours and performance, and with increased labour turnover (Guzzo et al., 1994; Robinson, 1995, 1996; Robinson & Morrison, 1995; Robinson & Rousseau, 1994). Table 7.1 summarizes the studies investigating the relationship between psychological contract breach and outcomes.

In terms of effect sizes it would appear that, in general, psychological contract breach is impressively associated with outcomes in both cross-sectional (in the region of 0.7 for trust and satisfaction for Rousseau's measure) and longitudinal (in the region of 0.3–0.5 for trust, satisfaction, and commitment for Rousseau's measure) studies. The outcomes that are best predicted by breach are inconclusive. When attitudes are measured at the same point in time, breach has a slightly higher correlation with trust ahead of satisfaction. Longitudinally, breach correlates most strongly with organizational commitment, then satisfaction, then trust, then civic virtue. When we consider the way the psychological contract breach has been operationalized, adaptations of Rousseau's measure, which specifically concentrate on promises, are more powerful predictors of outcomes than Guzzo et al.'s more general measure of fulfilled obligations focusing on what employees believe they "should" receive.

The very high correlations between psychological contract breach and job satisfaction raise some concerns about the discriminant validity between the two constructs. This issue has been investigated to some extent by Turnley & Feldman (2000), who found that while job satisfaction mediated the relationship between breach and the outcomes of the intention to quit, the neglect of in-role duties, and extra-role behaviours, breach remained significantly associated with the intention to quit and extra-role behaviours even after controlling for job satisfaction.

While the initial empirical support for psychological contract breach appears promising—in terms of the size of the associations found between breaches and outcomes—there are several reasons to regard these studies cautiously. First, very few studies have been carried out, and they are not independent from one another. For instance, five of the studies presented in the table emanate from the same longitudinal sample of recently employed MBA alumni (namely the studies by Robinson 1995, 1996; Robinson & Morrison, 1995, 2000; Robinson & Rousseau, 1994). Second, relatively few outcomes have been considered and the psychometric properties of some of the outcome measures are suspect. A number of single or two-item measures have been employed, and the psychometric properties of low-item measured constructs is widely known to be somewhat suspect. Third, measures of psychological contract breach are rather underdeveloped. The most widely used and adapted measure by Robinson & Rousseau (1994), for example, does not consider such factors as whether the promise is perceived as being important or not, who specifically broke the promise or when the promise was broken, and also assumes that a promise was made in the first place. Given the initial stage of research into psychological contract breach and violation, attempts to expand the repertoire of measures, for example in the work of Turnley & Feldman (1999) are welcome. Finally, a narrow range of methods has been used

Table 7.1 Relationship between psychological contract breach and outcomes: a summary of empirical findings

Psychological contract breach operationalisation	Correlation[a]	Dependent variable (operationalisation)	Reference
Transactional contract breach	−0.29	Perceived organizational support (Eisenberger et al., 1986)	Coyle-Shapiro & Kessler, 2000
Relational contract breach	−0.41		
Training contract breach[b]	−0.33		
Composite measure[c]	−0.29[d]	Trust in organization (Robinson & Rousseau, 1994)	Robinson, 1996
Composite measure[b]	−0.39[d]	Trust in organization (Robinson & Rousseau, 1994)	Robinson, 1995
Single item measure[e]	−0.79	Trust in organization (Robinson & Rousseau, 1994)	Robinson & Rousseau, 1994
Relational contract breach	−0.29[d]	Trust in organization (Robinson & Rousseau, 1994)	Robinson & Morrison, 1995
Transactional contract breach[b]	−0.29[d]		
Composite measure[c]	−0.18[d]	Performance (Robinson, 1996)	Robinson, 1996
Composite measure[c]	0.20[d]	Turnover (Robinson, 1996)	Robinson, 1996
Composite measure[b]	−0.44[d]	Job satisfaction (Kunin, 1955, and two ad hoc items by Robinson & Rousseau, 1994)	Robinson, 1995
Single item measure[e]	−0.76	Job satisfaction (Kunin, 1955, and two ad hoc items by Robinson & Rousseau, 1994	Robinson & Rousseau, 1994
Single item measure[e]	−0.72	Job satisfaction (three item measure)	Cavannaugh & Roe, 1999
Transactional contract breach	−0.38	Job satisfaction (Cook & Wall, 1980)	Coyle-Shapiro & Kessler, 2000
Relational contract breach	−0.46		
Training contract breach[b]	−0.46		
Composite measure[b]	−0.56	Job satisfaction (two items, Hackman & Oldman, 1976)	Turnley & Feldman, 2000
Global breach[f]	0.68	Feelings of violation (four items; Robinson & Morrison, 2000	Robinson & Morrison, 2000)
Composite measure[b]	−0.54[d]	Organizational commitment (Porter & Smith, 1970)	Robinson, 1995
Sufficiency of financial benefits	−0.23	Organizational commitment (Mowday et al., 1982)	Guzzo et al., 1994.
Sufficiency of support			
Sufficiency of family benefits	−0.28		
Composite of above three	−0.23		
(all measures designed by authors)[g]	−0.27		
Transactional contract breach			
Relational contract breach	−0.30 −0.27	Organizational commitment (Mowday et al., 1982)	Coyle-Shapiro & Kessler, 2000
Training contract breach[b]	−0.23		
Behaviours OCB			
Composite measure[c]	−0.25[d]	Civic virtue (Podsakoff et al., 1990)	Robinson, 1996
Relational contract breach	−0.29[d]		Robinson & Morrison, 1995
Transactional contract breach[b]	−0.23[d]		

continues overleaf

Table 7.1   *(continued)*

Psychological contract breach operationalization	Correlation[a]	Dependent variable (operationalization)	Reference
		EVLN behaviours:	
Composite measure[h]	0.38	Exit	Turnley &
	−0.32	Voice	Feldman, 1999
	−0.45	Loyalty	
	0.24 (ns)	Neglect	
Single item measure	−0.42	Intentions to remain (single-item measure)	Robinson & Rousseau, 1994
Sufficiency of financial benefits	0.07 (ns)	Intentions to quit (single-item measure)	Guzzo et al., 1994.
Sufficiency of support	0.23		
Sufficiency of family benefits	0.15 (ns)		
Composite of above three (all measures designed by authors)[g]	0.16		
Single item measure	0.27	Intentions to quit (single-item measure)	Cavannaugh & Roe, 1999
Composite measure[b]	0.48	Intentions to quit (six items; Weiss, 1967)	Turnley & Feldman, 2000

[a] All correlations are significant at the 5% level except those that are followed by (ns), indicating non-significance.
[b] Participants were asked the degree to which their employer had fulfilled their promises across a number of items such as: promotion and advancement, high pay, pay based on performance, training, long-term job security, career development, sufficient power and responsibility. The number of items varies across studies. In certain cases, factor analysis results are reported and the items are aggregated into subscales (see Coyle-Shapiro & Kessler, 2000; Robinson & Morrison, 1995).
[c] Difference score calculated through subtracting the degree to which a promise was fulfilled (at time 2) from the degree to which it was perceived to be highly obligated (at time 1, 18 months earlier) over seven items: promotion and advancement, high pay, pay based on performance, training, long-term job security, career development, and sufficient power and responsibility.
[d] Longitudinal study, time between violation and outcome measurement was 12 months.
[e] Single item measure, such as "How well, overall, has your employer fulfilled the promised obligations they owed you?" (Robinson & Rousseau, 1994).
[f] Example item, "So far my employer has done an excellent job in fulfilling their promises to me" (reverse scored).
[g] Participants were asked the extent to which what was being provided by their employer differed from what they thought should be provided on 43 items. Three factors emerged: financial benefits, general support and family benefits. Additionally, a composite of these three factors was used in the analysis.
[h] Psychological contract violation was assessed using a multiplicative measure: Respondents first indicated how important 16 items were, where the scale ranged from 1 (Not important) to 10 (Extremely important), then they were asked the extent to which they had actually received the item compared to which the organization committed to provide them, where the scale ranged from −2 (received much less than promised) to +2 (received much more than promised).

to examine breach, with existing studies being based to a very large extent on cross-sectional self-report questionnaire surveys.

While the conceptual distinction between breach and violation might be accepted, it may be far more difficult to establish the distinction empirically. Indeed to date only one study has explicitly examined the distinction between breach and violation. Robinson & Morrison, in a test of their model specifying the antecedents to breach and the moderators of the links between breach and violation, found that breach was highly correlated with feelings of violation ($r = 0.68$). They also found evidence that, despite the magnitude of the correlation, the two constructs were empirically distinct. Less support was found from the study for their model of the development of violation. Rather surprisingly, neither the perceived fairness of treatment following psychological contract breach nor the perception that the organization had purposely reneged (as opposed to a misunderstanding) significantly moderated the relationship between breach and violation. However, a three-way interaction was found, where the relationship between breach and violation was stronger under conditions of unfair treatment *and* attributions of deliberate reneging, suggesting that the interpretive process between breach and violation may be more complicated than initially specified.

In summary, to date only a small number of studies have considered breach or violation of psychological contracts and these have not explored outcomes directly related to health and well-being. Any conclusions are thus largely speculative and must be inferred from links to trust, satisfaction and labour turnover. Furthermore, the concepts of breach and violation are somewhat limited in increasing our understanding of affect. While violation may be useful in explaining negative affect, it does not lend itself readily to explaining positive affect (i.e. does absence of violation mean positive affect?) or to dealing with cases where no violations have taken place. To accommodate this we need a rather different model. One possibility is to develop the analysis of the *state* of the psychological contract.

7.6 A MODEL OF THE STATE OF THE PSYCHOLOGICAL CONTRACT AND INDIVIDUAL WELL-BEING

As already noted, one of the limitations of much of the research on the psychological contract is that it is relatively limited in its analysis of the antecedents and consequences. One reason for this has been the emphasis on identifying and measuring the dimensions and content of the contract. Where there has been some emphasis on consequences, the focus has been directed towards breach or violation and therefore almost entirely on negative outcomes. There is a prior empirical question about whether this is an appropriate focus. An alternative framework builds on what we describe as the *state* of the psychological contract. This is less concerned with the content of the contract and more concerned with its delivery. Therefore while the psychological contract may contain promises about a career, workload and job content, the state of the psychological contract is concerned with whether the promises have been kept. Since the promises may be limited and time constrained, the analysis incorporates fairness and trust. Fairness provides a sense of whether the promises that have been made are fair, both in themselves and in relation to those made to others. Trust is concerned with perceptions of whether those who have made the promises, or the organizations they represent, are likely to continue to keep them into the future. Since the model is concerned with whether the promises have been kept, the analysis of the content of the psychological contract—whether promises have been made—is subsumed within this framework. The model then builds in the antecedents and consequences of the psychological contract. It therefore broadens the analysis of the consequences of the psychological contract beyond violation. It now proposes that a poor state of the psychological contract, akin in certain respects to some level of breach or violation, will have negative consequences for attitudes and behaviour. But equally, a positive state of the psychological contract will be associated with positive outcomes for the individual and the organization. It should be noted that this analysis follows the emphasis recommended by Rousseau on employee assessments of the psychological contract. This is appropriate in the current context but it is important not to ignore the way in which the psychological contract is viewed by organizations and their representatives (Guest & Conway, 2001b).

The model informing the analysis of the state of the psychological contract is set out in Figure 7.1.

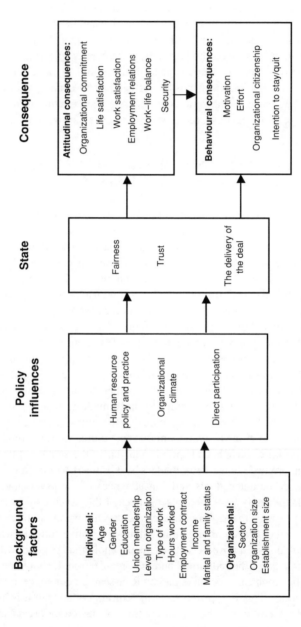

Figure 7.1 A framework for the state of the psychological contract

The model incorporates outcomes related to well-being. More specifically, it is hypothesized that a positive (state of the) psychological contract will be associated with lower levels of work-related stress, more positive emotional states, higher self-reported well-being and more positive life satisfaction, including work–life balance and reported health.

7.7 EVIDENCE ON THE STATE OF THE PSYCHOLOGICAL CONTRACT, HEALTH AND WELL-BEING

Each year in the UK, we undertake a national survey of the state of the psychological contract sponsored by the Chartered Institute of Personnel and Development. The survey normally covers 1000 workers, selected at random and interviewed by telephone. Each year the survey includes a number of standard questions and a set that address a specific theme. The standard questions cover topics identified in the model presented in Figure 7.1.

There is considerable consistency in the responses from year to year. Psychometric analysis confirms that the measure of the state of the psychological contract, incorporating the extent to which promises have been kept and the levels of trust and fairness, can be treated as a single factor and a single scale. Results show that for a large majority of UK workers, the state of the psychological contract is broadly positive but that for a sub-group of about 20%, it is poor. Looking at the antecedents, a more positive evaluation of the state of the psychological contract is consistently associated with a measure of the number of progressive human resource practices in place, with aspects of the organizational climate and with the scope for direct participation, all of which highlight the importance of organizational policy and practice. Background factors that are frequently associated with a positive psychological contract include working in a smaller organization and establishment and having a higher salary (Guest & Conway, 1998).

Over the years, the surveys consistently find that a positive state of the psychological contract is associated with higher levels of work satisfaction, organizational commitment, job security, satisfaction with employer–employee relations, motivation and intention to stay with the organization. It is not associated with individuals' self-assessments of performance, or with innovative behaviour, citizenship behaviour or with effort (which is externally driven, as opposed to motivation, which is more intrinsic). In other words, for employees there are positive work-related affective outcomes.

The survey regularly measures life satisfaction, including a measure of satisfaction with health. We should emphasize that this is a measure of satisfaction with life and with health, not an independent assessment; nevertheless, it is important in its own right. The results for 1998 are shown in Table 7.2. Results for individual items and for a composite measure of the various items is strongly associated with the state of the psychological contract. One of the potential problems concerns causality. In 1999, the survey consisted of a follow-up of the 1998 sample. This confirmed that the state of the psychological contract in 1998 predicted changes in life satisfaction between 1998 and 1999. In other words, those reporting a positive psychological contract were likely to report improvements in life satisfaction and those with a more negative psychological contract a deterioration. Interestingly, the state of the psychological contract in 1999 was an even stronger predictor of change in most attitudes between 1998 and 1999, including changes in life satisfaction. This suggests that the current state of the psychological contract has a stronger influence on attitude change than the state of the exchange a year earlier (Guest & Conway, 2001a)

Table 7.2 Satisfaction with life

	Satisfaction levels (%)				
	Low (1–3)	Medium (4–7)	High (8–10)	Don't know	Average
Satisfaction with:					
Life as a whole	4	41	55	1	7.37
Family	3	22	74	2	8.39
Friends	2	25	71	1	8.13
Health	4	30	66	0	7.87
Work	6	47	46	0	6.93
Finances	13	50	37	0	6.34

Responses are based on a random sample of 1000 workers in the UK interviewed by telephone during 1998. Responses were provided on a ten-point scale from totally dissatisfied (1) to totally satisfied (10).
Source: Guest and Conway (1998).

The 1997 survey examined the association between pressure at work and the state of the psychological contract. Asked how often they felt under excessive pressure at work, 9% said "all the time", 39% said "quite often", 38% said "every now and again", 9% said "rarely" and 5% said "never". In the regression analysis using pressure at work as the dependent variable, the factors showing the strongest association were, in order, working longer hours, having a poorer psychological contract, working in a job other than a blue-collar job, working in sectors other than the traditional industrial sector and being female. This confirms the strong relationship between the state of the psychological contract and reported pressures at work. (Guest & Conway, 1997).

The 1998 survey explored the association between the state of the psychological contract and the locus of emotional experience. This asked workers whether they were more likely to experience emotions such as feeling relaxed, excited, happy, in control, absorbed, valued, stressed and bored at home, at work, at both or at neither. The results are shown in Table 7.3. These indicate that for the typical worker, home is the main place for relaxation, elation and excitement while work is more likely to be the place where people are stretched, absorbed and stressed. It is debatable whether it is healthier for workers to locate their emotions at home or at work or both. In the event, the regression analysis reveals that those who tended to cite both are those with a more positive psychological contract. They are also more likely to be older, female, to report more human resource practices in place and to work on temporary contracts. Those reporting that work is the main locus of their emotional involvement are also likely to report a more positive psychological contract; in addition they are more likely to be divorced and/or single rather than married, to be older, to work in the public sector, and to believe they have the wrong balance between home and work. Those more emotionally involved at home report a poorer state of their (work-related) psychological contract, and are more likely to be male, younger and not to work on temporary contracts. The final group, who show low emotional involvement in both home and work, are likely to be older and to report less direct participation in their work.

Drawing these surveys together, they consistently show an association between subjective reports of the state of the psychological contract and reports of satisfaction with life as a whole, including satisfaction with health and with work–life balance. A positive assessment of the state of the psychological contract is also significantly associated with

Table 7.3 The locus of emotional experience

	Home %	Work %	Both %	Neither %	Don't know %
Relaxed	76	3	18	3	0
Elated	59	11	12	16	2
Excited	55	13	22	9	1
Happy	47	6	46	1	0
In control	32	26	38	3	0
Valued	42	22	34	2	1
Using abilities to the full	17	50	29	4	0
Absorbed in what you are doing	20	48	30	2	1
Stressed	13	58	15	13	0
Bored	27	28	9	36	0

Responses are based on 1000 workers in the UK selected at random and interviewed by telephone in 1998. The question asked whether the emotional experiences listed in the table were more likely to occur at home, at work, at both or at neither.
Source: Guest & Conway (1998).

lower reports of pressure at work. Finally, it is positively associated with a tendency to report that emotional experiences are gained both at home and at work. There is some evidence that it contributes to a possible over-involvement in work, reflected in a dominance of work as a source of emotional experience. Also, those who report more emotional involvement in activities at home may be reacting partly against a poor experience of work, indicated by a more negative state of their psychological contract. It seems that the state of the psychological contract, which can be described as a form of cognitive evaluation of the experience of work, is strongly associated with a range of emotional and well-being-related outcomes. The longitudinal analysis suggests that this is almost certainly a causal link.

One of the consistent but unexpected findings from this series of surveys is that there is no association between the state of the psychological contract and a range of behaviours. These include self-rated performance, organizational citizenship behaviour and innovative behaviour. These might legitimately be seen as part of the exchange. On the other hand, it is possible that those making a lower contribution are more likely to view the exchange as fair. Certainly the pattern of results suggests a stronger link between cognitive evaluation, reflected in the state of the psychological contract, and a range of affective outcomes than the link with behavioural outcomes. We might therefore expect a positive association between the state of the psychological contract and individual health and well-being.

We have suggested that while the interest in contract breach and violation has begun to address the outcomes of the psychological contract, it forces researchers to focus too much on the negative aspects and consequences of the exchange. Instead, a more balanced perspective can be obtained by concentrating on the state of the psychological contract. There appears to be empirical support for this in the generally positive state of the psychological contract reported by a majority of workers. This has some parallels with the data on job satisfaction, which continue to show that most workers are satisfied with their jobs. This is not to deny the pervasiveness of breaches of the psychological contract nor the seriousness for well-being of violations of the contract. But for most workers, the relationship is a more benign one, whether it is based on high or low mutual expectations and obligations, and we can expect this benign effect to be reflected in generally positive work-related well-being.

7.8 CONCLUSIONS AND A RESEARCH AGENDA FOR THE FUTURE

The psychological contract offers an increasingly accepted framework for exploring the employment relationship. As presented in this chapter, it can be studied in terms of both its antecedents and consequences, and it is plausible to expect that a positive psychological contract will be associated with lower stress and better well-being and health. At the same time, research on the consequences, and more particularly the positive consequences, of the psychological contract is in its infancy. We have presented the core findings of this research using a more balanced framework and it suggests a clear association between the state of the psychological contract and a range of relevant outcomes such as higher job satisfaction, lower perceived pressure at work, higher commitment to the organization and lower intention to quit and, in particular, higher levels of life satisfaction. Since a number of these indicators are strongly associated with measures of well-being such as the General Health Questionnaire, we can expect that the state of the psychological contract will also be positively linked to well-being.

Despite the growing interest in using the psychological contract to study the employment relationship, the research on outcomes is very under-developed. There is a need to develop and refine the research on breach and violation to examine its consequences for well-being. There is also scope to look more closely behind the finding that most people report a positive state of their psychological contract. If an employee expects very little and gets very little in return, the state of the psychological contract may be positive and the level of breach and violation very low. But it would be dangerous to equate this with positive well-being. Indeed, this is why the matching model is inherently unsatisfactory. In short, we need to go beyond the analysis of process and cognitive evaluation to assess the content of the psychological contract. A fuller model linking the psychological contract to well-being might then specify broad elements of both content and process of the contract. This offers a rich research agenda.

The focus of this chapter has been very much on the link between the psychological contract and outcomes related to well-being. It is important not to neglect the antecedents and to note that the research findings are reasonably consistent in highlighting the importance for a positive assessment by employees of the state of their psychological contract of having more progressive or high-commitment human resource practices in place and providing autonomy and control over day-to-day work, together with an organizational climate that emphasizes participation, friendliness and a degree of dynamism. These antecedents are all indicative of the importance of organizational policy and practice for the psychological contract. For example the presence of a range of human resource practices implies a large set of obligations on the part of the employer. The provision of scope for control and autonomy over day-to-day work decisions fits comfortably with notions of well-being. So, too, does a supportive and friendly climate. In other words, the research findings imply that a positive state of the psychological contract will invariably be one that is rich in promises, obligations and challenges and therefore likely to be consistent with most models of well-being and mental health. Somewhat paradoxically, the research has failed to show a consistent link between the state of the psychological contract and some core features of employee behaviour. This does not mean that employers should neglect the psychological contract. It remains strongly linked to organizational commitment, to motivation and to intention to stay with the organization. More research is needed to unravel the more complex link to organizational citizenship behaviour, innovation and performance. One possibility is that despite the indications of a causal link from the longitudinal research, the findings are bi-directional. For example, employees may engage in organizational citizenship in the hope or expectation of some reciprocation which is not always forthcoming, perhaps because of muddled signals about mutual expectations. Some support for this can be found in the generally positive evaluation of the state of the psychological contract reported by a number of professional and knowledge workers on fixed-term contracts. They have more transactional roles and appear to value the more explicit and bounded nature of these roles in preference to the ambiguities associated with the psychological contracts of many of their permanent counterparts.

In summary, advances in research and conceptualization of the psychological contract suggest that it can offer rich insights into the link between the employment relationship and well-being at work. This research is in its infancy and promises much for the future. We can therefore expect to see the kinds of framework outlined here gain more prominence as the research and analysis builds up a positive head of steam.

REFERENCES

Arnold, J. (1996). The psychological contract: a concept in need of closer scrutiny? *European Journal of Work and Organizational Psychology*, **5**(4), 511–20.

Blau, P.M. (1964). *Exchange and Power in Social Life*. New York: John Wiley & Sons.

Cavannaugh, M.A. & Noe, R.A. (1999). Antecedents and consequences of relational components of the new psychological contract. *Journal of Organizational Behavior*, **20**, 323–40.

Conway, N. (1996). The psychological contract: a metaphor too far? Paper presented at the British Academy of Management Conference, Birmingham, September.

Coyle Shapiro, J. & Kessler, I. (2000). Consequences of the psychological contract for the employment relationship: a large scale survey. *Journal of Management Studies*, **37**(7), 903–30.

Eisenberger, R., Huntingdon, R., Hutchison, S. & Sowa, D. (1986). Perceived organizational support. *Journal of Applied Psychology*, **71**(3), 500–7.

Freese, C. & Schalk, R. (1996). Implication of differences in psychological contracts for human resource management. *European Journal of Work and Organizational Psychology*, **5**(4), 501–9.

Guest, D. (1998). Is the psychological contract worth taking seriously? *Journal of Organizational Behavior*, **19**, 649–64.

Guest, D. & Conway, N. (1997). *Employee Motivation and the Psychological Contract. Issues in People Management*. London: IPD.

Guest, D. & Conway, N. (1998). *Fairness at Work and the Psychological Contract. Issues in People Management*. London: IPD.

Guest, D. & Conway, N. (2001a). *Change at Work and the Psychological Contract*. London: CIPD.

Guest, D. & Conway, N. (2001b). *The Employer's Side of the Psychological Contract*. London: CIPD.

Guzzo, R.A., Noonan, K.A. & Elron, E. (1994). Expatriate managers and the psychological contract. *Journal of Applied Psychology*, **79**(4), 617–26.

Herriot, P., Manning, W.E.G. & Kidd, J.M., (1997). The content of the psychological contract. *British Journal of Management*, **8**, 151–62.

Herriot, P. & Pemberton, C. (1995). *New Deals: The Revolution in Managerial Careers*. Chichester: John Wiley & Sons.

Kotter, J.P. (1973). The psychological contract: Managing the joining up process. *California Management Review*, **15**, 91–9.

McLean Parks, J.M. & Kidder, D.L. (1994). "Till death us do part..." Changing work relationships in the 1990s. *Trends in Organizational Behavior*, **1**, 111–36.

McLean Parks, J., Kidder, D. & Gallagher, D. (1998). Fitting square pegs into round holes: mapping the domain of contingent work arrangements onto psychological contracts. *Journal of Organizational Behavior*, **19**, 697–730.

Morrison, E.W. & Robinson, S.L. (1997) When employees feel betrayed: a model of how psychological contract violation develops. *Academy of Management Review*, **22**(1), 226–56.

Robinson, S.L. (1995). Violations of psychological contracts: impact on employee attitudes. In L.E. Tetrick & J. Barling (eds) *Changing Employment Relations: Behavioral and Social Perspectives*. Washington, DC: American Psychological Association, pp. 91–108.

Robinson, S.L. (1996). Trust and breach of the psychological contract. *Administrative Science Quarterly*, **41**, 574–99.

Robinson, S. L. & Morrison, E.W. (1995). Psychological contracts and OCB: the effect of unfulfilled obligations on civic behavior. *Journal of Organizational Behavior*, **16**, 289–98.

Robinson, S. L. & Morrison, E. W. (2000). The development of psychological contract breach and violation: a longitudinal study. *Journal of Organizational Behavior*, **21**, 525–46.

Robinson, S. L. & Rousseau, D. M. (1994) Violating the psychological contract: not the exception but the norm. *Journal of Organizational Behaviour*, **15**, 245–59.

Robinson, S.L., Kraatz, M.S. & Rousseau, D.M. (1994). Changing obligations and the psychological contract: a longitudinal study. *Academy of Management Journal*, **37**, 137–52.

Rousseau, D.M. (1989). Psychological and implied contracts in organizations. *Employee Responsibilities and Rights Journal*, **2**(2), 121–39.

Rousseau, D.M. (1990). New hire perceptions of their own and their employer's obligations: a study of psychological contracts. *Journal of Organizational Behavior*, **11**, 389–400.

Rousseau, D.M. (1995). *Psychological Contracts in Organizations*. Thousand Oaks, CA: Sage.

Rousseau, D.M. & Anton, R.J. (1991). Fairness and implied contract obligations in job terminations: the role of contributions, promises and performance. *Journal of Organizational Behavior*, **12**, 287–99.

Rousseau, D.M. & Schalk, R. (2000). *Psychological Contracts in Employment: Cross-National Perspectives*. Thousand Oaks, CA: Sage.

Schein, E.H. (1980). *Organizational Psychology*. Englewood Cliffs, NJ: Prentice Hall.

Turnley, W.H. & Feldman, D.C. (1999). The impact of psychological contract violations on exit, voice, loyalty, and neglect. *Human Relations*, **52**(7), 895–922.

Turnley, W.H. & Feldman, D.C. (2000). Re-examining the effects of psychological contract violations: unmet expectations and job dissatisfaction as mediators. *Journal of Organizational Behavior*, **21**, 25–42.

CHAPTER 8

Flexibility at Work in Relation to Employee Health

Töres Theorell

Karolinska Hospital, Stockholm, Sweden

8.1 PHYSIOLOGICAL FLEXIBILITY

From a medical perspective it is important to begin discussions about flexibility at work with individual physiological mechanisms underlying reaction patterns. A recent development in physiology is the formulation of "chaos theory" (Cotton, 1991; Goldberger, 1991), which can be regarded as the biological basis of flexible coping. It is, accordingly, of fundamental importance to the analysis of flexibility at work in relation to employee health. It postulates that the reactions in the healthy organism are unpredictable by means of conventional "linear" models because there are a large number of possible responses to demanding situations. This is mirrored in the fact, for example, that the healthy human being has a large number of cycles in its variation in heart rate. The most well-known cycle is the one that is associated with breathing: when we take in air the heart rate accelerates and vice versa. As we grow old or develop certain kinds of heart disorders this respiratory "sinus arrhythmia" disappears and so do several of the heart rate variability cycles. Most of our biological functions show variability that follows several cycles at the same time, and it seems to be true that ageing and sickness—for instance, heart disease—are associated with extinction of several of these cycles.

The unpredictable biological variability is also associated with the number of possible biological responses to demands in the environment. The larger the number of biological cycles, the larger the number of "ways out" from difficult situations. Perhaps this biological principle is also applicable in psychosocial processes.

8.2 PSYCHOLOGICAL FLEXIBILITY

Biological chaos theory has its counterpart in psychological coping theory. One way of summarizing this is to say that individuals who report that they have many different ways of responding to demands—coping strategies—at their disposal will do better in demanding

The Handbook of Work and Health Psychology. Edited by M.J. Schabracq, J.A.M. Winnubst and C.L. Cooper.
© 2003 John Wiley & Sons, Ltd.

situations. Shalit (1978) developed his "coping wheel" in order to predict which young men and women would be more able than others to stand the horrors of the Arab–Israeli wars during the 1960s and 1970s. His ideas were simple and straightforward. Those who report that they have many interests and areas of activity in life would do better than others. Furthermore, those who feel that they are in control of and have positive feelings about most of these activities—particularly those that are rated to have high priority—would be more likely to do better than others. According to these ideas, Shalit constructed a measurement technique that consists of a wheel with twelve segments. The subjects are asked to describe what activities they have in life. They only use one or two of their own words to describe the activity and they may use as many segments as they please. Afterwards they are asked to order the activities with regard to magnitude of importance (if they feel they are able to), and to rate them with regard to emotional feelings that they are associated with (from negative through neutral to positive) and with regard to the degree to which they feel they are in control. A recent study from our group has shown, for instance, that a programme for mental stimulation by means of pictures of pieces of art and discussion about the thoughts that these pictures evoke (exercises that take place for an hour once a week during four months) can increase the number of coping strategies and improve the pattern of coping in old people (Wikström et al., 1994). The effects of this programme were compared to the effects of ordinary conversations of the same frequency and amount. Improved emotional state and health were observed along with the improved coping patterns in the experimental group, but not in the control group.

In parallel with the observations on coping patterns in general, it might be speculated that flexible coping patterns could protect workers from poor health, and also that a work situation that enforces the development of such coping patterns stimulates the development of health in the workplace.

Another way of categorizing coping patterns is to group them into open and covert strategies. In a series of studies we have used a Swedish short version of a questionnaire measuring coping patterns (Harburg et al., 1973; Knox et al., 1985; Theorell et al., 1993). The person is asked what he or she would typically do if exposed to unfair treatment by the boss. Parallel questions are made about unfair treatment from a workmate. A number of fixed response categories are used, and the degree to which the person uses different strategies is rated on a four-graded scale. Factor analyses have shown that the responses can be grouped into open ("I would say immediately what I think" etc.) and covert ("I would not do anything", "I would brood about it at home" etc.) patterns. Covert coping is associated with sleep disturbance in both men and women (Theorell et al., 1993). This reaches statistical significance only for women in the study presented in Table 8.1. In a more recent study of 6000 employed women and men, however, a low decision latitude was statistically significantly related to a less open and a more covert coping pattern in both men and women although the relationship was stronger in women than in men (Theorell et al., 2000). In this later study we also found that covert coping pattern—at least in men—was associated with high blood pressure. This may indicate that there is a psychophysiological cost (long lasting energy mobilization) in covert coping.

The meaning and social context of flexibility may be markedly different for different groups. For instance, there are marked gender differences in the way in which psychosocial work organization correlates with individual coping patterns. Both intellectual discretion and authority over decisions increase significantly with age in men but not in women. This

Table 8.1 Correlations between self-reported coping patterns and self-reported work environment in randomly selected working men and women in Stockholm ($n = 80$–90 for both groups)

	Open coping	Covert coping	Psychological demands	Intellectual discretion	Authority over decisions	Social support
Men						
Covert coping	−0.16					
Psychological demands	0.07	−0.01				
Intellectual discretion	0.08	0.16	0.28*			
Authority over decisions	0.15	0.07	0.16	0.62*		
Social support	−0.10	−0.13	−0.22*	0.08	0.15	
Age	−0.03	0.13	0.01	0.23*	0.23*	0.07
Women						
Covert coping	−0.26*					
Psychological demands	−0.01	0.22*				
Intellectual discretion	0.15	0.17	0.07			
Authority over decisions	0.20*	−0.07	0.01	0.45*		
Social support	−0.04	−0.29*	−0.61*	0.06	0.04	
Age	−0.13	0.16	−0.05	−0.03	0.00	0.05

*Significant at least on the 5% level.

is consistent with findings in other countries. There are strong inverse correlations between social support, on the one hand, and psychological demands and the less covert coping, on the other, for women: the more support, the fewer demands and covert coping. In men, on the other hand, no relationship is found between covert coping and social support, whereas a weaker inverse relationship is found between social support and psychological demands. Social support at work stands out as a more significant buffer against stressful experiences for women than it does for men in this study.

But how do we stimulate flexible coping patterns in the work environment? In the following section I use Karasek's demand–control model (Karasek, 1979) to clarify my points.

8.3 ORGANIZATIONAL FLEXIBILITY

The organization—for example, of a workplace—can be regarded in the same way as that of a human being. According to most of the management literature, flexibility is an important ingredient in prosperous organizations (Anderson & King, 1993). There may, unfortunately, be a conflict between organizational flexibility and the individual's flexibility. This is one of the important themes in this review.

8.3.1   Flexibility from the Individual's Point of View in Relation to Health Risk

One of the most widely applied theoretical models for studying work organization in relation to individual health risks is the demand–control model. When Karasek introduced this model, it was an architect's synthesis of the stress research/psychology and the sociology research traditions (Karasek, 1979). Generating the concept "lack of control", or "lack of decision latitude", as Karasek labelled it, goes back to the old sociologists' question: "is the worker alienated from the work process?". It was assumed that the possibility to utilize and develop skills (*skill utilization*), a concept developed in work psychology, was closely related to *authority over decisions*. In factor analysis of responses to questions about work content these two factors are mostly positively related, and, accordingly, they have been summated to constitute *decision latitude* (Karasek & Theorell, 1990). The other dimension, psychological demands, included qualitative as well as quantitative demands.

It should be emphasized that the demand–control model was never intended to explain all work environment related illness. Thus, there was no element of individual variation introduced into its original construction. On the contrary, the model dealt with the way in which work is organized, and the way in which this relates to illness. This simplicity has made the model useful in organizational work. A model that tries to explain "all of the variance" would have to be more complicated and would be scientifically more, but educationally less, successful than the simple model that was introduced.

According to the model, there is interaction between high psychological demands and low decision latitude. If demands are regarded as the x-axis, and decision latitude as the y-axis in a two-dimensional system and the different combinations of high–low demands and high–low decisions are regarded, four combinations are recognized. The high demand/low decision latitude combination is regarded as the most relevant to illness development. Karasek uses a drastic analogy to describe this combination: if a person is crossing a street and he sees a truck approaching he may speculate that he will be able to cross the street without being hit by the truck—if he regulates his speed appropriately. However, if his foot gets stuck in the street his decision latitude diminishes dramatically and he is now in an extremely stressful situation. According to the theory, this kind of situation (not necessarily so dramatic), if prolonged and repeated for a long time, increases sympathoadrenal arousal and at the same time decreases anabolism, the body's ability to restore and repair tissues. The combination of high psychological demands and high decision latitude is defined as the active situation. In this situation the worker has more possibility to cope with high psychological demands because he or she can choose to plan working hours according to his or her own biological rhythm, and also has good possibilities for developing good coping strategies, facilitating feelings of mastery and control in unforeseen situations. The low demand/high decision latitude situation (relaxed) is theoretically associated with the smallest illness risks for the majority of subjects, whereas the low demand/low decision latitude situation, which is labelled "passive", may be associated to some extent with the development of psychological atrophy: skills that the worker had when he was employed may be lost (Karasek & Theorell, 1990).

The most important component in Karasek's demand–control model is perhaps *decision latitude*, since it is directly translatable into work redesign. Using our reasoning above regarding coping strategies, it can be stated that the two components of decision latitude both have major importance for the development of flexible coping strategies. A work site with a high degree of intellectual discretion will *stimulate* the development of such strategies in the employees and a high degree of authority over decisions will *allow* this to occur.

8.3.2 Introduction of Social Support to the Model

There have been two recent developments aimed at introducing social support to the demand–control model.

Iso-Strain

Firstly, Johnson has included social support in the theoretical model. A study of cardiovascular disease prevalence in a large random sample of Swedish men and women indicated that the joint action of high demands and lack of control (decision latitude) is of particular importance to blue-collar men, whereas the joint action of lack of control and lack of support is more important for women and white-collar men (Johnson & Hall, 1988). The multiplicative interaction between all the three aspects (iso-strain; demands × lack of control × lack of support) was tested in a nine-year prospective study of 7000 randomly selected Swedish working men. Interestingly, for the most favoured 20% of men (low demands, good suport, good decision latitude) the progression of cardiovascular mortality with increasing age was slow, and equally so in the three social classes. In blue-collar workers, however, the age progression was much steeper in the worst iso-strain group than it was in the corresponding iso-strain group in white-collar workers (Johnson et al., 1989).

Working Life Career

Secondly, attempts are now being made to use the occupational classification systems in order to describe the "psychosocial work career". Researchers have pointed out that an estimate of work conditions at only one point in time may provide a very imprecise estimation of the total exposure to adverse conditions (House et al., 1986). Therefore, in order to explore the effects of the total working career, a large group of randomly selected working men and women in Sweden were interviewed about occupations that they had had throughout their whole career. For each year the job description was translated to the Nordic classification of occupations. Occupational scores were subsequently used for a calculation of the "total lifetime exposure". These scores had been derived from the average scores (demands, control and support) calculated separately for a number of subgroups within each occupation. Thus, they were calculated separately for men and women, for those below and above 45 years of age, and for those with less than 5 years of employment, between 5 and 20 years and finally above 20 years of employment. The "total job control exposure" in relation to nine-year age-adjusted cardiovascular mortality in working Swedes was studied. It was observed for both men and women that the cardiovascular mortality differences between the lowest and highest quartiles were two-fold, even after adjustment for age, smoking habits and physical exercise. Furthermore, if the individual had had several large fluctuations in job control over the years, the risk of cardiovascular death during follow-up increased even more, up to almost three-fold compared to the high control group (Johnson et al., 1993). The index of psychological demands recorded in this study did not predict risk of cardiovascular death in the way that was expected. (The index consisted of two questions: "Is your work hectic?" and "Is your work psychologically demanding?"). For men it had no predictive value at all, and for women it predicted significantly in the reversed direction: the higher the psychological demands during the career, the lower the risk. These latter findings may indicate either that the index is not capturing psychological demands or that demands are associated with risk in different ways in the short term (according to previous studies) compared to the long term. They also illustrate differences between men and women in the patterns of correlations between psychosocial factors and cardiovascular disease risk (Hall, 1990).

A recent study has shown that the level of control inferred from the job title—after taking age, gender and time of exposure to the occupation into account—has a different development in working men who have developed a first myocardial infarction during the 10 preceding years than in a control group of age matched men without this experience (Theorell et al., 1998). The 25% of the employed men who had had the least favourable development with regard to decision latitude during the preceding ten years had a significantly elevated risk of developing a myocardial infarction. This was particularly true in the 45–54-year-old men, among whom the excess risk was 80% after adjustment for accepted biomedical risk factors and social class. This observation may illustrate that the timing of a first myocardial infarction in a working man may be related to falls in control level at work. In the near future there will be increasing numbers of lay-offs and changes in jobs. Due to the increasing pressures in the labour markets, individuals will have to accept jobs with much lower levels of decision latitude than they have been accustomed to. Thus, it is to be expected that the number of myocardial infarctions will show a further increase.

8.4 PHYSIOLOGICAL COUNTERPARTS OF THE DEMAND–CONTROL–SUPPORT MODEL

It has been hypothesized that working in an active situation stimulates the anabolic restoring and protective processes in the body (Karasek & Theorell, 1990), whereas working under job strain inhibits anabolism. In both active jobs and job strain, psychological demands are high. This means that mobilization of energy has a high priority. Long-lasting energy mobilization may lead to catabolism, the breakdown of protein for the provision of energy "at any cost". Due to the high level of anabolism taking place in the active jobs, the body will be able to stand these periods of energy mobilization well. In flexibility terms, this means that the active jobs enhance the body's capacity to stand periods of energy mobilization. This could be one way of describing flexibility in physiological terms. However, in the job strain situation, anabolism is inhibited and the body's capacity to stand periods of energy mobilization is therefore limited.

Anabolic processes correspond predominantly to certain hormones such as testosterone, growth hormone and insulin, which stimulate restoration and repair of worn-out tissue material in the body. The activity of this type of hormone typically peaks during deep sleep, when restoration and reparation activities are at maximum levels, whereas typical endocrine counterparts of energy mobilization are cate-cholamines and thyroid hormones.

Few studies have been published that have explored empirically the relationship between psychosocial job factors, on the one hand, and the balance between energy mobilization and anabolism, on the other. In a study performed by our group, working men and women were followed longitudinally during one year at three-month intervals, and spontaneous variations in job strain were recorded by means of questionnaires. It was shown that spontaneously occurring periods of job strain (according to the person's own standards) were associated with elevated blood pressure levels during working hours, increased sleep disturbance and lower testosterone concentration levels in plasma, findings compatible with increased energy mobilization and decreased anabolism (Theorell et al., 1988). These results illustrate that there may be physiological mechanisms linking an increased rigidity (from the employee's point of view) under demanding conditions to changes in health.

8.5 COMBINING THE INDIVIDUAL'S NEED FOR FLEXIBILITY WITH THAT OF THE WORK ORGANIZATION

The above review indicates that hard health outcome criteria, as well as mortality, covary with factors that are relevant to flexibility for the individual, and can be summarized under the heading of decision latitude with the two components:

1. Opportunity to develop and use one's own skills.
2. Opportunity to issue control over one's own situation.

Some of our empirical findings give a hint that long-term exposure to low decision latitude jobs creates even more pronounced health risks than does short exposure and, furthermore, that a sudden deterioration in decision latitude may be followed by increased health risks within a couple of years.

Although slightly less well established, good social support at work, which may be associated with flexible solutions from the individual's point of view (good social interactions may increase the number of options in difficult working situations), may protect the individual from the adverse effects of a rigid work environment. In at least two of our studies of personnel in adverse job conditions—prison personnel and airport freight handlers (Härenstam et al., 1988, Theorell et al., 1990)—it became evident that personnel working under bad conditions can stand low decision latitude more easily if they derive support from colleagues.

The central question in this contribution is how flexibility in the biological and psychological sense and from the perspective of the individual—in the long term, in particular—can be obtained in work organization. It is likely that organizational changes favouring the development of increased intellectual discretion and authority over decisions in individuals may stimulate flexibility in coping patterns.

Flexibility for the individual may not always be the same as flexibility for the organization. It is important to make this distinction. Organizational flexibility may mean, for instance, that employees should be able to change workplace and work hours at short notice. This may, of course, imply a lack of decision latitude for employees and their families. Such a development has been studied very recently by our research group in a large, prosperous international corporation with rapid technological development. In this company, expansion has made it impossible for the company to build sufficient office space for all employees. This has stimulated the development of alternative strategies for constructing offices. These alternative strategies are intertwined with changes in work organization. Employees do not work in jobs, but instead in projects, which last for only three months on average. As a consequence of their moves between projects, employees also make many geographical moves. Accordingly, it is meaningless for them to have offices of their own. In this situation, employees have a very stimulating work situation with good opportunities to develop and use their skills. They also feel that they have good opportunities to exercise control in their work situation. However, a basic sense of belonging and social support may be lost, and this may be a threat to the individual's possibility of exercising flexibility. Furthermore, we may be facing an era that goes too far in emphasizing the benefits of active work (see above). Our evidence does, indeed, indicate that active work is associated with good health. However, if demands are pushed excessively, with extreme working hours, for example, social support from the family may be lost; if this is combined with loss of continuous support from workmates, we may face serious problems.

In a pilot study of the consequences of the first version of these sociotechnical changes, two different departments were studied. The same change was perceived very differently by the staff in the two departments. In one case, the work contents suited the proposed organization; the staff had asked for the change and they felt mentally prepared for it. In the other case the management had decided that the change should take place, the staff had no mental preparation for it and the change did not suit the work contents. Obviously, the change was perceived as good in the first department and as bad in the second. This enforces the importance of good preparation and democratic processes preceding any change. However, the long-term consequences of these new ways of organizing work are largely unknown.

A large study of work sites in Sweden based upon line managers and personnel managers has shown that a number of changes have taken place in the management of Swedish working life during recent years (Edling & Sandberg, 1994). The analysis of the effects of decentralization in this study showed that the correlation between decentralization and skill utilization is highly complex. In Sweden, in general, the perceived skill utilization among employees has, contrary to expectations, become lower in work sites in which a flat hierarchy had been introduced than in those with a pyramidical hierarchy. This may reflect differences in management changes in different sectors of society. It may also illustrate that management interventions aiming at increased decision latitude for the employees cannot be achieved by one and the same solution in different sectors. This important result may also be due to too short a time perspective in the follow-up. It may take many years before the introduction of a flat hierarchy becomes functional, and in the Swedish case most of the work organizational changes have lasted for shorter periods. Furthermore, if the organizational changes are not paralleled by corresponding changes in the financial framework, the organizational changes may not function in an optimal way and complications may arise. Perhaps the disappointing results based upon randomly selected working Swedes may be explained on such grounds.

8.5.1 Work Organization Changes that Induce Flexibility

What characterizes work organization changes that induce flexibility, both for the company and for the individuals, and how does this relate to health? There are a few examples of work organization changes that have been evaluated in relation to changes in health or physiology of the employees. Some of these are described here, with the goal of exploring what characterizes changes that are successful for both the employees and the company.

One of the first controlled evaluations using a pre- and post-test design with two randomly selected groups of work sites was Jackson's (1983) study. The work change offered in the experimental group was aimed at improving both decision latitude and social support. No systematic changes were instituted in the control group. The groups studied were outclinic departments. Regular staff meetings every second week were instituted, with the specific aim of examining work organization and trying to improve it. These meetings may have affected both the employees' authority over decisions and the social climate in the ward. The other component of the evaluation was a teaching programme for solving interpersonal conflicts—a social support orientated measure. The results showed that the experimental outclinic wards had diminished sick-leave rates as well as decreased personnel turnover rates after the institution of these changes. There were also indications of improved quality of care. No similar changes took place in the comparison wards.

Another controlled evaluation was performed in a service institution for the elderly in Stockholm, by Arnetz et al. (1982). The basic idea underlying the intervention programme focused on one aspect of the quality of care given: it was felt that the elderly tenants were excessively passive and isolated from one another. The service institution was relatively new—only two years old—and the tenants, who had not known one another in advance, had been recruited from a large area, frequently with the implicit understanding that they would receive all kinds of service and "would have to do nothing" themselves. The first component in the method for changing this pattern was exploration of hobbies and interests among the tenants, with subsequent formation of activity groups. One activity group, for example, studied the history of the region; a second one grew plants during the summer and studied this topic during the winter; a third group jointly constructed a work of art; and a fourth went to theatre performances together. The other component was teaching the staff about various aspects of the importance of social activity among the elderly. The members of staff were also activated in the data collection for the evaluation of this programme. A longitudinal study was performed, with measurements of social activity, psychological states, and endocrinological and metabolic conditions in the tenants before, during and after the programme. Parallel measurements were performed in a comparable ward, which served as a control group.

The results indicated that the tenants in the experimental ward improved with regard to endocrinological and metabolic conditions (improved carbohydrate metabolism and anabolic/catabolic balance), social activity (more contacts with other tenants and more social activities for the elderly outside the home) and psychological state (less feelings of restlessness and more evidence of activity rather than passiveness, according to observations) (Arnetz, 1983; Karasek & Theorell, 1990). During the first year of follow-up an unfavourable trend with regard to sick-leave rates was broken in the staff in the experimental ward but not in the control ward. Personnel turnover was reported to decrease in the experimental ward but, again, not in the control ward. The experience in this case seemed to indicate that a more variable work content with increased mental stimulation and increased attention to the social activities of the tenants—which required more imagination and creativity on the part of the personnel—is associated with improved health among the employees.

Several other examples have been described. Karasek has summarized several recent efforts and analysed the characteristics of successful and unsuccessful programmes (Karasek, 1992).

8.6 PUBLIC HEALTH PERSPECTIVES

An observation of a more general nature was made by Karasek (1990) in a group of Swedish employees who had participated in a national longitudinal survey of living conditions in Sweden, with questionnaire measurements in 1968 and 1974. This particular study was focused on employed men and women who had gone through major changes in their job situation. As a group, these individuals had developed more health problems at the time of the second observation than at the time of the first one. However, when the group was divided according to reported changes in work organization leading to changes in decision latitude, it was shown that those employees who had had increased decision latitude did not report increased health problems. Deteriorating health was reported mainly among those employees who had reported decreased decision latitude at work to have been a consequence of the changes they had gone through. This observation indicates that spontaneously occurring, decreased decision latitude in working life may result in marked deterioration in public health. The Swedish nationwide longitudinal study of health and working life (Szulkin & Tåhlin, 1994) has indicated that job strain became an increasingly frequent problem from the 1970s to the end of the 1980s in working women—but not in men—in Sweden. During the same period sick-leave rates increased markedly in Swedish women but not in men. Multivariate analyses indicated that these findings could not be explained by increasing total work hours in women, and pointed at the interpretation that they were due to changes in work contents. The most pronounced changes were found in the health care and service sectors. Sweden underwent dramatic changes during the study period, with increasing emphasis on effectiveness and productivity in these sectors. Cardiovascular symptoms increased particularly in these groups of female employees.

Marked and frequent fluctuations in financial climate is an increasing worldwide problem for enterprise. As pointed out by Brenner (1983), recessions create problems, not only because enterprises may have to decrease the number of employees, but also because a period of marked financial activity may follow shortly after the recession, which means that the remaining employees in the enterprise will have to work very hard to meet the demands from the customers. These unpredictable short-cycle swings may be one of the more important mechanisms behind the relationship between rising unemployment in a country and subsequent rise in cardiovascular and other mortality. This relationship has been discussed extensively (see Janlert, 1991), and most authors claim that it exists, although the time lag between recession and mortality has been a point of debate. The important argument for the flexibility discussion in this chapter is that rising unemployment is a multifaceted problem, which affects not only those who become unemployed but also those who remain employed. It is one of the most important tasks for governments and management to find flexible solutions to this problem.

Unfortunately, a common belief in management is that during financial crisis there is a need to take more control—and hence to decrease the decision latitude of employees—and at the same time increase psychological demands in order to increase the company's ability to compete. The arguments that have been formulated in this chapter clearly speak against this common wisdom—in the long run, the ultimate result will be increasing health problems, and productivity will not increase.

The demand–control–support model has proved educationally useful. In an interactive process involving managers, unions and employees, it is a tool that can be used to initiate a dialogue. In this chapter I have given some examples indicating that it is the *balance* between the three components that is important. For instance, if demands are increased excessively, with extreme working hours, this may have secondary effects on the individual's total social support system. If the long working hours are combined with work outside the office, social support from workmates may be lost. This may jeopardize flexibility and may also be a threat to health. An excessive number of projects and activities will also decrease the individual's ability to experience control in his or her own situation, since the likelihood that complications will arise increases with the number of projects. When complications arise in one of the projects, this takes time and energy and the individual will have gross difficulties in managing all of the other activities. Thus, lack of flexibility is an inevitable consequence of an excessive number of activities (as well as of any form of task overload).

If biological chaos theory is correct, the human organism needs to play with as many possibilities as possible. Although highly speculative, if we limit the possibilities to respond by restricting the number of options, the number of spontaneous variations may decrease and health may deteriorate.

Finally, analyses of the national surveys in Sweden indicate that simplistic solutions aiming at increased authority over decisions for the employees—such as flattened hierarchy— may not always be a good way of achieving increased flexibility.

REFERENCES

Anderson, N. & King, N. (1993) Innovation in organizations. In C.L. Cooper & I.T. Robertson (eds) *International Review of Industrial and Organizational Psychology*, vol. 8, John Wiley & Sons, Chichester, pp. 1–34.

Arnetz, B.B. (1983) *Psychophysiological effects of understimulation in old age*. Thesis, Medical Faculty, Karolinska Institute, Stockholm.

Arnetz, B.B., Eyre, M. & Theorell, T. (1982) Social activation of the elderly, a social experiment. *Social Science and Medicine*, **16**, 1685–90.

Brenner, M.H. (1983) Unemployment and health in the context of economic change. *Social Science and Medicine*, **17**, 1125–38.

Cotton, P. (1991) Chaos, other nonlinear dynamics research may have answers: applications for clinical medicine. *Journal of the American Medical Association*, **266**(1), 12–18.

Edling, C. & Sandberg, Å, (1994) Är Taylor död och pyramiderna rivna? Nya former för företagsledning och arbetsorganisation [Is Taylor dead and are the pyramids torn down? New forms of management and work organization]. In C. Le Grand, R. Szulkin & M. Tåhlin (eds) *Sveriges arbetsplatser – organisation, personalutveckling, styrning* [*Swedish Work Sites – Work Organization, Personnel Development and Management*]. Prisma, Stockholm.

Goldberger, A.L. (1991) Is the normal heartbeat chaotic or homeostatic? *NIPS*, **6**, 87–91.

Hall, E.M. (1990) *Women's work: an inquiry into the health effects of invisible and visible labor*. Thesis, Karolinska Institute, Stockholm.

Harburg, E., Erfurt, J., Havenstein, L.S., Chape, C., Schull, W.J. & Schork, M.A. (1973) Socio-ecological stress, suppressed hostility, skin color and black–white blood pressure. *Psychosomatic Medicine*, **35**, 276–86.

Härenstam, A., Plam, U.-B. & Theorell, T. (1988) Stress, health and the working environment of Swedish prison staff. *Work and Stress*, **2**, 281–90.

House, J.S., Strecher, V., Metzner, H.L. & Robbins, C. (1986) Occupational stress and health among men and women in the Tecumseh Community Health Study. *Journal of Health and Social Behavior*, **27**, 62–77.

Jackson, S. (1983) Participation in decision making as a strategy for reducing job related strain. *Journal of Applied Psychology*, **68**, 3–19.

Janlert, U. (1991) Work deprivation and health, consequences of job loss and unemployment, thesis. Medical Faculty, Karolinska Institute, Stockholm.

Johnson, J.V. & Hall, E.M. (1988) Job strain, workplace social support and cardiovascular disease: a cross-sectional study of a random sample of the Swedish working population. *American Journal of Public Health*, **78**, 1336–42.

Johnson, J.V., Hall, E.M. & Theorell, T. (1989) Combined effects of job strain and social isolation on cardiovascular disease morbidity and mortality in a random sample of the Swedish male working population. *Scandinavian Journal of Work and Environmental Health*, **15**, 271–9.

Johnson, J.V., Hall, E. M., Stewart, W. & Theorell, T. (1993) Work stress over the life course, project report, Swedish Work Environment Fund, Stockholm.

Karasek, R.A. (1979) Job demands, job decision latitude and mental strain: implications for job redesign. *Administrative Science Quarterly*, **24**, 285–307.

Karasek, R.A. (1990) Lower health risk with increased job control among white-collar workers. *Journal of Occupational Behavior*, **11**, 171–85.

Karasek, R.A. (1992) Stress prevention through work reorganization: a summary of 19 international case studies. *Conditions of Work Digest*, **11**, 23–41.

Karasek, R.A. & Theorell, T. (1990) *Healthy Work*. Basic Books, New York.

Knox, S., Theorell, T., Svensson, J. and Waller, D. (1985) The relation of social support and working environment to medical variables associated with elevated blood pressure in young males: a structural model. *Social Science and Medicine*, **21**, 525–31.

Shalit, B. (1978) *The instrument, design, administration and scoring, report no. 1*. FOA-rapporter. Försvarets forskningsanstalt, Huvudavdelning 2, Stockholm.

Szulkin, R. & Tåhlin, M. (1994) Arbetets utveckling [The development of work]. In J. Fritzell and O. Lundberg (eds) *Vardagens villkor* [*Conditions of Everyday Life*]. Brombergs, Stockholm.

Theorell, T., Perski, A., Åkerstedt, T., Sigala, F., Ahlberg-Hultén, G., Svensson, J. & Eneroth, P. (1988) Changes in job strain in relation to changes in physiological state – a longitudinal study. *Scandinavian Journal of Work and Environmental Health*, **14**, 189–96.

Theorell, T., Ahlberg-Hultén, G., Sigala, F., Perski, A., Söderholm, M., Kallner, A. & Eneroth, P. (1990) A biomedical and psychosocial comparison between men in six service occupations. *Work and Stress*, **4**, 51–63.

Theorell, T., Perski, A., Orth-Gomér, K., Hamsten, A. & de Faire, U. (1991) The effects of the strain of returning to work on the risk of cardiac death after a first myocardial infarction before age 45. *International Journal of Cardiology*, **30**, 61–7.

Theorell, T., Michélsen, H., Nordemar, R. & Stockholm MUSIC Study 1 Group (1993) Validitetsprövning av psykosociala indexbildningar. In M. Haberg & C. Hogstedt (eds) *Stockholmsundersöknoningen*, vol. 1. MUSIC Books, Stockholm.

Theorell, T., Reuterwall, C., Hallquist, J., Emlund, N., Ahlbom, A. & Hogstedt, C. (1994) Metodstudier kring psykosociala faktorer i SHEEP. [Studies in methods used for measuring psychosocial factors in SHEEP]. *ONYX* (*Karolinska Hospital*), (1), 11–13.

Theorell, T., Tsutsumi, A., Hallqvist, J.J., Reuterwall, C., Hogstedt, C., Fredlund, P., Emlund, N., Johnson, J. & the Stockholm Heart Epidemiology Program (SHEEP). (1998) Decision latitude, job strain, and myocardial infarction: a study of working men in Stockholm. The SHEEP Study Group. Stockholm Heart Epidemiology Program. *American Journal of Public Health*, **88**(3), 382–8.

Theorell, T., Alfredsson, L., Westerholm, P. & Falck, B. (2000) Coping with unfair treatment at work—what is the relationship between coping and hypertension in middle-age men and women? *Psychotherapy and Psychosomatics*, **69**(2), 86–94.

Wikström, B.-M., Sandström, S. & Theorell, T. (1994) Emotional and medical health effects of mental stimulation of pictures of art. *Psychotherapy and psychosomatics*, **60**, 195–206.

PART II

Research and Diagnosis Issues

Work and Health Psychology as a Scientific Discipline: Facing the Limits of the Natural Science Paradigm

Amanda Griffiths
University of Nottingham, UK
and
Marc J. Schabracq
University of Amsterdam, The Netherlands

9.1 INTRODUCTION

As the 21st century begins, work in industrialised and post-industrialised societies is physically less arduous and dangerous than before. Other less tangible factors, largely concerning the design, management and organisation of work, now represent the most common threats to workers' health (Griffiths, 1998; Sauter et al., 1999). It is widely recognised that improving the design, management and organisation of work (often referred to as the "psychosocial" work environment) may be an important step in improving employee health and organisational productivity (World Health Organization, 1999). Broadly speaking, we are dealing here with the study object of work and health psychology.

This chapter reviews some issues in the conceptualisation and research methodology in the field of work and health psychology. It traces the origins of the discipline and examines well-being and health as objects of study that can be studied at various levels. Work and health psychology is conceived as an applied and pragmatic science primarily focused on maintaining and improving well-being and health, preferably by prevention. This chapter also addresses some problems inherent in the dominant experimental and quasi-experimental paradigm of the occupational health research establishment. It argues that the experimental paradigm, with its emphasis on identifying causal connections, focuses attention on outcome at the expense of process. However, we argue that interventions should be examined in terms of (i) their conceptualisation, design and implementation and

The Handbook of Work and Health Psychology. Edited by M.J. Schabracq, J.A.M. Winnubst and C.L. Cooper.
© 2003 John Wiley & Sons, Ltd.

(ii) the theoretical mediating mechanisms involved. These latter processes are likely to be more generaliseable than outcomes. Their examination may require the use of qualitative as well as quantitative methodologies. It is suggested that this approach holds promise for the healthier design, management and organisation of future work.

9.2   ORIGINS AND CONTRIBUTORY DISCIPLINES

The study of well-being and health in work and organisations is represented by a conglomeration of many disciplines without a tradition of close interdisciplinary cooperation. A short, and necessarily incomplete, overview of the main disciplines involved is presented below.

First, there are the contributions of the different branches of psychology that, history has shown, maintain a preference to remain as discrete sub-disciplines. General psychology has provided us with insights into psychological phenomena and processes such as emotion, cognition, perception, learning, personality, individual differences, fatigue, stress and coping (see Chapters 5 and 6), as well as with methodological principles for research and measurement purposes. Clinical psychology has focused on matters such as trauma and post-traumatic stress (Chapter 18), burnout (Chapter 19) and therapeutic interventions for individuals and groups (Chapter 25). Social psychology has taught us about group dynamics, social support and person–environment fit. Developmental psychology has contributed knowledge about life stages and career-related issues (Chapters 16 and 17). And finally, industrial, organisational and work psychology has examined matters such as work stress and fatigue, job characteristics (Chapter 20), and organisational issues and HRM interventions (Chapters 27 and 28).

There are also considerable influences from other disciplines such as engineering, management, administrative and business science, sociology, political science, cultural anthropology and, of course, biology and medical science. Engineering has contributed several systems designed to accomplish an optimal integration of technical systems on the one hand and individual workers and their social system on the other. Examples of such systems are ergonomics (focusing on the design of furniture, tools and machinery, attempting to accomplish optimal use for employees), occupational hygiene (focusing on the long-term health risks of jobs and work environments) and safety technology (focusing on the acute safety risks of tools, machines and other aspects of jobs and work environments). A major early contribution was provided by sociotechnical systems theory (an influential system, focusing on an optimal integration of the complete production system, consisting of a technical subsystem on the one hand and a social subsystem on the other), which gave rise to the development of so-called "autonomous task groups" (see Chapter 20). In addition, "action psychology" (*Handlungspsychologie*), a more individually oriented system with similar claims as sociotechnics, but less democratic in nature, devised in the former East Germany (Hacker, 1973), offers a goal-directed behaviourist approach reminiscent of the ideas in Tolman's book *Purposive Behavior in Animals and Men* (1932), which has been influential during the past decade in Germany and the Netherlands.

Managerial, administrative and business science have played an important role in shaping the study of work and organisations. As such, they have been very influential in issues of occupational health and well-being, both in positive and negative senses. Many of these approaches have not concerned themselves explicitly with occupational well-being and health. However, some of them, such as the "human relations" approach, have done and were highly significant in the development of work and health psychology. Sociology, political science and cultural anthropology produced insights into the concept of "roles", particularly important in the Michigan school (Chapter 20), the structural aspects of organisations and their surrounding societies, the dynamics of power, and the role of culture (see Chapter 3). Finally, biological and medical science have provided us with many insights into the physiology of health, well-being, stress, breakdown and illness, and medical treatments. In particular, biology contributed ethology, the study of animal behaviour, which taught us to study behavioural phenomena within their natural context and with minimum preconceptions.

All these approaches have resulted in a vast amount of information, methods and procedures. Though there has been some integration and cooperation, the resulting synergy has not been particularly impressive. There still is no generally accepted "unifying theory" of work and health psychology; the perspectives, concepts and practices of these different disciplines continue to be too different. Much of this is a result of the different levels at which these various sciences operate. Work and health psychology should feel at home at the levels of (i) individual employees and their differences, (ii) jobs and task characteristics, (iii) teams and groups, (iv) departments and (v) organisations (Schabracq, 1999). Moreover, it should also consider economical, juridical, political, technological, cultural and environmental influences (Gordon, 1991) and, at the other extreme physiological processes (Sapolsky, 1994). Of course, no one scientist can operate at all these levels and it is only logical that researchers in this area tend to become specialists. Nonetheless, questions about how to monitor developments at all levels, how to examine their effects on both individual and organisational health, and how, when necessary, to intervene, loom large in the horizons of researchers, practitioners and policy makers. Some of the answer lies in developing better ways of identifying trends and analysing problems, particularly in a climate of constant change. Another part of the solution lies in the careful design and thorough evaluation of interventions and in the education and training of relevant professional groups. In the Netherlands for instance, work and health psychologists should have been trained, and must have worked, in at least two of these levels for their professional certification.

9.3 THE STUDY OF MALFUNCTION, FUNCTION AND CHANGE

Work and health psychology has traditionally occupied itself predominantly with malfunction in work-related health and well-being, usually under the overall umbrella of stress. It has paid considerably less attention to normal functioning, well-being and health. This is not to deny that the study of malfunction is important. Stress phenomena, for instance, and their undesired consequences are not only important as such, but can teach us much about what goes wrong in organisations. However, there is currently an upsurge in interest in positive psychology (Seligman & Csikszentmihalyi, 2000). We suggest that work and health psychology would also do well to focus more on positive well-being and health. This avoids the trap of the classical medical model, focusing on curing manifest afflictions and illnesses rather than on prevention and proactivity (Illich, 1976). Further, focusing solely on acting against a phenomenon can inadvertently reinforce and reify that phenomenon, as people generally have difficulty dealing with negatives (Ofman, 1995). But more importantly, it is generally more rewarding for managers and entrepreneurs, many of whom sponsor research in this discipline, to invest money and effort in realising positive goals, such as greater effectiveness, motivation, and individual and organisational development.

In its concern for health and well-being, work and health psychology should ask, for instance, the following questions. What are the main characteristics of normal functioning? What does the ecology of normal functioning, well-being and health look like? Which environmental contingencies play an important part? How does organisational culture affect normal functioning and well-being? It is clear that we know far less about such matters than we should.

In such cases, because we have no clear theoretical framework or hypotheses, we should initially observe these phenomena and ask working people themselves for their views. We should use open questions about the status quo, its background, causes, opportunities for personal influence and possible improvements (Schabracq et al., 1996). Asking employees for their on views is based on several important assumptions. First, it is reasonable to assume that employees are the best experts on their own predicaments. They are the ones who have the greatest interest in improvements. They know best how they feel, what they want, what they are able and allowed to do, as well as what constitutes an improvement. Moreover, as experts in their own work, it is highly likely that they have valid ideas about the way improvements might be brought about. Of course, it is possible that they do not know the answers to such questions. And some have argued that they may not represent their views honestly. But experienced researchers have demonstrated convincingly that once employees are afforded opportunities to talk about their working situation and possible improvements, even given the methodological issues presented by aggregating "subjective" data from interviews or questionnaires, the general direction of these improvements is useful and feasible (Cox et al., 2000, 2002; Schabracq et al., 2000).

This is not to deny the role of researchers and consultants in this process—asking questions of any nature will influence respondents—and traditionally all efforts are used to minimise the enquirers' contribution and maximise the role of employees and their managers in efforts towards improving working conditions. But although such issues remain in applied research (Rosenthal & Rosnow, 1969), they need not always be "problems". Perhaps influencing the object of study may not always be undesirable: in itself, it can be an object of study. As a pragmatic and applied discipline, work and health psychology can also focus on ways to establish common meanings among those who study and those who are studied. These meanings may become common ground for working on improvements, a basis for new developments. As such, research in work and health psychology actively may contribute to signification, help to overcome resistance and facilitate the construction of a new reality, following the best traditions of constructionism (Davis, 1988; Gergen & Davis, 1985).

Work and health psychology, as an applied and pragmatic science, should strive towards understanding of the genesis, maintenance and development of its object—well-being and health in work and organisations—and produce applicable methods and techniques for continuous improvement. Therefore, the ultimate test of its worth lies in the effectiveness of its applications. Change might be designed and evaluated against the following criteria: effectiveness and efficiency, pleasure and motivation, creativity, individual and organisational development, social relations and organisational climate. In this sense, work and health psychology should be as the proverbial tree that is known by its fruits.

9.4 INTERVENTION STUDIES

The previous arguments underline the importance of evaluating interventions in work and health psychology. Many such evaluations are currently criticised because they do not have good control groups, because cause and effect cannot be safely ascribed, and because they are not generalisable. But these criticisms may in many cases be unwarranted, and "inadequate" evaluation in itself is not a sound reason to abandon interventions, although "pedantic scientists" would argue such a case, highlighting the practitioner–researcher divide (Anderson et al., 2001). Focusing exclusively on these issues might also be misguided in other ways as it conceals other important questions. In any case, attempts to confirm cause-and-effect relationships and allow prediction (maximise internal validity) are often at the expense of generalisability (external validity).

The current, dominant experimental paradigm in the current research establishment, with its emphasis on identifying causal connections, focuses attention on outcome at the expense of process. Interventions can be evaluated as "experiments", but at least they should also be examined in terms of their conceptualisation, design and implementation (macro-processes), and be explored via the detail of the nature of change (micro-processes). These micro-processes, or theoretical mediating mechanisms, are less context specific and hence more generalisable than outcomes. They hold unexplored promise for understanding interventions, and also offer possibilities for the healthier design, management and organisation of future work. These three dimensions of interventions—outcomes, macro-processes and micro-processes—are considered below.

9.4.1 Experiments and Quasi-Experiments

In work and health psychology organisational interventions to improve occupational health are usually treated as if these interventions were "experiments". Experiments are designed to discover whether or not desired changes occur as a result of the manipulation of some important variable or the introduction of a particular treatment. In other words, they are conceptualised as tests of cause-and-effect hypotheses. They originated largely as laboratory-based exercises in the natural sciences, where temporal priority, control over important variables and random allocation of subjects to treatment or control groups (the minimum necessary requirements for establishing causal connections) are generally feasible. However, experiments should be the last step, the ultimate test of a hypothesis well grounded in theory and research (e.g. De Groot, 1964), rather than a starting point.

Yet in organisations these conditions rarely apply. Researchers are guests, not autocrats. Causal relationships are not simple; they are embedded within complex contexts. Although temporal issues may be documented (for example, that treatment preceded change), interventions can rarely manipulate only one variable. And, when working within the operational constraints that characterise organisations, random allocation of subjects to groups is virtually impossible. Even with random allocation of subjects to groups, some alternative explanations for intervention outcomes exist (i.e. other than that the intended manipulation was responsible). But without random allocation, the number of alternative explanations increases considerably. For example, being members of control (or comparison) groups can represent threats to causal inference in organisational interventions. Cook & Campbell (1979) list four such threats. First, control groups may resent that other groups are receiving apparently more desirable treatment than they are, and this resentment may lead to increased dissatisfaction and decreased performance (resentful demoralisation). Second, control groups might respond by trying harder (compensatory rivalry). Both such effects would make subsequent intervention–control group differences hard to interpret. Third, if members of control groups learn about and become impressed with the interventions being provided elsewhere, they might implement them themselves (treatment diffusion). And fourth, intervention providers might become unwilling to tolerate what they perceive to be inequalities between intervention and control groups, and try to overcome such inequalities by whatever means at their disposal (compensatory equalisation). These four threats have all been observed in social experiments (Cook & Shadish, 1994).

In their influential book on research designs, Campbell & Stanley (1963) described various other threats to causal inference, such as the effects of history, maturation, selection, testing, instrumentation, regression to the mean and mortality. They argued that many of these threats to internal validity can be ruled out by careful research strategies. Various ingenious designs, commonly referred to as quasi-experiments, have been suggested, each of which deals with a different set of threats to causal inference. These designs may require, for example, a series of pre-intervention and post-intervention measurements, the sequential introduction of interventions, some groups having no pre-intervention measurements, some having no post-intervention measurements, some groups having no interventions at all, and various combinations of these situations. But in time it has become clear that these designs are rarely used (Cook & Shadish, 1994). While possible in many fields of social science (community health promotion, for example), within functioning organisations their realisation is extremely difficult.

Highlighting the difficulties and limitations of thoroughly evaluated "outcome" research is not meant to be an argument for its abandonment, particularly since research has shown that the more rigorous the design, the more modest the documented results of the intervention (e.g. Cohen & Ledford, 1994; Heaney & Goetzel, 1997). Rather, the acknowledgement of these challenges represents a plea to researchers, journal editors, practitioners and policy makers alike for more realistic expectations, more appropriate criticism, more in-depth interpretations and a greater awareness of alternative (but complementary) approaches. Researchers should frankly acknowledge the unavoidable constraints of their designs against ideal "experimental" principles, and attempt to explore some of the challenges in interpreting outcomes (the remaining threats to internal validity) by other means, such as demographic or attitudinal data (e.g. Cohen & Ledford, 1994) or by qualitative approaches. We shall return to this point, and the related issue of generalisation in Sections 9.4.4 and 9.4.5.

9.4.2   Process Evaluation

Though examining organisational interventions solely within (quasi-) experimental paradigms is probably unrealistic and unlikely to provide us with an optimal understanding, an exploration of the process of organisational change might enrich our understanding further. Researchers in different countries (notably in Finland, the USA, the UK and the Netherlands) have independently discovered that whatever the content of the intervention, the necessary implementation issues are similar, all resting heavily on participation of employees and other key stakeholders (e.g. Cox et al., 2000; Goldenhar et al., 1999; Kompier et al., 1998; Landsbergis & Vivona-Vaughn, 1995; Lindström, 1995; Schurman & Israel, 1995).

Careful documentation of the process of implementing interventions in both intervention and non-intervention groups is crucial. Without it, the interpretation of intervention outcomes is difficult. Exactly to what, for example, can "no-difference" findings be attributed? Was the analysis of the original problem wrong? Was the design of the intervention inappropriate? Was implementation deficient? In the absence of documentation about the integrity of the intervention, even positive results do not make it clear what role the intended processes played in bringing about the outcome (Cook & Shadish, 1994). Detailed questions should be asked about how the intervention was implemented. Did it reach the intended number of people? Did people comply with what they were supposed to do? If not, what appeared to be the barriers to compliance? If the intervention involved a planned increase in the amount of consultative meetings, did those meetings actually take place? How many people attended? Were training interventions mandatory? If not, was there anything different about the attendees and non-attendees? Did the training appear to make a difference to participants' subsequent knowledge, attitudes or behaviour? More generally, what were the views of key stakeholders about the implementation of the intervention? How did they conceptualise improvement? And, importantly, what were the unintended spin-offs? Much useful information about these kinds of issues can be revealed by qualitative methods. Such information facilitates judgements about why an intervention may or may not have had any impact; in other words, it informs the evaluation of outcome. It may also provide some indication of the nature of the underlying processes and mechanisms involved.

9.4.3 Mediating Mechanisms

Literature reviews point to many aspects of work design and organisation that are associated with health-related outcomes (e.g. Cooper & Marshall, 1976; Cox, 1993; Kristensen, 1999; NIOSH, 1988; Warr, 1992). Basic research, much of it epidemiological, provides a strong indication as to the broad type of intervention that would seem to have the greatest potential for improving employee well-being (Ganster, 1995). However, identifying these broad dimensions is one matter; identifying them in a local context, in one particular organisation, at one particular moment in time, and designing a concrete intervention to improve things, is quite another.

Let us take "control" as an example. There is now much agreement across many studies from various countries that people reporting low levels of control at work are at greater risk of coronary heart disease. It is also known that people in low employment grades have a higher incidence of coronary heart disease, and report less control, than higher status workers. These differences in perception of control alone may explain a substantial amount of the socioeconomic gradient in coronary heart disease (that is, in addition to differences in traditional risk factors and the effects of early environments). It has been suggested that control may play a role in the generation and maintenance of social inequalities in health (Marmot et al., 1997). Most investigations into work control have come from research-based, epidemiological perspectives, using broad-brush, standardised measures that can be applied to many different types of job situation. These measures are robust enough to reveal broad associations between working conditions (e.g. low control) and worker health (e.g. coronary heart disease, musculoskeletal disorders and minor psychiatric disorder). However, merely knowing that employees are experiencing low levels of control does not in itself provide sufficient information to facilitate change. Of course, there are clear advantages for researchers to keep the model simple, but these studies have thus far had little practical impact in the workplace. The concentration of effort to establish (and re-establish) causal connections, and hence to enhance general prediction, seems to be at the expense both of an exploration of mechanisms and, ultimately, of the effective translation of research to practice. So, what does "control" really look like?

Control has been widely used in the work and health psychology literature to represent a collection of overlapping constructs. Examples are participation in decision making, decision latitude, skill discretion (the breadth of skills a worker is allowed to use on the job), decision authority, autonomy, influence, challenge, empowerment, ownership, self-determination and workplace democracy. Control may be operationalised at many levels; for example, control over the task itself, control over the working environment, control over the organisation and management of work, control over the planning and achievement of career goals, or control over others. So, control has served as a convenient name covering several dimensions of work. Even the original authors of the "job control–job demands" model admit that "it is difficult to be precise" about which aspects of control (or demands) are important (Theorell & Karasek, 1996). Perceived lack of control (or any other undesirable aspect of work design and management) is likely to be a result of factors unique to each organisation at any one moment. We should ask what exactly does it mean when people report they have little control at work in terms of their feelings, decisions and behaviour. And, how does this translate into psychological and physical health outcomes? This level of analysis is currently rare and our lack of knowledge hampers attempts at intervention. Still, some of the answers may already be appearing in quite distinct literatures.

For example, studies concerning the health effects of participation in decision making at work are rarely mentioned in the literature on organisational development, or in the literature on distributive and procedural justice. Distributive justice refers to the outcome of decisions; procedural justice concerns the procedures that led to that outcome. Procedural justice, often the actual or perceived possibility to influence decision making, is seen as more important than distributive justice in determining people's overall judgements about work. People have less negative reactions to unfavourable outcomes when procedures are fair (Brockner & Wiesenfeld, 1996; Cohen, 1985). Various mechanisms have been proposed to account for the psychological phenomena that might underlie such results (Ehlen et al., 1999; Lind & Tyler, 1988). This approach to the study of behaviour at work may have much to offer to research which attempts to understand the micro-processes underlying the relation between control and health. However, as stated above, crossover between different branches of psychology is not particularly abundant.

Another important broad dimension in "healthy work" appears to be support, particularly from line managers or supervisors. But there is little in the literature (Leather et al., 1998) about the nature and origins of such support (although see Chapter 3), and even less about its precise function. How, precisely, does support affect people? Outside the work context, it has long been established that social support can reduce ill-health and psychological disturbance, but here too there is a lack of studies that examine possible intervening mechanisms (Thoits, 1995). Furthermore, it appears that the positive effects of social support depend on the nature of the measures used and, that effects are not always positive, particularly where there is a mismatch between support and individual coping requirements (Frese, 1999).

Attention to these assumed micro-processes underlying interventions is a crucial next step in our understanding of organisational interventions. It is these principles that will be generalisable, probably much more so than the outcome of any particular intervention. And it is this knowledge that may ultimately help us to design more effective interventions. This is particularly important in the world of work, where change is a constant feature. We should learn to predict the health effects of changes at the design stage. Cook and Shadish (1994, p. 574) give a neat illustration:

> The presumption is that once such knowledge has been gained, the crucial causal processes can be transferred to novel contexts of application. Cook and Campbell (1979) use the example of a light switch to illustrate this. Knowledge that flicking the light switch results in light is the type of descriptive knowledge about manipulanda that experiments promote; more explanatory knowledge requires knowing about switch mechanisms, wiring and circuitry, the nature of electricity, and how all these elements can be combined to produce light. Knowing so much increases the chances of creating light in circumstances where there are no light switches, providing one can reproduce the causal explanatory processes that make light in whatever ways local resources allow.

9.4.4   Paradigms and Methodologies

While carrying out experiments in organisations is probably impossible, even quasi-experiments, in many situations, are too much to ask for. Establishing the extent to which the intervention is the only systematic difference among the groups under study (i.e. providing internal validity) is simply too difficult. It is highly unlikely that the often-quoted "messiness" of human life can be fully understood in such terms. As Edgar Schein has described (quoted in Edmondson, 1996):

> The traditional research paradigm . . . has not worked very well . . . [it] has produced very reliable results about very unimportant things. . . . In that process, we have lost touch with some of the important phenomena that go on in organizations, or have ignored them simply because they were too difficult to study by the traditional methods available. (Schein, 1991, p.2)

Questions about the limitations of the natural science approach and its dominant methods of enquiry, and about the futility of "physics envy", have been noted by many distinguished academics from several social science disciplines. Many do not agree with extreme suggestions from socio-biologists that one day the social sciences will be made as rigorous as physics by grounding them in evolutionary theory, genetics and neuroscience (Horgan, 1998; Wilson, 1975). The anthropologist Clifford Geertz, describing the development of ideas over the past two decades among his fellow social scientists at the Institute for Advanced Study in Princeton, New Jersey, noted:

> We are hardly of one mind on everything and we have different interests and different problems before us; but we are all suspicious of casting the social sciences in the image of the natural sciences, and of general schemes which explain too much . . . Human beings, gifted with language and living in history are, for better or worse, possessed of intentions, visions, memories, hopes, and moods, as well as of passions and judgements, and these have more than a little to do with what they do and why they do it. An attempt to understand their social and cultural life in terms of . . . objectivised variables set in systems of closed causality, seems unlikely of success. (Geertz, 1995, p. 127)

Similarly, the psycholinguist Noam Chomsky (1988, p. 159) proposed that our verbal creativity may prove more fruitful than scientific skills for investigating human behaviour:

> It is quite possible—overwhelmingly probable, one might guess—that we will always learn more about human life and human personality from novels than from scientific psychology. The science-forming capacity is only one facet of our mental endowment. We use it when we can but are not restricted to it, fortunately.

There are many types of knowledge, and while scientific "truths" may be better than other truths in many respects, there are others which nonetheless are useful: historical facts, literature and "common sense". These types of knowledge are indeed "good enough" truths, which, in our attempts to understand people's reactions to changes in the world of work, should not be dismissed. Even methodologists as highly respected in the established (quantitative) research community as Cronbach (1982) propose that the qualitative methods of historians, ethnographers or journalists might be useful to generate and explore hypotheses about the micro-mediating processes involved in interventions. Nonetheless, as Cook & Shadish, equally respected as the "fathers" of quasi-experimental design, point out (1994, p. 575):

> Although we personally have a lot of sympathy for this qualitative approach, it is likely to fall on deaf ears in the social science community at large.

One set of basic problems inherent in the almost exclusive application of quantitative methods in evaluation studies in work and health psychology stems from the fact that generating data has often become equivalent to letting great numbers of subjects fill in standardised questionnaires. Sometimes the most readily available sources of data have been students: the fact that students rarely have much experience of working life has not been widely perceived as a great disadvantage. Issues concerning sampling have traditionally been neglected in favour of statistical considerations. Large data sets allow for the use of sophisticated statistical methods and the discovery of significant relations, differences and generalities. Exceptions are often removed from the data set. Thus, psychology is traditionally more focused on central tendencies than on variation or individuality. In organisational research, however, the individuality of people, teams, departments and organisations is often of paramount importance. Sometimes, the object of study cannot, by definition, involve large numbers of subjects: it may be team dynamics, or different management styles. And on occasion, it is not possible to predict in advance exactly what the important variables will be: they may not be found in general questions in standard questionnaires and may be context-dependent or specific. The "respectable" methods of academic psychology offer little in such cases.

Generally speaking, quantitative approaches demonstrate a preference for reliability over validity. Reliability is largely reduced to the internal consistency of questionnaire scales, as measured by coefficient alpha. Coefficient alpha appears to be the most important criterion by which scales and tests are judged. In practice, this often implies that questions have to be asked at least three times, in very slightly different ways, in order to be scientifically acceptable. This is not very appealing to most respondents, nor to their managers. The fundamental principle behind the desirability of high internal consistency is that a scale should be one-dimensional. However, most important concepts are not that simple. Moreover, even within a one-dimensional concept, different items may compensate for each other, such that a high score on one excludes a high score on the other: this would affect coefficient alpha negatively. Other disciplines such as economics do not mind adding up "apples and pears", as long as they add up to something valuable and meaningful.

While the strengths of quantitative methods have been appreciated by many in occupational health research, the advantages of qualitative methods have been as yet appreciated by few, and only relatively recently. Barbara Israel and her colleagues (e.g. Hugentobler et al., 1992; Israel et al., 1995, 1998), after many years engaged in public health interventions, have emphasised the importance of acknowledging that knowledge is socially constructed, rather than a static, objective body that is separate from the knower. Israel describes how a "constructionist" approach, acknowledging the social, cultural and historical contexts, requires specific research methods which are determined also by theoretical perspectives (including "local" theory), the purpose of the study, the context, the involvement of participants themselves and how the information is to be used. Under such conditions, both quantitative and qualitative methods may be used (Israel et al., 1998). In their review of the health-related outcomes of multi-component workplace health promotion programmes, Heaney & Goetzel (1997) also recommended that such qualitative evaluation methods could confer certain advantages. Clearly the same argument is pertinent for work organisation interventions: by definition, an organisational intervention cannot take place outside the participation and experience of the people under study.

Qualitative methodologies, based on people's verbal utterances or written reports, are interpretative in nature, use a smaller number of participants, and seek to identify the meaning of events in the social world. They ask "What is it like?" rather than "How much of it is there?". They are little used by most researchers interested in the implications of work organisation for employee well-being and performance. Still, they may provide a useful adjunct to traditional quantitative approaches for several reasons. First, they are useful as a stand-alone technique to examine the richness and significance of people's (context-dependent) experience, especially when used to investigate the process of the intervention. Experimental and quasi-experimental methods fail to capture the richness of the meaning of organisational interventions. They are only useful to establish intervention outcomes. Second, more qualitative methods, grounded in rich data, are helpful in the generation of new theories. As such, they are the appropriate approach in the early stages of problem analysis and project design. Organisational interventions, as examples of action research, are ideal situations for generating and testing new knowledge (Greenwood & Levin, 1998). At the same time, (quasi-) experimental methods have been criticised for their over-emphasis on testing existing theories (Henwood & Pidgeon, 1995). Some would say that this is the only purpose they serve (De Groot, 1964). The practice of doing experiments in the first stages of the hermeneutic cycle reminds one of a man casting very nicely carved stones over his shoulder in the full conviction that this will result, one glorious day, in a splendid cathedral—and not merely a pile of stones.

There is now a growing recognition for the need for qualitative approaches in psychology (e.g. Bannister et al., 1994; Cassell & Symon, 1994; Richardson, 1996; Symon & Cassell, 1998). Nonetheless, there is considerable reluctance in the academic community to use qualitative methods. Science too is embedded in its own social context (Gorman, 1996) and is fairly successful in fencing off threats to its status quo. Several influential institutions play a role in this, largely populated by like-minded personnel: decision makers in the funding agencies, board members of university departments and research institutes, as well as editors, reviewers and readers of the relevant journals. The mechanics are simple. Research institutes or university departments receive funds on proof of their scientific quality. Scientific quality is gained by publications in relevant scientific journals. These journals hold that in order to maintain high standards they only publish studies that use rigorous quantitative methods, preferably experimental or quasi-experimental. Notwithstanding sound arguments in the opposite direction (e.g. Symon & Cassell, 1998), many journals regard qualitative research as unworthy of publication. Moreover, methodologically diverse intervention studies are very time-consuming: they are not good for the survival of scientific institutions, nor for the careers of the individual researchers, whose performance is often judged simply on the number of publications. As a result, social science is heavily dominated by quantitative approaches. And the results, in the form of mindless empiricism or "pedantic science", are increasingly to be seen (Anderson et al., 2001). For example, the proliferating number of publications and conference presentations about the psychometric properties of various new self-report measures of the work environment (without actually using them in any way to provide external data) seems unlikely to advance the field very much (Kasl, 1999).

So, having considered how the over-zealous (i.e. natural science-based) evaluation of organisational intervention research may present a barrier to progress, how do we respond to the criticism that we cannot extrapolate the results of most organisational interventions, however obtained, to unstudied populations? We need to consider the question of external validity.

9.4.5   External Validity

A common knee-jerk reaction to organisational interventions, and hence a pronouncement of their unacceptability, is that "they're not generalisable". External validity can be defined as the extent to which experimental findings make us better able to predict real-world behaviour (Mook, 1989, p. 25). Notwithstanding the difficulties of carrying out experiments in organisations, and the fact that all such endeavours are highly context-specific, there is still much confusion over the need for research to be generaliseable (externally valid) or transferable to other situations. External validity is only important if we intend to make a decision on the basis of the outcome of the study in question: in other words, if prediction is our aim. But research is not always about predicting behaviour. Its purpose can be to help us understand the world in a different way. In such a case, external validity is much less relevant.

To take an example, Mook (1989) describes Johansson's classic study (1973) where participants observed films or still frames (photographs) of people walking in a dark room with small light bulbs attached to their major joints. Those who watched the movies saw people walking, whereas those who looked at stills saw meaningless patterns of dots:

> Could we find a more blatant case of external invalidity? Does your representative homo sapiens walk around in the dark with light bulbs on his knees? Does he watch other people doing so? Are we going to generalise these findings and attempt to predict how a population will react to ambulant Christmas trees? I do not think so. (Mook, 1989, p. 29)

The purpose of this investigation was an exploration of principles. And often:

> the generality of the principle rests on the diversity—not the representativeness—of subjects and settings in which instances arise. The external validity of individual studies, or the lack thereof, plays no part in this inductive proces. (Mook, 1989, p. 26)

Purposive sampling strategies to increase heterogeneity (to show that an intervention is robust in many different situations) or to select representative instances (to examine situations similar to the settings to which generalisation is sought) can help determine how broadly a principle or causal relationship can be generalised (St. Pierre & Cook, 1984). But, as pointed out above, it is the mediating processes underlying interventions that may be most usefully generaliseable.

9.5 CONCLUDING REMARKS

There are different types of scientific endeavour relevant to our interest in the effects of work organisation on health. The first aims to identify broad patterns in the relationship between work and health. Another aims to explain the underlying structures, mechanisms and mediating processes. And a third attempts to apply this knowledge, once gained. The latter tries to diagnose problems in the quality of work and to effect improvements for both employees and their organisations. A major task ahead in organisational intervention research is to further our understanding of the mediating processes involved in people's reactions to their working environment: for example, in modelling important general concepts such as control and support and exploring how they might serve as protective factors. Organisational interventions will play an important role in these more theoretical and practical endeavours. But:

> if our aim is to explain behaviour as it occurs in ordinary life, there is no escaping the ordinary description of behaviour and experience. Certainly causal mechanisms and structures discovered by experimental psychology or other sciences apply to such behaviour, but by themselves they do not provide sufficient explanation, and they certainly do not enable us to dispense with ordinary language and to substitute a pure language of behaviour. (Manicas & Secord, 1990, p. 410)

Partly as a result of the over-zealous imitation of the favourite methods of natural science, in order to please the current psychological establishment, those engaged in organisational intervention research may have sometimes put the cart before the horse. That is, methods have been put before problems, and prediction before understanding. This realisation, although not new, has had limited impact on the scientific community. In 1959, reviewing the contribution of psychology, Sigmund Koch wrote:

> From the earliest days of the experimental pioneers, man's stipulation that psychology be adequate to science outweighed his commitment that it be adequate to man. (p. 783)

We suggest, over 40 years later, that this criticism still holds true. In the real world, we cannot expect to achieve complete closure; we deal in patterns, probabilities, and of course, uncertainty. Understanding open systems demands more than experimental science alone can provide. It requires knowledge and acceptance of additional contexts and a variety of methods. We are confronted and disabled here by the heritage of behaviourism, with its logic of simple linear S–R relations, where the "R" is replaced by the summated scores of numerous questionnaires. According to Koestler (1967), when making such a remark, one should expect opposition from the SPCDH:

> The initials SPCDH stand for "Society for the Prevention of Cruelty to Dead Horses". It is a secret society with international ramifications and with a considerable influence on the intellectual climate of our time. . . . In the sciences, the SPCDH is particularly active.

> We are constantly assured that the crudely mechanistic nineteenth-century conceptions
> in biology, medicine, psychology are dead, and yet one constantly comes up against
> them in the columns of textbooks, technical journals, and in lecture rooms. In all this,
> behaviourist psychology occupies a key position. (Koestler, 1967, p. 391–2)

Although Koestler's criticism was made in 1967, and behaviourism itself has by-and-
large died, it appears that it has procreated quite successfully and has left its illegitimate
children in a number of psychological disciplines.

In summary, it may be timely to advocate a more modest but realistic approach, one that
is not so exclusively dominated by experimental and quasi-experimental designs, and one
that involves more flexible ways of collecting data. There is a need for the investigation of
new areas, with more descriptive research. Possible subjects might be emotional contagion,
sense-making, or how motivating factors are shaped within and by organisational culture.
Another possibility is exploring the role of historically oriented research. This might give
insights into the role of the "human factor" in the successes and failures of organisations.
What are the factors behind extreme indices of occupational health and well-being? Can we
analyse what exactly went well and what went wrong? What could have been done better?
Still another option is developing scenarios for several possible futures. Such an approach
would enable us to think through in advance how we can approach the opportunities and
difficulties inherent in each of these optional futures. Such an approach helped Shell to use
the oil crisis to become the biggest oil company in the world (De Geus, 1997).

The suggestions made above will require a more modest approach to research, one that
emphasises observational methods and the interviewing of strategically chosen stakeholders, in order to find out about their experience of reality, organisational culture and the
disturbances that are relevant to them. This kind of research can make use of the paradigms
and methods of ethology and cultural anthropology, without excluding other measures and
methods such as those employed in psychophysiological, clinical and social psychology.
And of course, where possible, statistical analysis can be used: there is no need to throw
the baby out with the bath water. But while new areas are being explored, conventional
testing of hypotheses may not have the highest priority. In principle, this approach can be
compared to the approach used by cultural anthropologists or by some consultants, where
the researchers might be viewed as a combination of scientist, detective, investigative jour-
nalist and change agent. Once employed, such approaches may enable us to understand far
more about how the design, management and organisation of work affect the health of both
employees and their organisations.

ACKNOWLEDGEMENT

Much of the latter part of this chapter is based on: Griffiths, A. (1999) Organizational
interventions: facing the limits of the natural science paradigm. *Scandinavian Journal of
Work, Environment and Health*, **25**, 589–96.

REFERENCES

Anderson, N., Herriot, P. & Hodgkinson, G. (2001) The practitioner–researcher divide in industrial,
    work and organizational (IWO) psychology: where are we now and where do we go from here?
    Journal of Occupational and Organizational Psychology, **74**, 391–412.

Bannister, P., Burman, E., Parker, I., Taylor, M. & Tindall, C. (1994) *Qualitative Methods in psychology.* Milton keynes: Open University Press.

Brockner, J. & Wiesenfeld, B.M. (1996) An integrative framework for explaining reactions to decisions: interactive effects of outcomes and procedures. *Psychological Bulletin,* **120**, 189–208.

Campbell, D.T. & Stanley, J.C. (1963) *Experimental and Quasi-Experimental Designs for Research.* Chicago, IL: Rand McNally.

Cassell, C. & Symon, G. (1994) *Qualitative Methods in Organisational Research: A Practical Guide.* London: Sage.

Chomsky, N. (1988) *Language and the Problems of Knowledge.* Cambridge, MA: MIT Press.

Cohen, R. (1985) Procedural justice and participation. *Human Relations,* **38**, 643–663.

Cohen, S.G. & Ledford, G.E. (1994) The effectiveness of self-managed teams: a quasi-experiment. *Human Relations,* **47**, 13–43.

Cook, T.D. & Campbell, D.T. (1979) *Quasi-Experimentation: Design and Analysis for Field Settings.* Chicago, IL: Rand McNally.

Cook, T.D. & Shadish, W.R. (1994) Social experiments: some developments over the past fifteen years. *Annual Review of Psychology,* **45**, 545–80.

Cooper, C.L. & Marshall, J. (1976) Occupational sources of stress: a review of the literature relating to coronary heart disease and mental ill health. *Journal of Occupational Psychology,* **49**, 11–28.

Cox, T. (1993) *Stress Research and Stress Management: Putting Theory to Work.* HSE Books: Sudbury.

Cox, T., Griffiths, A., Barlow, C., Randall, R., Thomson, T. & Rial-González, E. (2000) *Organisational Interventions for Work Stress: A Risk Management Approach.* Sudbury: HSE Books.

Cox, T., Randall, R. & Griffiths, A. (2002) *Interventions to Control Stress at Work in Hospital Staff.* Sudbury: HSE Books.

Cronbach, L.J. (1982) *Designing Evaluations of Educational and Social Programs.* San Fransisco, CA: Jossey Bass.

Davis, K.E. (1988) *Power Under the Microscope.* (dissertation). Amsterdam: Foris.

Edmondson, A.C. (1996) Three faces of Eden: the persistence of competing theories and multiple diagnoses in organizational intervention research. *Human Relations,* **49**, 571–95.

Ehlen, C.R., Magner, N.R. & Welker, R.B. (1999) Testing the interactive effects of outcome favourability and procedural fairness on members' reactions towards a voluntary professional organisation. *Journal of Occupational and Organizational Psychology,* **72**, 147–61.

Frese, M. (1999) Social support as a moderator of the relationship between work stressors and psychological dysfunctioning: a longitudinal study with objective measures. *Journal of Occupational Health Psychology,* **4**, 179–92.

Ganster, D.C. (1995) Interventions for building healthy organisations: suggestions from the stress research literature. In L.R. Murphy, J.J. Hurrell, Jr, S.L. Sauter & G. Puryear Keita (eds) *Job Stress Interventions.* Washington, DC: American Psychological Association, pp. 323–36.

Geertz, C. (1995) *After the Fact.* Cambridge, MA: Harvard University Press.

Gergen, K.J. & Davis, K.E. (eds) (1985) *The Social Construction of the Person.* New York: Springer-Verlag.

Geus, A. de (1997) *The Living Company.* New York: Longview.

Goldenhar, L.M., Landsbergis, P.A. & Sinclair, R.C. (1999) *The National Occupational Research Agenda (NORA) Intervention Research Team.* Poster presented at the APA/NIOSH Work, Stress and Health 99 Conference, Baltimore, MD, March.

Gordon, J.R. (1991) *A Diagnostic Approach to Organizational Behavior.* Boston, MA: Allyn & Bacon.

Gorman, M.E. (1996) Psychology of science. In W. O'Donohue & R.F. Kitchener (eds) *The Philosophy of Psychology.* London: Sage.

Greenwood, D.J. & Levin, M. (1998) *Introduction to Action Research: Social Research for Social Change.* London: Sage.

Griffiths, A.J. (1998) Work-related illness in Great Britain. *Work and Stress,* **12**, 1–5.

Groot, A.D. de (1964) *Methodologie [Methodology].* The Hague: Mouton.

Hacker, W. (1973) *Algemeine Arbeits and Ingenieurspsychologie.* [*General Work and Engineering Psychology*] Berlin: Verlag der Wissenschaften.

Heaney, C.A. & Goetzel, R.Z. (1997) A review of health-related outcomes of multi-component worksite health promotion programs. *American Journal of Health Promotion,* **11**, 290–308.

Henwood, K. & Pidgeon, N. (1995) Grounded theory and psychological research. *The Psychologist: Bulletin of the British Psychological Society,* **8**, 109–10.

Horgan, J. (1998) *The End of Science: Facing the Limits of Knowledge in the Twilight of the Scientific Age.* London: Abacus.

Hugentobler, M.K., Israel, B.A. & Schurman, S.J. (1992) An action research approach to workplace health: integrating methods. *Health Education Quarterly,* **19**, 55–76.

Illich, I. (1976) *Limits to Medicine.* London: Marion Bryars.

Israel, B.A., Cummings, K.M., Dignan, M.B., Heaney, C.A., Perales, D.P. et al. (1995) Evaluation of health education programs: current assessment and future directions. *Health Education Quarterly,* **22**, 364–89.

Israel, B.A., Schulz, A.J., Parker, E.A. & Becker, A.B. (1998) Review of community-based research: assessing partnership approaches to improve public health. *Annual Review of Public Health,* **19**, 173–202.

Johnasson, G. (1973) Visual perception of biological motion and a model for its analysis. *Perception and Psychophysics,* **14**, 201–11.

Karasek, R.A. & Theorell, T. (1990) *Healthy Work: Stress, Productivity and the Reconstruction of Working Life.* New York: Basic Books.

Kasl, S.V. (1999) Plenary speech, APA/NIOSH Work, Stress and Health 99 Conference, Baltimore, MD, March.

Koch, S. (1959) *Psychology: A Study of Science,* vol. 3. New York: McGraw-Hill.

Koestler, A. (1967) *The Ghost in the Machine.* London: Pan.

Kompier, M.A.J., Geurts, S.A.E., Grundemann, R.W.M., Vink, P. & Smulders, P.G.W. (1998) Cases in stress prevention: the success of a participative and stepwise approach. *Stress Medicine,* **14**, 155–68.

Kristensen, T.S. (1999) Challenges for research and prevention in relation to work and cardiovascular diseases. *Scandinavian Journal of Work, Environment and Health,* **25**, 550–7.

Landsbergis, P.A. & Vivona-Vaughn, E. (1995) Evaluation of an occupational stress intervention in a public agency.*Journal of Organizational Behaviour,* **16**, 29–48.

Leather, P., Lawrence, C. Beale, D. & Cox, T. (1998) Exposure to occupational violence and the buffering effects of intra-organizational support. *Work and Stress,* **12**, 161–78.

Lind, E. & Tyler, T. (1988) *The Social Psychology of Procedural Justice.* New York: Plenum Press.

Lindström, K. (1995) Finnish research in organizational development and job redesign. In L.R. Murphy, J.J. Hurrell, Jr, S.L. Sauter & G. Puryear Keita (eds) *Job Stress Interventions.* Washington, DC: American Psychological Association, pp. 283–93.

Manicas, P.T. & Secord, P.F. (1990) Implications for psychology of the new philosophy of science. *American Psychologist,* April, 399–413.

Marmot, M.G., Bosma, H., Hemingway, H., Brunner, E. & Stansfeld, S. (1997) Contribution of job control and other risk factors to social variations in coronary heart disease incidence. *Lancet,* **350**, 235–9.

Mook, D.G. (1989) The myth of external validity. In L.W. Poon, D.C. Rubin & B.A. Wilson (eds) *Everyday Cognition in Adulthood and Late Life.* New York: Cambridge University Press.

NIOSH (1988) *Psychosocial Occupational Health.* Washington, DC: National Institute of Occupational Safety & Health.

Ofman, D.D. (1995) *Bezieling en kwaliteit in organisaties.* [*Inspiration and Quality in Organizations*]. Cothen: Servire.

Richardson, J. (1996) *Handbook of Qualitative Research Methods for Psychology and the Social Sciences.* Leicester: BPS Books.

Rosenthal, R. & Rosnow, R.L. (eds) (1969) *Artifact in Behavioral Research.* New York: Academic Press.

Sapolsky, R.M. (1994) *Why Zebras Don't Get Ulcers.* New York: W.H. Freeman.

Sauter, S.L., Hurrel, J.J., Fox-Roberts, H., Tetrick, L.E. & Barling, J. (1999) Occupational health psychology: an emerging discipline. *Industrial Health,* **37**, 199–211.

Schabracq, M.J. (1999) De arbeids- en gezondheidspsycholoog. [The work and health psychologist]. In *Praktijkboek Gezond werken* [*Manual of Healthy Working*]. Maarsen: Elsevier.

Schabracq, M.J., Cooper, C.L. & Winnubst, J.A.M. (1996) Work and health psychology: towards a theoretical framework. In M.J. Schabracq, J.A.M. Winnubst & C.L. Cooper (eds) *Handbook of Work and Health Psychology.* Chichester: John Wiley and Sons, pp. 3–29.

Schabracq, M.J., Maassen Van den Brink, H., Groot, W., Janssen, P. & Houkes, I. (2000) *De prijs van stress* [*The Price of Stress*]. Maarsen: Elsevier.

Schein, E.H. (1991) Legitimating clinical research in the study of organizational culture. MIT working paper no. 3288-91-BPS.

Schurman, S.J. & Israel, B.A. (1995) Redesigning work systems to reduce stress: a participatory action research approach to creating change. In L.R. Murphy, J.J. Hurrell, Jr, S.L. Sauter & G. Puryear Keita (eds) *Job Stress Interventions*. Washington, DC: American Psychological Association, pp. 235–63.

Seligman, M. & Csikszentmihalyi, M. (2000) Happiness, excellence and optimal human functioning (positive psychology). *American Psychologist,* **55**, January, special issue.

St. Pierre, R.G. & Cook, T.D. (1984) Sampling strategy in the design of program evaluations. In R.F. Conner, D.G. Altman & C. Jackson (eds) *Evaluation Studies Review Annual,* **9**, 459–84.

Symon, G. & Cassell, C. (1998) *Qualitative Methods and Analysis in Organisational Research: A Practical Guide.* London: Sage.

Theorell, T. & Karasek, R.A. (1996) Current issues relating to psychosocial job strain and cardiovascular disease research. *Journal of Occupational Health Psychology,* **1**, 9–26.

Thoits, P.A. (1995) Stress, coping and social support processes: where are we? What next? *Journal of Health and Social Behaviour,* extra issue, 53–79.

Tolman, E.C. (1932) *Purposive Behavior in Animals and Men.* New York: Appleton-Century-Crofts.

Warr, P.B. (1992) Job features and excessive stress. In R. Jenkins & N. Coney (eds) *Prevention of Mental Ill Health at Work.* London: HMSO.

Wilson, E.O. (1975) *Sociobiology.* Cambridge, MA: Harvard University Press.

World Health Organization (1999) *Health 21: The Health for All Policy Framework for the WHO European Region.* Copenhagen: World Health Organization, Regional Office for Europe.

CHAPTER 10

A Risk Management Approach to the Prevention of Work Stress

Tom Cox, Amanda Griffiths and **Raymond Randall**

University of Nottingham, UK

10.1 BACKGROUND

In Europe, two developments in the early 1990s gave rise to an increased need for practical ways for managers to prevent and manage work stress: its apparent increasing incidence and the requirements of European and national legislation. In addition, in Britain, employers and their insurers were becoming increasingly concerned at the advance of employee litigation. In a landmark case in November 1994, John Walker, a social services manager, obtained a judgment against his former employers for failing to protect him from a health-endangering workload (*Industrial Relations Law Reports*, 1995). The judgment made it clear that there was no reason why *psychological* damage should be excluded from the scope of an employer's duty of care. Previously, "damage" was largely understood in terms of physical harm. Since the Walker case, there have been several other cases in Britain where employees have been awarded financial settlements in respect of stress-related claims.

Data from a variety of national and international surveys of working people, both in Europe and elsewhere in the developed world, identified work stress as a commonly reported cause of ill health. In Britain, for example, data from two government-run surveys (Hodgson et al., 1993; Jones et al., 1998) suggested stress and stress-related illness were second only to musculoskeletal disorders as the major cause of occupational ill health. At the time it was estimated that this resulted in about 6.5 million working days lost to industry and commerce in Britain each year. In terms of annual costs, estimated within the 1995–96 economic framework, the financial burden to society was £3.7–3.8 billion.

In 1989, the European Commission had published its Framework Directive on the Introduction of Measures to Encourage Improvements in the Safety and Health of Workers at Work (EC, 1989). These requirements had to be made law ("transposed") in each of the Member States of the European Union, within their national legislative framework within a specified time frame. The Directive required employers to avoid risks, evaluate the risks

The Handbook of Work and Health Psychology. Edited by M.J. Schabracq, J.A.M. Winnubst and C.L. Cooper.
© 2003 John Wiley & Sons, Ltd.

which cannot be avoided, to combat the *risks at source* (Article 6:2), to keep themselves informed of the "latest advances in technology and scientific findings concerning workplace design" (Article 10:1) and to "consult workers and/or their representatives and allow them to take part in discussions on all questions relating to safety and health at work" (Article 11:1). Employers were also charged to develop a "coherent overall prevention policy which covers technology, organization of work, working conditions, social relationships and the influence of factors related to the working environment" (Article 6:2). They were required to adapt "the work to the individual, especially as regards the design of workplaces, the choice of work equipment and the choice of working and production methods, with a view in particular, to alleviating monotonous work and work at a predetermined work-rate and to reducing their effect on health" (Article 6:2). In addition, employers were required to "be in possession of an assessment of the risks to safety and health at work" and to "decide on the *protective* measures to be taken" (Article 9:1).

In Britain, many of these provisions were already catered for under the Health and Safety at Work etc. Act 1974 (Health & Safety Executive, 1990), for example, in the general duty on employers to "ensure, so far as is reasonably practicable, the health, safety and welfare at work of all their employees". Some of the requirements, however, such as the duty to undertake assessments for all risks to health, were introduced in the Management of Health and Safety at Work Regulations 1992 (Health & Safety Commission, 1992) and their revision (Health & Safety Commission, 1999). A risk assessment involves "a systematic examination of all aspects of the work undertaken to consider what could cause injury or harm, whether the hazards could be eliminated, and if not what preventive or protective measures are, or should be, in place to control the risks" (European Commission, 1996). In other words, employers have a responsibility to take reasonable and practicable steps to protect their employees from those aspects of work or the working environment that are foreseeably detrimental to safety and health.

By the early 1990s therefore, it was clear in Britain and in other European countries, both that (i) work was widely thought to be giving rise to significant levels of stress, and was therefore a foreseeable risk, and (ii) employers were legally required to undertake risk assessments for known causes of ill health.

10.2 ADAPTING THE RISK MANAGEMENT PARADIGM FOR WORK STRESS

The use of risk management in health and safety has a substantial history. There are many texts that present its general principles and variants (Cox & Tait, 1998; Hurst, 1998; Stranks, 1996) and that discuss its scientific and sociopolitical contexts (Bate, 1997). Most models incorporate or otherwise recognise five important elements or principles: (i) a declared focus on a defined work population, workplace, set of operations or particular type of equipment, (ii), an assessment of risks, (iii) the design and implementation of actions designed to remove or reduce those risks, (iv) the evaluation of those actions, and (v) the active and careful management of the process.

It was proposed in 1993 that there was no convincing reason why the management of work stress should not be approached within this same paradigm (Cox, 1993). This was a framework that was already understood by managers, and one that had been widely in operation in Britain for some years with respect to the management of chemicals and other substances known to be hazardous to health. Much of the research and development work in Britain behind the adoption of this approach for the management of work stress over the past decade has been completed by the Institute of Work, Health & Organisations (I-WHO) at the University of Nottingham. This work has been funded by the British Government Health & Safety Executive, the British Medical Association and various unions, together with public sector and private sector organisations. It has been achieved by working hand-in-hand with many organisations, and is summarised, with case study examples, in the remainder of this chapter.

There cannot be an exact, point-by-point translation of models designed for the management of more tangible and physical risks to situations involving psychosocial risks and the experience of work stress. As such, the adaptation of the traditional risk management paradigm to deal with work stress is not "rocket science" in terms of the accuracy and specificity of its measures, nor the mechanisms underlying important decision making points. In finding a practical way forward for managers, the objective is not to seek an exhaustive, precisely measured account of all possible stressors for all individuals. There is no "ruler". Instead, the objective is to produce a reasonable account, with a sound scientific basis, of the major likely stressors for any given working group—an account that is "good enough" to enable employers and employees to decide on possible improvements, and one that will enable managers to comply with their legal duty of care. In other words, this is not an activity carried out for the benefit of researchers, but one pursued with the aim of making a difference to employees' working conditions within organisations. As Hernberg (1994) argued, "the fact that classical occupational diseases still occur does not automatically mean that more research is needed . . . what it really means is that we have failed to implement already existing knowledge".

A major objective of the I-WHO research, using existing knowledge about work stress, was the exploration and development of a feasible and generalisable *process* of risk management for work stress. It is understood that the *outcomes* of specific interventions are unlikely to be wholly generalisable to other organisations. The first stages of I-WHO's research and development work have focused largely on procedures for risk assessment. The later stages have explored how to help organisations engage in risk reduction and finally, in helping them learn how to manage the entire process themselves.

Before we describe the risk management process and present some case examples, we need to present: (i) a brief outline of the model of work stress that underpins this approach (in Section 10.3), and (ii) the defining characteristics of the approach—its participative nature and context-dependency (Section 10.4).

10.3 PSYCHOSOCIAL HAZARDS AND WORK STRESS

In adopting a health and safety model of work stress, as suggested in European law, we conceptualise stress as mediating between exposure to work hazards and some of their health outcomes. The question then becomes: which hazards are known to be associated with the experience of work stress? Apart from the stress-related consequences of anxiety about exposure to physical hazards (e.g. World Health Organization, 1995), the hazards best known for their association with stress concern the design and management of work. These psychological, social and organisational aspects of work have been the object of interest since the early 1950s (Barling & Griffiths, 2002; Johnson, 1996). Initially the focus

Table 10.1   Psychosocial hazards

Job content	Lack of variety or short work cycles, fragmented or meaningless work, underuse of skills, high uncertainty, continuous exposure to people through work
Workload and work pace	Work overload or underload, machine pacing, high levels of time pressure, continually subject to deadlines
Work schedule	Shift working, night shifts, inflexible work schedules, unpredictable hours, long or unsociable hours
Control	Low participation in decision making, lack of control over workload, pacing, shift working etc.
Environment and equipment	Inadequate equipment availability, suitability or maintenance; poor environmental conditions such as lack of space, poor lighting, excessive noise
Organisational culture and function	Poor communication, low levels of support for problem solving and personal development, lack of definition of, or agreement on, organisational objectives
Interpersonal relationships at work	Social or physical isolation, poor relationships with superiors, interpersonal conflict, lack of social support
Role in organisation	Role ambiguity, role conflict and responsibility for people
Career development	Career stagnation and uncertainty, under-promotion or over-promotion, poor pay, job insecurity, low social value to work
Home–work interface	Conflicting demands of work and home, low support at home, dual career problems

Source: Adapted from Cox (1993).

of research was employees' adaptation to their work and work environments, and individual differences in that process of adaptation and coping (Gardell, 1982). However, by the 1960s the focus of interest had begun to move away from how individual employees coped, towards concern for the design and management of their work (psychosocial factors) as one source of their problems.

The exploration of potential stressors used in the risk management approach to the management of work stress is based on one of the taxonomies of psychosocial factors in the literature (Cox, 1993; Cox et al., 2000 a, b), although there are other similar taxonomies that might be used (e.g. Cooper & Marshall, 1976; Warr, 1992). Cox (1993) identified nine categories of psychosocial factors that have been shown to be associated with the experience of stress and/or poor health outcomes, and labelled them "psychosocial hazards". They concern both the content of work, and its context. These hazards are summarised, together with examples, in Table 10.1. A hazard is an event or situation that has the potential for causing harm. Work hazards can be broadly divided into the *physical*, which include, among others, the biological, biomechanical, chemical, mechanical and radiological, and the *psychosocial*. The International Labour Office (ILO, 1986) identified psychosocial hazards in terms of the interactions among job content, work organisation and management, and other environ-mental and organisational conditions, on the one hand, and the employees' competencies and needs on the other. Those interactions that prove to be hazardous influence employees' health through their *perceptions* and *experience* (ILO, 1986). A simpler definition of psy-chosocial hazards might be "those aspects of the design and management of work, and its social and organisational contexts, that have the potential for causing psychological or physical harm".

There is a reasonable consensus in the literature of the nature of psychosocial hazards as presented in Table 10.1, but it should be noted that new forms of work give rise to new hazards—not all of which will yet be represented in scientific publications. In our experience, it is often very context-specific factors that prove to be associated with poor health. Factors such as poor feedback, inadequate appraisal and communication processes also appear to be important (Griffiths, 1998) but are not yet well represented in the scien-tific literature as being associated with the experience of stress or with poor well-being. Other factors such as performance visibility (where errors are highly visible), production responsibility (where the cost of errors is great) or employee interdependence may also prove to be problematic (Parker & Wall, 1998). Job insecurity, excessive working hours and a bullying managerial style have also been suggested as imminent concerns for many employees (Sparks et al., 2001). Any assessment of a particular working group's problems needs to be alert to the existence of new psychosocial factors, and to incorporate a process that allows for their discovery.

While risk assessments for stress clearly focus on psychosocial hazards, it is important to note that physical hazards also need consideration with a view to their possible ramifications for the experience of stress (Cox, 1993). Acceptance of the basic principle underpinning this argument takes us beyond "equivalence reasoning"; that is, only expressing concern for the direct physical actions of the more tangible physical hazards, or for the psychophysiological actions of psychosocial hazards. Different types of hazard can contribute to various forms of harm. For example, exposure to organic solvents may have a psychological effect on the person through their direct effects on the brain, through the unpleasantness of their smell and through fear that such exposure might be harmful (Levi, 1981). Physical hazards clearly can affect health through psychophysiological pathways (Levi, 1984). Violence, as a psychosocial hazard, may have a direct physical effect on its victim in addition to any psychological trauma or social distress that it causes. Furthermore, significant interactions can occur both between hazards and in their effects on health. Risk assessments for stress should take into account employees' concerns for any physical hazards inherent in their particular working environment.

10.4 PARTICIPATION AND CONTEXT DEPENDENCY

In this work on risk management, particular emphasis has been placed on the central status of workers as "experts" in relation to their own jobs. In this respect, data collection can be seen as an exercise in knowledge elicitation and modelling. Employees need to be educated about the process, to develop appropriate expectations, and to participate actively in both the risk assessment and risk reduction phases. At the start of any project, the researchers take the lead, whereas by its completion, a successful project will be led and managed by the workers themselves. In the more recent phases of this development work, the research team have trained workers to conduct and analyse risk assessments themselves and to assume leadership right from the project's inception.

It is this requirement, both ideological and practical, to empower workers to undertake the assessment and improvement of their own working conditions that drives the necessity for this approach to be "user-friendly". This is very different from most published attempts to examine work stress. There are a daunting number of research papers, reviews and books on work stress, covering almost every conceivable work setting. But the approach traditionally used in research into the nature and effects of work stress is neither appropriate nor adequate as a real-world, specific assessment of risk, let alone as a means of reducing that risk.

While there is a considerable amount of information to draw from the traditional academic approach to the study of work stress, there are significant limitations. Many studies provide an indication of a researcher's view of an association between various broadly defined work characteristics and particular employee health indices, usually driven by theoretical rather than practical interest. The measures used are often derived from macro-theories and models drawn from large populations in order to identify general laws, and are often used to provide comparisons across different forms of work. They ignore the context of work—aspects of work particular to any one type of working situation. Some focus on one type of job, but this still does not allow for a meaningful analysis of wide contextual issues. The research question has often been "what problems do different work groups share?" rather than "what are the problems of this particular work group?". As such, few studies have defined their samples adequately enough for the purposes of risk assessment, and few provide sufficient detail in their assessment of problems to enable any reduction of problems to be effected.

10.5 STAGES OF RISK MANAGEMENT

The stages to risk management are summarised in Figure 10.1. Before the process begins, however, there has to be a considerable consultation between stakeholders (including employee representatives) and experts. Setting appropriate expectations and time schedules, and identifying communication channels is vital. These stages are described more fully elsewhere (Cox et al., 2000a, 2002).

10.5.1 Stage I: Risk Assessment

The aim of the risk assessment stage is to identify, for a defined employee group, any significant potential sources of stress (psychosocial hazards) relating to its work and working conditions. This can be achieved, using the taxonomy described above as well as further open questions, by several methods—interviews, focus groups and organisational documentation—depending on the size of the group. Tailor-made questionnaires, based on interviews or focus group data, summarise the problems specific to that group, and provide sufficient detail to allow for the design and planning of specific interventions. Risk assessment is not an organisation-wide approach: such an approach would miss important details. The identification of psychosocial hazards relies on the expert judgement of groups of relevant working people about the adequacy of the design and management of their work. This information is treated at the group level and consensus is measured in those expert

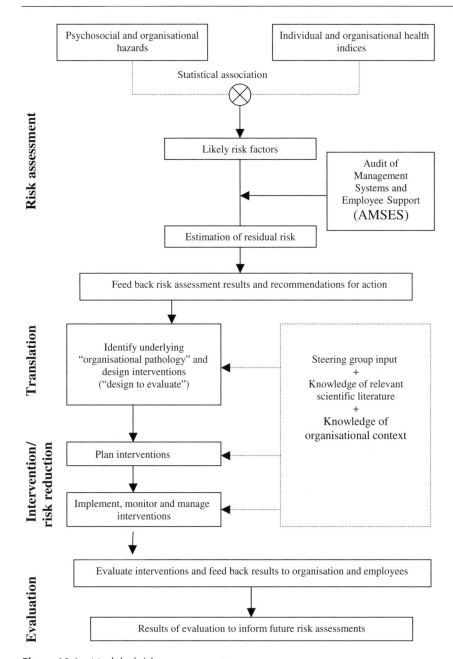

Figure 10.1 Model of risk management

judgements on working conditions. The method does not seek to catalogue individual views about work.

Information about the possible outcomes of work-related stress is collected both from the risk assessment and from otherwise available organisational records, such as absence data and occupational health referrals. The measure of employee well-being used by I-WHO is the General Well-being Questionnaire (Cox & Griffiths, 1995; Cox et al., 1983), developed in Nottingham for this purpose and used on a wide variety of occupational groups. This information is used to determine which of the psychosocial hazards (i.e. potential stressors) actually affects the health of those exposed to them or the healthiness of their organisation. This exercise, relating stressful hazards to their possible effects on health, can be formally investigated using simple statistical techniques such as odds ratios (Cox et al., 2002; Wang et al., 1995). In our experience, managers find odds ratios more acceptable than most other more sophisticated techniques, and can be easily trained to use them. In some cases, however, particularly with small samples, it is possible to rely on more informal analyses of association. This drawing together of information on hazards and harm allows for the identification of risk factors, which can be prioritised in various ways—the nature of harm, the strength of the relationship between hazard and harm, or the size of the group affected.

However, before action can be sensibly planned, it is necessary to establish what is already in place that deals with work-related stress and its effects on the individual or their organization. This involves audit of existing management practices and relevant employee support systems. This information, together with the risk assessment information, allows a notion of the residual risk to be formulated.

10.5.2   Stage II: Translation, Planning and Implementation of Interventions

One of the necessary developments from the traditional risk management model is the "translation" phase, where identified risk factors are discussed, prioritised and targeted by means of specifically designed actions. Usually, the discussion and exploration of likely risk factors involved in any case allows the discovery of any underlying organisational pathology—major problems that may be hidden. A medical analogy can be made where, by exploration of a patient's symptoms, a doctor discovers the underlying disease. This often facilitates intervention planning, since the underlying organisational pathology can be targeted, rather than symptoms (the likely risk factors). Often, more than one risk factor (several symptoms) may be targeted by one intervention: improving communication processes, for example, often deals with many specific problems.

A response to a risk assessment can be integrated into existing management plans for change, and this is shown clearly in our case studies. Risk reduction interventions need not be disruptive, nor need they be "different", or even revolutionary, when compared with everyday management practices. Primary prevention is about good management practice. It is about well-designed, organised and managed work in well-designed, organised and managed workplaces. This is clearly reflected in the nature of the interventions implemented. Most are simply examples of imaginative good management practice.

10.5.3   Stage III: Evaluation, Feedback and Organisational Learning

The key question in this phase is "did the actions achieve what was intended?". However, evaluation is a thread that runs though the entire risk management process. The evaluation of organisational interventions is not straightforward and this question is dealt with elsewhere in this volume (Chapter 9). However, I-WHO researchers have explored various methods of evaluating organisational interventions, with the stated aim of identifying a method that is good enough, yet also straightforward enough, for non-researchers to use. As well as documenting quantitative change in key outcome variables (well-being, for example), qualitative approaches such as stakeholder interviews are often found to be a cost-effective and satisfactory technique. In addition, because organisational interventions are not an "all-or-nothing" event, it is useful to explore how far any planned action was actually implemented, and whether or not it reached its intended audience. Exploring subtle variations in implementation (evaluating process as well as outcome) can provide a useful technique for evaluation research (Randall et al., 2001).

The evaluation of interventions is an important step, but one that is often overlooked or avoided. Not only does it tell the organisation how well actions have worked in reducing stress but it allows the reassessment of the situation, providing a basis for organisational learning. Essentially it establishes a process for continuous improvement. Managing work-related stress is not a one-off activity but part of an ongoing cycle of good management at work and the effective management of health and safety. In many ways, good management *is* stress management.

There are parallels between the risk management model and organisational intervention processes developed by other researchers around the world. When looking at the health effects of work design and management, and particularly when attempting to understand, to explain and to intervene (rather than simply describe), many applied psychologists have independently formulated an approach and have identified issues which have much in common (Goldenhar et al., 2001; Hugentobler et al., 1992; Israel et al., 1996, 1998; Kompier & Kristensen, 2000; Kompier et al., 1998; Landsbergis & Vivona-Vaughn, 1995; Lindström, 1995; Nytrø et al., 2000; Schurman & Israel, 1995). The major development with the I-WHO risk management approach is that it overtly attempts to construct a process based on legal requirements. With the data thus provided, employers should be able to (i) help promote the improvement and management of working conditions towards better employee and organisational health, (ii) provide opportunities for organisational development, (iii) reduce the likelihood of claims against organisations for breach of duty of care, and improve their defence against such claims, and (iv) strengthen the organisation's position with regard to employer liability insurance.

In Britain, the Regulations require employers to undertake a risk assessment that is "suitable and sufficient". Employers need to comply with legislative requirements within a feasible yet scientific and defensible framework, and are not charged with complying with the requirements of the more pedantic researcher. This is not to deny that several scientific challenges have been identified during the development of a risk management approach (Cox & Rial-González, 2000) but there is not space in the current chapter to cover them in detail. There is a debate, for example, as to whether self-report data on working conditions are better predictors of behaviour and (stress-mediated) health outcomes than objective measures (Bosma et al., 1997; Jex & Spector, 1996; Spector, 1987). Many would argue that they are, but this is not to deny that perceptions can be inaccurate or moderated by other factors. It is also far from straightforward deciding what constitutes a psychosocial hazard. Further, psychosocial hazards, unlike physical hazards, can often be conceptualised as part of a factor that is health-endangering at one end of its continuum, and health-enhancing at the other (for example, participation in decision making). It is also not easy to achieve a reliable classification of harm, or to measure degrees of harm when dealing with psychological and social outcomes. A further challenge is presented by estimating risk at the group level, although the objective of risk assessment is to identify the main risks for the majority of employees. This is not to deny that individual differences exist, or that employers have a duty of care to individuals.

We propose that it is unlikely that the average research-based "stress audit" would be regarded as good enough in law as a genuine attempt to assess and improve employee health and safety. However, the question is, do the actions as outlined above, within the risk management framework, constitute a good enough approach to the management of work stress? Is the process likely to identify the major stressors faced by any particular working group and assist managers to reduce them? The answer, we propose, is "yes". In the following section, several case studies are presented that demonstrate the risk management approach in action.

10.6   CASE STUDY EXAMPLES

Over the past ten years, I-WHO has undertaken a series of case studies in various types of organisation, with various groups of workers; for example, chemical manufacturing process operators, railway station supervisors, call centre operatives, nurses, doctors, senior managers, engineers, researchers, teachers, utility company field operatives, and supermarket, catering and warehouse staff. Space only permits a very brief account of some of these case studies here, but full accounts are available elsewhere (Cox et al., 2000a, 2002). These case studies have been published in a "warts-and-all" fashion. It has usually been the problems that have proved the most useful learning experiences and have promoted new developments in the process.

10.6.1   Case Study 1: Call Centre Employees

This case study was carried out with employees in the call centre of a large water utility dealing with telephone enquiries and written correspondence from customers. Many staff wanted to leave the company, their job satisfaction was low and well-being poor. Absence levels were fairly high, and a relatively large proportion of employees reported work-related musculoskeletal pain. The risk assessment stage identified the following risk factors: unrealistic performance targets and a lack of praise and recognition, poor communication with senior management, lack of support from line managers, slow movement of information around the organisation, lack of guidance on the prioritisation of tasks, lack of time to complete tasks, and inadequate time for taking breaks during the working day.

An extensive package of interventions was implemented that targeted risk factors and their underlying pathologies. The interventions included changes in the management of performance targets, the instigation of more regular, structured and purposeful team meetings, measures to improve organisational communication, the introduction of new training initiatives, the design of "Best Practice" guidelines in working procedures, a review and updating of staffing levels to meet increased public demand, formal break-taking arrangements and innovations in IT systems.

A number of positive findings emerged from the subsequent evaluation, with staff generally reporting that the interventions had improved their working life. Although some problems remained, fewer staff reported problems overall, fewer risks were identified, absence levels reduced and staff well-being improved.

10.6.2   Case Study 2: Accident and Emergency Nurses

This case study focused on a group of 35 nursing staff working in the Accident and Emergency Department of a medium-sized hospital. The department dealt with both minor and major injuries and disease conditions. The staff faced a number of problems. Once stabilised, patients were not being moved into the wards quickly, and this resulted in extra work for the department's staff when workload was already heavy. Many staff indicated that their "peripheral" workload (e.g., organising community-based work and dealing with paperwork) was a problem. Although communication was strong, staff indicated that consultation about change was weak. The availability of support for staff involved in distressing situations was rated as poor. There were some vacant posts in the department, and many staff reported that they were not notified of their working hours far enough in advance. Problems with training were also cited by the majority of staff. These problems appeared to impact on well-being of staff: although most found their job satisfying, they indicated that they were worn out and tense.

Interventions focused on addressing problems with staffing, reducing the peripheral workload placed on staff, and improving communications, training and the organisation of shifts. These included the recruitment of staff to fill vacancies, the introduction of an administration coordinator (to deal with many of the administrative tasks taken on by nurses) and the relocation of specialist and support staff into the unit (nurses who organised after-care for patients attending the ward such as places in residential homes), the introduction of in-house training sessions (run by the more highly qualified nursing staff), more regular and inclusive departmental meetings and the reorganisation of the off-duty rota. Interventions designed to reduce the peripheral workload placed on staff were seen as particularly effective, as was the recruitment of staff. The impact of the other interventions was more modest, but nonetheless important for a number of staff. It did appear, however, that persistent problems with the movement of stabilised patients to wards and its impact on workload, as well as problems in providing support for staff, tempered the impact of some of these interventions.

10.6.3   Case Study 3: Hospital-Based Outpatient Department Staff

This case study involved approximately 40 staff: nurses, health care assistants (direct staff) and administration staff. These groups of staff worked closely together to deliver outpatient care (treatment that does not involve overnight stays in hospital) in eye, ear, nose and throat departments. Risk assessments revealed that direct care staff regarded communication with administration staff as poor. Clinic time was pressured, clinics were over-booked and insufficient time was allocated for each patient. Treatments were often interrupted by administrators' requests to access patients' notes and test results, or to complete paperwork. There were problems with aggression from patients (staff also considered that patients were not given enough information when clinics were running behind schedule) and many reported that there was inadequate appreciation and recognition from consultants. They reported difficulties caused by covering the work of absent colleagues and problems with the physical working environment. There also appeared to be a specific problem with the inequitable distribution of late working hours. Nonetheless, staff well-being was relatively good. Administration staff identified a significant number of problems that suggested they were under real pressure. Staff turnover was high and this was having a significant impact on workload, ability to take up training opportunities and the overall ability of the section to deliver an effective service. Working relationships between administration staff and direct care staff were strained. The group reported poor well-being, low job satisfaction and high levels of intention to leave.

In response to the risk assessment a number of major interventions were implemented in the administration that led to fundamental change in the way work was organised. Staff were allocated to work with named consultants on the booking and management of particular clinics—this was designed to increase the ownership of information and to raise their level of expertise. A programme of training was set up to teach staff about the full capabilities of the patient administration computer system. A new management structure was implemented to give the section a more "hands-on" and influential management team. Regular staff meetings were also instigated. Special projects were run to help track down missing notes and files—a source of significant problems for all staff in the department.

A more modest package of interventions was implemented for direct care staff, whose good general well-being indicated a lower priority for action. A series of team-building sessions were introduced to allow direct care staff to meet and discuss issues with administration staff. A departmental clerk was appointed to ease the administration load placed on nursing staff. Some new clinics were run with a smaller number of patients. To improve the management of clinics and the information given to patients, one member of nursing staff was assigned to work as a clinic liaison nurse (to keep patients informed of delays and organise their passage through the clinic). Specific training courses were offered to help staff deal with aggression from patients.

Across the board, these interventions were well received. Problems with communication between administration staff and other staff in the department were virtually eliminated. Time pressures eased for many direct care staff as a result of a reduction in their peripheral workload—the introduction of the administrative coordinator was seen as particularly effective. Although many clinics remained very busy, restricting the sizes of clinics was seen as making a significant difference. Staff also indicated that late working was more equitably distributed. It was reported that the use of a clinic liaison nurse helped to make clinics run much more smoothly and eased a number of problems. The strong well-being of nursing staff was maintained. The administration section of the department responded well to the package of interventions. They reported significant improvements in communications and consultation (particularly with nursing staff), better working relationships with management and improved training. Job satisfaction had improved, absence dropped, and fewer staff indicated that they wanted to leave the department. Despite these improvements, the administrative staff's well-being had not improved significantly, the department was still very busy, new staff were being recruited, and managers were seeking to improve the situation further.

10.6.4   Case Study 4: Supermarket Staff

The study was carried out with two groups of employees from a major supermarket chain: customer services staff and staff working on night and evening shifts. Customer services staff reported relatively satisfactory levels of general well-being, but they had high levels of musculoskeletal disorders. A number of risk factors for health were identified that concerned excessive time pressures, concerns about performance monitoring, lack of support and lack of appreciation by management, and lack of training. The health profile of the night and evening shift staff contrasted sharply with that of the customer services staff. A relatively large proportion of these staff reported poor well-being, musculoskeletal disorders, a lack of sleep, job dissatisfaction, intention to leave the company and recent involvement in a workplace accident. A number of risk factors were identified: time pressures, unfair pay, poor communication with management, high demands from management, colleagues and cover staff, poor quality equipment, lack of support from store managers, absence among colleagues, lack of flexibility in hours, lack of communication about new procedures and intimidation at work.

Many of the interventions were broad-brush actions designed to impact upon more than one group of employees, more than one risk factor and on their underlying pathologies. These included the introduction of staff and management meetings, open surgeries with store managers, store newsletters, overlapping shifts, increased access to email, information on methods of best practice, harassment awareness and management training, "return to work" interviews for absentees, swap sheets for shift staff, flexi-hours for supervisors, separate customer services desks managed by an experienced member of staff, improvements in store equipment, and changes in customer complaints policies.

Although most case study interventions were evaluated some six months or a year after their implementation, due to the research funding arrangements, the interventions in this particular case study were evaluated less than six months after their implementation began. Inevitably, some stressors remained, but there were encouraging signs that where interventions had taken place, staff responded very positively to them, their perceptions of working conditions had improved and they reported better levels of general well-being.

10.7 CONCLUDING SUMMARY

There has been an increase in concern about work-related stress in relation to both individual and organisational health. Part of the experience of such stress and related health outcomes arises from the exposure of employees to psychosocial hazards at work. Organizations are required in law to assess the risks to employees arising from these hazards as well as those arising from the more tangible and physical hazards of work.

This chapter has introduced a framework, a methodology and procedures for conducting assessments for psychosocial hazards in the workplace, and for reducing them. These are based on the published work of the Institute of Work, Health and Organisations (I-WHO) at the University of Nottingham. This approach is set firmly within the risk management paradigm that is central to current European health and safety legislation and practice. It provides a positive framework for action, focused on the organisation as the generator of risk, and on prevention. The complex aetiology of work stress represents a major scientific challenge, and its mechanisms may never be fully understood. Nonetheless, there is a moral and legal imperative to act to reduce the harm caused by stress in the workplace. The assessment procedures and supporting instruments required to achieve this are still under development, most notably in an attempt to take the process forward out of the hands of researchers or consultants for use by workers themselves.

ACKNOWLEDGEMENTS

The authors gratefully acknowledge the support of the British Health and Safety Executive and other organisations in the funding of much of this research, and research colleagues for their contributions: notably, Claire Barlow, Margy McAfee, Karina Nielsen, Joanna Pryce, Eusebio Rial-González and Louise Thomson. They also extend their gratitude to the companies and employees who have worked with them in these efforts towards practical solutions. The views expressed here are those of the authors and do not necessarily reflect those of any other person or organisation.

REFERENCES

Barling, J. & Griffiths, A. (2002) A history of occupational health psychology. In J.C. Quick & L.Tetrick (eds) *Handbook of Occupational Health Psychology.* Washington, DC: American Psychological Association.

Bate, R. (1997) *What Risk?* Oxford: Butterworth-Heinemann.

Bosma, H., Marmot, M.G., Hemingway, H., Nicholson, A.C., Brunner, E. & Stansfeld, S.A. (1997) Low job control and risk of coronary heart disease in Whitehall II (prospective cohort) study. *British Medical Journal*, **314** (7080).

Cooper, C.L. & Marshall, J. (1976) Occupational sources of stress: a review of the literature relating to coronary heart disease and mental ill health. *Journal of Occupational Psychology*, **49**, 11–28.

Cox, S. & Tait, R. (1998) *Safety, Reliability and Risk Management.* Oxford: Butterworth-Heinemann.

Cox, T. (1993) *Stress Research and Stress Management: Putting Theory to Work.* Sudbury: HSE Books.

Cox, T. & Griffiths, A. (1995) The nature and measurement of work stress: theory and practice. In J. Wilson and N. Corlett (eds) *The Evaluation of Human Work: A Practical Ergonomics Methodology.* London: Taylor & Francis.

Cox, T. & Rial-González, E. (2000) *Risk Management, Psychosocial Hazards and Work Stress.* Copenhagen: World Health Organization, Regional Office for Europe.

Cox, T., Thirlaway, M., Gotts, G. & Cox, S. (1983) The nature and assessment of general well-being. *Journal of Psychosomatic Research*, **27**, 353–9.

Cox, T., Griffiths, A., Barlow, C., Randall, R., Thomson, T. & Rial-González, E. (2000a) *Organisational Interventions for Work Stress: A Risk Management Approach.* Sudbury: HSE Books.

Cox, T., Griffiths, A. & Rial-González, E. (2000b) *Research on Work-Related Stress.* European Agency for Safety & Health at Work. Luxembourg: Office for Official Publications of the European Communities.

Cox, T., Randall, R. & Griffiths, A. (2002) *Interventions to Control Stress at Work in Hospital Staff.* Sudbury: HSE Books.

European Commission (1989) Council Framework Directive on the Introduction of Measures to Encourage Improvements in the Safety and Health of Workers at Work. 89/391/EEC. *Official Journal of the European Communities*, **32** (L183), 1–8.

European Commission (1996) *Guidance on Risk Assessment at Work.* Brussels: European Commission.

Gardell, B. (1982) Work participation and autonomy: a multilevel approach to democracy at the workplace. *International Journal of Health Services*, **12**, 31–41.

Goldenhar, L.M., LaMontange, A.D., Katz, T., Heaney, C. & Landsbergis, P. (2001) The intervention research process in occupational safety and health: an overview from the NORA Intervention Effectiveness Research Team. *Journal of Occupational and Environmental Medicine*, **43**, 616–22.

Griffiths, A.J. (1998) The psychosocial work environment. In R.C. McCaig & M.J. Harrington (eds) *The Changing Nature of Occupational Health.* Sudbury: HSE Books, pp. 213–32.

Health & Safety Commission (1999) *Management of Health and Safety at Work Regulations: Approved Code of Practice and Guidance.* London: HMSO.

Health & Safety Commission (1992) *Management of Health and Safety at Work Regulations.* London: HMSO.

Health & Safety Executive (1990) *A Guide to the Health and Safety at Work etc. Act 1974.* Sudbury: HSE Books.

Health & Safety Executive (1995) *Stress at Work: A Guide for Employers.* Sudbury: HSE Books.

Hernberg, S. (1994) Editorial: 20th Anniversary Issue. *Scandinavian Journal of Work, Environment and Health,* **20**, 5–7.

Hodgson, J.T., Jones, J.R., Elliott, R.C. & Osman, J. (1993) *Self-Reported Work-Related Illness.* Sudbury: HSE Books.

Hugentobler, M.K., Israel, B.A. & Schurman, S.J. (1992) An action research approach to workplace health: integrating methods. *Health Education Quarterly,* **19**, 55–76.

Hurst, N.W. (1998) *Risk Assessment: The Human Dimension.* Cambridge: Royal Society of Chemistry.

Industrial Relations Law Reports (1995) *Walker v Northumberland County Council,* 35.

International Labour Office (1986) *Psychosocial Factors at Work: Recognition and Control.* Occupational Safety and Health Series no. 56. Geneva: International Labour Office.

Israel, B.A., Baker, E.A., Goldenhar, L.M., Heaney, C.A. & Schurman, S.J. (1996) Occupational stress, safety and health: conceptual framework and principles for effective preventions. *Journal of Occupational Health Psychology,* **1**, 261–86.

Israel, B.A., Schulz, A.J., Parker, E.A. & Becker, A.B. (1998) Review of community-based research: assessing partnership approaches to improve public health. *Annual Review of Public Health,* **19**, 173–202.

Jex, S.M. & Spector, P.E. (1996) The impact of negative affectivity on stressor–strain relations: a replication and extension. *Work and Stress,* **10**, 36–45.

Johnson, J.V. (1996) Conceptual and methodological developments in occupational stress research. An introduction to state-of-the-art reviews I. *Journal of Occupational Health Psychology,* **1**, 6–8.

Jones, J.R., Hodgson, J.T., Clegg, T.A. & Elliot, R.C. (1998) *Self-Reported Work-Related Illness in 1995.* Sudbury: HSE Books.

Kompier, M.A.J. & Kristensen, T.S. (2000) Organizational work stress interventions in a theoretical, methodological and practical context. In. J. Dunham (ed.) *Stress in Occupations: Past, Present and Future.* London: Whurr.

Kompier, M.A.J., Geurts, S.A.E., Grundemann, R.W.M., Vink, P. & Smulders, P.G.W. (1998) Cases in stress prevention: the success of a participative and stepwise approach. *Stress Medicine,* **14**, 155–68.

Landsbergis, P.A. & Vivona-Vaughn, E. (1995) Evaluation of an occupational stress intervention in a public agency. *Journal of Organizational Behaviour,* **16**, 29–48.

Levi, L. (1981) *Preventing Work Stress.* Reading, MA: Addision-Wesley.

Levi, L. (1984) *Stress in Industry: Causes, Effects and Prevention.* Occupational Safety and Health Series no. 51. Geneva: International Labour Office.

Lindström, K. (1995) Finnish research in organizational development and job redesign. In L.R. Murphy, J.J. Hurrell, Jr, S.L. Sauter & G. Puryear Keita (eds) *Job Stress Interventions.* Washington, DC: American Psychological Association, pp. 283–93.

Nytrø, K., Saksvik, P.O., Mikkelsen, A., Bohle, P. & Quinlan, M. (2000). An appraisal of key factors in the implementation of occupational stress interventions. *Work and Stress,* **3**, 213–25.

Parker, S. & Wall, T. (1998) *Job and Work Design: Organizing Work to Promote Well-Being and Effectiveness.* London: Sage.

Randall, R., Griffiths, A. & Cox, T. (2001) Using the uncontrolled work setting to shape the evaluation of work stress interventions. In C. Weikert, E. Torkelson & J. Pryce (eds) *Occupational Health Psychology: Europe 2001.* European Academy of Occupational Health Psychology Conference Proceedings Series. Nottingham: I-WHO Publications.

Schurman, S.J. & Israel, B.A. (1995) Redesigning work systems to reduce stress: a participatory action research approach to creating change. In L.R. Murphy, J.J. Hurrell, Jr, S.L. Sauter & G. Puryear Keita (eds), *Job Stress Interventions.* Washington, DC: American Psychological Association, pp. 235–63.

Sparks, K., Faragher, B. & Cooper, C. (2001) Well-being and occupational health in the 21st century workplace. *Journal of Occupational and Organizational Psychology,* **74**, 489–509.

Spector, P.E. (1987) Interactive effects of perceived control and job stressors on affective reactions and health outcomes for clerical workers. *Work and Stress*, **1**, 155–62.

Stranks, J. (1996) *The Law and Practice of Risk Assessment.* London: Pitman.

Wang, M., Eddy, J.M. & Fitzhugh, E.C. (1995). Application of odds ratio and logistic models in epidemiology and health research. *Health Values*, **19**, 59–62.

Warr, P. B. (1992) Job features and excessive stress. In: R. Jenkins and N. Coney (eds) *Prevention of Mental Ill Health at Work.* London: HMSO.

World Health Organization (1995) *Health Consequences of the Chernobyl Accident.* Geneva: World Health Organization.

PART III

Specific Issues in Work and Health Psychology

CHAPTER 11

New Technologies and Stress

Kai-Christoph Hamborg and **Siegfried Greif**
University of Osnabrück, Germany

11.1 INTRODUCTION

Technological innovation is important for industrial organizations trying to survive in competitive markets. However, innovation is never a simple nor a smooth process. Faced with major technological changes, people react differently; some seem to relish the challenge, but many show symptoms of stress. In the 1970s new computer technologies started to change nearly every workplace, and also influenced private life. People feared that stress and unemployment would be the future consequences of the technological revolution.

Scientists started empirical research that might support or contradict these expectations, and developed implementation strategies in order to reduce some of the potential negative consequences.

Nowadays computer systems have become standard, at least in modern industries and administration. The cycle of computer hardware and software innovation has accelerated. Every year or so new hardware and software systems are released, to which people have to adapt. The hardware components of new technologies are also changing more rapidly in our times. In the meantime, it has become evident that innovation and new technologies are not the source of unemployment or of low qualification requirements per se (Welsch, 1989). The question is how people react to such permanent innovation, whether it results in stress, and which practical psychological consequences should be drawn to help them cope with permanent technological innovation. One of the central psychological problems of all these different changes relates to highly complex interrelated systems and the resulting risk of errors. Complexity and error management, therefore, will be major problems that will have to be looked at in relation to stress and coping competencies.

This chapter gives a summary of research on new technologies and stress and discusses practical implications for the implementation process. It presents cross-sectional research and longitudinal studies. Following this, practical consequences concerning implementation strategies, job (re)design and software design are presented. The final section addresses the problem of permanent technological innovation and gives a vision of adaptive learning organizations.

The Handbook of Work and Health Psychology. Edited by M.J. Schabracq, J.A.M. Winnubst and C.L. Cooper.
© 2003 John Wiley & Sons, Ltd.

11.2 THE IMPACT OF NEW TECHNOLOGIES ON STRESS

11.2.1 Basic Stress Model

Faced with technological changes, not all people show stress reactions. According to the transactional stress model (Lazarus, 1976), the individual appraisal of the stressor, the resources, the reappraisal of the stressor and coping competences are important. Some people clearly seem to appreciate the challenge of technological novelty. Only subjects who expect a long-lasting aversive experience after an appraisal of the whole situation and its consequences will react with stress. Research into the impact of new technologies on stress therefore has to take into account many different factors and conditions that might affect the appraisal process and the stress reaction. In order to develop a systematic research overview we have to consider types of stressors, different resources, short- and long-term consequences, and also the means of measuring these consequences.

11.2.2 A Definition of Stress in the Context of New Technologies

We define stress as a state of intense and aversive tension, which the subject strongly wants to avoid. The sensation of stress depends on the expected persistence, closeness and lack of control of the situation (Greif, 1991a). The application of this definition implies several seemingly trivial, but often neglected, consequences. Stress is not suffered by people who before or after the implementation of new technologies neither show nor expect persistent aversive tension, nor want to avoid the change. Most people, apparently, do not worry about technological changes which may or may not come in the long run. People who are able to control the technological problems, either by avoiding or by learning to manage them, will show no stress reactions.

Stressors can be defined simply as factors that are assumed to release stress reactions with high probability (Semmer, 1984). The technology itself, but also the expected direct or mediated consequences of its implementation, may be a source of stress. Therefore, we have to take into account the whole range of different possible factors and sources known from stress research that elicit stress reactions. Following the transactional stress model and action theory, Semmer (1984) distinguishes three major groups of hypothetical stressors at work, which can be applied here:

1. Additional demands on the action regulation process or control of task performance (for example, long and unpredictable system response time, cumbersome handling, and indirect consequences such as time pressure following from higher work demands),
2. Regulatory insecurity or insufficient control of actions resulting from overload or ambiguous performance feedback (for example, complex hardware and software systems or incomprehensible handbooks, unclear wording and feedback, the program's error messages and, finally, higher complexity of the whole set of tasks).
3. Conflicting goals or lack of task and role clarity (for example, conflicts between time pressure and quality standards or unclear role changes resulting from the implementation of the technology).

In the scientific literature short-term and long-term consequences are differentiated. Examples of short-term consequences are biochemical and psychophysiological reactions such as increased blood pressure, pulse rate and catecholamine excretion. Moreover consequences like eye or musculoskeletal strain symptoms and lower performance efficiency (especially a higher rate of errors) are also short-term indicators that are found to be related to stress in some studies. The whole range of indicators mentioned above has also been applied in the research on stress induced by computer technology. Typical long-term consequences that have been examined in this field include reduced well-being, psychosomatic complaints and diseases. The following section gives a summary of research results on special factors or sources of stress possibly caused by new technologies. Field studies on the overall consequences of both the technology and the implementation process are summarized in Section 11.3.

11.2.3   Research on Different Factors and Sources of Stress

Several basic sources of organizational stress can be distinguished. Most of them have also been investigated in conjunction with work and new technologies: e.g. job demands, job control, job content as well as human factors constraints and career/future concerns (Briner & Hockey, 1988; Carayon, 1993; Carayon et al., 1995; Frese, 1991a).

Human factor constraints are related to hardware and software properties of computing environments. Important hardware components that have been studied in experiments and field studies are workstation layout, input devices (keyboards, mice etc.) and visual display units (VDUs). In the case of VDUs, results vary. Whereas Çakir (1981) and Zeier et al. (1987) found no properties directly related to physiological reactions and musculoskeletal discomfort Sauter et al. (1991) reported an association between work with VDUs and musculoskeletal complaints.

Furthermore, empirical evidence has been found on the impact of delayed or unpredictable system response times on stress (Johansson & Aronsson, 1984). In a summary of experimental research applying psychophysiological measures, Boucsein (1988) infers that system-response times that are either too long or too short may induce stress.

There is lack of evidence about the direct impact of software design on stress. Only particular problems such as system failures, especially crashes, definitely appear to cause stress. White-collar workers showed significantly different adrenalin excretion and diastolic blood pressure during a breakdown, in comparison to ordinary conditions, in an investigation by Johansson & Aronsson (1984). Zapf (1993) also identified the malfunctioning of computer systems as a typical "computer hassle" causing stress.

The impact that errors have on stress and emotional reactions has been investigated recently (Krone et al., 2000; Reason, 1990; Zapf, 1991, 1993). The practical relevance of the research on human errors is high. Observation shows that both novices and experts using standard software systems make mistakes or action slips every few minutes. This may lead to negative consequences for the organization and for the employees as well. There is empirical evidence that shows that errors are related to work and system complexity. For example, Zapf (1993) found an increase in errors related to high work complexity. Corresponding experimental results show that errors related to planning processes were particulary made by inexperienced users confronted with high task and system complexity (Hamborg, 1996).

Regarding the increasing complexity of software systems in office work, errors will become even more likely in the future. This effect is probably strengthened by faster hardware and software innovation. Today, most software systems and even hardware components are updated and replaced by new releases after one or two years. Very often the quality and stability of the first releases of new hardware and software systems remain insufficient. Shorter cycles of innovation require permanent learning and adaptation to new and potentially unstable changes.

How the resulting problems can be classified depends on the type of hardware and software malfunction and on individual coping competencies. If the problems are severe (for example, when tasks cannot be performed correctly, task achievement is impeded or information gets lost) such events may arouse high stress reactions and even states of panic. The frequent repetition of minor malfunctions, errors and action slips that users experience in their daily work with computers may be classified as "microstressors" or daily hassles.

Zapf (1991, 1993) has studied the cumulative effects of such computer hassles. He found that mental as well as physical workload and stress reactions are related to an observable number of performance errors. An increased workload and stress result in a substantial decrease of performance efficiency and quality. Moreover unsuccessful troubleshooting affects the emotional and motivational state and thus leads to frustration and irritation in the long run. Carayon (1997, p. 330f) points out that the cumulative effect of so-called acute stressors like slow computer performance and computer breakdowns can result in chronic symptoms of stress. Even though the technology may not cause any difficulties, the anticipation of errors due to lack of knowledge can, according to the above definition of stress, be enough to cause stress.

The design of workstations, hardware and software components, the furnishings and interior equipment are important factors related to stress. Scientific field research on ergonomic and usable design, arrangement of the hardware equipment (especially the screen, keyboards and furnishings) has been applied by industrial firms, and has become an essential aspect of their marketing strategy.

Research shows that it is insufficient to consider human factors constraints and the ergonomic design of the equipment as the only source of stress. Several authors emphasize that the type of work carried out at VDUs and the embedding organizational conditions seem to be the main causes of health complaints and stress reactions (Agervold, 1987; Briner & Hockey, 1988; Çakir, 1981; Frese, 1991a). New technology may lead to changes in work structure and human–machine redivision of labour (Buchanan & Boddy, 1982; Levi, 1994; Turner & Karasek, 1984). This may result in changes of work demands, e.g. work overload or underload, time pressure (Saupe & Frese, 1981; Schulz & Höfert, 1981) and interruptions (Johansson & Aronsson, 1984; Leitner et al., 1993), as well as anxiety (Mohr, 1991), uncertainty (Saupe & Frese, 1981; Turner & Karasek, 1984), lack of job control (Buchanan & Boddy, 1982, Sauter et al., 1983) and career concerns like uncertainty about job future and career advancement (Carayon, 1993). The following section briefly describes the role of intervening or moderating variables. Field studies on the overall consequences of new technologies and their implementation are addressed later.

11.2.4 Resources

It is well known from stress research that stress reactions and the resulting long- and short-term consequences are mediated by so-called intervening variables or resources, serving as buffers protecting the person from stress effects. Control, technological knowledge and competence, as well as support are the major resources that have been studied in this field.

Control

Control, defined as the subjective probability of reducing stress reactions, is often mentioned as an important buffering resource (cf. Frese & Brodbeck, 1989; Greif, 1991a; Johansson, 1989). This kind of control at work implies the possibility of successfully changing environmental conditions or one's own activities (cf. Frese, 1989). Low decision latitude and little control over scheduling of tasks may follow from the inadequate (re)design of jobs after the implementation of new technologies (Buchanan & Boddy, 1982; Frese & Zapf, 1987). Carayon (1993), however, has found that while job demands and career/future concerns are related to stress outcomes in office work, job control is not. According to Jones and Fletcher (this volume) the latter point seems not to be a clear cut issue.

Technological Knowledge and Competences

Technological knowledge and coping competences are very powerful resources meeting the challenge of technological change. Such changes require intensive, adaptive effort. Briner & Hockey (1988) supposed that in the short-term, differences between old and new work demands and the lack of competences are likely to be the main source of stress. Training and development of the necessary technological knowledge and skills provide security and self-confidence. Expert knowledge and competences reduce the probability of complex errors. Furthermore, the development of special error management competences appears to be an important resource preventing stress (Frese et al., 1991b). Therefore, the implementation of new technologies should be accompanied by the extensive training of novices. Methods of learning and error management training are considered in Section 11.4.

Social Support and Help

Social support and help by colleagues and experts is a well-known resource moderating stress reactions (Frese & Semmer, 1991; Udris, 1989). In the implementation process of new technologies the hardware and software retailers are normally expected to provide a guaranteed hotline to help the users. The development of an internal social support network within the work environment seems to facilitate individual learning, problem solving and error management beyond the initial period of formal training (Briner & Hockey, 1988; Dutke & Schönpflug, 1987; Greif, 1986). The results of some studies show that the implementation of new technologies may reduce social interaction (Buchanan & Boddy, 1982; Turner & Karasek, 1984; Stellman et al., 1987). Therefore, special investments in the development of personal help networks, and a positive social team and organizational climate may be necessary to compensate for an impairment of such resources. For example in training seminars, team development, reinforcement of supporting interactions between the participants and agreement to help each other when faced with problems in the workplace may be at least as important as filling any technological knowledge gaps that the participants may have.

11.3   RESEARCH ON THE IMPLEMENTATION
OF NEW TECHNOLOGIES

11.3.1   Cross-Sectional Studies

Studies on the overall influence of the implementation of new technologies show controversial results on strain and stress reactions. Some studies report an increase, others a
decrease and several no differences in stress-related reactions linked to the introduction of
new technologies.

The implementation strategy is an important variable that has to be considered. Often the
introduction follows a strategy of simply implementing the latest or the "best" hardware and
software system and "muddling through" the resulting problems of organizational change
(von Benda, 1990; Greif, 1991b). Here it is not predictable whether the technological
changes result in repetitious tasks and a loss of skill or in job enrichment. By following this
strategy it remains uncertain how the job demands and decision latitude will be affected. A
typical unsolved problem linked to the preference for "muddling through" seems to be the
lack of advanced knowledge about what computers can or cannot do and how the future
working situation may be affected by the new technology (Briner & Hockey, 1988). As a
consequence the fear of unemployment or negative job changes such as a lower position,
social isolation, role change and increasing supervision may arise (von Benda, 1990; Frese,
1991a; Frese & Brodbeck, 1989).

An increase in strain due to VDU usage, especially in connection with high workload
and repetitious tasks, is reported in a comprehensive study by Stellman et al. (1987). The
authors investigated more than 1000 female office clerical workers. They studied the differences between five groups: part-day typists, all-day typists, clerical workers, part-day
VDU operators and full-day VDU operators (as they call them). All-day terminal users
reported higher levels of job and physical environment stressors than part-day VDU users,
typists and other clerical workers. Musculoskeletal strain, symptoms such as eye strain, and
dissatisfaction were also highest among all-day users of terminals. However, no consistent
or significant differences in the levels of psychological symptoms (depression, anxiety,
hopelessness, irritation) were observed between the groups. Typists and clerical workers
who also held supervisory positions reported fewer stressors and greater job satisfaction
than workers with no supervisory tasks. However, there were no such differences between
supervisors and non-supervisors engaged in all-day VDU work with terminals.

Concerning full term VDU operators, the authors suppose that the potential advantage
of increased supervisory responsibilities may be annihilated when a worker is involved in
highly demanding, repetitive work. This group reported the highest mean levels of workload
demands and repetitiousness, and also the lowest mean levels of decision-making latitude,
ability to learn new things on the job, understanding of the overall work process, and the
meaning of the material dealt with. Furthermore, full term users of terminals reported the
highest level of ergonomic sources of stress, although they had a greater ability to adjust
the height and back of their chairs in comparison to other groups.

The results of Stellmann et al. (1987) correspond with a study on insurance staff by
Johansson & Aronsson (1984), which showed that the highest level of stress was found
among those doing repetitive tasks and constant work with VDUs.

Differing from these results, Agervold (1987) found, in an investigation of a representative sample of 907 white-collar workers, that the incidence of mental fatigue, stress and

psychosomatic complaints was the same in the sub-groups working with or without new technology. A close comparison was carried out. The results indicated there was no correlation between the impairment of the psychological work enviroment and new technologies. On the contrary, there seemed to be some improvement in the quality of work, although this was combined with an increase in workload (pressure of work and mental strain). Concerning psychological strain, the only effect of working with new technology was a tendency of higher levels of mental fatigue. Stress and psychosomatic reactions, however, seemed to remain unaffected.

Only where technological changes resulted in a deterioration of working conditions (e.g. less personal influence, fewer cognitive demands, greater isolation, more pressure at work, higher mental and physical workload) did the study of Agervold (1987) show a decrease in the quality of work related to the level of stress. Agervold concludes that "new technology seems only to have negative consequences in terms of stress if it is combined with changes in important psychological aspects of work" (Agervold, 1987, p. 149). The results of this study indicate that the consequences of the introduction of new technology concerning job content, quality of work, influence, satisfaction and stress are determined by the kind of job and the degree of change in the organization of work, combined with changes in work pressure.

In a study investigating the impact of computer technology on work content, feedback, job control and mental strain in text preparation in printing shops, Kalimo & Leppänen (1985) found that subjects working with the most advanced technology assessed their mental activity and self-determination at work more positively than subjects whose tasks involved less advanced technology. The former subjects were more satisfied with their work than the others. Their tasks demanded more decision making and were more complex. Even for subjects with minimal initial task variety and challenge, however, Kalimo & Leppänen found that computer technology and the application of VDUs may increase performance feedback and quality control. Therefore, this kind of work was associated with a positive impact on the whole work setting and positive changes in the daily workload as well. The results of this investigation show that new technologies may diminish stress even when combined with simple tasks.

The summarized studies demonstrate that the impact of new technologies on stress and its consequences can be extremely varied. We should be careful not to attribute observed increases of stress reactions to new technologies *per se*. The results of studies taking into account the design of task demands, performance feedback and other mediating organizational factors show that these are more critical factors, which have to be designed carefully in the implementation process (Briner & Hockey, 1988; Frese & Brodbeck, 1989; Greif, 1986). Moreover, new technology provides the "option" for an improvement in working conditions (Ulich et al., 1989). Stress is expected to decline as a consequence.

Cross-sectional field research has often been criticized in that it can be misleading when it comes to causal inferences. Correlations between hypothetical stressors and stress reactions may result from hidden factors or even from a reversed causal relation (for example, a stress reaction may increase time pressure). The same is true for observed mean differences between groups. It is impossible to control all relevant conditions and factors which may influence the results of field studies. Therefore, controversial results should not be surprising. Researchers prefer longitudinal studies because here, at least, the chronological order of hypothetical causes and effects can be partly controlled. Although longitudinal studies demand higher and longer research investments, several studies of this kind have been conducted especially in the past decade. The following section summarizes the results of several longitudinal studies on the consequences of implementing new technologies.

11.3.2 Longitudinal Studies

Frese & Zapf (1987) investigated the impact of new technologies on qualification demands, decision latitude and stress within a longitudinal design. The study used two measurement phases, before and after the technological changes. In 1979, before the changes, 218 blue-collar workers in the German car and steel industry participated in a comprehensive survey. At that time hardly any computer-aided machines or robots were used in the workplaces. Six years later, in 1985, 166 subjects of the first sample were studied again.

In the study the changes between the following five groups of technological demands were compared:

1. Traditional jobs which had not experienced technological changes.
2. Computer-supported work without programming tasks.
3. Computer-supported work with some influence on the programming (but not practised by the employees themselves).
4. Computer-suported work with programming tasks.
5. Operators of industrial robots.

In their statistical analysis of standard scales of job demands, stressors and hypothetical resources mediating possible stress reactions, the authors found only some minor changes and differences. One result was a low but significant increase of job decision latitude for all groups, from 1979 to 1985, and also a minor but significant general decrease in time pressure and concentration demands, with the exception of group 4. Job satisfaction increased significantly for groups 3 and 4 after the changes.

The results of the study show that job demands, stressors and their relations to resources have remained stable over time for the different groups. The authors conclude that new technology has only a very low—if any—impact on changes of stress and resources. Workers who had a high level of time pressure or job discretion and complexity before the implementation of the new technology were selected for jobs with similar attributes after the change.

The study of Frese & Zapf (1987) raises the problem of interactions between the implementation of new technologies and personnel selection by the organization or by the process of self-selection. When introducing new and expensive computer-based technologies, the organization typically selects experts or volunteers with high ability. Therefore also in longitudinal studies a comparison of mean values of selected sample groups may be completely misleading. Comparing individual changes in their longitudinal study, Majchrzak & Cotton (1988) have shown that stress reactions can be found only for subjects with unfavourable starting conditions who face strong technological changes. Kühlmann (1988), in his longitudinal study, assessed individual attitudes of employees facing the implementation of new technologies and their expectations of negative changes. Immediately before the change most employees developed an optimistic attitude and seemed to underestimate the possible negative job changes in comparison to their later observations. This tendency to simplify and belittle unpredictable future difficulties could be interpreted as an important type of cognitive coping with future uncertainty. Such a way of coping seems to be an important ability facing new and unpredictable situations. But as Kühlmann (1988) has found, a critical group of employees who, before the changes, are very concerned and worried about whether they will be able to cope with the changes should get special psychological support.

While Frese & Zapf (1987), Majchrzak & Cotton (1988) and Kühlmann (1988) investigated the impact of the change before and after implementation of new technologies, Korunka et al. (1993) also included a comparison of different types of implementation processes in their longitudinal study. In addition to the possible stress reactions related to new technologies, the authors suppose that the process of implementation can be an important source of strain. The authors applied a longitudinal design with three measurement phases: (i) prior to implementation, (ii) during implementation, and (iii) one year after implementation. Strain reactions and satisfaction were assessed for all three times. In particular, stress induced by job content, organizational aspects and physical conditions of the environment were considered. The sample consisted of 279 employees either using computer-aided design (CAD) software, doing clerical work or carrying out telephone information tasks. To assess the style of the implementation process, the authors distinguished three property classes: (i) organization of the project, (ii) participation of employees, and (iii) training and supervision.

The results of the study by Korunka et al. (1993) show a significant increase of subjectively experienced stress over the three phases. Paired comparisons of the phases showed a significant increase of subjectively experienced stress, as well as a significant increase of dissatisfaction in the interval between phase (i) ("prior to implementation") and phase (ii) ("during the implementation"). Furthermore, with the exception of eye problems, a significant increase in physical complaints (neck pains, shoulder pains, back pains, pains in the arms and arrhythmic heart rate) was registered from phase (i) ("prior to the implementation") to phase (ii) ("during the implementation") and from phase (ii) to phase (iii) ("one year after the implementation"). The authors suppose that the major cause for this increase is likely to be found in an insufficient provision of ergonomic furnishings.

To analyse the effect of project organization and inclusion—participation of employees— Korunka et al. (1993) classified the sample into different dichotomized subgroups. The results showed an interaction between stress and participation. Stress following implementation decreased significantly in those companies that practised more active employee participation in the change process. On the other hand, no differences over the same period were observed in companies with lower participation. Moreover, inclusion generally resulted in higher ratings of satisfaction with the technological changes. Across the three measurement phases, satisfaction showed an interaction effect too. High participation led to a decrease while low inclusion led to an increase in dissatisfaction. Furthermore, the overall extent of physical complaints is attenuated by participation. The authors conclude: "It seems to be that a participatory managerial style may counteract any negative effects of the new technologies" (Korunka et al., 1995, p. 138).

Furthermore four job clusters linked to qualification demands were distinguished and analysed with regard to the degree of participation and the impact of the introduction of the new technologies. Employees in the more highly ranked job clusters (using "computer aided drawing" as they call it, and also "Clerical work") had more opportunities to participate in the implementation process than personnel of the less qualified clusters (Korunka et al., 1993, 1995). In the cluster with the lowest qualification ("Extremely monotonous work") most psychosomatic complaints and decreased job satisfaction were observed. This result corresponds to a similar outcome of the study of Agervold (1987), cited above. On the other hand the employees in the highly technological qualified cluster ("Computer aided drawing") showed an increase in job satisfaction and only slightly increased psychosomatic complaints after the introduction of new technologies (Korunka et al., 1995).

Korunka et al. underline that their results fit the model of Karasek (Karasek & Theorell, 1990), who postulate that the most strain is associated with high demands and low decision latitude. High employee participation in the implementation process appears to generate a higher level of acceptance and leads to a high degree of attenuation of subjectively experienced stress and dissatisfaction. On the other hand, low participation results in an increase of these variables.

Furthermore, Korunka et al. (1997) report preliminary results of a follow-up study about the effects of continuous implementation (implementation in workplaces already equipped with computers) of new technologies on employees. In a longitudinal research design, strain and dissatisfaction of employees were investigated in 5 of 10 different companies (only in 5 organizations had new information technologies already been installed). Compared to a control sample, employees in the implementation sample showed (two weeks after the implementation) an increase in subjectively experienced stress but not in dissatisfaction. Regarding the implementation subsamples at the individual level of different organizations, all samples except one followed the general pattern of an increase in subjectively experienced stress. In only one organization, however, was this difference statistically significant. Dissatisfaction increased in two organizations significantly. The authors emphasize that the reported effects of implementation are preliminary as no data on organizational contextual factors (e.g. implementation style, participation, type of training) were available at this stage of the study. To analyse the effects of job profiles and external workload, the employees were grouped into persons performing jobs characterized by low versus high decision latitude and with regard to high versus low external workload. Subjectively experienced stress caused by implementation only seemed to increase in workplaces with low decision latitude and high external workload. The marked statistical trend corresponds with the results of the first longitudinal study (Korunka et al., 1993, 1995). It seems worth mentioning that the subjectively experienced stress in general was higher for participants with high decision latitude in contrast to low decision latitude in the pre-implementation period whereas dissatisfaction was lower in this group. The preliminary results of the study of Korunka et al. (1997) suggest that not only the initial introduction of new technologies but also the continuous changes of information technologies affect employees' strain and satisfaction.

In an advanced analysis of the above mentioned follow-up study, Korunka & Vitouch (1999) investigated the impact of personal factors (individual differences, external workload), situational factors like job design (e.g. job complexity, decision latitude), implementation content factors on strain (psychosomatic complaints, subjectively experienced stress) and satisfaction using structural equation modelling. Implementation content factors were (i) adaptational demands of the employees due to the new technology (qualification, duration of training and changes in program functionality), (ii) software-ergonomic changes and (iii) participation. Because in some of the 10 organizations implementation was delayed or was not yet in operation at the second measurement point, a "control sample" was available. Data were collected during a period of one and a half to five and a half months before implementation and three to six months after implementation of information technology. It was assumed that personal and situational factors at the job design level have general effects on users' strain and satisfaction. Implementation content factors were supposed to have causal effects in users' strain and satisfaction. In a two-step model testing procedure with a base model, (i) the factorial structure of the dimensions of strain and satisfaction and (ii) the measurements before and after the implementation were tested. Following the authors, the base model confirms the scales used to measure stress reactions and satisfaction to be solid markers for their latent factor and proves their factorial structure as unchanged over time. A general implementation factor showed no significant effect. However, as expected, a significant influence of personal dimensions on strain and satisfaction was found: internal locus of control, higher self-esteem and positive attitudes towards information technologies were associated with job satisfaction and less strain. In a second model the implementation content factors were included and revealed significant effects on the changes in users' strain and satisfaction at the second measurement point. The second model shows that participation, adaptational demands and ergonomic software design are relevant factors explaining employees' reactions to technological change. Ergonomic software design is related to the change of the user interface: software implementations retaining a character-based interface showed strong negative effects on strain and satisfaction compared to implementations changing from character-based to graphical user interfaces.

Adaptational demands like changes in the users' qualification, duration of training, and changes in the softwares' functionality are inversely related to strain measures. Concerning employee participation, the authors state that the study provides additional support for the positive effects of user participation in the case of the continous implementation of new technologies. They conclude that in the case of IT implementations, increased attention should be paid to current developments in user interface design and to active participation of employees. Furthermore, adaptational demands should accompany the enhancement of employee qualifications.

Slightly positive effects of the implementation of new technologies are reported in some longitudinal Scandinavian studies investigating the implementation process of new technologies. In his review of several longitudinal studies carried out in the field of public service (state institutions), a bank, a library and an insurance company, Huuhtanen (1997) summarizes a positive overall impact of new technology on work content experienced by employees in all occupation and age groups. He states that new technologies seem to have more often increased than decreased those characteristics that are important for mental well-being at work: "Compared with the expectations before the change, the work has become more interesting and the employees felt that they could use their abilities better" (p. 397), although office tasks have become somewhat more difficult, and the work pace has increased.

Mixed results are presented by Järvenpää (1997), who conducted a longitudinal study over a 4-year period on the implementation of office automation at a district court. After the implementation, office workers perceived their jobs as slightly more interesting than before the implementation. Short-term mental strain was also slightly lower after the implementation, but this positive effect seemed to decrease over time. On the other hand, a slight increase in office workers' long-term strain (e.g. stomach symptoms, chest pain, restlessness, fatigue and eye symptoms) was observed but no effect relating to job satisfaction was found.

An important aspect regarding results of longitudinal studies on job design and stress was given by Carayon et al. (1995). The results of their 3-year longitudinal study investigating the relationship between job design variables and strain of office workers from a public service organization indicate that the relationship between job design and strain changes over time. At the first point of measurement, quantitative workload, work pressure and supervisor support were related to most measures of worker strain. At the second point supervisor support was related to all of the strain measures as well as task clarity except for one. Job future ambiguity, quantitative workload and job control were respectively related to six and four of the eight measures of worker strain. Eventually, at the last point of measurement, task clarity was related to seven, attention and job future ambiguity to five and job control to four measures of strain. The authors suggest that the lack of stability of the correlations between work stressors and worker strain may be due to changes in management or, more generally, that work environments and people may change over time. Due to this assumption they conclude that in theories of job design and worker strain we have to take into account the flexibility of working environments.

Summarizing the results of the cross-sectional and longitudinal field studies on the implementation of new technologies, there is, as in the results of the reported cross-sectional studies, no definite support for the simple assumption that the computer technologies *per se* might excert stress. Malfunctions of systems that have not been tested sufficiently by the manufacturer, and poor ergonomic design of hardware, software and ergonomic furnishings are problems, which in most cases can be reduced to a tolerable level by professional experts by means of usability engineering. Where stress reactions are found, they seem to result from negative interactions between technology and job demands (especially monotony and time pressure; Carayon, 1997, p. 325) or sources of stress resulting from demands parallel to the technological changes or insufficient training.

However, the most difficult practical problem is an increase in stress that can be observed as a consequence of an indaquate implementation process of new technologies. Most experts recommend as remedies user participation during the implementation process (Briner & Hockey, 1988; Huuhtanen, 1997; Karasek & Theorell, 1990; Korunka & Vitouch, 1999), concrete information in advance, redesign of work, and training of the employees to manage the complex and cyclic technological changes (Korunka & Vitouch, 1999). Possible practical implications are presented in the following section.

11.4 PRACTICAL IMPLICATIONS

The research result shows that technologies result in changes in the overall job design, and in learning opportunities that enhance human development. They may even reduce stress at work in the long run. In several studies where an impairment of well-being and health was found, it could be traced to problems of the strategy and process of the implementation. The impairment does not primarily result from technology, but from job design changes and excessive demands, or insufficient knowledge and education of the users But from many studies we also know that the inadequate ergonomic design of hardware or software may lead to negative stress reactions. Therefore, a safe strategy seems to be to apply a holistic approach which integrates prevention of all major problems and risk factors, especially: (i) a participative design of the innovation tempo and implementation process, (ii) user oriented hardware and software design together with (iii) a stress reducing job design and (iv) an adequate training programme, a personal help network system and a self-organizing knowledge management concept. The ideal vision is a learning organization whose members are able to actively design and manage all current and future technological and job changes. In the following subsections we will outline important aspects of the four components of our holistic approach.

11.4.1   Implementation Strategies

Field surveys and practical observations show that systematic implementation strategies of new computer technologies are rare (Bjørn-Andersen, 1985; Dzida et al., 1984; Hirschheim et al., 1985). As mentioned above, organizations often simply try to buy and apply the "best" technological system and "muddle through" the resulting organizational problems (Greif, 1991b).

We advocate the following strategy for implementation:

1. detailed information in advance;
2. active partcipation in the selection and (re)design of hardware and software;
3. active participation in task and job redesign;
4. learning to master the changes.

Detailed Information in Advance

Planned technological changes put many people into a state of uncertainty which can be accompanied by strong emotional reactions. Many questions arise concerning the consequences of the changes. They should be answered by credible and concrete information which shows how it will be possible to manage the demands step by step successfully.

Typical concrete questions are:

- Is my job still safe after the change or will technological rationalization render it obsolete?
- Will I be able to master or learn the new technology?
- Who will help me if I need help?
- What will happen if I am unable to adapt to these changes or less able than my colleagues?
- Which of my basic tasks and responsibilities will change?
- How about stress at work? How can I cope with any problem while learning the new technology and doing my work, at the same time?
- Will time pressure increase?
- Is there enough space for the new hardware and where will it be placed?
- Will the firm buy good ergonomic and easy to use systems?

The management should be prepared to give clear and satisfactory answers to such questions at the start of the change process. Personal explanation by colleagues and illustrative models are better than written official announcements or information transfer in large conferences. Change anxiety and stress will not be reduced by information which is subjectively rated as not reliable and credible. To attempt to hush up existing high risks is itself a risky strategy. People do not forget false predictions in such situations. It is easy to lose long-term credibility after such an attempt. It would be better to give reliable information about risks and combine it with an optimistic and courageous personal statement saying that it will be possible to manage the risks. In cases where the future consequences are unpredictable and really dangerous, it is often better for the whole organization to find a small team of volunteers to start a pilot study to test the consequences.

Model launch in the car industry is an example of complex technological changes in the production lines. Since new car models in the past were normally kept top secret, the car workers were not informed about the future job changes. Hofmann & Bungard (1995) have demonstrated the advantages of giving concrete information in advance regarding car model changes at different automobile plants. Before the start all workers were invited to inspect the new model and plans (after signing an obligation of secrecy). The results were very convincing. Nearly all workers turned up and participated willingly in the change processes. Many were even filled with enthusiasm about the future changes. The whole process was less stressful, with fewer conflicts, and was substantially shorter than any technological change in the companies before. This example shows that investing in concrete information in advance pays, reducing typical insecurities and negative attitudes of the people involved.

Active participation in the Selection and (Re)design of Hardware and Software

Adequate information in advance and positive attitudes towards technological changes promote active participation in the start-up phase of change. If possible, the people affected should participate in the selection of hardware and software for their future tasks. A possible way is to send a delegation of workers to an engineering fair or invite companies to stage an exhibition of different hardware and software systems for the people in the enterprise. This procedure not only helps to reduce psychological uncertainty but also supports better decisions based on the practical knowledge of the people involved. The retail companies are confronted with the concrete practical demands of the users before the sale is effected. As a result, the hardware and software may have to be redesigned according to these demands before the application. Typical expenses for subsequent improvement services after purchasing are lowered (for concepts of partipative hardware and software design see Section 11.4.2).

Active Participation in Task and Job Redesign

The application of computer-based technologies, at least in the long run, is nearly always followed by changes of tasks, and sometimes even by changes of jobs and whole organization processes and structures. Active participation in job and task redesign is a strategy that helps to avoid insecurity and any opposition that may result from unknown future changes. A further advantage of active participation is that the practical expert knowledge of the people affected by the changes can be used in the process of job and task redesign (see Section 11.4.3).

Participation is rarely an easy process. Especially where the expected technological and organizational changes are large and where people see a risk of losing their acquired status, discussions between management and employees or group members with different interests can raise or enlarge conflicts. Our experience is that in such situations it seems to be preferable to apply a systematic strategy. The steps of the strategy have to be adapted to the management and to employee demands and competences. The following seven-step partcipation strategy gives an example which according to our experience works with an organization whose management and employees are open for participation.

1. Start-up information presented by the management and discussion of the goals, financial aspects and policy scope of the management decisions.
2. Individual interviews with active organizational members selected from all levels and departments involved (personal information, inventory and scaling of present tasks, expected advantages and disadvantages of new technology, threats and problems, suggestions for improvements and conflict resolutions).
3. Parallel workshop discussions about the interview results with the top management, the works council and the organizational members (problems, threats or conflicts and, especially, suggestions for their resolution should be described as clearly as possible).
4. Decision by top management on the redefinition of the goals and scope for the resulting participative problem solving process.
5. Establishment of one or more small problem solving groups (experts from all relevant departments and different opinions) for the development of solutions.
6. Parallel workshop discussions about of the solutions (management, works council and organizational members), leading to further suggestions for improvements.
7. Management decision on the planned changes and information of the employees.

The role of psychologists and consultants of other disciplines who accompany the process is that of process and project management coaches. They should try to help the participants to cope with stressful situations typical to many change processes: extreme complexity, high time urgency and power conflicts. They should also try to solve communication problems and should create the best possible team atmosphere to promote mutual information, trust, constructive participation, self-efficacy and common problem solving. Often for the survival of the organization in conjunction with the new technology very radical changes of key processes and structures in the organization are necessary which go beyond task and job changes. Important among other factors (Boonstra, in press; Greif et al., 1998) in complex change management processes are refined and effective change management team organizations, and specialized professional knowledge. The steps of the change management process may be similar to technology and task changes, but a systematic education in project management, instruments of analysis, problem solving techniques and perhaps stress management techniques would be useful for the team members.

Learning to Master the Changes

Early research results on success and failure of change management projects show that the risk of failing is very high. A study by Boonstra (2000) on change processes in the Netherlands showed that more than 70% of the change programmes that actually started led to insufficient results. Clegg (2000) reports that the majority of technological change projects do not reach their goals. Failure can result in existential crisis situations and is always an extremely stressful threat for all people involved. Nevertheless technological changes cannot be ignored. At least in the supplier industry, following the international ISO 9000 series, compatible new production and information technology are demanded by the industrial customers. Therefore, learning to master urgent and complex periodical or continuous changes becomes a core competence of the organization members. Where possible, to reduce stress reactions, the organization should start small and manageable change projects applied as pilot learning encounters for future changes.

As the research literature cited above shows, concrete information in advance and active participation in the design of hardware and software, as well as in the design of tasks, and new jobs will help to manage the threats of technological change and its consequences. However, individuals still may remain anxious and may doubt whether they will be able to master the change. Although there are no clear research results indicating substantial anxiety due to technological innovations (Kühlmann, 1988), people who fail to master technological change may be concerned about losing their jobs and therefore posssibly will hesitate to admit fears of making errors or of failure and avoid necessary training as long as possible. In Section 11.4.4 we describe learning approaches that have been successfully applied in training complex software systems and error management.

11.4.2   Hardware and Software Design

As mentioned above, inappropriate hardware and software design may lead to errors or regulation obstacles and consequently to stress reactions. Therefore the design of usable software may be considered as a means of stress prevention. The design of usable software is the topic of usability engineering (Nielsen, 1993).

Usability engineering is concerned with the systematic integration of methods and techniques of building usable software in the system development process. It can be characterized as a process which covers the definition and the measurement of product usability in general (Wixon & Wilson, 1997, p. 654). Usability engineering requires a software engineering model, which allows revisions and feedback loops. These models include prototyping approaches, iterative system design and user participation (Gould, 1988; Mayhew, 1999; Wixon & Wilson, 1997). Models of usability engineering are often subdivided into three phases (Gould, 1988; Mayhew, 1999; Nielsen, 1993).

Phase 1: Analysis and Specification

The first step—the "gearing-up" phase—starts with preparatory activities, such as choosing general principles for the design, for example, relevant standards, development models and tools. In the next step, the "requirements analysis" is concerned with the characterization of users and the set-up of user profiles; additionally, task and work flow have to be analysed. The obtained information is used to plan the activities of the "work re-engineering" and for the design of the user interface.

Phase 2: Iterative Development

The results of the preceeding phase are used to design the organizational and work flow part of the system. In this phase it should be remembered that the design and introduction of computer systems are considered as a part of job design and should therefore be seen in an organizational context (Zapf, 1995, S. 72; see above "Active participation in job and task design"). Conceptual models are developed which can be used to produce early prototyps, for instance paper and pencil prototypes or mock-ups. Using an iterative and participative design approach, the prototypes are evaluated and changed continuously by means of user testing (Rubin, 1994) or inspection methods (Nielsen & Mack, 1994). This helps to identify and remove major usability bugs. The evaluation–(re)design cycle is repeated until the goals of the user-centred design are fulfilled. It is recommended to utilize user participation in all phases of the design process (see ISO/DIS 13407). The product can be evaluated to ascertain whether it fulfils the user-orientated requirements and/or whether it is in accordance with other international standards such as ISO 9241 (for an overview on software evaluation, see Gediga et al., 2002).

Phase 3: System Installation

The final phase is concerned with system installation and user training. Furthermore, the acceptance of the system has to be assured, and system support and maintenance must be organized. Software evaluation procedures in the application phase have to be planned in order to obtain feedback about the usability of the system. This information can be used for the design of new releases. A revision of the system could be indicated after some time of application. In such a case a new version of the software should be designed corresponding to the principles of the phases of usability engineering.

Furthermore, the design of software and especially the human–computer interface should consider knowledge from the research field of human–computer interaction (Helander et al., 1997; Shneiderman, 1998; Wandmacher, 1993). We cannot give a detailed overview at this time but some important design aspects should be mentioned. The design—or redesign—of software systems should avoid too much complexity (Shneiderman, 1998). A reduction of complexity, while maintaining sufficient features of the system, may be achieved by the modularization of the system, for example, into task-related components. Complexity, moreover, may be decreased if software systems are adaptable to task and user requirements (Greif, 1994; Haaks, 1992). To anticipate and minimize errors, a consistent system structure and design, unambiguous and clearly available feedback about the state of the system, and reversiblity of actions should be realized (Brodbeck & Rupietta, 1994; Norman, 1983, 1988; Rasmussen & Vicente, 1989). Zapf (1995) emphasizes that tools supporting error handling can be a contribution to coping with stress. In particular he mentions backup files, undo functions and context-sensitive help.

Hardware and software system design has to be integrated with task, job and organization design. For example, task requirements have to be considered when the functionality of a system is defined. We have applied a combined technique for an intensive micro-analysis and redesign of individual tasks and software systems, called "heterarchic task analysis" (Greif,

1991b; Hamborg & Greif, 1999). Based on logfile records, video (up to three cameras) and self-confronting techniques, the individual mental model of a given task and of the software system, together with associated thoughts, emotional problems and design suggestions are assessed in an interview. The outcome of this analysis provides a starting point for the design or redesign of tasks and software systems. In the future electronic business economy, success of the whole organization will depend on a perfect customer-orientated internet design Especially the design of the human-interface will be crucial in this field. Furthermore, the customers using technologies like the internet will expect high-speed services. Peaks of unpredictable high runs of customers and high time pressure will pose a new challenge to concepts of flexible job and organization design solutions. Perhaps new technologies will be needed to reduce such time pressure in future electronic business firms.

11.4.3   Task and Job Design

Semmer (1984), as menioned in Section 11.2.2 identified three major groups of stressors at work. These can be applied to task and job design:

1. Additional demands on the action regulation process. For example, time pressure should be reduced to a manageable level. For complex tasks a compromise between accessibility to the customer and periods of uninterrupted work should be found.
2. Overload or blurred performance feedback which results in insecurity or insufficient control for the employees. Training the feedback behaviour of leaders is a standard solution to this problem. It is also useful to encourage the employees to demand clear feedback.
3. Conflicting goals or lack of task and role clarity. Sometimes it is a very difficult and time consuming task to design clear quality standards or decision rules in order to reduce conflicts between goals (like time pressure and quality). Total quality management handbooks as an ideal should define such standards and rules, and measurement criteria. But often these handbooks increase stress reactions by impractical demands. If the tasks require adaptive and flexible individual decisions or creativity, it would be better to admit that it is impossible to formulate clear rules. Here open heuristic rules explained by concrete examples and a supportive personal help network (people who can be asked to discuss a decision case) might be a possible solution.

Goal setting is a very well-known management technique, but in practice it is often difficult to operationalize adequate performance goals and therefore feedback becomes difficult too. Here, the construction and implementation of a behaviourally anchored performance feedback system (like ProMES; Pritchard, 1990) may be an optimal basis for both clear goals and feedback.

Warr (1987) in his *vitamin model* of general environmental influences of work upon mental health describes nine principal features which can be applied to task and job design:

1. Opportunity for control (decision latitude and influence of the employees, to choose their objectives, to schedule their tasks and rules of performance, and to predict the consequences of action).
2. Opportunity for skill use (the degree to which the utilization and development of skills is required by the job).

3. Externally generated goals (the degree to which the environment makes demands upon the employee).
4. Variety (occurence of repetitive and invariant routine actions or diverse and novel situations).
5. Environmental clarity (availability of feedback information about the results of one's actions, certainty and clarity of role expectations and requirements).
6. Availabilty of money (low or high income).
7. Physical security (protection against physical threat, security of tenure and job safety in the work market).
8. Opportunity for interpersonal contact (loneliness versus friendship contacts, social support, opportunities to compare one's opinions and abilities with other people).
9. Valued social position (esteem from other people within social networks).

Warr (1987) differentiates between two kinds of relationship between the environmental features and mental health: (i) the first group of features shows a positive effect on health up to a certain level, but not beyond it; (ii) the second group also has a positive effect on health up to a certain point. But after this point the features have a damaging effect on health. Features 6 (availability of money), 7 (physical security) and 9 (valued social position) belong to the first group. All other features can be classified into the second group. Depending on individual differences, these features should not be raised to an extreme demand level in order to avoid harmful consequences. For example, if the maximum individual capacity level of the opportunity for control or for skill is exceeded, this will result in difficult decision making or tasks. The individual will suffer from overload strain.

The research on stress and implementation of new technologies and task design mentioned in this chapter advocates participative strategies. Other authors developed methods and strategies of task and job design, which can be transferred to this field of application. Following Emery & Emery (1976), Ulich (1991) recommends a method called *Subjektive Arbeitsanalyse* (SAA) (subjective job analysis; Udris & Alioth, 1980). Here the whole process of analysis and task or job redesign is performed by the members of the work groups involved. The group members perform the following four steps, moderated by an expert:

1. Analysis and evaluation of the present work activities by using scales of psychological job dimensions (e.g. decision making, variety, learning, mutual support and respect, meaningfulness, desirable future);
2. development of individual suggestions for improvement;
3. assessment of training demands;
4. development of a group training programme.

Ulich and his co-workers (Ulich, 1991) have successfully applied this strategey of active participation to the implementation of team work by semi-autonomous work groups and also to technological changes. The basic assumption of their approach is a holistic design of task and work environments which results in highly motivativated work, efficient and flexible human performance and development, and also in the long run contributes to physical and mental health. The goal is not only to prevent harmful consequences. The vision is to study and support the development of positive human health resources. Rimann & Udris (1997) have constructed a special instrument called *Salutogenetische*

Subjektive Arbeitsanalyse (SALSA) (salutogenetic subjective job analysis, using the Italian word *salute*, meaning means "health") for this purpose. It combines typical scales applied in standard instruments of stress orientated job analysis questionnaires and scales for the assessment of organizational resources (task variety, learning demands, decision latitude and control, participation, individual influence on job design, scope to develop personal interests at work) and social resources (social climate, employee orientated leadership behaviour, social support by the leader, social support by the team). The authors recommend applying their instrument as a part of a holistic and multilevel analysis of the work system as well as a participative organizational development concept (Strohm & Ulich, 1997). Other authors also advocate the future integration of stress orientated job analysis and redesign into comprehensive preventive health strategies for the whole organization (Bamberg et al., 1998) or Total Quality Management (Zapf & Dormann, 2001).

11.4.4   Learning Environments, Error Management and Personal Help Networks

After implementation of new technologies, a routine procedure in most organizations is to send the employee to a training seminar in the field. The participants are expected to acquire the knowledge and skills by professional instruction and by feedback from a trainer. In addition, we recommend the design of psychological learning environments, which support active and successful self-organizing learning activities, self-efficacy and self-confidence when interacting with new and sometimes complex or permanently changing technologies. Studies on errors in human–computer interaction (Prümper, 1991) have shown that not only novices but also experts make errors. Errors give rise to quick emotional reactions like anger or even helplessness (Krone et al., 2000). Therefore, it is important to train employees in the detection and management of error situations (Frese, 1991b).

Novices should not always fall back upon their trainer or team when they meet a problem that they can try to manage by themselves. However, if the problem is too complex or if the consequences of errors cannot be eliminated, novices should ask for personal help. Social support is also a potential factor for reducing stress reactions. Like Carroll & Mack (1983), we tried to activate self-organized exploratory behaviour in the learning process using "minimal guidelines" for self-instruction instead of handbooks and teacher centred instruction methods. Since we concentrate especially on the exploration of error situations we call our learning concept "exploratory learning by errors" (Greif, 1986, 1994; for a description and empirical comparison of different error training approaches, see Irmer et al., 1991).

"Make mistakes! You can learn from your mistakes!" is our message at the beginning of a training session. By this we try to encourage our subjects to develop a more relaxed problem solving attitude to error situations and to learn by actively exploring these situations. How the trainer reacts to the first enquiries for help is very important. The learner should develop the impression that his or her errors are interesting and represent important learning opportunities.

It is very impressive to observe how radically the attitudes towards errors change in a course where the trainer reacts sensitively to errors, shows interest, comments on the problem solving strategies, and draws the attention of the other participants to an interesting error situation. The learner who makes an "interesting" error sometimes even seems to be proud of it, openly discussing the problem and testing different solutions without signs of stress. This can be supported by systematic instruction aimed at applying checklists or heuristic schemata for error diagnosis and problem solving or error management. The trainer is instructed not to help the learner by giving direct information on the solution of problems but to encourage the subjects to use these schemata autonomously. Following stress inoculation training (Meichenbaum, 1974) we prefer a gradual psychological immunization strategy. Learning to manage errors successfully reduces emotional strain (anxiety or anger reactions) and feelings of helplessness in unavoidable error situations. Instead of relying solely on online help systems in the program or on hotline telephone help, we try to establish mutual personal social support in the training courses and encourage the people to develop personal help networks at the workplace.

For practical use, the initial design of exploratory learning environments that are optimal for different learners is a rather difficult task. Our solution is to combine the design of minimal guidelines for self-instruction and exploratory learning tasks. We allow for individual differences. The individuals can choose between learning resources and can determine the level of system and task complexity and the speed of learning for themselves. According to theory (Greif & Keller, 1990), they have the opportunity to control the level of novelty and complexity in the exploration, facilitating the development of skills, and self-efficacy. This might encourage future exploratory learning, creativity and role innovation (Farr & Ford, 1990).

Exploratory learning by errors and self-organized learning approaches have been evaluated by several experimental studies and training courses for novices (different word processor software systems and multifunctional office packages; see Greif, 1994). The results show clearly that most novices, after exploratory learning by errors, are able to perform complex tasks successfully (see Irmer et al., 1991, for similar results relating to error management training). A clear advantage of self-organized learning is that it initiates personal help networks and social support between colleagues and autonomous exploratory learning on the job. Evidence from a follow-up study demonstrates that after the training most subjects were able to learn new complex software systems quickly on their own (Greif, 1994). The approach has been integrated into a broad self-organizing and organizational learning concept (Greif & Kurtz, 1998). It has been successfully applied to diverse application fields, including leadership and team learning, technological and communication skills.

For example, in team learning of call centre agents (Peukmann & Peukmann, 2001) we applied "minimal information" (short written information on special subjects, like fast internet connections; for a description of standards on how to write and design them, see Greif & Kurtz, 1998) instead of standard classroom instruction techniques. In order to stimulate active acquisition of technological knowledge the participants were asked to read the information and actively explore the technical system and to present it to the other team members in an entertaining way. Communication skills are trained by role playing through "minimal guidelines" (very short self-instructions or descriptions of heuristic procedures; see Greif & Kurtz, 1998) and video self-confrontation techniques. From the beginning of the seminar we stimulate the development of mutual help networks. The participants are encouraged to design minimal information and minimal guidelines for important and difficult tasks. They are accessible for everyone in the knowledge management system. The impressive results of the study show that there is a substantial increase of knowledge and communication skills assessed by calls of trained test customers, and also self-efficacy, team climate and mutual helping (Peukmann & Peukmann, 2001). In three teams apparently the situation changed from a general climate of stress and isolated helplessness to one of mutual support in the team. The test customers observed much more friendly, skilled and self-confident communication behaviour. The example shows that radical changes of helplessness are possible by adequate learning and supporting environments. It is not far from the ideal vision of a "salutogenic" (or healthiness supporting; see above) learning organization whose members are able to actively design and manage relevant current and future technological and job changes participatively, successfully and self-confidently.

11.5 CONCLUSIONS

In summary, the results of both experimental and field research show that new technology is not a source of stress *per se*. There is no study that would prove such a simple assumption. On the contrary, in many studies on different factors and on the overall impact of new technologies, we find groups of employees where stress remains constant or even declines following the implementation of new computer systems at work. However, stress may result from many concrete problems like malfunction and lack of usability of systems that have not been tested sufficiently, excessive complexity, poor ergonomic design of hardware and software equipment and furnishings, insufficient training or psychologically unsatisfying design of task demands and job roles.These problems in most cases can be reduced to a tolerable level by active participation in the (re)design of technological and organizational systems, and active self-organizing learning.

Cross-sectional and longitudinal studies on the overall impact of technological changes on mental health show that the basic problem is an inadequate implementation of the technological changes. It is essential to provide credible and concrete information in advance and to promote active employee participation. Participation should embrace the analysis and design of the job, the technology and the resulting changes. If the risk of negative consequences is high, small pilot tests should be carried out together with the promotion of active self-organizing learning processes, knowledge management and mutual help networks. Last but not least, enough time to adapt psychologically to the changes should be set aside.

We propose a holistic and participative implementation strategy to master all kinds of changes:

1. detailed information in advance;
2. active partcipation in the selection and (re)design of hardware and software;
3. active participation in task and job redesign;
4. design of active self-organizing learning environments and help systems.

The goal is to provide the employees with the necessary information, technology, task and organizational structures, knowledge and competences to manage the planned innovation. This prevents long-term stress reactions resulting from malfunctions, uncertainty, complexity and newness of the changes.

Learning how to manage technological or other changes in the organization by actively participating in the design of hardware and software, tasks and jobs, and learning environments is a very important investment of innovative organizations. It should be planned very carefully. The vision is a learning organization which is able to adapt to all relevant change demands, and which in the long run supports the development of human resources and health.

Today, computer systems are standard technologies in modern industries and administration, but technological innovation does not stop. The innovation tempo of computer hardware and software has accelerated. Therefore, "stress by permanent changes" is an emerging problem that should be observed carefully. From the results of the field studies cited above, we may infer that stress will be lower for those organizations that are able to manage quick adaptation processes with the active participation of their employees. The best practical recommendation to cope with the complexity and novelty of technological and organizational changes is to invest in the participation, competence and networks of the employees. Also exploratory and self-organized learning on the job appears to be a psychologically adequate solution. Still in the future new technologies and stress will remain a complex problem.

REFERENCES

Agervold, M. (1987). New technology in the office: attitudes and consequences. *Work and Stress*, **2**, 143–53.

Bamberg, E., Ducki, A. & Metz, A.-M. (eds) (1998). *Handbuch betriebliche Gesundheitsförderung*. Göttingen: Verlag für Angewandte Psychologie.

Benda, H. von. (1990). Information und Kommunikation im Büro. In C. Graf Hoyos & B. Zimolong (eds) *Enzyklopädie der Psychologie D III/2. Ingenieurpsychologie*. Göttingen: Hogrefe, pp. 479–510.

Bergmann, B. & Wiedemann, J. (1994). Lernbedarfsanalysen bei der Störungsdiagnose und -behebung in der flexibel automatisierten Fertigung. *Zeitschrift für Arbeitswissenschaft*, **48** (20NF), 217–24.

Bjørn-Andersen, N. (1985). Training for subjection or participation. In B. Shackel (ed.) *Human–Computer Interaction—Interact '84*. Amsterdam: North Holland, pp. 839–46.

Boonstra, J. (2000). De zinsloosheid van HRM bij organisatieverendering. *Tijdschrift voor HRM*, **3**, 25–51.

Boonstra, J.J. (in press). Dynamics of organizational change and learning.

Boucsein, W. (1988). Wartezeiten am Rechner—Erholung oder Streß? *Zeitschrift für Arbeitswissenschaft*, *42(4)*, 222–25.

Briner, R. & Hockey, R.J. (1988). Operator stress and computer-based work. In C.L. Cooper & R. Payne (eds) *Causes, Coping and Consequences of Stress at Work*. Chichester: John Wiley & Sons, pp. 115–40.

Brodbeck, F.C. & Rupietta, W. (1994). Fehlermanagement und Hilfesysteme. In: E. Eberleh, H. Oberquelle & R. Oppermann (eds) *Einführung in die Software-Ergonomie*. Berlin: de Gruyter, pp. 197–234.

Buchanan, D.A. & Boddy, D. (1982). Advanced technology and the quality of working life: the effects of word processing on video typists. *Journal of Occupational Psychology*, **55**, 1–11.

Çakir, A. (1981). Belastung und Beanspruchung bei Bildschirmtätigkeiten. In M. Frese (ed.). *Streß im Büro*. Bern: Huber, pp. 46–71.

Carayon, P. (1993). Job design and job stress in office workers. *Ergonomics*, **36**(5), 463–77.

Carayon, P. (1997). Temporal issues of quality of working life and stress in human–computer interaction. *International Journal of Human–Computer Interaction*, **9**(4), 325–42.

Carayon, P., Yang, C.-L. & Lim, S.-Y. (1995). Examining the relationship between job design and worker strain over time in a sample of office workers. *Ergonomics*, **38**(6), 1199–1211.

Carroll, J. (1985). Minimals design for the active user. In: B. Shackle (ed.), *Human–Computer Interaction—Interact '84*. Amsterdam: North-Holland, pp. 39–44.

Carroll, J.M. (ed.) (1991). *Psychological Theory in Human–Computer Interaction*. New York: Cambridge University Press.

Carroll, J.M. & Mack, R.L. (1983). Active learning to use a word processor. In: W.E. Cooper (ed.) *Cognitive Aspects of Skilled Typewriting*. Berlin: Springer-Verlag, pp. 259–82.

Clegg, C. (2000). Technological changes. Contribution to the Conference on Change Management organized jointly by the Unit Work and Organizational Psychology of Giessen University and Andersen Consulting. Giessen, 23 September 2000 (unpublished).

Dutke, S. & Schönpflug, W. (1987). When the introductory period is over: learning while doing one's job. In M. Frese, E. Ulich & W. Dzida (eds) *Psychological Issues of Human–Computer Interaction.* Amsterdam: North-Holland, pp. 295–310.

Dzida, M., Langenheder, W., Cornelius, D. & Schardt, L.P. (1984). Auswirkungen des EDV-Einsatzes auf die Arbeitssituation und Möglichkeiten einer arbeitsorientierten Gestaltung. St. Augustin: *GMD-Studie, no. 82.*

Emery, F.E. & Emery, M. (1976). *Democracy at Work.* Leiden: Martinus Nijhoff.

Farr, J. & Ford, C.M. (1990). Individual innovation. In M. West & J. Farr (eds) *Innovation and Creativity at Work: Psychological Approaches.* New York: John Wiley & Sons, pp. 63–80.

Frese, M. (1989). Human computer interaction within an industrial psychology framework. *Applied Psychology: An International Review,* **38**(1), 29–44.

Frese, M. (1991a). Streß und neue Techniken. Was ändert sich?. In S. Greif, E. Bamberg & N. Semmer (eds). *Psychischer Streß am Arbeitsplatz.* Göttingen: Hogrefe, pp. 120–34.

Frese, M. (1991b). Fehlermanagement: Konzeptionelle Überlegungen. In M. Frese & D. Zapf (eds) *Fehler bei der Arbeit mit dem Computer.* Bern: Huber, pp. 139–50.

Frese, M. & Brodbeck, F.C. (1989). *Computer in Büro und Verwaltung.* Heidelberg: Springer-Verlag.

Frese, M. & Semmer, N. (1991). Streßfolgen in Abhängigkeit von Moderatorvariablen: Der Einfluß von Kontrolle und sozialer Unterstützung. In S. Greif, E. Bamberg & N. Semmer (eds). *Psychischer Streß am Arbeitsplatz.* Göttingen: Hogrefe, pp. 135–53.

Frese, M. & Zapf, D. (1987). Die Einführung von neuen Techniken verändert Qualifikationsanforderungen, Handlungsspielraum und Stressoren kaum. *Zeitschrift für Arbeitswissenschaft,* **41**(13 NF) (1), 7–14.

Frese, M., Brodbeck, F., Heinbokel, T., Moser, C., Schleiffenbaum, E. & Thiemann, P. (1991a). Errors in training computer skills: on the positive function of errors. *Human–Computer Interaction,* **6**, 77–93.

Frese, M. Irmer, C. & Prümper, J. (1991b). Das Konzept Fehlermanagement: Eine Strategie des Umgangs mit Handlungsfehlern in der Mensch-Computer-Interaktion. In M. Frese, Chr. Kasten, C. Skarpelis & B. Zang-Scheucher (eds) *Software für die Arbeit von morgen.* Berlin: Springer-Verlag, pp. 241–52.

Gediga, G., Hamborg, K.-C. & Düntsch, I. (2002). Evaluation of software systems. In A. Kent & J. G. Williams (eds) *Encyclopedia of Computer Science and Technology,* vol. 45, supplement 30. New York: Marcel Dekker, pp. 127–53.

Gould, J. D. (1988). How to design usable systems. In M. Helander (ed) *Handbook of Human Computer Interaction,* 1st edn. Amsterdam. Elsevier, pp. 757–89.

Greif, S. (1986). Neue Kommunikationstechnologien-Entlastung oder mehr Streß? In K.-K. Pullig, U. Schäkel & J. Scholz (eds) *Streß im Unternehmen.* Hamburg: Windmühle GmbH Verlag, pp. 178–99.

Greif, S. (1991a). Streß in der Arbeit-Einführung und Grundbegriffe. In S. Greif, E. Bamberg & N. Semmer (eds) *Psychischer Streß am Arbeitsplatz.* Göttingen: Hogrefe, pp. 1–28.

Greif, S. (1991b). Organisational issues and task analysis. In B. Shackel & S. Richardson (eds) *Human Factors for Informatics Usability.* Cambridge: Cambridge University Press, pp. 247–67.

Greif, S. (1994). Fehlertraining und Komplexität beim Softwaredesign. *Zeitschrift für Arbeitswissenschaft,* **48**(20NF), 44–53.

Greif, S. & Keller, H. (1990). Exploratory behavior in human–computer interaction. In M. West & J. Farr (eds) *Innovation and Creativity at Work: Psychological Approaches.* New York: John Wiley & Sons, pp. 231–50.

Greif, S. & Kurtz, H.-J. (eds) (1998). *Handbuch Selbstorganisiertes Lernen* 2nd edn. Göttingen: Verlag für Angewandte Psychologie. 2nd edn

Greif, S., Schiffer, P., Bemmann, P., Offermanns, M., Kluge, S. Krone, Th. & Domcke, J. (1998). Erfolg und Misserfolg von Veränderungen nach Erfahrungen von Insidern. Bericht eines Studienprojekts, Universität Osnabrück, Fachbereich Psychologie, unpublished report http://www.psycho.uni-osnabrueck.de/fach/aopsych/www/profil.htm.

Haaks, D. (1992). *Anpaßbare Informationssysteme.* Göttingen: Verlag für Angewandte Psychologie.

Hamborg, K.-C. (1996). Zum Einfluß der Komplexität von Software-Systemen auf Fehler bei Computernovizen und Experten. *Zeitschrift für Arbeits- und Organisationspsychologie*, **40**(1), 3–11.

Hamborg, K.-C. & Greif, S. (1999). Heterarchische Aufgabenanalyse. In: H. Dunckel (eds) *Handbuch psychologischer Arbeitsanalyseverfahren*. Zürich: vdf, Hochschulverlag, pp. 147–77.

Helander, M., Landauer, T.K. & Prabhu, P. (eds) (1997). *Handbook of Human–Computer Interaction*, 2nd completely rev. edn. Amsterdam: Elsevier Science.

Hirschheim, R.A., Land, F.F. & Smithson, S. (1985). Implementing computer-based information systems in organisations: issues and strategies. In B. Shackel (ed.) *Human–Computer Interaction—Interact '84*. Amsterdam: North Holland, pp. 855–62.

Hofmann, K. & Bungard, W. (1995). Modellwechsel in der Automobilindustrie. In H.J. Warnecke (ed.) *Aufbruch in fraktalen Unternehmen—Praxisbeispiele für Denken und Handeln*. Heidelberg: Springer-Verlag.

Huuhtanen, P. (1997). Toward a multilevel model in longitudinal studies on computerization in offices. *International Journal of Human–Computer Interaction*, **9**(4), 383–405.

Irmer, C., Pfeffer, S. & Frese, M. (1991). Konsequenzen von Fehleranalysen für das Training: Das Fehlertraining. In M. Frese & D. Zapf (eds) *Fehler bei der Arbeit mit dem Computer*. Bern: Huber, pp. 151–65.

ISO (1997). EN ISO 9241-11. *Ergonomic requirements for office work with visual display terminals (VDTs)*. Part 11.

Järvenpää, E. (1997). Implementation of office automation and its effects on job charateristics and strain in a district court. *International Journal of Human–Computer Interaction*, **9**(4), 425–42.

Johansson, G. (1989). Stress, autonomy, and the maintenance of skill in supervisory control of automated systems. *Applied Psychology: An International Review*, **38**(1), 45–56.

Johansson, G. & Aronsson, G. (1984). Sress reactions in computerized administrative work. *Journal of Occupational Psychology*, **5**, 159–81.

Kalimo, R. & Leppänen, A. (1985). Feedback from video display terminals, performance control and stress in text preparation in the printing industry. *Journal of Occupational Psychology*, **58**, 27–38.

Karasek, R. & Theorell, T. (1990). *Healthy Work: Stress, Productivity and the Reconstruction of Working Life*. New York: Basic Books.

Korunka, C. & Vitouch, O. (1999). Effects of the implementation of information technology on employees' strain and job satisfaction: a context dependent approach. *Work and Stress*, **34**(4), 341–63.

Korunka, C., Weiss, A. & Karetta, B. (1993). Effects of new technologies with special regard for the implementation process per se. *Journal of Organizational Behavior*, **14**, 331–48.

Korunka, C., Weiss, A., Huemer, K.-H. & Karetta, B. (1995). The effect of new technologies on job satisfaction and psychosomatic complaints. *Applied Psychology: An International Review*, **44**(2), 123–42.

Korunka, C., Zauchner, S. & Weiss, A. (1997). New technologies, job profiles, and external workload as predictors of subjectively experienced stress and dissatisfaction at work. *International Journal of Human–Computer Interaction*, **9**(4), 407–24.

Krone, A., Hamborg, K.-C. & Gediga, G. (2000). *Untersuchungen zu emotionalen Reaktionen bei Nutzungsfehlern in der Mensch-Computer Interaktion*. Posterausstellung. 42. Kongress der DGP, Friedrich-Schiller-Universität Jena.

Kühlmann, T.M. (1988). *Technische und organisatorische Neuerungen im Erleben betroffener Arbeitnehmer*. Stuttgart: Enke.

Lazarus, R.S. (1976). *Patterns of Adjustment*. New York: McGraw-Hill.

Leitner, K., Lüders, E., Greiner, B., Ducki, A., Nierdermeier, R. & Volpert, W. (1993). *Analyse psychischer Anforderungen und Belastungen in der Büroarbeit*. Göttingen: Hogrefe.

Levi, L. (1994). Work, worker and wellbeing: an overview. *Work and Stress*, **8**, 79–83.

Majchrzak, A. & Cotton, J. (1988). A longitudinal study of adjustment to technological change: from mass to computer-automated batch production. *Journal of Occupational Psychology*, **61**, 43–66.

Mayhew, D. (1999). *The Usability Engineering Lifecycle. A Practitioner's Handbook for User Interface Design*. San Francisco, CA: Morgan Kaufmann.

Meichenbaum, D. (1974). *Cognitive Behavior Modification*. Morristown, NJ: General Learning Corporation.

Mohr, G. (1991). Fünf Subkonstrukte psychischer Befindensbeeinträchtigung bei Industriearbeitern: Auswahl und Entwicklung. In S. Greif, E. Bamberg & N. Semmer (eds) *Psychischer Streß am Arbeitsplatz.* Göttingen: Hogrefe, pp. 91–119.

Nielsen, J. (1993). *Usability Engineering.* Boston, MA: AP Professional.

Nielsen, J. & Mack, R. L. (1994). *Usability Inspection Methods.* New York: John Wiley & Sons.

Norman, D.A. (1983). Design rules based on analyses of human error. *Communications of the ACM,* **26**(4), 254–8.

Norman, D.A. (1988). *The Psychology of Everyday Things.* New York: Basic Books.

Peukmann, K. & Peukmann, J. (2001). Selbstorganisiertes Lernen in einem Call Center, University of Osnabrueck, Work and Psychology Unit, unpublished thesis, in preparation.

Pritchard, R.D. (1990). *Measuring and Improving Organizational Productivity: A Practical Guide.* New York: Praeger.

Prümper, J. (1991). Handlungsfehler und Expertise. In M. Frese & D. Zapf (eds) *Fehler bei der Arbeit mit dem Computer.* Bern: Huber, pp. 118–30.

Rasmussen, J. & Vicente, K.J. (1989). Coping with human errors through system design: implications for ecological interface design. *International Journal of Man–Machine Studies,* **31**, 517–34.

Reason, J.T. (1990). *Human Error.* New York: Cambridge University Press.

Rimann, M. & Udris, I. (1997). Subjektive Arbeitsanalyse: Der Fragebogen SALSA. In O. Strohm & E. Ulich (eds) *Unternehmen arbeitspsychologisch bewerten—Ein Mehrebenen-Ansatz unter besonderer Berücksichtigung von Mensch Technik und Organisation.* Zürich: vdf Hochschulverlag, pp. 281–98.

Rubin, J. (1994). *Handbook of Usability Testing.* New York: John Wiley & Sons.

Saupe, R. & Frese, M. (1981). Faktoren für das Erleben und die Bewältigung von Streß im Schreibdienst. In M. Frese (ed.) *Streß im Büro.* Bern: Huber, pp. 199–224.

Sauter, S.L., Gottlieb, M.S., Jones, K.C., Dodsen, V. & Rohrer, K.M. (1983). Job and health implications of VDT use: initial results of the Wisconsin NIOSH study. *Communications of the ACM,* **26**, 284–94.

Sauter, S.L., Schleifer, L.M. & Knutson, S.J. (1991). Work posture, workstation design and musculoskeletal discomfort in a VDT data entry task. *Human Factors,* **33**, 151–67.

Schönpflug, W. (1989). Streß bei Verwaltungsarbeiten. In S. Greif, H. Holling & N. Nicholson (eds) *Arbeits- und Organisationspsychologie. Internationales Handbuch in Schlüsselbegriffen.* München: PVU.

Schulz, P. & Höfert, W. (1981). Wirkungsmechanismen und Effekte von Zeitdruck bei Angestelltentätigkeiten. In M. Frese (ed.). *Streß im Büro.* Bern: Huber, pp. 72–95.

Semmer, N. (1984*). Streßbezogene Tätigkeitsanalyse: Psychologische Untersuchungen zur Analyse von Streß am Arbeitsplatz.* Weinheim: Beltz.

Shneiderman, B. (1998). *Designing the User Interface. Strategies for Effective Human–Computer Interaction,* 3rd edn. Reading, MA: Addison-Wesley.

Stellman, J.M., Klitzman, S., Gordon, G.C. & Snow, B.R. (1987). Work environment and the well-being of clerical and VDT workers. *Journal of Occupational Behaviour,* **8**, 95–114.

Strohm, O. & Ulich, E. (eds) (1997). *Unternehmen arbeitspsychologisch bewerten – Ein Mehrebenen-Ansatz unter besonderer Berücksichtigung von Mensch Technik und Organisation.* Zürich: vdf Hochschulverlag.

Turner, J.A. & Karasek, R.A. (1984). Software ergonomics: effects of computer application design parameters on operator task performance and health. *Ergonomics,* **27**(6), 663–90.

Udris, I. (1989). Soziale Unterstützung. In: S. Greif, H. Holling & N. Nicholson (eds) *Arbeits- und Organisationspsychologie. Internationales Handbuch in Schlüsselbegriffen.* München: PVU, pp. 421–5.

Udris, I. & Alioth, A. (1980). Fragebogen zur "Subjektiven Arbeitsanalysse" (SAA). In E. Martin, I. Udris, U. Ackermann & K. Oegerli (eds) *Monotonie in der Industrie.* Bern: Huber, pp. 61–8 & 204–7.

Ulich, E. (1991). *Arbeitspsychologie.* Stuttgart: Poeschel.

Ulich, E., Troy, N. & Alioth, A. (1989). Technologie und Organisation. In E. Roth (ed.) *Organisationspsychologie, Enzyklopädie der Psychologie,* B III/3. Göttingen: Hogrefe, pp. 119–41.

Wandmacher, J. (1993). *Software-Ergonomie.* Berlin: de Gruyter.

Warr, P. (1987). *Work, Unemployment and Mental Health.* Oxford: Clarendon Press.

Welsch, J. (1989). Technischer Wandel und Arbeitsmarkt-Ausgewählte Ergebnisse der META-Studie des Bundesforschungsministeriums. *WSI Mitteilungen*, **42**, 503–16.

Wixon, D. & Wilson, C. (1997). The usability engineering framework for product design and evaluation. In M. Helander, T. Landauer & P. Prabhu (eds) *Handbook of Human–Computer Interaction*, 2nd completely rev. edn. Amsterdam. Elsevier, pp. 653–88.

Zapf, D. (1991). Fehler, Streß und organisationaler Kontext. In M. Frese & D. Zapf (eds). *Fehler bei der Arbeit mit dem Computer*. Bern: Huber, pp. 106–17.

Zapf, D. (1993). Fehler in der Mensch-Computer Interaktion. Zum Einfluß von Komplexität, Kontrolle und Streß auf Fehler und Fehlerbewältigung. Habilitationsschrift, Justus-Liebig-Universität, Gießen.

Zapf, D. (1995). Stress oriented analysis of computerized office work. In J.M. Peiró, F. Prieto, J.L. Meliá & O.Luque (eds) *Work and Organizational Psychology: European Contributions of the Nineties. Proceedings of the Sixth European Congress of Work and Organizational Psychology*. Hove: Erlbaum, pp. 61–76.

Zapf, D. & Dormann, C. (2001). Gesundheit und Arbeitsschutz. In H. Schuler (ed.) *Lehrbuch der Personalpsychologie*. Göttingen: Hogrefe.

Zeier, H., Mion, H., Läubli, Th., Thomas, C. & Senn, E. (1987). Augen- und Rückenbeschwerden bei Bildschirmarbeit in Abhängigkeit von ergonomischen und biopsychosozialen Faktoren. *Zeitschrift für experimentelle und angewandte Psychologie*, **XXXIV**(1), 155–79.

CHAPTER 12

Women's Coping: Communal Versus Individualistic Orientation

Stevan E. Hobfoll
Kent State University, Ohio, USA
Pamela Geller
Hahnemann University, Pennsylvania, USA
and
Carla Dunahoo
Kent State University, Ohio, USA

12.1 STRESSORS IN THE WORKPLACE

Although women have been entering the workplace in steadily increasing numbers since the beginning of the twentieth century, the examination of how work affects people has continued to be conducted from a gender-segregated perspective. Studies of men at work have tended to focus on the influence of work itself on men. In contrast, studies of women at work have tended to focus on role strain that women experience from being torn between work and home (Barnett & Baruch, 1987; Simon, 1992; Thoits, 1992). This segregation was more reasonable when most working men had women at home shoring up the non-work related aspects of their lives. Hence, their stress may have been more clearly based on work itself. However, when the vast majority of couples (at least in the USA) have both partners working in the paid workforce, this distinction is no longer valid.

More recent research has attempted to compare men's and women's work experiences (Barnett et al., 1993), and there is much to be said for this approach. By comparing men and women who perform similar jobs and who have similar home lives, we might better understand the influence of work *per se*. In such tests, the limited number of studies conducted to date suggest that there are few differences in the stress experienced by men and women at work or in its influence on them (Barnett et al., 1993; Rodin & Ickovics, 1990; Wethington & Kessler, 1989).

The Handbook of Work and Health Psychology. Edited by M.J. Schabracq, J.A.M. Winnubst and C.L. Cooper.
© 2003 John Wiley & Sons, Ltd.

Nevertheless, this picture is also unsatisfying because although the effects of work on men and women who are directly comparable is one key focus for research, it does not represent the current picture of men's and women's experiences with work. Men tend to be in more senior positions, have greater autonomy, spend fewer hours on household labour, receive more pay, and hold more supervisory positions (Blumberg, 1991; Grossman & Chester, 1990; Powell, 1988). Even when they hold the same job, men tend to be given greater autonomy and are more likely to be given leadership roles, rather than maintenance tasks (Powell, 1988). Women are more likely to have to move to accommodate their partner's career opportunities, be subjected to sexual harassment, and have special demands related to the poor fit of their health issues with company policy (i.e. pregnancy considered a problem, whereas men's greater incidence of alcoholism and heart disease is not considered a gender-relevant concern). In addition, women are more likely to be expected to take time off work for care of an ill child or parent (even her spouse's parent), and are more likely to be expected to take time away from their careers for child rearing.

Psychology has further blurred the study of how women are affected by work through applying individualistic models of stress and coping to the study of women's workplace experiences. This chapter focuses on this theme and discusses the literature on women's stress and coping by introducing a communal perspective to our evaluation. In particular, there has been an almost exclusive emphasis on the study of the individual's perceived control in the workplace, to the point that few other psychological dimensions of either the work environment or people's response to it have been studied (Karasek et al., 1981, 1987).

This is not to say that the lack of control influences men, but not women. LaCroix (1984) and LaCroix and Haynes (1984) found that the situation of high demand and low control in the workplace increased women's risk of coronary heart disease (CHD), compared to women in job situations of low demand and high control. Men's CHD in these studies was not found to be differentially affected by levels of demand and control. High-demand/low-control work environments have similarly been associated with women's reports of greater cigarette smoking and chest pain (Biener et al., 1986; Haynes et al., 1987). These studies, however, tend to focus on clerical workers, a category in which women are over-represented and which may provide particularly low levels of autonomy and compensation. Hence, the studies may actually represent the risk of a given occupational category, and not of the general lack of control. Furthermore, studies have equated role ambiguity or clarity of supervisors as indicators of control, whereas many low-control situations are neither ambiguous nor unclear.

The primary question that we raise is whether control and individual action are the central variables to study in order to understand women's experience of stress in the workplace. Miller (1980) found that control was more a concern for men than for women. For men, job satisfaction was associated with positional authority, having decision making power, and not having close supervision. For women, high job satisfaction was associated with the use of thought and independent judgment, and the opportunity to utilize skills and ability.

Another way to look at the influence of work experiences on men's and women's lives is to take a cultural perspective. The workplace is traditionally dominated by a male culture, which is based not on the team model that is marketed by personnel departments, but on an individualistic, dominance-based model. Power and authority are the main themes in this culture. Even when people work together, status and hierarchical relationships predominate. To the extent that there exists a distinguishable women's culture, it does not seem to differ from the current workplace culture on the need for esteem or the value of success. Rather, women tend to both offer and receive support more often and more effectively than men (Hobfoll & Vaux, 1993; Kessler et al., 1985). They tend to be more willing to work with a team, rather than dominate the team (Powell, 1988; Radecki & Jennings, 1980), and they are more likely to consider others' needs, as well as their own. This is not to say that there is not appreciable overlap between men's and women's cultures. Even when collectivist and individualistic cultures that characterize Eastern versus Western cultures are compared, considerable overlap exists, at the same time that they are distinctive (Triandis et al., 1990).

In this chapter we examine how stress affects women and how coping may moderate the effects of that stress. We also explore the underlying assumptions of the individualistic model of stress and coping, and contrast them with a model that incorporates both individualism and communalism. Our own multiaxial model of coping is presented as an alternative structure that provides a different perspective on the experience of stress and how coping strategies may operate in response to stress.

12.2   EXAMINING THE MODEL OF RUGGED INDIVIDUALISM

Coping behaviors play an important role in people's response to stress (Endler & Parker, 1990; Lazarus & Folkman, 1984; McCrae & Costa, 1986). However, the influence of coping is still not well understood, and research regarding its influence has tended to be atheoretical (Carver et al., 1989; Schwarzer & Schwarzer, 1996). In particular, we criticize current methods as being tuned to an individualistic perspective that sociologically has been termed "rugged individualism". Rugged individualism pits man against the elements in his fight for survival. This perspective esteems control and action and ignores social and communal aspects of coping (Riger, 1993). Important gender and ethnic differences in coping are missed by adopting this Lone Ranger, "man against the elements" perspective.

Esteeming individualism asserts two underlying assumptions. As Riger (1993, p. 280) writes:

> A great deal of research in psychology rests on the assumption that the healthy individual is one who is self-contained, independent and self-reliant, capable of asserting himself and influencing his environment.

Coping research, particularly that conducted on stress in the workplace, has promoted this perspective, with an emphasis on active, problem-focused coping. That problem-focused efforts may even be antisocial and affect others negatively or sabotage potential support has been ignored (Lane & Hobfoll, 1992). Some coping scales even categorize such behaviors as "Visit a friend" and "Spend time with a special person" as types of avoidant coping (Endler & Parker, 1990). It is instructive that avoidant coping, as measured by this scale, was related to negative outcomes for men, but unrelated to negative outcomes for women.

Secondly, individualism denies the influence of the environment. Sampson (1993, p. 12) writes:

> Effort is expended in developing precise ways to measure and assess individual psychological states and perceptions and to evaluate individual behavior outcomes. The social context within which these individual perceptions and activities take place is put off to the side, occasionally alluded to, but rarely if ever systematically addressed.

Coping research suggests that when action is not chosen, the alternatives are either avoidance or "passive" attempts to reduce discomforting emotions (Lazarus & Folkman, 1984). These alternative strategies are the most strongly related to psychological outcomes, with more avoidance and emotion-focused coping producing greater psychological distress (Endler & Parker, 1990; Freedy et al., 1992). Research has suggested that men are more likely to adopt actions designed to alter the problem, whereas women are more likely to cope by managing their emotional responses to stress or by using avoidance (Billings & Moos, 1984; Endler & Parker, 1990; Stone & Neale, 1984). Some have suggested that these gender differences result from the action demands that men experience versus the emotional demands that women encounter because of the different role settings they typically occupy (Folkman & Lazarus, 1980; Roth & Cohen, 1986). However, we argue that, because the underlying models are based on individualism, the positive things that women are more likely to do are never measured.

12.3   THE STRESS OF WORK AND ITS INFLUENCE ON WOMEN

With more women entering the labor force, women are being confronted with workplace stressors that are shared with men, as well as stressors unique to their gender. Although they may share particular work-related stressors, men and women may perceive and re-act to these stressors differently according to their social support resources and coping orientation.

Both male and female employees experience stressors related to such variables as: (i) role ambiguity, involving a lack of clarity about job roles, expectations or criteria in order to perform adequately; (ii) role conflict, where directives are incompatible and conflicting, or when available resources are insufficient to meet job demands; (iii) role overload, which involves having too many demands, and may include time pressure; and (iv) lack of au-tonomy, resulting from significant supervisor control combined with limited opportunity to participate in decision making (Billings & Moos, 1982).

Although the specific ways in which men and women react to and choose to cope with these shared stressors may differ, in general, all can contribute to a sense of job dissatisfac-tion, and may have a variety of additional implications. For example, chronic job-related stress can result in job tedium, burnout, and reduced efficiency, motivation, and produc-tivity (Akabas, 1988; Maslach, 1982; Pines & Aronson, 1981). Physical health problems and somatic complaints, as well as various mental health problems (e.g. anxiety, depres-sion, marital discord) also have been linked to workplace stressors (House & Wells, 1978; Jackson & Maslach, 1982; LaRocco & Jones, 1978; LaRocco et al., 1980; Repetti et al., 1989).

When studies began to address the impact of employment specifically for women, research focused less on the specific workplace stressors mentioned above, and more on the addition of the employee role to those of wife and mother. Conceptualizations of multiple roles for women included the *scarcity hypothesis* (Goode, 1960), where a greater number of roles is likely to deplete limited resources, with negative consequences for women's health and well-being, and the *enhancement hypothesis* (Marks, 1977; Sieber, 1974), where an increased number of roles provides greater potential to access resources (e.g. self-esteem, social status, financial gains), and the ability to delegate obligations required by the various roles. More roles, therefore, provide expanded opportunities that are likely to result in greater health benefits (Gove & Zeiss, 1987; Thoits, 1983; Verbrugge, 1982).

When examining the health of women, the perceived quality of women's social roles has been found to be more important than the number of roles *per se* (Barnett & Baruch, 1985; Baruch & Barnett, 1986; Baruch et al., 1987). Therefore, it is essential when addressing coping orientation to look not only at the job-related stressors common among men and women, but also at the home and workplace stressors that are unique to working women. This provides information about how women assess the quality of their roles, and can give clues to the special support needs of employed women.

12.4   JOB-RELATED STRESSORS UNIQUE TO WOMEN

Management typically portrays the workplace as gender neutral, but there is ample evidence that gender bias exists on both overt and more subtle levels. This bias contributes to the special stressors facing working women. First, there is limited appreciable promotion of women to higher organizational ranks (Cowan, 1989; Grant, 1988; Kim, 1994). Hence, regardless of the fact that the opportunities for and acceptance of women in the workplace are improving, the glass ceiling effect remains, and women still are not well integrated in many organizational systems. Even where women work in traditional female professions, such as nursing, teaching, housekeeping, and food service, the management is male dominated (Powell, 1988). In some instances, a "men's club" mentality has resulted in outright discrimination and sexual harassment. The tendency is for managers to underrate and underreward women compared to men with identical credentials (Bhatnagar, 1988; Lott, 1985; Rosenfield & Stephan, 1978). Even with the same job, in the same occupation, women's earnings are typically lower than those of men (J. Kim, 1994; M. Kim, 1989; Powell, 1988). Indeed, this compensation gap *increases* as women ascend the corporate ladder into the executive ranks (J. Kim, 1994).

12.5   WORKPLACE SUPPORT

The existence of discrimination, sexual harassment, and the glass ceiling are factors that indicate an underlying lack of institutional support for women. An absence of support for women is further evidenced by the paucity of family-friendly initiatives, ranging from child-care assistance and leave for the caretaking of sick family members, to job-relocation for both members of dual-income families (Cowan, 1989). Provisions that have been developed such as flexitime and flexplace programs are not widespread and do not appear to ease the burden of work–family conflict for women with major family responsibilities (Beutell & Greenhaus, 1986).

In terms of access to workplace support on an interpersonal level, women have an apparent disadvantage when compared to men. Several studies have demonstrated that workplace support has been more effective in limiting work-related stress for men than for women (Baruch et al., 1987; Etzion, 1984; House, 1981). Geller & Hobfoll (1994) examined gender differences in the amount and effectiveness of interpersonal work support. Despite the fact that the men and women in this study reported receiving similar amounts of support from their co-workers and supervisors, men benefitted more from these support sources. It is possible that men benefit more from their work relationships because they may interact with their colleagues on a more informal level, which House (1981) suggests may be most effective in the prevention of work stress and its negative consequences. Because individualistic characteristics are so highly valued in the workplace, and because men are inclined toward this individualistic orientation, support may be provided more genuinely among men and may be more effective since it can involve mutual exchange and spontaneous acts, rather than role-required behavior. Some of the negative sequelae of women's limited access to effective, interpersonal work support include social isolation, difficulty finding mentors, and decreased status in the workplace (Bhatnagar, 1988).

12.6 EMPHASIS ON INDIVIDUALISTIC ORIENTATION IN THE WORKPLACE

The emphasis on individualistic characteristics as opposed to communal qualities may present a key obstacle to women obtaining necessary institutional, as well as interpersonal, workplace social support. Gupta et al. (1983) have argued that social problems such as women's social isolation and difficulty finding mentors may be tied to women's inability to gain access to the "old-boy network" of advancement, which involves off-the-job social and extracurricular activities essential for recognition, acceptance, and promotion in most organizations. In large part, this may stem from expectations for employees to act according to the individualistic-male model of managerial success, which includes agenic characteristics such as self-reliance and dominance. Simultaneously, there are covert messages punishing women for exhibiting these male gender role traits. At the same time, however, communal characteristics, such as nurturance, and interdependence, are not coping traits that are valued in most organizations (Grant, 1988). Put another way, women are paradoxically excluded from the one communal element of work—the old boys network—because their behavior is deemed too communal and not individualistic enough, but punished for exhibiting the esteemed traits more commonly exhibited by their male colleagues.

According to some authors, conflicting expectations at work place women in an irresolvable dilemma. If they want to retain people's approval, they must demonstrate such qualities of female gender role as warmth and expressiveness. If they want to succeed professionally, however, they must act according to the individualistic, power-centered model by being assertive, competitive, and firm (Bhatnagar, 1988; Grant, 1988).

Investigators assessing factors contributing to the provision of support found that assertive coping may attract support (Dunkel-Schetter & Skokan, 1990). Individuals who cope more actively and are less passive are given greater support in response to their efforts. This might suggest that assertive women demonstrating characteristics of agency would be best able to access workplace support. However, both men and women have been socialized to expect the gentle and empathic, communal role in women (Martin et al., 1983). In addition, if women's assertiveness is misread as aggressive, they may alienate and anger potential supporters.

Despite the fact that people prefer to interact with and support individuals whom they perceive to possess similar characteristics, women seem to be less positively evaluated by males, even when they exhibit traits of an individualistic orientation deemed necessary for business success (Eagly et al., 1992). Mathison (1986) found that *women* were actually more negative toward an assertive woman than were men. This phenomena may be attributed to the different goals that people believe are achieved by association with men and women in the work domain. In the interpersonal domain, both men and women prefer supportive relationships with women (Reis et al., 1985). If women are perceived as compassionate and sensitive, they can best provide interpersonal support. If men are perceived as competent and powerful, they are best able to provide work support (Bhatnagar, 1988), so their assertive orientation may be evaluated more positively in work settings.

In one of the few experimental investigations of how assertive men and women are evaluated in the workplace, Geller & Hobfoll (1993) found evidence of a double bias, with each gender preferring to mentor and offer support to their own gender. They suggest that this may represent a historical change in women's socialization. Due to increased awareness and sensitivity to problems such as the glass ceiling and lack of mentors, women may be recognizing a need for increased camaraderie. Women also may be developing increased understanding and acceptance of women adopting a more individualistic orientation. As men do not share women's plight, they either may not be experiencing this change, or may be experiencing it more slowly. However, since males hold the majority of key supervisory positions at this time, these findings support the fact that women are at a disadvantage in terms of organizational advancement.

12.7 STRESS AT HOME

The focus on stress in working women's home lives has been on inadequate household assistance from their partners. Women with families often have additional home burden since: (i) women's traditional core role has involved household responsibilities (Barnett & Baruch, 1987); and (ii) working men have been slow to pick up the slack at home. Typically, women take responsibility for much more of the family's home labor even when both members of a dual-career couple have full-time jobs (Cowan, 1989; Pleck, 1985; Powell, 1988). The most striking finding is that women spend more than twice as much time on housework and childcare than men. Although the husbands of employed wives are increasing their proportion of total family labor, the increase is due to wives' decreased participation, rather than to husbands' greater time commitments. Also, although men are increasing their number of child contact hours, women still perform the vast majority of childcare and household tasks. This unequal division of household labor contributes an average of 10 additional work hours each week to the schedules of employed women.

In addition to the roles of spouse and parent, it is women who typically take on additional family-related roles and responsibilities. For example, women's communal orientation makes them more likely than men (e.g. their husbands or brothers) to become the primary carer for an elderly or sick family member, even when the family member is more closely related to the woman's partner or spouse (e.g. mother-in-law). With the increasing number of aging Americans, there is a growing likelihood that more women will be in the position of primary caretaker for their children and their aging parents, in addition to holding a full-time job.

12.8 WORK–FAMILY ROLE CONFLICT

In the lives of both men and women, family life is usually the most important aspect (Barnett & Baruch, 1987), and, along with job satisfaction, is a significant predictor of general life satisfaction (Gutek et al., 1988). Yet, working women often feel conflicted about the combination of these roles. Since women have stronger personal, social and societal pressure to adhere to the roles focusing on family and household tasks, it is working women more so than working men who experience the strains of competing work and family demands (Barnett & Baruch, 1987; Beutell & Greenhaus, 1986).

Three different types of conflict that relate to the work–family role dilemma have been described (Beutell & Greenhaus, 1986; Gutek et al., 1988). The first, *time-based conflict*, involves the distribution of time, energy and opportunities between the occupational and family roles. Here, scheduling is difficult and time is restricted since the demands and the behaviors required to enact them are incompatible. Women often experience fatigue since the two roles compete for personal resources. The second conflict has been termed *strain-based conflict*, referring to the spillover of strain, or an emotional state that is generated in one role, into the performance of another role. *Behavior-based conflict*, the third type of work–family conflict, refers to the incompatible sets of behaviors an individual has for work and for family. Because of these separate set of behaviors, women often find it difficult to shift gears from one role to another.

For some women, their career commitment has resulted in changed priorities, in which equal priority for home and work roles replaces the traditional preference for the home role (Pines & Aronson, 1981). Some less traditionally minded women resolve the dilemma by giving the career precedence over their family whenever the two conflict. Other women, and they are increasing in number, are choosing to deal with this work–family conflict by not having a family at all (Gutek et al., 1988; Powell, 1988).

Most common, however, are women who cope with their conflict at the work–family interface by over-adhering to gender-role stereotypes at home. Due to their communal orientation, many women do not view their jobs as justification for attending less to their families and household work. Therefore, they feel personal pressure that causes them to feel guilt and anxiety when they cannot fulfill all of their responsibilities. "These women believe that in addition to being 'super-professionals,' they have to be 'super-mothers' and 'super-homemakers'" (Pines & Aronson, 1981). Because childcare is hard to find, expensive, and often breaks down, working women who are single parents or have children with a disability are likely to experience greater stress resulting from the work–family conflict (Goldberg et al., 1992).

12.9 HOME-BASED SUPPORT

Researchers have concluded that employment is associated with improved mental health for women only if partner support is received, as reflected by a favorable attitude toward women working and as demonstrated by an equitable division of household labor (Kessler & McRae, 1982; Ross et al., 1983). In addition, several studies have demonstrated that family support has been most effective in reducing work stress for women, while work-related sources of support have been most effective in the attenuation of these effects among men (Baruch et al., 1987; Etzion, 1984; House, 1981).

Geller & Hobfoll (1994) found that household assistance from partners was related to women reporting greater tedium and work-related stress—a counterintuitive finding that also has been noted in research by Baruch & Barnett (1986) and Hochschild & Machung (1989). There are several possibilities that may account for this finding. First, the support that is provided to women by their partners must correspond to their needs (Cohen & McKay, 1985; Cutrona, 1990). It may be that the household assistance women receive is too low to meet their needs, or that another aspect of support, such as emotional support, is needed and expected, but not provided. The stress experienced by many women may also be so great that the household support may come too late to be effective. When resources are overtaxed, social support reserves may be less effective. If partner assistance does not fit the needs of women adequately, this may actually result in greater strain. According to Parry (1986), employment can reduce the risk of psychological symptoms caused by stressful life events when support is sufficient, but results in increased symptoms when adequate support is unavailable. Another possibility is that women who report receiving the greatest amounts of household assistance may be receiving "high hassle support" (Geller & Hobfoll, 1994). Although women may be receiving assistance, the positive aspects my be associated with stress, and may overshadow the perceived helpfulness of the support. For example, if a woman must consistently remind her partner to complete household chores, or if he does them inadequately, frustration may develop and the woman may need to redo the task. Additionally, women may have difficulty accepting household assistance from their partners due to their communal orientation. Receiving a great deal of assistance may be interpreted by working women to mean they are failing at their "real" role as wife and mother. Feelings of guilt and failure may contribute to the experience of greater strain.

12.10 COMMUNAL ORIENTATION: DEVELOPING A COLLECTIVIST PERSPECTIVE

Despite the fact that the existing literature is filled with references to women being more communally-oriented as opposed to men, who tend to be more individualistic, few attempts have been made to study coping behavior in a way that considers both perspectives. The existing literature has persisted in portraying individualistic coping as the most desirable and most effective approach. Furthermore, despite the fact that investigators have repeatedly found that men and women cope in similar ways and report equal use of problem-focused coping (e.g. Folkman & Lazarus, 1980, 1985; Folkman et al., 1986a, b; Forsythe & Compas, 1987), the literature has persisted in portraying men as effective, individualistic copers and women as ineffective, emotional copers.

Women's active, direct coping has been ignored, as well as any results suggesting that men use ineffective means of coping. For instance, Parkes (1990) found that men reported more use of suppression coping than did women; in other words, men reported more use of withdrawal, restraint, compromise, and ignoring the problem. Carver et al. (1989) found that men were more likely than women to use alcohol and drug disengagement, and Hobfoll et al. (1994) found that men reported more aggressive rather than assertive coping. Despite these findings, men have been consistently portrayed as being good copers.

This bias is seen even more clearly in the workplace coping literature. The majority of this research has focused on Caucasian, middle-class males to the almost total exclusion of women (Long, 1990; Long et al., 1992). Even studies investigating the impact of unemployment have centered on men, despite the fact that women are more likely to lose their jobs. The impact of this has not been investigated because women are assumed to be less affected (Leana & Feldman, 1991).

Hobfoll and his colleagues have addressed this issue in a line of research presenting a new model of coping, and a companion coping instrument, developed to investigate coping from both individualistic and communal viewpoints, rather than emphasizing either approach. This work has allowed investigation of how well the traditional male-biased, individualistic assumptions regarding coping actually represent the realm of coping behavior.

12.11 THE MULTIAXIAL MODEL OF COPING

To study coping in a context that allows for both individualistic and communal orientations, we developed the multiaxial model of coping and a companion test instrument, the Strategic Approach to Coping Scale (SACS). We began with a dual-axis model (Hobfoll et al., 1994), the two axes representing active–passive and prosocial–antisocial dimensions. A communal orientation would suggest that the active–prosocial orientation would be the most effective. Active–antisocial action might be personally productive, but might also alienate others, be destructive to social networks, and eventually backfire on the individual. Passive–prosocial orientations could support others, but might not lead to goal-directed behavior for the individual. Passive–antisocial behavior could be the most destructive, both personally and socially, but might be adopted in a defensive strategy.

Expanding this model, we added another dimension, that of directness. The multiaxial model is depicted in Figure 12.1. A communal perspective suggests that, even when being active, behavior may be either direct or indirect. For example, in Japanese culture it is socially inappropriate to embarrass your business opponent. Hence, it is common practice to manipulate the environment indirectly so that your company gains an advantage without the other company losing face (Weisz et al., 1984). Such environmental manipulations demand great activity and a goal-directed posture, but they are performed indirectly and behind the scenes. Similarly, in African-American culture, people's actions may be aimed at altering settings to enhance others' well-being, rather than directly aiming actions at the people themselves (Dressler, 1985).

As depicted in Figure 12.1, not all octants of the model are believed to fully occur. Our prior research did not find appreciable evidence for people who are extremely passive to be either prosocial or antisocial, but relatively passive behavior was at times linked to prosocial or passive–antisocial coping (Hobfoll et al., 1994). This may be because when people become passive they become *a*social, rather than prosocial or antisocial. By being passive, one simply does not act toward others. We had expected a passive–aggressive kind of coping to occur, but this may be depicted better in our current model by being indirect and antisocial, rather than by seeing someone as passive and antisocial. As people become more active,

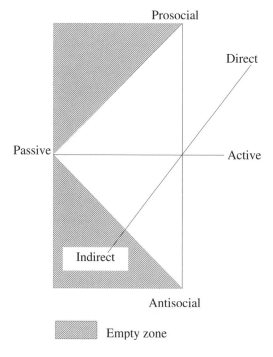

Figure 12.1   The multiaxial model of coping

their demeanor *vis-à-vis* the social environment becomes more relevant according to the model. Hence, people can be active and prosocial or antisocial in carrying out those actions.

12.12   HOW THE MULTIAXIAL MODEL OF COPING CHANGES COMMON COPING ASSUMPTIONS

Applying the multiaxial model of coping challenges certain assumptions that have been inherent in the basis of coping research to date.

Assumption 1: Perhaps one of the more commonly held assumptions is that it is best to approach goals through active problem-solving.

Particularly in Western cultures, attacking the problem is the valued approach to dealing with almost any situation. Any other approach would most likely be considered weak coping at best. This assumption is likely responsible for the existing literature's focus on problem-focused and emotion-focused coping. Folkman & Lazarus (1980) defined problem-focused coping as managing the stressor, while they defined emotion-focused coping as dealing with the emotional consequences of the stress. Although it was initially assumed that men were more likely to use problem-focused coping and women were more likely to use emotion-focused coping, subsequent research has failed to consistently support this (e.g. Folkman & Lazarus, 1980; Folkman et al., 1986a; Vitaliano et al., 1987).

Despite these findings to the contrary, the perception that men cope in problem-focused manners and women cope in emotion-focused manners has persisted. This perception has often been interpreted as suggesting that men cope actively and directly with whatever stressors they meet, while women cope passively, through only worrying about their feelings and thereby failing to cope. Thus, this focus on an individualistic perspective has lent support to positive attitudes toward the ways in which men cope and negative attitudes toward the ways in which women cope.

Approaching the same issue, that of how actively people cope, from a less individualistic perspective results in a less pejorative view of coping for women, while continuing to present men's coping in a positive way.

A more communal view of active coping would involve approaching goals through shared problem-solving. Shared problem-solving, as it implies, involves people addressing the stressor together, either through joint action or through joint planning. Turning to others for support, either primarily instrumental or primarily emotional, would be included in such efforts. In addition, offering support to others is part of shared problem-solving.

Research has supported the assertion that shared problem-solving can be an effective means of coping. Stone & Neale (1984) found that seeking social support was positively correlated with direct action. Hobfoll (1988) reported that perception of social support reinforces personal resources. Sarason et al. (1983) found that use of social support as a means of coping was associated with positive self-concepts, low anxiety, and higher perceived mastery. Thus, it is likely that social support allows those who utilize it to be better able to draw upon their own resources as well as relying on the assistance of others.

Further support for the effectiveness of shared problem solving is offered by other studies as well. Vitaliano et al. (1990) found that individuals with psychopathology tend to cope in maladaptive ways, which included less support seeking. McLaughlin et al. (1988) found that for women who hold dual roles (having both a career and a marriage), good marital adjustment was associated with more overall coping and less psychological distress. They suggested that one explanation for this finding may be that shared problem solving in a marriage leads to better outcomes. Additionally, Dunahoo et al. (1998) found that social joining as a means of coping was associated with less anxiety and depression.

Another alternative to the assumption that individualistic action aimed at problem solving is always best is the concept that it is better to be sensitive to the environmental constraints and choose one's responses according to the situation. The assumption that problem-focused forms of coping are always effective and emotion-focused forms of coping are always ineffective has been shown to be inaccurate. Although direct, individualistic approaches to problem solving may often be valued in a business setting, such approaches would be considered inappropriate in dealing with the types of stressors that typically occur in child-rearing, educational, and interpersonal settings. If team play is actually valued in work settings, these same behaviors may be equally counterproductive in the work domain.

Pearlin & Schooler (1978) suggest that some problems may not even be responsive to individualistic approaches and may in fact require communal approaches. Lazarus & Folkman have repeatedly asserted that stress and coping need to be considered with a transactional approach where the interaction between the person and the environment is recognized (e.g. Dunkel-Schetter et al., 1987; Lazarus, 1966). Researchers have found that, not only does coping differ by the situation in which the stressful event occurs (Folkman et al., 1986a; Hobfoll et al., 1994), but that the effectiveness of different means of coping differs by situation as well (Forsythe & Compas, 1987; Pearlin & Schooler, 1978). For example, problem-focused coping has been shown to be a particularly effective approach only in situations in which people have control or can change the situation (Compas et al., 1988; Folkman & Lazarus, 1980; Forsythe & Compas, 1987; Miller & Kirsch, 1987; Roth & Cohen, 1986). Thus, it appears to be more adaptive and effective for individuals to be flexible in the ways in which that they cope (Parkes, 1990). Gintner et al. (1989) investigated this issue and found that resourceful individuals varied their coping efforts according, to some degree at least, to situational characteristics. These individuals also reported fewer behavioral, cognitive, and physical symptoms of stress.

Assumption 2: An assumption that often goes along with the assumption that direct problem-solving is always the best approach is that it is best to be aggressive.

We contend that it is better to be assertive. Assertiveness is defined as behavior that shows confidence and firmness, without being unnecessarily aggressive or belligerent. Aggressiveness, in contrast, is typified by behavior that is both strong and hostile to others. Assertive responses to stressors allow effective coping while still considering the effects one's behavior has on others. Dunahoo et al. (1998) found that whereas use of assertive action was associated with lower levels of reported depression and anxiety, aggressive and antisocial action were associated with greater anger. In another study, confrontive coping was positively associated with the existence of psychological symptoms (Folkman et al., 1986b). Lending additional support to the need to consider coping from a communal perspective, Long (1990) found that active coping in the workplace was enhanced when accompanied by assertive action and the perception of interpersonal support in the workplace.

Substituting assertive coping strategies for aggressive ones allows people to cope with their own stressors without harming others in the process. In fact, assertive responding allows one to cope and still be supportive of others. This leads to better interpersonal relations with co-workers, possibly resulting in more opportunities for shared problem-solving in the future. In addition, better relations with co-workers are likely to result in more shared resources, both instrumental and emotional, being available to everyone in the future.

Hobfoll (1988) found that perceived social support reinforces one's own personal resources for dealing with stress. In addition, having the support of others provides the opportunity to benefit from the strengths and resources of others. Although social support has often been considered a strategy for coping only with problems outside the workplace, several investigators have found that it is an important component of dealing with workplace stress as well. For instance, Long et al. (1992) found that individuals who perceived high emotional support from co-workers reported lower levels of occupational stress, along with better physical and mental health. Lack of workplace social support, when coupled with high work demands, was found to be associated with high work-related stress (Parkes, 1990), while presence of workplace social support was found to enhance active coping strategies (Long, 1990). Similarly, Dunahoo et al. (1998) found that social joining acted as a buffer against depression in situations of high stress, thus leaving those who used social joining strategies to cope with high-stress situations less depressed than those who did not.

Assumption 3: Directness is another quality that is valued in individualistic, Western cultures, thus leading to the assumption that it is always best to be direct. Indirectness is often seen as synonymous with inaction.

However, as discussed earlier, in more communal cultures and subcultures, directness is often considered a negative quality. A more acceptable and valued approach to some problems would involve indirect approaches. Direct action is likely to dishonor or anger others.

Indirectness would, on the other hand, allow others to "save face" or maintain feelings of independence and self-sufficiency. The perception that indirectness is synonymous with inaction is inaccurate. Indirect approaches can, and often do, involve active coping. For instance, Dunahoo et al. (1998) found that indirectness was positively associated with active forms of coping.

In addition to approaching stressors indirectly because of differing social values, it is also important to recognize that, even in Western cultures, there are situations where direct action is either inappropriate or impossible. When subordinate employees disagree with their supervisors regarding the best approach for dealing with a workplace problem, it would be self-defeating for the employees to contradict their supervisors' wishes directly. However, there are indirect approaches that could lead to more successful resolution of the problems while still recognizing the supervisors' authority. In one study, coping with workplace stress through use of strategies such as withdrawal, restraint, compromise, and ignoring the problem was found to be associated with lower levels of somatic and affective symptomatology (Parkes, 1990). The author interpreted this as suggesting that these suppression strategies were adaptive in low-control situations. Although withdrawal and ignoring the problem would be considered avoidant or passive types of coping, it is possible that restraint and compromise represent indirect means.

There are also situations in which a supervisor may accomplish a lot by approaching a problem indirectly. If the problem is approached in a way that reinforces or increases self-esteem and mastery in the subordinate, while also illustrating appropriate responses, the supervisor can accomplish his or her goals and improve the chances of future problems being solved appropriately by the subordinate.

Assumption 4: It is also assumed that being bold and quick to respond is best. Cautious action is seen as weak.

However, a bold, quick response could also be considered impulsive. In a complicated social setting, cautious action is often the best course. Organizations often allude to sports teams as their model, and to the extent that the spontaneous, instinctive play that is necessary in football is carried to the workplace, this myth is perpetuated. Impulsive responses in situations for which all avenues of action have not been fully considered show poor judgment and may result in ineffective and possibly negative consequences.

On the other hand, cautiously considering one's options and proceeding only after weighing the alternatives is likely to result in more control over subsequent events and more efficient coping. Planful problem solving has been found to be negatively correlated with psychological symptomatology (Folkman et al., 1986b). Similarly, while cautious coping was positively associated with social joining and support-seeking, making it a prosocial–active coping strategy, it was negatively associated with avoidance, illustrating that being cautious is not the same thing as failing to act (Dunahoo et al., 1998). Furthermore, the same authors found that use of instinctive action as a means of coping was associated with higher levels of depression, while use of cautious action guarded against depression and anxiety at higher stress levels.

Assumption 5: The final assumption that will be addressed here is that people should not be too emotional. An implied component of this assumption is that women are too emotional.

Emotionality is typically assumed to interfere with rational responses. Thus, it follows that, if women are assumed to be too emotional, women are also irrational. However, we would contend that emotions are not always a handicap. Being aware of and comfortable with one's own emotions, as well as with the emotions of others, may allow one to cope more effectively with one's own problems. In addition, this awareness and comfort may permit one to better support others who are in distress, thus allowing everyone involved to participate more effectively in all types of interpersonal interactions, be they professional or social. In addition, consideration of the emotional side of an issue allows a broader conceptualization. Rather than limiting attention to only the cognitive and behavioral aspects of the situation, all three dimensions of people's lives receive consideration. This broader evaluation of stressful events may allow a more accurate assessment of the situational constraints, and thus result in more flexible, adaptive coping. Both of these issues have been addressed previously.

Although only a few assumptions regarding coping behavior have been presented here, it is hoped that the process of presenting alternative concepts to each of the assumptions presented has been illustrative. The assumptions in our society are often mirrored in scientific research. These assumptions are often as Eurocentrically-biased as they are male-biased, thus leading to pejorative portrayals of Afrocentric, Hispanic, and Asian cultures as well as women. Consideration of coping from both a communal as well as an individualistic perspective should allow the positive aspects of both perspectives to be valued, rather than valuing one perspective over the other.

12.13   IMPLICATIONS FOR INTERVENTION

A more communal perspective has indeed already entered the workplace, albeit in ways that have not been obviously attributed to this approach. These have already included such changes as flextime and flexplace. These programs are communal in that they recognize that individuals are not isolated from families, but rather are integral members of their family. They also tie the workplace and family into a common set of goals, recognizing that satisfaction and well-being in one sphere spread to the other sphere. Flextime allows workers to alter their schedules, usually insuring that the maximum number of employees are available at central times of the day in order to aid communication and meetings. Employees can come to work later and stay later, or come to work earlier and leave earlier. Flexplace has been afforded increased interest by employers with the increase of computers and because many employees can work out of their homes or satellite offices.

This reduces commuter time and also reduces workplace expenses for utilities (e.g. energy costs), square footage, and furnishings. The press for these changes has increased as women enter the workplace, but is advantageous for both men and women, especially given the high percentage of dual-career families. A study by Winett et al. (1982) indicated that employees derived increased satisfaction from such changes, and this can easily translate to less burnout and greater loyalty to their employers. Given expected ongoing shortage of skilled workers, employers should take heed of these changes, as maintaining a satisfied workforce is critical if employers taken the term *human resources* seriously.

Changes in laws in the USA allowing individuals to take leave time for care of an ill family member is another communally based policy. It allows employees to maintain their connections with the family and the workplace, rather than placing borders between them. It is instructive how aggressively businesses fought this change and lobbied against it. Increased attention to maternity leave, including fathers in maternity leave options, and protection of females who are pregnant from losing their positions are other policy changes that have been successfully instituted. This said, our experience with workers suggests that although such policies are allowed, employers often place those who take them (women or men) on a "mommy track" in which they are less seriously regarded for promotion and responsibilities that might increase the chances of promotion.

What has not changed in the workplace is the individualistic attitude that accompanies the "survival of the fittest" mentality. In this regard, there continues to be an emphasis placed on individualistic styles of coping related to aggressiveness and even antisocial action. Many Western companies, particularly in the USA, seem to subscribe to a policy of team play. However, it is unclear how they apply this. Rewards are almost uniformly given for individualistic effort and goal attainment, rather than goal attainment by the group. There appears to be very little "team play" in the team concept.

In basketball terms, it is clear how points for making baskets are tallied, but not how "assists" are recorded and rewarded. But it is assists that result in wins (Melnick, 2001).

In workshops, one of us (S.E.H.) often asks business executives when the basketball team, the Chicago Bulls used to win. Respondents, believing themselves knowledgeable about sports, uniformly answer, "when Michael Jordan scored points". The answer is incorrect, as the Bulls tended to lose when Jordan scored big. Rather, they won when he had a balance of points scored and assists made. Assists are when you set up another player to score. It is a critical statistic because it reflects not only points scored, but increasing team motivation. In discussions about how their business scores assists, executives usually state that this is done informally, or not at all. They want to play as a team, but do not apply the metaphor to practice. Yet, it is clear that supportive work climates which emphasize teamwork produce a less stressed and more involved workforce (Shadur et al., 1999).

Communal intervention implies teaching the use of "cautious action," where the feelings and honor of others is considered paramount. It implies the need to train workers in social joining. This form of coping encourages people to aid others and willingly seek aid of others. To the extent that individualistic models prevail, this will be viewed as a sign of weakness, rather than strength. The change from one way of coping to the other is fundamental to the cultural milieu of the workplace, and is not easily achieved without directed, thoughtful intervention.

Readers will note that some of these differences are already characteristic of the workplace in some European countries. In that regard, the more socialist leanings of the workplace in Europe have been feared in the USA, with its tradition of rugged individualism. The legal protections afforded workers in such countries as the Netherlands and Sweden are much more communally oriented than what is afforded in the US workplace. Comparing to Japan, these protections may be more cultural, and do not even require laws to uphold them (Fukuyama, 1995).

12.14 CONCLUSIONS

Future research on stress and coping among women in the workplace will need to change along with the changing roles that women are adopting. Just as the workplace will inevitably be altered by the increased representation of women, so psychological investigation will have to adopt new perspectives that change the basic assumptions of our approach to the study of workplace stress. Just as inevitably, this will also influence men's workplace coping and the way we look at men, as they will also need to adjust and adapt to new cultural imperatives.

Our principal thesis is that work will become more communal, and the communal aspects of work that have always existed will become more evident. Instead of viewing successful coping with the challenges of work as dependent on individualistic problem solving, we must gain a perspective that includes both individual and collectivist effort. Masquerading as an action orientation, there has been an accompanying set of behaviors that include aggressive and antisocial action, instinctive "shoot from the hip" response, and indirect, antisocial strategies. Whereas the action aspects of this orientation have been esteemed, the negative companion array of behaviors have been ignored. At the same time, communal action, sensitivity to emotions of the self and others, cautious planning, and reasoned action that takes others' needs into consideration has been demeaned. Even where past research evidence has been available to challenge the "men's club" climate in our literature review, it is apparent that this evidence has hardly influenced the way in which researchers construe coping in the workplace.

It appears that psychology has adopted the same agenic, male models of seeing the world as has the field of business. This has influenced not only our results and our interpretations, but also the very questions that we ask. When conducting workshops on these topics in business settings, we found that participants uniformly saw team play as integral to work success and productivity. However, when asked how their companies scored "assists" of others in meeting their objectives no one noted their company as evaluating this aspect of behavior. Similarly, when asked if supervisees were allowed to rate and give feedback to their supervisors (translate to team captains) on their supportive behavior (or lack thereof), a similar silence was experienced. Given this climate, it is no wonder that limited collectivist styles of coping are chanced by employees. Indeed, many participants reported that when they acted communally by covering for each other's absences or *faux pas*, it was done covertly, because such behavior was officially discouraged or even punished.

Finally, we raise an ethical, value-laden question. In studying the workplace, who is our client and what are our responsibilities? If we discover that communal aspects of coping are palliative for individuals and even lead to workplace productivity and satisfaction, are we bound to advocate these models and confront the male-dominated culture that is omnipresent? Is there a place for our role as social change agents? We cannot attempt to remain safely outside of the fray; failing to make a choice on this issue is not a value-free alternative, because it supports a certain set of values that exists in the status quo. Many psychological consultants have learned that to be invited back to the workplace we must please the purchaser of our services, i.e. senior management—almost uniformly composed of males of a certain social class, ethnicity, and culture. This potentially leads to our serving their value system. Because the senior echelons of our universities resemble the workplaces in which we study and consult in terms of their individualistic, male predominance, this is an especially sensitive issue. We must be introspective enough to realize that it has only been with the rise of women in academia that these questions have been posed.

REFERENCES

Akabas, S.A. (1988). Women, work and mental health: room for improvement. *Journal of Primary Prevention*, **9**, 130–40.

Barnett, R.C. & Baruch, G.K. (1985). Women's involvement in multiple roles, and psychological distress. *Journal of Personality and Social Psychology*, **49**, 135–45.

Barnett, R.C. & Baruch, G.K. (1987). Social roles, gender, and psychological distress. In R.C. Barnett, L. Biener and G.K. Baruch (eds) *Gender and Stress*. Free Press, New York, pp.122–43.

Barnett, R.C., Marshal, N.C., Raudenbush, S.W. & Brennan, R.T. (1993). Gender and the relationship between job experiences and psychological distress: a study of dual-earner couples. *Journal of Personality and Social Psychology*, **64**, 794–806.

Baruch, G.K. & Barnett, R.C. (1986). Role quality, multiple role involvement and psychological well-being in midlife women. *Journal of Personality and Social Psychology*, **5**, 578–85.

Baruch, G.K., Biener, L. & Barnett, R.C. (1987). Women and gender research on work and family stress. *American Psychologist*, **42**, 130–6.

Beutell, N. & Greenhaus, J. (1986). Balancing acts: work–family conflict and the dual career couple. In L.L. Moore (ed.) *Not As Far As You Think: The Realities of Working Women*. Lexington Books, Lexington, MA, pp. 149–62.

Bhatnagar, D. (1988). Professional women in organizations: new paradigms for research and action. *Sex Roles: A Journal of Research*, **18**, 343–55.

Biener, L., Abrams, D.B., Follick, M.J. & Hitti, J.R. (1986). Gender differences in smoking and quitting. Paper presented at the Society for Behavioral Research Meetings, San Francisco, CA.

Billings, A.G. & Moos, R.H. (1982). Work stress and the stress-buffering roles of work and family resources. *Journal of Occupational Behaviour*, **3**, 215–32.

Billings, A.G. & Moos, R.H. (1984). Coping, stress and social resources among adults with unipolar depression. *Journal of Personality and Social Psychology*, **46**, 877–91.

Blumberg, R.L. (ed.) (1991). *Gender, Family, and Economy: The Triple Overlap*. Sage, Newbury Park, CA.

Carver, C.S., Scheier, M.F. & Weintraub, J.K. (1989). Assessing coping strategies: a theoretically based approach. *Journal of Personality and Social Psychology*, **56**, 267–83.

Cohen, S. & McKay, G. (1985). Social support, stress and the buffering hypothesis: a theoretical analysis. In A. Baum, S. E. Taylor & J. Singer (eds) *Handbook of Psychology and Health*. Lawrence Erlbaum Associates, Hillsdale, NJ, pp. 253–67.

Compas, B.E., Malcarne, V.L. & Fondacaro, K.M. (1988). Coping with stressful events in older children and young adolescents. *Journal of Consulting and Clinical Psychology*, **56**, 405–11.

Cowan, A.L. (1989). Poll finds women's gains have been taking a personal toll. *New York Times*, 21 August, pp. 1, 8.

Cutrona, C.E. (1990). Stress and social support—in search of optimal matching. *Journal of Social and Clinical Psychology*, **9**, 3–14.

Dressler, W.W. (1985). Extended family relationships, social support and mental health in a southern black community. *Journal of Health and Social Behavior*, **26**, 39–48.

Dunahoo, C.L., Monnier, J., Hobfoll, S.E., Hulszier, M.R. & Johnson, R. (1998). There's more than rugged individualism in coping. Part 1: Even the Lone Ranger had Tonto. *Anxiety, Stress and Coping*, **11**, 137–65.

Dunkell-Schetter, C. & Skokan, L.A. (1990). Determinants of social support provision in personal relationships. *Journal of Social and Personal Relationships*, **7**, 437–50.

Dunkel-Schetter, C., Folkman, S. & Lazarus, R.S. (1987). Correlates of social support receipt. *Journal of Personality and Social Psychology*, **53**, 71–80.

Eagly, A.H., Makhijani, M.G. & Klonsky, B.G. (1992). Gender and the evaluations of leaders: a meta analysis. *Psychological Bulletin*, **111**, 3–22.

Endler, N.S. & Parker, J.D.A. (1990). Multidimensional assessment of coping: a critical evaluation. *Journal of Personality and Social Psychology*, **58**, 844–54.

Etzion, D. (1984). Moderating effect of social support on the stress–burnout relationship. *Journal of Applied Psychology*, **69**, 615–22.

Folkman, S. & Lazarus, R.S. (1980). An analysis of coping in a middle-aged community sample. *Journal of Health and Social Behavior*, **21**, 219–39.

Folkman, S. & Lazarus, R.S. (1985). If it changes, it must be a process: study of emotion and coping during three stages of a college examination. *Journal of Personality and Social Psychology*, **48**, 150–70.

Folkman, S., Lazarus, R.S., Dunkel-Schetter, C., DeLongis, A. & Gruen, R.J. (1986a). Dynamics of a stressful encounter: cognitive appraisal, coping, and encounter outcomes. *Journal of Personality and Social Psychology*, **50**, 992–1003.

Folkman, S., Lazarus, R.S., Gruen, R.J. & DeLongis, A. (1986b). Appraisal, coping, health, status, and psychological symptoms. *Journal of Personality and Social Psychology*, **50**, 571–9.

Forsythe, C.J. & Compass, B.E. (1987). Interaction of cognitive appraisals of stressful events and coping: testing the goodness of fit hypothesis. *Cognitive Therapy and Research*, **11**, 473–85.

Freedy, J.R., Shaw, D.L., Jarrell, M.P. & Maters, C.R. (1992). Towards an understanding of the psychological impact of natural disasters: an application of the conservation of resources stress model. *Journal of Traumatic Stress*, **5**, 441–54.

Fukuyama, F. (1995). *Trust: The Social Virtues and the Creation of Prosperity*. Free Press, New York.

Geller, P.A. & Hobfoll, S.E. (1993). Gender differences in preference to offer social support to assertive men and women. *Sex Roles: A Journal of Research*, **28**, 419–32.

Geller, P.A. & Hobfoll, S.E. (1994). Gender differences in job stress, tedium, and social support in the workplace. *Journal of Personal and Social Relationships*, **11**, 555–72.

Ginter, G.G., West, J.D. & Zarski, J.J. (1989). Learned resourcefulness and situation-specific coping with stress. *Journal of Psychology*, **123**, 295–304.

Goldberg, W.A., Greenberger, W., Hamill, S. & O'Neil, R. (1992). Role demands in the lives of employed single mothers with preschoolers. *Journal of Family Issues*, **13**, 312–33.

Goode, W. (1960). A theory of strain. *American Sociological Review*, **25**, 483–96.

Gove, W.R. & Zeiss, C. (1987). Multiple roles and happiness. In F. Crosby (ed.), *Spouse, Parent, Worker: On Gender and Multiple Roles*. Yale University Press, New Haven, CT, pp. 87–103.

Grant, J. (1988). Women as managers: what they can offer to organizations. *Organizational Dynamics*, **16**, 56–63.

Grossman, H.Y. & Chester, N.L. (eds) (1990). *The Experience and Meaning of Work in Women's Lives*. Lawrence Erlbaum Associates, Hillsdale, NJ.

Gupta, N., Jenkins A.D., Jr & Beehr, T.A. (1983). Employee gender, gender similarity, and supervisor–subordinate cross-evaluations. *Psychology of Women Quarterly*, **8**, 174–84.

Gutek, B.A., Repetti, R.L. & Silver, D.L. (1988). Nonwork roles and stress at work. In C.L. Cooper & R. Payne (eds) *Causes, Coping and Consequences of Stress at work*. John Wiley & Sons, New York, pp. 141–74.

Haynes, S.G., LaCroix, A.Z. & Lippin, T. (1987). The effect of high job demands and low control on the health of employed women. In J.C. Quick, R. Rasbhagat, J. Dalton and J.D. Quick (eds) *Work Stress and Health Care*. Praeger, New York, pp. 93–110.

Hobfoll, S. (1988). *The Ecology of Stress*. Hemisphere, New York.

Hobfoll, S.E. & Vaux, A. (1993). Social support: resources and context. In L. Goldberger and S. Breznitz (eds) *Handbook of Stress: Theoretical and Clinical Aspects*. Free Press, New York, pp. 685–705.

Hobfoll, S.E., Dunahoo, C.L., Ben-Porath, Y. & Monnier, J. (1994). Gender and coping: the dual-axis model of coping. *American Journal of Community*, **22**, 49–82.

Hochschild, A. & Machung, A. (1989). *The Second Shift: Working Parents and the Revolution at Home*. Viking, New York.

House, J.S. (1981). *Work Stress and Social Support*. Addison-Wesley, Reading, MA.

House, J.S. & Wells, J.A. (1978). Occupational stress, social support and health. In A. McLean, G. Black & M. Colligan (eds) *Reducing Occupational Stress: Proceedings of a Conference*, HEW publication no. 78-140. US Government Printing Office, Washington, DC, pp. 8–29.

Jackson, S.E. & Maslach, C. (1982). After-effects of job-related stress: families as victims. *Journal of Occupational Behavior*, **3**, 63–77.

Karasek, R., Baker, D., Marxer, F., Ahlbom, A. & Theorell, T. (1981). Job decision latitude, job demands, and cardiovascular disease: a prospective study of Swedish men. *American Journal of Public Health*, **71**, 694–705.

Karasek, R.A., Theorell, T., Schwartz, J.E., Schnall, P.L., Pieper, C. & Michela, J.L. (1987). Job characteristics in relation to the prevalence of myocardial infarction in the US Health Examination Survey and the First National Health and Nutrition Examination Survey, manuscript, Columbia University.

Kessler, R.C. & McRae, J.A., Jr (1982). The effect of wives' employment on the mental health of married men and women. *American Sociological Review*, **47**, 216–27.

Kessler, R.C., McLeod, J.D. & Wethington, E. (1985). The costs of caring: a perspective on the relationship between sex and psychological distress. In I.G. Sarason and B.R. Sarason (eds) *Social Support: Theory Research and Application.* Martinus Nijhoff, Dordrecht, pp. 491–506.

Kim, J. (1994). The executive wage gap: where women stand.*Working Woman*, January, 31.

Kim, M. (1989). Gender bias in compensation structures: a case study of its historical basis and persistence. *Journal of Social Issues*, **45**, 39–50.

LaCroix, A.Z. & Haynes, S.G. (1984). Occupational exposure to high demand/low control work and coronary heart disease incidence in the Framingham cohort, paper presented at the 17th Annual Meeting of the Society for epidemiologic Research, Houston, Texas. *American Journal of Epidemiology*, **120**, 481 (abstract).

Lane, C. & Hobfoll, S.E. (1992). How loss affects anger and alienates potential support. *Journal of Clinical and Consulting Psychology*, **60**, 935–42.

LaRocco, J.M. & Jones, A.P. (1978). Co-worker and leader support as moderators of stress–strain relationships in work situations. *Journal of Applied Psychology*, **63**, 629–34.

LaRocco, J.M., House, J.S. & French, J.R.P., Jr (1980). Social support, occupational stress, and health. *Journal of Health and Social Behavior*, **21**, 202–18.

Lazarus, R.S. (1966). *Psychological Stress and the Coping Process.* McGraw-Hill, New York.

Lazarus, R.S. & Folkman, S. (1984). *Stress, Appraisal and Coping.* Springer-Verlag, New York.

Leana, C.R. & Feldman, D.C. (1991). Gender differences in responses to unemployment. *Journal of Vocational Behavior*, **38**, 65–77.

Long, B.C. (1990). Relation between coping strategies, sex-typed traits, and environmental characteristics: a comparison of male and female managers.*Journal of Counseling Psychology*, **37**, 185–94.

Long, B.C., Kahn S.E. & Schutz, R.W. (1992). Causal model of stress and coping: women in management. *Journal of Counseling Psychology*, **39**, 227–39.

Lott, B. (1985). The devaluation of women's competence. *Journal of Social Issues*, **41**, 43–60.

Marks, S.R. (1977). Multiple roles and role strain: some notes on human energy, time and commitment. *American Sociological Review*, **41**, 921–36.

Martin, P.Y., Harrison, D. & Dinitto, D. (1983). Advancement for women in hierarchical organizations: a multilevel analysis of problems and prospects. *Journal of Applied Behavioral Science*, **19**, 19–23.

Maslach, C. (1982). *Burnout: The Cost of Caring.* Prentice Hall, Englewood Cliffs, NJ.

Mathison, D.L. (1986). Sex differences in the perception of assertiveness among female managers. *Journal of Social Psychology,* **126**, 559–606.

McCrae, R.R. & Costa, P.T. (1986). Personality, coping, and coping effectiveness in an adult sample. *Journal of Personality,* **54**, 385–405.

McLaughlin, M., Cormier, L.S. & Cormier, W.H. (1988). Relation between coping strategies and distress, stress, and marital adjustment of multiple-role women. *Journal of Counseling Psychology*, **35**, 187–93.

Melnick, M.J. (2001). Relationship between team assists and win–loss record in the National Basketball Association. *Perceptual and Motor Skills*, **92**, 595–602.

Miller, J. (1980). Individual and occupational determininants of job satisfaction, a focus on gender, differences. *Sociology of Work and Occupations*, **7**, 337–66.

Miller, S.M. & Kirsch, N. (1987). Sex differences in cognitive coping with stress. In R.C. Barnett, L. Biener & G.K. Baruch (eds) *Gender and Stress.* Free Press, New York, pp. 278–307.

Parkes, K.R. (1990). Coping, negative affectivity, and the work environment: additive and interactive predictors of mental health. *Journal of Applied Psychology*, **75**, 399–409.

Parry, G. (1986). Paid employment, life events, social support, and mental health in working-class mothers. *Journal of Health and Social Behavior*, **27**, 193–208.

Pearlin, L.I. & Schooler, C. (1978). The structure of coping. *Journal of Health and Social Behavior*, **19**, 2–21.

Pines, A.M. & Aronson, E. (with D. Kafry) (1981). *Burnout: From Tedium to Personal Growth.* Free Press, New York.

Pleck, J.H. (1985). *Working Wives/Working Husbands.* Sage, Newbury Park, CA.

Powell, G. N. (1988). *Women and Men in Management.* Sage, Newbury Park, CA.

Radecki, C. & Jennings J. (1980). Sex as a status variable in work settings: female and male reports of dominance behavior. *Journal of Applied Social Psychology*, **10**, 71–85.

Reis, H.T., Senchak, M. & Solomon, B. (1985). Sex differences in the intimacy of social interaction: further examination of potential explanations. *Journal of Personality and Social Psychology*, **48**, 1204–17.

Repetti, R.L., Matthews, K.A. & Waldron, I. (1989). Employment and women's health. *American Psychologist*, **44**, 1394–1401.

Riger, S. (1993). What's wrong with empowerment? *American Journal of Community Psychology*, **21**, 279–92.

Rodin, J. & Ickovics, J.R. (1990). Women's health: review and research agenda as we approach the 21st century. *American Psychologist*, **45**, 1018–34.

Rosenfield, D. & Stephan, W.G. (1978). Sex differences in attributions for sex-typed tasks. *Journal of Personality*, **46**, 244–59.

Ross, C.E., Mirowsky, J. & Huber, J. (1983). Dividing work, sharing work, and in-between. *American Sociological Review*, **48**, 809–23.

Roth, S. & Cohen, L.J. (1986). Approach, avoidance, and coping with stress. *American Psychologist*, **41**, 813–19.

Sampson, E.E. (1993). *Justice and the Critique of Pure Psychology*. Plenum Press, New York.

Sarason, I.G., Levine, H.M., Basham, R.B. & Sarason, B.R. (1983). Assessing social support: the social support questionnaire. *Journal of Personality and Social Psychology*, **44**, 127–39.

Schwarzer, R. & Schwarzer, C. (1996). Critical survey of coping instruments. In M. Zeidner and N. Endler (eds) *Handbook of Coping*. John Wiley & Sons, New York, pp. 107–32.

Shadur, M.A., Kienzle, R. & Rodwell, J.J. (1999). The relationship between organizational climate and employee perceptions of involvement: the importance of support. *Group and Organization Management*, **24**, 479–503.

Sieber, S.D. (1974). Toward a theory of role accumulation. *American Sociological Review*, **39**, 567–78.

Simon, R. (1992). Parental role strains, salience of parental identity and gender differences in psychological distress. *Journal of Health and Social Behavior*, **33**, 25–35.

Stone, A.A. & Neale, J.M. (1984). New measure of daily coping: development and preliminary results. *Journal of Personality and Social Psychology*, **46**, 892–906.

Thoits, P.A. (1983). Multiple identities and psychological well-being. *American Sociological Review*, **48**, 174–87.

Thoits, P.A. (1992). Identity structures and psychological well-being: gender and mental status comparisons. Sociology Department, Vanderbilt University, Nashville, TN.

Triandis, H.C., McCusker, C. and Hui, C.H. (1990). Multimethod probes of individualism and collectivism. *Journal of Personality and Social Psychology*, **59**, 1006–20.

Verbrugge, L.M. (1982). Women's social roles and health. In P. Berman and E. Ramey (eds) *Women: A Developmental Perspective*, publication no. 82-2298. US Government Printing Office, Washington, DC.

Vitaliano, P.P., Maiuro, R.D., Russo, J. & Becker, J. (1987). Raw versus relative scores in the assessment of coping strategies. *Journal of Behavioral Medicine*, **10**, 1–18.

Vitaliano, P.P., Maiuro, R.D., Russo, J., Katon, W., DeWolfe, D. & Hall, G. (1990). Coping profiles associated with psychiatric, physical health, work, and family problems. *Health Psychology*, **9**, 348–76.

Weisz, J.R., Rothbaum, F.M. & Blackburn, T.C. (1984). Swapping recipes of control. *American Psychologist*, **39**, 974–5.

Wethington, E. & Kessler, R.C. (1989). Employment, parental responsibility and psychological distress; a longitudinal study of married women. *Journal of Family Issues*, **10**, 527–46.

Winett, R.A., Neale, M.S. & Williams, K.R. (1982) The effects of flexible work schedules on urban families with young children: quasi-experimental, ecological studies. *American Journal of Community Psychology*, **10**, 49–64.

CHAPTER 13

Work Experiences, Stress and Health among Managerial Women: Research and Practice

Ronald J. Burke

York University, Ontario, Canada

13.1 INTRODUCTION

This chapter reviews research on work experiences, stress, and health among managerial women. This area is relatively new; most of the literature cited is less than 10 years old. One purpose of the chapter is to encourage more research on work and health of managerial women, since most of the available research findings are based on men (Chusmir et al., 1990; Greenglass, 1991). The focus on managerial women, a highly educated, motivated, and well-paid group, is taken because this group is growing in size and importance, serves both as an important model for younger women and as an indicator of women's progress towards equality, and may be frustrated with their relative lack of progress and increased stress (Nelson & Quick, 1985; Zappert & Weinstein, 1985). It goes without saying that other groups of women not included in this review may experience as much or even more work stress.

There are other reasons why this chapter makes an important contribution. First, the costs to organizations, women, and men resulting from stress-related illnesses is both large and growing (Matteson & Ivancevich, 1987). Second, there is evidence that the managerial job itself is a demanding one (Burke, 1988). Third, there is a growing consensus that work stressors are associated with a range of short-term quality of life and health outcomes (Repetti, 1993).

The chapter builds on established occupational stress research frameworks (Jex & Beehr, 1991); it extends them to incorporate work stressors and experiences unique to women. Figure 13.1 presents an organizing framework that provides a context for the review. It includes five panels of variables typically considered in stress and health research. This review focuses primarily on three panels: stressors, individual differences, and coping; the

The Handbook of Work and Health Psychology. Edited by M.J. Schabracq, J.A.M. Winnubst and C.L. Cooper.

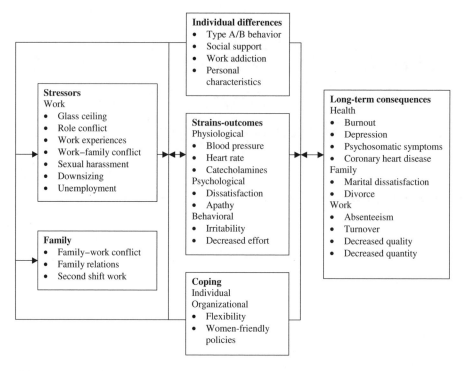

Figure 13.1 Work experiences, stress and health among managerial women

two remaining panels (strains and long-term consequences) illustrate a variety of emotional and physical health outcomes considered in one or more specific research studies. This chapter emphasizes the breadth and variety of research in this area rather than depth. A second purpose of this chapter is to spur organizational initiatives to reduce work and family stress and improve health. The field offers opportunities for both research and practice, which, if well conceived and undertaken, should improve the quality of life and health of managerial women (Ilgen, 1990; Keita & Jones, 1990; Nelson & Burke, 2001).

The following content areas are addressed:

- The glass ceiling
- Barriers to women's advancement
- Occupational stress
- Work and family
- Dual-career couples
- Sexual harassment
- Organizational downsizing
- Workaholism
- Unemployment
- Women-friendly organizations
- Intervention and policy implications
- Future research and action directions.

13.2   THE GLASS CEILING

There is considerable evidence that managerial women face a "glass ceiling" that limits their advancement to top management in large organizations (Morrison & von Glinow, 1990; Morrison et al., 1987). The glass ceiling refers to a subtle and almost invisible but strong barrier that prevents women from moving up to senior management levels. There is an emerging belief that the glass ceiling exists worldwide (Adler & Israeli, 1988, 1994), and may be at lower organizational levels than was first thought (Department of Labor, 1991).

Three hypotheses have been suggested to explain why this ceiling has remained impenetrable. The first builds on ways in which women are different from men. This hypothesis suggests that women's education, training, attitudes, behaviors, traits, and socialization handicap them in particular ways. Almost all research evidence shows little or no difference in the traits, abilities, education, and motivations of managerial and professional women and men (Powell, 1990).

A second hypothesis builds on notions of bias and discrimination by the majority towards the minority. It suggests that managerial and professional women are held back as a result of bias and stereotypes of women (Kanter, 1977; Marshall, 1984). Such bias or discrimination is either sanctioned by the labor market or rewarded by organizations, despite the level of job performance of women (Larwood et al., 1988). In addition, there is widespread agreement that the good manager is seen as male or masculine (Heilman et al., 1989; Schein et al., 1989). Thus, there is some research support for this hypothesis.

The third hypothesis emphasizes structural and systemic discrimination as revealed in organizational policies and practices, which affects the treatment of women and limits their advancement. These policies and practices include women's lack of opportunity and power in organizations, the existing sex ratio of groups in organizations, tokenism, lack of mentors and sponsors, and denial of access to challenging assignments. This hypothesis has also received empirical support (Burke & McKeen, 1992; Cox & Harquail, 1991; Jagacinski et al., 1987). The glass ceiling is the result of barriers to women's career advancement.

13.3   BARRIERS TO WOMEN'S ADVANCEMENT

There is considerable agreement on the barriers faced by managerial women. Morrison (1992) lists six as most important: (i) prejudice, treating differences as weaknesses, (ii) poor career planning and development (lack of opportunities for women), (iii) a lonely, hostile, unsupportive working environment, (iv) lack of organizational savvy on the part of women, (v) the old boys network (greater comfort men have in dealing with other men), and (vi) difficulty in balancing career and family (overload, conflict, stress). Mattis (1994) identifies the following: stereotyping and preconceptions about women's abilities and suitability for leadership positions; lack of careful planning and planned job assignments; exclusion from informal networks of communication; managers' aversion to placing women in line positions; absence of effective management training and the failure to hold managers accountable for developing and advancing female employees; absence of succession planning or succession planning processes that fail to identify and monitor the progress of high-potential women; inadequate appraisal compensation systems leading to inequities in salaries, bonuses, and perquisites; inflexibility in defining work schedules and work sites; and the absence of programs to enable employees to balance work–family responsibilities.

Morrison (1992) proposed a model of leadership development in which she suggest three critical components: challenge, recognition, and support. She observed that in many organizations, the barriers to advancement faced by women provided them with inordinate levels of challenge, without similar increases in recognition and support. Ohlott et al. (1994) provide empirical evidence that suggests this may in fact be the case. They surveyed male and female managers about developmental components in their current jobs. Their results suggested that men experienced some greater task-related developmental challenges, but women experienced greater developmental challenges resulting from obstacles that they faced in their jobs.

These studies have identified the barriers to women's advancement that commonly exist in organizations. In addition, women report greater obstacles to advancement than do men. One consequence of these additional barriers is heightened work and family stress.

13.4 OCCUPATIONAL STRESS

There is considerable evidence that the experience of work stress among managers is asso-ciated with undesirable consequences (Cooper & Payne, 1988). Most of this research has involved male managers since men have traditionally filled managerial roles (Burke, 1988). As more women have entered managerial jobs, they have increasingly become subjects of stress research (Barnett et al., 1987). With the appearance of this body of work, some researchers have begun asking whether women or men experience more work stress, exhibit more negative consequences, or have different coping or social support responses (Jick & Mitz, 1985; Nelson & Quick, 1985). Unfortunately there is not yet enough solid research on which to base firm conclusions to these questions (Martocchio & O'Leary, 1989).

Offermann & Armitage (1993), Davidson & Fielden (1999), and Langan-Fox (1998) reviewed the literature on stress and health outcomes among women managers. They noted that some stressors were shared by women and men (e.g. role conflict, overload, ambiguity), but that women experienced additional work stressors unique to them, as well as exhibit-ing different ways of interpreting and coping with the uniquely female and the common stressors. They categorized stressors experienced by women managers into three groups: (i) from society at large (work–family interface, off-the-job support, attitudes towards women in management, discrimination), (ii) from organizations (e.g. on-the-job support, sexual harassment, tokenism, sex discrimination, old boys network) and (iii) from women themselves (Type A behavior, personal control, self-esteem). The stress experienced by managerial women results from a combination of sources from all three groups, with health outcomes affected as a result. In addition, in keeping with previous work stress frameworks, individual differences operated at several places to influence the stress–health process.

Davidson & Cooper (1992) have contributed most to our understanding of the effects of work and extra-work stressors on managerial women. In addition, some of their research has compared the experiences of women and men. They propose a research framework in which demands (stressors) in three arenas (work, home and social, and the individual) serve as precursors of a wide range of stress outcomes. They review differences and similarities between female and male managers in relation to work stressors in the three arenas as well as stress outcomes. They report that female managers scored higher on both stressors and stress outcomes compared to their male counterparts. Women managers also reported significantly greater Type A behavior.

Cooper & Melhuish (1984) conducted a longitudinal study of stress and health involving 311 senior male and 171 senior female managers. They concluded that for male managers stress-related illness was more likely to be expressed in physical ill health, whereas for female managers, stress-related illness was more likely to be expressed in psychological illness (Jick & Mitz, 1985). They also found that Type A behavior was predictive of both cardiovascular risk and poor physical and psychological health for both women and men, but more strongly for women. Men scored more highly than women on more work stressors, but these were weak or modest predictors of cardiovascular risk or poor physical or emotional health.

Davidson & Cooper (1986) found that managerial women experienced more pressure at work than did men, and that more of this pressure came from external sources, unlike pressure on men, which came from internal sources. Women also experienced more pressure at home and received little support from their partners (Hochschild, 1989). These women felt isolated at work, were Type As, and exhibited greater manifestations of stress. Women in junior and middle management positions experienced the highest overall occupational stress levels. Furthermore, the stress vulnerability profiles of female and male managers most at risk of showing symptoms of stress were dissimilar.

Davidson et al. (1995) studied occupational stress in 126 female and 220 male under-graduate business majors. Similar to the earlier Davidson & Cooper (1986) study, female middle and junior-level managers reported being under greater pressure than their male counterparts. Women, not surprisingly, reported greater stress on gender issues, such as discrimination, prejudice and home–work conflict. Females also indicated more mental and physical ill health symptoms.

Burke & McKeen (1994), in a study of 792 managerial and professional women, built on the stress literature and extended it to include work and career experiences associated with career advancement of women (and men). The dependent variables were aspects of emotional well-being, which have long been a staple in stress research. Four groups of predictor variables were included: (i) individual demographics, (ii) organiza-tional demographics, (iii) work experiences associated with job and career satisfaction and progress (Morrison, 1992), and (iv) work outcomes. Specific work experiences (e.g. support and encouragement, challenging jobs, the absence of strain from conflict, overload and ambiguity) and work outcomes (considered as short-term responses to work conditions and work experiences that, over time, could affect emotional health) were fairly consis-tently and significantly related to self-reported emotional well-being in this large sample of managerial women.

This limited review of the occupational stress literature suggests that although women and men share some common work stressors, women also experience unique sources of stress. These emanate from discrimination and bias, role conflict, and work–family demands, resulting in overload.

13.4.1   Role Conflict

One of the most common occupational stressors is role conflict—that is, the simultaneous occurrence of two (or more) sets of pressures, such that compliance with one would make compliance with the other more difficult. Another type of role conflict is inter-role conflict with pressures from other group memberships. For example, pressures to spend long hours at the office may conflict with demands or expectations from family members to spend time at home. Role conflict can occur at work, within the family and between work and family roles.

Greenhaus & Beutell (1985) suggest that pressures from work or family can heighten conflict between work and family roles. They identified three ways in which role pressures can be incompatible: (i) time spent in one role may leave little time to devote to other roles, (ii) strain within one role may spill over into another role, and (iii) behavior appropriate to one role may be dysfunctional in another (e.g. shifting gears from work to family). Thus, variables that have an impact on time, strain, or behavior can heighten work–family conflict. The model proposes that any role characteristic that affects a person's time involvement, strain, or behavior within a role can produce conflict between that role and another role.

Greenglass et al. (1988) examined relationships between role conflict, work stress, and social support in women and men, and the psychological consequences of role conflict. Their results indicated that role conflict was higher in women than in men. Significant correlations between role conflict and work stress and social support, primarily in women, suggested a greater interdependence between work and family spheres in women.

13.5   WORK AND FAMILY

Work and family are the major life roles for most employed adults. Work–family conflict is experienced when pressures from work and family roles are incompatible, such that participation in one role makes it more difficult to participate in the other (Friedman & Greenhaus, 2000). Research evidence has shown that work–family conflict has negative effects on well-being in both work and family (Burke & Greenglass, 1987). Building on their earlier work, Greenhaus & Parasuraman (1994) propose two dominant forms of work–family conflict: time-based conflict and strain-based conflict. Time-based conflict is experienced when the time devoted to one role makes it difficult to fill the requirements of the other role. Strain-based conflict is experienced when the strain produced in one role spills over or intrudes into the other role. In addition, work interference with family may also have different antecedents and consequences than family interference with work.

The occupational stress literature indicates that the interaction of work and family may be an area of stress, particularly for managerial women (Etzion, 1988; Gutek et al., 1988). The assumptions that work and family are separate domains with little cross-impact has been increasingly questioned. Bedeian et al. (1988) found that parental demands interact to influence job, marital, and life satisfaction. The relationship between parental demands and life satisfaction was mediated by satisfaction with childcare arrangements for women, but not men, with young children at home. For men, time in professional work, work involvement, concerns about work competence, and time in family work during weekends were associated with higher levels of conflict. The latter was explained in terms of an encroachment hypothesis (Hochschild, 1997).

Work–family conflict is more likely to occur than family–work conflict (Greenhaus and Parasuraman, 1999) because the organization's demands on an individual's time are more important since the employer provides the salary needed to provide for one's family.

Extensive work–family conflict can lead to dissatisfaction and distress within the work and family domains (Frone et al., 1997; Netermeyer et al., 1996; Parasuraman et al., 1996). Such conflicts can also have negative impacts on parenting (Stewart & Barling, 1996).

13.6 DUAL-CAREER COUPLES

Most managerial women develop relationships with partners who are likely to be career-oriented, hence creating the dual-career couple (Gilbert, 1993; Sekaran, 1986). Experts predict that the number of dual-career couples will continue to increase (Hertz, 1986). This trend has obvious implications for managerial and professional women, who historically have been predominantly single (never married, separated, divorced) and childless (Brett et al., 1992). The effects on women of being in a dual-career situation are more pervasive since relatively more married managerial women than men are in such relationships. In addition, the impact of dual-career couple status is greater for women than for men (Lewis, 1994; White et al., 1992).

Hall & Hall (1980) indicate that stress among dual-career couples is caused by overload, conflict, and change. Overload arises from demand and pressures as a result of the number of roles played by the couple. Conflict results from interfering demands, such as a scheduled business trip conflicting with a spouse's birthday, or from the problems of meshing careers of two people such as scheduling vacations together. Another example of conflict results from unmet expectations or the feeling that one person is not living up to the standards the couple has set for itself. Change itself is a source of stress in that the couple must constantly adapt and respond to transitions in their work, personal, and family lives.

Rapoport & Rapoport (1976) identified various problems or dilemmas for dual-career couples: overload, normative, identity, social network, and role cycling. Overload dilemmas resulted from lack of time and energy when heavy scheduling demands prevented day-to-day domestic chores from being done. Normative dilemmas resulted from disparities between the personal norms of the dual-career couple and general societal norms. Identity dilemmas resulted from discontinuities between internalized early experiences and current wishes. Social network dilemmas resulted from problems experienced by dual-career couples in maintaining relationships outside their immediate family. They had limitations on the time available for interacting with friends because of overload dilemmas. Role cycling dilemmas refer to attempts by the dual-career couple to integrate their different individual career cycles with the cycle of their family. Each of the above created stress for dual-career couples (Gupta & Jenkins, 1985).

Organizations also have an important role to play, in cooperating with government agencies, in achieving a balance of childcare and careers through flexible work policies and childcare support, as well as through changes in organizational culture that come to place greater value on families. The formal policy changes required to ease work–family conflict include initiatives to assist with childcare and elder care, alternative patterns of work, part-time work with career opportunities and benefits, career breaks, enhanced maternity, parental and family leave, and changes in both relocation and anti-nepotism policies. These policy changes do not necessarily imply a fundamental change in organizational culture, however.

Kirchmeyer (1993) assessed a range of organizational practices addressing work/non-work issues using the concepts of boundary flexibility and boundary permeability as a framework. Flexibility refers to the extent to which time and location markers between domains are movable; permeability refers to the extent to which the psychological concerns of one domain enter the physical locations of others. She considered the effectiveness of three types of organizational responses to non-work:

- Separation: employers act as if workers' non-work worlds do not exist.
- Integration: employers treat work and non-work as related worlds that affect one another and try to reduce the gap between them.
- Respect: employers acknowledge and value the non-work participation of workers and commit to support it.

Most managers rated separation practices as most typical of their organizations. Organizations' use of separation practices were associated with lowered organizational commitment, while integration and respect practices were positively associated with organizational commitment. In addition, respect responses were associated with positive non-work-to-work spillover in women, but not in men.

13.7 SEXUAL HARASSMENT

Sexual harassment is a widespread problem in the workplace with estimates ranging from 28% to 90% for females and 14% to 18% for males (Fitzgerald et al., 1995; Schneider et al., 1997). What is sexual harassment? "Sexual harassment is any behavior of a sexual nature that an individual perceives to be offensive and unwelcome (whether or not it is legally or conceptually defined as such)" (Bowes-Sperry & Tata, 1999, p. 265). It has been proposed (Gelfand et al., 1995) that sexual harassment has three components: gender harassment (hostile or insulting attitudes or behaviors), unwanted sexual attention, and sexual coercion (sexual cooperation linked to job outcomes). One can also envision people being exposed to sexual harassment indirectly (the general level of sexual harassment in a work group).

Consequences of sexual harassment can be viewed as job-related, psychological/somatic and organizational. Fitzgerald et al. (1997) report a relationship between self-reported sexual harassment and headaches, sleep disturbances and psychosomatic symptoms (reduced self-esteem, increased stress, anger, fear, depression and anxiety).

The research program headed by Gutek (1985) has contributed much to our understanding of the impact of sexual behavior and harassment on women, men and organizations. She and her colleagues provide research support for the following conclusions. Social-sexual behavior at work is a widespread and common occurrence and has considerable impact (see also Fitzgerald, 1993). It creates significant problems for individuals and organizations as well as subtle yet strong effects on individuals and on work settings, in which tangible problems can develop. Social-sexual attitudes and behaviors at work are manifest in many ways, including sexual relationships between workers, flirtations, sexual teasing, pictures and posters, jobs, and styles of dress. Gutek and her colleagues found that social-sexual behavior at work resulted in part from sex-role spillover and in part from the amount of contact with the opposite sex. Sex-role spillover refers to sex roles undertaken by men and women in the broader society which interfered with (i.e. spilled over into) work roles.

In the area of sexual harassment, they found that women reported more sexual harassment than men, that male harassers were not demographically different from other men at work, that women who were harassed were usually afraid that they would be blamed for the incident, and did not lodge formal complaints because they did not want to ruin the harasser's career and believed that their organization would not do anything anyway. In contrast to women, who felt insulted, men were generally flattered by sexual overtures from women. Men used sex at work more frequently than women and talked about sex more. They used it to express a variety of feelings (friendship, caring, power, dominance, hostility) toward women and brag about their heterosexuality to other men. In contrast to men, women were hurt by sex in the workplace.

13.8 ORGANIZATIONAL DOWNSIZING

Significant reorganization or downsizing of firms has been commonplace throughout the past decade and will continue during the next. The accumulating evidence indicates that these changes typically have profound effects on both survivors and victims of job loss, almost always negative. It is also clear that women and men are likely to be affected in similar ways.

Women, however, may experience some unique issues associated with corporate restructuring. Interviews with senior women managers who voluntarily left a public sector organization in the midst of restructuring found that the most cited reasons were the lack of opportunities for career advancement and stress (Karambayya, 1998, 2001). In addition, these women commonly reported that the restructuring process had exacerbated existing gender issues. They also believed that the restructuring had created a backlash against women that would hinder their career prospects. Senior management appeared to close ranks, increasingly appearing to be an old boys club. Women were also over-represented in support functions, common targets of cost cutting. Women were also likely to be the most recent entrants to senior management ranks and did not have the personal and professional networks to protect them. The lean and mean values of the organization became increasingly antithetical to their personal values. The organizational culture placed increasing demands for commitment to career and organization. These preliminary findings suggest that managerial and professional women may be particularly vulnerable to the effects of organizational restructuring.

13.9 WORKAHOLISM

Workaholism has three main components: work involvement, feeling driven to work, and work enjoyment. Work addicts score high on work involvement and feeling driven to work and low on work enjoyment. Work enthusiasts score high on work involvement and work enjoyment and low on feeling driven to work. Enthusiastic workaholics score high on all three components.

Our first study examined the links between workaholism and non-work activities and psychological health. It also offered an opportunity to examine gender differences in workaholism and workaholism-related variables (Burke, 1996a, b). Data were obtained from 251 women and 279 men, all MBA graduates of the same university. There were some predictable gender differences on personal and situational characteristics. Males were older, more likely to be married, to be in longer marriages, more likely to have children, to have more children, had completed their MBA degrees earlier, were less likely to have gaps in their careers, earned higher incomes, and had been in their present jobs and with their present employers a longer period of time.

Women and men were different on one of the three workaholism components: Women were lower on work involvement but similar to men on work enjoyment and feelings of being driven to work. Women also devoted less time to their jobs, worked fewer hours and fewer extra hours, but reported greater job stress and greater perfectionism than did men. The fact that females worked fewer hours may reflect their typically greater time commitment to home and family responsibilities. Alternatively, the women may simply have been placed in low-power, low-opportunity jobs. Females reporting greater perfectionism and greater levels of job stress may reflect both work overload, greater work–family conflict, and aspects of personality (e.g. perfectionism) heightened by needs to prove themselves.

It is significant that females reported higher levels of job behaviors, such as perfectionism and job stress, likely to be associated with adverse work and well-being consequences. Women in particular professions may be as prone to exhibit workaholism as men. It may also be the case that workaholism among women may pose additional burdens, since women still shoulder the bulk of household responsibilities. Do ambitious women adopt the male model of the overwork ethic? Do managers function in ways that coerce some women to display workaholism?

13.10   UNEMPLOYMENT

Fielden & Davidson (2000) examined stresses experienced during unemployment in samples of women (N = 115) and men (N = 169) managers at different levels. Women managers reported greater stressors and more negative consequences of unemployment. Many of the stresses of unemployment among women were similar to the stresses women experience while working. Fielden & Davidson attribute this to the fact that women had a less well-developed occupational identity, a weaker sense of being a manager.

13.11   WOMEN-FRIENDLY ORGANIZATIONS

13.11.1   Workplace Flexibility

The findings related to unique workplace stressors experienced by managerial and professional women indicated that rigid work schedules and work overload interfered with women's satisfaction and family life (Burke & Greenglass, 1987). As a consequence, more organizations are currently experimenting with a variety of programs to provide employees with greater flexibility in work schedules (Rodgers & Rodgers, 1989).

Mattis (1990) investigated various types of flexible work arrangements for managers and professionals in major US corporations. She examined part-time work, job sharing and telecommuting. Part-time work has only relatively recently been made available to managerial and professional employees, although it has been available for clerical employees for some time. Part-time work includes reduced weekly hours, reduced annual hours and traditional part-time work (work full-time then no work). Job sharing is relatively new and has been used only on a small scale. It also has various forms: shared responsibility for one full-time job, divided responsibility (e.g. separate clients or projects), and unrelated responsibility (completely separate and unrelated tasks). Telecommuting includes work being done at a location other than the main office but being connected electronically.

She reported that most employees select flexible work arrangements to balance work and family responsibilities, and that telecommuting is chosen also to increase productivity and reduce costs as well as to avoid commuting. Although part-time work was the most common flexible work option in the companies studied, both job sharing and telecommuting showed increasing acceptance. Despite these findings, the number of employees on flexible work arrangements constitutes a small percentage of the total company workforce.

Nelson et al. (1990) found that organizational resources (e.g. flexible working hours, a mentor or role model) were associated with fewer symptoms of strain and greater job satisfaction in a sample of 195 female personnel professionals.

13.12   INTERVENTION AND POLICY IMPLICATIONS

It is important to target interventions relating to work stress and health since women have unique needs and experiences (Nelson & Burke, 2000a, b). For example, smoking is a distress symptom linked to work stress. Women encounter different problems than men do in trying to quit smoking (Chesney & Nealey, 1996).

Women may fare better in terms of lifestyle factors (e.g. alcohol consumption, healthy eating patterns). Lindquist et al. (1997), in a study of lifestyle stress and blood pressure, found that women were more likely to use healthy coping approaches (e.g. positive attitude) while men were more likely to use unhealthy eating, denial of stress and alcohol. Women may also use social support as a coping mechanism more than men (Matuszek et al., 1995).

13.12.1   Enhancing Executive Women's Health through Prevention

Because executive women have more resources at their disposal, it is tempting to argue that they should not be targets for organizational interventions. They may be healthier than women at lower levels of the organization, but it is especially important that they are healthy. As decision makers and policy setters, they hold the keys to the well-being of the organization. They also serve as models for the health-related behaviors of the people they lead. An awareness of the needs of different managerial groups can reshape the culture of the organization in healthy ways by broadening and enriching the majority culture. For example, changing an inflexible, long-working-hours culture benefits not only women but men as well.

For male and female executives alike, preventive management involves enhancing strengths and managing risks. Preventive management provides a three-part framework that can be used to develop interventions to improve the health of executive women. Within this framework, there are three levels of interventions: primary, secondary, and tertiary. Primary preventive efforts are directed at eliminating or reducing the sources of stress or the risk factors. Secondary preventive efforts focus on helping executive women manage their responses to the inevitable demands of work and home. Tertiary prevention involves healing executive women and organizations through appropriate professional care. There are guidelines at each level of intervention for organizations and for executive women.

Primary prevention efforts should focus on the stressors of politics, overload, barriers to achievement, sexual harassment and other social-sexual behaviors, and work–home conflict. For organizations, guidelines at the primary level include:

- Offer alternative work arrangements and assistance with childcare and elder care. Flexible work schedules, telecommuting, and company assistance with childcare and elder care can help women deal with overload and work–home issues. Patagonia, for example, has taken into consideration employees' needs for time for personal concerns, and offers flextime and the option of working at home for three hours per day. While childcare and elder care are offered more frequently by large corporations, most medium-sized and small organizations have yet to adopt these benefits.
- Develop zero-tolerance policies for social-sexual behaviors and sexual harassment. Victims of sexual harassment suffer depression, headaches, nausea, and other symptoms. Atlantic Richfield has a record of strong policies and has fired several highly placed managers who violated the policies.
- Ensure that development and reward systems promote equitable treatment of all employees. To address the wage differential issue, reward systems that promote equitable pay for women are necessary. In addition, audits of development programs should be conducted to see whether women are unfairly disadvantaged in terms of development opportunities. The Federal Government's commitment to equal opportunities for women has effectively shattered the glass ceiling in the Senior Executive Service, which consists of all top management positions except political appointments.
- Design programs that provide social support at work. Efforts to build social support, such as mentoring and networking programs, can be of special benefit to executive women. The phrase "lonely at the top" certainly applies in this case, and programs that foster connections with other executives can help female executives gain social support. Mentoring programs allow women to be either mentors or proteges, or both, and being a provider of social support to others also has beneficial health effects. Mentoring and networking efforts also benefit the organization by developing a diverse talent pool of future executives.

Executive women also have a responsibility for preventively managing their health. At the primary level, we propose the following guidelines for them:

- Identify your sources of stress and work toward managing or mitigating them. All executives suffer from stress of some form and often do not take the time to do a careful self-analysis to pinpoint exactly the causes of stress. A personal stress management plan, developed through careful introspection, is the best insurance against burnout.
- Take advantage of developmental opportunities and high-profile assignments. Women should recognize that top executives see a lack of experience as a barrier to women's achievement; therefore, high-visibility opportunities offer ways to enhance experience and gain exposure within the organization.
- Recognize the inevitability of work–home conflict and work to manage it. Women executives need to ask for programs like flexible work arrangements and for assistance from other family members such as spouses. They need to recognize that asking for help is a sign of strength and that they can overcome their own limitations by asking for help from others.
- Develop personal resilience by changing your perceptions. Part of primary prevention is changing the stressor. Alternatively, executive women can change their perceptions of stressors, which is also effective. Optimism and positive self-talk can transform a threat into a challenge that can be overcome.

Secondary prevention efforts focus on helping women manage their own responses to stress, and usually come in the form of exercise or ways to emotionally release tension. Organizations can assist women in several ways, including:

- Make exercise facilities and childcare options available. As noted earlier, women are less likely to utilize exercise as a coping technique than are men. This may be so because women have less discretionary time to pursue options like health club memberships, and often must find childcare to be able to exercise. Organizations can provide convenient exercise facilities with babysitting services, along with flextime, to help remedy this problem. On-site facilities with childcare would be ideal. Referrals to appropriate exercise facilities offer another alternative.
- Encourage networking groups to facilitate emotional release. Talking with trusted colleagues provides emotional ventilation. It allows executive women to reconstruct their experiences and move beyond them through verbal expression.
- Encourage training in yoga and meditation. There are a variety of methods for muscular and psychological relaxation. Training in relaxation methods can help women more effectively transition from the work into the home environment with less stress spillover.

Executive women must also take responsibility for secondary prevention. The suggestions for executive women parallel those for the organization.

- Make exercise a daily ritual. The best way to make exercise a priority is to schedule it on the calendar.
- Talk to others. Talking about experiences allows individuals to solve problems rather than ruminate or obsess about events. It allows executive women to work through their experiences and to benefit from input from others.
- Learn a meditation technique. Meditation has been found to be a powerful antidote to the stress of executive life. It has beneficial effects on both mind and body.

It must be noted, however, that secondary prevention alone is a palliative technique. Without accompanying primary interventions that focus on changing the stressors, little headway can be gained by executive women or organizations.

Tertiary prevention efforts are directed at symptom management or at healing the wounds of executive life. Organizations have a major role to play in this level of prevention.

- Ensure that employee assistance programs provide appropriate professional care. It is essential that employee assistance programs recognize the special needs of women in providing services or referrals to appropriate professional care. Certain behavioral distress symptoms, such as eating disorders, alcohol abuse, and smoking, may be more effectively treated with gender-specific interventions.

Executive women must also take responsibility for tertiary prevention.

- Develop a network of qualified professionals to rely on. This means establishing relationships with physicians, psychologists, and other trained professionals in advance of the need so that they will be available in times of crisis.

The three-level prevention framework provides ways of understanding what both executives and organizations can do to manage risks and enhance health. Care must be taken in these efforts to recognize that women at different life stages may have different needs. Childcare assistance, for example, may not be a high priority for mid-life women. Because they have spent many years putting others first—employees, co-workers, spouses, and children—they may need more personal time for putting themselves first. This raises the importance of dialogue between executive women and others in the organization. To develop interventions that improve the health and well-being of executive women, decision makers must listen to women's concerns and ascertain what they need. The perceptions of others concerning what might benefit executive women may not be accurate. A psychologist at the executive level can be an invaluable guardian of mental health and well-being. There are two models of this working relationship. The psychologist might be employed as a member of the CEO's staff, or might serve as an outside consultant.

The health and well-being of the organization is dependent on the health and well-being of all of its members. Women at the top of the organization are no exception. In a study mentioned earlier, company initiatives in general areas likely to address some of the demands experienced by managerial and professional women included work and family programs, flexible work arrangements, leadership and career development, mentoring programs, and total cultural change (Mattis, 1994). The most proactive approach organizations can take is to change the source of stress; that is, find out what is causing executive women's stress and modify the cause.

In addition to attacking the causes of stress, companies can help women manage their own responses to stress. As a final line of defense, organizations need to have employee assistance programs that recognize the health needs of women in providing services and referring women to professional care. The three-part preventive management framework proposes that interventions mainly consist of the primary level, supplemented by secondary and tertiary prevention. This framework provides an effective means for enhancing executive women's strengths and managing their health risks.

13.12.2   Implications for Interventions

The three-part preventive management framework provides a framework for integrating the preceding review into suggestions for interventions that would target the stress-related challenges of working women. Primary preventive efforts, directed at changing the source of stress, should focus on the stressors of politics, overload, barriers to achievement, sexual harassment and other social-sexual behaviors, and work–home conflict (Burke, 1996a, b). Flexible work schedules, alternative work arrangements like telecommuting, and company assistance with childcare and elder care can help women deal with overload and work–home issues (Mattis, 1994). Politics, barriers to achievement and sexual harassment can be effectively diminished by aggressive organizational efforts in terms of corporate policy, and a system of rewards that reinforces equitable treatment of all organizational members (Schwartz, 1992). Efforts to build in social support at work, such as in mentoring programs, can be of special benefit to working women (Kram, 1996).

Secondary prevention efforts focus on helping women manage their own responses to stress, and usually come in the form of exercise or ways to emotionally release tension. As noted earlier, women are less likely to utilize exercise as a coping technique than are men. Interventions that educate women about the stress management benefits of exercise and encourage them to engage in exercise are warranted. Support groups to facilitate emotional release and training in relaxation methods can help women more effectively with the transition from the work to the home environment with less stress spillover.

Tertiary prevention efforts are directed at symptom management. It is essential that employee assistance programs recognize the special needs of women in provision of services or referral to appropriate professional care. As mentioned above, certain behavioral distress symptoms, such as eating disorders, alcohol abuse and smoking, may be more effectively treated with gender-specific interventions.

One of the issues that must be addressed by organizations is how to alter employment demands so that they mesh more easily with family responsibilities. Unfortunately, most employers do not consider their employees' concerns as family members to be organizational concerns (Friedman, 1990). Policies and practices are designed as if responsibilities outside the job were subordinate to work demands. If, rather than ignoring these, companies were to acknowledge them and assist their employees, a great deal of employment–family conflict could be alleviated (Friedman et al., 1998).

Offermann & Armitage (1993) provide an inventory of stress management intervention options for women managers, categorizing them by target: society at large, organizations, and women themselves. Unfortunately, few examples of their application, and even fewer of their evaluation and effectiveness, are available. Some exceptions are Kossek (1990), Rushforth (1991), Miller (1984) and Goff et al. (1990).

One area in which the company could assist is childcare. Childcare is a demand on the family that poses conflict between work and family interests, particularly in the single-parent family. Other benefits could encourage men to take a more active role in the family through the provision of paternity leave. A second area in which organizations could take action involves the concept of what constitutes a career. Most organizations currently define career in a narrow sense in terms of progress and upward mobility, and in so doing preclude a lifestyle that deviates from the masculine one. For example, persons who move through the ranks efficiently and quickly are rewarded, and it is almost always assumed that the highly motivated person works his or her way upwards faster than the person who is minimally motivated. As a result, the part-time worker (whether part-time for one year or five) is tolerated rather than accepted, and may even be referred to as a casual worker. It is not recognized that individuals pursuing careers may have other commitments (e.g. family responsibilities and/or interests related to personal growth), which demand substantial time and energy. It is primarily during the years when women are experiencing pregnancy, childbirth, and rearing young children that societal institutions should acknowledge and accommodate alternative lifestyles to the one currently assumed for all members of society. Lack of 24-hour childcare, inadequately paid maternity leave, and the assumption that all committed employees should work an 8–12 hour day constitute discrimination against women (Greenglass, 1985). Moreover, organizations can introduce programs to promote a climate that is responsive to the needs of women and men, particularly when they are raising a young family (Schwartz, 1989). For example, flextime can be introduced such that workers can schedule their work in different time frames, depending on their needs and possibilities at particular stages in their life cycle.

13.13 FUTURE RESEARCH AND ACTION DIRECTIONS

There have been some pleasantly encouraging signs that research interest in the content examined in this chapter has increased. This is shown particularly in studies of work and family, and occupational stress experienced by managerial women (Freedman & Phillips, 1988).

On the other hand, several other areas are still under-researched (Repetti et al., 1989). These would include the effects of employment gaps on career satisfaction, consequences of the more varied patterns that women's careers reveal, gender proportions, and the effects of various work experiences (Morrison, 1992) on both career aspirations and emotional well-being.

Considerably more work needs to be done on the potential benefits of efforts of organizations to support the career aspirations of managerial and professional women through cultural change efforts and policy implementation (Morrison, 1992). There is an urgent need to document best practice in this area (Kraut, 1992). It is important to develop case studies of successful and less than successful change efforts to further our understanding of how best to bring about positive change. These case studies would also prove useful to organizations interested in creating a level playing field. Case studies would share the efforts of other organizations, a very persuasive and credible way to change attitudes and be helpful. In addition, more research attention needs to address the effectiveness of a variety of specific policies for creating a women-friendly environment (Galinsky & Stein, 1990; Kraut, 1990). These include policies in the areas of sexual harassment, flexible working hours, part-time work, and working at home. Without the active support by the top of the organizations, training in their understanding and use, and consistent and intelligent applications, well-conceived policies often fall considerably short. This seems particularly important because there has been recent speculation that companies may be less family-friendly in an increasingly competitive marketplace (Fierman, 1994).

ACKNOWLEDGEMENTS

Preparation of this chapter was supported in part by the School of Business, York University. I would like to thank Kelly LeCouvie and Rachel Burke for their help in collecting material for the chapter, and Louise Coutu for preparing the manuscript. This chapter has benefited from discussions with my friends and colleagues, Debra Nelson and Mary Mattis.

REFERENCES

Adler, N.L. & Israeli, D.N. (1988) *Women in Management Worldwide.* M.E. Sharpe, Armonk, NY.
Adler, N.J. & Israeli, D.N. (1994) *Competitive Frontiers: Women Managers in the Global Economy.* Basil Blackwell, Cambridge, MA.
Barnett, R.C., Biener, L. & Baruch, G.K. (1987) *Gender and Stress.* Free Press, New York.
Bedeian, A.G., Burke, P.J. & Moffett, R.G. (1988) Outcomes of work–family conflict among married male and female professionals. *Journal of Management,* **14**, 109–28.
Bowes-Sperry, L. & Tata, J. (1999) A multi-perspective framework of sexual harassment. Reviewing two decades of research. In G.N. Powell (ed.) *Handbook of Gender and Work.* Sage, Thousand Oaks, CA, pp. 263–80.
Brett, J.M., Stroh, L.K. & Reilly, A.H. (1992) What is it like being a dual-career manager in the 1990s? In S. Zedeck (ed.) *Work, Families and Organizations.* Jossey-Bass, San Francisco, CA, pp. 138–67.
Burke, R.J. (1988) Sources of managerial and professional stress in large organizations. In C.L. Cooper & R. Payne (eds) *Causes, Coping and Consequences of Stress at Work.* John Wiley & Sons, New York, pp. 77–114.
Burke, R.J. (1996a) Workaholism in organizations: gender differences. *Sex Roles,* **41**, 333–45.
Burke, R.J. (1996b) Workaholism among women managers: work and life satisfactions and psychological well-being. *Equal Opportunities International,* **18**, 25–35.

Burke, R.J. & Greenglass, E.R. (1987) Work and family. In C.L. Cooper & I.T. Robertson (eds) *International Review of Industrial and Organizational Psychology*. John Wiley & Sons, New York, pp. 245–83.

Burke, R.J. & McKeen, C.A. (1992) Women in management. In C.L. Cooper & I.T. Robertson (eds) *International Review of Industrial and Organizational Psychology*. John Wiley & Sons, New York, pp. 245–83.

Burke, R.J. & McKeen, C.A. (1994) Work and career experiences and emotional well-being of managerial and professional women. *Stress Medicine*, **10**, 65–79.

Chesney, M.A. & Nealey, J.B. (1996) Smoking and cardiovascular disease risk in women. In P.M. Kato & T. Mann (eds) *Handbook of Diversity Issues in Health Psychology*. Plenum Press, New York, pp. 199–218.

Chusmir, L.H., Moore, D.P. & Adams, J.S. (1990) Research on working women: a report card of 22 journals *Sex Roles: A Journal of Research*, **22**, 167–75.

Cooper, C.L. & Melhuish, A. (1984) Executive stress and health: differences between women and men. *Journal of Occupational Medicine*, **26**, 99–104.

Cooper, C.L. & Payne, R. (eds) (1988) *Causes, Coping and Consequences of Stress at Work*. John Wiley & Sons, New York.

Cox, T.H. & Harquail, C.V. (1991) Career paths and career success in the early career stages of male and female MBAs. *Journal of Vocational Behavior*, **39**, 54–75.

Davidson, M.J. & Cooper, C.L. (1986) Executive women under pressure. *International Review of Applied Psychology*, **35**, 301–26.

Davidson, M.J. & Cooper, C.L. (1992) *Shattering the Glass Ceiling: The Woman Manager*. Paul Chapman, London.

Davidson, M.J. & Fielden, S. (1999) Stress and the working woman. In G.N. Powell (ed.) *Handbook of Gender And Work*. Sage, Thousand Oaks, CA, pp. 413–26.

Davidson, M.J., Cooper, C.L. & Baldini, V. (1995) Occupational stress in female and male graduate managers. *Stress Medicine*, **11**, 157–75.

Department of Labor (1991) *A Report on the Glass Ceiling Initiative*. US Government Printing Office, Washington, DC.

Etzion, D. (1988) The experience of burnout and work/nonwork success in male and female engineers: a matched-pairs comparison. *Human Resource Management*, **27**, 163–79.

Fielden, S.L. & Davidson, M.J. (2000) Stress and the unemployed women manager: a comparative approach. In M.J. Davidson & R.J. Burke (eds) *Women in Management*, vol. II. Sage, London, pp. 192–204.

Fierman, J. (1994) Are companies less family-friendly? *Fortune*, 21, March, 64–7.

Fitzgerald, L.E. (1993) Sexual harassment: violence against women in the workplace. *American Psychologist*, **48**, 1070–6.

Fitzgerald, L.E., Gelfand, M.J. & Drasgow, F. (1995) Measuring sexual harassment: theoretical and psychometric advances. *Basic and Applied Social Psychology*, **17**, 425–45.

Fitzgerald, L.E., Drasgow, F., Hulin, C.L., Gelfand, M.J. & Magley, V.J. (1997) Antecedents and consequences of sexual harassment in organizations: a test of an integrated model. *Journal of Applied Psychology*, **82**, 578–89.

Freedman, S.M. & Phillips, J.S. (1988) The changing nature of research on women at work. *Journal of Management*, **14**, 231–51.

Friedman, D.E. (1990) Work and family: the new strategic plan. *Human Resource Planning*, **13**, 79–89.

Friedman, S.D. & Greenhaus, J.H. (2000) *Allies or Enemies? How Choices About Work and Family Affect the Quality of Men's and Women's Lives*. Oxford University Press, New York.

Friedman, S.D., DeGroot, J. & Christensen, P. (eds) (1998) *Integrating Work and Life: The Wharton Resource Guide*. Jossey-Bass, San Francisco, CA.

Frone, M.R., Yardley, J.K. & Markel, K.S. (1997) Developing and testing an integrative model of the work–family interface. *Journal of Vocational Behavior*, **50**, 145–67.

Galinsky, E. & Stein, P.J. (1990) The impact of human resource policies on employees: balancing work and family life. *Journal of Family Issues*, **11**, 368–83.

Gelfand, M.J., Fitzgerald, L.F. & Drasgow, F. (1995) The structure of sexual harassment: a confirmatory analysis across cultures and settings. *Journal of Vocational Behavior*, **47**, 164–77.

Gilbert, L.A. (1993) *Two Careers/One Family*, Sage, Newbury Park, CA.

Goff, S.J., Mount, M.K. & Jamison, R.L. (1990) Employer supported childcare, work/family conflict, and absenteeism: a field study. *Personal Psychology*, **43**, 793–809.

Greenglass, E.R. (1985) Psychological implications of sex bias in the workplace. *Academic Psychology Bulletin*, **7**, 227–40.

Greenglass, E.R. (1991) Burnout and gender: theoretical and organizational implications. *Canadian Psychology*, **32**, 562–72.

Greenglass, E.R., Pantony, K.L. & Burke, R.J. (1988) A gender-role perspective on role conflict, work stress and social support. *Journal of Social Behavior and Personality*, **3**, 317–28.

Greenhaus, J.H. & Beutell, N.J. (1985) Sources of conflict between workload and family roles. *Academy of Management Review*, **10**, 76–85.

Greenhaus, J.H. & Parasuraman, S. (1994) Work–family conflict, social support and well-being. In M.J. Davidson & R.J. Burke (eds) *Women in Management: Current Research Issues*. Paul Chapman, London, pp. 213–29.

Greenhaus, J.H. & Parasuraman, S. (1999) Research on work, family and gender: current status and future directions. In G.N. Powell (ed.) *Handbook of Gender and Work*. Sage, Thousand Oaks, CA, pp. 391–412.

Gupta, N. & Jenkins, G.D. (1985) Dual career couples: stress, stressors, strains and strategies. In T.A. Beehr & R.S. Bhagat (eds) *Human Stress and Cognition in Organizations*. John Wiley & Sons, New York, pp. 141–75.

Gutek, B.A. (1985) *Sex and the Workplace: The Impact of Sexual Behavior and Harassment on Women, Men and the Organization*. Jossey-Bass, San Francisco, CA.

Gutek, B.A., Repetti, R.L. & Silver, D.L. (1988) Nonwork roles and stress at work. In C.L. Cooper & R. Payne (eds) *Causes, Coping and Consequences of Stress at Work*. John Wiley & Sons, New York, pp. 141–73.

Hall, D.T. & Hall, F.S. (1980) Stress and the two-career couple. In C.L. Cooper & R. Payne (eds) *Current Concerns in Occupational Stress*. John Wiley & Sons, New York, pp. 243–66.

Heilman, M.E., Block, C.J., Martell, R.F. & Simon, M.C. (1989) Has anything changed? Current characterizations of men, women and managers. *Journal of Applied Psychology*, **74**, 935–42.

Hertz, R. (1986) *More Equal than Others: Women and Men in Dual-Career Marriages*. University of California Press, Berkeley, CA.

Hochschild, A. (1989) *The Second Shift: Working Parents and the Revolution at Home*. Avon Books, New York.

Hochschild, A.R. (1997) *The Time Bind*. New York: Metropolitan Books.

Ilgen, D.R. (1990) Health issues at work: opportunities for industrial/organizational psychology. *American Psychologist*, **45**, 273–83.

Jagacinski, C.M., Lebold, W.L. & Linden, K.W. (1987) The relative career advancement of men and women engineers in the United States. *Work and Stress*, **1**, 235–47.

Jex, S. & Beehr, T.A. (1991) Emerging theoretical and methodological issues in the study of work-related stress. *Research in Personnel and Human Resources Management*, **9**, 311–65.

Jick, T.D. & Mitz, L.F. (1985) Sex differences in work stress. *Academy of Management Review*, **10**, 408–20.

Kanter, R.M. (1977) *Men and Women of the Corporation*. Basic Books, New York.

Karambayya, R. (1998) Caught in the cross-fire: women and corporate restructuring. *Canadian Journal of Administrative Sciences*, **15**, 333–8.

Karambayya, R. (2001) Women and corporate restructuring: sources and consequences of stress. In D.L. Nelson & R.J. Burke (eds) *Gender, Work Stress and Health*. American Psychological Association, Washington, DC.

Keita, G.P. & Jones, J.M. (1990) Reducing adverse reactions to stress in the workplace: psychology's expanding role. *American Psychologist*, **45**, 1137–41.

Kirchmeyer, C. (1993) Managing the boundary between work and non-work: an assessment of organizational practices, paper presented at the Annual Meeting of the Academy of Management, Atlanta, GA.

Kossek, E.F. (1990) Diversity in childcare assistance needs: employee problems, preferences, and work-related outcomes. *Personnel Psychology*, **43**, 769–91.

Kram, K.E. (1996) A relational approach to career development. In D.T. Hall. (ed.) *The Career is Dead—Long Live the Career*. Jossey-Bass, San Francisco, CA.

Kraut, A.I. (1990) Some lessons on organizational research concerning work and family issues. *Human Resource Planning*, **13**, 109–18.

Kraut, A.I. (1992) Organizational research on work and family issues. In S. Zedeck (ed.) *Work, Families and Organizations*. Jossey-Bass, San Francisco, CA, pp. 208–35.

Langan-Fox, J. (1998) Women's careers and occupational stress. In C.L. Cooper & I.T. Robertson (eds) *International Review of Industrial and Organizational Psychology*. New York: John Wiley & Sons, pp. 273–304.

Larwood, L., Szwajkowski, E. & Rose, S. (1988) Manager–client relationships: applying the rational bias theory of managerial discrimination. *Sex Roles: A Journal of Research*, **18**, 9–29.

Lewis, S. (1994) Role tensions and dual career families. In M.J. Davidson & R.J. Burke (eds.) *Women in Management: Current Research Issues*. Paul Chapman, London.

Lindquist, T.L., Beilin, L.J. & Knuiman, M.W. (1997) Influence of lifestyle, coping, and job stress on blood pressure in men and women. *Hypertension*, **29**, 1–7.

Marshall, J. (1984) *Women Managers: Travellers in a Male World*. John Wiley & Sons, New York.

Martocchio, J.J. & O'Leary, A.M. (1989) Sex differences in occupational stress: a meta-analytic review. *Journal of Applied Psychology*, **74**, 495–501.

Matuszek, P.A.C., Nelson, D.L. & Quick, J.C. (1995) Gender differences in distress: are we asking the right questions? *Journal of Social Behavior and Personality*, **10**, 99–120.

Matteson, M.T. & Ivancevich, J.M. (1987) *Controlling Work Stress*. Jossey-Bass, San Francisco, CA.

Mattis, M.C. (1990) *Flexible Work Arrangements for Managers and Professionals: New Approaches to Work in US Corporations*. National Centre for Management Research and Development, University of Western Ontario, London, Ontario.

Mattis, M.C. (1994) Organizational initiatives in the USA for advancing managerial women. In M.J. Davidson & R.J. Burke (eds) *Women in Management: Current Research Issues*. Paul Chapman, London, pp. 241–76.

Miller, T.I. (1984) The effects of employer-sponsored childcare on employee absenteeism, turnover, productivity, recruitment or job satisfaction: what is claimed and what is known. *Personnel Psychology*, **37**, 277–89.

Morrison, A.M. (1992) *The New Leaders*. Jossey-Bass, San Francisco, CA.

Morrison, A.M. & von Glinow, M.A. (1990) Women and minorities in management. *American Psychologist*, **45**, 200–8.

Morrison, A.M., White, R.P. & van Velsor, E. (1987) *Breaking the Glass Ceiling*. Addison-Wesley, Reading, MA.

Nelson, D.L. & Burke, R.J. (2000a) Women executives: health, stress and success. *Academy of Management Executive*, **14**, 107–21.

Nelson, D.L. & Burke, R.J. (2000b) Women, work stress and health. In M.J. Davidson & R.J. Burke (eds) *Women in management*, vol. II. Sage, London, pp. 177–91.

Nelson D.L. & Burke, R.J. (2001) *Gender, Work Stress and Health*. American Psychological Association, Washington, DC.

Nelson, D.L. & Quick, J.C. (1985) Professional women: are distress and disease inevitable? *Academy of Management Review*, **10**, 206–18.

Nelson, D.L., Quick, J.C., Hitt, M.A. & Moesel, D. (1990) Politics, lack of career progress and work/home conflict: stress and strain for working women. *Sex Roles: A Journal of Research*, **23**, 169–85.

Netermeyer, R.G., Boles, J.S. & McMurrian, R. (1996) Development and validation of work–family conflict and family–work conflict scales. *Journal of Applied Psychology*, **81**, 400–10.

Offermann, L.R. & Armitage, M.A. (1993) Stress and the woman manager: sources, health outcomes and interventions. In E.A. Fagenson (ed.) *Women in Management: Trends, Issues and Challenges in Managerial Diversity*. Sage, Newbury Park, CA, pp. 131–61.

Ohlott, P.J., Ruderman, M.N. & McCauley, C.D. (1994) Gender differences in managers' developmental job experiences. *Academy of Management Journal*, **37**, 46–67.

Parasuraman, S., Purohit, Y.S., Godshalk, V.M. & Beitell, N. (1996) Work and family variables, entrepreneurial career success and psychological well-being. *Journal of Vocational Behavior*, **48**, 275–300.

Powell, G.N. (1990) One more time: do male and female managers differ? *Academy of Management Executive*, **4**, 68–75.

Rapoport, R. & Rapoport, R.N. (1976) *Dual-Career Families Reexamined*. Harper & Row, New York.

Repetti, R.L. (1993) The effects of workload and the social environment at work on health. In L. Goldberger & S. Breznitz (eds) *Handbook of stress,* 2nd edn. Free Press, New York.

Repetti, R.L., Mathews, K.A. & Waldron, I. (1989) Employment and women's health: effects of paid employment on women's mental and physical health. *American Psychologist*, **44**, 1394–1401.

Rodgers, F.S. & Rodgers, C. (1989) Business and the facts of family life. *Harvard Business Review*, **67**, 121–9.

Rushforth, D.M. (1991) Employee family programs pay off in lower absenteeism and higher retention, *Employment Relations Today*, **18**, 143–8.

Schein, V.E., Mueller, R. & Jacobson, C. (1989) The relationship between sex role stereotypes and requisite management characteristics among college students. *Sex Roles: A Journal of Research*, **20**, 210–19.

Schneider, K.T., Swan, S. & Fitzgerald, L.F. (1997) Job-related and psychological effects of sexual harassment in the workplace: empirical evidence from two organizations. *Journal of Applied Psychology*, **82**, 401–15.

Schwartz, F.N. (1989) Management women and the new facts of life. *Harvard Business Review*, **89**, 65–76.

Schwartz, F.N. (1992) *Breaking with Tradition*. Warner Books, New York.

Sekaran, U. (1986) *Dual-Career Families*. Jossey-Bass, San Francisco, CA.

Stewart, W. & Barling, J. (1996) Father's work-experiences effect children's behaviors via job-related affect and parenting behaviors. *Journal of Organizational Behavior*, **17**, 221–32.

White, B., Cox, C. & Cooper, C.L. (1992) *Women's Career Development*. Blackwell, Oxford.

Zappert, L.T. & Weinstein, H.M. (1985) Sex differences in the impact of work on physical and psychological health. *American Journal of Psychiatry*. **142**, 1174–8.

CHAPTER 14

Work/Non-Work Interface: A Review of Theories and Findings

Sabine A.E. Geurts
University of Nijmegen, The Netherlands
and
Evangelia Demerouti
University of Nijmegen, Utrecht University, The Netherlands

14.1 GENERAL INTRODUCTION

The meaning of and the relationship between "work" and "non-work" have been important topics in political, public and academic debate for a considerable period in Western history (Kabanoff, 1980). The awareness that the interface between the two domains may constitute a major problem for employees, families, organizations and society has particularly grown since the period of industrialization (Westman & Piotrkowski, 1999;). This period resulted in a major segregation of roles between workers and non-workers, with "work" being spatially, temporally and, to some extent, socially distinct from "non-work" (e.g. family, community, religion, politics and education) (Wilensky, 1960). A more contemporary viewpoint is that "work" and "non-work" are no longer separate domains, but highly interrelated. This changing perspective on the work/non-work interface[1] is directly related to the changing composition of the workforce. Whereas in the early days the segregation between "workers" and "non-workers" paralleled gender segregation, nowadays women form a substantial part of the active working force. Consequently, the numbers of dual-earner couples and of employed persons with care-giving responsibilities are rapidly growing (Gignac et al., 1996; Zedeck & Mosier, 1990).

Recent statistics show that these sociodemographic changes are not without a price. In fact, a high proportion of employed workers, and particularly of employed parents, has serious difficulty in combining obligations in the work domain and domestic obligations.

---

[1] The term "work/non-work interface" is used as a global concept referring to a the point where "work" and "non-work" meet each other, either in a negative or a positive way.

The Handbook of Work and Health Psychology. Edited by M.J. Schabracq, J.A.M. Winnubst and C.L. Cooper.
© 2003 John Wiley & Sons, Ltd.

For example, a survey among a national representative sample of the US workforce showed that 30% experienced major conflict between work demands and family responsibilities, often referred to as work–family conflict (Bond et al., 1998). This was true for an even higher proportion (40%) of employed American parents (Galinsky et al., 1993). In addition, the National Institute for Occupational Safety and Health (NIOSH) has identified work–family conflict as one of the 10 major stressors in the workplace (Kelloway et al., 1999). These precarious developments have captured the attention of social partners (employers and employees), public agencies and the academic community. Nowadays, it is generally agreed that a good work/non-work balance is of growing importance for the economic viability of organizations and for the welfare of families (Barnett, 1998).

The major purpose of the current chapter is to discuss the state of the art of research on the work/non-work interface and to develop an agenda for future research on this topic (see also Geurts et al., 2002). Although research in this area has its roots in a wide variety of disciplines (e.g. psychology, occupational health, sociology, gender and family studies), in order to conform to the scope of the present handbook, our focus will be particularly on studies in the field of occupational health psychology (OHP). We do not intend to provide an exhaustive overview of work/non-work studies that have been carried out during the past two decades. We will primarily discuss the most important theoretical issues and research findings by systematically answering the following questions:

1. What constitutes "work" and "non-work"?
2. What theoretical perspectives have been applied in research on the work/non-work interface?
3. What is the prevalence of (the various dimensions of) the work/non-work interface?
4. What are the possible antecedents of (the various dimensions of) the work/non-work interface?
5. What are the possible consequences of (the various dimensions of) the work/non-work interface?
6. What do we know about effective strategies to improve the work/non-work interface?
7. What are the limitations of current research on the work/non-work interface?
8. What conclusions and future suggestions can be derived from research on the work/non-work interface?

14.2   WHAT CONSTITUTES "WORK" AND "NON-WORK"?

Although there is agreement about the interdependence of "work" and "non-work", there is hardly any agreement about what constitutes both domains. The wide variety of disciplines from which the work/non-work interface has been studied is reflected in a wide range of topics that have been addressed (e.g. time schedule conflicts, household and care-giving responsibilities, marital conflict, children's development problems, and even community involvement; see Barnett, 1998). Whereas work (i.e. wage work) has generally been quite well defined, referring to a set of (prescribed) tasks that an individual performs while occupying a position in an organization, about non-work there has been much less consensus. Non-work may refer to activities and responsibilities within the family domain, as well as to activities and obligations beyond one's own family situation. Sociologists have often referred to the non-work domain as "leisure", interpreted in terms of "spare time". However, they have found it extremely difficult, if not impossible, to actually distinguish between work and leisure activities (Kabanoff, 1980). Also, the non-work domain involves activities (within and beyond the family domain) that cannot be simply considered leisure or spare time, because they involve (similar to the work domain) obligations and responsibilities (e.g. household activities, care-giving responsibilities, and social obligations). In other words, "leisure" is not simply "pleasure". Sociologists have long thought that the consideration of a particular activity as work or leisure should depend on one's mental state, that is, the feeling of pleasure, freedom or relaxation that is associated with the activity (Kabanoff, 1980). However, this would imply that in general work activities do not yield positive experiences of pleasure, freedom and even relaxation.

The question about what constitutes work and non-work has become even more complicated due to several irreversible changes in the context of work. A growing number of people work overtime (at their workplace or not and with more or less freedom of choice), work systematically one or more days at their home address (e.g. telework), and work often during hours beyond 'nine-to-five' (e.g. shift work, weekend work) (Merllié & Paoli, 2000; Paoli, 1997). Similarly, personal activities are often brought into the workplace by different kinds of employee benefits (e.g. the hairdresser at the workplace, fitness or child transport services offered by the company), and working hours are also spent on personal activities (e.g. personal phone calls and emails). Thus, the boundaries between work and non-work are fading. Classifying non-work simply as leisure or spare time does not do justice to reality. Individuals simply have multiple obligations and responsibilities to various others, both in their work domain (e.g. their employer, superior, colleagues, subordinates) and in their non-work domain (e.g. spouses, children, relatives and friends). Whereas the activities in the work domain are not *per se* obliged but may also be voluntarily chosen, the activities in the non-work domain do not *per se* reflect only freedom of choice, but may well involve obligations. We may conclude that whereas voluntarily chosen activities are most likely to be associated with a positive mental state (otherwise one would simply stop the activity), obliged activities (in both domains) are likely to yield negative and/or positive experiences, which may depend on the nature of the activity, individual characteristics (e.g. one's personality) and/or the moment in time (see also Kabanoff, 1980).

14.3 WHAT THEORETICAL PERSPECTIVES HAVE BEEN APPLIED IN RESEARCH ON THE WORK/NON-WORK INTERFACE?

14.3.1 Classical Hypotheses About the Work/non-Work Interface: Segmentation, Compensation and Spillover

Another approach to the difficult issue about what constitutes work and non-work has been to define non-work by its function in relation to work; that is, in terms of the work/non-work interface. Lots of (particularly sociological) scholars have tried to find out to what extent work activities (in terms of skill utilization and behaviour patterns) were copied or, just the opposite, were compensated in non-work activities. Classically, the relationship between the work and the non-work domain has been the basis of three different hypotheses (Cohen, 1997). The earliest hypothesis is the *segregation* (or segmentation) hypothesis (Dubin, 1956; Dubin & Champoux, 1977), postulating that no relationship exists between work and non-work. Both domains are considered (psychologically, physically, temporally and functionally) separate domains, whereby the activities in each domain

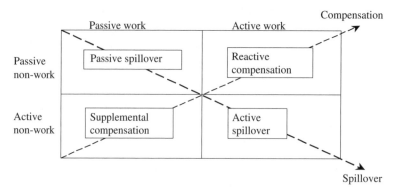

Figure 14.1   A model of four work/non-work patterns (based on Kabanoff, 1980)

are assumed to make unique demands on the individual. This view has been applied more frequently to blue-collar workers, who have more often unsatisfying and uninvolving jobs than white-collar workers (Lambert, 1990). Hardly any evidence exists for this approach and, as far as it does, it shows that segregation does not occur naturally, but may be the result of workers' active attempts to prevent work activities from intruding in their family life.

Besides the segregation hypothesis, Wilensky (1960) distinguished two major hypotheses about the work/non-work interface: (i) the *compensatory* hypothesis, representing attempts to make up for the deprivations experienced at work, and (ii) the *spillover* or generalization hypothesis, which posits the carry-over or generalization of alienation from work into alienation from non-work. As we notice, both hypotheses are based on a negative view of the work domain, whereby negative experiences at work are compensated for or carried over to the non-work domain. Both competing hypotheses have received some evidence (see Kabanoff & O'Brien, 1980). In some studies (Meissner, 1971; Rousseau, 1978), positive correlations were found between the sort of work people perform and their non-work activities. That is, a person in a repetitive and unchallenging job situation seemed to have similar routine non-work activities, supporting the spillover (or generalization) hypothesis. In other studies (Mansfield & Evans, 1975), negative correlations were found between work and non-work. That is, those with routine and unchallenging jobs seemed to choose varied and challenging non-work activities, supporting the compensatory hypothesis.

Kabanoff & O'Brien (1980) have built further on these competing hypotheses by analysing both work and non-work activities on five similar underlying dimensions: autonomy, variety, skill utilization, pressure and social interaction. They distinguished four work/non-work patterns (Figure 14.1) of which the first two correspond to Wilensky's classical hypotheses, and the latter two are based on more challenging job situations (see also Thierry & Jansen, 1998):

1. *Passive spillover/generalization*, whereby both work and non-work activities reflect low levels of autonomy, variety, skill utilization, pressure and social interaction.
2. *Supplemental compensation*, whereby work reflects a low level of the five dimensions mentioned above, whereas non-work activities reflect a high level of the five dimensions.

3. *Active spillover/generalization*, whereby all five dimensions are highly prevalent in both work and non-work activities.
4. *Reactive compensation*, which reflects a high level of the five dimensions in work but a low level of the five dimensions in non-work.

We should notice here, that the spillover hypothesis is in line with the hypothesis about active learning behaviour in the job demand–control model (Karasek & Theorell, 1990). The assumption is that the learning of new behaviour patterns and skills at work is associated with a higher variety in leisure activities. In a classic study among 1466 Swedish males, Karasek (1976) showed that active work was associated with high rates of participation in socially active leisure activities, whereas the opposite was true for passive work. Workers with passive jobs did *not* seem to compensate for their passive behaviour at work with being active in their leisure time, but appeared to carry over socialized patterns of passive behaviour from work to leisure.

Kabanoff & O'Brien (1980) showed that all four types of work/non-work patterns were prevalent but among different groups of people. For example, passive spillover was predominantly found among extrinsically motivated males with low income and low education, supplemental compensation among older females with a low income, active spillover among intrinsically motivated workers with a relatively high education and income, and reactive compensation among extrinsically motivated predominantly male workers. On the basis of his own and previous findings, Kabanoff (1980) concludes that there seems to be a number of different work/non-work patterns, some of which conform to the classical compensation and spillover hypotheses, and others which do not. However, the type of work/non-work pattern may depend on characteristics of the group studied, such as age, gender, education, income, work orientation and, more generally, life orientation. We therefore conclude that rather than concentrating on the development of ideal typologies or on the proving of the existence of a single work/non-work pattern, future research should focus on how people actually balance needs, aspirations and satisfactions across life spheres. In a similar vein, Lambert (1990) concluded on the basis of a literature review that both processes (spillover and compensation) may operate one way or the other to link work and non-work, and may even operate simultaneously.

14.3.2 The Role Strain Hypothesis

Within the field of OHP, the work/non-work interface has classically been studied from the perspective of role stress theory. From this perspective, it was basically assumed that managing multiple roles is difficult and inevitably creates "strain". Greenhaus & Beutell (1985) were one of the first to define work/non-work conflict, whereby non-work was interpreted in terms of "family" (and therefore excluding responsibilities and activities beyond the immediate family). Based on the perspective of role stress theory (also known as the Michigan Organization Stress Model; Kahn et al., 1964), they defined work–family conflict as "a form of inter role conflict in which the role pressures from the work and family domains are mutually incompatible in some respect. That is, participation in the work (family) role is made more difficult by virtue of participation in the family (work) role" (Greenhaus & Beutell, 1985, p. 77). They suggested that the type of work–family conflict could be based on role characteristics that affect time involvement, strain or behaviour in one domain (e.g. work) that are incompatible with fulfilling the role in the other domain (e.g. family). Therefore, they distinguished three forms of work–family conflict.

1. *Time*-based conflict, referring to (time) pressures from one domain (associated with the fulfillment of one role) that make it physically impossible to meet demands from the other domain, or produce a preoccupation with one role even when one is physically attempting to meet the demands of another role (Bartolome & Evans, 1979). An example of this type of conflict is when long working hours limit one's attendance and participation in family activities.
2. *Strain*-based conflict, referring to strain (e.g. tension, anxiety, fatigue, depression, irritability) created by the participation in one domain (role) that makes it difficult to comply with the demands from the other domain (another role). An example of this type of conflict is when fatigue built up during working hours spills over to the family domain and drains one's energy resources for family activities.
3. *Behaviour*-based conflict, referring to specific patterns of role behaviour that are incompatible with expectations regarding behaviour in another role. An example of this latter type of conflict is when one has difficulty in combining a professional, rational and business-like attitude at work with a personal, more open and sensitive attitude at home.

Within the area of OHP, most researchers have followed Greenhaus & Beutell (1985) in defining work–family conflict in terms of inter-role conflict and use their tripartite classification of the types of work–family conflict (see also Carlson et al., 2000). Due to difficulties in the operationalization of the last form of work–family conflict, there is little empirical evidence for the existence of behaviour-based work–family conflict.

Although during the 1980s research treated work–family conflict primarily as a unidimensional construct, in the early 1990s the reciprocal nature of the work–family conflict was recognized. Gutek et al. (1991) proposed that conflict between work and family might originate in either domain. Conflict can arise from work interfering with family (e.g. working overtime interferes with family activities) and from family interfering with work (e.g. illness of a child interferes with attendance at work). Evidence from different samples has consistently shown that work–family conflict and family–work conflict are two distinct aspects of the work/non-work interface that are at best only moderately correlated (Frone et al., 1992a, 1992b, 1997b; Netemeyer et al., 1996).

The role strain perspective on the work/non-work interface is based implicitly on the *scarcity* perspective on the fulfilment of multiple roles and human energy (see Marks, 1977). The basic assumption is that available time and energy resources are limited and that the fulfilment of multiple roles is likely to result in a depletion of these scarce resources. In order to prevent serious work/non-work conflict, individuals have to allocate their limited resources over multiple roles in both domains in such a way that role strain develops only in bearable proportions.

This role strain or scarcity perspective on the work/non-work interface cannot be unequivocally linked to the earlier distinction between spillover (active versus passive) and compensation (reactive versus supplemental) (see Figure 14.1). It may equally well be considered a form of "reactive compensation" (i.e. work requiring so much effort that leisure time is primarily used to relax from work) or as "spillover" of negative load effect built up at work. Psychologists have most often interpreted the work/non-work role conflict as a form of *negative spillover* of strain built up at work into one's family life (Lambert,

1990). It is important to notice here that whereas originally the spillover process involved mainly skills and behaviour patterns (i.e. type of activities), later researchers expanded on this by assuming that the spillover process might also involve strain, emotions, beliefs and attitudes.

14.3.3   The Role Enhancement Hypothesis

As opposed to the role strain hypothesis (and the related negative spillover perspective), a parallel line of theory suggests that energy or skills mobilized or developed in the work domain might also improve one's functioning in the non-work domain, a process often referred to as *positive spillover* or *role enhancement* (Grzywacz & Marks, 2000), or as *facilitation* (see Frone, 2002). The basic idea is that participation in multiple roles might provide a greater number of opportunities and resources to the individual that can be used to promote growth and better functioning in other life domains (Barnett, 1998). Following the idea of active spillover, Crouter (1984), for example, showed that workers who developed decision making skills at work began to use these newly developed skills to deal more effectively with their children. Also empirical reports from a variety of samples show that spouse support and having the opportunity to discuss work problems at home might enable workers to cope better with the pressures at work (Gattiker & Larwood, 1990; Weiss, 1990). Other sources consistently show that employed and married mothers experience greater happiness and better physical health than unemployed and married mothers or employed singles without children (CBS, 1999; Waldron et al., 1998).

The role enhancement hypothesis has its roots in Marks' *expansion* approach on the fulfilment of multiple roles and human energy (Marks, 1977). The basic assumption in this approach, which Marks presented as an alternative approach to the by then dominant scarcity approach, is that the fulfilment of multiple roles is not necessarily difficult and associated with the spending or depletion of energy resources and the development of role strain. On the basis of insights from human physiology, Marks stated that the process of consumption of human energy is inseparably related to the process of production of human energy. Activity is necessary to stabilize the production of human energy, and even while we are spending it we are also converting more of it for later use. In other words, adequately managing multiple roles may also create energy.

Although work/non-work research has long been dominated by the role strain or scarcity perspective, Marks (1977) as well as Kabanoff (1980) have laid the foundation for a more positive view on the work/non-work interface. In addition, recent perspectives on the work/non-work interface have moved away from the classical distinction between the processes of "compensation" and "spillover". The insight has grown that the two processes cannot be clearly distinguished (both conceptually and empirically), may operate simultaneously and may depend on individual differences (e.g. personal disposition, gender), family circumstances (e.g. parental status) and work characteristics (e.g. high strain jobs).

Recently, Edwards & Rothbard (2000) critically reviewed the classical approaches of the work/non-work interface. In addition to the earlier discussed hypotheses about how work and non-work are related (i.e. spillover, compensation, segregation and conflict), Edwards & Rothbard discuss the congruence model and the resource drain model. Hereby, congruence refers to similarity between both domains, due to a third variable that acts as a common cause (e.g. personality traits, behavioural styles, social and cultural forces). Resource drain refers to the transfer of limited personal resources (e.g. time, attention and energy) from one domain to the other. The congruence model is analogous to the spillover model, in that both lead to similarities between both domains. A difference is, however, that the similarities are not attributed to the effects from one domain that spill over to the other, but to a third variable that affects both domains. The resource drain model has similarities with the earlier discussed scarcity approach and related hypotheses (e.g. the role strain hypothesis). A greatest merit of the review of Edwards & Rothbard (2000) is their attempt to translate the various hypotheses about the work/non-work interface (often described in abstract and metaphoric terms) into causal relationships and concrete work and family constructs.

14.3.4   Recent Perspectives on the Work/non-Work Interface

Although the role strain hypothesis that work and non-work are two domains which are perpetually in conflict with each other is still quite dominant in work/non-work research (e.g. Frone et al., 1997b; Kinnunen & Mauno, 1998, Parasuraman et al., 1996; Stephens et al., 1997), recently researchers have build further on the idea that these two domains might also be in harmony. In addition to this more *positive* view of how work and non-work might relate, recent theoretical approaches no longer focus explicitly on the work/non-work interface (as did the classical hypotheses). In most empirical studies, conceptual models stem from more general sociological theories or general stress models (including the previously discussed role stress theory or Michigan Organization Stress Model). We will discuss five theoretical perspectives that have recently been used to improve our understanding of the work/non-work interface.

1. The *conservation of resources* (COR) theory (see Hobfoll, 1989) is one of the general stress models that has been applied frequently in research on stress and burnout. Recently Grandey & Cropanzano (1999) suggested that the COR theory may also offer an appropriate framework for work–family studies. The model proposes that individuals seek to acquire and maintain resources. The resources may include conditions (e.g. married status, tenure), personal characteristics (e.g. self-esteem) or energies (e.g. time, money and knowledge that allow one to acquire other resources). Stress reactions develop when there is a threat of loss of resources, an actual loss of resources, or lack of an expected gain in resources. The COR theory proposes that work–family conflict may lead to a wide variety of stress reactions (i.e. dissatisfaction, depression, anxiety or physiological tension), because valued resources are lost in the process of juggling both work and family roles. Grandey & Cropanzano (1999) tested a research model based on the COR theory on a sample of 132 American university professors and found supportive evidence that, however, cannot be simply generalized to other work settings or groups. A difference with the more traditional role stress theory is that the fulfilment of multiple roles is not inevitably related to the experience of higher levels of stress. Each role (e.g. being married or being parent) might also offer resources that help individuals to deal with other demands associated with the fulfilment of other roles (e.g. being employed).

2. Barnett's *fit model* (1998) stresses the importance of *fit* as a mediating process in the relationship between, for instance, the number of hours worked and psychological

health outcomes. "Fit" is conceptualized as "the extent to which workers realize the various components of their work–family strategies, that is, their plans for optimizing their own work and non-work needs as well as those of other members of their work–family/social system" (Barnett et al., 1999, p. 307). When available workplace options permit workers to realize their strategies, they experience compatibility and low distress. Otherwise, they experience conflict and high distress. For example, among people who work long hours, those whose strategies require significant time for family or other non-work activities would experience poor fit and, consequently distress, whereas those without such commitments would experience better fit and less distress. The fit construct does not assume an inherent conflict between work and family. Rather it assumes that adaptive strategies are formulated so as to simultaneously maximize employees' ability to meet the needs of the workplace and their ability to meet the needs of the family system. The fit construct goes beyond the notion of work–family conflict; it is about the family's adaptive strategies, the extent to which couples are able to optimize their family adaptive strategy. More concretely, Barnett et al. (1999) operationalized fit subjectively by asking employees on a 7-point scale (ranging from "extremely poorly" to "'extremely well") how well the number and distribution of their work hours and the flexibility of their work schedule met their needs. They were also asked to rate how well their own and their partner's schedules met their own, their partner's and their children's needs. Their results, based on a sample of 141 married physicians, provided support for the mediating role of fit in the relationship between work hours and burnout.

3. The *work/family border* theory is newly developed by Clark (2000). The basic idea is that "work" and "family" are different domains that are characterized by different cultures (i.e. different purposes, different language, different rules, different customs and behaviour). According to this theory, people are "border-crossers" who make daily transitions between the two domains. Hereby, individuals shape their goals, focus, language and behaviour to fit the unique demands of each domain. For some individuals, the transition (border-crossing) may be slight when, for instance, language and customs are highly similar in both domains. For others, the language and behaviour expected in the work domain are very different from what is expected in the family domain, thus requiring a more extreme transition. Notice here, the similarity with the earlier discussed behaviour-based conflict, based on the role strain hypothesis (see Section 14.3.2). The work–family border theory attempts to explain how individuals manage the borders between work and family in order to attain balance. Central to this theory is that individuals are largely proactive or enactive, meaning that they can essentially shape the nature of each domain, as well as the borders and bridges between both domains. A main proposition of the model is that weak borders (i.e. permeable and flexible) will facilitate work–family balance when domains are similar, while the opposite (i.e. strong borders) is more functional when domains are very different. According to the theory, "central participants" in a domain (i.e. those who have influence in that domain because of their competence, affiliation with central members within that domain and their internalization of the domain's culture and values) are very well able to control the border with the other domain and, consequently to attain a good balance between work and family. The opposite is true for so-called "peripheral participants", that is, those who have less influence within that domain because they ignore domain values, have not achieved full competence and do not interact sufficiently with other (central) members within that domain (e.g. supervisors in the work domain, and spouses in the home domain).

The work–family border theory, developed on the basis of qualitative information derived from interviews, provides an instructive insight into the process of managing work–family balance. However, the theory remains quite general in its concepts and is, therefore, difficult to test empirically. For instance, the theory postulates that with respect to the domains it is important to evaluate the degree of overlap of valued "ends" (i.e. benefits, such as close relationships) and "means" of attaining goals between both domains. However, the type of means and ends that should be taken into account and the way these concepts should be operationalized remains unclear. Furthermore, it is unclear how overload in one or both domains should be incorporated into this theory. For instance, whereas similarity with respect to the type and amount of close relationships in both domains will facilitate border-crossing, similarity in the amount of overload will not. Thus far, empirical studies testing this theory are lacking.

4. Grzywacz & Marks (2000) recently studied the work–family interface from the perspective of *ecological systems* theory. This theory goes beyond the individual and deterministic approach of role theory by assuming that the work–family interface is a joint function of "process", person, context and time characteristics. Each of these characteristics exerts an additive (and potentially interactive) effect on an individual's experience of the work–family interface, which is reflected by the adequacy of fit between the individual and his or her environment. Grzywacz & Marks (2000) hypothesized from this theoretical perspective that ecological resources at work (i.e. decision latitude, support from co-workers and supervisors) as well as at home (i.e. spouse support) would be associated with lower levels of negative spillover and higher levels of positive spillover between work and family. On the other hand, ecological barriers at work (i.e. pressure at work) as well as at home (i.e. spouse disagreement and family criticism/burden) would be associated with higher levels of negative spillover and lower levels of positive spillover between work and family. In line with this broader perspective, they have used a broader conceptualization of the work–family interface by distinguishing among positive and negative spillover from work to family as well as from family to work. However, Grzywacz & Marks did not define negative and positive spillover between both domains from the perspective of ecological systems theory (they only refer to it as work–family conflict and enhancement, respectively). Nor did they specify what attributes (e.g. emotions, attitudes, skills or behaviour) may be transferred from one domain to the other. Moreover, when we look at the operationalizations, positive family–work spillover mainly concerns whether family plays an alleviating role for the negative impact of work on the individual, for instance, as a support system or by providing relaxation and love. Positive work–family spillover, on the other hand, concerns the transference of, for example, skills and mood. In general, their empirical findings based on a representative sample of 1986 American employed adults are supportive of their hypotheses, and indeed provide evidence for a four-factor structure of the work–family interface.

5. Also Geurts and her colleagues have recently distinguished among four different dimensions underlying the work/non-work interface (Demerouti et al., submitted, Geurts, 2000; Wagena & Geurts, 2000). They have defined the work/non-work interface in terms of a process of interaction[2] between both domains, more specifically as a process whereby one's

---

[2] We preferred defining the work/non-work interface in terms of "interaction", rather than in terms of "conflict", because the former covers both negative and positive influence between both domains and clearly refers to the dynamics of this process. We

functioning (and behaviour) in one domain is influenced by (quantitative and qualitative) demands from the other domain (one's functioning is hereby dependent on both one's ability and one's motivation to invest time and effort into the work or the home domain). The interaction may be negative, for instance, when one's functioning at home is hampered by demands from the work domain ("work negatively influencing home") or the other way around ("home negatively influencing work"). The interaction between both domains can also be positive, for instance, when one's functioning at home is facilitated by demands from the work domain ("work positively influencing home") or the other way around ("home positively influencing work"). Based on the *effort–recovery model* (Meijman & Mulder, 1998), as well as the recently developed *job demands–resources model* (Demerouti et al., 2001) (the latter can be considered an elaboration of the well known demand–control–support model; Karasek & Theorell, 1990), the following assumptions were made. When job demands require too much effort and time (e.g. work overload, too tight deadlines) and job resources (e.g. social support, autonomy, performance feedback and career opportunities) are insufficient to fulfil the job requirements, energy and time resources are depleted. As a consequence, negative load effects build up and hamper one's functioning in the non-work domain ("work negatively influencing home"). On the other hand, when existing job resources are sufficient to deal with high job demands, individuals may be stimulated to learn from and "grow" in their job and energy will be mobilized rather than depleted. This will facilitate one's functioning in the non-work domain ("work positively influencing home").

Both processes might also initiate from the non-work domain. Thus, in a similar vein, it is assumed that home demands (e.g. household and care-giving tasks) that require too much effort and time and the lack of home resources (e.g. the lack of instrumental support from the spouse) to fulfil the task requirements will be associated with negative load effects that hamper one's functioning in the work domain ("home negatively influencing work"). The existence of home resources (e.g. a domestic help, domestic appliances, a babysitter, spouse support) that enable individuals to deal with the demanding aspects in their home situation, on the other hand, will be associated with positive load effects that will facilitate one's functioning at work ("home positively influencing work").

Recent empirical findings based on various occupational groups in the Netherlands were generally supportive of these hypotheses (Bakker & Geurts, submitted; Demerouti et al., submitted). Job and home demands were more strongly associated with negative interaction (initiating from the work domain and the home domain, respectively) than with positive interaction between both domains. Job and home resources, on the other hand, were more strongly related to positive interaction (initiating from the respective domain) than to negative interaction between both domains. In addition, and similarly to Grzywacz & Marks (2000), findings strongly supported the existence of the assumed four different (but empirically related) dimensions of work/non-work interaction.

---

also preferred the term "interaction" rather than "spillover", because the latter only seems to refer to attributes (e.g. emotions) that have *increased* to a certain level and, therefore, flow over to the other domain. The term "interaction", on the other hand, also covers attributes (e.g. time and energy) that have *decreased* to a certain level and, because of their scarcity, influence the other domain.

14.4   WHAT IS THE PREVALENCE OF (THE VARIOUS DIMENSIONS OF) THE WORK/NON-WORK INTERFACE?

Despite the use of different terms[3], definitions and measurements of the work/non-work interface, as well as the use of a wide variety of study samples, research in this area shows very consistently that "work negatively influencing home" is more prevalent than "home negatively influencing work" (e.g. Bond et al., 1998; Burke & Greenglass, 1999; Demerouti et al., submitted; Eagle et al., 1997; Frone et al., 1992b; Kinnunen & Mauno, 1998; Leiter & Durup, 1996). In fact, Frone et al. (1992b) found that negative work–family conflict was reported three times more frequently than negative family–work conflict by both male and female employed adults with a spouse and/or with children. Bond et al. (1998) reported similar results for a national representative sample of the American working population, with an even greater divergence in the prevalence. Whereas 32% of the American workers reported that during the last three months they had not had enough time for themselves because of their jobs, only 4% reported that during the same period family or personal life had kept them from getting paid labour done on time. The impact of non-work on working life is more often evaluated positively than negatively by both male and female workers (Demerouti et al., submitted, Grzywacz & Marks, 2000; Kirchmeyer, 1993). In fact, Demerouti et al. (submitted) showed that of all dimensions of work–home interaction, positive influence of the home situation on one's functioning at work ("home positively influencing work") is most prevalent among 751 employees from the Dutch Postal Services (see also Wagena & Geurts, 2000). Using an American population of around 2000 employees, Grzywacz & Marks (2000) showed that positive spillover from family to work was equally prevalent as negative spillover from work to family among both male and female workers.

14.4.1   Gender

Gender constitutes the sociodemographic characteristic that has been most frequently examined with respect to the prevalence of the various dimensions of the work/non-work interface. The reason is the generally believed gender role expectation that work is more important for men, and family life is more important for women (Pleck, 1977). However, competing hypotheses have been formulated on the basis of this gender role expectation. On the one hand, it has been hypothesized that because of higher family responsibilities, family factors intrude into the work situation more often for women than for men ("home negatively influencing work"), whereas work factors intrude into the family situation more often for men than for women ("work negatively influencing home") (e.g. Frone et al., 1992b; Pleck, 1977). On the other hand, it has been hypothesized that women experience more negative influence initiating from the work domain (rather than the home domain) compared to men, because of their higher involvement in the family domain. From the same

---

[3] The reader of this chapter will notice that in the following sections a variety of terms are used as conceptualizations of the work/non-work interface. More specifically, conflict, negative spillover, interference, negative influence and negative interaction are used to refer to the negative interface, and positive spillover, positive influence and positive interaction are used to refer to the positive interface. This variety in terminology is due to the fact that we describe empirical findings as much as possible in the terms that were originally used by the researchers who presented them.

perspective, one would expect men to experience more negative influence initiating from the family domain because of their higher work involvement (e.g. Higgins et al., 1994). The empirical evidence about gender most consistently shows that no (or hardly any) differences exist between males and females in their experience of negative interaction between work and family in both directions (Burke, 1988; Demerouti et al., submitted; Eagle et al. 1997; Frone, 2002; Frone et al., 1992b; Grzywacz & Marks, 2000; Kinnunen & Mauno, 1998; Kirchmeyer, 1993). Grzywacz & Marks (2000) did find that women reported slightly more positive spillover from work to family than men.

14.4.2   Age

The effect of age has been less systematically studied. Age has been found to be positively related to family–work conflict (Burke & Greenglass, 1999) or not related to any type of negative interaction between both domains (Kinnunen & Mauno, 1998; Frone et al.,1997a). Grzywacz & Marks (2000) showed that, after controlling for work and family characteristics, younger men reported higher negative spillover between work and home (in both directions) and less positive spillover from family to work than older men, whereas younger women reported more positive spillover from work to family and more negative spillover from family to work than did older women. Grzywacz & Marks (2000) did not provide an explanation for these differences.

14.4.3   Marital Status and Family Structure

The impact of marital status on the work/non-work interface is not so clearly investigated, since studies often include only married employees in their study sample. Grzywacz & Marks (2000) reported that being unmarried was associated with the experience of less negative work-to-family spillover, but also with the experience of less positive spillover from family to work. Grandey & Cropanzano (1999) failed to confirm an effect of marital status on conflict between work and family. Somewhat more consistent findings with respect to individual differences are observed for the number of home-living children, which is positively related to both work–family and home–family conflict (Grandey & Cropanzano, 1999; Kinnunen & Mauno, 1998; Netemeyer et al., 1996). There are indications that the age of the children does influence the experience of negative interaction between both domains differently for men and women. Working women with young children (<12 years) experience more negative spillover between both domains (in both directions), compared to both working women with older children and working men (e.g. Crouter, 1984; Higgins et al., 1994). These findings suggest that the experience of negative interaction between both domains is related to one's life stage (i.e. having young pre-school or school-age children), but only for women. In a similar vein, Higgins et al. (1994) showed that the experience of work–family conflict was dramatically lower for women with high-school children (>13 years) than for women with younger children, whereas for men the experience of work–family conflict was only slightly lower for those with high-school children than for men with younger children.

14.4.4   Educational Level, Income and Race

In the study of Grzywacz & Marks (2000) lower levels of education and income were robustly associated with a lower level of positive spillover from work to family among women, but were not associated with this outcome among men. The longitudinal study of Frone et al. (1997a), however, revealed non-significant relationships between both education and income on the one hand, and work–family conflict and family–work conflict on the other. Race has also been related to the work/non-work interface. According to Grzywacz & Marks (2000) black women reported less negative spillover from family to work than other women did, while Frone et al. (1997a) found no long-term relationships between race and conflict between both domains (see also Frone et al., 1992b).

14.4.5   Conclusion

With respect to the prevalence of the various dimensions of the work/non-work interface, empirical evidence shows quite consistently that negative influence initiating from the work domain is more prevalent than negative influence initiating from the non-work domain. In fact, the influence of non-work is more often evaluated positively than negatively. There are no indications that the prevalence of negative interaction initiating from both domains differs across genders. There are indications, however, that the experience of negative interaction between both domains depends on one's life stage (i.e. having young children), and that this relationship is gender-related (more specifically, female workers with young children seem to experience the highest levels of negative interaction between both domains, compared to males and to females with older children). With respect to the relationship of other individual differences and the work/non-work interface (i.e. age, educational level, income and race), empirical findings are inconsistent or not significant.

14.5   WHAT ARE THE POSSIBLE ANTECEDENTS OF (THE VARIOUS DIMENSIONS OF) THE WORK/NON-WORK INTERFACE?

The various possible antecedents of (negative and positive) interaction between work and non-work that have been found in different studies can be classified into personality characteristics, family-related factors, job-related factors and attitudes. As far as demographic characteristics are concerned, these have been discussed in the previous section.

14.5.1   Personality Characteristics

Most personality characteristics that have been related to the work/non-work interface are known from the general stress literature (see Chapter 5): neuroticism, extraversion, personal coping and Type A behaviour. Grzywacz & Marks (2000) found that a higher level of neuroticism was related to more negative interaction between work and non-work in both directions, while elevated levels of extraversion were associated with less negative spillover and more positive spillover in both directions (Grzywacz & Marks, 2000). It has also been observed that employees who rely on their own personal resources for reducing negative influence from non-work (i.e. who have an internal locus of control), instead of holding their employers largely responsible for work demands, experienced less negative influence from non-work (Kirchmeyer & Cohen, 1999). Finally, police officers with Type A characteristics (e.g. being impatient, being irritated easily, hasty eating or walking, and being competitive and ambitious) reported more work–family conflict than those without these characteristics (Burke, 1988).

14.5.2   Family Characteristics

Family–work conflict has been particularly related to several demanding aspects of the family situation. This concerns family life in general, as well as the relationship with one's partner and children. It has been found that family role conflict (i.e. receiving incompatible requests within the family domain) and family role ambiguity (i.e. not knowing exactly what the obligations towards the family are) are positively associated with experienced family–work conflict (Grandey & Cropanzano, 1999; Grzywacz & Marks, 2000), as well as with work–family conflict (Carlson & Perrewé, 1999; Grzywacz & Marks, 2000). However, it is also possible that the resulting relationship between family role conflict and the conflict between work and family can be explained by conceptual and operational overlap among these constructs.

One important family characteristic is social support provided by the family. In general this is negatively related to the experience of conflict between the work and the home domain (Frone et al., 1992a). Parasuraman et al. (1996) showed among 111 male and female entrepreneurs the beneficial effects of spouse support in enabling entrepreneurs to meet the dual demands of work and family roles. Informational and emotional support of one's spouse was directly and negatively linked with family–work conflict. Rosenbaum & Cohen (1999) also provided evidence for spouse support as an important resource for preventing work–family conflict. The importance of family social support is also underlined by Carlson & Perrewé's (1999) finding that support provided by the family was negatively related to family role ambiguity and family role conflict.

A low quality of the relationship with the spouse, on the other hand, has been found to be related to experiences of negative interaction between the two domains. For instance, personal conflict with family members has been found to be a predictor of work–family conflict over time (Leiter & Durup, 1996). Also Burke (1988) has shown that serious difficulties with one's spouse were related to the experience of work–family conflict. A lower level of spouse disagreement, on the other hand, has been associated with less negative spillover between the two domains (Grzywacz & Marks, 2000). Finally, Frone et al. (1992a, 1997b) studied parental stressors (i.e. parental workload and children's misbehaviour), which were positively related to family–work conflict. Also, the hours devoted to family activities have been found to be positively related to family–work conflict (Frone et al., 1997b; Grandey & Cropanzano, 1999; Gutek et al., 1991).

14.5.3   Job Characteristics

The amount of time required by the job (i.e. the pattern of working hours per week, working full- or part-time, and working overtime) has been frequently studied as an antecedent of negative work–family conflict, and obviously particularly of time-based conflict between the two domains (Greenhaus & Beutell, 1985). Here, the basic assumption is that the amount of time that is occupied by the job is one of the most obvious ways for occupational life to affect family life (Kanter, 1977). Several studies confirm that working longer hours per week is associated with a higher level of work–family conflict or negative work–family spillover (Frone et al., 1997b; Grzywacz & Marks, 2000; Gutek et al., 1991; Van der Hulst & Geurts, 2001; Wallace, 1997). Barnett (1998) questioned these findings after reviewing various studies that provide evidence that long work hours are associated with positive mental health indicators. Since the effect of long work hours is not as straightforward as expected, Barnett (1998) favoured the explanation that working long hours may be a risk factor for specific groups under specific conditions. Thus, the study of work hours alone seems to be insufficient in explaining interference from the work domain to the home domain.

Following a similar line of reasoning as for work hours, part-time work has been related to less work–family conflict primarily for women, that is, the group of employees who most frequently work part time (Higgins et al., 2000; Kinnunen & Mauno, 1998). As Barnett (1998) suggested, studying the direct effects of working full time or part time *per se* is less likely to yield consistent results because it might be confounded with other variables (e.g. the degree of flexibility in and control over the schedule, and the type of job that is performed). Moen & Yu (2000) found the most effective arrangement, in terms of a low level of work–family conflict and a high level of psychological life quality, among spouses who both work regular hours (39–45) and have full-time arrangements. However, when either or both spouses work longer hours (>45 hours per week), men and women report high levels of work–family conflict (Moen & Yu, 2000). This is in line with findings from Geurts et al., (1999) who showed among medical residents that having a spouse who frequently works overtime was related to a higher level of work–home interference by the resident.

Finally, the distribution of working hours has been related (although less frequently) with interference from the work domain. In this respect, Geurts et al. (1999; see also Pleck et al., 1980) found that those who evaluated their work time schedule unfavourably (e.g. work time schedules offering insufficient spare time during the week or at the weekend, or disturbing one's regular sleep/wake rhythm) reported higher levels of work–home interference. Also the shift-work of the husband makes considerable demands on the adaptability of the wife. However, wives complain less about their domestic problems than about reduced social life activities (Rutenfranz et al., 1981).

Another category of job characteristics that has been related to work–family conflict are the job stressors or job demands and requirements that might be incompatible with the family role (Greenhaus & Beutell, 1985). Among the job stressors, work overload is consistently found to be the most robust antecedent of work–family conflict (Frone et al., 1997b; Geurts et al., 1999; Wallace, 1997). Employees who experience a high level of work–family conflict are those who also report high work role conflict and work role ambiguity (Carlson & Perrewé, 1999; Grandey & Cropanzano, 1999), pressure at work (Frone et al., 1992a; Grzywacz & Marks, 2000) and work overload (Frone et al., 1997b; Geurts et al., 1999; Geurts et al., in press; Wallace, 1997). Burke (1988) utilized an index of several job stressors (doubts about competence, problems with clients, bureaucratic interference, lack of stimulation and collegiality) that had a substantial positive association with work–family conflict. In addition, Burke & Greenglass (1999) found that organizational restructuring and downsizing were consistently and strongly related to work–family conflict. In a similar vein, Kinnunen & Mauno (1998) showed that job insecurity was related to the experience of conflict between work and family (in both directions).

Besides these demanding aspects of the job, various dimensions of the work/non-work interface have also been related to positive job characteristics. It has been found that higher levels of decision latitude or job control are related to lower levels of work–family conflict or negative work–family spillover (Frone et al., 1992a; Grzywacz & Marks, 2000; Kinnunen & Mauno, 1998), to lower levels of family–work conflict (Parasuraman et al., 1996), and to higher levels of positive spillover in both directions (Grzywacz & Marks, 2000). Similarly, social support at the workplace is negatively associated with work–family conflict or negative work–family spillover (Carlson & Perrewé, 1999; Grzywacz & Marks, 2000; Kinnunen & Mauno, 1998; Kirchmeyer & Cohen, 1999; Moen & Yu, 2000). Higher levels of social support at the workplace also seem to contribute to higher levels of positive interaction between both domains (Demerouti et al., submitted; Grzywacz & Marks, 2000). In the study of Wallace (1997), motivators like promotion opportunities and the social value of work were negatively related to work–family conflict.

14.5.4 Attitudes

Among the possible antecedents of the work/non-work interface is also the importance and centrality of work or family respectively in one's life. The basic assumption is that the centrality of a particular domain in one's life might increase the amount of time and effort devoted to that domain, as well as the mental preoccupation when the demands in that domain are not fulfilled (Greenhaus & Beutell, 1985). This may make it difficult to devote time to and become engaged in activities that are required in the other domain (Frone, 2002). Results provide some support for this hypothesis. Specifically, Frone et al. (1992a) found a positive relationship between psychological involvement in the family domain and family–work conflict, though they did not find a similar relationship between psychological job involvement and work–family conflict. Frone et al. (1997b) did show, however, a positive relationship of work time commitment (i.e. the amount of time devoted to the work domain) with work–family conflict (and not with family–work conflict). Family time commitment (i.e. the amount of time devoted to parenting activities) was positively related to only family–work conflict (Frone et al., 1997b). Also, Parasuraman et al. (1996) showed that particularly time commitment to work, and to a lesser extent psychological job involvement (i.e. psychological importance of work in one's life), were related to work–family conflict. Family–work conflict, on the other hand, was more strongly related to psychological family involvement, and to a lesser extent to time devoted to household and childcare activities.

14.5.5 Conclusion

Among the job characteristics, particularly demanding aspects of the job seem to be responsible for negative influence of work on the non-work situation, and to a lesser extent for negative influence in the other direction. Among job demands, work overload is the most consistent and robust antecedent of interference from the work domain. The frequently studied relationship between working long hours and interference from the work domain is probably not so straightforward and may only be a risk factor under specific conditions. Demanding aspects of the family situation (e.g. parental load, family criticism and burden, spouse disagreement) are more consistently related to negative influence of non-work on the work situation, rather than the other way around. Motivational characteristics (i.e. "resources") of the job (particularly job control and social support) as well as in the home situation (i.e. spouse support) have been found to diminish negative interaction between both domains or, according to more recent studies, to evoke so-called positive interaction between both domains. Among personality characteristics, neuroticism and Type A behaviour have been positively associated with conflict between work and non-work, whereas extraversion and internal locus of control have been negatively associated with conflict between both domains. With respect to personal attitudes, there is some support for the hypothesis that high involvement in one domain (e.g. family) is associated with conflict originating from that domain (i.e. family–work conflict), due to (too) much time and effort devoted to the most central domain. Although we have pointed at some possible causal agents, we should note here that virtually all reported relationships between antecedents and the work/non-work interface derived from cross-sectional and self-report studies, which strictly speaking are inadequate research designs for testing causality (see Section 14.8.2).

14.6   WHAT ARE THE POSSIBLE CONSEQUENCES OF (THE VARIOUS DIMENSIONS OF) THE WORK/ NON-WORK INTERFACE?

The list of the possible consequences related to various dimensions of the work/non-work interface is increasing. Partly, these consequences, particularly of "conflict" between the two domains, parallel the outcomes of comparable experiences, such as "stress". However, the consequences of the work/non-work interface go beyond stress-related and organizational outcomes and also spread to a great extent to one's private life. We have categorized the consequences of the work/non-work interface into five major categories: physical, psychological, behavioural, attitudinal and organizational consequences.

14.6.1   Physical Consequences

In general, work–family conflict is positively related to overall self-reported poor physical health (Frone et al., 1997a; Grandey & Cropanzano, 1999). Allen et al. (2000) reported in their meta-analysis (based on 67 studies of which 17 included a measure of somatic or physical symptoms) a weighted mean correlation (r_w) of 0.29 with work–family conflict. Several specific physical outcomes have also been observed, such as headache, backache, upset stomach, fatigue, dizziness and pain in chest or heart area (Geurts et al., 1999). In addition, interference from the work domain seems to be associated to sleep deprivation (Geurts et al., 1999). However, contrasting results have also been reported. On the basis of a longitudinal study, Frone et al. (1997a) found that over a time of four years poor physical health was significantly related only to negative family–work conflict, and not to work–family conflict. This inconsistency with prior research was explained by the assumption that the causal impact of work–family conflict might occur during a shorter period of time, whereas family–work conflict might be more detrimental in the long run. However, the scale utilized to measure family–work conflict in this study had a low reliability ($\alpha = 0.54$).

14.6.2 Psychological Consequences

Consistent relationships have been found between conflict between work and non-work and psychological outcomes. These outcomes concern mainly psychological stress-related outcomes in both the work and the non-work domain. Allen et al. (2000) reported in their recent meta-analysis a weighted mean correlation of 0.29 between general psychological strain measures and work–family conflict. Much higher weighted mean correlations were found between work-related stress measures and work–family conflict ($r_w = 0.41$). Burnout is one of the frequently studied work-related psychological consequences of the work/non-work interface (e.g. Burke, 1988; Kinnunen & Mauno, 1998; Netemeyer et al., 1996). Allen et al. (2000) reported a weighted mean correlation of 0.42 between burnout and work–family conflict. Work–family conflict has also been consistently associated with family-related stress, for instance family distress ($r_w = 0.31$; Allen et al., 2000; Grandey & Cropanzano, 1999) and affective parental and marital stress (Guelzow et al., 1991).

Using the General Health Questionnaire (assessing, for example, mental health, coping with difficulties in life and enjoyment of daily activities), O'Driscoll et al. (1992) found a positive association between work/non-work conflict and general psychological strain. Also Parasuraman and her colleagues (Parasuraman et al., 1992, 1996) obtained positive relationships between work–family conflict and general life stress (including feelings of being upset or frustrated), whereas Beatty (1996) reported positive relationships with anxiety. Other domain-unspecific psychological consequences are negative feeling states, among which depression has been most frequently studied. Depressive complaints have been found to be positively related to both work–family conflict (Netemeyer et al., 1996) and family–work conflict (Frone et al., 1992a; Netemeyer et al., 1996). Similarly, Burke (1988) reported positive relationships between work–family conflict and negative affective states, including depression, the impulse and overt to aggression, anger, irritation, and insomnia.

14.6.3 Behavioural Consequences

An increased consumption of stimulants like coffee, cigarettes and alcohol among those who experience work–family conflict has been observed (Burke, 1988). Frone et al. (1997a) found that in the long run work–family conflict, but not family–work conflict, was related to heavy alcohol use. In addition, health habits like regular physical exercise and taking of medication were (respectively negatively and positively) related to work–family conflict (Burke, 1988). Burke & Greenglass (1999) found that not only work–family conflict, but also family–work conflict was positively related to medication use.

14.6.4 Attitudinal Consequences

Attitudinal consequences can be distinguished in work-related and non-work-related attitudes. Among the work-related attitudinal outcomes, job satisfaction is most frequently related to work–family conflict (see the meta-analyses by Allen et al., 2000; Kossek & Ozeki, 1998). It has been found that experienced conflict between work and non-work is negatively associated with job satisfaction, particularly when the latter is measured globally

(Parasuraman et al., 1989; Rice et al., 1992). Most studies provided evidence for a negative relationship of conflict between both domains with job satisfaction, with a weighted mean correlation of −0.23 found by Kossek & Ozeki (1998), and of −0.24 found by Allen et al. (2000). In some studies, however, no relationship has been found. This is true for the study of O'Driscoll et al. (1992), who used a composite measure of satisfaction with specific job facets, but also for the study of Wiley (1987), who used a global measure of job satisfaction. Organizational commitment, and particularly affective commitment, is another attitudinal outcome that has been associated with negative interaction between both domains. The results are highly comparable to those concerning job satisfaction. Conflict between both domains has been found to be negatively associated with organizational commitment ($r_w = -0.23$; Allen et al., 2000; Netemeyer et al., 1996), but also no relationship has been reported (O'Driscoll et al., 1992).

With respect to non-work-related attitudinal outcomes one can discriminate among different kinds of satisfaction, such as life satisfaction, marital satisfaction, family satisfaction and satisfaction with leisure activities. In general, work–family conflict is negatively related to satisfaction measures, irrespectively of the assessed aspect. According to the results of the meta-analysis of Allen et al. (2000), work–family conflict has a weighted mean correlation of −0.28 (−0.31 in the meta-analysis of Kossek and Ozeki, 1998) with life satisfaction, −0.23 with marital satisfaction and −0.17 with family satisfaction. Besides the studies that found significant associations of work–family conflict with the different types of satisfaction (e.g. Aryee et al., 1999; Beatty, 1996; Rice et al., 1992), there are also studies that failed to support a relationship with life satisfaction (Beutell & Greenhaus, 1983), marital satisfaction (Netemeyer et al., 1996) or family satisfaction (Parasuraman et al., 1996). Finally, in the study of Rice et al. (1992), leisure satisfaction was significantly and negatively related to conflict between work and non-work in both directions.

14.6.5 Organizational Consequences

There exists some limited longitudinal evidence that negative influence of work on non-work might cause actual turnover, absenteeism and reduced performance. Furthermore, most studies used self-reported measures of intentions with regard to turnover, performance and absenteeism. Among the organizational outcomes, turnover intentions had the strongest positive relationships with both work–family conflict and family–work conflict (Grandey & Gropanzano, 1999; Netemeyer et al., 1996). Allen and her colleagues (2000) reported in their meta-analysis a mean weighted correlation of 0.29 between intention to turnover and work–family conflict. Work–family conflict was not only positively related to turnover intentions, but also to actual turnover (Greenhaus et al., 1997). With respect to the relationship between conflict between both domains and absenteeism, results showed rather non-existent relationships ($r_w = -0.02$; Allen et al., 2000; Thomas & Ganster, 1995). Possibly, the impact of moderator variables (e.g. the work- and non-work-attachment; cf. Youngblood, 1982) might be responsible for the lack of a direct relationship of conflict between both domains and absenteeism rates. Finally, the influence of work–family conflict on performance rates is also not clear-cut. Netemeyer et al. (1996) found a negative relationship only between family–work conflict and self-rated performance, while Frone et al. (1997b) reported a negative relationship between conflict originating from both domains and a performance measure that corresponds basically to an evaluation of the overall in-role behaviour. Allen and her colleagues reported in their meta-analysis a mean weighted correlation of −0.12 between job performance and work–family conflict.

14.6.6   Conclusion

Even though the type of studies executed within work/non-work research inhibits us from making definitive conclusions about causality, our review shows that particular negative influence of work on non-work is related to many important consequences. These consequences vary from psychological and physical health to attitudes towards the job and behaviour within and outside the organization. The most extensively studied consequences, as well as the consequences with the most robust relationships with the work/non-work interface, have been found in three categories: psychological consequences (particularly work-related stress, burnout and to a lesser extent general psychological strain), physical consequences (e.g. somatic or physical symptoms) and attitudinal consequences (particularly job satisfaction and organizational commitment). Possible behavioural and organizational consequences of the work/non-work interface have received less attention.

14.7   WHAT DO WE KNOW ABOUT EFFECTIVE STRATEGIES TO IMPROVE THE WORK/NON-WORK INTERFACE?

In most European countries, national governments have been quite active to develop legislation that is aimed at facilitating the work/non-work interface for employees. Although European countries differ in their specific types of arrangements, generally the legislation involves three areas: (i) more flexible working time patterns, (ii) facilitation of leave arrangements, and (iii) provision of childcare facilities.

Governmental policy, however, can be very different from "real-life" organizational practice. In other words, whereas some organizations may be very active in the provision of facilities in the three areas mentioned above, other companies might be more backward. There are also national differences in the specific areas in which companies prefer to offer arrangements to their employees. Whereas, for example, Spanish companies tend to opt especially for flexible work time arrangements and leave permits (Poelmans & Chinchilla, 2001), Dutch companies are relatively active in the field of childcare, compared to similar organizations in the UK, Sweden and Italy (Den Dulk, 2001).

Despite these national differences, there are some similarities across the European countries with respect to what type of organizations are most active in the provision of work–family arrangements. In most European countries, for instance, organizations in the services sector are more likely to offer work–family arrangements than organizations in other sectors of industry. In the Netherlands, work–family arrangements are often part of collective agreements between employers and employees, and this, not surprisingly, also increases the likelihood that organizations actually offer these kinds of arrangements. Furthermore, as is the case with stress prevention in general within European countries, large companies are more active that smaller ones (Geurts & Gründemann, 1999). Besides the size of the companies, there are other factors that distinguish more active companies in this field from more passive ones. Factors that have been identified as triggering factors that motivate companies towards action are the percentage of female workers, the tightness of the labour market, and, most importantly, the extent to which companies wish to create a committed workforce (Poelmans & Chinchilla, 2001).

Although reliable statistics at cross-national level are lacking, probably quite a lot of companies in the European countries are active in providing work–family arrangements to their employees. There are, however, relatively few studies within the field of OHP that empirically address the question of which organizational strategies might be effective. The same is true for the question of which personal strategies are being used and are most effective in dealing with the work/non-work interface. As far as evidence exists, the results will be discussed briefly.

14.7.1 Organizational Strategies

In a Dutch study among 171 dual-earner couples with at least one child less than one year of age, it was shown that dual-earners benefited from a family-friendly workplace, that is, a workplace that allows or enables employees to combine work and family responsibilities (Kluwer et al., 1997). This study showed that this did not concern only the formal policies that were available in the workplace (e.g. flexible working hours, childcare arrangements, parental leave), but particularly the *informal* work environment. Male workers seemed to benefit most from a work environment that was characterized by a low pressure to work overtime, whereas women benefited most from a supportive supervisor and from part-time work. In general, these findings are in line with a study from Cohen (1997) among 300 employees of a school district in Canada. His study showed that organizational commit-ment of employees (particularly of those who find their non-work domains important) was particularly dependent on how organizations react to the non-work domains of employees (e.g. considering employees' personal lives when making important decisions about careers, accommodating employees' special non-work needs, having a flexible attitude with respect to employees' work schedules). Cohen's findings imply that organizations may increase positive attitudes among their employees by showing more respect for their non-work do-mains. Both studies discussed above suggest that people who struggle with balancing their work and family responsibilities might not only benefit from formal family-friendly policies, but particularly from an *informal* family-friendly organizational climate (see also Lambert, 2000; Lewis & Taylor, 1996; Thompson et al., 1999).

In addition, a study by Higgins et al. (2000) among employed women in career jobs (i.e. managerial or professional positions) and non-career jobs (i.e. clerical, administrative, retail or production jobs) showed that, for instance, simply making part-time work available was not enough to help employed women to deal with high work and family responsibilities. Their study illustrated that although non-career women benefited from working part time, career women did not. Whereas for non-career women, part-time work was associated with significant improvement of the work/non-work balance, career women reported high role overload and high family-to-work conflict regardless of their full-time or part-time status. The results suggest that offering part-time jobs may enable women to better manage a persistently demanding home domain (simply by making more time available there). However, as Higgins et al. (2000) conclude, in order to truly make a difference in the quality of life for employed women (especially working mothers) part-time work must also be made desirable and rewarding. The latter concerns again the informal organizational climate and the degree to which the different alternatives are incorporated in the daily practice and culture. Their research stresses the necessity for organizations to pay greater attention to some of the individual differences between career and non-career employed women in terms of the role that work plays in their lives and the rewards they are seeking through employment.

14.7.2 Personal Strategies

Beutell & Greenhaus (1983) have studied the effectiveness of three types of coping strategies for dealing with work/non-work conflict among 115 married women (with at least one child) who were attending college. Their study showed that *active* attempts to change the structural and/or personal definition of one's roles were more effective in dealing with work/non-work conflict than more passive and reactive role behaviour. Beutell & Greenhaus (1983) describe the active reaction pattern as attempts to lessen the conflict by discussing and finding mutual agreement with other people about what can be expected from them, as well as redefining one's own attitudes and perceptions in a more realistic way. The passive reaction pattern can be described as relying on existing role behaviours and trying to meet the unchanged expectations of others as well as of oneself (Beutell & Greenhaus, 1983). Kirchmeyer (1993) showed among professional men and women that, in contrast with her expectation, it was more than just having an active coping strategy that decreased negative spillover from non-work to work or facilitated positive spillover in the same direction. Important was the type of active coping strategy. More specifically, strategies that were aimed at changing one's *own* attitudes about what demands can realistically be met in both domains seemed to be more effective in coping with high demands from both domains than strategies aimed at changing the attitudes or behaviours of others. Men and women did not differ in the extent to which they used the various coping strategies.

14.7.3 Conclusion

Although empirical evidence is scarce, it quite consistently points at an important issue concerning the organizational strategy. Providing formal family-friendly arrangements (e.g. flexible work time patterns, leave arrangements and childcare facilities) is an important organizational strategy to enable employees to improve the balance between work and non-work demands, but it does not seem to be enough. In fact, "having a family-friendly policy" (i.e. the formal arrangements that are provided) is not identical to "being family-friendly" (i.e. the attitude of supervisors and colleagues towards the use of these arrangements). The missing link is the organizational climate. Only when the use of formal family-friendly arrangements is respected and accepted within the organization, might such arrangements be experienced as desirable ways of dealing with work/non-work conflicts. Consequently, companies need to strive for a family-friendly culture that goes beyond formal policies. The scarce empirical evidence concerning personal strategies suggests that the most successful strategy to deal with the work/non-work conflict is to actively change (particularly one's own) attitudes, expectations and behaviours in such a way that demands in both the work and non-work domains can be met.

14.8   WHAT ARE THE LIMITATIONS OF CURRENT RESEARCH ON THE WORK/NON-WORK INTERFACE?

Despite the fact that a lot of studies in the area of the work/non-work interface have contributed particularly to our understanding of antecedents and consequences of work–family conflict, many studies were based on rather weak theoretical grounds and were limited by some methodological issues (see also Barnett, 1998; Frone, 2002).

14.8.1   Theoretical Limitations

1. One of the most important theoretical limitations is the *conceptualization* of work and non-work. Among the variety of topics that have been studied in work/non-work research (see Section 14.2), the direction of influence (i.e. originating from the work or the non-work domain), the quality of impact (i.e. negative or positive) and the attribute of impact (i.e. time, strain, behaviours, skills, knowledge, emotions, or attitudes) change across studies. Most studies conceive the work/non-work interface as a situation of conflicting role pressures from the work and non-work domains that are mutually incompatible (i.e. time-, strain- or behaviour-based conflict; Greenhaus & Beutell, 1985) or as process of negative spillover of strain from one domain to the other (e.g. Frone et al., 1992a, b; Gutek et al., 1991; Netemeyer et al., 1996). This conception, however, ignores the possibility that both domains may also influence each other in a positive way by transferring positive attributes (e.g. learned skills, energy mobilized by rewarding activities, or personal attributes like self-esteem or self-efficacy).

2. A second limitation concerns the fact that it still remains unclear how work–family conflict should be theoretically embedded in the stressor–strain relationship. Work–family conflict is often considered as a *source* of stress, that together with other stressors, will have adverse effects on health and well-being (e.g. Cohen, 1997; Leiter & Durup, 1996). Rather than as a "stressor", work–family conflict has also been considered an *outcome* of stress (i.e. an indicator of strain), particularly caused by work-related stressors (Moen & Yu, 2000; Wallace, 1997). Instead of considering work–family conflict as a stressor or as a strain, various studies have provided evidence for a *mediating* role in the stressor–strain relationship, particularly between work-related stressors (e.g. work overload) and general (i.e. domain unspecific) indicators of impaired psychological health (e.g. psychosomatic health complaints, depressive complaints, sleep deprivation; Barnett et al., 1999, Geurts et al., 1999, in press; Kinnunen & Mauno, 1998; Kirchmeyer & Cohen, 1999; Stephens et al., 1997).

3. A (related) limitation is that a theoretical approach that enlightens the possible pathways of influence between work and non-work is merely lacking. To what extent, for example, are role overload and lack of recovery crucial in the work/non-work interface? Or, to what extent do work and non-work affect each other through affectively charged social interactions (e.g. conflict or withdrawal) among colleagues or among family members? Westman & Piotrkowski (1999) additionally suggest that some working conditions (e.g. shiftwork) may have direct effects on family members, independent of their impact on the worker. In sum, our understanding of the work/non-work interface would improve if more attention were provided to the main *mechanisms* that underlie the interaction between work and non-work.

4. A fourth limitation, as was also noticed by Barnett (1998), concerns the persistence of the researchers in studying employees in a *fragmented* way as if they have two or more separate and competing "selves" (like a "work self" and a "family self") rather than considering employees as human beings with one self that has co-existing needs and responsibilities in more than one domain. This limitation might be attributed to the substantial influence of role stress theory on work/non-work research, and its basic idea that participation in one domain is inevitably made more difficult by participation in another domain (Kahn et al., 1964). As has been discussed (see Section 14.3), only recently have researchers oriented themselves to other theoretical models that can broaden our understanding of the work/non-work interface, such as the conservation of resources theory, the fit model, the work–family border theory, the ecological systems theory, the effort–recovery model, and the job demands–resources model. However, a lot of work has still to be done in order to integrate the dynamic aspect of the functioning of human beings in various domains.

5. A final limitation, also discussed by Barnett (1998), is that most studies in the area of the work/non-work interface focus on the individual *worker* as the object of analysis, rather than on, for example, the *couple* or the *family*. The latter is important because what happens to the worker is also likely to affect his or her spouse or family (and even friends and relatives), and experiences of relevant others might also affect the worker and in turn the workplace (Bolger et al., 1990). Consequently, work/non-work research should not exclusively study the individual worker as if he or she does not take part in a broader social system, but should focus more on the combined work and non-work demands that couples or families are confronted with.

14.8.2   Methodological Limitations

1. First, most studies are *cross-sectional* and correlational by nature. This kind of study does not allow us to draw causal inferences about the correlates of the work/non-work interface. Moreover, they do not enable us to detect how the work/non-work interface may change over time, for example, due to developments in one's career, changes in one's family situation, or changes in one's perspective on life in general. Not surprisingly, we still do not definitely know whether the work/non-work interface reflects a stable or a changing experience.

2. Second, the majority of the studies rely solely on *self-report measures* (often based on questionnaires) addressing simultaneously the workplace, the family situation and outcome variables. The use of only one method of data collection increases the danger that the associations are spurious and trivial, and reflect cognitive consistencies in the responses (Kelloway et al., 1999) or, in other words, are contaminated due to common method variances.

3. Third, most work/non-work research has been conducted among white-collar, professional, and relatively highly educated employees of large organizations (Westman & Piotrkowski, 1999), as well as among female employees (Barnett, 1998). These biases reflect some beliefs such as, for example, that segmentation (and not conflict) between work and non-work would occur for blue-collar workers (cf. Westman & Piotrkowski, 1999), or that female workers would experience more work–family conflict due to their higher family responsibilities than male workers (cf. Barnett, 1998). The *selective groups* that have been studied thus far partly explain, among other things, the inconsistent findings across studies. Moreover, this limits our ability to generalize findings to the working population in general,

and to develop a comprehensive conceptual model that is applicable to a variety of job settings and groups of workers.

4. A fourth limitation that is related to the previously discussed high variety in the conceptualization of the work/non-work interface, is the diversity of *measures of the work/non-work interface* that have been used. This limitation makes it often impossible to compare the prevalence of the various dimensions of the work/non-work interface, as well as their relationships with correlates, across studies and across groups.

5. A final limitation is that variables in the non-work domain empirically explain far less variance of the work/non-work interface than variables in the work domain. This might reflect reality, but it might also be caused by the *lack of adequate measures* of what truly matters in the *non-work* domain. As far as non-work variables have been studied in work/non-work research, too often they are limited to some objective home characteristics (e.g. marital status, number and age of children, and dual career). These characteristics alone do not provide adequate information about, for instance, what tasks in the non-work domain individuals are actually involved in (e.g. specific household activities, taking care of children or parents, organizing and planning) and what responsibilities they actually have. What pressures do they experience from the non-work domain (e.g. expectations from relevant others, time pressures), and what resources, besides spouse support, do they have? As long as we do not assess people's home situation in the same precise way as we assess their work situation, we will not have a clear picture of the true antecedents of the work/non-work interface.

14.9   WHAT CONCLUSIONS AND FUTURE SUGGESTIONS CAN BE DERIVED FROM RESEARCH ON THE WORK/NON-WORK INTERFACE?

With this review we have shown that the work/non-work interface, though difficult to conceptualize, is an important topic to study, not only because an increasing number of workers have difficulty in combining work and non-work demands, but also because the effects of work are not restricted to the workplace, and the effects of the non-work domain affect employees' behaviour and experiences at work. Our review has made clear that the work/non-work interface is a multifaceted phenomenon: work and non-work mutually influence each other, and this can be in a negative as well as in a positive way. We have shown that the more classical hypotheses about the mechanisms through which work and non-work influence each other, that is, either spillover or compensation, cannot be (conceptually and empirically) distinguished and may very well operate simultaneously. We have discussed the more recent perspectives on the work/non-work interface that are characterized by a more positive view on it.

Our review has shown that work negatively influences non-work more often than the other way around. The prevalence of negative interaction between both domains does not differ across genders. It does, however, seem to depend on one's life stage (i.e. having young children). Even though the type of studies executed within work/non-work research inhibits us from making definitive causal conclusions, our review shows that demanding aspects in the work domain are primarily related to negative influence of work on non-work. Demanding aspects of the family domain, on the other hand, are more consistently related to negative influence of non-work on work. There is also some support for the hypothesis that high psychological involvement in one domain (in terms of many hours devoted to that domain and/or a high psychological importance of that domain in the person's life) is associated with conflict originating from that domain. Motivational aspects (i.e. "resources") in the work as well as in the non-work situation seem to diminish negative interaction between both domains or, according to more recent studies, to evoke so-called positive interaction between both domains.

Our review further shows that particularly negative influence originating from the work domain is related to many relevant consequences, varying from physical and psychological health to job attitudes and behaviour within and outside the organization. Finally, our review revealed that our knowledge about organizational and personal strategies to enhance work/non-work balance is limited. Scarce evidence indicates that, besides the provision of formal work–family arrangements, the organizational climate is important. The most successful personal strategy to cope with work/non-work conflict is to actively change (one's own) attitudes, expectations and behaviours, rather than to keep trying to meet the unrealistic expectations from oneself and others.

On the basis of the theoretical and methodological limitations in current research on the work/non-work interface, the following suggestions are made.

14.9.1   Research on the Positive Interface

It is vital to expand our understanding of the phenomenon of the work/non-work interface. In addition to the investigation of how work negatively influences non-work and the other way around, it is functional to consider how work positively affects the non-work domain and how non-work (e.g. family) can facilitate functioning at work. This can be seen also as an expression of a more general trend towards positive psychology that focuses on human strengths and optimal functioning rather than on weaknesses and malfunctioning. In this respect, it is possible that some characteristics of work (e.g. overload) or of the home situation (e.g. death of a family member) will only negatively affect the functioning in another life domain, while others (e.g. job control or good living conditions) may only have positive effects. This would agree with the findings of Demerouti et al. (2001) that excessive job demands were mainly related to health impairment, while job resources evoked primarily positive experiences (e.g. motivation). A recent study by Demerouti and Geurts (submitted) shows that negative and positive interaction between both domains may even occur simultaneously within the same persons.

14.9.2   Theory-Guided Research: Definitions and Instruments

The identification of the main characteristics or constellations of characteristics at work and at home is the first step, which should be followed by the identification of the mechanisms that underlie the interaction between work and non-work. Important questions are, for instance: "Under what conditions do which specific job characteristics influence families?" "How are negative (stressful) experiences and positive experiences (e.g. motivation and learning) transmitted?" and "What different types of outcomes are observed?"

(Perry-Jenkins et al., 2000). The role of the individual with his or her preferences and priorities, needs, abilities and coping efficiency is no doubt a key factor. Thus, research should move towards more sophisticated theoretical models that go beyond the stress–strain idea. An important merit of future research would be that the work/non-work interface is clearly defined from a theoretical perspective, and that measurements are based on this perspective. Recently, Geurts and her colleagues at the University of Nijmegen (Demerouti et al., submitted; Geurts, 2000; Wagena & Geurts, 2000) have defined the work/non-work interface in terms of a process of interaction between both domains. Based on the perspective of the previously discussed effort–recovery model (Meijman & Mulder, 1998), they have developed a questionnaire (SWING, Survey Work–home Interaction—Nijmegen) that aims to measure both positive and negative interaction between work and non-work.

14.9.3 Home Characteristics

To find out which demands and resources in the home situation affect one's functioning at work, it is important to assess the home situation with the same preciseness as the workplace assessment. This means that work–family researchers should move beyond the investigation of primarily objective family characteristics, such as marital and parental status. One suggestion is to search for subjective demanding and rewarding aspects in the home situation (e.g. time pressure, conflict with family members, support from family members, and rewarding aspects of household, care-giving or other activities). Another suggestion is to make a more objective and detailed analysis of people's social, mental and physical activities in the home situation, and what consequences this might have in terms of energy mobilization (i.e. energy consumption or energy production; Marks, 1977), recovery and accumulation of load effects (see, for instance, the diary study of Sonnentag, 2001). Such finer grained analysis of the home situation may not only be instrumental to better understand how work and non-work are related to each other, but also how they might be influenced by specific work–family policies.

14.9.4 Longitudinal Research Designs with Multiple Sources of Information

As is also true for other research in the area of OHP, studies on the work/non-work interface need to move towards better methodological and research design approaches. Instead of asking only employees themselves about their experiences and therefore running the danger of measuring cognitive consistencies in the response patterns, it is important to have multiple sources of information from both domains, for instance, from the partner and adolescent children, from supervisors or observers. The use of several research methods and data sources to test the same hypothesis or finding is often called *triangulation* (see Babbie, 1995).

The use of longitudinal designs can further improve our insight into the possible causal relationships of the work/non-work interface and its correlates. Moreover, longitudinal studies could provide insight into the question of whether the work/non-work interface reflects a more *stable* situation over time, or whether it is highly influenced by sudden and *fluctuating* experiences in the work and home situation. The effect of these so-called "critical events" on the work/non-work interface as compared to the effects of stable characteristics (at work and at home) has virtually never been estimated. "Critical incidents" can be described as events or incidents that do not occur every day, but have a more sudden and unexpected character (e.g. interpersonal conflicts, accidents and unexpected successes). If research does show that the work/non-work interface is affected more by stable aspects of the work and home situation, rather than by critical incidents in both domains, it will have important practical implications for the prevention of negative interaction and the promotion of positive interaction between both domains (e.g. by job redesign or individual training).

14.9.5   "Natural Experiments" and Intervention Studies

As our review has shown, studies that investigate the impact of work–family policies or, more generally of workplace interventions, on the work/non-work interface have been scarce. We agree with Westman & Piotrkowski (1999, p. 304) who suggest that "we need to look for opportunities to conduct 'natural experiments' when people are changing or starting jobs, or when corporate restructuring occurs". With respect to interesting interventions, one could think of the introduction of flexible work time schedules or other family-friendly practices, like leave permits, special benefits or services (e.g. child transport services), so that we can assess whether or not these changes reduce negative interaction and/or facilitate positive interaction between both domains. Important in this respect is to analyse the impact of the various work–family measures for different subgroups, because what is helpful for, for instance, working women with young children is not necessarily beneficial for working women without (young) children or for male workers. As stated before, individual preferences are no doubt, again, a key factor.

14.9.6   Organizational Culture

Our review has shown that besides the importance of formal work–family policies, the organizational climate (i.e. the degree to which policies are incorporated and accepted in the daily practice and culture) also seems to be of crucial importance (cf. Thompson et al., 1999). Some recent American studies have focused on factors influencing managers' decisions to grant flexible working arrangements to their subordinates (Powel & Mainiero, 1999) or to take up flexible working arrangements themselves (Kossek et al., 1999). Because managers may be crucial to more fundamental changes in organizational culture, further research is needed on the role of managers. They are not only the ones who actually implement policies, they may also function as role models in terms of their own work/non-work balance.

14.9.7   Variety in Nations, Occupations and Samples

Last but not least comes the necessity for the investigation of various occupations and various family situations, including persons with different individual characteristics. If working conditions that are *not* unique for a specific occupational group are indeed related to the work/non-work interface, then these conditions are potentially relevant for every occupation and the observed restriction to white-collar professionals has no ground. Thus, the investigation of heterogeneous populations with respect to work situation, the family situation and/or individual characteristics is important for reasons of generalization, extension of variance range, and consequently for better estimation of the effects. An additional necessity is the comparison across nations with respect to the prevalence of the various dimensions of the work/non-work interface, as well as the possible antecedents and consequences. Thus far, this type of cross-national comparative study is absent from the work–family literature.

14.9.8 To Conclude

To conclude, the value of these suggestions for future research lies in their ability to provide guidelines for the design of effective strategies for improving the integration of work and private life (see also Lambert, 1990). Research on the work/non-work interface has consistently shown that the influence of work on non-work is evaluated more often negatively, rather than positively (Demerouti et al., submitted; Grzywacz & Marks, 2000). Therefore, the most promising strategy to reduce conflict and facilitate balance between both domains is to create a healthy and motivational workplace that respects workers who have responsibilities and interests outside the workplace that they consider important for their quality of life. This organizational strategy can be expected to have a positive and profound impact on people's functioning within and outside the workplace, which is beneficial not only for employees themselves, but also for their families, organizations and society.

ACKNOWLEDGEMENT

This study has been carried out within the framework of two programmes that are financially supported by The Netherlands Organization for Scientific Research (NOW): The Priority Program "Fatigue at work" (580-02-104) and the programme "ASPASIA" (015.000.027).

REFERENCES

Allen, T.D., Herst, D.E., Bruck, C.S. & Sutton, M. (2000). Consequences associated with work-to-family conflict: a review and agenda for future research. *Journal of Occupational Health Psychology*, **5**, 278–308.

Aryee, S., Luk, V., Leung, A. & Lo, S. (1999). Role stressors, interrole conflict, and well-being: the moderating influence of spousal support and coping behaviours among employed parents in Hong Kong. *Journal of Vocational Behavior*, **54**, 259–78.

Babbie, E. (1995). *The Practice of Social Research*. Toronto: Wadsworth.

Bakker, A.B. & Geurts, S.A.E. (submitted). Towards a dual-process model of work–home interference.

Barnett, R.C. (1998). Toward a review and reconceptualization of the work/family literature. *Genetic, Social, and General Psychology Monographs*, **124**, 125–82.

Barnett, R.C., Gareis, K.C. & Brennan, R.T. (1999). Fit as a mediator of the relationship between work hours and burnout. *Journal of Occupational Health Psychology*, **4**, 307–17.

Bartolome, F. & Evans, P.A.L. (1979). Professional lives versus private lives—shifting patterns of managerial commitment. *Organizational Dynamics*, **7**(4), 3–29.

Beatty, C.A. (1996). The stress of managerial and professional women: is the price too high? *Journal of Organizational Behavior*, **17**, 233–51.

Beutell, N.J. & Greenhaus, J.H. (1983). Integration of home and non-home roles: women's conflict and coping behavior. *Journal of Applied Psychology*, **68**, 43–8.

Bolger, N., DeLongis, A., Kessler, R.C. & Wethington, E. (1990). The microstructure of daily role-related stress in married couples. In J. Eckenrode & S. Gore (eds) *Stress between Work and Family*. New York: Plenum Press, pp. 95–114.

Bond, J.T., Galinsky, E. & Swanberg, J.E. (1998). *The 1997 National Study of the Changing Workplace*. New York: Families and Work Institute.

Burke, R.J. (1988). Some antecedents and consequences of work-family conflict. *Journal of Social Behavior and Personality*, **3**, 287–302.

Burke, R.J. & Greenglass, E.R. (1999). Work–family conflict, spouse support, and nursing staff well-being during organizational restructuring. *Journal of Occupational Health Psychology (Special issue: Relationship between Work and Family Life)*, **4**, 327–36.

Carlson, D.S. & Perrewé, P.L. (1999). The role of social support in the stressor–strain relationship: an examination of work–family conflict. *Journal of Management*, **25**, 513–40.

Carlson, D.S., Dacmar, M.K. & Williams, L.J. (2000). Construction and validation of a multidimensional measure of work-family conflict. *Journal of Vocational Behavior*, **56**, 2, 249–76.

CBS (Central Bureau for Statistics) (1999). Tevreden moeders [Satisfied mothers]. *Webmagazine* (11-3-99). Voorburg/Heerlen: CBS.

Clark, S. (2000). Work/family border theory: a new theory of work/family balance. *Human Relations*, **53**(6), 747–70.

Cohen, A. (1997). Personal and organizational responses to work–nonwork interface as related to organizational commitment. *Journal of Applied Social Psychology*, **27**(12), 1085–1114.

Crouter, C. (1984). Spillover from family to work: the neglected side of the work–family interface. *Human Relations*, **37**, 425–42.

Demerouti, E. & Geurts, S.A.E. (submitted). Towards a typology of work-home interference.

Demerouti, E., Bakker, A.B., Nachreiner, F. & Schaufeli, W.B. (2001). The job demands–resources model of burnout. *Journal of Applied Psychology*, **86**(3), 499–512.

Demerouti, E., Geurts, S. & Kompier, M. (submitted). *Positive and negative interaction between work and home*.

Den Dulk, L. (2001). *Work–Family Arrangements in Organisations. A Cross-National Study in the Netherlands, Italy, the United Kingdom and Sweden*, Doctoral thesis, University of Rotterdam. Amsterdam: Rozenberg.

Dubin, R. (1956). Industrial workers' world: a study in the central life interests of industrial workers. *Social Problems*, **4**, 3–13.

Dubin, R. & Champoux, J.E. (1977). Central life interests and job satisfaction. *Organizational Behavior and Human Performance*, **18**, 366–77.

Eagle, B.W., Miles, E.W. & Icenogle, M.L. (1997). Interrole conflicts and the permeability of work and family domains: are there gender differences? *Journal of Vocational Behavior*, **50**, 168–84.

Edwards, J.R. & Rothbard, N.P. (2000). Mechanisms linking work and family: clarifying the relationship between work and family constructs. *Academy of Management Review*, **25**(1), 178–99.

Frone, M.R. (2002). Work–family balance. In J.C. Quick & L.E. Tetrick (eds) *Handbook of Occupational Health Psychology*. Washington, DC: American Psychological Association.

Frone, M.R., Russell, M. & Cooper, M.L. (1992a). Antecedents and outcomes of work–family conflict: testing a model of the work–family interface. *Journal of Applied Psychology*, **77**, 65–78.

Frone, M.R., Russell, M. & Cooper, M.L. (1992b). Prevalence of work–family conflict: are work and family boundaries asymmetrically permeable? *Journal of Organizational Behavior*, **13**, 723–9.

Frone, M.R., Russell, M. & Cooper, M.L. (1997a). Relation of work–family conflict to health outcomes: a four-year longitudinal study of employed parents. *Journal of Occupational and Organizational Psychology*, **70**, 325–35.

Frone, M.T., Yardley, J.K. & Markel, K.S. (1997b). Developing and testing an integrative model of the work–family interface. *Journal of Vocational Behavior*, **50**, 145–67.

Galinsky, E., Bond, J.T. & Friedman, D.E. (1993). *The Changing Workforce: Highlights of the National Study*. New York: Families and Work Institute.

Gattiker, U.E. & Larwood, L. (1990). Predictors of career achievement in the corporate hierarchy. *Human Relations*, **43**(8), 703–26.

Gignac, M.A., Kelloway, E.K. & Gottlieb, B.H. (1996). The impact of caregiving on employment: a mediational model of work–family conflict. *Canadian Journal on Aging*, **15**(4), 525–42.

Geurts, S.A. (2000). SWING: Survey Work–Home Interaction—Nijmegen. Background information and Dutch and English version. Internal research report, University of Nijmegen.

Geurts, S.A. & Gründemann, R. (1999). Workplace stress and stress prevention in Europe. In M.A.J. Kompier & C. Cooper (eds) *Preventing Stress, Improving Productivity*. London: Routledge, pp. 9–32.

Geurts, S.A.E., Rutte, C. & Peeters, M. (1999). Antecedents and consequences of work–home interference among medical residents. *Social Science and Medicine*, **48**, 1135–48.

Geurts, S.A.E., Kompier, M.A.J., Roxburgh, S. & Houtman, I.L.D. (in press). Does work-home interference mediate the relationship between workload and well-being? *Journal of Vocational Behavior*.

Geurts, S.A.E., Taris, T., Demerouti, E., Dikkers, J., & Kompier, M.A.J. (2002). Waar werk en privé elkaar raken: de stand van zaken [Where work and nonwork meet: The state of the art]. *Gedrag & Organisatie,* **15**(3), pp. 163–183.

Grandey, A.A. & Cropanzano, R. (1999). The conservation of resources model applied to work–family conflict and strain. *Journal of Vocational Behavior*, **54**, 350–70.

Greenhaus, J.H. & Beutell, N.J. (1985). Sources of conflict between work and family roles. *Academy of Management Review*, **10**, 76–88.

Greenhaus, J.H., Collins, K.M., Singh, R. & Parasuraman, S. (1997). Work and family influences on departure from public accounting. *Journal of Vocational Behavior*, **50**, 249–70.

Grzywacz, J.G. & Marks, N.F. (2000). Reconceptualizing the work–family interface: an ecological perspective on the correlates of positive and negative spillover between work and family. *Journal of Occupational Health Psychology*, **5**, 111–26.

Guelzow, M.G., Bird, G.Q. & Koball, E.H. (1991). An exploratory path analysis of the stress process for dual-earner men and women. *Journal of Marriage and the Family*, **53**, 151–64.

Gutek, B.A., Klepa, L. & Searle, S. (1991). Rational versus gender role explanations for work–family conflict. *Journal of Applied Psychology*, **76**, 560–8.

Higgins, C., Duxbury, L. & Lee, C. (1994). Impact of life-cycle stage and gender on the ability to balance work and family responsibilities. *Family Relations*, **43**, 144–50.

Higgins, C., Duxbury, L. & Johnson, K.L. (2000). Part-time work for women: does it really help balance work and family? *Human Resource Management*, **39**(1), 17–32.

Hobfoll, S.E. (1989). Conservation of resources a new attempt at conceptualising stress. *American Psychologist*, **44**(3), 513–24.

Kabanoff, B. (1980).Work and nonwork: a review of models, methods and findings. *Psychological Bulletin*, **88**(1), 60–77.

Kabanoff, B. & O'Brien, G. (1980). Work and leisure: a task attributes analysis. *Journal of Applied Psychology*, **65**(5), 596–609.

Kahn, R.L., Wolfe, D., Quinn, R., Snoek, J. & Rosenthal, R. (1964). *Organizational Stress: Studies in Role Conflict and Ambiguity*. New York: John Wiley & Sons.

Kanter, R.M. (1977). *Men and Women of the Corporation*. New York: Basic Books.

Karasek, R.A. (1976). The impact of the work environment on life outside the job, doctoral thesis, Massachusetts Institute of Technoloy. Springfield: National Technical Information Service, Department of Commerce.

Karasek, R. (1979). Job demands, job decision latitude, and mental strain: implications for job redesign. *Administrative Science Quarterly*, **24**, 285–307.

Karasek, R.A. & Theorell, T. (1990). *Healthy Work: Stress, Productivity and the Reconstruction of Working Life*. New York: Basic Books.

Kelloway, E.K., Gottlieb, B.H. & Barham, L. (1999). The source, nature and direction of work and family conflict: a longitudinal investigation. *Journal of Occupational Health Psychology*, **4**, 337–46.

Kinnunen, U. & Mauno, S. (1998). Antecedents and outcomes of work–family conflict among employed women and men in Finland. *Human Relations*, **51**, 157–77.

Kirchmeyer, C. (1993). Nonwork-to-work spillover: a more balanced view of the experiences and coping of professional women and men. *Sex Roles*, **28**, 531–52.

Kirchmeyer, C. & Cohen, A. (1999). Different strategies for managing the work/non-work interface: a test for unique pathways to work outcomes. *Work and Stress*, **13**, 59–73.

Kluwer, E.S., Boers, S.A., Heesink, J.A.M. & Vliert, van der, E. (1997). Rolconflict bij tweeverdieners: De invloed van een "zorgvriendelijke" werkomgeving [Role conflict among dual-earners: the impact of a "family-friendly" workplace]. *Gedrag en Organisatie*, **10**, 223–41.

Kossek, E.E. & Ozeki, C. (1998). Work–family conflict, policies, and the job–life satisfaction relationship: a review and directions for future organizational behavior-human resources research. *Journal of Applied Psychology*, **83**, 139–49.

Kossek, E., Barber, A. & Winters, D. (1999). Using flexible schedules in the managerial world: the power of peers, *Human Resource Management*, **38**(1), 33–46.

Lambert, S. (1990). Processes linking work and family: a critical review and research agenda. *Human Relations*, **43**(3), 239–57.

Lambert, S.J. (2000). Added benefits: the link between work-life benefits and organizational citizenship behavior. *Academy of Management Journal*, **43**(5), 801–15.

Leiter, M.P. & Durup, M. J. (1996). Work, home, and in-between: a longitudinal study of spillover. *Journal of Applied Behavioral Science*, **32**, 29–47.

Lewis, S. & Taylor, K. (1996). Evaluating the impact of family-friendly employer policies: a case study. In S. Lewis & J. Lewis (eds) *The Work–Family Challenge: Rethinking Employment*. London: Sage, pp. 112–27.

Mansfield, R. & Evans, M.G. (1975). Work and non-work in two occupational groups. *Industrial Relations*, **62**, 328–34.

Marks, S.R. (1977). Multiple roles and role strain: some notes on human energy, time and commitment. *American Sociological Review*, **42**, 921–36.

Meijman, T.F. & Mulder, G. (1998). Psychological aspects of workload. In P.J.D. Drenth, H. Thierry & C.J. de Wolff (eds) *Handbook of Work and Organizational Psychology*, 2nd edn. Hove: Psychology Press/ Erlbaum, pp. 5–33.

Meissner, M. (1971). The long arm of the job: a study of work and leisure. *Industrial Relations*, **10**, 239–60.

Merllié, D. & Paoli, P. (2000). *Ten Years of Working Conditions in the European Union*. Dublin: European Foundation for the Improvement of Living and Working Conditions.

Moen, P. & Yu, Y. (2000). Effective work/life strategies: working couples, work conditions, gender, and life quality. *Social Problems*, **47**, 291–326.

Netemeyer, R.G., Boles, J.S. & McMurrian, R. (1996). Development and validation of work–family conflict and family–work conflict scales. *Journal of Applied Psychology*, **81**, 400–10.

O'Driscoll, M.P., Ilgen, D.R. & Hildreth, K. (1992). Time devoted to job and off-job activities, interrole conflict, and affective experiences. *Journal of Applied Psychology*, **77**, 272–9.

Paoli, P. (1997). *Second European Survey on Working Conditions 1996*. Dublin: European Foundation for the Improvement of Living and Working Conditions.

Parasuraman, S., Greenhaus, J.H., Rabinowitz, S., Bedeian, A.G. & Mossholder, K.W. (1989). Work and family variables as mediators of the relationship between wives' employment and husbands' well-being. *Academy of Management Journal*, **32**, 185–201.

Parasuraman, S., Greenhaus, J.H. & Granrose, C.S. (1992). Role stressors, social support, and well-being among two-career couples. *Journal of Organizational Behavior*, **13**, 339–56.

Parasuraman, S., Purohit, Y.S., Godshalk, V.M. & Beutell., N.J. (1996). Work and family variables, entrepreneurial career success, and psychological well-being. *Journal of Vocational Behavior*, **48**, 275–300.

Perry-Jenkins, M., Repetti, R.L. & Crouter, A.C. (2000). Work and family in the 1990s. *Journal of Marriage and the Family*, **62**, 981–98.

Pleck, J.H. (1977). The work–family role system. *Social Problems*, **24**, 417–42.

Pleck, J.H., Graham, L.S. & Lang, L. (1980). Conflicts between work and family life. *Monthly Labor Review*, **103**, 29–32.

Poelmans, S. & Chinchilla, N. (2001). The adoption of family-friendly HRM policies. Competing for scarce resources in the labour market, research paper no. 438, IESE Research Division, IESE Business School, University of Navarra.

Powel, G. & Mainiero (1999). Managerial decision making regarding alternative working arrangements. *Journal of Occupational and Organizational Psychology*, **72**(1), 41–57.

Rice, R.W., Frone, M.R. & McFarlin, D.B. (1992). Work–nonwork conflict and the perceived quality of life. *Journal of Organizational Behavior*, **13**, 155–68.

Rousseau, D,M. (1978). Relationship of work to nonwork. *Journal of Applied Psychology*, **63**, 513–17.

Rosenbaum, M. & Cohen, E. (1999). Equalitarian marriages, spousal support, resourcefulness and psychological distress among Israeli working women. *Journal of Vocational Behavior*, **54**(1), 102–13.

Rutenfranz, J., Knauth, P., Küpper, R., Romahn, R. & Ernst, G. (1981). Pilot project on the physiological and psychological consequences of shift work in some branches of the service sector. In *Effects of Shift Work on Health, Social and Family Life*. Dublin: European Foundation for the Improvement of Living and Working Conditions.

Sonnentag, S. (2001). Work, recovery activities, and individual well-being: a diary study. *Journal of Occupational Health Psychology*, **6**(3), 196–210.

Stephens, M.A.P., Franks, M.M. & Atziena, A.A. (1997). Where two roles intersect: spillover between parent care and employment. *Psychology and Aging*, **12**, 30–7.

Thierry, H. & Jansen, B. (1998). Work time and behaviour at work. In P.J.D. Drenth, H. Thierry & C.J. de Wolff (eds) *Handbook of Work and Organizational Psychology*, 2nd edn, vol. 2. Hove: Psychology Press Erlbaum, pp. 89–119.

Thomas, L.T. & Ganster, D.C. (1995). Impact of family-supportive work variables on work–family conflict and strain: a control perspective. *Journal of Applied Psychology*, **80**, 6–15.

Thompson, C.A., Beauvais, L.L. & Lyness, K.S. (1999). When work–family benefits are not enough: the influence of work–family culture on benefit utilization, organizational attachment, and work–family conflict. *Journal of Vocational Behavior*, **54**, 392–415.

Van der Hulst, M. & Geurts, S. (2001). Associations between overtime and psychological health in high and low reward jobs. *Work & Stress*, **15**(3), 227–240.

Wagena, E. & Geurts, S. (2000). SWING: Ontwikkeling en validiering van de "Survey Werk-thuis Interferentie-Nijmegen" [SWING: Development and validation of the "Survey Work–Home Interference—Nijmegen']. *Gedrag en Gezondheid*, **28**, 138–58.

Waldron, I., Weiss, C.C. & Hughes, M.E. (1998). Interaction effects of multiple roles on women's health. *Journal of Health and Social Behavior*, **39**, 216–36.

Wallace, J.E. (1997). It's about time: a study of hours worked and work spillover among law firm lawyers. *Journal of Vocational Behavior*, **50**, 227–48.

Weiss, R.W. (1990). Bringing work stress home. In J. Eckenrode & S. Gore (eds) *Stress between Work and Family*. New York: Plenum Press, pp. 17–37.

Westman, M. & Piotrkowski, C.S. (1999). Introduction to the special issue: work–family research in occupational health psychology. *Journal of Occupational Health Psychology*, **4**(4), 301–6.

Wilensky, H. (1960). Work, careers and social integration. *International Social Science Journal*, **12**, 543–60.

Wiley, D.L. (1987). The relationship between work–nonwork role conflict and job related outcomes: some anticipated findings. *Journal of Management*, **13**, 467–72.

Youngblood, S.A. (1982). Work, leisure and absence: an approach–avoidance view of withdrawal. Texas: University of Business Administration.

Zedeck, S. & Mosier K.L. (1990). Work in the family and employing organization. *American Psychologist*, **45**, 240–51.

CHAPTER 15

Alcohol and Drug Misuse and the Organization

Andrew Guppy
Middlesex University, Enfield, UK
and
John Marsden
Institute of Psychiatry, London, UK

15.1 DEGREE OF OCCURRENCE OF ALCOHOL AND DRUG USE IN ORGANIZATIONS

15.1.1 Use, Misuse and Problems

One of the most vexing questions addressed in the literature concerned with alcohol and drugs involves the distinction between different patterns of substance use and their associated problems. However, it seems clear that contemporary practitioners and researchers tend to regard such behaviour as existing on a continuum reflecting problem severity (e.g. Edwards & Unnithan, 1992).

Beyond what may be viewed as non-problem use, a first problem category could be labelled "substance misuse". This could include substance-related behaviour that may cause trouble in the short term through accidents, and social or legal problems. However, such behaviour need not have formed a regular pattern for the individual. In DSM-IV (American Psychiatric Association, 1994), a detailed definition is given for two other categories: "substance abuse" (recurrent and continued misuse of a substance over the past 12 months) and "substance dependence" (presence of tolerance, withdrawal and control loss features as well as those of abuse).

Clearly alcohol, which is legally available for adults in most states, can be consumed in patterns fulfilling the criteria for any of the above labels from use to dependency. Among many prescribed medicines a similar pattern of use, misuse, abuse and dependency may also exist (e.g. benzodiazepines). However, for illicit drugs some would argue that there can be no legitimate non-medical "use" and therefore all use without prescription is misuse (American Medical Association, 1987). We feel that there remains value in distinguishing degrees of use and misuse within all substances, even those currently classed as unlawful.

The Handbook of Work and Health Psychology. Edited by M.J. Schabracq, J.A.M. Winnubst and C.L. Cooper.
© 2003 John Wiley & Sons, Ltd.

15.1.2   Population Use of Alcohol and Other Drugs

The use of substances such as alcohol and other drugs is a very common occurrence among people of working age in most cultures across the world. In the developed world, the most easily available drugs that are associated with health problems are probably alcohol and nicotine (tobacco). However, there are many powerful prescription drugs that may also be associated with problems (e.g. morphine, benzodiazepines). In addition to these, there are a range of illicit and semi-licit substances that perhaps are more popularly known as "drugs" such as cocaine, cannabis, heroin, amphetamines and ecstasy (methylenedioxymetham-phetamine, MDMA). To assist readers, a basic briefing of the most commonly encountered drugs is provided in Table 16.1. While a brief review of the prevalence of use of these substances is provided in the following paragraphs, it is emphasized that all figures are estimates. Under-reporting of alcohol consumption is well documented, and it is felt that reporting of use of illicit drugs is also likely to be somewhat biased.

The use of alcohol is deeply rooted in the customs and culture of a majority of societies throughout the world. In the UK each year 90–95% of the adult population consume alcoholic beverages on an occasional or regular basis (Goddard, 1991; Wilson, 1980). These surveys revealed that average weekly consumption in the UK was around 20 drinks per week for males and around 7 drinks for females (a standard drink being equivalent to a single whisky, a small glass of table wine or a half pint of beer, all containing roughly 8–10 g or between 0.28 and 0.35 ounces of ethanol).

For the USA, Dawson (1993) reported that the average daily consumption was 0.73 ounces (21 g) of ethanol for men and 0.37 ounces (10.5 g) for women, based on a sample of 22 102 current drinkers from the 1988 National Health Interview Survey. These figures roughly equate to consumption of 15–17 drinks per week for men and 7–9 drinks for women.

More usefully, surveys like these suggest that around 5% of men and 2% of women report alcohol-related problems in health, social and economic areas of life functioning (Wilson, 1980). Estimates of population fractions evidencing alcohol-related problems are similar for a number of countries similar in culture and development to the UK, such as the USA, though may vary slightly depending on cultural factors associated with the patterns of consumption (e.g. wine-drinking versus beer-drinking countries; Haphus et al., 1993) and historical factors such as the influence of temperance movements (e.g. Scandinavia). The proportion of a nation's population reporting misuse behaviours may also depend on how such behaviour is legally defined and how such legislation is enforced and sanctioned (Ross, 1982). For example, Pfafferott (1993) and Guppy & Adams-Guppy (1995) have reported considerable differences across international samples in terms of reported drink-driving behaviour, some of which related to differing definitions of the legal drink-driving limit.

A significant empirical contribution to information concerning alcohol use within an occupational group has been provided by the Whitehall II study (Marmot et al., 1993). In this study a cohort of over 10 000 civil servants provided self-report information about their drinking habits and a number of other relevant factors (including psychological well-being), which were then linked with subsequent sickness absence.

Marmot et al. reported that alcohol consumption was significantly related to employment grade within this white-collar sample, with lower grades having higher proportions of both sexes reporting no alcohol consumption. Grade differences in terms of moderate to heavy consumption were more marked for females in higher grades. Overall, they found that 29.5%

Table 15.1 Drugs: a basic briefing

Alcohol	A depressant drug contained in beer (usually 3–4% alcohol), wine (10–12% alcohol) and spirits (40–50% alcohol); adult use legalized in most countries. Intoxication effects: initially relaxed feelings, reduced inhibition, later impaired psychomotor skill, followed by unconsciousness. Long-term heavy use: psychological and physical dependence possible; associated with various health and social problems. Prevalence: 90% of British adults drink. Around 10% of male and 5% of female workers may be defined as "heavy" drinkers. Detectable in urine for several hours depending on amount consumed.
Nicotine	A stimulant contained in tobacco, adult use legalized in almost all countries. Short-term effects may include feelings of arousal or increased concentration. Long-term heavy use is associated with dependence and a cluster of physical problems and is linked to over 100 000 premature deaths annually in the UK, mainly from cancer and circulatory problems. Prevalence: around 30% of UK adults smoke.
Amphetamines	Stimulants; prescribed use possible, illicit use common. Short-term use results in feelings of energy and arousal. Long-term and/or heavy use may result in delusions, hallucinations and feelings of persecution. Psychological dependence possible, tolerance effects common. Prevalence among workers may be less than 1%. Detectable for up to 3 days after use.
Lysergic acid diethylamide (LSD)	Illicit hallucinogen. Short-term effects include heightened visual and auditory sensations, may include mystical, ecstatic or frightening experiences, true hallucinations rare, impairment of psychomotor and cognitive performance likely. Long-term effects relate to mental rather than physical well-being, prolonged serious disorders are rare.
Ecstasy (MDMA)	Stimulant-like drug. Short term use may be similar to LSD (calming, heightened senses) without hallucinations, larger doses may produce effects similar to amphetamines. Prevalence not known, assumed to be similar to amphetamines.
Cocaine (including crack)	Stimulant; rarely prescribed, usually occurs illicitly. Produces feelings of well-being, exhilaration. Long-term and/or heavy use may result in feelings of restlessness, sleeplessness and persecution. Prevalence in US military studies 1–2%, US general population may have 1 million regular users. The UK has over 1000 registered abusers; the Netherlands estimates 75 000 occasional users. Metabolite (benzoylecgonine) detectable for 3–5 days.
Cannabis	Mild depressant-hallucinogen; rarely prescribed, has "decriminalized" status in some countries, is illicit in most. Short-term relaxant, enhances perceptions, impairs psychomotor skills. Heavy use may result in perceptual distortions. Prevalence of 1 million users in the UK, with 7 million regular users in the USA, though maybe current use for less than 10% of employees. Detectable for between 3 and 30 days, depending on use.
Opiates (including heroin)	Depressant-sedative drugs. Morphine and codeine commonly prescribed, heroin usually illicit. Short-term use: feelings of contentment and warmth. Long-term heavy use: dependence may result. Physical harm usually related to needle use. Prevalence: probably less than 0.1% in the UK workforce, US Navy estimate 0.1%. Detectable for up to 72 hours.
Minor tranquilizers	Sedative drugs. Benzodiazepines are the most commonly prescribed (include Valium, Librium, Ativan). Short-term use depresses mental activity and alertness; can impair psychomotor skills. Withdrawal effects common, as is psychological dependence. Prevalence: 1 in 7 British adults occasional users, 1 in 40 long-term users. Detectable usually for 3–10 days,.

Prevalence sources: UK Central Office of Information (1993), United Nations Economic and Social Council (1993). Detection periods from Macdonald et al., (1992).

of men and 18.3% of women reported drinking "almost daily", while 4.3% of men and 1.6% of women reported drinking "twice a day or more". In terms of amount of drinking over the 7 days prior to the survey, the number of drink units reported consumed was used, where a unit was taken as equivalent to a half pint (284 ml) of beer, lager or cider, a single measure of spirits or a glass of wine. From the self-reported weekly consumption, Marmot et al. classified heavy drinking as over 30 units for men and over 20 units for women. Almost 10% of male and 5% of female civil servants were classed as heavy drinkers within this sample. These findings are broadly similar to those reported in a more recent study reported by Davies et al. (1997) from a survey of over 2000 British employees across a wide range of companies, with approximately 11% of males consuming over 30 units per week and 7% of females consuming over 20 units of alcohol per week.

Thus, based on general population surveys, one could expect that 5–10% of male workers and 2–5% of female workers may have consumption patterns that may be associated with problem drinking (misuse, abuse and dependency).

For substances other than alcohol, the estimates vary considerably depending on legality, availability and reason for use. Illicit drugs are the ones that grab the headlines and in this category we find heroin and other opiates, LSD, cannabis, cocaine and amphetamines. Generally speaking, the estimates on prevalence of use of illicit drugs in the United Kingdom are far from satisfactory and provide a tremendous range of possible values (Sutton & Maynard, 1993). In many other countries, similar problems with prevalence estimation exist, with data coming mainly from enforcement agencies and self-report surveys (United Nations Economic and Social Council, 1993). For example, Backer (1987) suggested that nearly one in five Americans between the ages of 20 and 40 had used an illicit drug at least once over a period of one month prior to being interviewed.

In the USA, there has been considerable experience with urine screening for illicit drug use in many working environments and therefore it is possible to provide reasonably informed estimates of the prevalence of drug use, particularly in relation to those applying for jobs and in some cases for job incumbents.

Needleman & Romberg (1989), for example, reviewed the urine analysis results of nearly 1.8 million subject specimens analysed over the five years to March 1988 for US Navy personnel. Their study focused on four illicit drug types: cocaine, marijuana, amphetamines and opiates. The average rate of positive marijuana specimens for Navy recruits over this period was 6.2%, and for Marine recruits it was 3.2%. Much lower positive specimen rates were observed among Navy and Marine service school members (1.1% and 1.3% respectively). The highest rate of positive cocaine metabolite (benzoylecgonine) specimens in one year over the period studied was 2.2% for Navy recruits in 1988, with the average rates for these recruits being 1.2% over the period. Amphetamine-related positive specimens were generally much lower, with the highest rate (of only 0.11%) being for Navy service school members in 1988. For opiates, changes to screening cutoffs meant that only the 1987/88 figures can be deemed appropriate. A rate of just above that for amphetamines (0.12%) was the highest one observed and occurred among Marine service school members. Interesting points in the Needleman & Romberg paper highlight that no distinction was possible within these data sets between different opiates (particularly the medicinally common codeine). Also, the change in cutoff in 1987 was "to correct for possible non-abuse ingestion through poppy seeds".

An indication of the usership likely within non-military employment can be provided from the research in the US Postal Service (Normand et al., 1990). In this work, the results from over 5000 new recruits who underwent pre-employment urine screening for drugs were described. It was found that 12.2% tested positive for "drugs"—7.4% for marijuana, 2% for cocaine, and 2.7% for other drugs, including morphine, codeine and benzo-diazepine.

In other countries outside the USA, the picture seems relatively consistent across developed nations in showing lower misuse patterns than the USA (e.g. Alvarez et al., 1992) and consistently vague across developing nations with a general lack of reliable statistical evidence. Obviously, there are many factors in operation that mean that reliable pictures of the prevalence of both use and misuse of illicit drugs are not commonly available. Additionally, the methods of estimating prevalence seems to vary internationally, rendering comparisons across countries an inexact science to say the least (United Nations Economic and Social Council, 1993).

Thus it would seem clear that, generally, drug use is less common than that of alcohol among the majority of nations. Among the illicit substances, it would appear that cannabis is usually the most commonly occurring.

15.2   SUBSTANCE MISUSE IN RELATION TO OTHER ORGANIZATIONAL PHENOMENA

15.2.1   Alcohol Misuse and Occupation

Although sex and age variables are perhaps the most important influences on alcohol consumption (Knupfer, 1989), both occupational status and other organizational factors have been reported to be associated with consumption levels and alcohol-related problems.

Indeed, over 100 years ago, it was acknowledged that there were aspects of some jobs that predisposed employees to alcohol-related problems: "Again, railway employees, from their liability to night work, irregular hours, exposure to all kinds of weather, and from the expensive and foolish custom of 'treating', are exposed to much danger and many temptations" (Gustafson, 1884, p. 446).

More recently, the survey reported by Goddard (1991) found construction workers were the most likely to have drunk more than the recommended maximum weekly drinking level of 21 units and whose average consumption was the highest across the various occupational groups.

Another study, reported by Casswell & Gordon (1984), highlighted that there may be differences in drinking patterns rather than overall consumption across occupational groups. They found a high frequency of drinking but lower consumption of alcohol reported by men in professional, technical and managerial positions as compared with semi-skilled and unskilled men, where the pattern was reversed, with lower frequency of drinking but greater consumption on drinking occasions.

A very interesting comparison across a number of quite different occupational groups was described by the Royal College of Psychiatrists (1979). This comparison was based on liver cirrhosis mortality data for England and Wales and thus is likely to relate to more serious patterns of misuse. Compared to a population average, publicans and innkeepers were reported to be 15 times more likely to die of cirrhosis. Other working groups with a professional proximity to alcohol (bar staff, hoteliers, restaurateurs and cooks) were also clearly over-represented in cirrhosis deaths. The next main "at risk" group included seamen and military personnel and seemed to reflect the removal from normal social relationships as a factor contributing to problem drinking. A third factor linking several occupational groups (journalists, general practitioners and some transportation workers) seemed related to freedom from supervision (Chivers, 1987).

One of the most detailed studies of occupational risks for alcohol-related problems was conducted by Plant (1979). In an investigation of possible selection factors influencing levels of problem drinking in the alcohol production industry, structured personal interviews were held with a total of 300 newly recruited employees: 150 brewers and distillers and 150 recruits to a comparison group within non-drinks trade industries. The average amount of alcohol consumed during the 7 days prior to interview by the drinks producers was 33 units, compared with just over 21 units for the comparison group. Of note was the finding that alcohol producers were significantly more likely than the comparison group to state that they had begun to drink more since starting their new jobs. In addition, the alcohol producers were significantly more likely to have poorer employment records, reporting more than five jobs in the previous 5 years, or previously holding jobs of higher status. Equal numbers of subjects in the two groups reported having previously worked in a "high-risk" job, such as the armed forces, merchant navy or as bar staff. Plant interpreted these data as suggesting that both selection and workplace effects operate within high-risk industries, with alcohol producers found to be "sliding down the social scale" (p. 622) and entering an environment in which the drinking norms are conducive to heavy drinking.

One year after their initial interviews, 80 respondents were re-interviewed, and between two and three years later, all 300 respondents were sought of which 70% were assessed. Plant (1979) separated the outcome status of the cohort into three groups:

1. the "stables", who were still in the same type of job at follow-up;
2. the "leavers", those who had left the drink trade and had moved to low-risk jobs or were unemployed;
3. the "entrants", those who had left the low-risk comparison group and had moved into high-risk jobs.

For the stable group, 57% of the alcohol producers and 76% of the comparison sample reported being in the same type of work. However, older alcohol producers, aged 45 or more, continued to report heavy drinking while their lower risk counterparts reported reduced drinking levels. Moreover, stable high-risk respondents reported higher levels of alcohol-related problems than the comparison group. Forty-six men had left the drink trade and were either working in low-risk jobs or were unemployed; they reported a decrease of 31% in alcohol consumption during the 7 days prior to interview. There are problems, however, with the reliance on the stability of two weekly measures which may fluctuate considerably over time.

Plant concluded that the results overall suggested that high-risk industries may attract a disproportionate percentage of workers who are already heavy drinkers, but that drinking levels and experience of alcohol-related problems are strongly influenced by the working environment. Overall, Plant (1979) suggested that although a number of aspects of the work environment have been reported to identify certain occupations at risk of drinking problems, there is no compelling evidence to support a "syndrome of risk factors" (p. 315). Moreover, even if certain risks can be described, it is difficult to determine the direction of causality—that is, whether some occupations attract people predisposed to excessive drinking or whether some occupations can be said to cause drinking problems.

Some further indication that there may be a self-selection mechanism acting in certain at-risk occupations comes from recent research on alcohol use in the service industry described by Larsen (1994). Larsen found that, compared to other service industry employees, restaurant workers had higher scores on the Alcohol Use Disorders Identification Test (AUDIT; Claussen & Aasland, 1993). However, Larsen also identified that college students studying hotel management were higher scorers on the AUDIT alcohol problems checklist. This would suggest that problems may be developing before entering the profession and this tends to support the hypothesis that there is a strong self-selection component underlying differences across occupations.

15.2.2 The Misuse of Other Drugs and Organizational Features

One of the results of the restriction of availability of drugs other than alcohol means that an even narrower band of workers may be at particular risk because of their type of job. An interesting and obvious group with a high degree of availability of prescribable drugs are doctors. Brooke et al. (1991) reported an investigation of 144 British doctors with dependency problems. Of the cohort, 26% were described as currently misusing drugs, with 31% misusing both alcohol and drugs, while the remaining 42% were identified as just alcohol-related at the time of treatment. After alcohol, the most frequently misused drugs were opiates (used by 30% of the sample), barbiturates (24%), benzodiazepines (21%) and amphetamines (15%). The main access to the misused substance was found to be primarily through self-prescription, highlighting the factor of availability peculiar to this group and to other professions who work with drugs.

Apart from availability, the factor of beneficial use would seem an important one for linking drug use to certain professional groups. Beneficial use in this instance could refer to performance enhancement gained through the use of illicit drugs or medicines. An often highlighted instance would be that of drug use among professional athletes in order to enhance performance either in the long term (steroids) or shorter term respiratory aids (see Fuller & LaFountain, 1987; VanHelder, 1991). Another group highlighted in various media forms could be seen as the long-distance truck drivers and their use of amphetamines and other stimulants to increase wakefulness over long journeys (Lund et al., 1989).

Another possible example of beneficial use comes from the case studies reported by Lacoursiere et al. (1980), where veterans who had suffered combat trauma seemed to be using alcohol to overcome PTSD symptoms of intrusive thoughts. However, for active combat personnel, illicit drugs were probably more useful than alcohol because they were easier to carry. In general, there would seem little doubt of the over-representation of post-discharge substance misuse among combat-involved Vietnam veterans (Fischer, 1991), though Helzer (1984) has suggested the possibility of this being associated with a pre-service history of misuse.

For military personnel not involved in combat, the study by Cook et al. (1976) would seem to suggest a strong link between regular drug use (40% of the sample reported recent cannabis use) and low morale and job satisfaction. However, this association is not peculiar to drugs as other researchers have linked heavy alcohol use to higher job stress (Romelsjo et al., 1992) and low job satisfaction (Marsden, 1992).

15.2.3 Summary of Substance Misuse in Relation to Organizational Phenomena

It would seem that there are several strong occupational features that are regularly associated with an increased tendency to misuse substances. The first relates to a removal from "normal" social environments. This may be evidenced for military personnel on station, seamen and oil-rig workers.

The second relates to the "reduced supervision" factor, associated with journalists, physicians, shift workers, some transportation workers and travelling salespeople. Obviously, for some, reduced supervision is accompanied by an abnormal social life.

The strongest occupational feature, though, would seem to be that linked to availability of the substance in question. The high proportion of heavy drinkers within the drinks trade seems to be readily understandable. However, the possibility that relatively unsupervised access to certain drugs may be a factor predisposing physicians to substance misuse perhaps is less appreciated.

That "high-stress" environments may also facilitate substance misuse also seems to be supported by the literature and is an important clue. Within modern stress theories, the selection and use of coping strategies are important components in predicting psychological well-being following stressful experiences (e.g. Folkman et al., 1986). In this context, substance use and misuse may be seen as the selection and repeated selection of an avoidance-related coping strategy. Such strategies may be more frequently used in stressful work encounters perceived as being beyond one's control (Dewe, 1991).

However, the evidence seems strong that for more serious misusers, there may be an already existing predisposition to such ways of coping. For this sub-group, it may be natural to migrate to occupations where substances are more easily obtained or excessive consumption seems less out of place.

15.3 WORKPLACE COSTS OF SUBSTANCE MISUSE

There is general agreement that the costs of substance misuse in the workplace are primarily related to absenteeism, lost productivity, safety and health care cover (DuPont, 1990; Macdonald et al., 1992; Osterloh & Becker, 1990; Seymour and Smith, 1990). However, these and other authors have also acknowledged that the research establishing the associations between substance misuse and these cost elements is far from robust in many respects (Guppy & Marsden, 1995).

The major difficulty in this area lies in clearly identifying that problems with safety and productivity are caused by or are directly related to substance use. The identification of causation is a scientifically demanding task and would usually involve two stages:

1. The identification of the increase in relative risk of adverse consequences derived from specific patterns of drug use.
2. The identification of causative relationships from behavioural evidence.

These two stages are seen as the beginning of the scientific approach necessary in the area of drug misuse at work as well as other related areas (Guppy, 1994). Without a clear identification of a causal association between substance use and a problem outcome, no true cost estimate can be scientifically validated.

15.3.1   Alcohol Use and Workplace Safety

A review of alcohol-related occupational injuries was reported by Stallones & Kraus (1993). They concluded that this area had not been accurately assessed and that a reasonable description of the role of alcohol in relation to work injuries was not available from current evidence. The particular problem with the literature covered by Stallones & Kraus relates to the first of the stages mentioned above. While data were available concerning the blood alcohol concentrations (BACs) of accident-involved workers in some studies, there was a general absence of reliable estimates of the distribution of BACs across control samples of non-accident-involved workers. However, there was some suggestion from the study by Baker et al. (1982) that the proportion of accident-involved workers with a positive BAC (15.3%) was around eight times higher than the estimated level of drinking on the job. Generally speaking, from the studies reviewed by Stallones & Kraus, it would appear that, for non-motor-vehicle work-related accidents, one might expect 7–11% of the injuries to involve a positive BAC. The estimates for work accidents involving motorized vehicles (including boats, cranes and other non-road vehicles) may be somewhat higher at up to 27%. Further estimates of the role of alcohol in work accidents were provided by Harrison et al. (1993) covering Australian data. They found that 13–15% of work-related road fatalities involved alcohol impairment (BACs above 50 mg/100 ml), compared with around 6% of other workplace fatalities. Interestingly, they reported that road-related accidents accounted for 24% of all work-related fatalities in their database and nearly 40% if commuting deaths were included.

Although the weaknesses of the workplace research linking accidents and alcohol misuse would seem problematic, the field of alcohol and road safety has a considerable wealth of scientific evidence associating causal links between drinking and accident involvement (Guppy, 1994). The research from this field would largely support the estimates provided above and would certainly implicate alcohol intoxication as a significant causal factor in work-related accidents.

15.3.2   Drug Use and Workplace Safety

There has been some published research suggesting associations between drug use and increased probability of accidents at work, though reliable empirical evidence is not common. In a study of Utah Power and Light employees, Crouch et al. (1989) found that drug (predominantly cannabis) users had higher accident rates than non-drug users. However, it should be noted that the accident data was from a somewhat limited population and that there were problems estimating employee culpability.

Epidemiological evidence from the field of road safety would seem to implicate several drugs in terms of being over-represented in drivers involved in serious accidents. Stoduto et al. (1993) reported results of tests on nearly 500 Canadian motor vehicle collision victims. They reported that, other than alcohol, the most frequently detected drugs in drivers were cannabinoids (14%), benzodiazepines (13%) and cocaine (5%). Accident data such as this seems supported by behavioural evidence for drugs such as cannabis (Dauncey et al., 1993) and benzodiazepines (Berghaus & Fleermann, 1993). However, experimental evidence of impairment from low doses of cocaine may not be so strong (Burns, 1993).

In a comprehensive examination of the value of pre-employment drug testing, Normand et al. (1990) reported a study of over 4000 US Postal Service workers. New employees were classified as drug positive or negative depending on their pre-employment urine analysis results and their employment records were monitored over the next couple of years. No significant differences in subsequent accident and injury records were found between employees who had tested positive and those testing negative for drugs. Although the Postal Service data provide useful insight into this area, it is obviously not the case that all those testing positive pre-employment would have continued to use drugs throughout the monitoring period.

Other research has indirectly commented on the association of drug use and accidents through examination of accident trends around drug use policy implementation (e.g. Taggart, 1989). However, the absence of any rigorous control procedures prevents such data from ascribing accident rate improvements to any one cause. Indeed, in their recent review, Macdonald Kapur et al. (1992) emphasized that major system changes had occurred within the railroad environment that was the focus of the report by Taggart, which may well have accounted for much of the observed improvement in accident rates.

Thus there would only appear to be a weak association between very general patterns of drug use and accident involvement. In particular, most of the research does not distinguish between the different drugs used and very rarely attempts to examine degrees of use that may be associated with impairment. From behavioural evidence and road safety research, it would seem possible that drug misuse has a role in workplace accidents. However, the problem of relatively low incidence means that this role does not seem to be a very large one in comparison with alcohol.

15.3.3 Alcohol Use and Productivity

In the Whitehall II study described by Marmot et al. (1993), measures of reported alcohol consumption were linked to recorded rates of short and long spells of absence (up to one week and greater). Marmot et al. found that there was a significant quadratic (U-shaped) relationship between alcohol intake and frequency of short spells of absence for male civil servants, even after adjusting for age and grade. Non-drinkers and those drinking more than once a day had significantly higher rates of short spells of absence. The difference between the very frequent drinkers and those drinking once or twice a week was reported as corresponding to almost 240 extra short spells of absence per 1000 men per year. Similarly, for male heavy drinkers (more than 30 drinks per week) the results suggested an extra 160 short spells of absence per 1000 men per year. For longer spells of absence, frequent drinkers had 12% more absence spells than light drinkers, though this difference was not significant. For the female sample, neither rates of short nor longer spells of absence were linked to the drinking measures, though this may be explained by the generally lower consumption patterns of the female employees with very few cases in the higher drinking categories.

Several studies have identified a relationship between workplace problems and the very heavy alcohol use indicative of problem drinker status. Pell & D'Alonzo (1970) suggested that suspected problem drinkers had nearly twice the rate of sickness absences of a comparison group.

A detailed investigation of work performance in a cohort of 140 problem drinking employees was reported by Guppy and Marsden (1997a). Over the 6-month period prior to involvement in a company-based treatment programme, these clients had an average of 29.4 days absence compared to a matched employee control group average of 4.5 days absence.

15.3.4   Drug Use and Productivity

Several recent studies have provided general evidence of associations between drug use and workplace performance measures such as absenteeism and turnover. The assumptions of causal mechanisms existing between drug use and absenteeism may be most easily justified as there is evidence to suggest that long-term heavy use of certain substances can also have serious effects on mental and physical well-being (e.g. Allgulander & Evanoff, 1990). The existence of direct causal mechanisms between low-order drug use and health may be more difficult to determine. Similarly, there may not be explanations for the direct causal association between drug use and turnover, though this does not rule out indirect mechanisms.

In terms of absenteeism, the results reported by Normand et al. (1990) suggested that, after an average of nearly 1.5 years employment, employees who had tested positive for "illicit" drugs had an absenteeism rate 60% higher than employees who had tested negative. It should be noted, though, that the drug user group in this study did include instances of morphine, codeine and benzodiazepine which may be used to treat some illnesses, which in turn could be related to inflated absenteeism among those clients. Normand et al. also found that employees who had tested positive for drugs had a 50% higher rate of involuntary turnover than employees who had tested negative, a finding similar to that of Blank & Fenton (1989) performed on military personnel.

In another study, McDaniel (1989) examined self-reported drug use among a sample of over 10 000 military recruits and compared responses with a gross indicator of job performance, discharge (classified as "failure to meet minimum behavioral or performance criteria"). McDaniel reported that the relative risk of discharge increased with more frequent drug use, though some care with interpretation was required owing to small cell sizes within certain drug/frequency categories. It is worthy of note, however, that often the distinction between the relative risk of discharge for non-users versus infrequent users was quite small and may not have been significant. In the discussion, McDaniel identified that there were some statistical as well as theoretical problems with using the discharge variable as a gross measure of job performance. However, it was suggested that "the limited operational validity of pre-employment drug use measures found in the present research suggests that employers who presently rely solely on drug use measures as predictors of on-the-job suitability will be doing less than an optimal job of applicant screening". McDaniel went on to suggest that increased use of more standard predictors of job performance would be more likely to provide utility than drug use screening.

15.3.5   Summary of Workplace Research

The general criticisms of this area of research have been detailed in previous reviews (e.g. Gust & Walsh, 1989; Macdonald et al., 1992). One of the main problems that is apparent in the research covering drugs other than alcohol is the often used creation of a simple dichotomy between users and non-users. This approach is simply inadequate for scientific purposes as it confuses some very important issues. First, drug types that are combined may differ considerably in terms of their potential effects (e.g. stimulants versus depressants). Second, there is rarely information available to validly differentiate the kinds of use (e.g. medicinal, recreational and dependent). Third, there is usually no information concerning the likely impairment of work functions that may have occurred in relation to the drug use. It may be the case that the dose levels concerned may have caused the individual no impairment, or that the impairment was limited to non-work hours. All these factors combine to make it difficult to say with certainty that drug use directly caused the observed problems (Macdonald & Dooley, 1991).

However, the research reviewed here would suggest that alcohol impairment plays a strong causal role in 5–10% of serious work-related accidents. Also heavy alcohol use among men is associated with a 12% increase in short spells of absence. For those with consumption patterns indicative of abuse or dependency, the increases in terms of sickness rates could be as high as 200–500% over matched groups of employees.

As mentioned, the evidence for the direct costs of problems relating to other drugs is not so strong. Increased accident risks are hard to determine, though behavioural evidence favours the existence of such effects even though they are rare. There seems to be firm evidence of productivity costs associated with drug use, though it is not clear that drug use alone is the causal factor. However, the estimates from Normand et al. would suggest that 60% increased absenteeism may be expected among illicit drug users.

15.4 WORKPLACE MANAGEMENT OF SUBSTANCE RELATED PROBLEMS

15.4.1 Types of Interventions for Alcohol and Drug Problems Available within the Workplace

In the field of alcohol and drug use, there are available various models that can be used to classify potential interventions within the workplace. Simple models of systems for deterring substance misuse have been described for the specific scenario of drinking and driving (e.g. Guppy, 1984; Ross, 1982). Similarly, models for the development of workplace policies and procedures for limiting problems of alcohol misuse at work have been available for some time. For example, Trice & Roman (1972) suggested the following as components of an Occupational Alcoholism Programme:

1. A written policy statement by the employer that accepted the concept of alcoholism as a treatable health problem.
2. Specific procedures for handling and referring employees experiencing work performance impairment/deterioration.
3. "Constructive confrontation" procedures for supervisors to use with employees who are experiencing work deterioration.
4. Supervisor training for "constructive confrontation" and implementation of the company policy on alcoholism.
5. Formal procedures that guarantee access by impaired workers to treatment facilities and self-help groups.
6. Procedures for guaranteeing the confidentiality of the individual employee.

7. Provision of the third-party payment for the treatment of alcoholic employees in their group health insurance policies or other compensatory benefits.
8. Diffusion of information about the programmes to the entire workforce.

The basic principles of such models can be described within a deterrence theory framework. This allows us to view the general process of how such activities function. The three main stages of such a process are prevention, detection and rehabilitation.

1. Prevention. The primary stage involves the prevention of alcohol- and drug-related problems within the workplace and operates through several related mechanisms. A mechanism of health promotion is commonly utilized within organizations discouraging substance misuse. An associated mechanism of general deterrence can be seen in terms of attempting to prevent substance misuse through the construction and advertisement of policies, rules and regulations. The goals are to explain why such action is necessary, what behaviour is expected and what the consequences are for incorrect behaviour. The use of pre-employment screening for alcohol and drug misuse indicators to either discourage or reject substance misusing applicants may also be seen as a method of preventing such problems from existing within the workforce, though obviously has no direct role in the prevention of substance use problems *per se*.

2. Detection. The detection of misuse generally constitutes the secondary level of such models. It is at this level that policies and procedures are formulated to allow identification of misuse when it occurs. Activities that occur at this level include supervisor monitoring of work performance indicators, readiness to perform testing (Gilliand & Schlegel, 1993) and drug screening programmes.

Drug screening programmes can be introduced into the work domain in a number of different ways (Macdonald & Dooley, 1991; Macdonald et al., 1992). Perhaps the most commonly used procedures are:
  i. Pre-employment screening. This involves screening of applicants for all or sensitive posts prior to employment.
 ii. Testing employees following specific behaviours or events ("for cause" testing). While in some countries there would appear to be a framework for "probable cause" testing following serious accidents, it is not clear that such a framework exists for minor accidents and incidents or for more general aspects of poor work performance (Daintith & Baldwin, 1993).
iii. Testing without prior cause. This would include testing on a periodic basis (e.g. at an annual medical) or on a random basis. This form of testing would seem to include the most opposed procedures where employees are tested without any prior significant event or even, in the case of random screening, without prior warning.

The impact of procedures at this level of the model is twofold in that not only does detection allow the process of specific deterrence to begin, but also feedback from this level impacts at the primary level of the model, affecting general deterrence through perceptions of the probability of detection (Guppy, 1984).

3. Rehabilitation. The tertiary level of intervention generally is seen as the provision of mechanisms for the reduction of recidivism within the individual detected of misuse. In other words, actions are taken to attempt to prevent further instances of substance misuse. These actions may be punitive or rehabilitative in nature and may often represent mixtures of both. Commonly within the context of Occupational Alcohol Programmes, efforts would be made to address potential dependency problems faced by clients, generally through

counselling while remaining within the boundaries of traditional disciplinary processes (Guppy & Marsden, 1997).

Thus the general model described above should act to deter most of the target population from indulging in the proscribed behaviour, either through health-related education, or through the threat of detection and associated sanctions. The second level concerns the detection of misuse and its goal is to elevate both the real and the perceived likelihood that misuse will be identified. The final level of intervention attempts to limit the repetition of the misuse within the individual.

The scientific evidence in support of the activities covered by these intervention levels is relatively limited, largely through practical difficulties of conducting carefully designed research within workplace environments (Kurtz et al., 1984; Marsden, 1992). However, the following case examples provide an insight into the levels of activity described above and will hopefully demonstrate the need for action research at each level.

15.4.2 Case Study: A London Model

This case concerns a public transport organization which employed over 40 000 staff working in and around London. The organization had an established internal employee assistance programme, implemented as a confidential counselling and advisory service for employees. In the early 1980s, aware of the potential problem of alcohol misuse to the health and safety of its operations, the executive, after negotiations with staff representatives and unions, formulated a policy statement on alcohol. The policy statement had both a control element—concerning the consumption of alcohol during work hours, and an assistance element—which aimed to offer assistance to employees experiencing alcohol-related problems. The central tenets of the original policy statement were as follows:

1. The consumption of alcohol while on duty is forbidden. Further, staff who present themselves for duty, evidently having consumed alcohol, will not be permitted to commence duty, and such behaviour will be considered as a breach of discipline.
2. Staff who are absent from duty through sickness, or injury due to excessive consumption of alcohol may forfeit the right to sick leave and sick pay. However, staff who have a drink problem, and who take appropriate action will not necessarily forfeit these benefits.
3. Any employee who believes that they have an alcohol-related problem should inform management via their supervisor. The medical or welfare services will be made available at the request of staff at this stage or the employee may establish direct contact with these services. Any approach of this nature will be dealt with in confidence.
4. Staff must show that they are taking, or are prepared to take, such steps as are necessary to obtain and adhere to specialist advice.
5. Any employee who seeks help under this procedure will not have disciplinary action taken against them or be dismissed from service simply on the grounds that they have a drink problem, provided that the employee observes any conditions under paragraph 4 (above) and in general observes the policy statement. However, there can be no immunity from disciplinary action for a breach of discipline.

Accompanying the implementation of the alcohol policy, the executive also issued guidance for managers and supervisors for the appropriate management of problem drinking employees. The guidelines sought to distinguish between employees who might be found intoxicated while on duty and who would be managed by existing disciplinary procedure and employees with an identifiable alcohol-related or dependency problem, who would be regarded as having a treatable illness and would be eligible for appropriate treatment assistance.

Following implementation of the alcohol policy, management identified the need for a specialist resource within the organization to complement existing medical and welfare departments to provide an information, training and assistance service for management and problem drinking staff. A pilot Alcohol Education Project (AEP) was designed and implemented with two explicitly stated aims:

1. To improve the productivity and reliability of employees who have alcohol-related problems by effective assessment and, where appropriate, referral to treatment services outside the organization, such as hospital-based detoxification programmes and community based advisory services.
2. To assist management and supervisory staff via education and training programmes to identify alcohol-related problems within the workforce and ensure an appropriate and effective response.

The early aim of the programme was thus not to offer an in-house treatment service for alcohol problems *per se*, but rather to forge links with existing specialist alcohol treatment agencies who would deliver counselling and assistance. Thus, the AEP would serve a monitoring function of the employee's progress and act as a resource to management in the monitoring of work performance.

The programme developed in two main areas. The first area of work concerned the development of a service orientation for the programme. This involved firstly the identification of assistance materials and approaches for counselling problem drinkers. The approach taken was to provide a brief intervention service which embraced a range of non-abstinent treatment goals using self-monitoring and relapse prevention materials developed by controlled drinking programmes (Robertson & Heather, 1986). This approach, although supporting abstinent treatment goals as appropriate, also reflected the range of moderate dependency and problematic drinking within an employment setting. Thus, the philosophy of the service acknowledged that attenuated drinking may be a realistic and effective objective for employed problem drinkers. The second area of work involved a structured programme of seminars directed at supervisors and management to discuss the company policy and the basic managerial intervention skills required to work successfully with problem drinking staff members.

Dearing (1989) described the impact of an element of the extensive management training programme on a cohort of 160 supervisor grade staff. Primarily, the training programme concerned educational elements focusing on alcohol effects, and the details of the company policy and procedures. The training programme also contained elements addressing factors which may be indicative of an employee developing an alcohol problem and a discussion of strategies for successful intervention. It was found that initially participants had relatively little alcohol-related knowledge and showed little awareness regarding the company alcohol policy. It was also revealed that there was a tendency for the supervisors to feel hesitant about identifying, confronting and referring employees with suspected alcohol problems. To some extent, this reflected feelings of inadequacy in terms of their practical skills, though such perceptions improved after training. It was concluded that improving the swift referral of clients to the specialist unit for assessment (rather than "treatment") could provide benefits for both client and hesitant supervisors.

A detailed longitudinal investigation of the impact of the assessment and counselling support intervention was reported by Guppy & Marsden (1997a). They examined the short-term treatment and management outcomes associated with referral to the company programme. Using a core group of 104 employees assessed at 6-month follow-up, a repeated-measures design was used to analyse scores on self-report scales of alcohol, health and work-related functioning, with additional work absence data obtained from personnel records and supervisors providing ratings of work performance. The results revealed that there was a significant improvement in the problem drinker group in terms of work performance as rated by both employees and their surpervisors. There was a significant reduction in absenteeism from an average of nearly 30 days absence over 6 months prior to counselling to an average of 15 days absence in the 6 months following intervention. Context-free psychological well-being was also shown to have significantly improved over this period. However, there were no significant changes in job satisfaction or job commitment measures over this time. It was noted that there was strong support for the efficacy of this particular intervention approach from the perspective of individual change. The addition of a disciplinary component (with implied coercion towards assistance) to a brief counselling intervention seemed to work very well. However, it was observed that although the clients improved significantly in themselves, they still remained significantly higher than controls in terms of absenteeism at the 6-month follow-up (average absence of 15 days versus 5 days for controls). This would suggest that the overall cost-effectiveness of such interventions "may be demonstrated only when it is assumed that poorly performing employees are expensive to remove and replace" (Guppy and Marsden, 1997a, p. 349).

15.4.3 Summary of Workplace Interventions

There would seem to be a fairly straightforward way of categorizing intervention efforts aimed at substance misuse in the workplace: prevention, detection and rehabilitation. It would seem that most effort in relation to alcohol misuse is directed at prevention through health promotion activities. Most intervention activity focusing on illicit drugs is currently at the level of detection, while prevention is largely a deterrent by-product of these detection activities. Rehabilitation efforts seem quite successful in relation to alcohol misusing employees, while the picture remains less clear in relation to illicit drug using employees.

15.5 SUMMARY AND CONCLUSIONS

From the research covered in the previous sections, it would seem clear that the main drug of concern in terms of safety and productivity is alcohol. Alcohol intoxication has a significant role in accident causation and heavy drinking patterns are linked with increased sickness absence. Thus there is reasonable motivation for the development of policies and interventions that assess and assist employees with alcohol related problems.

In terms of successful interventions, there is clear evidence that workplace interventions can assist alcohol abusing employees and bring work performance measures into normal range. It is also the view of a number of authors that the workplace provides a useful early indicator of the development of serious problems and provides an environment rich with motivators for the client to work hard at rehabilitation (Guppy & Marsden, 1997b).

For all the efforts and activities concerning the implementation of drug testing programmes, there has been very little firm evidence indicating a major problem in terms of safety and productivity as a direct result of the misuse of drugs other than alcohol. Thus it should not be surprising that there is little evidence establishing a sizeable impact on safety and productivity as a result of illicit drug-specific measures. This is not to say that policies and procedures for minimizing drug misuse in the workplace should be ignored. It is more the case that substance-related policies and procedures should be developed with alcohol primarily in mind and concern for other drugs should be placed within this context. This does suggest, however, that procedures aimed primarily at illicit drug use (such as urine testing) may be extravagant and misdirected. Certainly, urine testing generally represents a poor method of indicating impairment by any substance and is one of the least favoured methods of assessing alcohol intoxication. However, at least partly because of directed legislation in the USA (Reagan, 1986), urine testing remains a major activity in this field. While this is so, there will be much debate concerning the legal and ethical issues surrounding urine testing (e.g. Ontario Law Reform Commission, 1992; Zwerling, 1993) and the technical questions of its value against more traditional methods of selection and assessment (McDaniel, 1989). It is sincerely hoped that empirical research will be given the opportunity to contribute to the debate within such a politically and morally sensitive area.

Finally, it is suggested that the future development of alcohol and drug interventions probably includes the acknowledgement of the links between substance misuse and appraisal and coping mechanisms seen within mainstream stress research (e.g. Cooper et al., 1988, 1990). Although substance use may be simply categorized with other escape–avoidance coping methods (Lazarus & Folkman, 1984), it may be that chronic misuse may be more difficult to place within the appraisal–coping framework. However, movement of the addiction scene towards a more unified well-being model has been supported by a number of authors (e.g. Marlatt & Gordon, 1985; Moos, 1994) and seems particularly appropriate in the workplace, where less severe substance-related problems are likely to be found.

REFERENCES

Allgulander, C. & Evanoff, B. (1990) Psychiatric diagnoses and perceived health problems in a sample of working Swedes treated with psychoactive medications. *Journal of Psychoactive Drugs*, **22**, 467–78.

Alvarez, F.J., Quiepo, D., Del Rio, M.C. & Garcia, M.C. (1992) Patterns of drug use in Castille and Leon (Spain). *British Journal of Addiction*, **87**, 1153–60.

American Medical Association (1987) Issues in employee drug testing. *Journal of the American Medical Association*, **258**, 2089–96.

American Psychiatric Association (1994) *Diagnostic and Statistical Manual of Mental Disorders*, 4th edn (DSM-IV). American Psychiatric Association, Washington, DC.

Backer, T.E. (1987) *Strategic Planning for Workplace Drug Abuse Programs*. National Institute for Drug Abuse Publication ADM-87–1538, US Government Printing Office, Washington, DC.

Baker, S., Samkoff, J., Fisher, R. & Van Buren, C. (1982) Fatal occupational injuries. *Journal of the American Medical Association*, **64**, 692–7.

Berghaus, G. & Fleermann, T. (1993) Benefits of a databank on empirical studies on drugs and driving. Results on some hypnotics, sedatives as an example. In H-D. Utzelmann, G. Berghaus & G. Kroj (eds) *Alcohol, Drugs and Traffic Safety—T92*. Verlag TUV Rheinland, Cologne, pp. 546–51.

Blank, D.L. & Fenton, J.W. (1989) Early employment testing for marijuana: demographic and employee retention patterns. In S.W. Gust & J.M. Walsh (eds) *Drugs in the Workplace: Research and Evaluation Data*, NIDA research monograph 91. NIDA, Rockville, MD.

Brooke, D., Edwards, G. & Taylor, C. (1991) Addiction as an occupational hazard: 144 doctors with drug and alcohol problems. *British Journal of Addiction*, **86**, 1011–16.

Burns, M. (1993) Cocaine effect on performance. In H.-D. Utzelmann, G. Berghaus & G. Kroj (eds) *Alcohol, Drugs and Traffic Safety—T92*. Verlag TUV Rheinland, Cologne, pp. 612–19.

Casswell, S. & Gordon, A. (1984) Drinking and occupational status in New Zealand men. *Journal of Studies on Alcohol*, **45**, 144–8.

Central Office of Information (1993) *Drug and Solvent Misuse: A Basic Briefing*. Department of Health, London.

Chivers, C.P. (1987) Recognition of alcohol problems in the workplace. *British Journal of Clinical Practice*, **49**, 2–7.

Claussen, B. & Aasland, O.G. (1993) The Alcohol Use Disorders Identification Test (AUDIT) in a routine health examination of long term unemployed. *Addiction*, **88**, 363–8.

Cook, R., Walizer, D. & Mace, D. (1976) Illicit drug use in the army: a social-organizational analysis. *Journal of Applied Psychology*, **61**, 262–72.

Cooper, M.L., Russell, M. & George, W.H. (1988). Coping, expectancies, and alcohol abuse: a test of social learning formulations. *Journal of Abnormal Psychology*, **97**, 218–30.

Cooper, M.L., Russell, M. & Frone, M.R. (1990). Work stress and alcohol effects: a test of stress-induced drinking. *Journal of Health and Social Behaviour*, **31**, 260–76.

Crouch, D.J., Webb, D.O., Peterson, L.V., Buller, P.F. & Rollins, D.E. (1989) A critical evaluation of the Utah Power and Light Company's substance abuse management program: absenteeism, accidents and costs. In S.W. Gust & J.M. Walsh (eds) *Drugs in the Workplace: Research and Evaluation Data*, NIDA research monograph 91. NIDA, Rockville, MD.

Daintith, T. & Baldwin, R. (1993) *Alcohol and Drugs in the Workplace. A Review of Laws and Regulations in the Member States of the European Communities*. Draft Report for the International Labour Office & the Commission of the European Communities. Institute of Advanced Legal Studies, London.

Dauncey, H., Chesher, G., Crawford, J., Adena, M. & Horne, K. (1993) Alcohol and marijuana, a less than additive interaction? In H.-D. Utzelmann, G. Berghaus & G. Kroj (eds) *Alcohol, Drugs and Traffic Safety—T92*. Verlag TUV Rheinland, Cologne, pp. 620–4.

Davies, J.B., Wright, L.B., Hutcheson, G.D., Henderson, M.M., Hepburn, A., McPherson, A. & Fox, A. (1997) *Alcohol in the Workplace: Results of an Empirical Study*. HSE Books/HMSO, Norwich.

Dawson, D.A. (1993) Patterns of alcohol consumption: beverage effects on gender differences. *Addiction*, **88**, 133–8.

Dearing, M. (1989) An evaluation of an alcohol training programme for supervisors, MSc thesis, Cranfield Institute of Technology, Bedford.

Dewe, P. (1991) Primary appraisal, secondary appraisal and coping: their role in stressful work encounters. *Journal of Occupational Psychology*, **64**, 331–51.

DuPont, R.L. (1990) Medicines and drug testing in the workplace. *Journal of Psychoactive Drugs*, **22**, 451–9.

Edwards, G. & Unnithan, S. (1992) *Epidemiologically Based Needs Assessment*. DHA Project, research programme report no 7. NHS Management Executive, London.

Fischer, V.J. (1991) Combat exposure and the etiology of postdischarge substance abuse problems among Vietnam veterans. *Journal of Traumatic Stress*, **4**, 251–77.

Folkman, S., Lazarus, R.S., Gruen, R.J. & DeLongis, A. (1986) Appraisal, coping, health and status, and psychological symptoms. *Journal of Personality and Social Psychology*, **50**, 571–9.

Fuller, J.R. & LaFountain, M.J. (1987) Performance-enhancing drugs in sport: a different form of drug abuse. *Adolescence*, **22**, 969–76.

Gilliland, K. & Schlegel, R.E. (1993) *Readiness to Perform Testing: A Critical Analysis of the Concept and Current Practices*, Federal Aviation Administration report no. DOT/FAA/AM-93/13. US Dept. of Transportation, Washington, DC.

Goddard, E. (1991) *Drinking in England and Wales in the Late 1980s*. Office of Population Censuses and Surveys, HMSO, London.

Guppy, A. (1984) Perceived and real likelihood of the detection of drinking and driving, PhD thesis, Cranfield Institute of Technology, Bedford.

Guppy, A. (1994) At what blood alcohol concentration should drink-driving be illegal? *British Medical Journal*, **308**, 1055–6.

Guppy, A. & Adams-Guppy, J.R. (1995) Behaviour and perceptions related to drink-driving in an international sample of company vehicle drivers. *Journal of Studies on Alcohol*, **56**, 348–55.

Guppy, A. & Marsden, J. (1995) Drug related problems in the workplace: a British perspective. In *Proceedings of the Occupational Psychology Conference*. British Psychological Society, Leicester, pp. 73–8.

Guppy, A. & Marsden, J. (1997a) Assisting employees with drinking problems: changes in mental health, work performance and job perceptions. *Work and Stress*, **11**, 341–50.

Guppy, A. & Marsden, J. (1997b) Counselling substance related problems in the workplace. In C. Feltham (ed.) *The Gains of Listening*. Open University Press, Milton Keynes.

Gust, S.W. & Walsh, J.M. (1989) Research on the prevalence, impact and treatment of drug abuse in the workplace. In S.W. Gust & J.M. Walsh (eds) *Drugs in the Workplace: Research and Evaluation Data*, NIDA research monograph 91, NIDA, Rockville, MD.

Gustafson, A. (1884) *The Foundation of Death*. Kegan Paul, Trench & Co, London.

Haphus, C.L., Knibbe, R.A. & Drop, M.J. (1993) Alcohol consumption in the European Community: uniformity and diversity in drinking patterns. *Addiction*, **88**, 1391–1404.

Harrison, J.E., Mandryk, J.A. & Frommer, M.S. (1993) Work-related road fatalities in Australia, 1982–1984. *Accident Analysis and Prevention*, **25**, 443–51.

Helzer, J. (1984) The impact of combat on later alcohol use by Vietnam veterans. *Journal of Psychoactive Drugs*, **16**, 183–91.

Knupfer, G. (1989) The prevalence in various social groups of eight different drinking patterns, from abstaining to frequent drunkeness: analysis of 10 US surveys combined. *British Journal of Addiction*, **84**, 1305–18.

Kurtz, N.R., Googins, B. & Howard, W.C. (1984) Measuring the success of occupational alcoholism programmes. *Journal of Studies on Alcohol*, **45**, 33–45.

Larsen, S. (1994) Alcohol use in the service industry. *Addiction*, **89**, 733–41.

Lacoursiere, R., Godfrey, K. & Ruby, L. (1980). Traumatic neurosis in the etiology of alcoholism: Viet Nam combat and other trauma. *American Journal of Psychiatry*, **137**, 966–8.

Lazarus, R.S. & Folkman, S. (1984) *Stress, Coping and Adaptation*. Springer-Verlag, New York.

Lund, A.K., Preusser, D.F. & Williams, A.F. (1989) Drug use by tractor-trailer drivers. In S.W. Gust & J.M. Walsh (eds) *Drugs in the Workplace: Research and Evaluation Data*, NIDA research monograph 91. NIDA, Rockville, MD.

Macdonald, S. & Dooley, S. (1991) The nature and extent of EAPs and drug screening programs in Canadian transportation companies. *Employee Assistance Quarterly*, **6**, 23–40.

Macdonald, S., Kapur, B. & Sorenson, M. (1992) *Drugs and Alcohol in the Maritime Industry*. International Labour Office, Geneva.

Marlatt, G.A. & Gordon, J.R. (eds) (1985) *Relapse Prevention: Maintenance Strategies in the Treatment of Addictive Behavior*. Guilford Press, New York.

Marmot, M.G., North, F., Feeney, A. & Head, J. (1993) Alcohol consumption and sickness absence: from the Whitehall II study. *Addiction*, **88**, 369–82.

Marsden, J.R. (1992) Employees with drinking problems: short-term evaluation of treatment and management outcomes, PhD thesis, Cranfield Institute of Technology, Bedford.

McDaniel, M.A. (1989) Does pre-employment drug use predict on-the-job suitability? In S.W. Gust & J.M. Walsh (eds) *Drugs in the Workplace: Research and Evaluation Data*, NIDA research monograph 91. NIDA, Rockville, MD.

Moos, R.H. (1994) Treated or untreated, an addiction is not an island unto itself. *Addiction*, **89**, 507–9.

Needleman, S.B. & Romberg, R.W. (1989) Comparison of drug abuse in different military populations. *Journal of Forensic Sciences*, **34**, 848–57.

Normand, J., Salyards, S.D. & Mahoney, J.J. (1990) An evaluation of preemployment drug testing. *Journal of Applied Psychology*, **75**, 629–39.

Ontario Law Reform Commission (1992) *Report on Drug and Alcohol Testing in the Workplace.* Ontario Government Publications Service, Toronto.

Osborn, C.E. & Sokolov, J.J. (1989) Drug use trends in a nuclear power company: cumulative data from an ongoing testing program. In S.W. Gust & J.M. Walsh (eds) *Drugs in the Workplace: Research and Evaluation Data,* NIDA research monograph 91. NIDA, Rockville, MD.

Osterloh, J.D. & Becker, C.E. (1990) Chemical dependency and drug testing in the workplace. *Journal of Psychoactive Drugs,* **22**, 407–17.

Pell, S. & D'Alonzo, C.A. (1970) Sickness absenteeism of alcoholics. *Journal of Occupational Medicine,* **12**, 198–210.

Pfafferott, I. (1993) Drinking and driving at different legal BAC limits in Europe. In H.-D. Utzelmann; G. Berghaus & G. Kroj (eds) *Alcohol, Drugs and Traffic Safety—T92,* Verlag TUV Rheinland, Cologne, pp. 1068–73.

Plant, M.A. (1979) Occupations, drinking patterns and alcohol-related problems: conclusions from a follow-up study. *British Journal of Addiction,* **74**, 267–75.

Reagan, R. (1986) *Executive order 12564.* Federal Register 51 (180), September 17.

Rick, J. (1994) Perceptions of stress, coping behaviour and the impact of a low level intervention amongst white collar public sector employees, PhD thesis, Cranfield University, Bedford.

Robertson, I. & Heather, N. (1986) *Let's Drink to Your Health! A Self-Help Guide to Sensible Drinking.* British Psychological Society, Leiester.

Roman, P.M. (1989) The use of EAPs in dealing with drug abuse in the workplace. In S.W. Gust & J.M. Walsh (eds) *Drugs in the Workplace: Research and Evaluation Data,* NIDA research monograph 91. NIDA, Rockville, MD.

Romelsjo, A., Hasin, D., Hilton, M., Bostrom, G., Diderichsen, F., Haglund, B., Hallqvist, J., Karlsson, G. & Svanstrom, L. (1992) The relationship between stressful working conditions and high alcohol consumption and severe alcohol problems in an urban general population. *British Journal of Addiction,* **87**, 1173–83.

Ross, H.L. (1982) *Deterring the Drinking Driver.* Heath & Co. New York.

Royal College of Psychiatrists (1979) *Alcohol and Alcoholism.* Tavistock, London.

Seymour, R.B. & Smith, D.E. (1990) Identifying and responding to drug abuse in the workplace: an overview. *Journal of Psychoactive Drugs,* **22**, 383–405.

Stallones, L. & Kraus, J.F. (1993) The occurrence and epidemiologic features of alcohol-related occupational injuries. *Addiction,* **88**, 945–51.

Stoduto, G., Vingilis, E., Kapur, B., Sheu, W.-J., McLellan, B.A. & Liban, C.B. (1993) Alcohol and drug use among motor vehicle collision victims admitted to a regional trauma unit: demographic, injury and crash characteristics. *Accident Analysis and Prevention,* **25**, 411–20.

Sutton, M. & Maynard, A. (1993) Are drug policies based on fake statistics? *Addiction,* **88**, 455–8.

Taggart, R.W. (1989) Results of the drug testing programme at Southern Pacific Railroad. In S.W. Gust & J.M. Walsh (eds) *Drugs in the Workplace: Research and Evaluation Data,* NIDA Research Monograph 91. NIDA, Rockville, MD.

Trice, H.M. & Roman, P. (1972) *Spirits and Demons at Work: Alcohol and Other Drugs on the Job.* ILR paperback no. 11, Cornell University, Ithica, New York.

United Nations Economic and Social Council (1993) *Examination of the World Situation with Respect to Drug Abuse.* Commission on Narcotic Drugs, report no. E/CN.7/1993/4, United Nations, Vienna.

VanHelder, W.P., Kofman, E. & Tremblay, M.S. (1991) Anabolic steroids in sport. *Canadian Journal of Sport Sciences,* **16**, 248–57.

Wilson, P. (1980) *Drinking in England and Wales.* Office of Population Census and Surveys, HMSO, London.

Zwerling, C. (1993) *Current Practice and Experience on Drug and Alcohol Testing in the Workplace.* International Labour Office, Geneva.

CHAPTER 16

Issues of the Second Career Half

Marc J. Schabracq
University of Amsterdam, The Netherlands

16.1 INTRODUCTION

This chapter examines a number of factors that may negatively affect the functioning of senior employees. This necessarily involves some over-generalizing. As such, this may be a risky undertaking: it seems only one step away from stereotyping and passing the responsibility for these problems to the senior employees involved. Of course, this is not what is intended. The idea behind the chapter is to give an overview of the threats that senior employees are confronted with. In the next chapter, interventions and possible solutions are discussed.

The growing interest in senior employees primarily stems from demographically based economic concerns. Employees aged from 45 to 65 years make up an increasing proportion of the population in the OECD countries. If they are allowed to choose, many of these employees would prefer the freedom of early retirement to a working existence, which apparently is not very rewarding to them. And many organisations, up until recently, were not particularly reluctant to let them go. Older employees are often considered to be a source of problems on variables such as productivity, flexibility, innovation, stress, fatigue and health. Though this clearly is a case of stereotypical exaggeration, there are many senior employees who do experience difficulties in these areas to support this view.

Massive early retirement is no solution. It is simply unaffordable, and not only for financial reasons. Well-trained, younger replacements are increasingly hard to find, and there is a growing understanding that the premature removal of senior employees represents an unacceptable waste of useful knowledge, competence and talent, as well as of all investments in their training and career development. As a result, it is to be expected that the number of senior employees will increase further. In this respect, it may be useful to turn to the senior employees who are still working and to look at how they are doing.

Though this may come as a surprise, research results indicate that work performances of senior employees in most jobs are, on average, not very different from those of younger ones (Cascio & McEnvoy, 1989; Sterns and Alexander, 1988; Waldman & Avolio, 1986; Warr,

The Handbook of Work and Health Psychology. Edited by M.J. Schabracq, J.A.M. Winnubst and C.L. Cooper.
© 2003 John Wiley & Sons, Ltd.

1993). The same holds more or less for sick leave: though the average length of absence due to sick leave tends to be somewhat higher, the mean frequency of sick leave tends to be lower. Although these findings may be reasoned away as a consequence of a massive selection effect—employees with poor performance or health would retreat at an earlier age from the labour market—they still demonstrate that many senior employees do perform at an appropriate level.

When one looks at work satisfaction, the data, at first sight, are even more surprising: senior employees, on average, are somewhat more satisfied with their work than their younger colleagues (Broersen et al., 1993; Haasnoot, 1993; Mottaz, 1987; Warr, 1992; White & Spector, 1987). Selection undoubtedly plays an important role here too, as well as probably the response shift stemming from adaptation, i.e. altering one's standards to the changed circumstances. Still, these data likewise show that many senior employees indicate that they are reasonably happy in their jobs.

The data on work performance and satisfaction on the one hand and the enthusiasm for early retirement on the other illustrate the huge variation in functioning of senior employees, and of older people in general. Though this variability runs counter to the popular stereotype of the elderly as a more or less uniform group of problematic people, it is a key characteristic of the functioning and cognitive abilities of older people (Baltes and Baltes, 1993; Belsky, 1990; Rabbitt, 1993; Ventis, 1992). Such diversity is only to be expected, because people lead divergent lives. People not only enter the last stage of their working life from completely different positions, but they do not enter it being of the same developmental status either. As a consequence, not everyone is equally ready, willing and able to take on the challenges of the last stage. The problem is, however, that those who are the least ready, willing and able appear to have determined the overall picture.

16.2   THE AGEING PROCESS

Ageing is not a simple matter of decline of faculties and functions, but also of growth and development. This leads to complex individual patterns of consistencies and change (Thomae, 1993). Moreover, before the age of 65, much functional decline does not meet the eye because there still is considerable latent reserve capacity (Baltes & Baltes, 1993), notwithstanding the decrease of these reserves.

Horn (1982) makes a distinction between crystallised and fluid mental abilities. Of these two, only the latter show significant decline with ageing, while the former tend to show further growth and development. Generally speaking, crystallised abilities are largely automatic, knowledge-based and procedural in character. They demand little effort and tend to increase throughout one's working life. So, Schroots & Birren (1993) state that "One of the most reliable patterns of ageing is the increase of verbal information with age" (p. 19). In this respect, Hess (1992) stresses the importance of well-ramified, domain-bound "scripts", cognitive structures that steer the memory of domain-relevant information and make it possible to handle that domain in a more or less automatic fashion. Such scripts hardly age, but presuppose the presence of a more or less stable, familiar environment (Hoyer & Rybash, 1992), a condition that in our organisations is becoming increasingly rare. Though scripts obviously are necessary, they may have drawbacks also. Apart from difficulties with change, their use is also at the expense of one's awareness of one's actions in the domain, which may lead to forgetfulness in this respect (Plude & Murphy, 1992).

Fluid mental abilities are characterised by more conscious information processing and rely upon factors such as processing speed, spatial functions and connecting pieces of new information. These factors do tend to deteriorate with ageing. Also, older people have, on average, more difficulties with divided, alternating and sustained attention (Cremer, 1995). In addition, they tend to become slower in most of their actions, due to an impaired synchronisation of the constituent processes (Salthouse, 1992). This is also a matter of limitations of the working memory, though not necessarily of its diminished capacity. For example, Kemper et al. (1993) point to the possibility of a "revision or re-evaluation of inhibitory mechanisms that control access to the working memory" (p. 138) as the causal factor, which would result in better judgements and decisions. As we have seen before, the impairment of the fluid abilities does not, as a rule, affect work performance in most jobs, because the decay is compensated for by the use of more sophisticated crystallised abilities. Problems may arise, however, when radical changes occur.

Also in the second career half, there are some definite bodily changes that indicate that youth is over. So, there are changes in skin, hair and general physique, as well as declines in muscular strength, stamina and sensory functioning, changes that are often associated with a loss of physical attractiveness. In addition, women are confronted with menopause and the loss of their reproductive potential (Janssen & Gerrichhauzen, 1995).

In summary, many senior employees may have to cope with one or several of the following problems:

- smaller mental and physical reserves;
- slower functioning;
- declining fluid abilities;
- declining muscular strength and stamina.

In spite of the above-mentioned mixed data, employees over 45 are often, and for the greater part erroneously, seen as a uniform, problematic group of employees. The next sections examine some of the backgrounds of these ideas. We start with some issues around the so-called midlife and mid-career issues.

16.3   MIDLIFE AND MID-CAREER

Approaching our life course as a succession of more or less fixed stages is one of our culturally determined ways of giving us the idea that we actually have some control in this respect (Schroots & Birren, 1993). So, we speak of a "normalised biography" (*Normalbiographie* in German; Kohli, 1985, in Baars, 1988). This tradition goes back to classical antiquity and is associated with names such as Hippocrates and Shakespeare. More recently, developmental and organisational psychologists have described working lives also as a series of typical stages and transitions. Examples are the models of Super (1957), Hall (1976), Schein (1978) and Levinson et al. (1978). The concepts of midlife and mid-career stem from this very tradition. Separate stages are each thought to be characterised by relative stability and gradual change, while transitions are associated with more sudden and more radical change and adaptation to a new life stage. As such, transitions provide us with typical developmental tasks (Havighurst, 1972).

In everyday life, we hold on to our own versions of these frames of reference. So, we usually can describe ourselves and others as "early", "late" or "on time" with regard to the transitions in our life (Kimmel, 1990, in Merriam, 1994; Neugarten, 1976). This provides us with some predictability. In middle age for instance, we know we are confronted with the necessity of re-assessing our position and functioning and that we have to cope with that.

Middle age comes with changes in career perspective. Middle-aged employees have become seniors. Rebellion has lost its attraction. They are supposed to have acquired an established position by now. Following the line of reasoning inherent in the notion of a normalised biography, employees are supposed to reach the summit of their career in middle age. Though most people, at least in principle, subscribe to this notion, everyday life often teaches otherwise. As organisations have become flatter, the number of management jobs has decreased. At the same time, the percentage of middle-aged employees, competing for higher level jobs, has increased considerably in most Western countries and in Japan (Offerman & Gowing, 1990; Schlüter & Schabracq, 1994). As a result, many middle-aged employees see their expectations and dreams thwarted. To them it may appear that their efforts and adaptations have been in vain. Some of them may see themselves as trapped in their present jobs, experiencing themselves as victims of over-specialisation or other plateauing effects. At the same time, it is pretty obvious that their jobs and organisations at large will significantly change in the near future, changes demanding further adaptations from them.

Also, there are the developments in the non-work domain: children growing up and leaving the parental home, marital adjustments, divorce, sickness and death of parents, the loss of other family members and friends, new affiliations and changes in leisure activities. These events imply role changes and demand new perspectives and fundamental adaptations.

Another issue is that people in middle age are confronted with a change of culture at large. As members of the baby boom generation cohort (Becker, 1992), they were raised in the affluent 1960s and early 1970s. This generation, more than the preceding one, has established its identity within the context of a youth culture, which intentionally set itself apart from mainstream culture. As such, it is often strongly influenced by the moral ideas and ideals of that youth culture, such as the emphasis on peace, communication, (sexual) freedom, self-actualisation, democratic relationships, malleability of social structures, small-scale "alternative" enterprises and the essential goodness of mankind. At the same time, many of them have learned to be suspicious of economic motives and business life in general.

Since then, however, the cultural pendulum has swung back. As a result, the baby boom generation is often seen as somewhat childish, irresponsible and soft by the members of the older generation, while many members of the younger generation look upon them as overly idealistic, inefficient and self-righteous. So, many middle-aged people are now confronted with what they see as a reactionary culture, characterised by materialism, dubious morality and a lack of meaning and purpose. They are rather reluctant to adapt in this respect, because the adaptations go against their beliefs and convictions. Problems are bound to arise in the following areas:

- As a generation that shaped its identity within a youth culture, youth itself is to them an important constituent of that identity. This can make the transition to "proper" midlife roles a difficult enterprise.
- The emphasis on freedom and democratic relationships, and pleasant, human-relations-oriented ways to settle conflicts and solve problems may lead to problems with accepting and exercising authority and leadership without questioning.

- The emphasis on self-actualisation and meaningful activities may interfere with performing in a less meaningful way. As such, members of this generation may be particularly prone to burnout symptoms. In other domains (family relationships, leisure activities, personal health) this emphasis may lead to a strongly felt responsibility to live up to high standards. Apart from consuming much time and energy, these activities may be a source of negative feelings when one performs less well in one of these areas.
- The rise of the second feminist wave, with its ideas of economic independence of women and the performance of household and child rearing tasks by men, took place within the baby boom generation. However, as its convictions and ideals are not to the same degree incorporated by all members of the generation, it has created considerable turbulence and tension in the division of gender roles. For many women of this generation, it has led to a double task load. As far as feminism has been really successful, the same applies to some of the men. For both groups, this double task load can interfere with career opportunities.

Another point is that middle-aged employees are confronted with the finite character of their future and their own impending death. Time suddenly appears to have become a scarce commodity. Before midlife, death seems far away and many people do not spend much time wondering about their own mortality. They feel they have more important things to do, i.e. to chase their short-term daily goals. In this respect, Jaques (1970) speaks of the "manic denial" of death during the first half of life. The denial can take several forms—for instance, becoming a workaholic or entertaining a secret belief of personal "invulnerability" or "being protected" (Yalom, 1980). While these forms of denial vary in their energy consumption, all of them result in an unnecessarily restricted and fragmented personal reality. This can obscure certain options and interfere with optimal functioning.

Combinations of these processes can lead to existential feelings of uncertainty, anger, conflict, despair and anxiety. These feelings indicate that things obviously are not as they should be: some serious changes have to be made. So, people in midlife face radical developmental tasks. Though most people accomplish some or most of these tasks, some are confronted with some serious risks and threats.

16.4   THE LAST CAREER STAGE

The oldest cohort of employees, consisting of those born between 1935 and 1945, belong to the so-called silent generation (Becker, 1992). Though many of them already have left the labour market, this generation still is a powerful one, as its members still occupy key positions in the upper layers of our societies. To the degree that senior employees in the upper layers experience problems, they often are in a position to solve these themselves or to find someone who can.

The silent generation grew up in the era of the Great Depression, the Second World War and the first ten post-war years. Consequentially, they have been exposed in their formative years to more hardship and misery than the younger generations. Also, they have had more models that taught them to cope with these circumstances by perseverance, denial and identification with the aggressor. On average, they complain less and show fewer emotions than their younger colleagues. Also, they seem less seriously affected by traumatic events and carry on longer when they do not feel too well. This makes them less visible to their superiors: their being there becomes a self-evident datum, similar to the presence of a familiar peace of furniture. When they do experience serious difficulties, this may go unnoticed for a long time. This is probably one of the causes of the pattern of low average frequency and long mean duration of sick leave, which is characteristic of many senior employees.

Senior employees have, again on average, learned to accept authority without much critical questioning. In addition, they were taught that age in itself is something that deserves respect. And though many senior employees realise that much has changed in this regard, they may still expect more respect than they usually get from their younger colleagues, superiors and subordinates.

The next issue is that the members of the silent generation see themselves on average as less changeable than their younger colleagues. They allowed their identity to be determined by being born into a certain family, social class, church and political party, while their younger colleagues made more choices in this respect. Such choices, however, have become more and more important in dealing with the ongoing changes in today's—and tomorrow's—world. Besides, members of the silent generation often have some vaguely unpleasant feelings about such an approach: though obviously not a forbidden course of action, it is felt not to be completely right either.

Though men and women are still far from being evenly represented in the higher levels of organisations, nowadays it is not uncommon to come across a female superior. Senior employees, male and female, often find it more difficult to work under a female, and often younger, superior. This goes back to implicit, deeply anchored assumptions about the nature of reality.

Apart from the fact that the value orientation and attitudes of the silent generation can interfere with their well-being, health and adaptation, these also may set this generation apart from the younger generations, which can lead to mutual, stereotyped perceptions and conflicts.

In their last career stage, most employees have come to realise that they only have a finite time to go. So on the one hand, they are more focused on the value of their present tasks and products, and the general quality of their present working life, including the social contacts. However, on the other hand, this awareness makes the reality and meaning of their work more relative. This sense of relativity is also reinforced by the disappearance of the illusionary dreams and goals, which used to make work into a logical route toward a better future.

Many employees in their last career stage are no longer primarily focused on increasing their income. Besides that substantial increases are not to be expected, most of the senior employees are more or less satisfied with their present lifestyle. In addition, as their children live independent lives now, their expenses have become lower. A similar loss of interest usually applies to other work objectives such as promotion or increases in status, prestige and power. In addition, as senior employees are more directed to their present activities, they often are rather weary of the prospect of another radical organisational change. Another consequence may be that, as their jobs have insufficiently enabled them to realise their objectives, senior employees have turned more to their leisure time for this purpose.

In many organisations, superiors tend to see this change in work objectives as a decrease of motivation, which interferes with the perceived organisational interests. However, this may be a very counterproductive perspective. Apart from causing unnecessary misery to many senior employees, it misses the point that employees who mind the quality of their work and products obviously can be very useful to the organisation. However, this presupposes an organisational culture that is not hostile toward senior employees, as well as a well-established form of human resource management, including a careful policy of career planning and guidance. Within such a context, objectives of individual senior employees and the organisation can be integrated with the help of periodical job interviews.

16.5 DEVELOPMENTAL RISKS

In everyday working life, as in the rest of our life, we develop our integrity, a system of relevant meanings, images, assumptions, goals, rules, procedures, skills, resources and instruments, which enables us to control our personal functioning and its outcomes (see Chapter 2). Developing integrity can be described as an active and creative process of exploration, reinvention, representation and reconstruction (Moscovici, 1984). By observational learning, trial and error, and some moments of insight, we assemble our individual integrity. In the process, we get acquainted with the opportunities and limits of the pre-existing cultural formats. In an organisation, the process of developing integrity also implies going through all kinds of role transitions, and this may hold some risks.

To start with, role transitions are not always easy (Allen & Van der Vliert, 1984; Schabracq & Winnubst, 1992). First, we have to leave behind the former role with its familiar ways of functioning and its, often highly valued, outcomes. Often, this also implies some separation from individuals who are very important to us. So, we have to say goodbye to friends, mentors and colleagues, while the common realities we shared with them and their outcomes disappear also. This is sometimes experienced as a serious loss, which can activate a corresponding emotional process. Second, mastering the new role may be a stressful process in itself: we have to find our way in a new territory, acquire new ways of functioning and be constantly alert in order to avoid all kinds of pitfalls. Of course, the pain of a transition depends on the degree to which it is voluntary and whether it is experienced as an improvement or deterioration. However, in the worst case, transition may lead to stagnation and depression, when we do not want to let go the former position (Marris, 1974).

Moreover, some people hold on to coping styles that have proven their usefulness in previous roles, but that are clearly inappropriate now. As such, these styles often are basic elements of their integrity. These coping styles are so self-evident and "logical" to them that they do not question or even notice them. Examples are habitually suppressing emotional expression, reacting defensively or avoiding authority figures. These once successful coping styles can hamper the development of a new integrity, because they interfere with the behavioural style that is deemed appropriate in the new domain.

In addition, taking on a new role sometimes means forcing ourselves—or allowing ourselves to be forced—into a kind of behavioural and emotional mould that confines us too much. Often, however, we take the unpleasant aspects of these adaptations for granted. We accept these in order to achieve future (career) goals that, at the moment, appear to be so valuable that they are thought to make up for the present inconveniences. For the time being, we deal with these inconveniences mostly by some form of denial (Breznitz, 1983), often combined with some degree of identification with the oppressor to prevent feelings of alienation (Freud, 1936).

Apart from some temporary hardship, this kind of role transition can demand complete abolition of certain ways of functioning. However, the abolished areas may have been essential parts of our integrity. By abolishing them, we are left with an impoverished form of integrity, which is no longer connected to our basic needs (Bolen, 1989).

Things can become even worse when individuals go through a series of such transitions. As a result, people may be left with a highly conventionalised and emotionally bleak form of integrity, reminiscent of the second stage of a stress process (see Chapter 2). They may feel "empty", "hollow" and alienated. They do what they have to do, but not with much zeal. Sometimes, they feel bored and find it difficult to concentrate, while rewards become less meaningful to them. At the same time, behaviour may become more rigid and ritualistic in character, without serving a clear functional purpose. From the point of view of ethology, the biology of animal and human behaviour (Eibl-Eibesfeldt, 1989), such behaviour can be described as displacement behaviour. It probably functions as a coping mechanism moderating the overall arousal level (Dantzer, 1993; Vrugt and Schabracq, 1991; Wiepkema, 1985). An example is the performance of all kinds of make-work (Goffman, 1961). Though this kind of ritualistic functioning certainly has arousal-reducing qualities, it also keeps us away from acquiring new options and learning in general.

Usually, the ones involved find nothing abnormal in this way of being. However, problems may arise when they have to adapt to fundamental changes. Managing change may ask for ways of functioning that are no longer part of their repertoire. The new situation then becomes unmanageable and threatening, which may activate stress reactions.

16.6   GETTING STUCK

The phenomenon of getting stuck in our job partially stems from our own identification with that job, but there are also organisational influences, such as an overly friendly climate with a taboo on mutual competition, where people do not hold each other responsible for their performances and failures. Anyhow, many people grow old in functions that do not appeal to them any longer. They let themselves be condemned to a role that does not fit them any more, a state of affairs that leads to serious health risks.

Except for the costs of inefficient functioning and sick leave, such a development impairs the organisation's flexibility. Moreover, younger employees see the advancement of their careers blocked and may decide to leave. Several variants of getting stuck are described below, their common characteristic being that those involved apparently do not dare to give up their job security and the false feeling of safety resulting from it (Chapter 3). Often, several of these effects are at work at the same time.

16.6.1   Experience Concentration

In general, we want to be good at our jobs. That is why we invest in skill development: we specialise. This gives us a stable repertory of successful behaviour, appropriate thoughts and feelings, which all are felt to be our own. As a result, however, we develop ourselves solely within the narrow limits of our job: we learn more and more about less and less, and are seen as persons who cannot be deployed elsewhere any more, a process called "experience concentration" (Thijssen, 1988). On the one hand, this may lead to rut, make our job less captivating and lead to qualitative task underload. On the other, we lose our career opportunities, as we cannot rise higher than our jobs or—in the best of cases— the top of our department. This becomes especially consequential when the organisation changes so that our job disappears. Essentially, this is also a consequence of failing career policies that do not pay sufficient attention to horizontal mobility, further training and education.

16.6.2   The Golden Cage Syndrome

The golden cage syndrome implies that, when we earn a high income, it is often impossible for us to make the same amount of money elsewhere. Often, this makes us stay in a position that does not really challenge us any more. As a result, it becomes less easy to keep our mind on our work, which may activate a stress process.

16.6.3   The Peter Principle

The Peter principle refers to a scenario of being promoted as long as we do well in our successive jobs, and getting stuck in the first odd job where we are not doing so well, because it asks too much of us. If this actually were the case, it would result in the long run in a situation where incompetent people would occupy all key positions in the organisation. Though organisations exist where this has played a part, this principle probably is not so realistic in most organisations, as it is based on rather obsolete propositions. For instance, it sees careers as a strictly vertical affair. It also sees a job as an unchangeable datum that we cannot adapt to our needs. Moreover, it takes proven competence as the sole determinant of promotion. Lastly, it passes over the possibility of appointing a competent assistant who can do the things that we cannot do. As such, the principle is based on a rather absolute faith in the rationality of organisations designed on a drawing board.

16.6.4   Being Kicked Upstairs

Some organisations solve problems with incompetent or unpopular employees by promoting them to formally higher, but factually empty, positions, because they cannot do much harm there. Seemingly, there is no loss of face. After all, they are promoted and get a higher salary. However, everybody involved knows that they have been sidetracked. Though such a position offers, in principle, great opportunities to somebody who flourishes best in freedom and loves to design his or her own job, in practice, it often leads to many stress complaints.

16.6.5   The Glass Ceiling

This refers to the phenomenon that it is nearly impossible for certain groups of employees (women, employees of minority subcultural, religious, racial or ethnical backgrounds) to rise above a certain level in the organisation. This was not at all clear to them beforehand. The word "glass" refers to the ceiling's invisibility: the unreachable levels are clearly visible and also seem easily reachable. The phenomenon stems from deeply rooted cultural premises about the underlying division of power and roles (Chapter 3). Employees troubled by the glass ceiling often have the capacities as well as the ambition to work at a higher lever. They work hard and perform well, to find out later that this was not as important as they were told. At the same time, they witness how colleagues and subordinates who come from the right group do progress in their careers. In the longer run, this often leads to all kinds of stress reactions (Schabracq & Van Vugt, 1993).

16.7   LACK OF ADDITIONAL TRAINING

Many employees over 40 get little or no additional training (Boerlijst et al., 1993; Groot & Maassen van den Brink, 1997). At the same time, technology in the workplace and the ways in which the work is organised are changing faster than ever. As a result, the skills of senior employees may become obsolete rapidly. As the obvious thing to do is to give these senior employees additional training, the question arises as to why this does not happen at the largest scale possible.

The omission of additional training, typically, is a matter of organisational culture and its stereotypes and self-fulfilling prophecies. On the one hand, training older employees is often, and mostly erroneously, considered a bad investment. On the other, there sometimes does exist among senior employees some persistent reluctance against additional training.

Several motives can be mentioned here. Some senior employees mistrust the reasons of the management. They associate additional training with an unwanted change in their job. Often this resistance is a collective phenomenon: old hands supporting each other in their resistance against the change forced upon them. Apart from that, some senior employees fear they are lagging behind so far that it will be impossible to catch up. This particularly applies to employees with a low level of formal schooling, a poor economical background and a lack of possibilities in other areas. This then can be the start of a vicious circle of uninteresting jobs, little personal development (Bourdieu, 1986; Kohn and Schooler, 1983; Lee, 1991; Schaie & Schooler, 1989) and stereotyping (Vrugt & Schabracq, 1996).

Other motives have to do with the nature of the courses and the way they are given. For example, most training courses are not adapted to the specific needs of senior employees. Some courses may conflict with their value systems and some provide insufficient opportunities to practise their newly acquired skills and knowledge.

If lack of additional training is not properly confronted, problems will arise. Sometimes, this will initially result in some form of qualitative overload, as the work has become too difficult. However, in most cases, someone else is appointed for the new and difficult parts of the task, leaving the senior employee with an impoverished function, stripped of much of its meaning and structure. As a result, the older employee may face a work situation of qualitative underload, while at the same time, the organisation is burdened with the presence of an unproductive, overpaid and, probably, poorly motivated senior employee.

16.8   AGEING OF NETWORKS

As described in Chapter 3, employees develop social networks of familiar and trusted people, with whom it is pleasant to be with and who make everyday affairs workable. Such a network is important for one's integrity and power position in the organisation, and it helps to prevent stress, makes stress less harmful and facilitates the recovery from stress-related complaints.

However, social networks age too: senior employees are confronted with the loss of the ones who are of importance for their integrity. This loss also is an emotional matter, involving feelings such as grief, anxiety, depression and bereavement. Because many elderly people do not make new friends as easily as they used to, such losses leave the senior employees with an impoverished network. This leads, apart from a loss of structure of their working environment, to a partial loss of the yields of the network. Apart from the obvious, negative consequences for the individuals involved, this process also affects the communication within the organisation at large in a negative way.

16.9 MANAGERIAL UNEASINESS

Managers sometimes experience some uneasiness in dealing with their senior employees. On the one hand, managers tend to have a rather low opinion of many of them. On the other, they have to take into consideration that these same employees have acquired a certain status, based upon their seniority and contributions in the past. Because this entitles these employees to a certain respect, it becomes more complicated for the managers to deal appropriately with problems with them. Disciplining and correcting senior employees may activate feelings of uneasiness and guilt. Managers may avoid doing this and, consequentially, the employees in question get little or no feedback about their performance and are exposed to a greater risk of role ambiguity. This can be regarded as an instance of loss of role structure.

16.10 STEREOTYPING

People in the Western world do not look forward to being old. Americans, for example, tend to see old age as the worst life stage (Bennett & Eckman, 1973). This attitude goes together with a stereotyped perception of old age. This, at least, goes back to classical antiquity, as can be concluded from Cicero's 'an Old Age', which actually is a discourse against such a way of perceiving, as well as Greek and Roman mythology. The god of old age—Kronos in Greek, Saturn in Latin—was seen as cold, dry and unfriendly, and was traditionally associated with melancholy, prisons and long-lasting loneliness (Biedermann, 1989).

Notwithstanding the huge individual variability of senior employees, stereotyped perception ensues that older employees are regarded as a more or less uniform group, characterised by low flexibility, strength, speed and productivity, as well as by conservatism, bitterness, dependency and passivity (Belsky, 1990; Foner & Schwab, 1981; Krijnen, 1993; Vrugt & Schabracq, 1996). In addition, old age is also associated with functional deficits, which may only be bettered by medical interventions (Baars 1988). This kind of stereotyping can be very damaging to senior employees. Two processes are important here.

First, as a case of blaming the victim, this kind of stereotyping leads attention away from solutions such as technological, organisational and ergonomic adaptations of the workplace, job redesign, training programmes and better career policies. Because blaming the victim makes it possible to hold on to a favourable image of the organisation, these solutions may disappear out of sight altogether. In these circumstances, removing the senior employee from the organisation may start to look like the only feasible "solution".

Second, this kind of stereotyping tends to act like a self-fulfilling prophecy: senior employees may learn to see themselves as problematic persons and may learn to find some compensation in it (less responsibility, lower standards, less demands, more claims for support on other parties). This process may add considerably to the gravity of the problem, because it may disturb the integrity, self-esteem and well-being of senior employees. In the longer run, it also may lead to impoverishment of their functioning and their jobs.

16.11   THE INCREASE IN CHANGE

As described in Chapters 3 and 29, our organisations are being confronted by an unprecedented acceleration of societal, cultural, technological and economic change. Organisations have to adapt to these changes by changing themselves. As a rule, older employees find more difficulty with such changes than younger ones.

Changes in an organisational culture imply changes in the prominence and priority of prevailing values and objectives. Objectives as quantity of output, flexibility and being client- or market-oriented may become more prominent, while technical perfection and professional freedom may lose their dominant roles. However, these last ones may have been the very reason for senior employees to join this particular organisation. Changes in this respect may leave them behind with work that, in their eyes, has been stripped of most of its challenges and intrinsic meaning. This may lead to qualitative job underload and stress. Also, they are confronted with demands to learn new skills that do not appeal to them. Though it is easy enough to discuss such a development in terms of a personal motivation problem, and to act accordingly, it is important to realise that its causes lie in the area of cultural change.

As stated in Chapter 3, our culture gives its members environments that are changing at an accelerating rate. As a result, already several generations see the former generation as somewhat lagging behind and old-fashioned (Schabracq, 1994). So, we look upon our (grand)parents with some weariness when they try to operate a ticket machine or to extract some money from a cash machine, and we preferably avoid queues with an high percentage of elderly people in it. Though this is, in the case of most senior employees, a typical case of stereotyped exaggeration, such perceptions are very common.

The content of much organisational change also causes problems for senior employees. Organisations nowadays have become flatter, more flexible, less product-oriented, more market-oriented, more quality-oriented, and so on. People working in these organisations have to become more autonomous, more decisive, more creative and more entrepreneurial. Also, they have to accept change as the normal state of affairs. In order to accomplish all this, they are asked to use all their powers to the fullest. In fact, they are asked to behave as if they were completely free beings, who were working for themselves, and not for an organisation owned by other persons. To senior employees this remains more of a contradiction. The main issue, however, is that many of them have effectively unlearned to act in a way such as is asked of them now: until now, many organisations have consistently aimed at minimising the power of individual workers. So, many senior employees come to work in an organisation in which they can only partly believe. This can be seen as another impairment of the role structure available to them.

16.12   CONCLUDING REMARKS

In summary, it may be said that many senior employees have to cope with one or several of a number of problems. Most of these problems can be characterised as a lack or loss of control and a corresponding lack or loss of role structure (Schuyt & Van de Klinkenberg, 1988): older people have to resign from certain ways of functioning (Rümke, 1947). Consequentially, the main developmental tasks of senior employees can be described as graceful resignation and creating new, meaningful role structures. This means, among other things, that senior employees are confronted by problems that are relatively unstructured and ill-defined. According to Featherman et al. (1993), this is part of a general trend: throughout the life course, developmental tasks tend to become less well structured (Wood, 1983).

Making a successful transition into retirement can serve as an example of such an ill-structured task. First, this task is characterised by an ill-defined goal state, as, beforehand, no one knows what comprises an ideal form of retirement. Second, there is no such thing as a fixed path toward that goal state, nor in the initial stage, nor later on. So, one has to design such a goal state oneself and one also has to find one's own path toward it. However, in most organisations, as well as in most educational institutions, most people do not get much training and practice in such design tasks, as is rightfully pointed out by De Bono (1990). Still, this is an important developmental task that has to be successfully accomplished in order to live a satisfactory life. It will not come as a surprise that many people fail in this respect. They do not succeed in dealing adequately with the constriction in economic and cultural participation inherent in retirement. They do not succeed in building a new supportive context that is necessary for maintaining and further developing their cognitive abilities. Consequently, many of them experience corresponding declines in cognitive functioning in their late 60s to early 70s. The good news, however, is that many other people do manage to make a successful transition into retirement.

The same kind of remarks can be made about other developmental tasks within the last career stage, such as renewing one's social network, carving out an adequate function for one's last working years, maintaining functional independence and carrying out a successful life review (Featherman et al., 1993).

REFERENCES

Allen, V.L. & Vliert, E. van der (eds) (1984) *Role Transitions.* New York: Plenum Press.

Baars, J. (1988) De sociale constitutie van de ouderdom. [The social constitution of old age]. In C.P.M. Knipscheer, J. Baars & M. Severijns (eds) *Uitzicht op ouder worden: een verkenning van nieuwe rollen* [*A View of Growing Old: An Exploration of New Roles*]. Assen: Van Gorcum, pp. 21–36.

Baltes, P.B. & Baltes, M.G. (1993) Psychological perspectives on successful aging. In P.B. Baltes & M.G. Baltes (eds) *Successful Aging. Perspectives from the Social Sciences.* Cambridge: Cambridge University Press, pp. 1–34.

Becker, H.A. (1992) *Generaties en hun kansen* [*Generations and their Chances*]. Amsterdam: Meulenhoff.

Belsky, J.K. (1990) *The Psychology of Aging,* 2nd edn. Pacific Grove, CA: Brooks/Cole.

Bennett, R. & Eckman, J. (1973) Attitudes towards aging. In C. Eisendorfer & M.P. Lawton (eds) *The Psychology of Adult Development and Aging.* Washington, DC: APA.

Biedermann, H. (1989). *Knaurs Lexicon der Symbole* [*Knaur's Lexicon of Symbols*]. Munich: Knaur.

Boerlijst, J.G., Heyden, B.I.J.M. van der & Assen, A. van (1993) *Veertig-plussers in de onderneming* [*People Over 40 in the Corporation*]. Assen: Van Gorcum.

Bolen, J.S. (1989) *Gods in Every Man.* New York: Harper & Row.

Bourdieu, P. (1986) The Forms of Capital. In J.G. Richardson (ed.) *Handbook of Theory and Research for the Sociology of Education.* New York: Greenwood Press.

Breznitz, S. (1983) The seven kinds of denial. In S. Breznitz (ed.) *The Denial of Stress.* New York: International Universities Press, pp. 257–80.

Broersen, J.P.J., Zwart, B.C.H. de, Meijman, T.F., Dijk, F.J.H. van, Veldhoven, M. van & Schabracq, M.J. (1993) *Atlas Veroudering, Werk en Gezondheid* [*Atlas of Ageing, Working and Health*]. Amsterdam: University of Amsterdam.

Cascio, W.F. & McEnvoy, G.M. (1989) Cumulative evidence of the relationship between employee age and job performance. *Journal of Applied Psychology*, **74**, 11–17.

Cremer, R. (1995). Mental belasting en veroudering [Mental load and ageing]. In J.A.M. Winnubst, M.J. Schabracq, J. Gerrichhauzen & A. Kampermann (eds) *Arbeid, levensloop en gezondheid* [*Work, Life Course and Health*]. Heerlen: Open Universiteit, pp. 63–82.

Dantzer, R. (1993) Coping with stress. In S.C. Stanford & P. Salmon (eds) *Stress. From Synapse to Syndrome*. London: Academic Press, pp. 167–89.

De Bono, E. (1990) *I am Right, You are Wrong*. London: Viking.

Eibl-Eibesfeldt, I. (1989) *Human Ethology*. New York: Aldine.

Featherman, D.L., Smith, J. & Patterson, J.G. (1993) Successful aging in a post-retired society. In P.B. Baltes & M.G. Baltes (eds) *Successful Aging. Perspectives from the Social Sciences*. Cambridge University Press, Cambridge, pp. 49–93.

Foner, A. & Schwab, K. (1981) *Aging and Retirement*. Belmont, CA: Wadsworth.

Freud, A. (1936) *The Ego and the Mechanisms of Defence*. New York: International Universities Press.

Goffman, E. (1961) *Asylums*. Garden City, NY: Doubleday.

Groot, W. & Maassen van den Brink, H. (1997) *Bedrijfsgerelateerde scholing en arbeidsmarktflexibiliteit van oudere medewerkers*. (*Corporation-Related Education and Labour Market Flexibility of Senior Employees*) Den Haag: Welboom.

Haasnoot, M. (1993) *Leeftijd en arbeidssatisfactie* [*Age and Work Satisfaction*]. Amsterdam: University of Amsterdam.

Hall, D.T. (1976) *Careers in Organizations*. Pacific Palisades: Good Year.

Havighurst, R. (1972) *Developmental Tasks and Education*, 3rd edn. New York: McKay.

Hess, T.M. (1992) Adult age differences in script content and structure. In R.L. West & J.D. Sinnott (eds) *Everyday Memory and Aging*. New York: Springer-Verlag, pp. 87–100.

Horn, J.L. (1982) The aging of human abilities. In B.B. Wolman (ed.) *Handbook of Developmental Psychology*. Englewood Cliffs, NJ: Prentice Hall, pp. 847–70.

Hoyer, W.J. & Rybash, J.M. (1992) Knowledge factors in everyday visual perception. In R.L. West & J.D. Sinnott (eds) *Everyday Memory and Aging*. New York: Springer-Verlag, pp. 215–27.

Janssen, P. & Gerrichhauzen, J. (1995) De middenloopbaan- en middenleven-fase [The midcareer and midlife stage]. In J.A.M.Winnubst, M.J. Schabracq, J. Gerrichhauzen & A. Kampermann (eds) *Arbeid, levensloop en gezondheid* [*Work, Course of Life and Health*]. Heerlen: Open Universiteit, pp. 159–247.

Jaques, E. (1970) *Work, Creativity and Social Justice*. London: Heinemann.

Kemper, S., Kynette, D. & Norman, S. (1993) Age differences in spoken language. In R.L. West & J.D. Sinnott (eds) *Everyday Memory and Aging*. New York: Springer-Verlag, pp. 138–52.

Kimmel, D.C. (1990) *Adulthood and Aging*, 3rd edn. New York: John Wiley & Sons.

Kohli, M. (1985) Die Institutionalisierung des Lebenslaufs [The Institutionalising of the Life Course]. *Kölner Zeitschrift für Soziologie und Sozialpsychologie*, **37**, 1–29.

Kohn, M.L. & Schooler, C. (1983) *Work and Personality: A Study. An Inquiry into the Impact of Social Stratification*. Norwood, NJ: Ablex.

Krijnen, M.A. (1993) *Beeldvorming over ouderen* [*Representations of the Elderly*]. Amsterdam: University of Amsterdam.

Lee, J.S. (1991) *Abstraction and Aging. A Social Psychological Analysis*. New York: Springer-Verlag.

Levinson, D.J., Darrow, C.N., Klein, E.B., Levinson, M.H. and McKee, B. (1978) *The Seasons of a Man's Life*. New York: Ballantine.

Marris, P. (1974) *Loss and Change*. New York: Pantheon.

Merriam, S.B. (1994). Learning and life experience: the connection in adulthood. In J.D. Sinnott (ed.) *Interdisciplinary Handbook of Adult Lifespan Learning*. Westport, CT: Greenwood Press, pp. 74–89.

Moscovici, S. (1984) The phenomenon of social representation. In R.M. Farr & S. Moscovici (eds) *Social Representations*. Cambridge: Cambridge University Press, pp. 3–69.

Mottaz, C.J. (1987) Age and work satisfaction. *Work and Occupations*, **14**, 387–409.

Neugarten, B.L. (1976) Adaptation and the life cycle, *Counseling Psychologist*, **6**, 16–20.

Offerman, L. & Gowing, M. (1990) Organizations of the future. *American Psychologist*, **45**, 95–108.

Plude, D.J. & Murphy, L.S. (1992) Aging, selective attention, and everyday memory. In R.L. West & J.D. Sinnott (eds) *Everyday Memory and Aging*. New York: Springer-Verlag, pp. 235–45.

Rabbitt, P.M.A. (1993) Methodological and theoretical lessons from the University of Manchester longitudinal studies of cognitive changes in normal old age. In J.J.F. Schroots (ed.) *Aging, Health and Competence*. Amsterdam: Elsevier, pp. 199–219.

Rümke, H.C. (1947) *Levenstijdperken van de man* [*Life Stages of the Male*]. Amsterdam: De Arbeiderspers.

Salthouse, T.A. (1992) *Mechanisms of Age–Cognition Relations in Adulthood*. Hillsdale, NJ: Lawrence Erlbaum.

Schabracq, M.J. (1994) On the origins of trouble: motivational and cultural factors underlying dysfunctioning of older employees. In J. Snel & R. Cremer (eds) *Work and Aging. A European Perspective*. Basingstoke: Taylor & Francis.

Schabracq, M.J. & Van Vugt, P.M. (1993) Psychotherapeutische interventies: een voorbeeld van een AGP-praktijk [Psychotherapeutic Interventions: An Example of a Work and Health Psychology Practice]. In M.J. Schabracq & J.A.M. Winnubst (eds) *Handboek "Arbeid en Gezondheid"-Psychologie. Toepassingen* [*Handbook of Work and Health Psychology: Applications*]. Utrecht: Lemma, pp. 259–73.

Schabracq, M.J. & Winnubst, J.A.M. (1992) Rolovergangen [Role transitions]. In J.A.M. Winnubst & M.J. Schabracq (eds) *Handboek "Arbeid en Gezondheid"-Psychologie. Hoofdthema's* [*Handbook of Work and Health Psychology: Main Themes*]. Utrecht: Lemma.

Schaie, K.W. & Schooler, C. (eds) (1989) *Social Structure and Aging*. Hillsdale, NJ: Lawrence Erlbaum.

Schein, E. (1978) *Career Dynamics.: Matching Individual and Organizational Needs*. Reading, MA: Addison-Wesley.

Schlüter, C.J.M. & Schabracq, M.J. (1994) *Ouder worden in organisaties* [*Becoming Older in Organizations*]. Deventer: Kluwer Bedrijfswetenschappen.

Schroots, J.J.F. & Birren, J.E. (1993). Theoretical issues and basic questions in the planning of longitudinal studies of health and aging. In J.J.F. Schroots (ed.) *Aging, Health and Competence*. Amsterdam: Elsevier, pp. 4–34.

Schuyt, T. & Klinkenberg, T. van de (1988) Helpen en de zuigkracht van de macht [Helping and the pull of power]. In C.P.M. Knipscheer, J. Baars & M. Severijns (eds) *Uitzicht op ouder worden: een verkenning van nieuwe rollen* [*A View of Growing Old: An Exploration of New Roles*]. Assen: Van Gorcum, pp. 53–64.

Sterns, H. and Alexander, R. (1988) Performance appraisal of the older worker. In H. Dennis (ed.) *Fourteen Steps in Managing an Aging Work Force*. Lexington, MA: Lexington Books, pp. 85–93.

Super, D.E. (1957) *The Psychology of Careers*. New York: Harper & Row.

Thijssen, J.G.L. (1988) *Bedrijfsopleidingen als werkterrein* [*In-company Training as a Field of Work*]. Den Haag: Vuga.

Thomae, H. (1993) Foreword. In J.J.F. Schroots (ed.) *Aging, Health and Competence*. Amsterdam: Elsevier, pp. XI–XIII.

Ventis, D.G. (1992) Individual differences in everyday memory aging: implications for theory and research. In R.L. West & J.D. Sinnott (eds) *Everyday Memory and Aging*. New York: Springer-Verlag.

Vrugt, A.J. & Schabracq, M.J. (1991) *Vanzelfsprekend gedrag. Opstellen over non-verbale communicatie* [*Behaviour that Goes without Saying. Essays on Nonverbal Communication*]. Amsterdam/Meppel: Boom.

Vrugt, A. & Schabracq, M.J. (1996). Stereotypes with respect to elderly employees: the contribution of attribute information and representativeness. *Journal of Community and Applied Social Psychology*, **6**, 287–92.

Waldman, D. & Avolio, B. (1986) A meta-analysis of age differences in job performance. *Journal of Applied Psychology*, **71**, 33–8.

Warr, P. (1992) Age and occupational well-being. *Psychology and Aging*, **7**, 37–45.

Warr, P. (1993) *Age and job performance*. Amsterdam: European Symposium on Work and Aging, University of Amsterdam, p. 17.

Wiepkema, P.R. (1985) Abnormal behaviours in farm animals: ethological implications. *Netherlands Journal of Zoology*, **35**, 279–99.

White, A.T. & Spector, P.E. (1987) An investigation of age-related factors in the age–job-satisfaction relationship. *Psychology and Aging*, **2**, 261–5.

Wood, P.K. (1983) Inquiring systems and problem structure: implications for cognitive development. *Human Development*, **26**, 249–65.

Yalom, J. (1980) *Existential Psychotherapy*. New York: Basic Books.

CHAPTER 17

Policies and Strategies for the Second Career Half

Marc J. Schabracq
University of Amsterdam, The Netherlands

17.1   INTRODUCTION

In organisations in the industrialised world, senior employees represent a steadily increasing reserve of high-quality human capital, in which much money has been invested. This reserve can be of strategic importance, certainly in times of scarcity of personnel. At least, it would be if it were used more appropriately. As it is, management tends to pay insufficient attention to the possibilities of most senior employees, at the expense of these individual employees as well as the organisation as a whole. When nothing changes, the value of this capital will diminish. This is not an inevitable natural phenomenon, but a consequence of the implemented policies and the self-fulfilling prophecies induced by these policies. This makes the development of senior employees who work in the same jobs for a long time an important challenge and chance for organisations. Though absolute success may be improbable, doing better than the competition in this respect may well be a crucial strategic factor in organisational survival, as well as in employees' well-being and health.

The question now is: what can be done to help senior employees to develop their potential contributions to the organisation? Several points are important here.

In Chapter 16 it was concluded that most problems experienced by senior employees could be reduced to a lack or loss of personal power and role structure. Using this conclusion as the point of departure, it is only logical to focus solutions on increasing or giving back individual power to these employees by allowing them to build up new role structures.

As senior employees differ so strongly from each other, interventions should take these variations into account. Put more strongly, the great individual variety among senior employees makes it impossible to use generally applicable measures. So the general approach focuses on the available potential of adaptation and coping of the individual employees. Making senior employees aware of the necessity of their further development and then allowing them sufficient freedom, means and responsibility to shape their own further career is probably the best guarantee that they will make a successful effort in this respect. After all, they are the experts as well as the main stakeholders with respect to their own destiny.

The Handbook of Work and Health Psychology. Edited by M.J. Schabracq, J.A.M. Winnubst and C.L. Cooper.
© 2003 John Wiley & Sons, Ltd.

The focus is on jointly optimising outcomes for the individual employees and the organisation. This boils down to creating optimal room for the employees involved to design their own jobs and to provide them with appropriate possibilities to develop their abilities and skills, in a way that is geared to their own developmental tasks (Havighurst, 1972). This is primarily a matter of training and education, but essentially all HRM instruments can play a part here (see also Chapter 28).

Such an approach demands a certain attitude of the employees involved. First of all, they should be aware of the necessity of their own further development and the efforts this demands from them. Moreover, this awareness should also be translated into willingness to act accordingly and take on the responsibility demanded by the approach. This implies that they must have sufficient trust in the organisation. A serious lack of trust can be considered as a clear contraindication of the approach.

The approach also implies serious demands for the organisation. First, this is about a leadership and management style based on subsidiarity (Handy, 1994) and trust, resulting in sufficient decision latitude and room to move for the employees. In addition, this approach should be embedded in a thorough overall HRM approach, aiming at prevention of problems with future senior employees. Another issue is that an organisation should have a clear vision of its own purpose and desired future, which provides individual employees with clear guidelines for their own actions (Collins & Porras, 1994). A mission statement stemming from a clear organisational philosophy, which—among other things—includes the rationale behind the policies under consideration, is of help too. This provides the individual senior employees involved with an overall picture. It helps them to tailor their activities optimally to the organisational demands, without any need for directives from other persons such as managers. A last issue is the transparency of the organisation to the employees involved. It is important that employees know the consequences of their actions for their evaluation and further careers. This is a matter of providing and receiving the right information. More generally, the organisation should give the employees involved sufficient time, information and attention (Doeglas & Schabracq, 1992).

The remainder of the chapter consists of a number of attention points and interventions, in which the emphasis lies initially wholly on the individual senior employee, to shift gradually to the organisation. The points and interventions that are primarily directed at the individual employees may be part of a special self-management training programme for senior employees.

17.2   DEVELOPMENTAL TASKS OF SENIOR EMPLOYEES

17.2.1   Becoming Aware of One's Own Predicaments

> Midway this way of life we're bound upon,
> I woke to find myself in a dark wood,
> Where the right road was wholly lost and gone.

This often cited opening strophe of the *Divina Comedia* (Dante Alighieri, 1969, p. 71) is said to refer to the loss of perspective many people experience sometime during midlife. To many people, midlife is a life stage to take stock of their situation. Certain illusions and some prospects have grown thin, the future has become a finite affair and not everybody finds themselves in a place they want to be. So, we have to ask ourselves: "Where am I heading for? Do I want to go to that place?". And if not: "Can I do something about it?". Assessment does not have to be limited to work-related areas such as function, products, career and work-related social network, but can also be directed to other life domains, such as family life, personal development, leisure activities and health matters. As the third strophe of the *Divina Comedia* (p. 71) points out, all this may be a painful, but rewarding, undertaking:

> It is so bitter, it goes nigh to death;
> Yet there I gained such good, that, to convey
> The tale, I'll write what else I found therewith.

Actually, writing a diary of such events—or better still, writing an autobiography—can be a useful method to get a grip on our life again (for an elaborate example see Schroots and Van Dongen, 1995). However, before going into these issues, many of us have to finish some unfinished business. On the one hand, this is a matter of self-examination, as well as of attending to and "minding" our functioning. On the other, it boils down to trying out new ways of functioning and practising.

So, it may be useful to turn our attention to what went wrong in our personal past and still needs mending now. This can be regarded as a case of catching up with overdue maintenance. In midlife, many of us look back at some more or less traumatic events. As far as these are still actual to us and continue to demand or to divert our attention, the event in question needs to be addressed, maybe even with the help of a professional therapist. Another issue may be that we may still respond with coping styles that used to be adaptive once, but obviously are obsolete now. So, we have to unlearn dysfunctional tactics and strategies, and to explore and to re-integrate options that we once split off. Sometimes, a good conversation with our partner or a friend will be helpful here. In some cases, consultation of a professional is needed, especially when there is a serious problem that goes back to our early youth:

> The kind of crisis that may occur during midlife is one where the most primitive, infantile reaches of the psyche are explored and exposed for reworking. This can result in an acute disorganization and tremendous feelings of pain and loss. The feelings that emerge are likely to be inexplicable, because of their preverbal, infantile nature. (Kramer & Bacelar, 1994, p. 41)

However, it is important to stress that, most of the time. midlife issues do not take such serious proportions.

One of the typical developmental tasks of midlife is accepting certain facts of life. For example, we have to accept conflicts, guilt and suffering as inevitable and necessary elements of life (Rümke, 1947). The same applies to the acceptance of the loss of youth and the decay of physical strength, speed and sensory acuity. Only if we accept these facts of life fully, does it become possible to stop avoiding the experience of them, and only then are we able to deal with them. Another very important developmental task is learning to accept our mortality and the certainty of our death.

This last task is often considered to be a very difficult one, because it may activate intense anxiety. However, accepting our death as a reality and being able to tolerate the feelings activated by that acceptance can have a powerful positive effect. When we have come to terms with our own death, it becomes possible to appreciate more fully the preciousness of life. Only then can we fully grasp the once-only character of each moment, and only then the relevance of mindfully making choices and decisions becomes obvious (Schabracq, 1991).

Heidegger (1962) speaks in this respect of *Sein zum Tode*, being-towards-death, which he sees as a *sine qua non* for becoming an authentic (in German *eigentlich*) person, one who can become one's true self (see also Spinelli, 1992). In addition, one can state that—as denial often takes the form of compulsively focusing attention elsewhere when death threatens to become an issue—the removal of denial of death may facilitate more integrated functioning.

Coming to terms with death is a typical developmental task of midlife. Accepting our mortality and making it a part of our integrity (Chapter 2) can be an important condition to be able to embrace the above-mentioned attitudes and convictions that are necessary for a radical reorientation. At the same time, acceptation can generate a salutary sense of freedom: as we have to die anyway, the petty anxieties, which steer our decisions in everyday life and hold us back from interesting options that imply a change, lose their significance and urgency. As a result, we acquire more autonomy to realise options that truly correspond with our basic needs, motives and goals, i.e. options that are the most meaningful and purposive to us. Typically, this sense of freedom is accompanied by a pleasant feeling of excitement, of being fully alive, of being in control over our resources and opportunities. The effects of near-death experiences can be regarded as extreme cases in this respect. People who have gone through such an experience often report the disappearance of the threatening quality of death, as well as fundamental changes in their perspective on life along the lines described above. This is not an admonition to organise our own near-death experience in a physical way, but a thought experiment about this matter would do no harm.

17.2.2   Coming to Terms with Painful Events in the Organisation

Most senior employees have experienced one or more painful events during their working life. Some of them still hold grudges, and still feel offended, frustrated or disappointed about such events. This often leads to distrust and resistance when it comes to implementing changes that actually would improve their situation. These employees often have become very cynical about their own possibility to change things as well as about the organisational intentions in this respect. They know one or two things for sure: they want satisfaction for what is done to them and they are not going to be hurt again. This often takes the form of a collective attitude of cynical indifference, shared by a number of employees, who reinforce each other in this attitude. This often leads to a situation of deadlock and paralysis.

An obvious form of wisdom in this respect is to realise that you cannot change the past. Maybe, you can learn something from it for designing your future, but remaining frustrated and resentful is clearly counterproductive. In such a case, it is often useful to find out in individual and group discussions what has happened. This boils down to discussing "unspeakables", raking up cold conflicts, bringing up what is swept under the carpet and opening closets which everybody involved knows or suspects that they house "old skeletons".

All parties involved must have considerable courage, and there has to be sufficient trust that the organisation is willing to actually do something about the issues that show up. To achieve this, we must allow the nasty events from the past to "get" to us sufficiently. This enables us to give these events their deserved place in the common organisational history and to free ourselves from their influence. Only then are we able to occupy ourselves with some faith with a better future. In mutual discussion, we can then determine how to continue, without ignoring what has happened (see Ryan & Oestreich, 1988; Schabracq et al., 2001).

17.2.3 Coming to Terms with the Threats to Occupational Functioning

Apart from the task of performing at an adequate level and showing specific expertise (Schein, 1978), which in itself is a considerable assignment, people in midlife have to reorient themselves towards the threats that were discussed in Chapter 16. Coming to terms with these threats can also be considered to be a developmental task. So, employees have to become aware of the following threats.

- experience concentration
- lack of additional training
- ageing of networks
- motivational factors and value orientation
- insufficient managerial feedback
- generation gaps and stereotyping.

Experience Concentration

"Concentration of experience" and other plateau effects, such as the "golden cage syndrome", Peter's principle, being "kicked upstairs" and the glass ceiling are threats to look out for. Some senior employees have adapted too strongly to a way of working that is intrinsically too limiting to be pleasant and healthy. This may have led to impoverished development and abolishing of certain ways of functioning. Though it may appear as if the abolished ways of functioning and their underlying needs have simply vanished altogether, they are only out of awareness and, usually, can be reactivated by some focused reflection. This means that the persons involved have to go back mentally to a time when the particular way of functioning was still part of their integrity. This, however, may take some form of counselling or psychotherapy (for example Bolen, 1989; Schabracq & Van Vugt, 1993). In any case, becoming aware of such a difficulty is a necessary condition to be able to do something about it. This also is or should be an organisational or, more specifically, an HRM responsibility. The focus of interventions in this respect should be on bringing about greater flexibility and horizontal mobility. Job redesign, training, an active career policy, including creating enough possibilities for job rotation, special projects and posting employees to sister or client organisations, are normal elements of such an approach. Older employees, however, may need considerably more time and attention in this respect than others, involving a self-management programme.

Baltes & Baltes (1993) advocate a more careful strategy for the oldest group of employees, which they call "selective optimisation". This strategy, at first sight, runs counter to the approach just mentioned. Baltes & Baltes recommend a purposive, selective restriction of one's life world, combined with efforts to increase one's resources and reserves, including finding good replacements for lost resources. This strategy can be regarded as an alternative when the normal HRM approach proves to be no longer possible: for some older employees who have been in the same function for too many years, it may not be a viable option any more to deal with much change. However, such a strategy demands a high degree of overall organisational stability, and this has become a rare commodity in many organisations.

Lack of Additional Training

Apart from becoming aware of one's own individual lacunas in this respect, proper additional training programmes for the senior employees in question is the obvious solution when it comes to dealing with a lack of additional training. However, what does "proper" mean in this respect? The following list is a compilation of characteristics mentioned by Laird (1985), Goldstein (1986), Cranton (1989), Thijssen (1991), Schabracq & Boerlijst (1992), Thompson (1992), Sinnott (1994), Schlüter & Schabracq (1994) and Cremer (1995). Though most of these characteristics may apply to all kinds of training programmes, they are especially important to older employees. In order for additional training to be maximally effective, it is important to:

- have a clear picture of what is needed in terms of knowledge and skills;
- create special training courses for older employees, characterised by a non-competitive, cooperative and supportive learning climate;
- explain and stress the necessity and use of the learning tasks, as well as their connection with pre-existing values, motives, experiences and skills of older workers;
- generate an active learning attitude by giving the trainees responsibility for the learning agenda (pace, number and dates of sessions), creating opportunities for dialogue and discussion, and stressing the importance of active processing of information, including fact-finding, creativity and synthetic operations;
- use concrete examples and provide for systematic forms of supportive feedback, in order to prevent fear of failure;
- provide possibilities for individual contacts between trainer and trainee, and create intervision groups for trainees;
- provide possibilities to practise the newly acquired knowledge and skills in real-life working situations.

In general, it can be stated that the additional training issues mentioned here can easier be prevented than cured. A careful HRM approach, including a good career policy and ample training opportunities, is probably the best way to accomplish this. However, when change occurs, it is important to realise that older employees, on average, do need more time, information and attention (Doeglas & Schabracq, 1992).

Ageing of Networks

Besides becoming aware of the decay of one's network, it is also necessary to face— and deal with—some senior employees' rejecting attitude toward deliberate networking and instrumentally making new contacts. Possible interventions are forms of training and coaching that focus on these attitudes as well as on deliberate development of a network. Such a programme usually also pays attention to assertiveness issues. At the same time, an organisational policy to create the opportunities for this can be of help too. Elements of such a policy may involve increasing internal mobility and opportunities for contact.

Motivational Factors and Value Orientation

Attempts to solve problems around motivational factors stemming from a particular value orientation of senior employees should focus on bringing about a greater awareness of their own ways of functioning, in order to increase the number of behavioural options. This can be accomplished within the context of a training programme or in individual coaching sessions. However, to the degree that such an approach is successful, it also implies that the basic convictions and assumptions that steered their life up until now become more relative. As such, this can lead to feelings of uncertainty, though the graceful acceptance of this relativity can be regarded as the development of a form of wisdom as well.

Insufficient Managerial Feedback

Insufficient managerial feedback is a common problem encountered by senior employees, because managers often experience some uneasiness in this respect, which induces them to be reticent in their feedback. Special training programmes for the managers involved can be of help in this respect. Such a training programme should address stereotypical perception and can teach managers to solve their problems in dealing with senior employees by exercises and role play techniques. On the other hand, senior employees can play an important role too by explicitly asking their managers for feedback if their managers do not provide it spontaneously. Here too, some assertiveness issues may need to be addressed.

Generation Gaps and Stereotyping

Another point that emerged from the previous chapter is that stereotyping reinforces the lack or loss of power of senior employees. Stereotyping leads to a one-sided and incorrect image of these employees as a uniform group of people characterised by diminished possibilities with respect to employability and flexibility. Apart from the fact that such stereotyping tends to become a self-fulfilling prophecy, it tends also to obscure possible solutions for all parties involved. An effective approach will have to do something about this stereotyping. Special training courses can, to a certain extent, neutralise these processes. One can learn to become aware of the way in which stereotypes operate through one's own functioning and that of the other parties involved. Role playing exercises, including exaggeration of role behaviour and different forms of role reversal, can be effective techniques (French & Bell, 1984). Ideally, this kind of training starts in the highest organisational level and successively goes down to all organisational levels. It is important to realise that management has an important modelling function. Apart from training programmes, provision of relevant information by the organisation can be of help as well.

17.3 WISDOM

Success in all the developmental tasks mentioned in the previous section—that is, accomplishing a state of maturity—enables us to lead a life that is better geared to our own basic needs and talents, more focused on the here and now, and on putting things in perspective. In general, successful accomplishment of these developmental tasks helps us to get a view of the greater picture and a taste of the feelings of easy functioning associated with wisdom. Whether these objectives actually are accomplished depends, of course, on the employee in question.

Wisdom is one of the few concepts associated with ageing that has a positive connotation. However, is it at all possible to define wisdom in a simple way? Probably not, but some remarks can be made.

For instance, wisdom is more about perception than about logic: it leads to a "greater picture" and "sense of coherence" (Antonovsky, 1991). Wisdom is about concerning ourselves with the mutual determination of our functioning and our surroundings, i.e. with our integrity (Chapter 2). As such, it is about systems and subsystems, allowing insight, a helicopter view and reflexivity, as well as options to act in a more deliberate and effective way.

Also, wisdom is about potentiality, exploration and creativity; it is an antidote to prejudice and fossilised thinking. As such, it refers to recognising the possibility of different "logical bubbles", i.e. localised domains of reality with their own frames of reference of axioms, rules, meanings, morality and emotionality (De Bono, 1996). In this way, wisdom often focuses on design and designing (De Bono, 1996), and can result in prevention, repair and replacement of losses of structure. Wisdom then can be conceived as a conglomerate of coping techniques to counteract the effects of the threats of ageing (see Section 17.2 and also Chapter 16), as far as these result in a loss of structure and integrity, by designing a new and more flexible reality.

Lastly, wisdom results in a pleasant feeling state of equanimity and awareness of relativity, as well as a certain ease of functioning and goal accomplishment. In such a state, emotions can be trusted and used as a compass for action. This feeling state is incompatible with strain and stress, and, as such, may be an excellent point of departure for preventing and counteracting stress. However, when stress takes over, wisdom tends to wither away.

Most of the elements and aspects of wisdom are inextricably connected to each other and often show considerable overlap. In this section, the following elements and aspects are described:

- detachment
- inward turn
- identifying and developing personal themes
- improved integration of diverse information
- motivating
- life plan.

17.3.1 Detachment

Wisdom is characterised by a basic attitude of detachment. Detachment implies a sense of peace and serenity, stemming from a flexible but solid integration in the here and now. The persons involved are not blindly engaged in pursuing future goals, knowing that goals can be altered or given up when they turn out to be unattainable or when more attractive options turn up. Neither are detached persons involved in fruitless attempts to undo the past, as they understand that the past and even the present stemming from it are not subject to change, and can only serve as learning material for future actions. So, detachment means accepting the responsibility for the status quo as the point of departure for shaping the future.

This state allows people to toss around thoughts, put things in perspective, ask themselves questions, look for and explore inconsistencies and contradictions, and change at will their own point of view. So, they can search, design and execute alternatives, and they can accept all of them, alternate between them, combine them, pick only one etc. (De Bono, 1996). In short, they can open up new opportunities, chances and challenges (Cavanaugh & McGuire, 1994), in order to create appropriate niches for designing new, more adapted roles. Also they can intentionally practise looking at things from different perspectives. So they can try to look through the eyes of a more or less powerful person, or of a person they love or hate. Also, they can look at things as if they were perfectionists, pleasers, performers, romantics, rationalists, pragmatics, thrill-seekers, bosses or peacekeepers.

Detachment is not *per se* something exotic that is out of reach of normal mortals. Detachment can be taught and practised, for instance within the context of a self-management programme. Practising some method of "thinking of nothing in particular" (via meditation, relaxation exercises, hypnosis, alpha training, yoga, running) helps to produce a state of mental calm which allows for the thinking processes mentioned above.

17.3.2 Inward Turn

Another important element of wisdom is the so-called inward turn, a concept that found its place in a number of prominent theories of adult development (Sinnott, 1994). The inward turn consists of a form of gradual cognitive restructuring, which is supposed to take place during and after midlife (Baltes & Baltes, 1993; Jepson & Labouvie-Vief, 1992). The inward turn implies that the persons involved live more in their thoughts and fantasies, and somewhat less in the outer world at hand. Two factors are important here.

First, older persons can apply more elaborated scripts and schemas. This allows them to handle many tasks and situated roles almost automatically, which leaves them with sufficient processing capacity to turn their attention inward. Another factor with the same effect is the loss of role structure that senior employees may go through. As a result, the employees involved may find themselves in situations that provide insufficient cues to bind their attention.

The inward turn implies that senior employees spend more time musing, thinking of nothing in particular. From a different perspective, this can be described as a way of functioning which is related to meditation or contemplation. Such a way of mental functioning can also be used in a more focused and goal-directed way, for instance to refresh and centre oneself.

Other applications, described by Stokvis (1946) as a form of self-suggestion, are techniques of programming oneself to reinforce a more goal-directed and effortless way of working, without interference from disturbing thoughts or feelings. Variants of such an approach are also applied in sports psychology under the denominator of mental training. As such a way of working provides optimal outcomes at low costs in effort, they are especially appropriate for older employees who have to be sparing in energy expenditure.

The combination of detachment and inward turn can also lead to more attention for one's own integrity, to self-reflection and self-monitoring. Pursued in a systematic way, it may contribute to a better quality of choices, decisions and goal-setting. A useful method in this respect is the focusing technique (Gendlin, 1981) and all kinds of variants (e.g. Hendricks, 1998). Explicating internal dialogue, as practised in *Gestalt* therapy, can be of help here too.

Another aspect of the inward turn is an increased inclination to reflexivity. This can be about one's own functioning, but also about the functioning of others and the work process in itself. This can lead to questions such as (Schabracq et al., 2001):

- How are we doing?
- Where are we now, and what has to be done yet?
- How can we do this better, nicer and smarter?

17.3.3   Identifying and Developing Personal Themes

As far as socialisation leads to the underdevelopment of basic personal themes, it may result in an impoverished life of senior employees. Being a misfit or leading a bleak life of conformism and little creativity are possible outcomes here. Learning about our basic themes, finding better outlets for them and reactivating them, often with the help of a professional, can re-energise our integrity (Bolen, 1989; Schabracq & Van Vugt, 1993).

The underdevelopment of themes can also be a consequence of overdevelopment of other themes, resulting in too narrowly focused activity. As the underdevelopment of these other themes may lead to some critical limitations in our behaviour repertory, developing them can help to enrich our repertory of actions and reinforce our freedom of action. Learning about our basic themes and motives is important here.

Assessment of themes and motives is an important issue in self-management programmes. Essentially, this can be considered as an instance of the inward turn. This can be done in different ways. Practising some detachment, reflecting, applying focusing techniques, writing a conscientious autobiography, counselling, and discussing results of paper-and-pencil personality tests can all be of help here. Identifying our personal themes provides us with more insight into personal assumptions and underlying values, as well as a better understanding of our group roles, personal pitfalls based upon an exaggeration of a certain theme, and typical theme-bound sources of stress (Ofman, 1992; Ofman & Van der Weck, 2000; Palmer, 1988).

Once the most important themes are identified, these may serve as a safe home base, from which we can explore other ways of functioning. Formulating a concise wording of our main reason, motive or goal for living can be useful here. Once formulated, it may be used as a yardstick or touchstone for evaluating our actions. Moreover, identifying our main personal theme may also lead to a clarification of our value orientation. As this orientation determines our room to move and main guidelines, such a clarification can be crucial in shaping our future.

Learning about such themes may also lead to a more precise perception of the habitual conduct of other people. Their attitudes and behaviour become more predictable and one can come to a better understanding of what moves them and what may be their most effective rewards and punishments.

An example of actualising an underdeveloped part in some men is an increase in attention to the relational sides of life, such as giving attention and care (which, according to Baltes &

Baltes, 1993, may be due to decreased production of male hormones). Such a development is conducive to better relationships, a better social network and more social support, and can prevent or soften the occurrence of stress. It may take place spontaneously, but often can be furthered by extra instruction and attention.

17.3.4 Improved Integration of Diverse Information

The "inward turn" enables some persons to integrate different domains of knowledge and competence in a better way. This can be a matter of making better connections between abstract suppositions on the one hand and concrete issues, needed for dealing with the situated state of affairs, on the other (Jepson & Labouvie-Vief, 1992). This can only be accomplished if they are completely immersed in their thoughts and there are no intruding thoughts, feelings or blanks. A useful technique here is lowering their own activation to a level of alpha EEG waves, and to take it from there to explore certain lines of thought without interference (Silva & Goldman, 1988). Such a state of mind is also more appropriate for dealing with fuzzy sets (De Bono, 1996).

Another aspect relevant here is that people when they grow older become more involved in finding and defining problems, and less in solving well-specified problems (Featherman et al., 1993). According to Featherman et al., creatively designing a problem is of crucial importance in solving the ill-structured and ill-defined problems inherent in elderly employees' developmental tasks. It is also the first step in designing new structures.

Because the effects of these forms of integration depend on the quality and quantity of one's knowledge, wisdom has more meaning when actors have a broad general knowledge, enabling them to relate knowledge from different disciplines (Kramer & Bacelar, 1994). An improved integration of information can have several positive effects on the quality of mental functioning and integrity (De Bono, 1996).

First, the view may become broader (helicopter view). A broader picture implies a shift from focusing on separate events and simple cause–effect attributions to a more systems-oriented way of thinking (Senge, 1992). This allows actors to get a grip on underlying mechanisms, which may provide them with the leverage to steer some of their outcomes. Also, it allows them to determine where they are right now in the ongoing project and what has yet to happen.

Second, the view may become deeper. First, it becomes richer in detail. Moreover, as the persons involved are more aware of different values and assumptions, they can distinguish, enter and leave different individual or group-bound realities (De Bono's logical bubbles), experiencing their points of view and logic without losing the overall picture. In addition, the time horizon widens (Jaques, 1986). Exploring different options, people can think in greater time entities. This is particularly useful for designing strategies and fundamental changes that encompass many years, an activity that—at least in principle—is highly important for every organisation.

Third, the view may become richer, in the sense that more potential alternatives are taken into account. This faculty is one of the outcomes of greater detachment, described above.

The improved integration of information has its costs in processing capacity and time. For instance, Kemper et al. (1993, p. 138) point out that the lower working memory thresholds for all kinds of cognitive material may very well be a cause of the well-documented slowing down of the working memory (Salthouse, 1992).

A valuable technique to improve the integration of knowledge is asking ourselves explicit and relevant questions (Schabracq & Cooper, 2001). This may be combined with specially prepared pauses (Von Oech, 1992), such as a state of mental rest just before falling asleep or by concentrating on bodily sensations (Gendlin, 1981; Hendricks, 1998).

17.3.5   Motivating

As mentioned in Section 17.3.3, the development of wisdom implies that the persons involved develop a different attitude to and a better understanding of others. Also, goal-setting may improve as a result of more self-reflection, while the processes underlying seemingly separate events are said to be better understood as well. Together, this attitude and these abilities enable one to motivate others for common causes. Motivating can take place by providing an inspiring future vision and by stimulating others to develop initiatives to realise this attractive vision (Senge, 1992). The latter is primarily a matter of asking questions, creating challenges and opportunities, and giving responsibility (Aubrey & Cohen, 1995). Though ability to motivate others may be useful to anybody, this applies even more when people get older and somewhat less energetic and strong.

17.3.6   Life Plan

During the latter career stages, it becomes clearer which goals can and cannot be reached. The persons involved may reorient themselves and say goodbye to what proved to be unattainable. This asks for a new life plan, based on who they really are and want to be, and on the options and limitations afforded by external reality.

The elements of wisdom described so far can be integrated in such a plan. The persons involved have to draw up the balance of their life (Featherman et al., 1993) in order to determine what they still want to pursue. This is about what they can and want to do, within what they are allowed and allow themselves to do. This is first a matter of self-assessment to find out about their most basic themes and motives. This may be done with the help of a personality questionnaire such as the MMPI, MBTI or an Enneagram measure. Its outcomes can then be used as the point of departure for reflection and self-questioning. As stated before, an autobiography can be helpful too. All this results in developing and scrutinising personal goals, as well as a plan for accomplishing these goals (Schabracq & Cooper, 2001). Essentially, this is the subject matter of a good self-management course focusing on the second career half. Techniques such as self-suggestion (Stokvis, 1946), imagination and visualisation (Lazarus, 1977), as well as formulating affirmations (Knoope, 1998), may be useful here as well. Essentially, formulating and executing a life plan can be seen as redesigning our integrity: redesigning priorities, main issues and the value orientation for our further development. The concise wording of our main life themes can be a helpful tool here too.

A good life plan usually is not confined to job, career and professional development. Relationships with other people and other societal institutions play a crucial role too. Questions one should ask are: "What can I contribute?", "What can I mean to others?". The reward then consists of the relationships one chooses and their outcomes, such as, for instance, all forms of social support (see Chapter 3).

Another feature of a good life plan is that it is not harmful to their well-being and health. So, it must be well-balanced over the different life domains. People should learn to get enough pleasure and rest, and to deal with their own and others' stress processes. They should seek some form of physical exercise (swimming, running, etc.) and make enough time to keep up their general knowledge, and to get some form of mental quiet (swimming and running are appropriate here too). Furthermore, there should be enough room to plan, to think things over and to make some sense of it all. Essentially, a plan such as this is a general coping programme. It allows for a life of further development, without unnecessary stress. As such, it can be an outcome of a self-management programme that also pays attention to the elements of wisdom described in this section.

Lastly, a life plan must be used with sufficient detachment: sometimes there are impossibilities and sometimes a more promising vista will appear. Both cases may call for an adaptation of the plan.

All in all, wisdom can be considered as a set of abilities to shape the second half of our life and career in a way that is satisfying to us and the others we relate to. As such, wisdom is about coping with change and loss. As organisations themselves have to cope with more change than ever, wisdom essentially should be very valuable to them. The same holds for the employees in which this commodity is most likely to be present, i.e. their senior employees.

17.4 ORGANISATIONAL POLICY

What can an organisation do to jointly optimise the productivity and the well-being of its senior employees? How can it help them to succeed in the developmental tasks mentioned before and what can it do to promote the development of wisdom? This section describes a great number of possible interventions. A combination of some of these interventions may constitute a viable, tailor-made approach to optimisation.

17.4.1 Development of Objectives

First, the management team itself should formulate an unambiguous global vision on the future of their senior personnel. This vision then can be elaborated in well-defined objectives and a strategy. A special workshop with an external expert can be useful. Several points have to be taken in account.

The main objective is to ensure that employees—younger and senior—develop their abilities and skills so that they are able to adapt in their own way to the changes the organisation is going through. This means that they have to pursue a career that capitalises on their own talents and (age-bound) competencies, in a way that is compatible with the greater organisational picture. Such a career should provide challenging tasks, with enough room for further development, but without undue stress and health risks.

An important element—because it is the main basis of the problem—is facing how stereotyping of older employees and its silent effects on organisational policy have contributed substantially to the present problems. One of the indications of possible stereotyping is a—probably justified!—concern that special policies focusing on older employees will lead to stigmatisation. Though becoming aware of stereotyping is a matter for the whole company, the management team here has a clear modelling function. Moreover, most management teams are not composed of the youngest people in the organisation. Later, this becomes primarily a task for middle management, which has to implement the policy. Still later, all personnel, younger and older, get involved in this.

Another element of the objective is the individualised character of the policy to be followed. Such a policy can only be successful if it is geared to the existing individual differences. The simplest way to realise this is to give employees enough information, time and attention to enable them to make their own decisions and set their own goals in a way compatible with the organisational goals and rules. So, employees have to take care of their own development and employability. Obviously, such an approach can only be successful if the organisation gives enough freedom and opportunities to learn and practise.

In order to be able to successfully implement such a policy, an organisation has to take stock of where it wants to go in the near future and what this implies for its demands in the area of future jobs and tasks. Only when the organisation has some valid ideas about its needs in this respect can it determine whether a certain activity is useful or not.

17.4.2   Interventions

When the management team has agreed on objectives and strategy, they should communicate them immediately and clearly to the organisation at large. This can be accomplished in special meetings, circular letters, special attention to the issue in team discussions of progress and periodical one-to-one meetings with one's superior, and so on.

The most important policy modification often may consist of executing human resource management with more consistency for all age groups (see Chapter 28). This also prevents interventions being seen as stigmatising. It can help to speak about diversity policies instead of policies for senior personnel. Also, it may be of help when the management team elaborates and communicates a clear organisational vision and mission as a context for individual development.

It is recommended to institute a special task force, which includes key representatives of all parties—and age groups—involved (management team, internal HR professionals, middle management, shop floor) and an external facilitator. Such a task force is responsible for the design and implementation of the policy, and reports periodically to the management team.

The first task for the project team is studying the status quo, its causal factors and the options and limitations it offers for improvement. On the one hand, this is about objective data, such as the division of employee age over the organisation, resulting in a breakdown based on variables such as department, gender, profession and job level. Other crucial variables here are the number of years in the last job and the sick leave data of the last years, as well as an inventory of the additional training programmes followed during the past ten years and of experience outside the present job and organisation. On the other hand, such a study should map the resistance to change in this respect, opportunities to improvement that the employees point out themselves and the possibilities for other interventions. The objective of such a study is not only to generate knowledge about these issues, but also to create support for interventions by creating a shared reality among all parties involved.

Though such a policy essentially addresses all age groups in the same way, it may imply considerable changes for employees over 40. For instance, as the latter group will be the target of real career policy now, they will be involved (again) in:

- periodical meetings with the immediate superior about performance, well-being, changes, training needs and career;
- individualised job and task changes jointly devised by employee and organisation, such as:
  - job redesign, including other forms of working together and organising support;
  - creating completely new tasks and jobs (such as acting as a co-manager or mentor, or developing, coordinating and describing new products, scenarios, strategies, policies etc.);
  - job rotation;
  - secondment to another department or organisation;
  - temporary projects;
- changes in terms of employment:
  - individualized working hours;
  - study leave and sabbatical leave;
  - cafeteria plans for pay, fringe benefits and pensions;
  - teleworking;
  - outsourcing;
  - outplacement;
- additional work-related training and education programmes:
  - intervision (peer group counselling);
  - work-related training programmes, including training on the job of and by colleagues from different age groups;
  - general training programmes focusing on self-management, as mentioned before in this chapter;
  - training programmes focusing on stereotyping for senior personnel and management;
  - training programmes for managers focusing on implementing this policy and learning to act as a coach.

Chapter 28 provides a more elaborate discussion of these interventions.

17.5 CONCLUDING REMARKS

Again, when an organisation wants to jointly optimise the productivity and well-being of its senior employees, it is of crucial importance that these employees have a big say in designing their own development, job and career. Only then does it become possible to make optimal use of their specific strong points, to minimise the influence of possible weaker points and to allow for their optimal individual development. And also again, applying existing HRM instruments with more consistency to all age groups is the main approach. Though all this may sound logical or even self-evident to an external observer, such an approach may constitute a major change in the cultures of most organisations involved. So, it is advisable to be prepared for all kinds of resistance. After all, most people rise to the tops of their creativity and willpower when it comes to drumming up and defending reasons why they do not need to change.

REFERENCES

Antonovsky, A. (1991) The structural sources of salutogenic strengths. In C.L. Cooper & R. Payne (eds) *Personality and Stress: Individual Differences in the Stress Process*. Chichester: John Wiley & Sons, pp. 67–104.

Aubrey, R. & Cohen, P.M. (1995). *Working Wisdom*. San Francisco, CA: Jossey-Bass.

Baltes, P.B. & Baltes, M.G. (1993) Psychological perspectives on successful aging. In P.B. Baltes & M.G. Baltes (eds) *Successful Aging. Perspectives from the Social Sciences*. Cambridge: Cambridge University Press, pp. 1–34.

Bolen, J.S. (1989) *Gods in Every Man*. New York: Harper & Row.

Cavanaugh, J.C. & McGuire, L.C. (1994). Chaos theory as a framework for understanding adult lifespan learning. In J.D. Sinnott (ed.) *Interdisciplinary Handbook of Adult Lifespan Learning*. Westport, CT: Greenwood Press, pp. 3–21.

Collins, J.C. & Porras, J.I. (1994) *Built to Last: Successful Habits of Visionary Companies*. New York: HarperCollins.

Cranton, P.A. (1989) *Planning Instruction for Older Adult Learners*. Toronto: Wall & Thompson.

Cremer, R. (1995). Mentale belasting en veroudering [Mental load and ageing]. In J.A.M. Winnubst, M.J. Schabracq, J. Gerrichhauzen & A. Kampermann (eds) *Arbeid, levensloop en gezondheid* [*Work, Course of Life and Health*]. Heerlen: Open Universiteit.

Dante Alighieri (1969) *Divina Commedia* (trans. D.L. Sayers). Harmondsworth: Penguin.

De Bono, E. (1996) *Textbook of Wisdom*. Harmondsworth: Penguin.

Doeglas, J.D.A. & Schabracq, M.J. (1992) Transitiemanagement [Transition Management]. *Gedrag en Organisatie* [*Behaviour and Organisation*], **5**, 448–66.

Featherman, D.L., Smith, J. & Patterson, J.G. (1993) Successful aging in a post-retired society. In P.B. Baltes & M.G. Baltes (eds) *Successful Aging. Perspectives from the Social Sciences*. Cambridge: Cambridge University Press, pp. 49–93.

French, W.L. & Bell, C.H. (1984) *Organization Development*. Englewood Cliffs, NJ: Prentice Hall.

Gendlin, E.T. (1981). *Focusing*. New York: Bantam Books.

Goldstein, I.L. (1986) *Training in Organizations*, 2nd edn. Monterey, CA: Brooks-Cole.

Handy, C. (1994) *The Age of Paradox*. Boston, MA: Harvard Business School Press.

Havighurst, R. (1972) *Developmental Tasks and Education*, 3rd edn. New York: McKay.

Heidegger, M. (1962) *Being and Time* (trans. J. Macquarrie & E. Robinson). New York: Harper & Row.

Hendricks, G. (1998) *The Ten-Second Miracle*. San Francisco, CA: Harper.

Jaques, E. (1986) The development of intellectual capability: a discussion of stratified systems theory. *Journal of Applied Behavioral Science*, **22**, 361–83.

Jepson, K.J. & Labouvie-Vief, G. (1992). Symbolic processing of youth and elders. In R.L. West & J.D. Sinnott (eds) *Everyday Memory and Aging*. New York: Springer-Verlag, pp. 124–37.

Kemper, S., Kynette, D. & Norman, S. (1993). Age differences in spoken language. In R.L. West & J.D. Sinnott (eds) *Everyday Memory and Aging*. New York: Springer-Verlag, pp. 138–52.

Knoope, M. (1998) *De creatiespiraal* [*The Creation Spiral*]. Nijmegen: KIC.

Kramer, D.A. & Bacelar, W.T. (1994). The educated adult in today's world: wisdom and the mature learner. In J.D. Sinnott (ed.) *Interdisciplinary Handbook of Adult Lifespan Learning*. Westport, CT: Greenwood Press, pp. 31–50.

Laird, D. (1985) *Approaches to Training and Development*, 2nd edn. Reading, MA: Addison-Wesley.

Lazarus, A.A. (1977) *In the Mind's Eye*. New York: Rawson.

Oech, R. von (1992) *A Whack on the Side of the Head*, rev. edn. Menlo Park, CA: Creative Think.

Ofman, D. (1992). *Bezieling en kwaliteit in organisaties* [*Inspiration and Quality in Organisations*]. Cothen: Servire.

Ofman, D. & Weck, R. van der (2000) *De kernkwaliteiten van het enneagram*. [*The Core Qualities of the Enneagram*]. Schiedam: Scriptum.

Palmer, H. (1988). *The Enneagram*. New York: HarperCollins.

Rümke, H.C. (1947) *Levenstijdperken van de man* [*Life Stages of the Male*]. Amsterdam: De Arbeiderspers.

Ryan, K.D. & Oestreich, D.K. (1988). *Driving Fear out of the Workplace*. San Francisco, CA: Jossey-Bass.

Salthouse, T.A. (1992) *Mechanisms of Age–Cognition Relations in Adulthood*. Hillsdale, NJ: Lawrence Erlbaum.

Schabracq, M.J. (1991) *De inrichting van de werkelijkheid* [*The Design of Reality*]. Meppel/ Amsterdam: Boom.

Schabracq, M.J. & Boerlijst, J.G. (1992) Oudere medewerkers (Older Employees). In J.A.M. Winnubst & M.J. Schabracq (eds) *Handboek "Arbeid en Gezondheid"-Psychologie. Deel I: Hoofdthema's* (*Handbook of Work and Health Psychology. Part I: Main themes*). Utrecht: Lemma, pp. 92–105.

Schabracq, M.J. and Cooper, C.L. (2001) *Stress als keuze* [*Stress as a Choice*]. Schiedam: Scriptum.

Schabracq, M.J & Van Vugt, P.M. (1993) Psychotherapeutische interventies: een voorbeeld van een AGP-praktijk [Psychotherapeutic interventions: an example of a "work and health psychology" advisory practice]. In M.J. Schabracq & J.A.M. Winnubst (eds) *Handboek "Arbeid en Gezondheid"-Psychologie. Toepassingen* (*Handbook of Work and Health Psychology: Applications*). Utrecht: Lemma, pp. 259–73.

Schabracq, M.J., Cooper, C.L., Travers, C. & Maanen, D. van (2001) *Occupational Health Psychology: The Challenge of Workplace Stress*. Leicester: British Psychological Association.

Schein, E. (1978) *Career Dynamics: Matching Individual and Organizational Needs*. Reading, MA: Addison-Wesley.

Schlüter, C.J.M. & Schabracq, M.J. (1994) *Ouder worden in organisaties* [*Becoming Older in Organizations*]. Deventer: Kluwer Bedrijfswetenschappen.

Schroots, J.J.F. & Van Dongen, L. (1995) *Birren's ABC*. Assen: Van Gorcum.

Senge, P.M. (1992). *The Fifth Dimension*. London: Century Business.

Silva, J. & Goldman, B. (1988). *The Silva Mind Control Method of Mental Dynamics*. New York: Pocket Books.

Sinnott, J.D. (ed.) (1994) *Interdisciplinary Handbook of Adult Lifespan Learning*. Westport, CT: Greenwood Press.

Spinelli, E. (1992) *The Interpreted World: An Introduction to Phenomenological Psychology*. London: Sage.

Stokvis, B.B. (1946). *Psychologie der suggestie en autosuggestie* [*Psychology of Suggestion and Autosuggestion*]. Lochem: De Tijdstroom.

Thijssen, J.G.L. (1991). Een model voor het leren van volwassenen in flexibele organisaties [A Model of Adult Learning in Flexible Organizations]. In H.P. Stroomberg, J.G.L. Thijssen, L. Simonis-Tabbers & H.W.A.M. Coonen (eds) *Didactiek en volwasseneneducatie* [*Didactics and Adult Education*]. Assen: Dekker and Van der Vegt.

Thompson, D.N. (1992) Applications of psychological research for the instruction of elderly adults. In R.L. West & J.D. Sinnott (eds) *Everyday Memory and Aging*. New York: Springer-Verlag, pp. 173–84.

CHAPTER 18

Acute Stress at Work

Rolf J. Kleber
Utrecht University, The Netherlands
and
Peter G. van der Velden
Institute of Psychotrauma, Zaltbommel, The Netherlands

18.1 INTRODUCTION

A bank employee becomes the victim of a hold-up. A large company is suddenly confronted with the suicide of one of its co-workers. A moment of inattentiveness and suddenly a schoolteacher has to deal with a serious accident affecting a pupil. Fire-fighters discover in a burned house the corpse of one of their colleagues. These are all forms of acute stress in work situations. Unsuspectedly, an employee has to cope with an overwhelming experience at work which he or she can hardly handle.

The consequences of acute stress at work can be serious and sometimes long lasting for those involved. One can discern direct emotional reactions, like dismay, shock and disbelief. These are followed by reactions like fear, anger, depression and tiredness. The employee concerned will be angry for some time that such a thing happened to him or her, or will fear that it might happen again. Sometimes victims blame themselves for not having done enough. All of these reactions influence work performance and functioning at home. The employee finds it difficult to concentrate, suffers from forgetfulness and has difficulties in communicating with others. After some time tensions at work may develop, which become apparent through deterioration of work performance, irritations, fatigue, burnout and absenteeism.

The interest of scientists in the consequences of acute and extreme stress has a long history. Already in the second half of the nineteenth century scientists and clinicians dealt with the psychological reactions after train accidents (for example, Erichsen in 1866; for an overview see Trimble, 1981). The studies into the consequences of war stress during and after the Second World War (Grinker & Spiegel, 1945) and into the effects of brief, taxing circumstances (Basowitz et al., 1955) are also examples of this interest. However, in the domain of work and health the attention of researchers has been directed mainly to chronic stress, as is shown by the many studies on work overload and role insecurity. Only recently scientists as well as practitioners have turned their attention to the impact of acute stressors in the workplace.

The Handbook of Work and Health Psychology. Edited by M.J. Schabracq, J.A.M. Winnubst and C.L. Cooper.
© 2003 John Wiley & Sons, Ltd.

In this chapter we deal with the characteristics and consequences of acute stress in the work situation—especially confrontations with violence—and with aspects of victim assistance and organizational health care. Acute stress phenomena will be analysed in this chapter from a trauma perspective. Many painful and extraordinary experiences have been associated with traumatic stress: rape, criminal violence, sexual abuse of children, torture, combat, natural disasters, technological disasters and traffic accidents (Van der Kolk et al., 1996). Findings and concepts concerning various consequences of traumatic stress and disturbances in the process of adaptation with traumatic experiences will be used in this chapter, as well as insights on mental health care with regard to traumatic events, in particular trauma counselling.

18.2   WHAT IS ACUTE STRESS?

Whenever persons are required to do something which they cannot, may not or do not want to do, this is called stress. Using the well-known transactional definition of stress (Lazarus, 1981), the concept refers to a discrepancy between the demands of the environment and the resources of the individual. This discrepancy generally takes the form of the demands taxing or exceeding the resources.

"Acute" means that this discrepancy occurs suddenly. The term does not imply that the stressor should necessarily be an extreme event. However, this is usually the case. A short argument at work does not get attention, unless it leads to intense emotions or is part of a long-slumbering conflict.

The following forms of acute stress at work can be discerned:

1. Extreme experiences during work, such as confrontations with violence or with accidents. Examples of persons who experience the former are employees of banks, money transport companies, supermarkets and shops, but also prison guards and police officers. Examples of people who experience the latter are fire fighters (Wagner et al., 1998), ambulance service workers (Clohessy & Ehlers, 1999) and railway employees who have to deal with traffic accidents and suicide attempts, and employees of industrial plants confronted with explosions, fires and other calamities.
2. Radical changes in company structure—reorganization, collective discharge, bankruptcy—resulting in a situation in which persons suddenly lose their security with regard to work and have to deal with a completely changed situation.
3. Extreme experiences in social networks. A dramatic example is the suicide of a co-worker in a situation in which it may be supposed that the reasons for the suicide are related to problems in the work setting.
4. Extreme experiences from outside, like technical, natural and environmental catastrophes. For instance, rescue workers have been sent to catastrophes, such as the sinking of the ferries the *Herald of Free Enterprise* and the *Estonia*, a disaster on a drilling platform (Holen, 1993), aeroplane crashes, and the ruins of buildings demolished by fires or by terroristic actions, such as the gross attack on the World Trade Center in New York. These workers are confronted with diverse stress reactions during and after their work (Paton & Violanti, 1996).

In this chapter we focus especially on the category of extreme experiences which were mentioned first, in particular the confrontation with acts of violence in the work situation.

Bank robberies or hold-ups (Gabor, 1987; Leyman, 1988) may serve as the prototypical examples here, but it should be kept in mind that hold-ups also occur in other settings, for instance petrol stations, hotels, catering industries and shops. Other examples of the confrontation with violence are sexual assault at the workplace and aggressive clients who attack paramedics, doctors or the nursing staff of psychiatric institutions (Haller & Deluty, 1988; Van der Velden & Herpers, 1994). Violence is inherent in our society, and there are many situations, also at work, in which one is confronted with it. It is remarkably to notice that, nevertheless, research on the impact of work-related violence and trauma has only been sparsely conducted.

18.3 THEORETICAL BACKGROUND

Well-known scientific approaches to job stress can hardly be used for the analysis of acute stress. The Michigan approach (French & Caplan, 1973) or the job demand–control model (Karasek & Theorell, 1990) are directed almost solely to long-existing sources of problems and their consequences. That is why we start from a comprehensive perspective on coping with extreme stress which is based on cognitive perspectives on trauma combined with concepts from social and cognitive psychology (Kleber & Brom, 1992).

An extreme event characteristically causes an intense powerlessness. During a violent crime a person is reduced to a thing, an object used by the perpetrator to attain something. This experience disrupts the normal certainties of existence. It contrasts with our functioning as an independent individual, which is based partly on obvious and mostly implicit expectations and suppositions. For instance, everybody implicitly assumes invulnerability: "something like this will not happen to me" (Perloff, 1983). Daily life generally seems to be predictable and secure. There is an expectation of being treated honestly. These implicit ideas are useful and meaningful. They prevent continuous vigilance for all possible hazards, which would constitute high levels of enduring distress.

Then suddenly an actual threat takes place, against which one is almost powerless. The normal control over one's life is disrupted and feelings of security are superseded by feelings of (death) anxiety. At once the victim realizes that he or she can be confronted with a violent crime again and again. Certainties and suppositions which constitutes basic trust and stability vanish after traumatic events. The core beliefs or basic assumptions—which could also be called illusions—are shattered (Janoff-Bulman, 1992; McCann & Pearlman, 1990).

Incidents like violent crimes and disasters are followed by a variety of psychological processes that are labelled as "coping with traumatic stress" (Kleber & Brom, 1992). This is a form of coping that is typical for these kinds of events, during which mainly intra-psychic ways of dealing with the stressor are important. After all, the incident has already taken place. Nothing can change that. The person has to learn to live with what has happened to him or her. He or she has to regain or restore feelings of security, control and trust in one way or another.

18.4 THE PROCESS OF COPING

The process of coping with acute stress develops in the following way. During an extreme situation the person concerned will first react with disbelief and bewilderment, although usually acting reasonably adequately at the same time. Panic and aggressive resistance, for instance, do not often occur. It is as if victimized employees automatically respond in such a way that possible escalations are minimized. In some cases a total blocking of emotions is reported; that is, the overwhelming emotions are directly inhibited and the person responds with derealization, depersonalisation and disorientation. This phenomenon is called peritraumatic dissociation (Shalev et al., 1996).

When the event is over and the person concerned begins to realize what has happened, various kind of emotions emerge, predominantly emotions of fear, anger, despair and self-blame. These emotions are often accompanied by physical reactions, such as headache, trembling or the inclination to vomit. In some cases these reactions occur a few days after the event when there are no special commands any more. This is seen especially in victims who have to deal with all kinds of matters directly after the event, like the management of a bank confronted with a robbery.

The alternation between two central psychological processes—intrusion and denial—is typical of the psychological coping process after extreme events (Creamer, 1995; Horowitz, 1997). Intrusion refers to re-experiencing the traumatic event. It takes a number of forms, the most common being the involuntary recollection of the stressor. A person continuously deals with what has happened. Memories and emotions come up again and again. Nightmares and repetitive dreams are also a common way in which thoughts, feelings and images related to the event are re-experienced. At night one sleeps restlessly and has bad dreams about the event. Finally, there are startle reactions in situations that resemble the original situation. For instance, employees victimized by an industrial disaster report distress triggered by the smell of gasoline or by loud noises. The psychological process of denial has to do with a general numbing of psychic responsiveness. It is expressed by not wanting to talk about it, by avoiding the location of the event and other avoidance behaviours, by diminished interest in significant activities, and by emotional numbness.

In itself, this alternation between denial and intrusion can be regarded as a normal and necessary process. After all, old certainties and expectations which have been overthrown by the event need to be replaced by new ones. This cannot be done at once: the victim would be overwhelmed by emotions. The person lets, as it were, the experience permeate bit by bit. That is why intrusion—being preoccupied by the event—is alternated by denial; that is, avoiding memories about the event. Very often this intrusion is expressed by victims as "looking at fragments of a picture".

An important element in the coping process is the search for meaning. That is, the victim looks for a way to understand the situation by means of interpretations of what has happened to him or her (Silver et al., 1983). For instance, victims ask themselves: "why has this happened to me?" or "how could this happen?". They may also blame themselves for having made mistakes. In these ways, they try to regain control over their own life (Thompson et al., 1998). Especially in cognitive oriented approaches to coping with traumatic stress, much attention has been paid to this process of attributing meaning and replacing old ideas by new ones (Kleber & Brom, 1992; McCann & Pearlman, 1990).

The coping process furthermore effects the energy level of a person. He or she becomes tired and exhausted after even small activities at work or at home. The normal interest in significant others or activities decreases, and minor problems with the spouse or the children easily evoke impatience and aggression. Irritation about the unsafe work situation is vented off on colleagues and relatives.

Hypervigilance and jumpiness after violent events are other prominent reactions. These are often of a specific nature—that is, they are connected with the characteristics of the violent situation. For a prison guard who has been beaten up, a screaming prisoner again evokes the fear of aggression. A bank employee who has been involved in a hold-up approaches every client suspiciously and feels continuously on his or her guard. Intrusive thoughts are provoked in the same way. Watching a television programme about a hostage induces painful memories of the colleague who was used as a hostage. The smell of burned food provokes images of the dead child who was found by a fire fighter.

Adaptation takes time. After a few weeks to a few months the symptoms of intrusion and denial as well as the various emotional, behavioural and somatic reactions decrease in frequency and intensity. Sometimes it takes longer, much longer even, as research on the aftermath of war and violence has shown (Bar-On et al., 1998). Gradually the extreme experience is fitted into the life of the person concerned. The coping process is completed when the person only suffers occasionally or not at all from intrusion and avoidance as well as other symptoms related to the event. The person can think of the event without being overwhelmed by emotions, and the memory of what has happened does not have to be avoided any more.

18.5   RISK FACTORS

In acute stress, more than in chronic stress, the nature of the stressor appears to play a predominant role. However, this is only partly true. Also with acute stress an interactive approach is necessary. The nature and seriousness of the consequences of an acute stressor are moderated or mediated by several social and psychological variables. A distinction could be made here between risk factors present before, during and after the event (Foa & Meadows, 1998; Kleber & Brom, 1992).

Earlier stressful life events or similar recently experienced critical events are a major risk factor for long-lasting coping disturbances (Breslau, 1998). It was found that some bank employees fell victim to several hold-ups in a period of a few months (Van der Velden et al., 1991). This accumulation of violence causes permanent damage to the feeling of security of the persons concerned. Repeated violence enhances the feeling of powerlessness and fear (Rothbaum et al., 1992). Pre-existing psychological problems can also augment health problems after critical incidents (Breslau, 1998; McFarlane, 1989).

Risk factors during the event are the severity of the stressor itself as well as so-called peritraumatic factors, such as sustained physical harm, vehement negative emotions and the already mentioned dissociative responses. It has been shown that injuries as well as immense powerlessness and anxiety can be important risk factors (Kilpatrick et al., 1985). The victim's perception of the seriousness of the threat may even be of more significance that the objective circumstances (Foa et al., 1989; Van der Velden et al., 1991). Furthermore, peritraumatic dissociation had been found to be a leading determinant of later disturbances (Marmar et al., 1996).

Besides personal factors and the seriousness of the incident, social factors after the event play an important part in the coping process. On the one hand the support from the social network (family, relatives, friends, colleagues) may have a positive influence on the coping process (Ullman, 1995). On the other hand, negative interventions of others (like police, media, insurance companies, medical authorities) can aggravate the consequences (Figley & Kleber, 1995), a process that is called "secondary victimization" (Symonds, 1980). Victims of violence are often not adequately informed about the procedures of the police or the justice department. When employees of banks and money transport companies are questioned, they often get the impression they are under suspicion themselves. Most people regard this as a serious breach of confidence.

18.6 LONG-TERM CONSEQUENCES

Some persons who are struck by an extreme incident suffer from permanent psychological problems. Overviews of empirical studies into the consequences of extreme events (Breslau, 1998; Kleber & Brom, 1992) show that about 10–30% of all victims have to deal with malfunctioning. This can take the form of a mood disorder (which is manifested in—among others—major depression), a post-traumatic stress disorder (PTSD), substance abuse, burnout or other mental disturbances.

PTSD is the well-known and well-established diagnostic term for mental problems after extreme experiences. The lingering and painful effects of the Vietnam war in the United States led to the introduction of this concept in the *Diagnostic and Statistical Manual of Mental Disorders* of the American Psychiatric Association. The distinctive criteria of the disorder are (1) an extreme stressor, (2) persistent intrusive and re-experiencing symptoms, (3) permanent avoidance of stimuli associated with the traumatic experience and numbing symptoms, (4) symptoms of persistent hyperarousal, and (5) a duration of the symptoms of at least one month (American Psychiatric Association, 1994). Since the introducion in 1980, a vast amount of articles and books has been published on the aetiology and diagnostics of PTSD as well as on the various forms of counselling and psychotherapy. There is also a growing stream of publications indicating that PTSD is associated with abnormalities in psychobiological processes, in particular mechanisms in neurotransmitter and neurohormonal systems (Kleber, 1997).

However, the absence of a disorder such as PTSD does not imply the absence of disturbances in the adaptation with acute stress or the absence of ongoing health problems. It does not mean that the remaining people—the majority of 70–80%—do not suffer from the consequences of violence and other traumatic events. Above we have shown that a large part of victimized persons at some time experience specific symptoms which interfere with work, such as irritations, sleeping disturbances, fatigue in the workplace and concentration difficulties. Nevertheless, in most cases these problems disappear after some duration and the person's functioning will return to an adequate level.

Damage to the victim's health also becomes manifest in an increase of sick leave, in enduring stress at work and in burnout. For example, it has been established that the social atmosphere in many police departments deteriorated because of inadequate support after shooting incidents (Anshel, 2000; Gersons, 1989). In the same way that chronic stress may be associated with financial costs and with decreases of production and identification with the organization, acute stress may be followed by these negative consequences.

18.7 INTERVENTION

Those who are confronted with acute stress suffer with various reactions, such as sleeplessness, irritability, absenteeism, feelings of insecurity and lower work performance. Undoubtedly, personality characteristics play a part, but it should be remembered that the victim has hardly any responsibility for what has happened. Banks and supermarkets happen to get robbed and employees of social welfare services are sometimes confronted with clients who threaten them (or members of their family) physically. Because the incident has to do with the nature of the work setting itself, intervention at the work level is appropriate.

Intervention can take different forms. First, there is primary intervention. This ensures that situations of acute stress occur as infrequently as possible. Such an approach is, of course, justified, but many unpleasant and extreme incidents can hardly be prevented. Accidents and violent crimes do take place, however adequate the prevention policy of the company.

It is also possible to make sure that the employees are optimally prepared for the event and its consequences. This is the aim of training in the field of "stress management" and "aggression regulation" (for instance, Mitchell & Dyregrov, 1993). Bank employees are prepared for hold-ups, police officers for shooting incidents and railway employees for suicide attempts or accidents involving trains. However, one should not overestimate the efficacy of this preparedness: anticipation is only useful when the stressor is reasonably expectable and not too complex (Sarason et al., 1979). For instance, if a hold-up takes place two years after the training, the content of the whole training programme may have faded away.

This is the reason why secondary prevention is important. The organization should explicitly pay attention to the consequences of acute stress at work and to the possibilities of direct assistance afterwards, so that employees will feel supported and will be better prepared to deal with the aftermath of the overwhelming experience. An example of this approach is the intervention programme developed for employees victimized by violence or other calamities, which is described below.

18.7.1 An Intervention Programme for Victimized Employees

Many organizations are confronted with employees victimized by some kind of violence, such as robberies, hijackings, hold-ups and physical abuse. Intervention programmes for employees within the company, such as a bank or a police department, have been developed in the Netherlands by representatives of the Institute for Psychotrauma (Brom & Kleber, 1989; Brom et al., 1993; Kleber & Brom, 1986; Van der Velden et al., 1999).

Based on the theoretical approach of coping with extreme experiences described above, a number of intervention elements can be discerned. First, organizations have to offer support to the employee. The person needs recognition and attention after the extreme experience. The importance of these elements cannot be overestimated. Recognition is a highly relevant element in the support of victims. Often this is what victims are looking for: recognition that they have gone through a very unpleasant situation.

Support from the organization and especially from superiors is often limited. In several investigations (Van der Ploeg et al., 2000) it was indicated how much victimized employees appreciated support and recognition, and how little of this support was received, especially from superiors. The reason why colleagues and superiors pay little attention is often due to misunderstandings about the coping process and social support. They assume that attention and questions about what happened will increase the psychological problems of the victims concerned, or, instead of serious attention, they make jokes about the event with the intention of distracting the victim.

Supplying information is also important. The person concerned wants to know what can be expected. People who fall victim to violence while performing their work have to deal with all kinds of judiciary and business consequences afterwards. Help with this is necessary. However, information not only concerns practical matters and juridical affairs, but also psychological aspects; that is, the characteristics of the coping process and stress reactions. Rendering this information while stressing the normality of the psychological reactions provides rest and assurance. It prevents victims (and their families) from getting upset about the stress reactions that they did not expected.

Another important goal is to create the opportunity to express the thoughts and feelings which accompanied the critical event. The person is encouraged to vent personal thoughts with regard to the event and emotions like fear, anger and sorrow. In individual or group meetings he or she gets the chance to talk about the experience of the hold-up, the related thoughts and feelings, and the influence it all has had on work and personal life. Experimental studies in social psychology have shown that disclosure about traumatic experiences (e.g. talking or writing abour one's own experience) has a strong positive effect on various indicators of physical and mental health (Pennebaker, 1997). The disclosure has to do with all aspects of the experience, not only the emotional aspects. Recent publications on acute interventions after trauma (Solomon, 1999) have emphasized that one should be careful with the ventilation of emotions. Too much emphasis can be harmful.

This brings us to another goal of the intervention programme: confrontation with what has happened. The person has to recognize what he or she has been through. It is important to recollect the event as precisely as possible. In this way the person concerned has less chance of avoiding or restraining the unpleasant feelings of the shock. Such a confrontation enhances the coping process and the integration of the experience in personal life.

An intervention programme is different in principle from psychotherapy. It is focused on stimulating normal coping with extreme stress, not on disturbances in these coping processes. Such a programme of crisis counselling consists of a broad range of intervention tools. It is concerned not only with psychological support, but also with information supply, practical advice and assistance from the management of the company. Nevertheless, psychotherapy may be necessary, namely in cases of employees who suffer from serious disorders, for instance after a very dangerous incident or after repeated violence. Such treatments usually are of short duration (usually 10 to 15 sessions of therapy), and demand a rather directive attitude from the therapist. Nowadays, various effective short-term psychotherapies for the treatment of PTSD, such as cognitive-behavioural therapy (e.g. exposure), eye movement desensitization and reprocessing (EMDR) and brief psychodynamic therapy, are available (Brom et al., 1989; Foa & Meadows, 1998).

18.7.2   Starting Points for Intervention After Violence at Work

Intervention programmes for victimized employees are a development of the 1980s and 1990s. Traditionally, companies had the idea that it was not useful or even necessary to pay attention to these kinds of matters. At the same time psychiatry and clinical psychology emphasized that extreme incidents would lead almost automatically to mental disorders, which would make psychotherapeutic treatment necessary.

Stress reactions are not interpreted as symptoms of mental disorders in modern intervention programmes after extreme incidents. Instead, the normal character of the reactions to an acute stress-situation is emphasized. Going through an experience of violence can be seen as a job risk. One should avoid the medicalization of reactions to such an event and the resulting danger of stigmatizing the person(s) concerned. Employees should be taken seriously. People should be supported in such a way that they will not get stuck in their problems, but will be able to function again at work and in their personal lives as before.

In principle an intervention programme for victimized employees is directed at all people who were involved in the event. Such a standardized approach is of an active or "outreaching" nature. Studies into victim support (for example, Maguire & Corbett, 1987; Van der Ploeg & Kleijn, 1989) have shown that this kind of health care is usually more appropriate than a more passive approach. Risk groups are also reached better in this way. Stress reactions and disorders have been found to appear especially with victims who would rather avoid (professional) assistance (Weisaeth, 1989). The goal of this standardized outreaching approach is also to avoid an association between victim assistance and personal weakness. In this way, one can contribute to the victim's coping with the experience and to the prevention of disorders.

Intervention programmes can be offered by people from within the company, like social workers and personnel officers, after the required specialized training. Such support programmes find themselves on the intersection of volunteer assistance and professional assistance. When, after the introduction of an intervention programme in an organization, everything is going as it is supposed to, professionals from outside the company are only called in during or after large-scale disasters and, of course, in case of serious disorders that necessitate specialized assistance.

Assistance to victimized employees can only be successful if one starts with explicit principles. Such guidelines have been formulated (Dunning, 1988; Mitchell & Dyregrov, 1993; Van der Velden et al., 1999) during the development and implementation of various intervention programmes in organizations. The goal of these interventions is to stimulate normal coping and recognition of problems (both with adjustment and with reactions of the environment). These principles are as follows:

1. Everybody who has been involved in some way with the acute stressor takes part in the intervention programme (except those who explicitly refuse; participation is not mandatory). A standardized approach assistance is offered to all employees concerned.
2. The assistance is offered directly after the event. Directly after a hold-up police and management have to deal with other matters, which usually is not in accordance with the employees' interest. Support of the employees during contact with the police is useful to protect the victim. For instance, an employee of a money transport company immediately becomes a suspect when his van has been robbed.
3. It is necessary to have several contacts during a longer period with the victimized persons, since the coping process stretches over a long period of time. It is important to follow the employee in this process, also because the concern from the near environment soon tends to ebb away. At the Institute for Psychotrauma (Kleber & Brom, 1986) an intervention programme often consists of four contacts over a period of two to three months. The differences between the four meetings are described below.
4. The organization appoints a employee who is explicitly responsible for the intervention programme. This employee may be a member of the personnel department, a social worker or a clinical psychologist, but this is not necessarily the case. Sometimes, a close colleague or direct supervisor is better suited for this task. Preferably, this person receives training in the field of social skills and assistance to victimized persons. It is important to

notice that this person should be accepted by the other employees and should be available at any moment.

5. The intervention programme is introduced formally as a programme within the organization. This also means that all procedures should be laid down in an explicit plan or intervention strategy. Explicit rules make clear who in the organization is responsible for the intervention programme and what rules exist within the organization for it.
6. The organization allows certain changes in the work situation, for instance special rules if an employee needs extraordinary leave after an extreme incident.
7. In the case of serious mental disorders one should be able to refer the employees concerned to specialized assistance, such as a psychotherapist.

Most often the intervention programme consist of meetings lasting for about 1 or 2 hours, although group meetings can take longer. The aims of the various contacts differ. During the first contact mainly structure and social support should be offered. Victims are invited to disclose their experiences and feelings during the event, but not too deeply. Furthermore concise information is provided about the stress reactions that can be expected, for instance about nightmares and sleeping problems that may appear during the first night.

A couple of days after the first contact the second meeting should be scheduled. Again victims are invited to disclose their experiences, thoughts and feelings. To a greater extent than during the first contact, victims are asked about specific and significant moments during or immediately after the event, and what has frightened them the most. Attention is paid to the initial stress symptoms and the responses of colleagues or significant others after the event. Information is given about possible other negative reactions and their impact. General education about stress symptoms and the coping process after critical incidents is focused on the particular event. This information is usually provided while the victims talk about their own stress reactions.

The third contact should be arranged 14 days later. The content of this meeting is partly the same as the second one, but now the development of the coping process can be monitored. Attention towards the coping process prevents dominant avoidance tendencies. Furthermore, positive and negative reactions are discussed and ways to counteract sceptical and obnoxious responses from the environment are explored.

During the fourth and last meeting, approximately 2–3 months after the event, the coping process is evaluated; that is, the presence of the aforementioned avoidance reactions, intrusive thoughts and other stress reactions is systematically assessed. The period of 2–3 months is chosen—note that the diagnosis of PTSD can be made after one month—because it gives a better insight into presence or absence of long-lasting coping disturbances. In case most stress reactions have dissipated, possible changes in personal values and attitudes towards work and family life are investigated and discussed. If various stress reactions are still very intense and normal functioning has not yet returned, psychotherapy is proposed to the victim. This offer should be made carefully because victims often associate therapy with personal weakness or "being mad". These ideas are often accompanied with feelings of shame and fear that it will jeopardize their career.

One has to realize that a concrete assistance programme is never a direct copy of the model described above. Any model for company-directed assistance has to be specified in an actual programme, depending on the specific characteristics of the organization and the work setting.

18.7.3 Organizational Culture

It has become clear in the course of the development of in-company intervention programmes for victims of violence and calamities that the organizational context is much more important than anticipated. Nevertheless, organizations sometimes hesitate to introduce programmes of psychological assistance. Ideas that problems are only evoked by offering assistance, and that it would be best to do as little as possible are still persistent.

Many companies pay no attention to matters which do not fit directly into the business-like atmosphere which characterizes the work climate. This usually applies to organizations with a technical character. Not only do they resent spending money on assistance, they also assume that assistance is not wanted or even that it is senseless. The organization is opposed to the introduction of intervention programms, because they "only evoke problems" and because "the employees will be too much preoccupied by their own problems". If such organizations decide to develop an intervention programme, they prefer to keep this programme within the company and not to draw in external experts.

A striking element of such an organizational climate is the so-called "macho culture", which is also called "John Wayne" culture. This attitude may be present in organizations in which employees are confronted with violence or other critical incidents. Examples are police forces, rescue workers, prison guards and public traffic workers. Colleagues who do show their emotions after experiencing violence are sometimes publicly called "wimps": "If you can't cope with it, you shouldn't have taken this job." It will be clear that in this macho culture victims often are treated disagreeably. For example, a policeman returning, still affected, to his work after an incident during which he had to shoot at someone is faced with colleagues who dive behind their desks and mockingly warn the others about this trigger-happy cowboy. People in these organizations often prefer to keep their contacts with social workers or other professionals a secret.

It is therefore of vital importance that the introduction of an intervention programme is supported by management. Information material and meetings can be very useful for this. It is not surprising that adequate victim assistance often profits from change of the organizational culture: a change of values and suppositions should take place within the organization.

18.7.4 Self-Help

Another form of assistance may be offered by self-help teams, for instance, at police departments for the assistance of colleagues after shooting incidents. After such an incident, those who have experienced a similar event visit the person concerned and assist him or her.

In these self-help groups the assistance is organized with as little help from outside as possible. However, this cannot always be realized. The organization may be too small; there are no trained employees available; or for some reason an external specialist is preferred. Manton & Talbot (1990) developed a crisis intervention approach to victims in Australia in which a bank permanently hires specialists. In the assistance programme of some Dutch organizations external specialists train employees to perform specific kinds of assistance; if desired they will also supply the necessary assistance themselves.

18.7.5   Psychological Debriefing

Rescue workers have to do their work under high pressure and in difficult circumstances. Acute stress is part of their work. Moreover, they sometimes do not work in a permanent organization and soon disperse after the event. For assistance to various categories of rescue workers after calamities Mitchell developed a group-directed assistance programme, called Critical Incident Stress Debriefing, in the early 1980s (Mitchell, 1983; Mitchell & Everly, 1995).

Maximally three days after an extreme situation, a team of rescue workers comes together in a debriefing session, headed by a specialized helper, for "emotional ventilation" and "stress education". The event as well as the resulting thoughts, reactions and emotions it has evoked are discussed in the peer group. The specialized helper emphasizes that such reactions and stress reactions are normal after extreme events and informs the participants about the various consequences. Usually there is only one such a group meeting, although it preferably should be followed by a follow-up meeting some time after the event.

The method of debriefing, as developed by Mitchell, as well as the term debriefing itself became immensely popular in the 1990s. However, in the second half of the decade strong criticisms were directed at this method. The central point of this disapproval is that the effects of debriefing are rather poor or even non-existing. Debriefed rescue workers may not suffer from PTSD to a lesser extent than comparable non-debriefed groups. This criticism is indeed justifiable. Controlled studies on one-session forms of counselling have shown that this kind of help does not have any effect or only very minor effects (Rose & Bisson, 1998).

However, the debate on debriefing also showed that the term itself was used in an improper way. Nearly all kinds of early intervention were called debriefing and the specific criticisms on debriefing were therefore also generalized to these other types of assistance. This generalization is not justifiable. First of all, research had shown that brief forms of psychotherapy are quite successful (Bryant et al. 1998; Foa & Meadows, 1998). Furthermore, expectations with regard to debriefing have been quite exaggerated. One can hardly expect that people will recover from a horrible experience in just one session. Next, it is also questionable whether early forms of interventions should focus so much on emotion ventilation and on the prevention of PTSD. Research findings in experimental social psychology (Rimé et al., 1998) indicate that people show positive improvements with regard to job satisfaction, social support, general outlook on life and physical health, but not so much with regard to emotional recovery. "Sharing an emotion cannot change the emotional memory" (Rimé, 1999, p. 177).

The debate on debriefing is still going on, but it is by now clear that one-session forms of trauma counselling should be avoided. People need aftercare. It has also become clear that proper counselling is not the same as just talking about one's emotions and finally that it is extremely important to pay attention to the context of the people involved.

18.8   CONCLUSIONS

Acute stress at work can take different forms, one of which is confrontation with violence during work. Victimized employees experience a severe impact on their personal autonomy and their confidence in others. The diversity of reactions is usually large: bewilderment, anger, fear, listlessness, absenteeism. Employees experience a general feeling of insecurity; often people in the near environment who were not victimized themselves suffer from this as well (Figley & Kleber, 1995). In general, these psychological reactions take longer than was expected beforehand.

Fighting the causes of violence in the company is of course necessary, as is preparation for the possible occurrence of these extreme events, but acute stress can not always be prevented. Intervention after the event is useful, in order to enable employees to realize the meaning of what they have been through, to express their thoughts and emotions, and to prevent, as far as possible, undesired stress reactions. This chapter described the premises for such interventions.

In many organizations a structured assistance approach nowadays exists for victims of acts of violence and other calamities. The experiences with it are positive; employees are mostly quite satisfied with it. The target groups of these approaches have been broadened in the past decade: first the banking business, then the police, later supermarkets, fire fighters and rescue workers. The introduction of the assistance mostly takes place in an ad hoc fashion, usually in response to a violent incident that has drawn attention to the problem.

An integral approach to acute stress is essential. An approach that is only directed at the individual side has little use if the care is not accepted and stimulated by the management of the organization. It is necessary to formulate and execute a policy for intervention after extreme incidents, while the climate within the organization should be such that the assistance after the violent incident and the victim's taking up work again afterwards can take place optimally. Investigations (Day & Livingstone, 2001; Van der Ploeg et al., 2000) have shown that the consequences of extreme experiences such as violent crimes are connected to chronic sources of stress, like work overload. Both enforce each other in a negative way: the greater the workload, the more serious and longitudinal the reactions to acute stressors. That is the reason why intervention at different levels of the organization is essential.

REFERENCES

American Psychiatric Association (1994) *Diagnostic and Statistical Manual of Mental Disorders, 4th edn (DSM-IV)*. APA, Washington D.C.

Anshel, M.H. (2000) A conceptual model and implications for coping with stressful events in police work. *Criminal Justice and Behavior*, **27**, 375–401.

Bar-On, D., Eland, J., Kleber, R.J., Krell, R., Moore, Y., Sagi A., Soriano, E., Suedfeld, P, Velden, P.G. van der & IJzendoorn, M.H. van (1998) Multigenerational perspectives of coping with the Holocaust experience: an attachment perspective for understanding the developmental sequelae of trauma across generations. *International Journal of Behavioral Development*, **22**, 315–38.

Basowitz, H., Korchin, S.J., Persky, H. & Grinker, R.R. (1955) *Anxiety and Stress*. McGraw-Hill, New York.

Breslau, N. (1998) Epidemiology of trauma and posttraumatic stress disorder. In R. Yehuda (ed.) *Psychological Trauma*. Washington, DC: American Psychiatric Press, pp. 1–30.

Brom, D. & Kleber, R.J. (1989) Prevention of posttraumatic stress disorders. *Journal of Traumatic Stress Studies*, **2**, 335–51.

Brom, D., Kleber, R.J. & Defares, P.B. (1989) Brief psychotherapy for posttraumatic stress disorders. *Journal of Consulting and Clinical Psychology*, **57**(5), 607–12.

Brom, D., Kleber, R.J. & Hofman, M.C. (1993) Victims of traffic accidents: incidence and prevention of posttraumatic stress disorder. *Journal of Clinical Psychology*, **49**, 131–40.

Bryant, R.A., Harvey, A.G., Dang, S.T., Sackville T. & Basten, C. (1998) Treatment of acute stress disorder: a comparison of cognitive behavioral therapy and supportive counselling. *Journal of Consulting and Clinical Psychology*, **66**, 862–6.

Clohessy, S. & Ehlers, A. (1999) PTSD symptoms, response to intrusive memories and coping in ambulance service workers. *British Journal of Clinical Psychology*, **38**, 251–65.

Creamer, M. (1995) A cognitive processing formulation of posttrauma reactions. In R.J. Kleber, Ch.R. Figley & B.P.R. Gersons (eds) *Beyond Trauma: Societal and Cultural Dimensions*. Plenum Press, New York, pp. 55–74.

Day, A.L. & Livingstone, H.A. (2001) Chronic and acute stress among military personnel: do coping styles buffer their negative impact on health? *Journal of Occupational Health Psychology*, **6**, 348–60.

Dunning, C. (1988) Intervention strategies for emergency workers. In M.L. Lystad (ed.) *Mental Health Response to Mass Emergencies: Theory and Practice*. Brunner/Mazel, New York, pp. 284–307.

Figley, Ch.R. & Kleber, R.J. (1995) Beyond the "victim": secondary traumatic stress. In R.J. Kleber, Ch.R. Figley & B.P.R. Gersons (eds) *Beyond Trauma: Cultural and Societal Dimensions*. Plenum Press, New York, pp. 75–98.

Foa, E.B. & Meadows, E.A. (1998) Psychosocial treatments for posttraumatic stress disorder. In R. Yehuda (ed.) *Psychological Trauma*. American Psychiatric Press, Washington, DC, pp. 179–204.

Foa, E.B., Steketee, G. & Rothbaum, B.O. (1989) Behavioral/cognitive conceptualizations of post-traumatic stress disorder. *Behaviour Therapy*, **20**, 155–76.

French, J.R.P. & Caplan, R.D. (1973) Organizational stress and individual strain. In A.J. Marrow (ed.) *The Failure of Success*. Amacom, New York.

Gabor, T.M. (1987) The victim's perspective. In T. Gabor, M. Baril, M. Cusson, D. Elie, M. Leblanc & A. Normandeau (eds) *Armed Robbery: Cops, Robbers and Victims*. C.C. Thomas, Springfield, IL, pp. 86–120.

Gersons, B.P.R. (1989) Patterns of PTSD among police officers following shooting incidents: a two-dimensional model and treatment implications. *Journal of Traumatic Stress*, **2**, 247–58.

Grinker, R.R. & Spiegel, J.P. (1945) *Men under Stress*. Blakiston, Philadelphia, PA.

Haller, R.M. & Deluty, R.H. (1988) Assaults on staff by psychiatric in-patients. *British Journal of Psychiatry*, **152**, 174–9.

Holen, A. (1993) The North Sea oil rig disaster. In J.P. Wilson and B. Raphael (eds) *International Handbook on Traumatic Stress*. Plenum Press, New York, pp. 471–8

Horowitz, H.J. (1997) *Stress Response Syndromes, 3rd edn.* J. Aronson, New York.

Janoff-Bulman, R. (1992) *Shattered Assumptions: Towards a New Psychology of Trauma*. Free Press, New York.

Karasek, R.A. & Theorell, T (1990) *Healthy Work: Stress, Productivity and the Reconstruction of Working Life*. Basic Books, New York.

Kilpatrick, D.G., Veronen, L.J, Amick, A.E., Villeponteaux, L.A. & Ruff, G.A. (1985) Mental health correlates of criminal victimization: a random community survey. *Journal of Consulting and Clinical Psychology*, **53**, 866–73.

Kleber, R.J. (1997) Psychobiology and clinical management of posttraumatic stress disorder. In J.A. den Boer (ed.) *Clinical Management of Anxiety: Theory and Practical Applications*. Marcel Dekker, New York, pp. 295–319.

Kleber, R.J. & Brom, D. (1986) Opvang en nazorg van geweldsslachtoffers in de organisatie [A mental health care program for victimized employees]. *Gedrag en Gezondheid*, **14**, 97–104.

Kleber, R.J. & Brom, D. in collaboration with Defares, P.B. (1992) *Coping with Trauma: Theory, Prevention and Treatment*. Swets & Zeitlinger, Amsterdam.

Lazarus, R.S. (1981). The stress and coping paradigm In C. Eisdorfer, D. Cohen, A. Kleinman & P. Maxim (eds) *Models for Clinical Psychopathology*. Spectrum, New York, pp. 177–214.

Leyman, H. (1988) Stress reactions after bank robberies: psychological and psychosomatic reaction patterns. *Work and Stress*, **2**, 123–32.

Maguire, M. & Corbett, C. (1987) *The Effects of Crime and the Work of Victim Support Schemes*. Gower, Aldershot.

Manton, M. & Talbot, A. (1990) Crisis intervention after an armed hold-up: guidelines for counsellors. *Journal of Traumatic Stress*, **3**, 507–22.

Marmar, C.R., Foy, D., Kagan, B. & Pynoos, R.S. (1993) An integrated approach for treating post-traumatic stress. *Review of Psychiatry*, **12**, 239–72.

Marmar, C.R., Weiss, D.S., Metzler, T.J. & Delucchi, K. (1996) Characteristics of emergency services personnel related to peritraumatic dissociation during critical incident exposure. *American Journal of Psychiatry*, **153**, 94–102

McCann, I.L. & Pearlman, L.A. (1990) *Psychological Trauma and the Adult Survivor*. Brunner/Mazel, New York.

McFarlane, A.C. (1989) The aetiology of posttraumatic morbidity: predisposing, precipitating and perpetuating factors. *British Journal of Psychiatry*, **154**, 221–8.

Mitchell, J.T. (1983) When disaster strikes . . . : The critical incident stress debriefing process. *Journal of Emergency Medical Services*, **8**, 36–9.

Mitchell, J.T. & G.S. Everly (1995) Critical Incident Stress Debriefing (CISD) and the prevention of work-related traumatic stress among high risk occupational groups. In G.S. Everly & J.M. Lating (eds) *Psychotraumatology: Key Papers and Core Concepts in Post-Traumatic Stress*. Plenum Press, New York, 267–80.

Mitchell, J.T. & Dyregrov, A. (1993) Traumatic stress in disaster workers and emergency personnel: prevention and intervention. In J.P. Wilson & B. Raphael (eds) *International Handbook of Traumatic Stress*. Plenum Press, New York, pp. 905–14.

Paton, D. & Violanti, J.M. (1996) *Traumatic Stress in Critical Occupations: Recognition, Consequences and Treatment*. C. C. Thomas, Springfield, IL.

Pennebaker, J.W. (1997) *Opening Up: The Healing Powers of Expressing Emotions*. Guilford Press, New York.

Perloff, L.S. (1983) Perceptions of vulnerability to victimization. *Journal of Social Studies*, **39**, 193–210.

Rimé, B. (1999) Expressing emotion, physical health, and emotional relief: a cognitive-social perspective. *Advances in Mind–Body Medicine*, **15**, 175–9.

Rimé, B., C. Finkenhauer, O. Luminet, E. Zech & P. Philippot (1998) Social sharing of emotion: new evidence and new questions. In W. Stroebe and M. Hewstone (eds) *European Review of Social Psychology*, vol. 9. John Wiley & Sons, Chichester, pp. 225–58.

Rose, S. & J. Bisson (1998) Brief early psychological interventions following trauma: a systematic review of the literature. *Journal of Traumatic Stress*, **11**, 697–710.

Rothbaum, B.O., Foa, E.B., Riggs, D.S., Murdock, T. & Walsh, W. (1992) A prospective examination of posttraumatic stress disorder in rape victims. *Journal of Traumatic Stress*, **5**, 455–75.

Sarason, I.G., Johnson, J.H., Berberich, J.P. & Siegel, J.M. (1979) Helping police officers to cope with stress: a cognitive-behavioral approach. *American Journal of Community Psychiatry*, **7**, 593–603.

Shalev, A.Y., Peri, T., Canetti, L. & Schreiber, S. (1996) Predictors of PTSD in injured trauma survivors: a prospective study. *American Journal of Psychiatry*, **153**, 219–25.

Silver, R.L., Boon, C. & Stones, M.H. (1983) Searching for meaning in misfortune: making sense of incest. *Journal of Social Issues*, **39**, 81–102.

Solomon, S. (1999) Interventions for acute trauma response. *Current Opinion in Psychiatry*, **12**, 175–80.

Symonds, M. (1980) The "second injury" to victims and acute responses of victims to terror. *Evaluation and Change*, **1** (special issue), 36–41.

Thompson, S.C., Armstrong, W. & Thomas, C. (1998) Illusions of control, underestimations and accuracy: a control heuristic explanation. *Psychological Bulletin*, **123**, 143–61.

Trimble, M.R. (1981) *Post-Traumatic Neurosis: From Railway Spine to the Whiplash*. John Wiley & Sons, Chichester.

Ullman, S.E. (1995) Adult trauma survivors and postraumatic stress sequelae: an analysis of reexperiencing, avoidance and arousal criteria. *Journal of Traumatic Stress*, **8**, 179–88.

Van der Kolk, B, McFarlane, A.C. & Weisaeth, L. (eds) (1996) *Traumatic stress: The overwhelming experience on mind, body and society*. New York: Guilford Press.

Van der Ploeg, E., Kleber, R.J. & Velden, P.G. van der (2000). Acute en chronische werkstress: Implicaties voor psychische gezondheid [Acute and chronic work stress: Implications for mental health]. *Gedrag & Gezondheid*, *28*, 172–185.

Van der Ploeg, H.M. & Kleijn, W.C. (1989) Being held hostage in The Netherlands: a study of long-term aftereffects. *Journal of Traumatic Stress*, **2**, 153–171.

Van der Velden, P.G. & Herpers, T.M.M. (1994) Agressie in een psychiatrisch ziekenhuis [Violence by psychiatric patients: a controlled study of frequency and impact on victimized personnel], *Gedrag & Gezondheid*, **5**, 209–218.

Van der Velden, P.G., Burg, S. van der, Bout, J. van den & Steinmetz, C.H.D. (1991) *Risk factors for health problems after a bank robbery*, Paper presented on the annual meeting of the International Society for Traumatic Stress Studies, Washington, D.C. October 1991.

Van der Velden, P.G, Hazen. K. & Kleber, R.J. (1999). Traumazorg in organisaties [Trauma care in organizations]. *Gedrag & Organisatie*, **12**, 397–412.

Wagner, D., Heinrichs, M. & Ehlert, U. (1998) Prevalence of posttraumatic stress disorder in German professional firefighters. *American Journal of Psychiatry*, **155**, 1727–1732.

Weisaeth, L. (1989) Importance of high response rates in traumatic stress research. Special Issue. Traumatic stress: empirical studies from Norway. *Acta Psychiatrica Scandinavica*, **80**, 131–137.

CHAPTER 19

Burnout: An Overview of 25 Years of Research and Theorizing

Wilmar B. Schaufeli
Utrecht University, The Netherlands
and
Bram P. Buunk
University of Gromingen, The Netherlands

19.1 THE SHORT HISTORY OF AN ANCIENT PHENOMENON

Burnout is a metaphor that is commonly used to describe a state or process of mental exhaustion, similar to the smothering of a fire or the extinguishing of a candle. The dictionary defines "to burn out" as "to fail, wear out, or become exhausted by making excessive demands on energy, strength, or resources". As such, the experience of burnout is likely to be universal and of all times. Probably the earliest written example in which "to burn out" is related to exhaustion comes from Shakespeare, who wrote in 1599 in *The Passionate Pilgrim*: "She burnt with loue, as straw with fire flameth. She burnt out loue, as soon as straw out burneth" (cited in Enzmann & Kleiber, 1989, p. 18). More recently, but long before the "discovery" of burnout in professional settings, individuals who suffer from it have been portrayed in great detail. For instance, Graham Greene's 1960 novel *A Burnt-Out Case* tells the sad story of the world famous architect Querry, a gloomy, spiritually tormented, cynical and disillusioned character. The most illustrious example of burnout *avant-la-lettre* is the case-study of a psychiatric nurse, Miss Jones, published by Schwartz & Will (1953).

19.1.1 The "Discovery" of Burnout

Although the term "staff burnout" was first mentioned by Bradley (1969) in an article about probation officers who ran a community-based treatment programme for juvenile delinquents, Herbert Freudenberger (1974) is generally considered to be the founding father of the burnout syndrome. His influential paper on "staff burn-out" set the stage for the

The Handbook of Work and Health Psychology. Edited by M.J. Schabracq, J.A.M. Winnubst and C.L. Cooper.
© 2003 John Wiley & Sons, Ltd.

introduction of the concept. As an unpaid psychiatrist Freudenberger was employed in a New York Free Clinic for drug addicts that was mainly staffed by young, idealistically motivated volunteers. Freudenberger observed that many of them experienced a gradual energy depletion and loss of motivation and commitment, which was accompanied by a wide array of mental and physical symptoms. To label this particular state of exhaustion that usually occurred about one year after the volunteers started working in the clinic, Freudenberger chose a word that was being used casually to refer to the effects of chronic drug abuse: *burnout*.

At about the same time, Christina Maslach (1976), a social psychological researcher, became interested in the way people in the human services cope with emotional arousal on the job. She noticed that the term "burnout" was colloquially used by Californian poverty lawyers to describe the process of gradual exhaustion, cynicism and loss of commitment in their colleagues. Maslach and her co-workers decided to adopt this term as it was easily recognized by the interviewees in their study among human services professionals.

In a way, the almost simultaneous "discovery" of burnout by the clinician Freudenberger and by the researcher Maslach marks the beginning of two different traditions that approach burnout from a practical and from a scientific point of view, respectively. The former focuses primarily on assessment, prevention and treatment, whereas the latter is mainly concerned with research and theory. Both traditions have developed relatively independent from each other; initially in the so-called pioneering phase the clinical approach prevailed, while in the empirical phase the accent shifted towards a more scientific approach.

19.1.2   The Pioneering Phase

After the introduction of the concept by Freudenberger (1974) and by Maslach and her colleagues (Maslach, 1976, 1982a, b; Pines & Maslach, 1978), burnout soon became a very popular topic. Apparently, the appropriate name had been given to something that was "in the air". The first publications on professional burnout appeared primarily in journals, magazines and periodicals for a variety of professionals such as teachers, social workers, nurses, correctional officers and police officers. The mass media eagerly picked up the burnout concept, and public interest in this topic grew enormously, making burnout a buzz word in the late 1970s and early 1980s. At the same time, a tremendous proliferation of workshops, training materials and interventions took place.

Initially, mainly practitioners and the general public were interested in burnout and the conceptual development was influenced by pragmatic rather than by scholarly concerns (Maslach & Schaufeli, 1993). This resulted in a blurred, all-encompassing meaning of burnout. Many authors stretched the concept of burnout to encompass far more than it did originally, so that in the end it ran the risk of hardly meaning anything at all. Furthermore, the early burnout literature was descriptive and not empirical, and relied heavily on unsystematic observations. An early review indicated that only 5 of the 48 articles included empirical data that went beyond an occasional anecdote or personal case history (Perlman & Hartman, 1982). These narrative papers mainly emphasized the importance of individual factors, such as over-commitment, idealism and perfectionism.

The image of burnout as a popular term used by journalists and practitioners hampered the serious scientific study of this phenomenon. This is illustrated by the rejection of the psychometric article that introduced the Maslach Burnout Inventory (MBI), which later was to become the most widely used and best validated instrument to assess burnout. The journal editor returned the manuscript with a short note that it had not even been read "because we do not publish 'pop' psychology" (Maslach & Jackson, 1984, p. 139).

19.1.3   The Empirical Phase

Despite the fact that professional burnout was initially not viewed as a serious scientific topic, empirical research on this phenomenon started to flourish from the beginning of the 1980s. Between 1975 and 1980, the yearly number of publications on burnout increased steadily from 5 to over 200 and since 1980 the average publication rate remained stable at about 200 per year, with an additional increase of 300 at the end of the 1980s (Schaufeli & Enzmann, 1998, p. 69–71). By the turn of the century more than 6000 publications on burnout had appeared. A major impulse came from the introduction of short and easy to administer self-report questionnaires to assess burnout—particularly the MBI, which was first published in the early 1980s (Maslach & Jackson, 1981). Academic interest was also stimulated by scholarly books that offered comprehensive social psychological (Maslach, 1982a; Pines & Aronson, 1981) and organizational (Cherniss, 1980a, b; Golembiewski et al., 1986) perspectives on burnout.

In the so-called empirical phase, which started in the mid-1980s, seven trends may be observed. First, the MBI was almost universally used, which highly structured the field. In fact, this instrument is used in over 90% of the empirical publications on burnout (Schaufeli & Enzmann, 1998, pp. 71–7). Second, burnout started to draw attention in countries outside the USA, beginning with English-speaking countries such as the UK and Canada, but soon followed by countries from the European continent (e.g. Germany, France, Sweden, Finland, Norway, Spain, Poland, Italy and The Netherlands) and from Asia (e.g. Israel, Jordan, China, Taiwan and Japan). It is illustrative that Golembiewski et al. (1996) in the subtitle of their book *Global Burnout* use the phrase "a worldwide pandemic". Third, initially most research focused on people-oriented, human services occupations. According to Schaufeli & Enzmann (1998, pp. 72), 34% of the research papers on burnout that appeared before 1996 included health professionals and 27%, 7%, 4% and 3% pertained to teaching and education, social work, administration and management, and law enforcement, respectively (25% included other or unspecific samples). However, since the publication of the MBI–General Survey (MBI-GS; Schaufeli et al., 1996a), which allows burnout to be studied independently from its specific job context, the number of studies carried out outside the traditional realm of the human services has increased. Fourth, research in the empirical phase tended to focus more on job and organizational factors than on individual factors. Fifth, the methodological rigor of burnout research has improved over the years, for instance, by using longitudinal instead of cross-sectional designs in order to study the development of burnout over time. Sixth, traditionally most burnout research was rather atheoretical, but a growing number of comprehensive conceptual approaches have proposed to link burnout to mainstream psychological theories. And last but not least, in recent years the concept of burnout is being supplemented and enlarged by the positive antithesis of job engagement so that currently the full spectrum of workers' well-being is studied, running from negative (burnout) to positive (engagement) states (Maslach et al., 2001).

19.2   DEFINITIONS OF BURNOUT

In most early writings, burnout was "defined" by merely summing up the symptoms (e.g. Freudenberger, 1974). Such "laundry lists" are problematic because they are inevitably selective and because they tend to ignore the dynamic aspect of the syndrome. These drawbacks are avoided by either selecting the most characteristic core symptoms of burnout, as is done in state definitions, or by describing the process of burnout, as is done in process definitions. Of course, both types of definitions are not mutually exclusive. Even more so, in a certain sense, they are complementary, because state definitions describe the end-state of the burnout process.

19.2.1   State Definitions of Burnout

Probably the most often cited definition of burnout comes from Maslach & Jackson (1986, p. 1): "Burnout is a syndrome of emotional exhaustion, depersonalization, and reduced personal accomplishment that can occur among individuals who do 'people work' of some kind". Its popularity is due to the fact that the most widely used self-report questionnaire, the MBI, includes the three dimensions that are mentioned in this definition. Emotional exhaustion refers to the depletion or draining of emotional resources caused by interpersonal demands. Depersonalization points to the development of negative, callous and cynical attitudes toward the recipients of one's services. The term depersonalization may cause some confusion since it is used in a completely different sense in psychiatry, namely to denote a person's extreme alienation from the self and the world. However, in Maslach & Jackson's definition, depersonalization refers to an impersonal and dehumanized perception of *recipients*, rather than to an impersonal view of the self. Finally, lack of personal accomplishment is the tendency to evaluate one's work with recipients negatively. Burned-out professionals believe that their objectives are not achieved, which is accompanied by feelings of insufficiency and poor professional self-esteem. Initially, Maslach & Jackson (1981, 1986) claimed that burnout exclusively occurs among professionals who deal directly with recipients (e.g. students, pupils, clients, patients or delinquents). Hence, in their view burnout is restricted to the helping professions. But in the third edition of the MBI test manual (Maslach et al., 1996), the concept of burnout is broadened and defined as a crisis in one's relationship with work *in general* and not necessarily as a crisis in one's relationship with *people* at work. As a consequence, the three original burnout dimensions are redefined. Exhaustion now refers to fatigue irrespective of its cause. Cynicism reflects an indifferent or distant attitude towards work instead of other people. Lastly, lack of professional efficacy encompasses both social and non-social aspects of occupational accomplishment.

Pines & Aronson (1988) present a somewhat broader definition of burnout. They include physical symptoms as well, and do not restrict burnout to the helping professions as Maslach and her colleagues initially did. They describe burnout as "a state of physical, emotional, and mental exhaustion caused by long-term involvement in situations that are emotionally demanding" (p. 9). Physical exhaustion is characterized by low energy, chronic fatigue, weakness, and a wide variety of physical and psychosomatic complaints. Emotional exhaustion involves feelings of helplessness, hopelessness and entrapment. Finally, mental exhaustion refers to the development of negative attitudes towards one's self, work and life itself. Since excessive emotional demands are not restricted to the human services, burnout may, according to Pines (1993, 1996), also occur in occupational settings such as managerial jobs, as well as in such diverse settings as love and marriage, and even political activism.

Finally, a less well known but more precise definition of burnout has been proposed by Brill (1984, p. 15): "Burnout is an exceptionally mediated, job-related, dysphoric and dysfunctional state in an individual without major psychopathology, who has (1) functioned for a time at adequate performance and affective levels in the same job situation and who (2) will not recover to previous levels without outside help or environmental rearrangement". Accordingly, distress from lay-offs or economic hardship is not interpreted as burnout, since it is not exceptionally mediated. Moreover, burnout can occur in every type of job but not outside the occupational context. In addition, incompetent individuals are excluded as well as those who suffer from mental illness. Finally, individuals who either experience a temporary decrement in their performance or who are able to recover on their own are not considered burnt-out.

To summarize, although state definitions of burnout differ in scope, precision and dimensionality of the syndrome, they seem to share five common elements: (i) dysphoric symptoms, and most notably emotional exhaustion, are predominant; (ii) the accent is on mental and behavioural symptoms, although atypical physical symptoms are sometimes mentioned as well; (iii) burnout is generally considered to be work-related; (iv) symptoms are observed in "normal" individuals; and (v) decreased effectiveness and poor work performance occur because of negative attitudes and behaviours.

19.2.2 Burnout as a Dynamic Process

More than a decade ago, Cherniss (1980a, p. 5) was among the first to propose a straightforward description of the burnout process: "Burnout refers to a process in which the professionals' attitudes and behaviour change in negative ways in response to job strain". More specifically: "The first stage involves an imbalance between resources and demands (stress). The second stage is the immediate, short-term emotional tension, fatigue, and exhaustion (strain). The third stage consists of a number of changes in attitude and behaviour, such as a tendency to treat clients in a detached and mechanical fashion, or a cynical preoccupation with gratification of one's own needs (defensive coping)" (Cherniss, 1980b, p. 17). Thus, Cherniss considered excessive job demands as the root cause of burnout, fostered by a defensive coping strategy characterized by avoidance and withdrawal.

Other process definitions have emphasized the gradual development of burnout. For instance, Edelwich & Brodsky (1980) described burnout in the helping professions as a process of increasing disillusionment, i.e. the "progressive loss of idealism, energy, and purpose experienced by people in the helping professions as a result of conditions in their work" (1980, p. 14).

According to Etzion (1987), burnout is a slowly developing process that starts without warning and evolves almost unrecognized up to a particular point. Suddenly and unexpectedly, one feels exhausted and one is not able to relate this devastating experience to any particular stressful event. Etzion (1987, pp. 16–17) suggested that "continuous, barely recognizable, and for the most part denied, misfits between personal and environmental characteristics are the source of a slow and hidden process of psychological erosion. Unlike other stressful phenomena, the mini-stressors of misfit do not cause alarm and are rarely subject to any coping efforts. Thus the process of erosion can go on for a long time without being detected".

Hallsten (1993) presented a more complex framework for the process of burning-out. He defined burnout "as a form of depression that results from the process of burning out, which is a necessary cause of burnout" (p. 99). Accordingly, not the outcome (i.e. a particular depressive state) is considered to be specific for burnout but its aetiology: the process of burning-out that develops in several phases. Hallsten (1993, p. 99) assumed that the process of burning-out occurs "when the enactment of an active, self-definitorial role is threatened or disrupted with no alternative role at hand".

To conclude, most process definitions of burnout maintain that burnout starts out with stress that results from the discrepancy between on the one hand the individual's expectations and ideals, and on the other hand the harsh reality of everyday occupational life. This stress may be consciously observed by the individual or it may remain unnoticed for a long time. Gradually, the individual starts to feel emotionally strained, and begins to change his or her attitudes towards the job and the people he or she works with, finally resulting in burnout. The way in which the individual copes with stress is in most process definitions considered crucial for the development of burnout.

19.2.3   A Synthetic Definition of Burnout

An overarching definition of burnout that includes both state as well as process characteristics of burnout was proposed by Schaufeli & Enzmann (1988, p. 36): "Burnout is a persistent, negative, work-related state of mind in 'normal' individuals that is primarily characterized by exhaustion, which is accompanied by distress, a sense of reduced effectiveness, decreased motivation, and the development of dysfunctional attitudes and behaviours at work. This psychological condition develops gradually but may remain unnoticed for a long time for the individual involved. It results from a misfit between intentions and reality at the job. Often burnout is self-perpetuating because of inadequate coping strategies that are associated with the syndrome". This synthetic definition of burnout specifies its general symptomatology, its preconditions, as well as the domain in which it occurs. More specifically, one core indicator (exhaustion) and four accompanying, general symptoms are identified: (i) distress (affective, cognitive, physical and behavioural symptoms); (ii) a sense of reduced effectiveness; (iii) decreased motivation; and (iv) dysfunctional attitudes and behaviours at work. Furthermore, frustrated intentions and inadequate coping strategies play a role as preconditions in the development of burnout, and the burnout process is considered to be self-perpetuating despite the fact that it may not be recognized initially. Finally, the domain is specified: symptoms are work-related and burnout occurs in "normal" individuals who do not suffer from psychopathology.

19.3   OLD WINE IN NEW BOTTLES?

Job burnout has been equated with a myriad of terms. Most of them are plagued by the same sort of definitional ambiguity: tedium, stress, job dissatisfaction, depression, alienation, low morale, anxiety, strain, tension, feeling "worn-out", "nerves", boredom, chronic fatigue, poor mental health, personal crisis, professional melancholia, and vital exhaustion (cf. Maslach & Schaufeli, 1993). Accordingly, the distinctiveness of burnout from other related and more familiar psychological constructs is an important issue. In particular, questions have been raised about the extent to which burnout can be distinguished from job stress, depression and chronic fatigue.

19.3.1 Burnout and Job Stress

Occupational stress occurs when job demands do not match the person's adaptive resources. Stress is a generic term that refers to the temporary adaptation process that is accompanied by mental and physical symptoms. In contrast, burnout can be considered as a final stage in a breakdown in adaptation that results from the long-term imbalance of demands and resources, thus from prolonged job stress (Brill, 1984). A related conceptual distinction between burnout and stress is that the former includes the development of negative attitudes and behaviours towards recipients, the job and the organization, whereas job stress is not necessarily accompanied by such attitudes and behaviours (Maslach, 1993). This assertion was empirically supported by Schaufeli & Van Dierendonck (1993), who showed the discriminant validity of burnout, as measured with the MBI (particularly depersonalization and reduced personal accomplishment), and generic mental and physical symptoms of job stress. Roughly speaking, emotional exhaustion shares about 30% of the variance with these two stress responses, whereas for depersonalization and reduced personal accomplishment the shared variance is only 14% and 10%, respectively. Finally, it has been claimed that anybody can experience stress, while burnout can only be experienced by those who entered their careers enthusiastically with high goals and expectations. For example, Pines (1993) has argued that specifically individuals who expect to derive a sense of significance from their work are susceptible to burnout (see Section 19.6.1). Those without such expectations would experience job stress instead of burnout. Accordingly, burnout is a specific type of job stress that is characterized by its chronic and multifaceted nature. Moreover, it includes the development of negative attitudes, and it occurs among initially highly motivated individuals.

19.3.2 Burnout and Depression

According to Freudenberger (1983), burnout tends, at least initially, to be job-related and situation-specific rather than pervasive. Instead, a "real" depression generalizes across situations and other spheres of life. In a similar vein, according to Warr (1987), depression concerns *context-free* affective well-being, whereas burnout concerns *job-related* affective well-being. This was recently illustrated in a study among teachers that showed that a work-related stressor (i.e. lack of reciprocity in the relationship with students) predicted burnout (and not depression), whereas a similar non-work stressor (i.e. lack of reciprocity in the relationship with one's partner) predicted depression (and not burnout) (Bakker et al., 2000a). Nevertheless, although burnout and depression are different phenomena, they also overlap to a certain extent. Empirical research on the discriminant validity of both concepts shows that particularly the emotional exhaustion component of burnout is substantively related to depression. Based on 12 studies, Schaufeli & Enzmann (1998, p. 86) calculated that both concepts share on average 26% of their variance. The relationships with other burnout components such as depersonalization and personal accomplishment are much weaker, sharing 13% and 9% of their variance, respectively. It may be noted that the fact that depression is differently related to different components of burnout underlines the validity of a multidimensional model of burnout. After an extensive qualitative review, Glass & McKnight (1996, p. 33) concluded: "Burnout and depressive symptomatology are not simply two terms for the same dysphoric state. They do, indeed, share appreciable variance, especially when the emotional exhaustion component is involved, but the results do not indicate complete isomorphism. We conclude, therefore, that burnout and depressive symptomatology are not redundant concepts". It is unlikely that the relatively strong association between emotional exhaustion and depressive symptomatology is due to overlap in item content of the scales used because factor-analytic studies show that burnout and depression factors emerge as different factors when the items of the burnout and depression instruments are pooled (Bakker et al., 2000a; Leiter & Durup, 1994; McKnight, 1993). Furthermore, some research suggests that burnout may under certain conditions develop into depression rather than the other way around (Glass et al., 1993), and that burnout will result in depression in particular when it becomes accompanied by feelings of inferiority (Brenninkmeyer et al., 2001).

19.3.3   Burnout and Chronic Fatigue

The most prominent symptom of the chronic fatigue syndrome (CFS) is persistent unexplained fatigue, whereas other symptoms commonly reported include mild fever or chills, sore throats, painful lymph nodes, unexplained generalized muscle weakness, muscle discomfort, prolonged generalized fatigue after levels of exercise, generalized headaches, joint pain, neuropsychiatric complains and sleep disturbances (Jason et al., 1995). Unlike burnout, CFS is pervasive, it can affect virtually all major bodily systems: neurological, immunological, hormonal, gastrointestinal and musculoskeletal problems have been reported (Jason et al., 1995). Burnout symptoms are primarily psychological, although accompanying physical symptoms are not uncommon. Contrarily, CFS primarily includes physical symptoms, although accompanying psychological symptoms are observed as well. Therefore, some authors propose to use physical criteria (i.e. low-grade fever, nonexudative pharyngitis, tender cervical or axially lymph nodes) in addition to debilitating fatigue to diagnose CFS (Jenkins, 1991, p. 36). However, others maintain that there are no objective abnormal physical signs that can by used diagnostically (Royal Colleges of Physicians, Psychiatrists and General Practitioners, 1996). Although the debate about the proper diagnostic criteria continues, it is clear that physical symptoms are much more prominent in CFS than in burnout. Furthermore, burnout is job related, whereas the CFS is not restricted to a particular life sphere. Generally, burnt-out workers blame their jobs for the condition they are in, whereas for patients who suffer from CFS, the origin of their symptoms is unclear. In fact, severe *unexplained* fatigue and exhaustion is a hallmark of CFS. That is precisely what makes CFS such a bewildering experience. Finally, while exhaustion is a common denominator of CFS and burnout, the development of negative, dysfunctional attitudes and behaviours characterize the latter, but not the former. To date, no empirical studies exist on the relationship between burnout and CFS.

19.3.4   Conclusion

It seems that burnout is a separate phenomenon, and that researchers of burnout are not just putting "old wine in new bottles". Burnout is, more than depression, a multidimensional phenomenon, but is at the same time, unlike depression, restricted to the job setting. More-over, burnout is different from job stress in several ways: it refers more to a breakdown in adaptation as a result of prolonged job stress, it is characterized by a multidimensional symptomatology, particularly specific attitudes, and it seems partly the result of a high initial level of motivation. Finally, unlike CFS, burnout is a multidimensional, work-related, and primarily mental syndrome, whereas CFS is generic and predominantly characterized by unexplained fatigue and additional physical symptoms.

19.4 MEASUREMENT AND PREVALENCE OF BURNOUT

Many different instruments to assess professional burnout have been proposed (for a review see Schaufeli & Enzmann, 1998, pp. 43–54). Most of these instruments are self-report measures, particularly designed to assess the level of burnout in the human services professions. Although all measures focus in one way or another on the individual's depletion of emotional resources as the core meaning of burnout, less agreement exists about the number and the nature of the other burnout dimensions involved.

19.4.1 Maslach Burnout Inventory

Despite the variety of burnout measures, two instruments are used most frequently. The most popular instrument is the MBI (Maslach et al., 1996), of which three versions exist: the Human Services Survey (HSS), the Educators Survey (ES) and the General Survey (GS). The HSS and the ES are virtually identical except that "recipients" is replaced by "students". Both contain three scales: emotional exhaustion, depersonalization and (reduced) personal accomplishment. The MBI-GS is more generic and includes exhaustion, cynicism and (reduced) professional efficacy. The psychometric quality of the MBI is encouraging: the three scales are internally consistent and the three-factor structure has been confirmed in various studies (Schaufeli & Enzmann, 1998, pp. 51–3). The core symptom of burnout—emotional exhaustion—is the most robust scale of the MBI that is strongly related to other burnout measures (convergent validity). Paradoxically, as noted before, it is also the least specific scale, that cannot easily be distinguished from related concepts such as depression (discriminant validity). Similar positive psychometric results have been obtained with the French (Dion & Tessier, 1994), German (Büssing & Perrar, 1992; Enzmann & Kleiber, 1989), Dutch (Schaufeli & Van Dierendonck, 1993, 2000) and Swedish (Söderfeldt et al., 1996) versions of the MBI. Moreover, the cross-national validity of the MBI–HSS has been demonstrated across German, French and Dutch samples (Enzmann et al., 1994) and of the MBI–GS across Finnish, Swedish and Dutch samples (Schutte et al., 2000).

19.4.2 Burnout Measure

The second most widely employed burnout questionnaire is the Burnout Measure (BM) (Pines & Aronson, 1988), originally denoted the Tedium Measure (Pines et al., 1981). The BM is used in about 5% of all studies on burnout (Schaufeli & Enzmann, 1998, pp. 71–2). Although the authors of the BM define burnout as a three-dimensional construct that comprises physical, emotional and mental exhaustion, they conceive their instrument as a one-dimensional questionnaire for which a single composite burnout score is computed. The BM is a reliable and reasonably valid research instrument that indicates the individual's level of exhaustion, which is not necessarily job-related. Its factorial validity is not beyond question, though. Instead of one dimension that reflects various aspects of exhaustion, there appear to be two strongly related dimensions, exhaustion and demoralization (Enzmann et al., 1998). In addition, a third dimension—loss of motive—is likely to be an artefact, since it is substantially affected by inconsistent answering patterns of the respondents. Not surprisingly, associations between the BM and the MBI are rather strong, particularly as far as emotional exhaustion and depersonalization are concerned—shared variance between 25% and 50% (Schaufeli & Enzmann, 1998, p. 50).

19.4.3   Stability and Change

Burnout scores are rather stable across time. Schaufeli & Enzmann (1998, pp. 96–8) analysed 15 longitudinal studies with the MBI and found that for emotional exhaustion between 24% and 67% of the variance of the second measurement is explained by the first measurement. Regarding the other burnout dimensions, stability values are similarly high: 12% – 61% of variance for depersonalization, and 20% – 62% for personal accomplishment. For a construct that is meant to assess a state that is influenced by current situational characteristics, these values are rather high. Remarkably, the length of the time interval seems to be unrelated to the stability of burnout: correlations across a six-month interval are similar to those across a two-year period or even a five-year interval. Hence, burnout seems to be a chronic rather than a transient condition. Despite these high stability coefficients significant changes of mean burnout scores over time may be observed. This might seem contradictory at first glance, but it should be noted that stability is based on correlations across time, which are statistically speaking independent from changes in mean values.

19.4.4   Levels of Burnout

Except for the Netherlands, there are no clinically valid cut-off points available for the MBI (or the BM) that allow differentiation between levels of burnout. The MBI test manual only presents numerical cut-off points based on arbitrary statistical norms. The test authors divided the normative sample into three equally sized groups of 33.3%, assuming that the top, intermediate and bottom thirds of the samples would experience "high", "average", and "low" levels of burnout, respectively (Maslach et al., 1996, p. 5). Although they—correctly—warn that this classification should not be used for diagnostic purposes, there is a strong temptation to do so, especially for practitioners. Clearly, this is an inappropriate approach, not only because the cut-off points are based on arbitrary statistical norms, but also because they are computed from a composite convenience sample that is not representative for US human services professions. Schaufeli & Van Dierendonck (1995) showed that— as expected—levels of burnout are significantly higher in a patient sample that received psychotherapeutic treatment for burnout compared to working samples. Moreover, levels of emotional exhaustion, depersonalization and (reduced) personal accomplishment were significantly higher in the American normative MBI sample than in the Dutch normative sample. Accordingly, extreme caution is required when cut-off points are used to classify subjects according to their level of burnout: only nation-specific and clinically validated cut-off points should be employed.

19.4.5   The Prevalence of Severe Burnout

Recently, Schaufeli et al. (2001) used a Dutch sample of burned-out employees who were psychotherapeutically treated in an outpatient clinic in order to develop clinically validated cut-off points for the three MBI scales. It appeared that this group, suffering from severe "clinical" burnout, exhibited levels of exhaustion, depersonalization and reduced personal accomplishment that correspond with the 95th, 75th and 75th percentiles, respectively, of the normal distribution of the Dutch normative sample. Based on these clinically validated cut-off points, it was estimated that 4% of the Dutch working population (about 250 000 persons) suffer from clinical burnout. That is, they have MBI burnout levels that are comparable to those who receive psychotherapeutic treatment for burnout (Bakker et al., 2000c). The prevalence of clinical burnout was particularly high among occupational physicians (11%), psychiatrists (9%), teachers (9%), general practitioners (8%) and social workers (7%). Relatively low levels of burnout were found among police officers (1%), hospice workers (2%), staff working with the mentally retarded (2%) and correctional officers (3%). Probably, the low level of burnout in law enforcement is caused by a selection effect because police officers and correctional officers are screened psychologically: those who score high on neuroticism are excluded and drop out. As we shall see later (in Section 19.5.1), neuroticism is positively correlated with burnout.

19.4.6   Occupation-Specific Burnout Profiles

It seems that occupation-specific burnout profiles exist. Schaufeli & Enzmann (1998, pp. 60–6) analysed 73 US studies that were conducted in various occupational fields. They found that, in the US, levels of emotional exhaustion were clearly highest among teachers. Intermediate levels were found in the social services and in medicine, whereas workers in mental health and post-secondary education experienced the lowest levels of emotional exhaustion. For depersonalization, the picture is slightly different. Social workers and teachers report the highest levels, whereas levels in post-secondary education and in mental health professions are lowest. Two professions exhibit particularly high levels of depersonalization: physicians and police officers. Perhaps, this reflects their occupational socialization, which is characterized by emphasis on objectiveness and distance, as in the prototypical "John Wayne syndrome" in police officers—playing the tough guy who is not moved or touched by anything he gets involved in during his duty. An alternative explanation would be that these are typically male-dominated professions with relatively few females. It is known that, as a rule, males experience more depersonalization than females (see Section 19.5.1). Finally, reduced personal accomplishment is especially found in the social services, and among nurses, police officers, and probation and correction officers. Not surprisingly, the most highly trained professionals (i.e. physicians and psychologists) experience the strongest sense of accomplishment in their jobs.

In addition, Schaufeli & Enzmann (1998, pp. 63–5) analysed 27 Dutch studies and it appeared that, compared to the US, profiles of law enforcement (police officers and prison officers), medicine, and teaching are strikingly similar in the Netherlands. The authors conclude therefore: "it seems that despite absolute differences in levels of burnout between countries, similarities in burnout-profiles are larger than differences" (p. 65).

19.4.7   Conclusion

Burnout can be reliably and reasonably validly measured, particularly with the MBI. Burnout scores tend to be relatively stable across time, even after longer periods. If clinically validated cut-off points are available, the MBI can be used as an individual assessment tool. A relatively small proportion of the working population, roughly ranging from 1% to 10%, suffers from severe burnout symptoms that are comparable to the symptom levels of those who receive psychotherapeutic treatment. Occupation-specific patterns of burnout that are similar across countries seem to exist.

19.5   CORRELATES, CAUSES, SYMPTOMS AND CONSEQUENCES OF BURNOUT

In the past decades, many different factors have been found to be related to burnout in one way or another. Below, the empirical evidence for these associations is discussed briefly. It should be noted that most studies are cross-sectional in nature, so that no causal inferences can be made. Hence, we prefer to talk about possible causes and consequences. Furthermore, various variables have been studied that are neither causes nor consequences, such as demographic characteristics and personality traits. We start our review of empirical evidence with these so-called correlates, followed by a discussion of the possible causes, manifestations and possible consequences. For reasons of clarity, not all references are included. Sometimes, only the most recent or methodologically most rigorous studies are mentioned (for more detailed reviews see Burke & Richardsen, 1996; Cordes & Dougherty, 1993; Kahill, 1988; Lee & Ashforth, 1996; Maslach et al., 2001; Schaufeli & Enzmann, 1998; Shirom, 1989).

19.5.1   Correlates of Burnout

Demographic Characteristics

Most studies do not systematically investigate demographic differences in burnout. Nevertheless, burnout seems to occur most frequently—at least in the USA—among young employees aged under 30, who have relatively little work experience (e.g. Maslach et al., 1996). However, this finding must be interpreted with some caution because of selective dropout. It is quite likely that employees who burnt-out have left their jobs, so that the remaining group of older and more experienced employees—the survivors—is relatively healthy. This so-called "healthy worker effect" has often been observed in studies on job stress (Karasek & Theorell, 1990). Quite remarkably, in European countries such as the Netherlands burnout is more prevalent in older age groups (Schaufeli & Van Dierendonck, 2000). Probably, European employees are more reluctant to change jobs because cultural values and social security systems restrict labour market mobility more than in the US.

Generally speaking, compared to Europe, burnout levels in North America are somewhat higher. For instance, after controlling for age, gender, work experience, number of working hours and type of school, Canadian teachers report significantly higher levels of exhaustion and depersonalization than their Dutch colleagues (Van Horn et al., 1997). One can only speculate about the explanation of this generally observed difference. Perhaps working conditions are poorer in North America or North American respondents are less reluctant to give unfavourable answers.

Initially, it was claimed that women report higher burnout levels then men (e.g. Etzion & Pines, 1986). However, as Greenglass (1991) has pointed out, gender is often confounded with occupational role and hierarchical position. For instance, compared to men, women occupy supervisory roles less often in organizations and therefore have less access to job-related rewards such as high income, social status and autonomy. When these confounding variables are taken into account, no significant gender differences in burnout are observed, except for depersonalization. It is consistently found that males report higher depersonalization scores than females, a finding that is in line with other gender differences such as higher prevalence of aggression among males and higher interest in the nurturing role among females (Ogus et al., 1990).

Burnout is associated with higher levels of education (e.g. Maslach et al., 1986). This is quite remarkable since most stress-related problems seem more prevalent among workers with low status and poor education (Fletcher, 1988). Finally, most studies show that singles have an increased risk of burning-out compared to those who are living with a partner (e.g. Maslach & Jackson, 1985). It is claimed that social support from the partner might alleviate stress.

Personality Characteristics

Most personality characteristics associated with burnout are known from the general stress literature (see Chapter 5). It is estimated that burnout and hardiness (i.e. involvement in daily activities, a sense of control over events, and openness to change) share about 10%–25% of their variance, whereby the highest correlations are found with emotional exhaustion (Schaufeli & Enzmann, 1998, p. 78).

Compared to internals, externals are more emotionally exhausted, depersonalized, and experience reduced feelings of personal accomplishment. That is, a review of eleven studies showed that external locus of control explains about 10% of the variance of emotional exhaustion and about 5% of depersonalization and reduced personal accomplishment (Glass & McKnight, 1996).

A review of twelve studies revealed that those who are burned-out cope with stressful events in a rather passive, defensive way, whereas active and confronting coping is associated with less burnout (Schaufeli & Enzmann, 1998, p. 78). Both confronting coping and avoiding coping share an equal amount of about 5%–10% of the variance of emotional exhaustion and depersonalization. With respect to personal accomplishment, confronting coping explains about 15% of the variance, whereas the relationship with avoidant coping is clearly weaker (less than 5%).

In their meta-analysis of 26 samples, Pfennig & Hüsch (1994) found significant negative correlations of all three burnout dimensions with self-esteem, and self-appraisal of competence and personal worth. The explained average variance ranged from 14% (emotional exhaustion) to 10% (depersonalization) and 9% (reduced personal accomplishment). The only longitudinal study that investigated the causal relationship of burnout and self-esteem found no conclusive evidence about their causal order (Rosse et al., 1991).

In a similar vein, Pfennig & Hüsch (1994) summarized twelve studies on burnout and anxiety, showing that this trait correlates most highly with emotional exhaustion (shared variance 23%), followed by depersonalization (17%) and reduced personal accomplishment (12%).

The "Big Five" personality factors show a particular pattern of relationships with burnout which is illustrated by the study of Deary et al. (1996). Their study was re-analysed by Schaufeli & Enzmann (1998, p. 80) in order to evaluate the relative contribution of all five factors to the variance shared with burnout. It appeared that emotional exhaustion is positively related with neuroticism and openness (shared variance 33%). Depersonalization is positively related with neuroticism and negatively related with agreeableness (shared variance 20%). Lastly, lack of personal accomplishment is positively related with neuroticism, extraversion and openness, and negatively related with conscientiousness (shared variance 25%). Piedmont (1993) predicted burnout seven months later, controlling for situational factors: neuroticism and agreeableness at time 1 explained 42% of emotional exhaustion at time 2.

A small set of personality characteristics that pertain to the relationship with recipients seems to be typical of burnout. For instance, Garden (1989) found that burnout is associated with the Jungian "helping type", which is over-represented in the human services and is characterized by a need for affiliation, a capacity for warmth, and a desire for harmony (see Section 19.6.1). Furthermore, positive associations with burnout have been found with empathy (Williams, 1989) and with poor communal orientation; that is, with a low desire to give and receive benefits in response to the needs of others (Van Yperen et al., 1992; see also Section 19.6.2).

Already in the earliest theoretical accounts, high or unrealistic expectations had been made responsible for the development of burnout. However, Schaufeli & Enzmann (1998, pp. 80–1) analysed twenty studies and found inconclusive results. Ten studies reported a positive correlation of expectations with burnout, but in seven studies the correlation was not significant. Furthermore, in the remaining three studies a *negative* correlation was reported that contradicted the idealism → burnout hypothesis. Interestingly, the only longitudinal study showed that optimistic and idealistically motivated social workers reported lower levels of burnout at the one-year follow-up compared to their less optimistic and idealistic fellows (Kirk & Koeske, 1995). Thus, rather than leading to burnout, high expectations may function as a buffer against burnout.

19.5.2   Possible Causes of Burnout

Quantitative Job Demands

A meta-analysis by Lee & Ashforth (1996) showed that experienced workload and time pressure share on average 42% (six studies) and 25% (five studies) of variance with emotional exhaustion, respectively. Relationships are much weaker with both of the other MBI dimensions. The high correlations with workload must be qualified, however, because this stressor is often operationalized in terms of experienced strain so that considerable overlap in item content exists, especially with emotional exhaustion. Other, more objective, job demands such as number of hours worked per week, amount of direct client contact, caseload, and the severity of clients' problems, are only studied occasionally. Generally, correlations with burnout are lower but nevertheless in the expected directions: employees experience more burnout when they work more hours per week, interact frequently with recipients, have high caseloads, and have to deal with severe client problems.

Role Problems

Role conflict and role ambiguity are moderately to highly correlated with burnout. Role conflicts occur when conflicting demands at the job have to be met. For instance, correctional officers are expected to facilitate the delinquent's rehabilitation—educational role—as well as guard them—disciplinary role (Schaufeli & Peeters, 2000). Role ambiguity occurs, for instance, when no adequate information is available to do the job well. For example, nurses may be deprived of essential medical information that should be provided by physicians. Whereas role conflict results in conflicting goals and behaviours, role ambiguity precludes the development of goals that direct work behaviour. According to a meta-analytic study of Pfennig & Hüsch (1994), role conflict (49 studies) shares 24% of variance with emotional exhaustion, 13% with depersonalization, and only 2% with personal accomplishment; the percentages for role ambiguity (38 studies) are 14%, 8% and 10%, respectively.

Lack of Social Support

Clear evidence exists for a positive relationship between lack of social support and burnout. Especially, lack of social support from *supervisors* is related with burnout. On the average, lack of support from supervisors explains 14% of the variance of emotional exhaustion, 6% of depersonalization, and 2% of personal accomplishment (13 studies; Lee & Ashforth, 1996). These results, however, could not be replicated in longitudinal studies on social support and burnout (e.g. Dignam, 1986). For lack of social support from co-workers the amounts of variance are 5%, 5% and 2%, respectively (14 studies; Lee & Ashforth, 1996). Independently of a direct effect on burnout, social support might buffer the effects of stressors in such a way that employees who receive more support are better able to cope with their job demands. However, to date, the results of studies on the existence of such a buffer effect of social support are equivocal (e.g. Himle et al., 1991). Small but significant longitudinal effects were found for peer-cohesion, which was related to a decrease in burnout across 1 year (Wade et al., 1986).

Lack of Self-Regulatory Activity

A particular set of job resources fosters self-regulatory activity, which is instrumental in achieving one's work goals. Examples are participation in decision making, autonomy and feedback, which all seem to be negatively associated with burnout. For instance, a meta-analysis of six studies revealed that participation in decision making shares 10% of the variance of emotional exhaustion, 3% of depersonalization and 9% of reduced personal accomplishment, whereas the percentages for autonomy (11 studies) are 2%, 2%, and less than 1%, respectively (Lee & Ashforth, 1996).

Moreover, lack of feedback is positively related to all three burnout dimensions. Although there are only a few studies available, their results are quite consistent. A meta-analysis of six studies showed that lack of feedback explains 18% of the variance of emotional exhaustion, 12% of depersonalization and 9% of reduced personal accomplishment (Pfennig & Hüsch, 1994).

Client-Related Demands

The above-mentioned job characteristics relate not only to burnout, but also to a variety of other health-related outcomes (Warr, 1987). It was claimed from the very beginning that burnout is specifically associated to client-related stressors (see Section 19.1.1). Schaufeli & Enzmann (1998, p. 84) compared the results of 16 studies and found that, overall, and contrary to expectations, common job-related stressors such as workload, time pressure and role conflicts correlate *higher* with burnout than client-related stressors. Examples of such stressors are interaction with difficult clients, problems in interacting with clients, frequency of contact with chronically or terminally ill patients, or confrontation with death and dying. The authors conclude: "Hence, it seems that on empirical grounds the assertion that burnout is particularly related to emotionally charged interactions with clients has to be refuted" (p. 84). It may be that those who are frequently confronted with "difficult" patients develop adaptive mechanisms that prevent negative long-term effects such as burnout.

19.5.3   Symptoms and Possible Consequences of Burnout

Some confusion exists about the difference between the symptoms and the consequences of professional burnout. For example, is reduced personal accomplishment a symptom or a consequence of burnout? This type of confusion was particularly obvious in the pioneer phase, when clinical observations prevailed. In the empirical phase, when standardized instruments were used to assess burnout, this distinction was implicitly made since the assumed symptoms of burnout constituted the instrument. Hence, distinction between symptoms and consequences remains rather arbitrary since it depends on the conceptualization and operationalization of burnout. Therefore we prefer to speak about manifestations of burnout that cover both symptoms as well as consequences.

More than 100 symptoms and possible consequences have been associated with burnout, ranging from anxiety to lack of zeal (Schaufeli & Enzmann, 1998, pp. 21–4). Although the number and the variety of these phenomena look rather impressive at first glance, it should be noted that many symptoms come from uncontrolled clinical observations or from interview studies with an impressionistic or unspecified analysis of the data.

Manifestations of burnout are grouped for convenience into five major categories: affective, cognitive, physical, behavioural and motivational. Typically, manifestations not only appear at the individual level, but also at the interpersonal and organizational level.

Affective Manifestations

Usually, a gloomy, tearful and depressed mood is observed among those who suffer from burnout. Although moods may change quickly, generally spirits are low, and a sad and dim mood prevails. The person's emotional resources are exhausted because too much energy has been used for too long a time. Earlier in this chapter (see Section 19.3.2.) we argued that burnout and depression are different yet overlapping constructs. The second type of affective symptom relates to aggression and anxiety (Kahill, 1988). The burnt-out person's frustration tolerance is diminished, he or she is irritable, oversensitive, and behaves in a hostile and suspicious manner, not only towards recipients, but also towards colleagues and superiors (Maslach, 1982b; Freudenberger, 1980).

Cognitive Manifestations

First and foremost, burnt-out individuals feel helpless, hopeless and powerless. Sometimes, there is even the fear of "going crazy" because one feels out of control. Work has lost its meaning and after being unsuccessful in influencing one's work situation, the person now feels "trapped" (Kahill, 1988). A sense of failure is experienced as well as a feeling of insufficiency, impotence and poor job-related self-esteem (Rossse et al., 1991). Moreover, particular cognitive skills such as memory and attention might be impaired and thinking becomes more rigid, schematic and detached.

One of the most characteristic symptoms of burnout at the interpersonal level is the decreased involvement with recipients. This negative attitude is particularly striking since initially the relationship with recipients has been characterized by involvement, empathy, concern and understanding (Pines & Kafry, 1978). Cognitively, this is reflected by a cynical and dehumanizing perception of recipients characterized by negativism, pessimism, lessened empathy and stereotyping. By derogating, stereotyping and blaming recipients, a psychological distance is created which protects or enhances the self (Maslach, 1982a).

On the organizational level, burnt-out employees neither feel appreciated by their supervisors nor by their colleagues. They lose their concern for the organization and become hypercritical—distrusting management, peers and supervisors. Recently, Schaufeli & Enzmann (1998, pp. 89–91) re-analysed the findings of Lee & Ashforth's (1996) meta-analysis, adding 15 more studies on the relationships of burnout with job satisfaction, organizational commitment and intention to leave. They found that job satisfaction correlates comparatively highly with all three burnout dimensions but most highly with depersonalization (shared variance: 27%), followed by emotional exhaustion and reduced personal accomplishment (20% and 16% shared variance, respectively). Although less strongly than job satisfaction, organizational commitment consistently correlates negatively with emotional exhaustion and depersonalization (shared variance 16%). The relationship with reduced personal accomplishment is clearly weaker (shared variance 5%). Similar results are found with respect to the intention to quit, which shares 20% of variance with emotional exhaustion, 12% with depersonalization, and 6% with reduced personal accomplishment.

Physical Manifestations

A few studies are available that show a consistent positive correlation between psychosomatic complaints and burnout, most clearly with emotional exhaustion. Based on these studies Schaufeli & Enzmann (1998, p. 87) estimate that both constructs share between 20% and 46% of their variance. The relationships with depersonalization (between 6%

and 21%) and personal accomplishment (between 3% and 18%) are much weaker. Unfortunately, virtually no study employed an adequate longitudinal design. An exception is Wolpin (1986), who showed that, after one year, burnt-out teachers report significantly more somatic complaints than teachers who were not considered burnt-out.

It is noteworthy that those complaints that may more easily be verified by objective diagnoses correlate less strongly with burnout. Unfortunately, only one study exists that investigated more or less objectively diagnosed health indicators in relation to burnout. Hendrix et al. (1991) observed a small but significant relationship between emotional exhaustion and the frequency of self-reported cold or flu episodes (1% of explained variance). Finally, results concerning physiological health indicators are inconclusive. For instance, Melamed et al. (1999) found higher cholesterol levels—a risk factor for cardiovascular disease—in burnt-out employees, whereas Pruessner et al. (1999) found lower levels and Hendrix et al. (1991) failed to observe any relationship between burnout and cholesterol levels. Based on the observation that levels of cortisol—also known as the stress hormone—are usually elevated in depression, one could expect this to be the case in burnout as well since this is a related kind of affective syndrome (see Section 19.3.2). Indeed, Melamed et al. (1999) observed higher levels of cortisol in burnt-out employees compared to non-burnt-out employees. However, Pruessner et al. (1999) observed lower cortisol levels.

As far as self-reported frequency of various illnesses is concerned, Corrigan et al. (1995) reported a shared variance with emotional exhaustion plus depersonalization of 10%. A similar relationship between emotional exhaustion and a self-report measure of the frequency of serious illness (12% of shared variance) was found by Bhagat et al. (1995); depersonalization was only marginally related (2%) and reduced personal accomplishment was unrelated to serious illness. Finally, Landsbergis (1988) found a significant positive relationship between self-reported symptoms of coronary heart disease and emotional exhaustion (3% shared variance) and depersonalization (4%). The relationship with reduced personal accomplishment was not significant (2%). Thus, convincing empirical support for the often claimed relationship of burnout with (objectively diagnosed) health problems is still lacking, although significant correlations with self-report measures were found.

Behavioural Manifestations

At the individual level, behavioural symptoms are mainly caused by the person's increased level of arousal. Landsbergis (1988) observed no significant relationship between smoking behaviour and burnout. In a study of police officers, Burke (1994) found no relationship between coffee consumption, smoking, alcohol use, consumption of medication or drug use and any of the burnout dimensions. One study found slightly more substance use (composite measure of alcohol, cigarettes, drugs) among women who scored higher on depersonalization (Nowack & Pentkowski, 1994). In a similar vein, Ogus et al. (1990) reported a small but significant correlation between depersonalization and the use of pain medication among male teachers (explained variance 3%). Hence, it seems that—if at all—substance use is weakly related to depersonalization, probably because this burnout dimension is linked with psychological withdrawal and palliative coping behaviour.

At the organizational level, the most important manifestations of burnout are absenteeism, job turnover and impaired performance. Based on the available studies Schaufeli &

Enzmann (1998, p. 91) estimated that in general the relationship of absenteeism with emotional exhaustion is most consistent (2% explained variance on the average), followed by depersonalization (1%). In contrast, only very few studies have found that reduced personal accomplishment is related to absenteeism, with an average explained variance of less than 1%. Thus, despite the popular assumption that burnout causes absenteeism, its effect is rather small and can best be confirmed with respect to emotional exhaustion. In a similar vein, the relationship between actual turnover and burnout (exhaustion and depersonalization) is rather weak, with effects in terms of shared variance ranging between 1% and 5% (Schaufeli & Enzmann, 1998, p. 91). No effects were found with respect to reduced personal accomplishment. The fact that the relationship between turnover intentions and burnout (see above) is much stronger than with actual turnover, suggests that a large percentage of burnt-out professionals stay in their jobs involuntarily.

It is important to distinguish between self-ratings of performance and objective measures or ratings by others such as co-workers or supervisors. Based on six studies Schaufeli & Enzmann (1998, pp. 91–2) conclude that self-rated performance correlates weakly with burnout: on the average 5% of variance is shared with emotional exhaustion, 4% with depersonalization, and 6% with reduced personal accomplishment. With respect to other-rated or objectively assessed performance, results are inconsistent and disappointing. Three studies found no significant or even positive correlations with burnout, whereas four studies found the expected significant negative correlations, at least with some burnout dimensions. However, on the average the explained variance is less than 1%, irrespective of the dimension of burnout.

Motivational Manifestations

Typically, the burnt-out professional's intrinsic motivation has vanished: zeal, enthusiasm, interest and idealism are lost (Maslach, 1976). Contrarily, disillusionment, disappointment and resignation set in, and physical as well as mental withdrawal from others is observed (Maslach & Pines, 1977). At the interpersonal level this deeply rooted motivational crisis is expressed by a loss of genuine interest in recipients, indifference and discouragement (Pines & Maslach, 1978). One of the most obvious characteristics of burnout is the decreased involvement with recipients. This is illustrated by the so-called "John Wayne syndrome" that is observed among police-officers (see Section 19.4.6) The employee's present poor and/or inappropriate motivation stands in sharp contrast to his or her initial idealism and drive. Initially, it was argued that burnt-out individuals might take home their work problems. Because of this negative transfer, these problems were thought to come to dominate family life and might increase interpersonal conflicts with spouse and children (Jackson & Maslach, 1982). However, after reviewing the studies involved, Schaufeli & Enzmann (1998, p. 89) conclude: "Taken together, there is *no* conclusive evidence on negative spillover of burnout to private life".

19.5.4 Conclusions

Results from empirical research on the correlates and manifestations of burnout are rather difficult to interpret because the field is rather scattered and the research findings often contradict each other. Most probably, this is due to sampling bias, the use of poorly validated measures, inadequate research designs, and, last but not least, the complexity of the relationships involved. Nevertheless, five general conclusions can be drawn:

1. Comparing the relative importance of correlates of burnout, it seems that anxiety, neuroticism and lack of hardiness are the most prominent personality characteristics. At the same time, workload, time pressure and role conflict seem to be the most important possible causes, while depression, psychosomatic complaints and job dissatisfaction are the most important concomitants or consequences. Quantitative demands such as time pressure and workload are clearly more strongly related with burnout than qualitative demands such as problems in interacting with clients or the confrontation with death and dying. This contradicts the popular assertion that interaction with clients and the confrontation with their emotional needs is at the heart of burnout.
2. As far as the three dimensions of the MBI are concerned, emotional exhaustion is most strongly related to various correlates of burnout. This applies especially to work-related stressors (e.g. workload, role conflict) neuroticism, depression and psychosomatic symptoms. Generally, correlations with depersonalization are weaker. On balance, personal accomplishment is least strongly related to potential correlates. Exceptions are the "Big Five" factors of personality, confronting coping behaviour and subjective performance. These results confirm the validity of personal accomplishment as a burnout dimension that reflects professional self-efficacy (Cherniss, 1993; Maslach & Leiter, 1997).
3. The least strong or most inconsistent relationships of potential correlates of burnout were found with respect to high or unrealistic expectations, objective health problems, physiological markers, spillover to private life and objectively assessed performance.
4. Self-report measures correlate much more highly with burnout than data based on records, physiological measures, observations or assessments by others such as supervisors or co-workers. This may explain at least partly why organizational consequences that are mostly not based on self-reports are only weakly related with burnout.
5. When controlling for the initial status of burnout, longitudinal studies do not usually replicate the findings of cross-sectional studies as far as the effects of job demands on burnout are concerned.

19.6   THEORETICAL APPROACHES

Initially, most theorizing was rather speculative and eclectic, borrowing concepts from various psychological theories. In the previous decade, more systematic theoretical approaches have been developed some of which are—at least partly—confirmed by empirical studies. Nevertheless, a comprehensive theoretical framework for burnout is still lacking. Probably, a single general and valid theory of burnout will always remain an illusion in view of the complexity of the phenomenon.

This section distinguishes three theoretical approaches to burnout. First, individual approaches emphasize the role of intra-personal processes. Second, interpersonal approaches particularly focus on the unbalanced relationships that exist between caregivers and recipients. Third, organizational approaches stress the relevance of the wider organizational context for understanding burnout. Of course, these three types of approaches are not mutually exclusive; they mainly differ in the extent to which they stress the importance of a particular type of factor in the development of the burnout syndrome.

19.6.1   Individual Approaches

Without exception, the eight individual approaches below are speculative, since none of them is supported by robust empirical evidence. The first two approaches are mainly descriptive. The remaining individual approaches are attempts to analyse burnout from more general psychological perspectives that are either traditional (psychoanalysis, existential psychology and learning theory) or more recent (action theory and conservation of resources theory). In one way or another, all individual approaches emphasize the relevance of the discrepancy between expectations and reality.

Burnout as Failure to Retain One's Idealized Self-image

According to Freudenberger (1980), burnout ("the super-achiever sickness") develops when individuals firmly believe in their idealized images of themselves as charismatic, dynamic, inexhaustible and super-competent persons. As a result, they lose touch completely with their other more fallible "real" selves. In vigorously trying to hold up their idealized self-images, burnout candidates typically use the wrong strategies that further deplete their emotional resources. These "false cures" are summarized by Freudenberger in four Ds: Disengagement, Distancing Dulling and Deadness.

Burnout as Progressive Disillusionment

The basic tenet of Edelwich & Brodsky's (1980) approach is that the idealistic expectations of the "helpers" are frustrated. Although they recognize several other built-in sources of frustration in the human services (e.g. lack of criteria for measuring accomplishment, low pay, poor career prospects, inadequate institutional support, low social status), the crucial role of initial unrealistic expectations and noble aspirations is highlighted. According to Edelwich & Brodsky, four stages of progressive disillusionment characterize the burnout process: (i) enthusiasm; (ii) stagnation; (iii) frustration; and (iv) apathy.

Burnout as a Narcistic Disorder

According to Fischer (1983), individuals who have idealized their jobs and suffer subsequent disillusionment could either reduce their ideals or leave the situation. However, neither option is acceptable to the burnout candidate. Instead of giving up or reducing their ideals or looking for another job, they redouble their efforts in order to achieve their unrealistic objectives. They are motivated by the fear of having to give up their narcistic "illusion of grandiosity", the erroneous notion of being special and superior. The burnout candidate's basic sense of self-esteem is grounded in this narcistic illusion. Accordingly, when a choice has to be made between giving up the illusion of grandiosity or exhausting one's resources, the burnout candidate opts for the latter.

Burnout as an Imbalance between Conscious and Unconscious Functions

Based on the psychodynamic theory of Jung, Garden (1991) developed a model of burnout in which the distinction between two opposite personality types plays a central role: "feeling types", who are tender-minded and are characterized by concern and awareness for people, and "thinking types", who are hard-boiled, achievement-oriented and tend to neglect others. In fact, these two types represent psychic functions that are simultaneously present in each individual. One of these functions is usually preferred and the ego identifies with that preferred—and conscious—function, whereas the opposite function remains largely unconscious. People tend to choose jobs that are compatible with their personality type. For instance, in the human services the proportion of feeling types to thinking types is 4:1, whereas in occupations such as engineering, or in management this proportion is reversed: 1:4 (Garden, 1991). According to Jungian theory, feeling types are better in handling emotional demands, whereas thinking types cope better with mental demands. Garden (1989) observed that regardless of the type of job, emotional demands predict burnout in feeling types, while mental demands are predictive for burnout in thinking types. Thus, burnout is most strongly associated with the kind of demand each personality type is "naturally" adapted with. This observation that burnout is related to the *fit* between job and personality type and not to *lack* of fit, is explained by a particular psychodynamic self-regulatory process. According to Jungian theory, relying too much on one function (e.g. "feeling") creates an imbalance in the psyche that is counteracted by a likewise increase of its opposite (e.g. "thinking") in the unconscious opposite sphere. Thus, relying too much on one's feeling functions has the paradoxical effect of fuelling the unconscious thinking reservoir (and vice versa). But if the repressed function emerges, its negative effect will be all the more devastating. Accordingly, the dropping of conscious functions into the unconscious and the simultaneous emergence of actively repressed unconscious functions are considered the root causes of burnout since this is a highly energy consuming process that depletes the individual's mental resources.

Burnout as a Failed Quest for Existential Meaning

Drawing upon existential psychology, Pines developed a motivational approach to burnout in which the individual's basic need for meaning and significance plays a crucial role (Pines 1993, 1996; Pines & Aronson, 1988). The underlying assumption of the model is that only highly motivated individuals burnout: "In order to burn out, one has first to be 'on fire'. A person with no such initial motivation can experience stress, alienation, depression, an existential crisis, or fatigue, but not burnout" (Pines, 1993, p. 41). Essentially, according to Pines, burnout is the final result of a gradual process of disillusionment in the quest to derive a sense of existential significance from work. "Idealistic people work hard because they expect their work to make their lives matter in the larger scheme of things and give meaning to their existence" (Pines, 1996, p. 83). So, basically, employees burnout because their experiences do not match their intentions and expectations. In other words, the existential perspective on burnout illustrates that the employee's deeply rooted goals and expectations are instrumental in the development of burnout. In her more recent work, Pines (1996) extends the concept of burnout to other spheres of life such as marriage ("couple burnout").

Burnout as a Pattern of Wrong Expectations

From the perspective of learning theory, burnout results from wrong expectations with re-spect to: (i) reinforcements; (ii) outcomes; and (iii) efficacy (Meier, 1983). Reinforcement expectations are descriptions about whether certain work outcomes will meet one's goals. For instance, a teacher might prefer to work with motivated students who frequently ask questions. If these goals are too high, reinforcement expectations are not met and burnout might develop. Outcome expectations are defined as descriptions about which behaviours will lead to certain outcomes. For instance, a teacher may experience burnout because of experiences that create the expectation that a class of students "simply cannot learn the ma-terial", thus drowning any hope for positive reinforcement from that class. Finally, efficacy expectations refer to personal competence in executing the desired behaviour. For instance, teachers may burnout because they feel that they lack the personal competence necessary to teach adequately. Meier (1983) emphasizes that these three expectations strongly depend on social and personal factors. For instance, group norms and personal beliefs have a major impact on a person's expectations, and thus—indirectly—on the burnout process.

Burnout as Disturbed Action Process

Following German action theory, Burisch (1993) considers the action episode as the basic unit of analysis of his action model of burnout. The individual's latent motives and the situation at hand lie at the core of action episodes that are activated by some perceived situation. In order to reach the incentive, the actor engages in some action (i.e. goal-directed behaviour). When the necessary cognitive and behavioural steps are taken and the goal is attained, the motive becomes temporarily satiated. In that case, the action episode is considered satisfactorily completed. However, according to Burisch, action episodes may be disturbed in four different ways. Some obstacle may interfere with goal attainment, either calling for unexpected high investments (goal impediment) or blocking the goal altogether (motive thwarting). Alternatively, the goal may be obtained, but the rewards fail to meet expectations (insufficient reward). Finally, unexpected negative side effects may occur. Disturbed action episodes result in "first-order stress" that may develop into "second-order stress" when attempts to remedy the situation repeatedly fail. Coping with second-order stress and the concomitant loss of autonomy may be successful and lead to personal growth, enhanced competence, and so on. On the other hand, when coping fails a burnout process is triggered: motives (e.g. of being an effective helper) may inflate or extinguish, action planning may become inadequate, aspiration levels may shift downwards, feelings of self-efficacy may decrease, and demoralization may set in.

Burnout as Loss of Coping Resources

Conservation of resources (COR) theory is a basic motivational theory that postulates that stress occurs: (i) when resources are threatened; (ii) when resources are lost; or (iii) when in-dividuals invest in resources without the expected pay-off (Hobfoll, 1989). Resources are de-fined rather broadly as valued objects (e.g. clothing, furniture), conditions (e.g. employment, successful marriage), personal characteristics (e.g. social skills, hardiness), and energies (e.g. stamina, knowledge). Since the basic tenet of COR theory is the utilization of resources and burnout is characterized by resource depletion, the COR perspective seems quite relevant for understanding burnout. According to Hobfoll & Freedy (1993), burnout is more likely to occur when resources are lost than when resources are not gained. They call this the "primacy of loss" and the "secondary importance of gain", respectively. For instance, for teachers, negative interactions with pupils, parents and administrators—which imply losses on the interpersonal level—are more salient than the everyday gains they receive from their job. When loss occurs, or when resources are threatened, people are motivated to use their coping skills in order to regain resources or to prevent losses. Viewed from this perspective, burnout—the depletion of emotional resources—can be considered the ultimate price that has to be paid for the individual's active attempts to regain resources or to prevent their loss.

Conclusion

Virtually all individual approaches emphasize that a strong conscious or unconscious motivation (to help)—including concomitant highly valued goals, expectations and aspirations—is a necessary condition for the emergence of burnout. Furthermore, these approaches assume that often these individual psychological characteristics do not match the employee's experiences on the job, and that thus a mismatch between intentions and reality exists. As a result of this poor fit, job stress occurs that eventually may lead to burnout when inadequate coping strategies are adopted and/or when the appropriate individual or organizational coping resources are lacking. For most individual approaches empirical evidence is rather sparse.

19.6.2 Interpersonal Approaches

The next two interpersonal approaches highlight the importance of emotional demands in relationships with recipients, and the dynamics of social relationships in the workplace, respectively. Traditionally, emotionally demanding interpersonal relationships of professional caregivers with recipients have been considered to be the root cause of burnout. However, it is important to broaden the social context and to include relationships with others at the workplace as well, such as superiors and co-workers. Both interpersonal approaches are described in somewhat more detail because they have received—at least partly—empirical support.

Burnout as a Phased Reaction to Emotional Demands

According to Maslach (1982a, 1993), the burnout syndrome is initiated by emotionally demanding relationships between caregivers and their recipients. Particularly in the human services these relationships are stressful by their very nature because professionals are confronted with people's needs, problems and suffering. This puts a heavy psychological burden on them which may drain their emotional resources, eventually leading to emotional exhaustion, the first phase in the burnout process. In order to cope with the emotional stresses, professionals generally develop an attitude of "detached concern"; they learn to distance themselves from recipients in order to help them better. Unfortunately, this survival

strategy, which in fact is a professional skill, does not adequately develop in every professional. Some of them overreact and develop an impersonal, negative, callous and cynical
attitude, in which initial concern has given way to complete detachment. This so-called
depersonalization constitutes the second phase of the burnout process. It is considered to be
a defensive coping strategy to deal with feelings of emotional exhaustion. This strategy further deteriorates the relationships with recipients since instead of reducing emotional strain,
depersonalization increases exhaustion. At that point, when the professional is continuously
unsuccessful in achieving his or her professional goals, because relationships with recipients are impoverished, feelings of reduced personal accomplishment may develop. This
third and final phase completes the downward spiral: diminished accomplishment further
increases emotional exhaustion, and, consequently, depersonalization.

The results of three earlier cross-sectional studies partly agree with this sequential model
of burnout (Leiter, 1988; Leiter & Maslach, 1988; Leiter & Meechan, 1986). More particularly, the expected positive associations between emotionally demanding relationships with
recipients and emotional exhaustion, and between emotional exhaustion and depersonalization have been confirmed. Byrne (1994), who employed causal modelling techniques to
test the sequential model of burnout on cross-sectional data, confirmed the model in three
independent teacher samples. However, recent work of Leiter (1990, 1991, 1993) supports
a mixed sequential *and parallel* model of burnout. His "developmental model" defines
emotional exhaustion as a reaction to occupational stressors, of which work overload and
interpersonal conflict are among the most prominent. In Leiter's model, depersonalization is
a function of emotional exhaustion, as outlined above. This means that emotional exhaustion
mediates most of the impact of environmental conditions on depersonalization. In contrast to
the original phased reaction model of Maslach (1982a), Leiter's developmental model does
not depict personal accomplishment as a function of depersonalization. Rather, personal
accomplishment is positively influenced by the presence of resources such as social support,
opportunities for skill enhancement, and participative decision making. Accordingly, two
processes seem important: (i) a sequential process in which interpersonal work demands
play a major role, leading to depersonalization through exhaustion; and (ii) a parallel process
that is dominated by lack of resources, leading to diminished personal accomplishment. A
longitudinal study across eight months confirmed the first process, as well as the somewhat
independent role of personal accomplishment (Lee & Ashforth, 1993). Moreover, it appeared among physicians that depersonalization—across a five-year period—deteriorates
the relationship with patients and thus increases emotional demands, which in their turn
lead to emotional exhaustion (Bakker et al., 2000b). Finally, in their meta-analysis, Lee &
Ashforth (1996) found that emotional exhaustion is particularly related to interpersonal job
demands, whereas poor personal accomplishment is related to lack of resources and depersonalization appears to be related to both job demands and lack of resources. Essentially,
these findings agree with both processes that are assumed in Leiter's model.

Burnout as a Result of Social Comparison and Social Exchange Processes

Basing themselves on social comparison theory (Schachter, 1959) and equity theory (Walster
et al., 1978), the central thesis of Buunk & Schaufeli (1993) is that burnout develops primarily in the social context of a work organization. In order to understand burnout, attention

has to be paid to the way in which individuals evaluate their psychological outcomes of, and investments in, the relationships with the recipients, the way in which individuals compare their own responses and feelings with those of others at work, and the way in which they are influenced by the burnout symptoms in their colleagues. Within this general social-psychological framework, three different approaches can be distinguished.

Burnout as a Lack of Reciprocity

By definition, the relationship between caregiver and recipient is complementary, which is semantically illustrated by the terms caregiver and recipient; the former gives, the latter receives. However, according to equity theory, people pursue reciprocity in interpersonal relationships: what they invest and gain from a relationship should be proportional to the investments and gains of the other party in the relationship. Clearly, this is not the case in the human services: the caregiver–recipient relationship is unbalanced in terms of costs and benefits or investments and outcomes. Hence, it is likely that over time a lack of reciprocity develops, whereby caregivers feel that they continuously put much more into relationships with their recipients than they receive back in return. As Buunk & Schaufeli (1999) have pointed out, reciprocity plays a central role in human life, and establishing reciprocal social relationships is essential for the individual's health and well-being. They argue that the strong universal preference for reciprocal interpersonal relationships is deeply rooted because it may have fostered survival and reproductive success in our evolutionary past. Lack of reciprocity—in their evolutionary view—not only leads to negative emotions, but it also motivates attempts to restore reciprocity. This lack of reciprocity, whereby caregivers continuously put much more into relationships with their recipients than they receive back in return, may eventually deplete the professional's emotional resources. It can be inferred from equity theory that this lack of reciprocity and the resulting emotional exhaustion can be dealt with—among others ways—by lowering the recipients' outcomes—that is, by responding to them in a depersonalized way.

   Indeed, significant correlations have been found between lack of reciprocity and burnout (particularly exhaustion and depersonalization) in several occupational groups such as nurses, general practitioners, hospital doctors, police officers, teachers, staff working with the mentally handicapped, and correctional officers (for a review see Buunk & Schaufeli, 1999; Schaufeli & Enzmann, 1998, pp. 120–1). Although most studies are cross-sectional, there is some longitudinal evidence for a curvilinear relationship between lack of reciprocity and emotional exhaustion: feeling more deprived as well as feeling more advantaged results in higher exhaustion levels (Van Dierendonck et al., 2001). Furthermore, the relationship between lack of reciprocity and burnout seems to be moderated by personality factors. For instance, Van Yperen et al. (1992) found that nurses who felt they invested highly in the relationships with patients showed elevated levels of burnout only when they were low in communal orientation, a personality characteristic that refers to a general responsiveness to the needs of others. This finding was replicated by Van Yperen (1996).

   According to equity theory, similar social exchange processes that are observed in interpersonal relationships govern the relationship of the employee with his or her organization. Therefore, Schaufeli et al. (1996b) have proposed a dual-level social exchange model assuming that in addition to an unbalanced relationship at the interpersonal level, burnout is also caused by lack of reciprocity at the organizational level. They argue that in addition to the usually observed cognitive and behavioural withdrawal reactions (job dissatisfaction, reduced organizational commitment, turnover and absenteeism), lack of reciprocity at the organizational level may also lead to burnout. The dual-level model was tested successfully in samples consisting of student nurses, teachers, therapists from a forensic psychiatric clinic, staff working with the mentally disabled, and police officers (for a review see Buunk & Schaufeli, 1999; Schaufeli & Enzmann, 1998, p. 122). That is, it was confirmed that burnout is related to perceptions of inequity at the interpersonal as well as at the organizational level.

In sum, it seems that lack of reciprocity is a key concept for understanding burnout. Instead of simply working too long, too hard with too difficult recipients—as is assumed in most traditional models of burnout—it appears that the *balance* between investments and outcomes is crucial for the development of burnout. It looks like this mechanism is working in similar ways at the interpersonal level of caregiver and recipients and at the organizational level of employee and organization.

Burnout as Related to Social Comparison

In addition to emphasizing the importance of social exchange processes, Buunk & Schaufeli (1993) argued on the basis of social comparison theory that human services professionals, who—by the nature of their work—are faced with high emotional demands, tend to compare their own emotional reactions to those of their co-workers. Individuals under stress, particularly when they are uncertain about their own responses, will seek out others for reasons of self-evaluation in order to assess the appropriateness of their own reactions (Buunk, 1994; Schachter, 1959). Buunk & Schaufeli (1993) found—as predicted—that nurses who felt uncertain at work showed an increased *desire* to affiliate with others, but at the same time their actual affiliation decreased. They explain the latter tendency towards social isolation, which is typical of burnout, by pointing to the fear of embarrassment: talking about one's doubts and uncertainties may be felt as admitting inferiority.

According to social comparison theory, a crucial feature of social comparison is its direction. Individuals may compare themselves with others who are better off (upward comparison) or with others who are worse off (downward comparison). In general, it is assumed that particularly engaging in upward comparisons and interpreting such comparisons in a non-defensive way serve an adaptive function by fostering effective performance and by promoting subjective well-being (e.g. Aspinwall, 1997; Collins, 1996). Vice versa, interpreting upward comparisons in a negative, defensive way will be accompanied by poor well-being and will hinder effective functioning. Indeed, a number of studies have shown that engaging in comparison with others who are better off, and particularly deriving positive feelings from such comparisons, is associated with less emotional exhaustion (Buunk et al., 1994, 2001a, b). In addition, compared to those low in burnout, those high in burnout have been found to respond with higher levels of negative affect to upward comparisons, and to derive more positive affect from downward comparisons (Buunk et al., 2001b). This last finding is in line with Wills' (1991) downward comparison theory. This theory states that individuals faced with lower well-being, such as those experiencing work stress, may temporarily feel better by deriving positive feelings from comparisons with others who are still worse off. However, recent research suggests that under certain conditions, individuals high in burnout may view the situation of others worse off as a potential future for themselves, and thus feel bad when they are confronted with such others (Buunk et al., 2001a). Thus, in general these findings suggest that individuals who use more competent co-workers as positive role models, who provide information on how to deal effectively with problems at work, may have a lower risk of developing burnout than those who identify with others who are doing worse. Furthermore, those who experience burnout may, as a form of emotional coping, derive positive feelings from the idea that others are still worse off.

Burnout as an Emotional Contagion

The contagious nature of burnout has been observed in case studies (Schwartz & Will, 1953) as well as in field surveys (Golembiewski et al., 1986, pp. 159–64; see also Section 19.6.3). That is, burnout tends to concentrate in particular task groups, wards or departments, whereas at the same time it is virtually not observed in comparable other groups. Of course, this concentration of burnout in particular groups may also be explained by higher workloads in these groups, which would contradict a symptom contagion explanation. However, this alternative hypothesis was rejected in a study that included almost eighty European intensive care units (Bakker et al., submitted). It appeared that—after controlling for job autonomy, subjective workload and objectively assessed workload (i.e. complexity of nursing tasks)—nurses' levels of experienced burnout remained higher in some units compared to others. Moreover, nurses from these units observed more burnout complaints among their colleagues then their fellows did in the other units. These intriguing results support the contagion hypothesis of burnout.

Buunk & Schaufeli (1993) have suggested that colleagues may act as models whose symptoms are imitated through a process of emotional contagion. That is, individuals under stress may perceive symptoms of burnout in their colleagues and automatically take on these symptoms. Emotional contagion is defined as "The tendency to automatically mimic and synchronize facial expressions, vocalizations, and movements with those of another person, and consequently, to converge emotionally" (Hatfield et al., 1994, p. 5). The emphasis in this definition is clearly on non-conscious emotional contagion. There is, however, an alternative way in which people may "catch" emotions from others. Contagion may also occur through a conscious cognitive process by "tuning in" to the emotions of others. This will be the case when an individual tries to imagine how he or she would feel in the position of another, and, as a consequence, experiences the same feelings. The professional attitude of human services workers that is characterized by empathic concern is likely to foster such a process of consciously tuning in to the emotions of others.

Few studies suggest that emotional contagion may play a role in the development of burnout. Westman & Etzion (1995) studied about 100 couples of male military officers and their wives and found that burnout transferred from husbands to wives and vice versa. In a similar vein, Miller et al., (1995) found among professionals who work with homeless people that emotional contagion was directly as well as indirectly—through communicative responsiveness—related to burnout. Recently, two studies with general practitioners (Bakker et al., 2001) and teachers (Bakker & Schaufeli, 2000) showed that those who perceived burnout complaints among their colleagues reported higher levels of emotional exhaustion and subsequent negative attitudes (depersonalization and reduced personal accomplishment) than those who did not perceive such complaints. In addition, in both studies individual susceptibility to emotional contagion was positively related to burnout, particularly in combination with the perception of burnout symptoms in their colleagues. That is, doctors and teachers who perceived burnout complaints among colleagues and who were susceptible to emotional contagion reported the highest exhaustion scores.

Conclusion

In a way, both interpersonal approaches are complementary. The first approach assumes that burnout results from emotionally charged relationships between caregivers and recipients. Furthermore, a dynamic process is stipulated in which depersonalization is considered to be a dysfunctional attempt to deal with feelings of emotional exhaustion. However, it remains unclear *why* the relationship between caregiver and recipient is so demanding. This is where the second approach links in by emphasizing that this relationship is often characterized by a lack of reciprocity from the perspective of the caregiver. And it is this lack of reciprocity, not only in interpersonal relationships but also in the relationship with the organization, that lies at the core of the burnout syndrome. In addition, social psychological processes, such as social comparison and emotional contagion, seem to play a role in perpetuating burnout in work groups.

19.6.3 Organizational Approaches

Organizational approaches to burnout interpret the syndrome in terms of undesired organizational behaviour, which not only affects the individual but the organization as well. Three approaches are described that differ in scope and in the degree to which they are supported by empirical evidence. The first approach focuses on burnout among young professionals. The second approach describes a phase model of progressive burnout that has been successfully tested in various organizational settings and countries. The final approach considers burnout as the result of a mismatch between person and job.

Burnout as Reality Shock

Cherniss (1980a, 1995) proposed a model of early career burnout that was based on interviews with human service professionals at the beginning of their careers. The basic tenet of his model is that particular work-setting characteristics interact with person characteristics to produce particular stressors. Whether burnout develops or not depends on the way professionals cope with these stressors. Active problem solving is superior to defensive strategies such as avoiding. Accordingly, burnout is a process that develops over time and represents one way of adapting to particular sources of organizational stress.

Cherniss distinguishes between eight negative work-setting characteristics:

1. the absence of an orientation or introduction programme for novices;
2. high workload;
3. understimulation;
4. limited scope of client contact;
5. low level of autonomy;
6. discrepancy between institutional goals with personal values;
7. inadequate leadership and supervisory practices;
8. social isolation.

In addition, two kinds of personal characteristics are mentioned: resources outside of work and career orientation. The latter includes "social activists" (who want to change the world), "careerists" (who want to make money), "artisans" (who are intrinsically motivated), and "self-investors" (for whom the job is a necessary evil). According to Cherniss, the major sources of stress that are brought about by the interaction of work setting and person are:

1. uncertainty and doubts about one's competence;
2. problems with recipients;
3. bureaucratic infringement on one's autonomy;
4. lack of challenge and fulfillment;
5. lack of collegiality.

In the process of adapting to these stressors, which are rather typical for the human services, Cherniss observed in young professionals negative changes in attitudes and outlook that are indicative of burnout: reduced aspirations and responsibility, loss of idealism, increased cynicism and pessimism, increased emotional detachment, withdrawal from work and growing concern with the self.

Cross-sectional studies among police officers (Burke et al., 1984) and teachers (Burke & Greenglass, 1989) support the validity of the model. As expected, path-analysis showed two significant indirect paths from work-setting characteristics and personal characteristics to burnout, both mediated through experienced sources of stress. In addition, significant direct paths were found from work-setting and personal characteristics to burnout. Furthermore, Burke & Greenglass (1988) showed that teachers who described themselves as "social activists" had the highest burnout scores. This is compatible with the view of burnout as a process of progressive disillusionment.

Cherniss (1989, 1995) re-interviewed the same professionals ten years after he developed his model in order to explore the relationship between the degree of burnout experienced during the first year of the career and career adaptation during the next decade. His results show that those who were more burnt-out early in their careers were less likely to change careers and were more flexible in their approach to work. So, the follow-up study suggests that early career burnout does not lead to any significant negative long-term consequences.

Burnout as a Virulent Process

Essentially, the approach of Golembiewski and his colleagues is rather straightforward (Golembiewski & Munzenrider, 1988; Golembiewski et al., 1996). They consider burnout as a virulent process that develops progressively through eight phases. It is claimed that the burnout process might be set in motion by various different job stressors (e.g. work overload, lack of autonomy, conflicts with co-workers or supervisors). Moreover, it is assumed that burnout leads to poor physical health, reduced productivity and poor work performance. Golembiewski agrees with the three-dimensionality of the burnout syndrome as proposed by Maslach (1982a), but does not agree with her sequential model. Instead, he distinguishes eight progressive phases of burnout. Depersonalization is considered the least important contributor to burnout, followed by lack of personal accomplishment and emotional exhaustion. Dichotomizing the distribution of MBI scale scores at the median as high and low generates eight phases of burnout (Table 19.1). It is important to note that, although the virulence of burnout increases from phase I to phase VIII, individuals do not necessarily need

Table 19.1 Progressive phases of burnout

	I	II	III	IV	V	VI	VII	VIII
DEP	Low	High	Low	High	Low	High	Low	High
PA(r)	Low	Low	High	High	Low	Low	High	High
EE	Low	Low	Low	Low	High	High	High	High

DEP = MBI-depersonalization; PA(r) = MBI-personal accomplishment (reduced); EE = MBI-emotional exhaustion.
Source: Golembiewski & Munzenrider, R.F. (1988, p. 28). Reprinted by permission of Greenwood Publishing Group Inc., Westport, CT.

to follow the successive stages. Since no theoretical rationale is presented, Golembiewski's approach remains purely descriptive.

The categorization into eight phases boils down to reducing all possible (80 000!) combinations of MBI scores on an eight-point scale. When depersonalization, reduced personal accomplishment and emotional exhaustion are assigned weights of 1, 2 and 4, respectively, and these weights are added for every phase, an eight-point rating scale emerges ranging from 0 (phase I) to 7 (phase VIII) (Burisch, 1989, p. 20). Accordingly, the phase model is heavily biased towards emotional exhaustion (Leiter, 1993).

Research based on the phase model in organizations followed three lines. Most studies have attempted to validate the notion of progressive phases of burnout. Overall, these attempts have been quite successful. Individuals in more advanced phases almost always report more negative work experiences (e.g. greater stress, less autonomy, more conflicts and role problems, less support) and more negative outcomes (e.g. job dissatisfaction, psychosomatic symptoms, higher turnover intentions, less job involvement, decreased productivity). For extensive reviews see Golembiewski & Munzenrider (1988) and Golembiewski et al. (1996). In addition, most of these results have been replicated in cross-national studies.

A second stream of research indicates that the incidence of burnout in various phases differs across organizations (see Golembiewski et al., 1996). For instance, the range of respondents in phase VIII varies from 6% to 29%. Moreover, burnout tends to cluster in particular work groups: 83% of the employees in the most advanced phase are employed in work groups where more than 50% of their colleagues are assigned to an advanced phase as well. As we have seen (in Section 19.6.2), this might be explained by a process of symptom contagion. Finally, phase assignments are fairly stable across time: 40% are assigned to the same phase one year later, whereas 55% move only one phase up or down. Individuals moving to a lower burnout phase reported corresponding improvements in antecedents (i.e. work-setting characteristics) and consequences (greater job satisfaction and fewer psychosomatic symptoms) (Burke & Greenglass, 1991).

Burnout as Mismatch between Person and Job

Recently, Maslach & Leiter (1997) argued that burnout results from a situation of chronic imbalance in which the job demands more than the employee can give and provides less than he or she needs. This mismatch between person and job is independent of the specific content of the job. It may occur in the human services as well as outside this occupational field. Emotional overload resulting from working with recipients, which was considered the root cause of burnout in their previous model (Leiter, 1993; Maslach, 1993; see also Section 19.6.2), is now regarded as a particular aspect of the person–job mismatch. Instead of a single root cause for burnout (i.e. emotional overload), six types of person–job mismatches are considered to be potential sources of burnout:

1. work overload (i.e. having to do too much in too little time with too few resources);
2. lack of control (i.e. having no opportunities to make choices and decisions, using one's abilities to think and solve problems);
3. lack of rewards (i.e. inadequate monetary rewards as well as internal rewards such as recognition appreciation);
4. lack of community (i.e. a loose and non-supportive social fabric, social isolation and chronic and unresolved problems);
5. lack of fairness (i.e. employees are treated inequitably, and respect and self-worth are not confirmed);
6. value conflict (i.e. the requirements of the job do not agree with personal principles).

Maslach & Leiter (1997) argue that these six person–job mismatches are pervasive in modern organizational life. They illustrate these mismatches with case materials and use their approach to put burnout research in perspective.

Conclusion

Despite large differences, the three approaches agree that similar organizational factors (e.g. qualitative and quantitative job demands, lack of autonomy or control, lack of rewards, incongruent institutional goals or values, and lack of social support or community) are important correlates of burnout. Moreover, they point to the fact that burnout not only has negative effects for the individual but that it is also detrimental to the organization in terms of lowered productivity and efficiency, and poor quality of service.

19.7   INTERVENTIONS

From the moment burnout was introduced in the early 1970s, there has been a vivid interest in interventions. There is an extensive, albeit kaleidoscopic and rather scattered, literature on burnout interventions that suggests that virtually every approach from the occupational stress area can be used to prevent or reduce burnout. Essentially, two general approaches can be distinguished: individual interventions and workplace interventions. Although almost every author on the subject acknowledges that a combination of both approaches would be most effective, the vast majority of burnout interventions have been conducted on the individual level. However, a strictly individual approach to burnout creates the danger that a "blame the victim" situation is created.

   This concluding section first briefly reviews individual and workplace interventions that have been applied to burnout (for a more extensive review see Schaufeli & Enzmann, 1998, pp. 144–83). Next, the results of empirical studies on the effectiveness of stress management and burnout interventions are discussed.

19.7.1 Individual and Workplace Interventions

Individual approaches to prevent or reduce burnout include cognitive-behavioural techniques such as stress inoculation training, rational emotive therapy, cognitive restructuring
and behavioural rehearsal (Edelwich & Brodsky, 1980). A cognitively oriented approach
is relevant because burnout often involves "wrong" cognitions such as unrealistic expectations and false hopes. In addition, relaxation techniques and didactic stress management are
often used to reduce burnout (e.g. Jaffe & Scott, 1989). The latter involves the presentation
of practical information about burnout and includes techniques such as self-monitoring.
Time management, balancing work and private life, physical training, dieting and increasing one's social skills—particularly assertiveness—have been recommended to combat
burnout (Maslach, 1982b). In order to counteract the reality shock that is experienced
by many professionals at the start of their careers, preparatory training programmes may
provide them with more realistic images of their profession, instead of fostering wrong
expectations (Cherniss, 1995). Mutual aid groups are advocated for self-help (Spicuzza &
De Voe, 1982). Preferably these groups should be initiated by the professionals themselves,
rather than by their management (Cherniss & Dantzig, 1986). Specialized counselling and
psychotherapy programmes have been developed for burnt-out patients that are not only
directed towards symptom reduction but also towards work resumption and rehabilitation
(Schaufeli & Enzmann, 1998, pp. 160–64).

Many of the aforementioned techniques to reduce burnout are combined in so-called
burnout workshops that rest on two pillars: increasing the participants' awareness of their
work-related problems and augmenting their coping resources by cognitive and behavioural
skills training and by establishing support networks. More specifically, workshops may
include self-assessment, didactic stress management, relaxation, cognitive and behavioural
techniques, time management, peer support, and the promotion of a healthy lifestyle and
a more realistic image of the job. In other words, the burnout workshop combines many
rather general strategies for one specific purpose: preventing and combating burnout.

Only occasionally, workplace interventions are explicitly carried out in order to reduce
stress or burnout. Generally, other purposes are targeted such as increased productivity and
efficiency, cost-effectiveness, smooth communication or organizational flexibility. Nevertheless, there is an increasing awareness that preventing stress at the workplace is important
because of the high direct and indirect costs that are associated with it (European Commission, 1999). As far as burnout is concerned, workplace interventions are even less specifically
described than individual approaches.

Work redesign (i.e. job enlargement, job rotation and job enrichment) is mentioned as
a major tool to decrease quantitative and qualitative workload (Pines & Maslach, 1980).
Another way to reduce qualitative workload is to follow additional training courses (e.g.
"How to deal with violent clients"). Since many burnout candidates feel "locked in" to their
careers, career development programmes and career counselling would be other organizational approaches to prevent burnout. Especially in order to avoid early career burnout,
Cherniss (1980a) proposed an introductory mentorship system. Bi-directional communication between management and employees, adequate procedures for conflict management
and participative decision making have also been proposed as antidotes to burnout (Cherniss,
1980a). Moreover, social support from colleagues and superiors should be institutionalized
in the form of regular consultations and meetings (Pines & Maslach, 1980). In addition,
"time-outs" and sabbatical leaves have been suggested in order to enhance the recuperation

from the daily stresses of the job (Pines & Kafry, 1982). Finally, Golembiewski et al. (1987) describe an organizational development (OD) approach to burnout that strengthened the workers' social network for participatory change through problem confrontation, group consolidation around problems, and building consensus for change. According to Karasek & Theorell (1990, pp. 239–41), this approach essentially reduces job demands and increases worker control.

19.7.2   The Effectiveness of Interventions

Recently, Van der Klink et al. (2001) performed a meta-analysis of 48 (quasi-) experimental studies on the effectiveness of interventions for work-related stress. They distinguish four intervention types, three of which are individual-focused, that are also often used to combat burnout: (i) cognitive-behavioural (18 studies), (ii) relaxation (17 studies) (iii) multimodal (8 studies)—a combination of (i) and (ii). Workplace-focused intervention programmes (5 studies) constitute the fourth type of intervention. It appeared that all individual-focused programmes had significant effects but that cognitive-behavioural interventions and mutimodal programmes are more effective than relaxation training. In terms of effect size, the impact of cognitive-behavioural and mutimodal programmes is "medium", whereas the impact of relaxation is "small". In contrast, workplace interventions showed no significant effects.

In addition to studies evaluating the effectiveness of general stress management interventions, there have also been a number of studies examining the effects of specific anti-burnout programmes. While most of these studies exclusively involve individually oriented programs, Pines & Maslach (1980) describe a successful workplace intervention to reduce burnout by redesigning the jobs of professionals who worked at a day-care centre for children. Unfortunately, they do not present quantitative data. In contrast, Golembiewski et al. (1987) were able to show a positive effect on burnout and turnover rates of their organizational development programme that was conducted in the human services department of a pharmaceuticals company. Unfortunately, the effect on burnout was not retained after the firm went through a process of reorganization. The introduction of a system of planned nursing care in a Swedish psychogeriatric clinic, in which each patient was assigned a particular nurse who was responsible for all nursing tasks, led to a reduction of burnout at the one-year follow up compared to the traditional ward system where one patient was nursed by many different nurses (Berg et al., 1994). Unfortunately, two Dutch studies on similar job redesign projects among psychiatric nurses failed to confirm these positive results (Melchior et al., 1996, 1997). To conclude, it seems that in general, the results of workplace intervention programmes to reduce burnout are somewhat disappointing.

The effectiveness of individual approaches to combat burnout has been established somewhat more firmly that that of organizational approaches. For instance, Freedy & Hobfoll (1994) used stress inoculation training among nurses to enhance their social support and individual mastery resources. Participants experienced significant enhancements in social support and mastery compared to the no-intervention control group. Particularly, nurses with low initial levels on both resources showed significant reductions in emotional exhaustion and depression. Similar positive results were obtained by West et al. (1984), who used didactic stress management, training in coping skills (i.e. relaxation, assertiveness, cognitive restructuring and time management), and exposure via role-playing. A four-month follow-up showed that burnout (i.e. emotional exhaustion and reduced personal accomplishment) decreased significantly, as did anxiety and systolic blood pressure. More detailed analysis revealed that coping skills were the main ingredient of the programme. In another controlled study, Higgins (1986) showed that learning palliative coping skills (i.e. progressive relaxation and systematic desensitization) was equally effective as cognitive and behavioural skills training (i.e. time management, assertiveness training and rational emotive therapy) in reducing levels of emotional exhaustion. However, Corcoran & Bryce (1983) showed that a behaviourally oriented "Human Resource Development Program" was slightly superior to a more cognitively oriented "Microcounseling Training Program" in reducing levels of emotional exhaustion.

Pines & Aronson (1983) evaluated a one-day burnout workshop for employees of two social services that combined several individual approaches: e.g. relaxation techniques, cognitive stress management, time management, social skills training, didactical stress management and attitude change. The participants' level of exhaustion decreased slightly but not significantly. However, compared to the control group that did not participate in the workshop, satisfaction with co-workers went up significantly in the experimental group. Schaufeli (1995) evaluated a somewhat similar burnout workshop for community nurses but found that only the symptom levels (i.e. emotional exhaustion, psychological strain and somatic complaints) of the participating nurses decreased significantly. However, *no* significant changes were observed in levels of the attitudinal component of burnout (depersonalization and reduced personal accomplishment). In addition, it was observed that nurses who were rather resistant to stress benefited most from the workshop. Van Dierendonck et al. (1998) evaluated a three-day burnout workshop for staff working in direct care with mentally disabled people. The workshop was strongly cognitive-behaviourally oriented and included such aspects as cognitive restructuring, didactic stress management and relaxation. In addition, a strong accent was put on career development. Participants analysed their strengths and weaknesses and drew up a plan of action for the time ahead. After six months and one year, follow-up meetings were organized in order to evaluate this plan. The study included two non-treated control groups, one from the same organization (the internal control group) and one from another similar organization (the external control group). Results showed that emotional exhaustion dropped significantly for the experimental group compared to both control groups at each follow-up, but no effects were observed for depersonalization and personal accomplishment. Finally, registered absenteeism significantly decreased in the experimental group, whereas it increased in the internal control group. In another study, the effects of mutual aid groups were evaluated by two studies that consistently showed that levels of burnout did not decrease (Brown, 1984; Larson, 1986). However, participants were satisfied about the programme and about the group experience, and had become more content with their co-workers and superiors.

Conclusion

It seems that individual stress management interventions work. However, it is rather difficult to draw general conclusions about the effectiveness of specific individual burnout intervention programmes because the evaluation studies use different samples, procedures, time frames, measurement instruments and training methods. In addition, some studies suffer from methodological inadequacies such as the lack of control groups and small numbers of participants. Nevertheless, one major conclusion emerges: the core symptom of burnout—exhaustion—can be reduced by training professionals to use particular coping skills, most notably relaxation techniques and cognitive restructuring. On the other hand, personal accomplishment, and particularly depersonalization seem rather resistant to change. The fact that depersonalization and reduced personal accomplishment do not change is not very surprising because most techniques that are employed in burnout workshops focus on reducing arousal and not on changing attitudes (depersonalization) or on enhancing specific professional skills or resources (personal accomplishment). Besides, most burnout models assume that depersonalization results from exhaustion. Providing social support—as in staff-support groups—does not seem to have a positive impact on burnout, although these programmes are evaluated positively and satisfaction with colleagues seems to increase.

19.8   FINAL REMARKS

More than 25 years after its introduction, burnout developed into a prospering research area in work and health psychology. The concept—which was initially recognized as a social problem—has successfully penetrated from practice into the realm of academic psychology—and from there back to practice again. Some major achievements have been made in the past quarter of a century. Most importantly, a consensual agreement has developed on an operational definition of burnout, which is exemplified by the almost universal use of the MBI. In addition, this chapter has shown that much progress has been made on the empirical as well as on the conceptual level. However, much work remains to be done. There is still a great need for research that is theory-driven, longitudinal and includes other than self-report measures. Moreover, valid tools for individual assessment have to be developed as well as specific—organization-based—interventions.

The overview presented in this chapter is based for a large part on North American studies that were carried out among human services professionals, although the growing number of studies from other countries and outside the human services was also considered. In the years ahead researchers have to take up the challenge to further expand burnout research outside North America as well as beyond the human services in order to investigate whether or not the findings summarized in this chapter generalize to different countries and occupational fields. A final challenge originates from the recent expansion of the burnout construct into the direction of its positive pole, job engagement—an energetic state in which one is dedicated to excellent performance (Maslach et al., 2001). Do the findings from this chapter also apply to engagement, except—of course—that the direction of the relationships is reversed, or does engagement has its own specific causes, correlates and consequences? How does one move from burnout to engagement, and from engagement to burnout? These and other new questions are on the research agenda for the years to come.

REFERENCES

Aspinwall, L.G. (1997) Future-oriented aspects of social comparison. In B.P. Buunk & F.X. Gibbons (eds) *Health, Coping, and Well-Being: Perspectives from Social Comparison Theory.* Mahwah, NJ: Lawrence Erlbaum, pp. 125–66.

Bakker, A.B. & Schaufeli, W.B. (2000) Burnout contagion processes among teachers. *Journal of Applied Social Psychology*, **30**, 2289–308.

Bakker, A.B., Schaufeli, W.B., Demerouti, E., Janssen, P.M.P., Van der Hulst, R. & Brouwer, J. (2000a) Using equity theory to examine the difference between burnout and depression. *Anxiety, Stress and Coping*, **13**, 247–68.

Bakker, A., Schaufeli, W.B., Sixma, H.J., Bosveld, W. & Van Dierendonck, D. (2000b) Patient demands, lack of reciprocity, and burnout: a five-year longitudinal study among general practitioners. *Journal of Organizational Behaviour*, **21**, 425–41.

Bakker, A., Schaufeli, W.B. & Van Dierendonck, D. (2000c) Burnout: prevalentie, risicogroepen en risicofactoren [Burnout: prevalence, risk groups and risk factors]. In I.L.D. Houtman, W.B. Schaufeli & T. Taris (eds). *Psychische vermoeidheid en werk: Cijfers, trends en analyses.* Alphen a/d Rijn: Samsom, pp. 65–82.

Bakker, A.B., Schaufeli, W.B., Sixma, H. & Bosveld, W. (2001) Burnout contagion among general practitioners. *Journal of Social and Clinical Psychology*, **20**, 82–98.

Bakker, A.B., Le Blanc, P.M. & Schaufeli, W.B. (submitted) Burnout contagion among nurses who work at intensive care units: a European study.

Berg, A., Welander-Hansson, U. & Hallberg, I. R. (1994) Nurses' creativity, tedium and burnout during 1 year of clinical supervision and implementation of individually planned nursing care: comparisons between a ward for severely demented patients and a similar control ward. *Journal of Advance Nursing*, **20**, 742–9.

Bhagat, R.S., Allie, S.M. & Ford, D.L. (1995) Coping with stressful life events: an empirical analysis. In R. Crandall & P.L. Perrewe (eds) *Occupational Stress: A Handbook*. Philadelphia, PA: Taylor & Francis, pp. 93–112.

Bradley, H.B. (1969) Community-based treatment for young adult offenders. *Crime and Delinquency*, **15**, 359–70.

Brenninkmeijer, V., Van Yperen, N.W. & Buunk, B.P. (2001) Burnout and depression are not identical twins: is superiority a distinguishing feature? *Personality and Individual Differences*, **30**, 873–80.

Brill, P.L. (1984) The need for an operational definition of burnout. *Family and Community Health*, **6**, 12–24.

Brown, L. (1984) Mutual help staff groups to manage work stress. *Social Work with Groups*, **7**, 55–66.

Burisch, M. (1989) *Das Burnout-Syndrom: Theorie der inneren Erschöpfung* [*The Burnout Syndrome: Theory of Internal Exhaustion*]. Berlin: Springer-Verlag.

Burisch, M. (1993) In search of theory: some ruminations on the nature and etiology of burnout. In W.B. Schaufeli, C. Maslach & T. Marek (eds) *Professional Burnout: Recent Developments in Theory and Research*. Washington, DC; Taylor & Francis, pp. 75–94.

Burke, R.J. (1994) Stressful events, work–family conflict, coping, psychological burnout, and well-being among police officers. *Psychological Reports*, **75**, 787–800.

Burke, R.J. & Greenglass, E.R. (1988) Career orientations and psychological burnout in teachers. *Psychological Reports*, **63**, 107–16.

Burke, R.J. & Greenglass, E.R. (1989) Psychological burnout among men and women in teaching: an examination of the Cherniss model. *Human Relations*, **42**, 261–73.

Burke, R.J. & Greenglass, E.R. (1991) A longitudinal study of progressive phases of psychological burnout. *Journal of Health and Human Resources Administration*, **13**, 390–408.

Burke, R.J. & Richardsen, A.M. (1996) Stress, burnout, and health. In C.L. Cooper (ed.) *Handbook of Stress, Medicine, and Health*. New York: CRC Press, pp. 101–17.

Burke, R.J., Shearer, J. & Deszca, E (1984) Correlates of burnout phases among police officers. *Group and Organizational Studies*, **9**, 451–66.

Büssink, A. & Perrar, K.M. (1992) Die Messung von Burnout. Untersuchung einer deutschen Fassung des Maslach Burnout Inventory (MBI-D) [The measurement of burnout: an investigation with the German version of the Maslach Burnout Inventory]. *Diagnostica*, **38**, 328–53.

Buunk, B.P. (1994). Social comparison processes under stress: towards an integration of classic and recent perspectives. In W. Stroebe & M. Hewstone (eds) *European Review of Social Psychology*, vol. 5. Chichester: John Wiley & Sons, pp. 211–41.

Buunk, B.P. & Schaufeli, W.B. (1999) Reciprocity in interpersonal relationships: an evolutionary perspective on its importance for health and well-being. In W. Stroebe & M. Hewstone (eds) *European Review of Social Psychology*, vol. 10. Chichester: John Wiley & Sons, pp. 260–91.

Buunk, A.P & Schaufeli, W.B. (1993) Burnout: a perspective from social comparison theory. In W.B. Schaufeli, C. Maslach & T. Marek (eds) *Professional Burnout: Recent Developments in Theory and Research*. Washington, DC: Taylor & Francis, pp. 53–73.

Buunk, A.P., Schaufeli, W.B. & Ybema, J.F. (1994) Burnout, uncertainty and the desire for social comparison among nurses. *Journal of Applied Social Psychology*, **24**, 1701–18.

Buunk, B.P., Ybema, J.F., Gibbons, F.X. & Ipenburg, M.L. (2001a) The affective consequences of social comparison as related to professional burnout and social comparison orientation. *European Journal of Social Psychology*, **31**, 1–15.

Buunk, B.P., Ybema, J.F., Van der. Zee, K., Schaufeli, W.B. & Gibbons, F.X. (2001b) Affect generated by social comparisons among nurses high and low in burnout. *Journal of Applied Social Psychology*. **31**, 1500–20.

Byrne, B.M. (1994) Burnout: testing for validity, replication and invariance of causal structure across elementary, intermediate, and secondary teachers. *American Educational Research Journal*, **31**, 645–73.

Cherniss, C. (1980a) *Staff Burnout: Job Stress in the Human Services*. Beverly Hills, CA: Sage.

Cherniss, C. (1980b) *Professional Burnout in Human Service Organizations*. New York: Praeger.

Cherniss, C. (1989) Career stability in public service professionals: a longitudinal investigation based on biographical interviews. *American Journal of Community Psychology*, **17**, 399–422.

Cherniss, C. (1993) Role of professional self-efficacy in the etiology and amelioration of burnout. In W.B. Schaufeli, C. Maslach & T. Marek (eds) *Professional Burnout: Recent Developments in Theory and Research*. Washington, DC: Taylor & Francis, pp. 135–49.

Cherniss, C. (1995) *Beyond Burnout: Helping Teachers, Nurses, Therapists and Lawyers Recover from Stress and Disillusionment*. New York: Routledge.

Cherniss, C. & Dantzig, S.A. (1986) Preventing and managing job related stress. In R.R. Kilberg, P.E. Nathan and R.W. Thoreson (eds) *Professionals in Distress: Issues, Syndromes, and Solutions*. Washington, DC: American Psychological Association, pp. 255–73.

Collins, R. L. (1996) For better or worse: the impact of upward social comparison on self-evaluations. *Psychological Bulletin*, **119**, 51–69.

Corcoran, K.J. & Bryce, A.K. (1983) Intervention in the experience of burnout: effects of skill development. *Journal of Social Service Research*, **7**, 71–9.

Cordes, C.L. & Dougherty, T.W. (1993) A review and an integration of research on job burnout. *Academy of Management Review*, **18**, 621–56.

Corrigan, P.W., Holmes, E.P. & Luchins, D. (1995) Burnout and collegial support in state psychiatric hospital staff. *Journal of Clinical Psychology*, **51**, 703–10.

Deary, I.J., Blenkin, H., Agius, R.M., Endler, N.S., Zealley, H. & Wood, R. (1996) Models of job-related stress and personal achievement among consultant doctors. *British Journal of Psychology*, **87**, 3–29.

Dignam, J.T. (1986) Social support, job stress, burnout and health among correctional officers: a longitudinal analysis. *Dissertation Abstracts International*, **47**, 4646-B (order no. DA8704509).

Dion, G. & Tessier, R. (1994) Validation de la traduction de l'Inventaire d' épuisement professionnel de Maslach et Jackson [Validation of the translation of the burnout inventory of Maslach and Jackson]. *Canadian Journal of Behavioral Science*, **26**, 210–27.

Edelwich, J. & Brodsky, A. (1980) *Burn-out: Stages of Disillusionment in the Helping Professions*. New York: Human Services Press.

Enzmann, D. & Kleiber, D. (1989) *Helfer-Leiden: Stress und Burnout in psychosozialen Berufen* [*Helper Ordeals: Stress and Burnout in the Human Services*]. Heidelberg: Asanger Verlag.

Enzmann, D., Schaufeli, W.B. & Girault, N. (1994) The validity of the Maslach Burnout Inventory in three national samples. In L. Bennett, D. Miller & M. Ross (eds) *Health Workers and AIDS: Research, Interventions and Current Issues*. London: Harwood, pp. 131–50.

Enzmann, D., Schaufeli, W.B., Janssen, P. & Rozeman, A. (1998) Dimensionality and validity of the Burnout Measure. *Journal of Occupational and Organisational Psychology*, **71**, 331–51.

Etzion, D. (1987) Burnout: The hidden agenda of human distress, IIBR series in Organizational Behavior and Human Resources, working paper no. 930/87), The Israel Institute of Business Research, Faculty of Management, Tel Aviv University, Israel.

Etzion, D. & Pines, A. (1986) Sex and culture in burnout and coping among human service professionals: a social psychological perspective. *Journal of Cross-Cultural Psychology*, **17**, 191–209.

European Commission (1999) *Guidance on Work Related Stress. Spice of Life or Kiss of Death.* Luxembourg: Office for Official Publications of the European Communities.

Fischer, H.J. (1983) A psychoanalytic view on burnout. In B.A. Farber (ed.) *Stress and Burnout in the Human Service Professions.* New York: Pergamon Press, pp. 40–6.

Fletcher, B. (1988) The epidemiology of occupational stress. In C.L. Cooper & R. Payne (eds) *Causes, Coping and Consequences of Stress at Work.* Chichester: John Wiley & Sons, pp. 3–52.

Freedy, J.R. & Hobfoll, S.E. (1994) Stress inoculation for reduction of burnout: a conservation of resources approach. *Anxiety, Stress and Coping,* **6**, 311–25.

Freudenberger, H.J. (1974) Staff burnout. *Journal of Social Issues,* **30**, 159–65.

Freudenberger, H.J. (1980) *Burnout: The Cost of High Achievement.* New York: Anchor Press.

Freudenberger, H.J. (1983) Burnout: Contemporary Issues, Trends, and Concerns. In B.A. Farber (ed.) *Stress and Burnout in the Human Service Professions.* New York: Pergamon Press, pp. 23–8.

Garden, A.M. (1989) The effect of psychological type on research findings. *Journal of Occupational Psychology,* **62**, 223–34.

Garden, A.M. (1991) The purpose of burnout: a Jungian interpretation. *Journal of Social Behavior and Personality,* **6**, 73–93.

Glass, D. C. & McKnight, J. D. (1996) Perceived control, depressive symptomatology, and professional burnout: a review of the evidence. *Psychology and Health,* **11**, 23–48.

Glass, D.C., McKnight, J.D. & Valdimarsdottir, H. (1993) Depression, burnout and perceptions of control in hospital nurses. *Journal of Consulting and Clinical Psychology,* **61**, 147–55.

Golembiewski, R.T. & Munzenrider, R. (1984) Active and passive reactions to psychological burnout: toward greater specificity in a phase model. *Journal of Health and Human Resources Administration,* **7**, 264–8.

Golembiewski, R.T. & Munzenrider, R.F. (1988) *Phases of Burnout: Developments in Concepts and Applications.* New York: Preager.

Golembiewski, R.T., Munzenrider, R. & Carter, D. (1983) Phases of progressive burnout and their work site covariates: critical issues in OD research and practice. *Journal of Applied Behavioral Science,* **19**, 461–81.

Golembiewski, R.T., Munzenrider, R.F. & Stevenson, J.G. (1986) *Stress in Organizations.* New York: Praeger.

Golembiewski, R.T., Hilles, R. & Rick, D. (1987) Some effects of multiple OD interventions on burnout and work site features. *Journal of Applied Behavioral Science,* **23**, 295–313.

Golembiewski, R.T., Boudreau, R.A., Munzenrider, R.F. & Luo, H. (1996) *Global Burnout: A Worldwide Pandemic Explored by the Phase Model.* Greenwich, CT: JAI Press.

Greenglass, E. (1991) Burnout and gender: theoretical and organizational implications. *Canadian Psychology,* **32**, 562–74.

Hallsten, L. (1993) Burning out: a framework. In W.B. Schaufeli, C. Maslach & T. Marek (eds) *Professional Burnout: Recent Developments in Theory and Research.* Washington, DC: Taylor & Francis, pp. 95–112.

Hatfield, E., Cacioppo, J.T. & Rapson, R.L. (1994) *Emotional Contagion.* New York: Cambridge University Press.

Hendrix, W.H., Steel, R.P., Leap, T.L. & Summers, T.P. (1991) Development of a stress-related health promotion model: antecedents and organizational effectiveness outcomes. *Journal of Social Behavior and Personality,* **6**, 141–62.

Higgins, N.C. (1986) Occupational stress and working women: the effectiveness of two stress reduction programs. *Journal of Vocational Behavior,* **29**, 66–78.

Himle, D.P., Jayaratne, S.D. & Thyness, P.A. (1991) Buffering effects of four social support types on burnout among social workers. *Social Work Research and Abstracts,* **27**, 22–7.

Hobfoll, S.E. (1989) Conservation of resources. A new attempt at conceptualising stress. *American Psychologist,* **44**, 513–24.

Hobfoll, S.E. & Freedy, J. (1993) Conservation of resources: a general stress theory applied to burnout. In W.B. Schaufeli, C. Maslach & T. Marek (eds) *Professional Burnout: Recent Developments in Theory and Research.* Washington, DC: Taylor & Francis, pp. 115–29.

Jackson, S.E. & Maslach, C. (1982) After-effects of job related stress: families as victims. *Journal of Occupational Behavior,* **3**, 63–77.

Jaffe, D.T. & Scott, C.D. (1989) *Self-Renewal: A Workbook for Achieving High Performance and Health in a High-Stress Environment*. New York: Simon & Schuster.

Jason, L.A., Wagner, L., Taylor, R., Ropacki, M.T., Shlaes, J., Ferrari, J.R., Slavich, S.P. & Stenzel, C. (1995) Chronic fatigue symdrome: a new challenge for health care professionals. *Journal of Community Psychology*, **23**, 143–64.

Jenkins, R. (1991) Introduction. In R. Jenkins and J. Mowbray (eds) *Post-Viral Fatigue Syndrome: Myalgic Encephalomyelitis and Chronic Fatigue Syndrome*. Chichester: John Wiley & Sons, pp. 3–39.

Kahill, S. (1988) Symptoms of professional burnout: a review of the empirical evidence. *Canadian Psychology*, **29**, 284–97.

Karasek, R. & Theorell, T. (1990) *Healthy Work: Stress, Productivity and the Reconstruction of Working Life*. New York: Basic Books.

Kirk, S.A. & Koeske, G.F. (1995) The fate of optimism: a longitudinal study of case managers' hopefulness and subsequent morale. *Research on Social Work Practice*, **5**, 47–61.

Landsbergis, P.A. (1988) Occupational stress among health care workers: a test of the job demands–control model. *Journal of Organizational Behavior*, **9**, 217–39.

Larson, D.G. (1986) Developing effective hospice staff support groups: pilot test of an innovative training program. *The Hospice Journal*, **2**, 41–55.

Lee, R.T. & Ashforth, B.E. (1993) A longitudinal study of burnout among supervisors and managers: comparisons between the Leiter and Maslach (1988) and Golembiewski et al. (1986) models. *Organizational Behavior and Human Decision Processes*, **54**, 369–98.

Lee, R.T. & Ashforth, B.E. (1996) A meta-analytic examination of the correlates of the three dimensions of job burnout. *Journal of Applied Psychology*, **81**, 123–33.

Leiter, M.P. (1988) Burnout as a function of communication patterns: a study of multidisciplinairy mental health team. *Group and Organization Studies*, **13**, 111–28.

Leiter, M.P. (1990) The impact of family resources, control coping and skill utilization on the development of burnout: a longitudinal study. *Human Relations*, **43**, 1067–83.

Leiter, M.P. (1991) Coping patterns as predictors of burnout: the function of control and escapist coping patterns. *Journal of Organizational Behavior*, **12**, 123–44.

Leiter, M.P. (1993) Burnout as developmental process: consideration of models. In W.B. Schaufeli, C. Maslach and T. Marek (eds) *Professional Burnout: Recent Developments in Theory and Research*. Washington, DC: Taylor & Francis, pp. 237–50.

Leiter, M.P. & Durup, J. (1994) The discriminant validity of burnout and depression: a confirmatory factor analytic study. *Anxiety, Stress and Coping*, **7**, 357–73.

Leiter, M.P. & Meechan, K.A. (1986) Role structure and burnout in the field of human services. *Journal of Applied Social Science*, **22**, 47–52.

Leiter, M.P. & Maslach, C. (1988) The impact of interpersonal environment on burnout and organizational commitment. *Journal of Organizational Behavior*, **9**, 297–308.

Maslach, C. (1976) Burn-out. *Human Behavior*, **5**, 16–22.

Maslach, C. (1982a) Burnout: a social psychological analysis. In J.W. Jones (ed.) *The Burnout Syndrome: Current Research, Theory, Interventions*. Park Ridge, IL: London House, pp. 30–53.

Maslach, C. (1982b) *Burnout: The Cost of Caring*. Englewood Cliffs, NJ: Prentice Hall.

Maslach, C. (1993) Burnout: a multidimensional perspective. In W.B. Schaufeli, C. Maslach & T. Marek (eds) *Professional Burnout: Recent Developments in Theory and Research*. Washington, DC: Taylor & Francis, pp. 19–32.

Maslach, C. & Jackson, S.E. (1981) The measurement of experienced burnout. *Journal of Occupational Behavior*, **2**, 99–113.

Maslach, C. & Jackson, S. E. (1984) Burnout in organizational settings. In S. Oskamp (ed.) *Applied Social Psychology Annual*, vol. 5. Beverly Hills, CA: Sage, pp. 133–53.

Maslach, C. & Jackson, S. E. (1985) The role of sex and family variables in burnout. *Sex Roles*, **12**, 837–51.

Maslach, C. & Jackson, S.E. (1986) *MBI: Maslach Burnout Inventory; Manual Research Edition*. Palo Alto, CA: Consulting Psychologists Press.

Maslach, C. & Leiter, M. P. (1997) *The Truth About Burnout: How Organizations Cause Personal Stress and What to Do About It*. San Francisco, CA: Jossey-Bass.

Maslach, C. & Pines, A. (1977) The burn-out syndrome in the day care setting. *Child Care Quarterly*, **6**, 100–13.

Maslach, C. & Schaufeli, W.B. (1993) Historical and conceptual development of burnout. In W.B. Schaufeli, C. Maslach & T. Marek (eds) *Professional Burnout: Recent Developments in Theory and Research*. Washington, DC: Taylor & Francis, pp. 1–16.

Maslach, C., Jackson, S. E. & Leiter, M. (1996) *Maslach Burnout Inventory. Manual*, 3rd edn. Palo Alto, CA: Consulting Psychologists Press.

Maslach, C., Schaufeli, W.B. & Leiter, M.P. (2001) Burnout. *Annual Review of Psychology*, **52**, 397–422.

McKnight, J.D. (1993) Perceived job control, burnout and depression in hospital nurses: longitudinal and cross-sectional studies. *Dissertation Abstracts International*, **54**(12), 6499B.

McKnight, J.D. & Glass, D.C. (1995) Perceptions of control, burnout, and depressive symptomatology: a replication and extension. *Journal of Consulting and Clinical Psychology*, **63**, 490–4.

Melamed, S., Ugarten, U., Shirom, A., Kahana, L., Lerman, Y. & Froom, P. (1999) Chronic burnout, somatic arousal and elevated salivary coritsol levels. *Journal of Psychosomatic Research*, **46**, 591–8.

Melchior, M.E.W., Philipsen, H., Abu-Saad, H.H., Halfens, R., Van den Berg, A.A. & Gassman, P. (1996) The effectiveness of primary nursing on burnout among psychiatric nurses in long-stay settings. *Journal of Advanced Nursing*, **24**, 694–702.

Melchior, M.E.W., Van den Berg, A.A., Halfens, R., Abu-Saad, H.H., Philipsen, H. & Gassman, P. (1997) Burnout and the work-environment of nurses in psychiatric long-stay care settings. *Social Psychiatry and Psychiatric Epidemiology*, **32**, 158–64.

Meier, S.T. (1983) Toward a theory of burnout. *Human Relations*, **36**, 899–910.

Miller, K.I., Birkholt, M., Scott, C. & Stage, C. (1995). Empathy and burnout in human service work: an extension of a communication model. *Communication Research*, **22**, 123–47.

Nowack, K.M. & Pentkowski, A.M. (1994) Lifestyle habits, substance use and prediction of job burnout in professional working women. *Work and Stress*, **8**, 19–35.

Ogus, E.D., Greenglass, E.R. & Burke, R.J. (1990) Gender-role differences, work stress and depersonalization. *Journal of Social Behavior and Personality*, **5**, 387–98.

Perlman, B. & Hartman, A.E. (1982) Burnout: summary and future research. *Human Relations*, **35**, 283–305.

Pfennig, B. & Hüsch, M. (1994) Determinanten und Korrelate des Burnout-Syndroms: Eine meta-analytische Betrachtung [Determinants and correlates of the burnout syndrome: a meta-analytic approach], unpublished thesis, Freie Universität Berlin, Psychologisches Institut.

Piedmont, R.L. (1993) A longitudinal analysis of burnout in the health care setting: the role of personal dispositions. *Journal of Personality Assessment*, **61**, 457–73.

Pines, A. (1993) Burnout: an existential perspective. In W.B. Schaufeli, C. Maslach & T. Marek (eds) *Professional Burnout: Recent Developments in Theory and Research*. Washington, DC: Taylor & Francis, pp. 33–51.

Pines, A.M. (1996) *Couple Burnout: Causes and Cures*. New York: Routledge.

Pines, A. & Aronson, E. (1981) *Burnout: From Tedium to Personal Growth*. New York: Free Press.

Pines, A. & Aronson, E. (1983) Combating burnout. *Children and Youth Services Review*, **5**, 263–75.

Pines, A. & Aronson, E. (1988) *Career Burnout: Causes and Cures*. New York: Free Press.

Pines, A. & Kafry, D. (1978) Occupational tedium in the social services. *Social Work*, **23**, 499–507.

Pines, A. & Kafry, D. (1982) Coping with burnout. In J.W. Jones (ed.) *The Burnout Syndrome*: Current Research, Theory, Interventions. Park Ridge, IL: London House, pp. 139–50.

Pines, A. & Maslach, C. (1978) Characteristics of staff burn-out in mental health settings. *Hospital and Community Psychiatry*, **29**, 233–7.

Pines, A. & Maslach, C. (1980) Combating staff burnout in a day care setting: a case study. *Child Quarterly*, **9**, 5–16.

Pines, A.M., Aronson, E. & Kafry, D. (1981) *Burnout: From Tedium to Personal Growth*. New York: Free Press.

Pruessner, J., Hellhammer, D.H. & Kirschbaum, C. (1999) Burnout, perceived stress and salivary cortisol upon awakening. *Psychosomatic Medicine*, **61**, 197–204.

Rosse, J.G., Boss, R.W., Johnson, A.E. & Crown, D. F. (1991) Conceptualizing the role of self-esteem in the burnout process. *Group and Organization Studies*, **16**, 428–51.

Rountree, B.H. (1984) Psychological burnout in task groups. *Journal of Health and Human Resources Administration*, **7**, 235–48.

Royal Colleges of Physicians, Psychiatrists and General Practitioners (1996) *Chronic Fatigue Syndrome*. London: Royal Colleges of Physicians, Psychiatrists and General Practitioners.

Schachter, S. (1959) *The Psychology of Affiliation*. Palo Alto, CA: Stanford University Press.

Schaufeli, W.B. (1995) The evaluation of a burnout workshop for community nurses. *Journal of Health and Human Services Administration*, **18**, 11–31.

Schaufeli, W.B. & Enzmann, D. (1998) *The Burnout Companion to Study and Research: A Critical Analysis*. London: Taylor & Francis.

Schaufeli, W.B. & Peeters, M.C.W. (2000) Job stress and burnout among correctional officers: a literature review. *International Journal of Stress Management*, **7**, 19–48.

Schaufeli, W.B. & Van Dierendonck, D. (1993) The construct validity of two burnout measures. *Journal of Organizational Behavior*, **14**, 631–47.

Schaufeli, W.B. & Van Dierendonck, D. (1995) A cautionary note about the cross-national and clinical validity of cut-off points for the Maslach Burnout Inventory. *Psychological Reports*, **76**, 1083–90.

Schaufeli, W.B. & Van Dierendonck, D. (2000) *Handleiding van de Utrechtse Burnout Schaal (UBOS)* [Test manual Utrecht Burnout Scale—UBOS]. Lisse: Swets & Zeitlinger.

Schaufeli, W.B., Leiter, M.P., Maslach, C. & Jackson, S.E. (1996a) The MBI—General Survey. In C. Maslach, S.E. Jackson & M. Leiter (eds) *Maslach Burnout Inventory*, 3rd edn. Palo Alto, CA: Consulting Psychologists Press, pp. 19–26.

Schaufeli, W.B., Van Dierendonck, D. & Van Gorp, K. (1996b) Burnout and reciprocity: towards a dual-level social exchange model. *Work and Stress*, **3**, 225–37.

Schaufeli, W.B., Bakker, A., Hoogduin, C.A.L., Schaap, C. & Kladler, A. (2001) On the clinical validity of the Maslach Burnout Inventory and the Burnout Measure. *Psychology and Health*. **16**, 565–82.

Schutte, N., Toppinnen, S., Kalimo, R. & Schaufeli, W.B. (2000) The factorial validity of the Maslach Burnout Inventory—General Survey (MBI-GS) across nations and occupations. *Journal of Occupational and Organizational Psychology*, **73**, 53–66.

Schwartz, M.S. & Will, G.T. (1953) Low morale and mutual withdrawal on a hospital ward. *Psychiatry*, **16**, 337–53.

Shirom, A. (1989) Burnout in work organizations. In C.L. Cooper & I. Robertson (eds) *International Review of Industrial and Organizational Psychology*. New York: John Wiley & Sons, pp. 25–48.

Söderfeldt, M., Söderfeldt, B., Warg, L.E. & Ohlson, C.-G. (1996) The factor structure of the Maslach Burnout Inventory in two Swedish human service organization. *Scandinavian Journal of Psychology*, **37**, 437–43.

Spicuzza, F.J. & De Voe, M.W. (1982) Burnout in the helping professions: mutual aid groups as self help. *The Personnel and Guidance Journal*, **61**, 95–9.

Van der Klink, J.J.L., Blonk, R.W.B., Schene, A.H. & Van Dijk, F.J.H. (2001) The benefits of interventions for work related stress. *American Journal of Public Health*, **91**, 270–6.

Van Dierendonck, D., Schaufeli, W.B. & Buunk, B.P. (1998) The evaluation of an individual burnout intervention program: the role of inequity and social support. *Journal of Applied Psychology*, **83**, 392–407.

Van Dierendonck, D., Schaufeli, W.B. & Buunk, A.P. (2001) Burnout and inequity among human services providers: a longitudinal study. *Journal of Occupational Health Psychology*, **6**, 43–52.

Van Horn, J.E., Schaufeli, W.B., Greenglass, E.R. & Burke, R.J. (1997) A Canadian–Dutch comparison of teachers' burnout. *Psychological Reports*, **81**, 371–82.

Van Yperen, N.W. (1996) Communal orientation and the burnout syndrome among nurses: a replication and extension. *Journal of Applied Social Psychology*, **26**, 338–54.

Van Yperen, N.W., Buunk, A.P. and Schaufeli, W.B. (1992) Imbalance, communal orientation and the burnout syndrome among nurses. *Journal of Applied Social Psychology*, **22**, 173–89.

Wade, D.C., Cooley, E. and Savicki, V. (1986) A longitudinal study of burnout. *Children and Youth Services Review*, **8**, 161–73.

Walster, E., Walster, G.W. & Berscheid, E. (1978) *Equity: Theory and Research*. Boston, MA: Allyn & Bacon.

Warr, P.B. (1987) *Work, Unemployment and Mental Health*. Oxford: Clarendon Press.

West, D.J., Horan, J.J. & Games, P.A. (1984) Component analysis of occupational stress inoculation applied to registered nurses in an acute care hospital setting. *Journal of Consulting Psychology*, **31**, 209–18.

Westman, M. & Etzion, D. (1995). Crossover of stress, strain and resources from one spouse to another. *Journal of Organizational Behavior*, **16**, 169–81.

Williams, C.A. (1989) Empathy and burnout in male and female helping professionals. *Research in Nursing and Health*, **12**, 169–78.

Wills, T.A. (1991). Similarity and self-esteem in social comparison. In J. Suls & T.A. Wills (eds) *Social Comparison. Contemporary Theory and Research*. Hillsdale, NJ: Lawrence Erlbaum, pp. 51–78.

Wolpin, J. (1986) Psychological burnout among Canadian teachers: A longitudinal study, PhD thesis, York University, Toronto.

PART IV

Preventive and Curative Interventions

CHAPTER 20

Job Design and Well-Being

Michiel Kompier
University of Nijmegen, The Netherlands

20.1 INTRODUCTION

The focus of this chapter is on the design of the psychosocial work environment. First, seven important theoretical approaches in the field of stress and well-being, job satisfaction and job design are characterized in order to find the factors in work that affect stress and psychological well-being. We restrict ourselves to those factors that are related to the job content—that is, the job itself, including its functional and social contacts, i.e. the field of "psychosocial factors" (Johnson & Johansson, 1991; Levi, 1987). While doing so, however, we should bear in mind that these are not the only factors in the working situation that may cause psychological harm. There is much evidence that poor physical working conditions affect the experience of stress and the psychological and physical health of employees (Cox et al., 2000; Warr, 1992). Noise, for example, can act as a physical and psychological stimulus (Evans & Johnson, 2000; Smith, 1991). In addition to auditory health effects such as impaired hearing capacity, noise may produce non-auditory effects, such as fatigue, the experience of stress, and impaired performance. Apart from direct "physical" effects, working conditions may cause stress because they may hinder employees in performing their tasks or because they cause fear in employees, e.g. for infections or radiation.

There is also ample evidence that factors in the terms of employment and with respect to the social relations at work may exert a negative influence on (mental) health (Cox et al., 2000; Levi, 1984; Scheuch & Schreinicke, 1989). Examples of the first category are precarious employment, system of remuneration, shiftwork, work and rest schedules, and poor career prospects. Poor leadership, bad management style and low support are examples of the latter category. For a thorough discussion of how, i.e. by what potential pathways and mechanisms, physical and psychosocial elements of the work environment may interrelate to affect human health, we refer to Evans et al. (1994).

There are at least seven theoretical approaches that offer relevant information with respect to the requirements of well-designed "healthy" work:

1. The job characteristics model (JCM)
2. The Michigan organization stress (MOS) model
3. The job demands–control model (DC)

The Handbook of Work and Health Psychology. Edited by M.J. Schabracq, J.A.M. Winnubst and C.L. Cooper.
© 2003 John Wiley & Sons, Ltd.

4. The sociotechnical (ST) approach
5. The action-theoretical (AT) approach
6. The effort–reward imbalance (ERI) model
7. The vitamin model (VM)

Each of these seven approaches will be characterized by discussing (i) its content—that is, the way it relates job characteristics to stress and/or well-being and/or job satisfaction—(ii) its level of analysis (task, position, group or organization), (iii) possible principles of job (re)design, and (iv) its empirical status and (methodological) criticisms (Section 20.2).

In the next three sections, attention shifts from theory and research to policy and practice. The focus in Section 20.3 is on the legal aspects of the design of the psychosocial work environment, as these are part of national and European legislation on working conditions. Examples are given of two countries with prominent legislation with respect to job design and well-being. Section 20.4 discusses the extent to which occupational stress prevention programmes incorporate these theoretical and legal requirements with respect to job design and psychological well-being. Section 20.5 is directed at the implementation of effective job stress intervention programmes and at those process factors that can make (re)design of the psychosocial work environment successful.

20.2   WELL-DESIGNED JOBS: SEVEN THEORETICAL APPROACHES

20.2.1   The Job Characteristics Model

In the 1960s motivational problems arose in industrial and other work settings, due to an increasing imbalance between, on one hand, employee educational levels and employee participation needs and, on the other hand, traditional concepts of organization and control. Against this background, the job characteristics model was developed. It relates characteristics of the job content to the motivation and satisfaction of (individual) employees. Pioneering work was done by Turner & Lawrence (1965). They defined six job characteristics, which were measured independently of the employee: variety (e.g. in speed of work and in working aids), autonomy (e.g. with respect to the working method), required interaction (required contacts), optional interaction (both at the workplace and outside), knowledge and skill, and responsibility.

Based on this early study and the work of, among others, Hackman & Lawler (1971), Hackman & Oldham (1975, 1976, 1980) defined the JCM (Figure 20.1). It describes the relations between "core job dimensions", "critical psychological states", and some personal and work outcomes, such as motivation, job satisfaction, employee work effectiveness, absenteeism and turnover. Also, some individual moderator variables, such as the growth need of the employee, are part of the model.

With the JCM as their theoretical framework, Hackman & Oldham (1975) developed the job diagnostic survey (JDS) for job analysis. The target for analysis is a group of jobs or positions. Individual data are aggregated at the group level. This questionnaire is not meant for the diagnosis of individual jobs. Hackman & Oldham (1980) developed five principles with regard to the (re)design of tasks: (i) combining tasks, (ii) the formation of "natural" work units, (iii) the formation of a client-centred structure, (iv) job enrichment

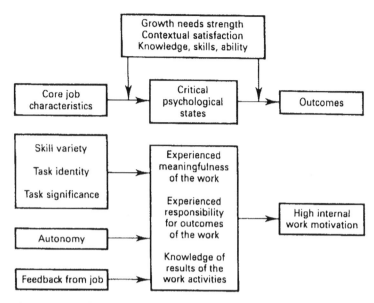

Figure 20.1   The job characteristics model. Adapted from Hackman & Oldham (1976, p. 256)

and (v) creating feedback channels. There is no detailed design theory. An early review of JCM-inspired job redesign studies was published by Richard Kopelman (1985).

Algera (1991) summarizes various critical reviews of empirical research around the JCM (Algera, 1989; Fried & Ferris, 1987; Roberts & Glick, 1981). He mentions several short-comings. A first point relates to its theoretical basis (number of core dimensions, nature and causality of its relations). A second point relates to the operationalization of the concepts that are measured. Third, he questions the extent to which questionnaires measure "objective" task characteristics or merely perceptions (see also Ilgen & Hollenbeck, 1991). In general, these points also relate to the Michigan organizational stress model (see Section 20.2.2). Despite these criticisms, there exists an impressive literature that relates the dependent variables motivation and satisfaction to (combinations of) five core job dimensions. These five job characteristics are: (i) skill variety (the degree to which a job requires a variety of different activities, requiring the use of a number of different skills and abilities), (ii) task identity (the degree to which a job requires completion of a whole and identifiable piece of work), (iii) task significance (the importance of the job), (iv) autonomy (the degree to which the job provides substantial freedom, independence and discretion in scheduling the work and in determining work procedures) and (v) feedback (from the job itself and from others).

Some of these variables are also included in the Michigan organizational stress model, in the job demands–control model, and in the vitamin model (see also Section 20.2.8).

20.2.2   The Michigan Organizational Stress Model

In stress research, the MOS model (Caplan et al., 1975; Kahn et al., 1964) has been very influential. It offers a framework for the (causal) relations between stressors and stress reactions and the moderating influence of personality characteristics and social support.

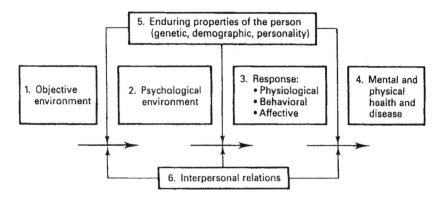

Figure 20.2 The Michigan organizational stress model. Reproduced from French & Kahn (196, p. 2) by permission of the Society for the Psychological Study of Social Issues

This approach is also known as the "role-stress approach", due to the central position of the concepts of role conflict, role ambiguity and role expectations. Its emphasis is not on the "objective" environment, as for instance in the model of Karasek (Section 20.2.3), but on the environment as it is perceived by the employee. Stressors in this "subjective environment" are role ambiguity, role conflict, lack of participation, responsibility for others, job future ambiguity, workload, tension in relations, and under-utilization of skills and abilities. A first basic version of this model is shown in Figure 20.2.

Data are often collected from individual employees, mostly by means of questionnaires. These individual data are then aggregated at a group level, which is the primary unit of analysis.

This model is primarily of an explanatory nature. A design theory is lacking. Still, it provides several indications for (re)design, pointing at the importance of participation, skill utilization, responsibility, feedback, task identity and social support. Empirical support for the model is strong as far as relations between perceived work characteristics and stress reactions are concerned (see also Chapter 4). The empirical support for the relations between the other boxes in the model is weaker. A criticism towards the application of this model is that often too little attention is paid to the "objective" work environment, and that stress is seen too much as a subjective individual phenomenon (Karasek & Theorell, 1990; Kompier et al., 1990). Accordingly, when it comes to stress prevention, the emphasis is often directed at recruitment policies, personnel selection and improving coping behaviours, and not so much at changing the work environment in order to make it less stressful.

20.2.3   The Job Demands–Control Model

In occupational health psychology, the job demands–control model is the most influential stress model at the moment. The model, developed by Robert Karasek (1979) and expanded by Karasek & Theorell (1990) and Karasek (1998), builds upon (criticisms of) the JCM and MOS approaches, from which several concepts have been borrowed. In its original format, the model defines two independent dimensions of stress risks: psychological demands and decision latitude. Decision latitude is also labelled as job control, which is a combination of task authority and skill discretion.

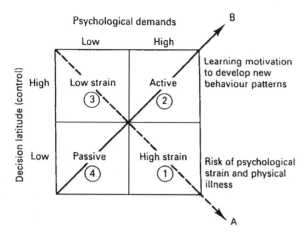

Figure 20.3 Job demands–control model. Reproduced from Karasek (1979) by permission of Cornell University

Stimulated by Johnson (1986) and Johnson & Hall (1988), the original two-dimensional model was adapted by Karasek & Theorell (1990). As a third dimension, "social support" was added. This expanded version is also known as the demands–control–support (DCS) model. Despite his criticism of more cognitive and person-based stress theories, Karasek (1998) acknowledges that person-based perceptions are an important part of the process by which environments affect individuals. He also acknowledges that there are long-term differences in personal responses to environments. Therefore, a "time dynamic, integrated environment and person-based" version of the DC model was also developed (Karasek, 1998). This enlarged version integrates environmental effects with person-based phenomena such as self-esteem development and long-term exhaustion. In this chapter, we will restrict ourselves to the core of the model, as depicted in Figure 20.3.

The model predicts that stress-related health problems increase, depending on the increase of job demands and the decrease of job control (and social support). This hypothesis, the strain hypothesis (cf. dis-stress) is reflected by diagonal A in Figure 20.3. High-strain work is characterized by a combination of high psychological demands and low job control (and low support).

The model also predicts that, when both job demands and job control (and social support) increase, work becomes more challenging and provides more opportunities for learning and developing one's abilities (cf. eu-stress). Diagonal B in Figure 20.3 reflects this second "learning" or "active–passive" hypothesis.

Individually collected data are aggregated at group level. The unit of analysis is often a homogeneous group of jobs or positions.

Although a detailed design theory and redesign strategy is lacking, clearly several several principles for job (re)design have been deduced from the model: preventing demands from becoming too excessive, increasing control and increasing support. It is also emphasized that employees should be provided with opportunities for learning. In their theorizing, Karasek & Theorell explicitly relate redesigning to the productivity of organization. This is also illustrated by the title of their book *Healthy Work. Stress, Productivity, and the Reconstruction of Working Life* (1990). Theorell (1998) summarizes the yet limited but increasing evidence that the demand–control–support model may be used successfully in job redesign (see also Ganster, 1995; Kristensen, 1995). In doing so, he also points at the need for "local" and more focused information specific to the examined organization (Theorell, 1998, p. 215) and the potential impact of contextual variables (see also Section 20.5).

Studies into the DC(S) model can roughly be divided into (i) epidemiological studies in multi-occupation groups, (ii) cross-sectional studies in homogeneous or heterogeneous groups, (iii) psychophysiological studies and (iv) intervention studies (De Jonge & Kompier, 1997). Epidemiological studies offer the most support for the DCS model, and for the strain hypothesis (diagonal A in Figure 20.3) in particular. Schnall et al. (1994) and Kristensen (1995) published reviews with cardiovascular diseases as outcome variables. In a recent review of 51 studies on the DC(S) model in relation to physical health outcomes, Van der Doef & Maes (1998) not only studied these cardiovascular health outcomes but also other indicators of physical health. Overall, with respect to cardiovascular diseases, the strain hypothesis of the DC(S) model receives substantial support. Firm conclusions on other physical outcomes, such as musculoskeletal symptoms and general (psycho)somatic complaints seem premature, considering the limited number of studies in these areas. In a second review of 63 studies in the period 1979–1997, Van der Doef & Maes (1999) examined the relations between combinations of demands, control and support and psychological well-being (general psychological well-being, job-related well-being and job satisfaction, burnout, job-related psychological well-being). It can be concluded, that, all in all, these studies provide considerable support for the strain hypothesis.

Several authors have made critical comments with respect to the content and methodology of the DCS model (see, for example, De Jonge & Kompier, 1997; Kasl, 1996; Kristensen, 1995). Here we will restrict ourselves to two critical issues: (i) the under-utilization of the learning or active–passive hypothesis, and (ii) the existence of curvilinear instead of linear relationships. One core assumption of the model, the learning or active–passive hypothesis (see Figure 20.3), has received remarkably little attention in the job stress literature (De Jonge & Kompier, 1997; Karasek, 1998). This is regrettable. As a result, the empirical basis under this hypothesis is still rather small. Referring to the second issue, the DCS model presupposes linear relationships. This assumption is not without problem. Warr (1990, 1994), for example, has pointed out that not only too little decision latitude, but also too much of it can lead to strain. As a result, the relationship might be (inverted) U-shaped (see also Section 20.2.7).

In conclusion, there is substantial empirical evidence for the model, although mainly for the strain hypothesis. Furthermore, the attraction of the DC(S) model is primarily in its simplicity and in its emphasis on structural characteristics of the working environment, as "objective" determinants of stress.

20.2.4 The Sociotechnical Approach

Classical sociotechnics is rooted in the Tavistock Institute of Human Relations in London. Its pioneers (among others, Trist and Bamforth, Emery, Miller and Rice) were committed to rebuilding the post-war society by combining economic profits and industrial democracy. Their work was founded in the open systems approach. The aim of the work reconstruction experiments (up until the 1970s) was the joint optimization of two system components in organizations: the technical and the social system. The working group is the main target of classical sociotechnics. Therefore, its scope was somewhat restricted (Kuipers, 1989).

In modern sociotechnics, the total organization is the unit of analysis (De Sitter, 1989). Its aim is the reconstruction of work organizations in order to cope effectively with modern demands like flexibility, order control, product quality, innovative capacity, and the quality of working life (Kuipers & Van Amelsvoort, 1990). The nucleus of modern sociotechnics stress theory is that insufficient job control is the most important stress risk. Stress risks and opportunities for learning are depending on the company's structure of the division of labour. In this respect, the theory heavily leans upon Karasek's DC model.

Modern sociotechnics is a typical design theory. Cherns (1976, 1987) was one of the first who offered a set of principles of sociotechnical design. Against the background of the work of Cherns, Clegg (2000) formulated a set of sociotechnical principles to guide system design, and some considerations of the role of these principles. The principles are for use by system managers, users and designers, and by technologists and social scientists.

The sociotechnical approach is directed at the "integral" reconstruction of the total production organization. Minimal division of labour is its leading principle (Kuipers, 1989). This puts the theory in diametric opposition to the classical theory of Frederick Taylor (1911), with its vigorous division between mental work and manual work. The building blocks of new organizations are working groups with a (semi-)autonomous status.

The empirical position of the sociotechnical approach is not very strong. This is partly due to its "integral objectives", which make it difficult to test empirically. To date a well-documented review and meta-analysis of important case studies and experiments is not available. Critical remarks with respect to the sociotechnical approach point at its preference for (mass) production branches of industry, its preference for the autonomous group as a "standard solution" and its conception of job control as "never enough" (cf. our discussion of U-shaped relations between control and health outcomes; see also Section 20.2.7). Furthermore, sociotechnics deals with the formal organization structure and does not pay much attention to the informal ("real") organization, nor to aspects of organizational culture or individual preferences of employees.

20.2.5 The Action-Theoretical Approach

In Germany, work psychology is not just seen as a descriptive science of work behaviour, but as a prescriptive science that should contribute to work design (Frese & Zapf, 1994). To justify design work, German-speaking work psychology has developed an action theory. Central variables in this theory are the completeness of action (*vollstandige Tätigkeit*), the increase of regulation requirements, the increase of control (*Handlungsspielraum*; Semmer, 1984; Ulich, 1972), the reduction of regulation problems, and the concept of personality enhancement (*Personlichkeitsforderlichkeit der Arbeit*; Hacker, 1984, 1986; Volpert, 1989). According to this theory, the essence of work is its goal-directed behaviour: the ultimate purpose of work is to produce a product or service. A goal constitutes a set-point to which action outcomes are compared. The core of action is the feedback cycle (Volpert, 1971). The theory describes an action process, consisting of goals, information integration, plans, monitoring and feedback (Frese & Zapf, 1994). In addition, action regulation is hierarchically structured (Hacker, 1973; Semmer & Frese, 1985). There are four levels of regulation: (i) the sensorimotor level (largely unconscious, automatic information processing), (ii) the flexible patterns level (ready-made action programmes, rule based), (iii) the intellectual level (controlled information processing, complex analyses, new solutions) and (iv) the heuristic level ("metacognitive heuristics", abstract reasoning). Action theory promotes completeness of action (Hacker, 1985). This implies that work is designed well (i) when it provides opportunities to the worker to carry out all steps in the action process (goal setting, plan development, plan decision making, monitoring and feedback processes), and (ii) when all levels of regulation are used. When an employee can regulate his or her actions "automatically" (e.g. at an assembly line), the action is not complete, indicating poor job design. Also, when an employee has to spend all of his or her time trying to find solutions for very complicated problems (intellectual and heuristic levels), the action is incomplete.

Based on action theory, various job analysis instruments have been developed in order to be able to design and change workplaces. These instruments claim to measure objective rather than subjective representations of work characteristics (Frese & Zapf, 1994). They have several characteristics in common: (i) they are related to the objective environment; (ii) they are based on the concept of the ideal typical ("average") worker; (iii) they make use of "observational interviews", in which the observer, who is familiar with the underlying theory, both observes the work actions and asks questions to understand his or her observations; and (iv) they do not deal with individual qualities and inter-individual differences of employees. One of these instruments is VERA (*Verfahren zur Ermittlung von Regulationserfordernissen in der Arbeitswelt*), which identifies regulation requirements in work. Two other instruments are RHIA (*Regulationshindernisse in der Arbeitstätigkeit*), an instrument to identify regulation problems in industrial work, and TBS (*Tätigkeitsbewertungssystem*), an instrument for evaluating the chances for personality enhancement in a job (see Frese & Zapf, 1994, for a characterization of these three instruments).

The instruments mentioned above can be used to analyse single jobs. In action theory, the unit of analysis is primarily the job, consisting of various tasks. According to action theory the following principles are important for job design:

- work should allow employees to choose their own work strategy;
- work should encompass complete actions (see above);
- outside events that do not belong to the task (obstacles and interruptions often stemming from poor work organization) should be minimized;
- people should be allowed to be active in their work;
- people need control because control helps them to act more adequately, choosing appropriate strategies to deal with the situation;
- well-designed jobs need well-qualified workers;
- qualifications can only be upheld if work has a certain complexity;
- work should provide feedback.

Furthermore, action theory stresses the importance of strong relationships between job design and the engineering sciences, like machine construction and computer sciences.

The empirical basis of action theory is still restricted (Roe & Zijlstra, 1991). According to Frese & Zapf (1994), "Action theory has not been clearly defined or as well tested as some cognitive theories. At times action theorists seem to have been content with being able to use a concept in the field rather than to verify it independently".

However, the amount of empirical research is increasing. One of the main advantages of this theory is its clear emphasis on job redesign.

20.2.6 The Effort–Reward Imbalance Model

The concept of (lack of) reciprocity from equity theory inspired German medical sociologist Johannes Siegrist and his co-workers. Their ERI model's starting point is that effort at work is spent as part of a socially organized exchange process, in which this effort is (or is not) compensated by occupational rewards. These rewards are distributed by three transmitter systems: money, esteem (cf. social support) and career opportunities, including job security. The central hypothesis of the ERI model is that lack of reciprocity between costs and gains (i.e. high-cost/low-gain conditions) defines a state of emotional disstress with special propensity to autonomic arousal and associated strain reactions (Siegrist, 1996, 1998). Two sources of effort are distinguished: (i) an extrinsic source, the demands on the job, and (ii) an intrinsic source, the motivations of the individual worker in a demanding situation (Peter et al., 1998). The extrinsic source strongly resembles the concept of job demands in the DC model. The intrinsic source has been given several labels: "need for control" (Peter et al., 1998), "critical coping" (Siegrist 1998), "immersion" (Peter et al., 1998; Siegrist, 1998) and "overcommitment" (Siegrist, 2000). Siegrist (1998) explains how this person-specific component evolved from a critical analysis of the rather global pattern of Type A behaviour.

Empirical evidence for the ERI model is increasing. In various cross-sectional and prospective studies it has been demonstrated that employees whose working situation is characterized by the combination of high effort and low reward are at higher risk for cardiovascular health, sickness absence and subjective health complaints (e.g. De Jonge et al., 2000; Marmot et al., 1999; Siegrist, 1996, 1998, 2000; Siegrist et al., 1990). So far, empirical evidence suggests that the ERI model provides a fruitful framework for examining work stress and its contribution to the development of physical and psychological disease.

As with most other discussed models, various comments can be made and questions formulated with regard to its conceptualization and methodology. A first point relates to the ratio that usually is calculated in ERI data analyses between a sum score of items measuring effort (nominator) and a sum score of items measuring reward (denominator) (Siegrist, 1998). When effort is high and rewards are high, this effort–reward (ER) ratio is 1. When effort and reward are both low, the ER ratio is also 1. In data analysis both combinations (high–high, low–low) are treated as if they fit the same category. One might, however, question whether it makes theoretical sense that the model poses the same value for two "objectively" quite distinct work situations.

A second point is the way extrinsic and intrinsic scores are combined in one category, both in the nominator and in the denominator. For example, Siegrist & Peter (1994; also Siegrist, 1998) define a high effort condition as "immersion" (upper tertile of critical intrinsic effort as measured by "need for control") *and/or* "high work pressure". From a more theoretical point of view one might question how valid such an "and/or" category is. A third point relates to the conceptual lack of clarity of the personal characteristic of overcommitment. This variable seems to be primarily conceived as an independent variable in ERI research; that is, as a predictor, or as a moderating variable, influencing the relation between (extrinsic) effort and demands (Siegrist, 2000, p. 56), and stress outcomes. However, it may well be that this overcommitment is (also) a dependent variable; that is, an effect of (high) effort and (low) rewards. Therefore, one should be cautious in interpreting associations between overcommitment scores and indicators of stress, especially when self-reported (risk of spurious correlations; Kasl, 1987, p. 308). It may also be argued that the various and changing labels for the same dimension have not contributed to a clear conceptualization of this personality dimension.

ERI research has not developed a detailed (re)design theory, but the model clearly has some important (re)design principles (Marmot et al., 1999; Siegrist, 1998, 2000). The reduction of high-cost/low-gain situations includes actions at three levels: (i) the individual level (e.g. reduction of excessive need for control), (ii) the interpersonal level (e.g. improvement of esteem reward), and (iii) the structural level (e.g. adequate compensation, increased job security) (Marmot et al., 1999, p. 126).

As to the unity of analysis in ERI research, data are collected at individual level and analysed at group level.

20.2.7   The Vitamin Model

In thinking about employee well-being, according to Warr (1996), it is important to distinguish between three principal axes: (i) from displeasure to pleasure (e.g. job satisfaction), (ii) from anxiety to comfort (e.g. job-related anxiety), and (iii) from depression to enthusiasm (e.g. burnout, depression). These axes are significantly intercorrelated, but have partially different causes and outcomes (Warr, 1996). Warr (1987, 1994, 1996) identified nine main groups of job characteristics which may affect one or more of these three axes:

1. opportunity for personal control;
2. opportunity for skill use;
3. externally generated goals (job demands);
4. variety;
5. environmental clarity (feedback, job security);
6. opportunity for interpersonal contact (social support);
7. availability of money;
8. physical security (good working conditions);
9. valued social position (e.g. occupational prestige).

These characteristics include the five JCM factors as well as the main factors from the DC model (see also Section 20.2.8). Warr assumes that the first six job characteristics affect mental well-being in a curvilinear (inverted U-shaped) way, similar to the way AD vitamins may affect health. Very high levels of job autonomy, to give an example, are potentially harmful since they imply uncertainty, difficulty in decision making, and high responsibility on the job (Warr, 1987). The last three job characteristics (7–9) are supposed to follow a linear pattern (the way vitamins C and E affect health): the higher the job characteristic, the higher the level of mental well-being. Furthermore, Warr points at the role of personal characteristics and outside work factors in explaining differences in (work-related) mental well-being. The role of personality receives more attention in later expositions of the model (Foster, 2000). Warr (1996, p. 235) comments that "people's feelings about their work are thus a function both of that work itself and also of their own personality".

De Jonge & Schaufeli (1998) and Le Blanc et al. (2000) discuss empirical support for the vitamin model. Warr (1987, 1994) showed that his nine job characteristics do act as predicted in isolation. Taken together, the results of the few studies that have—partially—tested the VM are mixed and inconclusive (De Jonge & Schaufeli, 1998). Indeed, it has been demonstrated that job demands and job autonomy are curvilinearly related to some aspects of employee mental health (De Jonge & Schaufeli, 1998; Fletcher & Jones, 1993; Warr, 1990). A more comprehensive empirical test of the VM is yet lacking. Longitudinal studies have not been reported yet.

As to the unit of analysis, data are often collected at the individual level and analysed at the group level. Although there is no clear redesign theory, implications for designing and redesigning jobs are obvious. As Warr (1987, p. 298) states: "The vitamin model can provide a useful basis for determining the goals of intervention at the level of both the job and the organization". With respect to the first six job characteristics (AD factors), optimal levels should be neither too low nor too high. With respect to the last three job characteristics (CE factors), one should strive for high levels. To our knowledge, hardly any VM work redesign studies have been reported yet. One of the main strenghts of this model is its emphasis on potential curvilinear associations between job features and mental health.

20.2.8   Comparable Requirements with Respect to Tasks and Jobs

In the following subsections, the main similarities and dissimilarities of the seven theoretical approaches are summarized with respect to their content, level of analysis, design theory, and the amount of empirical support.

Content

All approaches define characteristics of the environment and the worker, and define the interaction between the environment and the worker. In identifying "critical job features", there is a remarkable overlap between these approaches, as is demonstrated in Table 20.1. This table identifies the main job characteristics (assumed situational determinants of job related well-being) in the seven theoretical approaches.

The most prominent job features are skill variety (six out of seven theories, not in ERI), autonomy (six out of seven theories, not in ERI) and job demands (six out of seven theories, not in JCM). As for skill variety, it is interesting to note that some theories conceive this concept in terms of job content (i.e. choose the perspective of the job, job variety), whereas other theories define this construct in terms of (under-)utilization of skills (i.e. choose the perspective of the person). Only in the vitamin model are both factors included separately. Social support (or strongly related concepts) is part of four theories (MOS, DC, ERI, VM). Feedback (or proxy constructs) is part of three theories (JCM, AT, VM). Task identity is also a component of three theoretical approaches: JCM, ST and AT. In the latter two theories the factor is not mentioned as such, but is part of a broader task requirement, namely minimal division of labour and "completeness of action", respectively. Job future ambiguity (or related constructs such as job security) is also part of three theories (MOS, ERI, VM; the latter theory uses the broader construct of environmental clarity, which includes both job insecurity and role ambiguity). Pay (money rewards, availability of money) as an aspect of terms of employment is an important factor in two theories (ERI, VM).

Despite these strong parallels, there are clear differences as well. The first difference relates to the emphasis on either the subjective appraisal of the environment or on the "objective (or collective) environment", i.e. relatively irrespective of the individual evaluation.

Table 20.1 Job design and well-being: main job characteristics in seven theoretical approaches

JCM	MOS	DC	ST	AT	ERI	VM
Skill variety	Underutilization of skills/abilities	Skill discretion	{ Minimal division of labour	{ Completeness of action	–	Opportunity for skill use, variety
Task identity	–	–			–	–
Task significance	Responsibility for others	–	–	–	–	Valued social position
Autonomy	Lack of participation	Task authority	Job control	Handlungsspielraum	–	Opportunity for personal control
Feedback	–	–	–	Feedback cycle	–	Environmental clarity
–	Workload	Job demands	Regulation problems	Regulation problems	Extrinsic effort	{ Externally generated goals
–	Role conflict	–	–	–	–	
–	Tension in relations	Social support	–	–	Esteem rewards	Opportunity for interpersonal contact
–	–	–	–	–	Money rewards	Availability of money
–	Job future ambiguity	–	–	–	Career opportunities (including job security)	{ Environmental clarity
–	Role ambiguity	–	–	–	–	
–	–	–	–	–	–	Physical security

The JCM and the MOS model emphasize perceptions and cognitions. These two models are more directed at the "subjective" individual. ST, DC, AT and VM emphasize the role of the environment. These four theories are more directed at the "objective" environment. The ERI model, with its emphasis on both extrinsic and intrinsic sources, holds an in-between position. The second difference relates to the role that personality factors are assumed to play. In JCM, MOS and ERI, personality is primarily taken as an independent variable. The DC model and AT more or less turn the issue around, in the sense that it is believed that work enhances personality. The DC model and AT in a way thus transform personality to (also) a dependent variable. The VM seems to combine both perspectives, whereas ST merely neglects the issue of individual differences and preferences.

Level of Analysis

In action theory, the scope is primarily on the analysis of single jobs and their various tasks. The other approaches aggregate individually collected data to a group level.

Design Theory

The most pronounced design principles are found in the sociotechnical approach and in action theory. The first approach defines the total production organization with its different jobs or positions as its target. Action theory chooses the job or the task as target. Design principles can be derived from the other approaches, but detailed intervention strategies and theories are generally lacking. One might add that, in view of the extensive literature that concentrates on job characteristic–mental health outcomes, surprisingly few theoretical and empirical studies have been performed in the field of interventions and job redesign (see Sections 20.4 and 20.5).

Empirical Support

The approaches under study refer to rather complex relations between task characteristics, personal characteristics and outcomes such as fatigue, job satisfaction, subjective health, sickness absenteeism and turnover. In this field there are many methodological pitfalls (Frese, 1985; Kasl, 1978, 1987; Kompier & Kristensen, 2000). Furthermore, it is difficult to perform well-designed studies in "ordinary" companies (Griffiths, 1999; Kompier & Kristensen, 2000). Most extensive studies have been performed around the JCM, the MOS model and the DC model. As a general conclusion it can be stated that substantial support has been found for all theories that have been described.

Despite the differences, it is remarkable that seven differing research schools, research traditions and research models, to a large extent, define comparable requirements for tasks and jobs. These can be summarized as follows (Gardell, 1981):

> Three factors seem to be at the core of work motivation and enjoyment of work: (a) influence in the job world and self-determination over work pace and working methods, (b) overview and meaningfulness in the working role and (c) cooperation and fellowship with other people. (p. 66)

> Work should be arranged in a way which allows the individual worker to influence his own working situation, working methods and pace. Work should be arranged in a way which allows for an overview and understanding of the work process as a whole. Work should be arranged in a way which gives the individual worker possibilities to use and develop all his human resources. Work should be arranged in a way that allows for human contacts and co-operation in the course of work. Work should be arranged in a way which makes it possible for the individual worker to satisfy time claims from roles and obligations outside work, e.g. family, social, and political commitments, etc. (p. 73)

These quotations can be regarded as the essence of diagnosis, of interventions and of prevention of stressful work: stimulating control (over work pace, among other things), meaningfulness and feedback, and cooperation at the workplace. Gardell also points out that the qualitative and quantitative workload should be in accordance with the possibilities and capacities of the employees. This means that, apart from optimizing the work organization, recruitment and training ("human resources management") are also important.

20.3   LEGAL REGULATIONS WITH RESPECT TO JOB DESIGN AND WELL-BEING

To a considerable extent, Gardell's conclusions are compatible with European legislation with respect to the psychosocial work environment. The most important regulation in this area is the European Framework Directive on Health and Safety at Work (89/391/EEC), which came into force on 1st January 1993. Although stress and well-being at work as such are not elements that are central to the Framework Directive, it is quite clear that this directive does apply to psychosocial job design and work-related well-being (see also Levi, 2000).

This framework states, among other things, that the employer has:

> a duty to ensure the safety and health of workers in every aspect related to the work, following general principles of prevention:
>
> - avoiding risks;
> - evaluating the risks which cannot be avoided;
> - combating the risks at the source;
> - adapting the work to the individual, especially as regards the design of work places, the choice of work equipment and the choice of work and production methods, with a view, in particular, to alleviating monotonous work and work at a predetermined work rate and to reducing their effects on health;
> - developing a coherent overall prevention policy which covers technology, organisation of work, working conditions, social relationships and the influence of factors related to the working environment.

As Lennart Levi (2000, p. 28) concludes, "clearly 'avoiding risks', 'combating the risks at the source', and 'adapting the work to the individual' all relate to primary prevention". It is also clear that the formulation "in every aspect related to the work" includes the psychosocial work environment. In addition, Levi (2000) draws attention to the European Commission's (1996) Guidance on "Risk assessment at work", which points out the need to review "psychological, social and physical factors which might contribute to stress at work, how they interact together and with other factors in the work organisation and environment". Also the European Parliament's Resolution A4-0050/99 (of 25 February 1999) takes this position (see also Levi, 2000). In this Resolution, the European Parliament, inter alia:

- considers that work must be adapted to people's abilities and needs and not vice-versa, and notes that by preventing a disparity from arising between the demands of work and the capacities of the workers, it is possible to retain employees until retirement age; considers that new technologies should be used in order to achieve these aims;
- urges the Commission to investigate the new problem areas which are not covered by current legislation: i.e. stress, burn-out, violence and the threat of violence by customers, and harassment at the workplace;
- notes that muscular-skeletal diseases and psycho-social factors constitute the greatest modern threat to worker's health;
- draws attention to the problems resulting from a lack of autonomy at the workplace, monotonous and repetitive work and work with a narrow variety of content, all features which are typical of women's work in particular, and calls attention to be paid to the importance of ergonomics to the improvement of health and safety conditions at the workplace;
- draws attention to the health and safety at work of groups which now largely fall outside the scope of legislative protection, such as home workers and the self-employed; and
- recommends the principle of safety management whereby the management of the risks of the working environment and development of the safety and welfare of workers are regarded as part of the normal activity of the workplace, and that this should be done in cooperation with the management and workforce.

In addition to this European legislation, several European countries have developed legislation with respect to the design of the psychosocial work environment (see also Kompier & Cooper, 1999; Kompier et al., 1994). For example, the Dutch Working Conditions Act states that (for more details, see Schaufeli & Kompier, 2001):

- The workplace, the working methods, the used tools, machines and appliances and other aids as well as the work content should—as far as may reasonably required—be in accordance with the personal characteristics of the employees;
- Monotonous and repetitive work should be avoided, as far as may reasonably required.

In Sweden, chapter 2, section 1 of the amended Work Environment Act (version 1, January 2001) is of special relevance to stress and well-being at work. This section states:

- Working conditions shall be adapted to people's differing physical and mental aptitudes.
- The employee shall be given the opportunity to participate in designing his own working situation and in processes of change and development affecting his work.
- Technology, work organization and job content shall be designed in such a way that the employee is not subjected to physical or mental strains which can lead to illness or accidents. Forms of remuneration and the distribution of working hours shall also be taken into account in this connection. Closely controlled or restricted work shall be avoided or limited.
- Efforts shall be made to ensure that work provides opportunities for variety, social contact and cooperation, as well as coherence between different working operations.
- Furthermore, efforts shall be made to ensure that working conditions provide opportunities for personal and vocational development, as well as for self-determination and professional responsibility.

Regulations in other nordic countries, for instance in Norway, resemble Swedish regulations.

20.3.1   The Mutual Relationships between Theory and Legal Requirements

Of course theoretical and legal developments have not taken place independently of each other. In Sweden, for instance, the work of scientists like Gardell and Levi, whose endeavour was and is to narrow the gap between theory and research on the one hand, and policy and practice on the other hand, has had an influential impact on legislation with respect to psychosocial factors at work. In the Netherlands, the legislation regarding psychological well-being has been formulated in accordance with the state of the art in this field and the political opportunities (Geurts et al., 2000; Schaufeli & Kompier, 2001). On the one hand, legislation has been influenced by theory. On the other hand, scientific approaches can benefit from practical in-company experiences and experiments, which are being based on this legislation.

20.4   DO STRESS PREVENTION PROGRAMMES BUILD UPON JOB DESIGN PREREQUISITES?

In this section, a framework for stress prevention and intervention is introduced and job (re)design is placed in this framework. Next, we will question to what extent stress prevention programmes incorporate central job design prerequisites as introduced in the previous sections.

Interventions may be directed at either the work environment (changing the work situation) or at the coping capacity of the employee (changing the individual). In the second place, interventions may be aimed at (i) eliminating, reducing or altering stressors in the working situation (primary prevention), or (ii) at preventing employees who are already showing signs of stress from getting sick and to increase their coping capacity (secondary prevention), or (iii) at treating those employees who show serious stress consequences and rehabilitation after sickness absenteeism (tertiary prevention). By combining these two axes, "changing work versus changing the person" and "eliminating risks versus preventing reactions from becoming worse", a conceptual framework can be developed that indicates four types of prevention and intervention (Figure 20.4).

Examples of measures in the first quadrant are changing the job content (job redesign), ergonomic improvements, the introduction of autonomous teams, new working and resting arrangements, career development activities, and increasing social support within the organization. For a recent overview of studies into such interventions we refer to Semmer (2002).

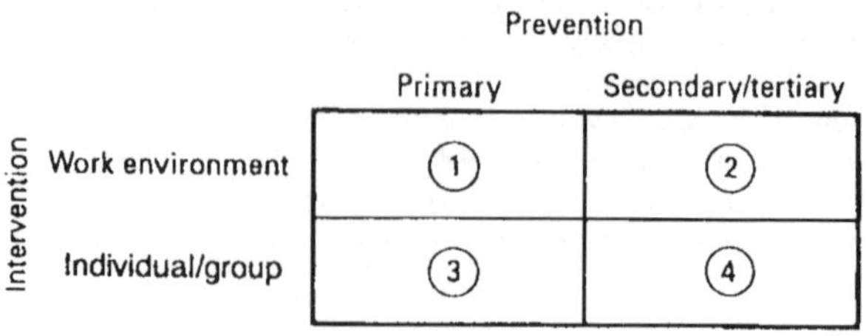

Figure 20.4   Framework for stress prevention and intervention

Examples of the second quadrant are comparable measures directed at those employees who already show signs of stress, for instance special work schedules for older employees or workers recovering from a long-term sickness spell. Examples of the third quadrant are selection, pre-employment medical examination, health promotion and wellness programmes, and training programmes. Examples of the fourth quadrant are rehabilitation after sick leave, post-traumatic stress assistance programmes, response- or symptom-directed techniques such as relaxation, and also psychotherapy. When compared to the more "collective" measures from quadrant 3, quadrant 4 measures are more "tailor-made". With the help of Figure 20.4, it is possible to search systematically for effective strategies against work stress. The model facilitates the systematic consideration of possible changes in the work situation and in the worker, and forces us to consider both "the healthy" and "the sick". We should keep in mind that the same type of intervention may fit into more than one quadrant. Sometimes a given intervention (e.g. the introduction of autonomous teams) may be seen as primary prevention for one person (who is healthy) and as secondary prevention for another person (who has stress-related health complaints) (Kompier & Kristensen, 2000).

It is obvious that job design and job redesign, when dealing with central task characteristics as discussed in the previous sections, primarily relate to the first quadrant in the framework presented in Figure 20.4. Also the working condition legislation described in Section 20.3 puts primacy on the first quadrant, that is prevention at the source.

The crucial question now is: "Do occupational stress prevention programmes also put primacy on prevention at the source?". The answer to this question is "no". Given the remarkable consensus in theories on the psychosocial work environment (Section 20.2), and given the legal emphasis on risk assessment and risk management ("rooting out the risks") (Section 20.3), one might expect a flourishing field of research into organizational-level stress interventions, i.e. studies that aim at changing work in order to make it less stressful and to increase well-being. This, however, is not the case. Unfortunately, there is a large gap between theory and practice, as follows from an overview of the past two decades in the field of work stress prevention. Based on the literature (see, for example, Cox, 1993; Cox et al., 2000; Cooper & Payne, 1988; DeFrank & Cooper, 1987; Kahn & Byosiere, 1992; Kompier et al., 1998; Murphy, 1986, 1996; Van der Hek & Plomp, 1997; Van der Klink et al., 2001), six interrelated conclusions may be drawn (see, for a more detailed discussion, Kompier & Kristensen, 2000):

1. Occupational stress is a rapidly expanding field and so is occupational stress management. There is a great deal of activity.
2. "This activity is concentrated disproportionally on reducing the effects, rather than reducing the presence of stressors at work" (Kahn & Byosiere, 1992, p. 623). In terms of the model depicted in Figure 20.4, stress interventions mainly constitute secondary and tertiary prevention, i.e. they are of a post hoc (reactive) nature, such as counselling of stressed employees, individual psychotherapy, relaxation or biofeedback. Primary prevention ("rooting out the risks"), and especially measures in the first quadrant in Figure 20.4, are scarce.
3. Related to this, the main target is the individual employee rather than the workplace or the organization. Most programmes aim at the reduction of the cognitive appraisal of stressors and their subsequent effects, rather than at the reduction or elimination of the stressors themselves. A worker-oriented approach (quadrants 3 and 4) prevails over a work-oriented approach (quadrants 1 and 2).

4. The majority of the programmes have a "one size fits all" character. Stress management programmes are often "off the shelf" programmes. Many practitioners offer sovereign remedies regardless of the presenting symptoms (Kahn & Byosiere, 1992). This stands in the way of a systematic risk assessment identifying risk factors and risk groups. Such a stress audit is often lacking in stress intervention studies.

5. There is a lack of evaluation research, and of strong designs in evaluation research. Many interventions are not evaluated in a systematic way, and, in case of evaluations, study designs are often characterized by serious methodological flaws.

6. Finally, the role of contextual and process variables, such as the introduction and implementation of measures, receives insufficient attention in evaluation research and in the literature.

Given this somewhat disappointing present status of the core of stress intervention research, it is still hard to provide clear and "evidence-based" answers to questions such as: Under what circumstances does organizational stress prevention work? Which components are effective? Why and how, i.e. through which psychological mechanisms, do they work? What are the intended and unintended side effects? What are the costs and benefits? What are the stimulating and obstructing factors?

This present status has been well summarized by Cox and colleagues (2000, p. 73):

> There is an obvious need to encourage theoretically exciting and methodologically adequate research in this area of practice. The main problems, which again are widely recognized, relate to: the lack of application of theory to practice, the lack of a framework for practice, the lack of adequately designed and meaningful evaluation studies, and the lack of balance between the number of individually—and organizationally—focused interventions.

In their thorough review of the research on work-related stress, including the evidence on the effectiveness of stress management interventions, Cox and colleagues draw two important conclusions (Cox et al., 2000, pp. 10–11):

> First there is a wealth of scientific data on work stress, its causes and effects, and some of the mechanisms underpinning the relationships among these. *More general research is not needed* [M.K.'s emphasis]. What is required is an answer to the outstanding methodological questions, and to more specific questions about particular aspects of the overall stress process and its underpinning mechanisms. Second, although this wealth of scientific data exists, it still needs to be translated into practice, and the effectiveness of this practice evaluated. This is another set of needs, and one that will only be settled outside the laboratory and through the development of consensus and eventually common practice.

20.5 INTERVENTIONS

20.5.1 Studying Examples of good Preventive Practice

One of the ways to contribute to answering the questions "How well, why and when do stress prevention programmes work?" is to study examples of (good) preventive practice. Kompier & Kristensen (2000) argue that such multiple case studies may constitute an adequate research strategy for several reasons:

1. They may provide an alternative to the "true experimental approach", which, for both practical and theoretical reasons, is hard to realize in "real companies" (see also Griffiths, 1999), and to the great majority of cross-sectional questionnaire studies with very limited evidence regarding the causal role of work characteristics for health outcomes (Kasl, 1978).
2. They may function as alternatives to many of the post hoc individual-biased studies that now dominate the literature on work stress interventions.
3. They may provide information on the role of contextual and process factors in stress prevention programmes.
4. Finally, there is the argument of "the power of the good example".

A multiple case study approach is an adequate research strategy "when how and why questions are being posed, when the investigator has little control over events, and when the focus is on a contemporary phenomenon within some real-life context" (Yin, 1994, p. 1). In this respect, occupational stress is the contemporary phenomenon, and the organization is the "real-life context", in which stress researchers are guests with restricted "control over events". In multiple case studies, research data can be treated cumulatively. Multiple cases should be considered as multiple experiments or multiple surveys (i.e. follow a replication logic), instead of as multiple respondents in a survey (Yin, 1994). Since 1990, research in this field has been increasing (Burke, 1993; Karasek, 1992; Kompier et al., 1998, 2000a, b; Semmer, 2002).

To illustrate this approach, we shall summarize the three studies of Kompier et al. A total of 30 case studies were analysed in these reports: 9 in the Netherlands (1998), 12 international intervention projects in bus companies (2000a) and 9 European cases in stress prevention (2000b). The cases cover a wide range of branches of industry and include small, medium-sized and large companies. Each case received a research design rating, according to a procedure proposed by Murphy (1996). One study had a randomized control group, five studies a control group without randomization. The other 24 studies included an intervention and evaluation, but lacked a control group. Each study was analysed in a step by step approach. In the first step (preparation) the motives for starting these projects were studied. The most common motives related to high sickness absence figures, the prevention of health problems, the aim to improve both work and productivity, and shortages at the labour market. Obviously, there were both "internal" motives (e.g. health problems, sickness absenteeism) and "external" motives, i.e. motives in the context of the organization, such as the goal to be an attractive employer.

From the second step (analysis), it appears that these organizations often used a combination of more simple instruments, such as checklists and interviews, and more "professional" instruments, such as instruments for task analysis. Larger organizations often used questionnaires to identify risk factors and risk groups, and analysed administrative data (sickness absenteeism, working overtime, work disability). In many cases, a combination of instruments and a type of benchmarking were used: companies or departments compared their scores with those of comparable organizations to define their relative position.

The most important interventions (step 3) from these 30 projects can be divided into three categories (the number in brackets relates to the number of cases with this type of measure). The first category comprises work-directed measures (quadrants 1 and 2 in Figure 20.4): work redesign (16; e.g. job enrichment, work planning, team-based work), ergonomics and technology (14), social work environment and management style (14), and work time schedules (10).

The second category comprises person-directed measures (quadrants 3 and 4 in Figure 20.4): training employees (17), promoting a healthy lifestyle (9) and training of management (6). The last category "Other measures", includes among others things better registration of sickness absences and managing the sickness absence reports (7).

From the fourth step, implementation, it appears that most organizations have chosen to integrate the interventions in the regular company and management structure. This implies that (line) management is responsible and that stress prevention (for example, introducing the interventions) belongs to their "normal daily duties". In many cases principles of worker participation were explicitly chosen. Needless to say, the implementation did not always run smoothly, systematically and according to plan. There were various stimulating and hindering factors.

The fifth step comprises the evaluation of the project. It is not easy to present a neat picture of the effects of these intervention programmes, given the variety of interventions, outcome measures, and the ways the projects were evaluated (e.g. time interval of evaluation). To structure the assessment of possible effects of these intervention programmes, they were classified into more "objective" and more "subjective" effects. With respect to the first category, mainly changes in sickness absenteeism were studied. In the first study (Kompier et al., 1998) sickness absenteeism (absence percentage) significantly ($p < 0.05$) decreased in five cases, often equal to or below the average score for that branch of industry. In three cases, the change in absence percentage was in the expected direction, but this effect was not significant. In one case data on absenteeism could not be provided. In the study of interventions in bus companies (Kompier et al., 2000a), half of the cases used absence figures as an effect parameter. From a scientific point of view these analyses are not very satisfying (methodological flaws). Nevertheless, there are clear indications that these preventive programmes were related to decreases in sickness absenteeism. In the third study (Kompier et al., 2000b), changes in sickness absence were measured in four cases. The decrease was significant in three cases. In the fourth case the change was in the expected direction but not significant, probably due to small sample size.

Regarding "subjective", i.e. self-reported, effects, more data are available and the overall picture is quite positive. Subjective evaluations were recorded in most cases. Mostly, these data relate to (changes in) subjective evaluations of work factors, to evaluations of changes that were implemented, and to (changes in) health complaints. In various cases comparable questionnaires were administered pre-intervention and post-intervention. In general, positive self-reported results are found in these evaluations. In addition, there are clear indications from various cases that these projects may be regarded as successful from a financial perspective, often due to the decrease in sickness absenteeism.

Against the background of these results, generally speaking, these cases may be regarded as successful. Can these predominantly positive effects be attributed to the interventions? In various cases there are possible threats to internal validity (e.g. history, regression to the mean, selection) and to external validity (e.g. interaction of selection and intervention). Still, our general conclusion is that—given the systematic assessment of risks and risk groups, and the "tailor-made" interventions—it is at least plausible that the positive outcomes can largely be attributed to the intervention programmes. External and construct (theoretical) validity are a matter of replication and variations of these "experiments", and especially a matter of more theoretically developed and well-designed intervention studies. In addition, it would make sense to learn from less successful cases in prevention.

20.5.2 Success Factors in Prevention: Content and Context

A crucial question is: "Which interventions work?". That is, what specific measure had what specific effect? It is not easy to answer this question. Not only the starting situation but also the remedies and the outcome variables differ in these cases. In these studies, most cases preferred a cocktail of medicines, often combining work-directed and worker-directed measures. It is the paradox of field intervention research that those intervention programmes offering the best preventive potential (e.g. addressing the real problems, multimodal treatments directed at work and the worker) make it difficult to answer the question "What

Table 20.2   Questions to be addressed in a stress prevention quality approach

Content:
- Is there a problem? (risk assessment: risk factors and risk groups)
- Is an intervention necessary? (risk evaluation)
- Does the intervention theoretically "fit in" with the problem? (cf. theoretical validity/mechanisms: is it theoretically plausible that it will cause certain effects?)
- Does the intervention cover/address the real problem? (cf. content validity)
- Do the outcome measures (dependent variables) theoretically "fit in" with the problem?
- Does the intervention address work and/or the worker? (quadrants in Figure 20.4)
- Does the intervention have serious impact? (duration, intensity, frequency of intervention)
- Does the intervention address those who need it? (is it directed at primary, and/or secondary, and/or tertiary prevention)

Design:
- Is the study design adequate? (preferably with control condition)
- Are instruments reliable and valid? (risk assessment, evaluation-effect parameters)
- Are both "subjective" and "objective" data collected? ("soft" and "hard" data, "triangulation")
- Is the time interval theoretically valid (adequate time span, not too short follow-up)?
- Is selective drop-out studied (attrition, biased response)?
- Can differential analyses be performed (sub-group analyses, e.g. between those with high, medium and low complaints)?
- Are statistical analyses adequate?

Context:
- Is the change process and the intervention systematically/well organized (introduction, implementation)?
- Is it participatory? (is there serious participation by those whose work and stress is at stake?; communication, feedback)
- Is there sustained top management support?
- "Did the patient take the pill?" (feasibility, prevention effectiveness)
- Which "competing" developments took place during the project? ("plausible rival hypotheses", analysis of competing causes or artefacts that may otherwise account for observed outcomes)
- What were obstructing and stimulating factors during the project? (How) were problems overcome?

works?". In addition, we want to emphasize that the success of stress prevention depends not only on the content of the intervention ("what", i.e. the specific measure taken), but also on the process ("how", e.g. introduction and implementation). These content and process variables are often intertwined. With Amanda Griffiths (1999), we hypothesize that such processes (in terms of conceptualization, design and implementation of interventions) are likely to be more generalizable than outcomes. Therefore, against the background of these 30 cases and the literature (e.g. Goldenhar & Schulte, 1994; Karasek, 1992), it is our hypothesis that a "stress prevention quality approach" should address the following questions from three partially overlapping domains. These three domains are: (i) content ("what"), (ii) methodological context (study design), and (iii) organizational context (process: "how", "who", "when") (Table 20.2).

It is our conviction that one of the main challenges of occupational health psychology is to transform the impressive existing body of knowledge on the psychosocial work environment, stress, health and well-being into prevention. We hope that these "success factors in prevention" will play a stimulating role in coping with this challenge. Scientific work in this area is still somewhat scarce. However, multiple case studies such as those presented suggest that occupational stress prevention that combines adequate interventions and proper implementation may be beneficial for both the employee and the company.

REFERENCES

Algera, J.A. (1989) Taakkenmerken [Task characteristics]. In P.J.D. Drenth, Ch.J. de Wolff and Hk. Thierry (eds) *Nieuw Handboek Arbeids- en Organisatiepychologie* [*New Handbook of Work and Organizational Psychology*]. Deventer: Van Loghum Slaterus, pp. 2.2.-1–2.2-30.

Algera, J.A. (1991) Arbeidsanalyse ten behoeve van motivatie en satisfactie [Job analysis on behalf of motivation and satisfaction]. In J.A. Algera (ed.) *Analyse van arbeid vanuit verschillende perspectieven* [*Work Analysis from Different Perspectives*]. Amsterdam: Swets & Zeitlinger, pp. 143–78.

Burke, R.J. (1993) Organizational-level interventions to reduce occupational stressors. *Work and Stress*, **7**, 77–87.

Caplan, R., Cobb, S., French, J. & Harrison, R. (1975) *Job Demands and Worker Health, Main Effects and Occupational Differences*. Washington, DC: NIOSH.

Cherns, A.B. (1976) The principles of sociotechnical design. *Human Relations*, **29**, 783–92.

Cherns, A.B. (1987) Principles of sociotechnical design revisited. *Human Relations*, **40**, 153–62.

Clegg, C.W. (2000) Sociotechnical principles for system design. *Applied Ergonomics*, **31**, 463–77.

Cooper, C.L. & Payne, R. (eds) (1988) *Causes, Coping and Consequences of Stress at Work*. Chichester: John Wiley & Sons.

Cox, T. (1993) Stress research and stress management: putting theory to work, HSE Contract Research report, no. 61/1993.

Cox, T., Griffiths, A. & Rial-Gonzalez, R. (2000) *Research on Work-Related Stress*. Bilbao: European Agency for Safety and Health at Work.

DeFrank, R.S. & Cooper, C.L. (1987) Worksite management interventions: their effectiveness and conceptualization. *Journal of Managerial Psychology*, **2**, 4–10.

De Jonge, J. & Kompier, M. (1997) A critical examination of the demand–control–support model from a work psychological perspective. *International Journal of Stress Management*, **4**, 235–58.

De Jonge, J. & Schaufeli, W.B. (1998) Job characteristics and employee well-being: a test of Warr's vitamin model in health care workers using structural equation modelling. *Journal of Organizational Behavior*, **19**, 387–407.

De Jonge, J., Bosma, H., Peter, R. & Siegrist, J. (2000) Job strain, effort-reward imbalance and employee well-being: a large scale cross-sectional study. *Social Science and Medicine*, **50**, 1317–27.

De Sitter, L.U. (1989) Moderne sociotechniek [Modern sociotechnics]. *Gedrag en Organisatie*, **2**, 222–51.

Evans, G.W. & Johnson, D. (2000) Stress and open-office noise. *Journal of Applied Psychology*, **85**, 779–83.

Evans, G.W., Johansson, G. & Carrere, S. (1994) Psychosocial factors and the physical environment: inter-relations in the workplace. In C.L. Cooper & I.T. Robertson (eds) *International Review of Industrial and Organizational Psychology*, vol. 9. Chichester: John Wiley & Sons.

Fletcher, B. & Jones, F. (1993) A refutation of Karasek's demand-discretion model of occupational health with a range of dependent measures. *Journal of Organizational Behavior*, **14**, 319–30.

French, J.R.P., Jr & Kahn, R.L. (1962) A programmatic approach to studying the industrial environment and mental health. *Journal of Social Issues*, **18** (3), 1–47.

Frese, M. (1985) Stress at work and psychosomatic complaints; a causal interpretation. *Journal of Applied Psychology*, **70**, 314–28.

Frese, M. & Zapf, D. (1988) Methodological issues in the study of work stress: objective versus subjective measurement of work stress and the question of longitudinal studies. In C. Cooper & R. Payne (eds) *Causes, Coping and Consequences of Stress at Work*. Chichester: John Wiley & Sons, pp. 375–414.

Frese, M. & Zapf, D. (1994) Action as the core of work psychology: a German approach. In H.C. Triandis, M.D. Dunnette & L.M. Hough (eds) *Handbook of Industrial and Organizational Psychology*, 2nd edn, vol. 4. Palo Alto, CA: Consulting Psychologists Press, pp. 271–340.

Fried, Y. & Ferris, G.R. (1987) The validity of the job characteristics model: a review and meta-analysis. *Personnel Psychology*, **40**, 287–322.

Foster, J.J. (2000) Motivation in the workplace. In N. Chmiel (ed.) *Introduction to Work and Organizational Psychology*. Oxford: Blackwell, pp. 302–26.

Ganster, D.C. (1995) Interventions for building healthy organisations: suggestions from the stress research literature. In L.R. Murphy, J.J. Hurrell, S.L. Sauter & G.P. Keita (eds) *Job Stress Interventions*. Washington, DC: American Psychological Association, pp. 323–36.

Gardell, B. (1981) Psychosocial aspects of industrial product methods. In L. Levi (ed.) *Society, Stress and Disease*, vol. 4. Oxford, Oxford University Press, pp. 65–75.

Geurts, S.A.E, Kompier, M.A.J. & Grundemann, R.W.M. (2000) Curing the Dutch disease? Sickness absence and work disability in the Netherlands. *International Social Security Review*, **53**(4), 79–103.

Goldenhar, L.M. & Schulte, P.A. (1994) Intervention research in occupational health and safety. *Journal of Occupational Medicine*, **36**, 763–75.

Griffiths, A. (1999) Organizational interventions. Facing the limits of the natural science paradigm. *Scandinavian Journal of Work, Environment and Health*, **25**, 589–96.

Hacker, W. (1973, 1978) *Allgemeine Arbeits- und Ingenieurspsychologie*. Berlin: Deutscher Verlag der Wissenschaften.

Hacker, W. (1984) *Arbeidsgestaltungsmassnahmen*. Berlin: Springer-Verlag.

Hacker, W. (1985) Activity: a fruitful concept in industrial psychology. In M. Frese & J. Sabini (eds) *Goal Directed Behavior: A Concept of Action Psychology*. Hillsdale, NJ: Lawrence Erlbaum, pp. 262–83.

Hacker, W. (1986) *Arbeitspsychologie*. Bern: Huber.

Hackman, J.R. & Lawler, E.E. (1971) Employee reactions to job characteristics. *Journal of Applied Psychology*, **55**, 259–86.

Hackman, J.R. & Oldham, G.R. (1975) Development of the Job Diagnostic Survey. *Journal of Applied Psychology*, **60**, 159–70.

Hackman, J.R. & Oldham, G.R. (1976) Motivation through the design of work: test of a theory. *Organizational Behavior and Human Performance*, **16**, 250–79.

Hackman, J.R. & Oldham, G.R. (1980) *Work Redesign*. Reading, MA: Addison-Wesley.

Ilgen, D.R. & Hollenbeck, J.R. (1991) The structure of work: job design and roles. In M.D. Dunnette & L.M. Hough (eds) *Handbook of Industrial and Organizational Psychology*, 2nd edn, vol. 2. Palo Alto, CA: Consulting Psychologists Press, pp. 165–207.

Johnson, J.V. (1986) The impact of the workplace social support, job demands, and work control under cardiovascular disease in Sweden, PhD thesis, Johns Hopkins University. Department of Psychology, University of Stockholm, Stockholm, report no. 1–86.

Johnson, J.V. & Hall, E.M. (1988) Job strain, workplace social support and cardiovascular disease: a cross-sectional study of a random sample of the Swedish working population. *American Journal of Public Health*, **78**, 1336–42.

Johnson, J.V. & Johansson, G. (eds) (1991) *The Psychological Work Environment: Work Organization, Democratization and Health*. Amityville, NY: Baywood.

Kahn, R.L. & Byosiere, P. (1992) Stress in organizations. In M.D. Dunnette and L.M. Hough (eds.) *Handbook of Industrial and Organizational Psychology*, 2nd edn, vol. 3. Palo Alto, CA: Consulting Psychologists Press, pp. 571–650.

Kahn, R.L., Wolfe, D., Quinn, R., Snoek, J. & Rosenthal, R. (1964) *Organizational Stress: Studies in Role Conflict and Ambiguity*, New York: John Wiley & Sons.

Karasek, R.A. (1979) Job demands, job decision latitude, and mental strain: implications for job redesign. *Administrative Science Quarterly*, **24**, 285–308.

Karasek, R.A. (1992) Stress prevention through work reorganization: a summary of 19 international case studies. In *Conditions of Work Digest, Preventing Stress at Work*, vol. 11, no. 2, Geneva: International Labour Office, pp. 23–41.

Karasek, R.A. (1998) Demand/control model: a social, emotional, and physiological approach to stress risk and active behaviour development. In J. Stellman (ed.) *Encyclopaedia of Occupational Health and Safety*. Geneva: International Labour Office, pp. 34.6–34.14.

Karasek, R.A. & Theorell, T. (1990) *Healthy Work. Stress, Productivity and the Reconstruction of Working Life*. New York, Basic Books.

Kasl, S.V. (1978) Epidemiological contributions to the study of work stress. In C.L. Cooper & R. Payne (eds) *Stress at Work*. New York: John Wiley & Sons, pp. 3–48.

Kasl, S.V. (1987) Methodologies in stress and health: past difficulties, present dilemmas, future directions. In S.V. Kasl & C.L. Cooper (eds) *Stress and Health: Issues in Research and Methodology*. Chichester: John Wiley & Sons, pp. 307–18.

Kasl, S.V. (1996) The influence of the work environment on cardiovascular health: a historical, conceptual, and methodological perspective. *Journal of Occupational Health Psychology*, **1**, 42–56.

Kompier, M.A.J. & Cooper, C.L. (eds) (1999) *Preventing Stress, Improving Productivity: European Case Studies in the Workplace*. London: Routledge.

Kompier, M.A.J. & Kristensen, T.S. (2000) Organizational work stress interventions in a theoretical, methodological and practical context. In J. Dunham (ed.) *Stress in the Workplace: Past, Present and Future*. London: Whurr.

Kompier, M. & Levi, L. (1994) *Stress at Work: Causes, Effects and Prevention. Guide for Small and Medium-Sized Enterprises*. Dublin: European Foundation for the Improvement of Living and Working Conditions.

Kompier, M., De Gier E., Smulders, P. & Draaisma, D. (1994) Regulations, policies and practices concerning work stress in five European countries. *Work and Stress*, **8**, 296–318.

Kompier, M.A.J., Geurts, S.A.E., Grundemann, R.W.M., Vink, P. & Smulders, P.G.W. (1998) Cases in stress prevention: the success of a participative and stepwise approach. *Stress Medicine*, **14**, 155–68.

Kompier, M.A.J., Aust, B., Van den Berg, A.-M. & Siegrist, J. (2000a) Stress prevention in bus drivers: evaluation of 13 natural experiments. *Journal of Occupational Health Psychology*, **5**, 11–31.

Kompier, M.A.J., Cooper, C.L. & Geurts, S.A.E. (2000b) A multiple case study approach to work stress prevention in Europe. *European Journal of Work and Organizational Psychology*, **9**, 371–400.

Kopelman, R. (1985) Job design and productivity: a review of the evidence. *National Productivity Review*, Summer, 237–55.

Kristensen, T.S. (1995) The demand–control–support model: methodological challenges for future research. *Stress Medicine*, **11**, 17–26.

Kuipers, H. (1989) Zelforganisatie als ontwerpprincipe [Self organization as design principle]. *Gedrag en Organisatie*, **2**(4/5), 199–221.

Kuipers, H. & Amelsvoort, P. van (1990) *Slagvaardig organiseren. Inleiding in de sociotechniek als integrale ontwerpleer [Effective Organizing. Introduction to Modern Sociotechnics]*. Deventer: Kluwer Bedrijfswetenschappen.

Le Blanc, P., Jonge, J. de & Schaufeli, W.B. (2000) Job stress and health. In: N. Chmiel (ed.) *Introduction to Work and Organizational Psychology*. Oxford: Blackwell, pp. 148–75.

Levi, L. (1984) *Stress in Industry. Causes, Effects and Prevention*. Geneva: International Labour Office.

Levi, L. (1987) Fitting the work to human capacities and needs; improvement in the content and organization of work. In R. Kalimo, M. El-Batawi & C.L. Cooper (eds) *Psychological Factors at Work and their Relation to Health*. Geneva: World Health Organization, pp. 168–84.

Levi, L. (2000) *Guidance on Work-Related Stress. Spice of Life or Kiss of Death?* Luxembourg: Office for Official Publications of the European Communities.

Marmot, M., Siegrist, J., Theorell, T. & Feeney, A. (1999) Health and the psychosocial environment at work. In M.G. Marmot & R. Wilkinson (eds) *Social Determinants of Health*. Oxford: Oxford University Press, pp. 105–31.

Murphy, L.R. (1986) A review of organizational stress management research. *Journal of Organizational Behavior Management*, **8**, 215–27.

Murphy, L.R. (1996) Stress management in work settings: a critical review of the health effects. *American Journal of Health Promotion*, **11**, 112–35.

Peter, R., Alfredsson, L., Hammar, N., Siegrist, J., Theorell, T. & Westerholm, P. (1998) High effort, low reward and cardiovascular risk factors in employed Swedish men and women—baseline results from the WOLF study. *Journal of Epidemiology and Community Health*, **52**, 540–7.

Roberts, K.H. & Glick, W.H. (1981) The job characteristics approach to task design: a critical review. *Journal of Applied Psychology*, **66**, 193–217.

Roe, R.A. & Zijlstra, F.R.H. (1991) Arbeidsanalyse ten behoeve van (her)ontwerp van functies: een handelingstheoretische invalshoek [Work analysis in behalf of job (re)design: an action theoretical perspective]. In J.A. Algera (ed.) *Analyse van de arbeid vanuit verschillende perspectieven* [*Work Analysis from Different Perspectives*]. Amsterdam: Swets & Zeitlinger, pp. 179–244.

Schaufeli, W.B. & Kompier, M.A.J. (2001) Managing job stress in the Netherlands. *International Journal of Stress Management*, **8**, 15–34.

Scheuch, K. & Schreinicke, G. (1989) *Stress, Gedanken, Theorien, Probleme*. Berlin: VEB Verlag Volk und Gesundheit.

Schnall, P.L., Landsbergis, P.A. & Baker, D. (1994) Job strain and cardiovascular disease. *Annual Review of Public Health*, **15**, 381–411.

Semmer, N. (1984) Stressbezogene Arbeitsanalyse. In S. Greif, E. Bamberg & N. Semmer (eds) *Psychischer Stress am Arbeitsplatz*. Gottingen: Hogrefe, pp. 57–90.

Semmer, N. & Frese, M. (1985) Action theory in clinical psychology. In M. Frese & J. Sabini (eds) *Goal Directed Behavior: The Concept of Action in Psychology*. Hillsdale, NJ: Lawrence Erlbaum, pp. 296–310.

Semmer, N. (2002) Job stress interventions and organization of work. In J.C. Quick & L.E. Tetrick (eds) *Handbook of Occupational Health Psychology*. Washington, DC: American Psychological Association.

Siegrist, J. (1996) Adverse health effects of high effort-low reward conditions at work. *Journal of Occupational Health Psychology*, **1**, 27–43.

Siegrist, J. (1998) Adverse health effects of effort–reward imbalance at work. In C.L. Cooper (ed.) *Theories of Organizational Stress*. New York: Oxford University Press, pp. 190–204.

Siegrist, J. (2000) A theory of occupational stress. In J. Dunham (ed.) *Stress in the Workplace: Past, Present and Future*. London: Whurr, pp. 52–66.

Siegrist, J. & Peter, R. (1994) Job stressors and coping characteristics in work related disease: issues of validity. *Work and Stress*, **8**, 130–40.

Siegrist, J., Peter, R., Cremer, P. & Seidel, D. (1990) Low status control, high effort at work and ischaemic heart disease: prospective evidence from blue-collar men. *Social Science and Medicine*, **31**, 1127–34.

Smith, A. (1991) A review of the non auditory effects of noise on health. *Work and Stress*, **5**, 49–62.

Taylor, F.W. (1911) *Scientific Management*. New York, Harper & Brothers.

Theorell, T. (1998) Job characteristics in a theoretical and practical health context. In C.L. Cooper (ed.) *Theories of Organizational Stress*. Oxford: Oxford University Press, pp. 205–19.

Turner, A.N. & Lawrence, P.R. (1965) *Industrial Jobs and the Worker. An Investigation of Response to Task Attributes*. Boston, MA: Harvard Graduate School of Business Administration.

Ulich, E. (1972) Aufgabenwechsel und Aufgabenerweiterung. *REFA-Nachrichten*, **25**, 265–75.

Van der Doef, M. & Maes, S. (1998) The job demand–control (–support) model and physical health outcomes: a review of the strain and buffer hypotheses. *Psychology and Health*, **13**, 909–36.

Van der Doef, M. & Maes, S. (1999) The job demand–control (–support) model and psychological well-being: a review of 20 years of empirical research. *Work and Stress*, **13**, 87–114.

Van der Hek, H. & Plomp, N. (1997) Occupational stress management programmes: a practical overview of published effect studies. *Journal of Occupational Medicine*, **47**, 133–41.

Van der, Klink, J. Blonk, R.W.B., Schene, A.H. & Dijk, F.J.H. van (2001) The benefits of interventions for work-related stress. *American Journal of Public Health*, **91**, 270–6.

Volpert, W. (1971) *Sensumotorisches Lernen. Zur Theorie des Trainings in Industrie und Sport*. Frankfurt: Limpert.

Volpert, W. (1989) Work and personality development from the viewpoint of the action regulation theory. In H. Leymann & H. Kornbluh (eds) *Socialization and Learning at Work: A New Approach to the Learning Process in the Work Place and Society*. Aldershot: Avebury, pp. 215–32.

Warr, P. (1987) *Work, Unemployment and Mental Health*. Oxford: Clarendon Press.

Warr, P.B. (1990) Decision latitude, job demands, and employee well-being. *Work and Stress*, **4**, 285–94.

Warr, P.B. (1992) Job features and excessive stress. In R. Jenkins & N. Coney (eds) Prevention of Mental Ill Health at Work. London: HMSO.

Warr, P. (1994) A conceptual framework for the study of work and mental health. *Work and Stress*, **8**, 84–97.

Warr, P. (1996) Employee well-being. In P. Warr (ed.) *Psychology at Work*, 4th edn. Chichester: John Wiley & Sons.

Yin, R.K. (1994) *Case Study Research: Design and Methods*, 2nd edn. Thousand Oaks, CA: Sage.

CHAPTER 21

Organizational Learning

Joan L. Meyer
University of Amsterdam, The Netherlands

21.1 INTRODUCTION

Many theorists have already pointed out that it is not too hard to teach people new skills and competencies, and that the same holds true at a group or organizational level. In other words, people, groups and organizations can master a new technique or a new technology with relative ease, *as long as* it remains within a clearly defined cognitive system. However, a new technique, technology or product is no guarantee of succes, as we learn from the countless campaigns, hopes for succes, change efforts and disappointments at every level in the firm. In modern business it is the result that counts, and so the assignment is not just a question of completing a product and offering and delivering it to the customers. Even in the simplest of situations, as in delivering a hamburger to a hungry customer, it is the total situation, the interaction from before the first pangs of the clients' hunger until well after the final satisfied belch, which is under consideration if a professional orientation is adopted.

By a professional orientation, we mean an orientation that is directed towards results, and that is able to distinguish between techniques, routines and basic competencies that can be deployed towards the desired end, between application problems, where techniques, routines and competencies are applied to a new problem, in a new situation or in a new fashion, and complex problems, where aim, specifications and approach are unclear at the starting point. It is the last type of problem that forms a special challenge for the professional, because this is where his or her creative abilities are brought to bear. The realization "I should be able to do this, but I don't know how (yet)", spurs the professional to greater heights. The concept of "effort" in this context is relatively meaningless—the desired results are the criterion for succes.[1]

Moreover, we are increasingly dealing with knowledge-intensive business, with professionals, and with complex processes. More and more, the "product", if we continue to use this term, is actually something that is produced *in the interaction* between the "producer" and the "customer". The question of organizational learning thereby shifts from learning in a traditional sense (as learning in school) to producing new and desired results through new forms of interaction. In other words, the emphasis has shifted to the communication

---

[1] I wish to thank Dr Rob Halkes of Bouman, MIM & van Spaendonck for providing these insights.

The Handbook of Work and Health Psychology. Edited by M.J. Schabracq, J.A.M. Winnubst and C.L. Cooper.
© 2003 John Wiley & Sons, Ltd.

process between people, groups and firms. What is at stake is their shared ability to define, enable and realize desirable situations, in shifting coalitions that co-produce and reframe.

In this chapter we will deal first with learning organizations as products. Levels of learning are described for the individual and, subsequently, forms of organizational learning are defined and analysed. Next, learning is viewed as process, and different ways of understanding the processes involved in organizational learning are put forward. Finally, we discuss the general factors obstructing the learning process, and conditions necessary to create learning in organizations. Throughout the chapter we will deal with implications of learning for stress.

21.2   LEARNING AS PRODUCT

Learning can apply to both process (how one learns) and product (what is learned). Individuals learn in many ways: by accumulating knowledge, which is dealt out in specific forms and tested in educational institutions, by implicitly following the example of others ("modelling") and from experiences that are either pleasing or unpleasant. For individuals to learn from experience, it is necessary that they can reflect on, become aware of themselves as a person and watch retrospectively from a point in the distance what they actually did to achieve the pleasant or unpleasant results. Then, using the available knowledge and reasoning, they can construct a theory (my behaviour x led to consequence y) and either test this theory directly (if the consequence was pleasing) or, if the consequence was unpleasant and they wish to avoid it, develop alternatives (if I do z, p or q, I might avoid unpleasant consequence y) and test those.

Learning is stressful. Although people are intrinsically motivated to learn, the learning situation leads to high levels of arousal, sometimes ending in frustration and aggression, as many of us know from personal experience. On the other hand, the learning situation appeals to us, and challenges us to test and develop our skills and competencies. In the proper proportions, the tensions associated with learning and mastery can lead to the rewarding experience of "flow" (Csikszentmihalyi, 1990; 1997).

21.2.1   Products of Individual Learning

When can we say that learning has taken place at an individual level, and what kind of learning are we speaking about? If people are interviewed about their "most important learning experience" they most frequently describe an experience which resulted in "throwing a new light on things". Or, as one of the interviewees put it, "It is as though you were given better eyes, or new ears. Finally something new has happened and what was in a haze has become clear". The circumstances by which this result comes about can vary widely, depending on content and learning context, but people's interpretations converge in the sense that really important learning experiences do not happen every day and are occasions that are remembered and referred to.

The products of learning are generally divided into different levels or dimensions:

1. First-order knowledge, or direct sensory knowledge of that which is happening around us. Example: seeing the sun rise.

2. Second-order knowledge. This type of knowledge presupposes the first type. After seeing the sun rise several times, one comes to order these experiences as of a similar nature, and to build theories around them. We expect to see the sun rise on a new day, in fact, we *know* that the sun rises every day and will continue to do so even after we are gone. From second-order knowledge, knowledge building can take place, leading for instance to the knowledge that the sun does not rise at all, but that our direct sensory perception is the result of our earth turning and revolving around the sun.

3. Third-order knowledge is of another kind again. This type of knowledge is *integrative*. It involves the building of a conceptual world, and making sense out of the first- and second-order knowledge. This sense-making takes the form of assumptions about the world in which one has been placed and one's relation to this world. These (basic) assumptions determine how people deal with each other and with the environment. Third-order knowledge is resistant to change, in contrast to second-order knowledge. To put this another way, people are quick to accommodate new techniques and insights, as long as these do not touch on their conceptual world and their personal identity. Change of third-order knowledge is painful, and people can go to great lengths to avoid it. The story of Galileo's treatment by his contemporaries is well known and illustrates the point. One can also ask how many people in our time have actually incorporated Galileo's findings into their basic assumptions. Some findings stay in the cognitive realm (we know the sun does not rise, but continue to see it), others come to be incorporated in our basic reality (open the curtains and say "Look, the world has turned again!").[2]

4. To strive for change in third-level knowledge, it is necessary to presuppose a fourth level, from which this could be done. Fourth-order knowledge approaches the limits of what is conceivable for human beings at this time. There is hardly any conscious knowledge *about* this level. It is the realm of intuition, of identification and creation, of the *Aha-Erlebnis* (eureka!). It is also the level where subjective and objective knowledge become one. The harmony that is experienced when they merge forms a significant life event.

It is important to dwell on the relations between the levels of knowledge, and the relation between product and process. Direct sensory perception is relatively unperturbed by second-level knowledge. However, from time to time, second-level knowledge building leads to paradigm shifts that have consequences for third-level knowledge. Such shifts may be seen as threats and suppressed, or as enlightment and welcomed. However, thanks to the process of organization, the *products* of such paradigm shifts can be deployed by a wide range of individuals who would never have been able to construe them. In this way the products of advanced technology can be applied within primitive conceptual worlds, leading to awesome consequences. The coexistence of widely disparate levels within one and the same society is one of the great problems of our time.

To illustrate the above points, imagine the consequences of widespread availability of products like atom bombs and the technology to clone human beings, in combination with a primitive world view (third-order knowledge) that includes only good–bad differentiations (the good being situated inside, and the bad being situated in the outer world).

For individuals, groups and organizations, stressful situations arise when they attempt to communicate in a meaningful way with others whose world view is at a different level

---

[2] The point being that practically nobody can say this convincingly.

of knowledge (third-order). This effect is even more pronounced when one (mistakenly) expects the other party to share the same view of the world. However, one cannot take it for granted that people will have sophisticated world views simply because they are in positions of power; neither can one take this for granted regarding groups holding advanced technological know-how or products. Moreover, it is virtually impossible to bring about the development of third-order knowledge in a forceful way, or on demand. Through dialogue, one can attempt to gain insight into the world view of the other party. By empathy, one can attempt to find a common ground for communication. But it will be the more sophisticated party who makes this effort—the more primitive his "opposite numbers" are, the less they will be able to reciprocate.

21.2.2   Collective Learning

In the psychology of learning, both the products and processes of learning are conceived of as something in the head of an individual. Collective learning is seldom an issue. When Argyris and Schön launched their theories on organizational learning in the 1970s, there was quite a bit of resistance among the established scientists. In their own words, "organizational learning seemed to smell of some quasi-mystical, Hegelian, personification of the collectivity. Surely, they felt, it is individuals who may be said to learn, just as to think, reason, or hold opinions. To them, it seemed paradoxical, if not perverse, to attribute learning to organizations" (Argyris & Schön, 1996, p. 4).

However, there is nothing mystical about the learning of organizations. In everyday conversation, but also in scholarly discourse, people attribute thinking, reasoning, remembering and similar processes to teams, departments or organizations. For instance, the remark that "Sales departement has only just realized that we have been on the wrong course" is not an unusual statement. It does, however, tacitly take for granted a number of considerations or givens, which are listed below.

First of all, a collectivity can be said to act or think in so far as individual members do this *on behalf of* the collectivity. This is only possible if the following conditions are met:

1. There must be agreed-upon procedures for making decisions in the name of the collectivity.
2. Authority needs to be delegated to individuals, so that they can act for the collectivity.
3. There need to be boundaries between the collectivity and the rest of the world (Argyris & Schön, 1996).

With reference to point 1, these procedures can vary in shape from explicit rules and regulations, to "rule of thumb" procedures that have evolved in a group and never really been challenged enough to merit explicit discussion. In content, they can vary from extremely dictatorial to extremely democratic. What is important is that it is understood by all that at a certain point the group or organization will move, and that the "critical mass" for this movement is generated in a fashion that is implicitly or explicitly agreed upon.

With reference to point 2, authority can be delegated to individuals or to groups; what is important is that it is clear when individuals or groups act for the collectivity. Such distinctions are also made in everyday speech, such as: "The group feels that x is important, but personally I feel we should redefine the issue".

With reference to point 3, in an organization there are boundaries between teams, departments and the rest of the organization. At the same time, teams, groups and departments belong *to* the organization, and there are boundaries between the organization and the rest of the world. A learning process in an organization might start out with an individual, move on to the team, eventually be taken over by the department, ultimately become part of the standard procedure in an organization, or ultimately influence other organizations and environments. It is important to note that the relations *between* organizations are subject to change: driven sometimes by the high cost of expertise, sometimes by the dynamics of takeovers and mergers, organizations are coming to share specific R&D facilities, or designing joint knowledge structures, instead of jealously guarding their own facilities and protecting "their knowledge" from outsiders.

A special case of organizational learning is the learning that takes place in scientific disciplines. Disciplines form communities of learning. Individuals contribute significantly, but progress is measured in terms of the discipline.

Although the development of sciences can be concentrated at certain points in time and at certain centres of excellence, basically, the discipline is the community, not the department or the university. Outsiders from other parts of the world can join in the formation of knowledge if they have something to contribute. Of necessity, development and interchange depend heavily on published material; however, the "live" exchange of ideas is important too. The community of the discipline is made up of individuals and groups who accept and play by the same rules and theories. In the case of science, challenge is an inherent part of the scenario. This idea is more accepted here than in other communities of knowledge (Kuhn, 1962). In the past decade the easy transmission of information and exchange of ideas through the internet is encouraging the coming into being of virtual environments where communities of learning can thrive. However, there is no documentation available as yet on the extent, content and success of these communities.

21.2.3   Organizational Knowledge

In order to determine what organizations learn, it is necessary to take stock of organizational knowledge. What kind of knowledge do organizations possess?

First of all, of course, there is knowledge in the minds of individuals—this knowledge may be vital to the organization, but it is not necessarily collective. It may not be used at all, and it may depart with the individuals leaving the organization, leaving no trace.

Second, knowledge is stored in files (both physical and virtual, although the latter are still more vulnerable to accidents), records, libraries, knowledge systems and other explicit environments built and maintained by the organization for the explicit purpose of storing and distributing knowledge.

A special form of the storage of knowledge is the way in which the physical environment is used to underline and guide chains of action—these signs and chains help different parties to fullfil their roles as these have been outlined in the past. Examples are the way in which the check-in counters and security systems in airports are translated into the environment (regulating the behaviour of officials, personnel and passengers), or the lay-out of a hospital However, the most important form of organizational knowledge consists of the routines and practices which have evolved to tackle the problems which form the raison d'être of the firm. In this sense, one can view an organization as a task system, a collective vehicle for the performance of recurrent tasks and new tasks related to or derived from the recurrent ones. The problems that have been encountered in the past have led to solutions. These solutions have become embodied in "due procedure" practices of which not everyone knows or needs to know the origin. Occasionally, a newcomer might question some aspect of these routines or practices. This might lead to insight and the adoption by the newcomer of the routine, or alternatively it might start a new learning process. The embodied solutions, which exist not as theory but are enacted by the organization's members as they go about their business, have been labelled "theory-in-use" by Argyris and Schön, and "structuration" by Giddens. Both contrast this aspect of knowledge with the explicit, verbalized forms of knowledge in which people explain what to do or how to do it. The underlying idea is the same in both cases: what is enacted is not necessarily the same as what people verbalize. Ideas, norms, ideals all belong to the realm of theory and cognition, whereas the results achieved by an organization depend ultimately on what is put into practice or action.

Perhaps, at this point, it is helpful to bring to mind the experiment with the chimpanzees in a cage, which showed the process of social conditioning. A banana was introduced in the cage, high up on a string. By standing on a box, the chimpanzees could reach the banana and eat it. But the experimenter started to give them an electric shock when they reached for the banana. After a few times, this started a process of social learning. The chimpanzees prevented each other from going after the banana, thereby protecting their cage-mates from the experience of shock. Even long after all chimpanzees that had actually experienced the shock were no longer in this cage, and no shocks had been delivered, all animals, including the newcomers, still refrained from reaching for the banana. For them, it had become "due procedure" to stay off the banana.

In a similar fashion, organizational knowledge becomes stored in practices and routines. Practices and routines function as anchors against stress. They help people maintain a "steady state", a quasi-equilibrium in which they feel rewarded by peace of mind for practising a manageable behavioural repertoire.[3]

And as with the chimps, sometimes routines stick with us much longer than their actual usefulness. At what point they will be questioned, and a new process of collective learning will be sparked off, is hard to predict. Usually the occasion will be some kind of mismatch, for instance between what is expected and what is actually achieved. Initially, this mismatch will lead to a stressful situation. However, if adequate adjustments and coping strategies can be found (or learned), a new steady state will be achieved which is more effective.

21.2.4   Levels of Organizational Learning

With the description of levels of knowledge in Section 21. 2.1 in mind, what can we say about levels of organizational learning? First of all, all levels are potentially involved. However, since involvement of the third and fourth levels are rare in individuals, they will be rare in organizational learning. Most organizational learning takes place in second-order knowledge. Present-day forms of organization are themselves the result of second-order knowledge building. So, for instance, in pre-industrial Asian societies, trees were felled to be used as building material only at the moment they were needed and were then transported

---

[3] Obviously, for some people this "manageable behavioural repertoire" can become a psychological prison or lead to work underload.

to where the building would take place. However, the colonizing by industrialized countries led to mechanized felling, supplemented by planting with the aim of felling, pre-fell cutting, the mass transportation of felled trees making use of rivers and waterfalls, the storage of wood and global transportation, in order to exact maximum prices worldwide. All this knowledge is built within one knowledge system, that of maximizing profit and amassing wealth. Within this paradigm, it is possible to go extremely far in refining methods and specific procedures, until the system of getting money from wood from nature is hard to perfect. From the perspective of a different paradigm, for instance a long-term view of global stewardship, this system, now called deforestation, has long outlived its usefulness and turned into a detriment—but to endorse that perspective, one needs to adopt the viewpoint of the broader paradigm, integrating different knowledge systems, sense making and values.

A second example is the case of fishing. Consider the technology used to kill sea creatures. This technology has made it possible to kill more and more sea creatures, using less and less people and equipment; in addition, the techniques for storing dead fish and keeping them edible have been improved. The system of getting money from fish from the sea has been perfected to the point where the putting into effect of what is technically possible would mean that the sea would quickly be emptied of fish, since humans can kill at a much faster rate than fish can multiply. Again, a possibly valuable ore of knowledge has burned itself out, by remaining for too long within the same knowledge system. Now, the press bemoans the fate of fishermen having to seek new employment on account of the quota systems—to guarantee the long-term existence of fish in the sea, agreements are made that stipulate the amount of each type of fish a country is allowed to catch (the limits come from the new paradigm, since the old one sets no limits).

In modern organizations, people work together who have widely disparate world views. It is rarely necessary for all of them to share third-level understanding in every way. However, some common ground is necessary, especially at the level of teams, groups and organizational leadership responsible for strategy development. At some point also, it will be necessary to communicate to a broader circle (of clients, providers, general public) what position the organization takes regarding important issues.

The common ground is offered by the organizational reality, the interpretations on which the organization formed and grew. The important question then regards that organizational reality: To what extent and how has it expanded? Has it broadened to take in new perspectives, or has it closed in upon itself, cementing a too-narrow "reality", in the course of its life? And if the latter is the case, who or what is to correct the situation?[4]

21.3 LEARNING AS PROCESS

Depending on the metaphor underlying your concept of organization, the relation between the individual and the group or organization takes on a different shape. So, for instance, in the machine metaphor, the individual becomes a cog in the wheel and learning remains restricted to routines and competencies.[5]

---

[4] Up to a point, paying clients, voters and interest groups can act as safeguards, since they vote with their feet and ultimately determine the fate of many organizations. But obviously, this is not sufficient.

[5] That is, unless one moves to the designer of the machine, but he or she is outside the metaphor.

In the models or metaphors used by advocates of organizational learning the basic metaphor varies (Morgan, 1986). Sometimes it is a biological one, with the individual as a cell, containing specific, changing knowledge relating to the whole and developing in interaction with the whole, which is also dependent on these individual particles. Sometimes the metaphor offers more scope to actually describe and analyse the learning processes and relations involved. Here I will discuss the culture metaphor, the "brains" metaphor and the "flux and transformation" metaphor.

21.3.1   The Culture Metaphor

Culture in this context is defined as the total of solutions worked out by a group or community in answer to two basic problems: the problem of dealing with the environment (including environmental change) and the problem of integrating the group members into a more or less coherent whole. This definition gives us scope to apply the culture metaphor to organizational learning, since organizations likewise have to find "satisficing" anwers to these two basic questions. The domain of culture is a broad domain, encompassing, as it does, not just formal learning or cognitive material, but also behavioural codes, values, taken-for-granted assumptions, beliefs, dogma and, last but not least, emotions and feelings. The culture metaphor is probably the hardest nut to crack in organizational learning, since the relation between individual and collectivity is both the central focus and the most problematic aspect of culture.

Organizations as cultures define learning as "learning the ropes" or in other words, acculturation;[6] nevertheless, culture can also be said to be moulded by individuals and groups. In cultural change, taken-for-granted norms, values and behavioural codes are called into question, resulting in periods of general confusion and debate. Eventually, new norms begin to take shape, a form of consensus can be discerned, and in the long run, the new norms can become as much taken-for-granted as the old ones. Culture change is slow-moving and intrusive, and can indeed form the occasion for conflict and war. Cultures can adapt to changing environments and circumstances, and cultures can become rigid and be the cause of destruction. Cultures vary in their tolerance towards deviations. It is typical for modern cultures to allow pockets to form where minorities adhere to their own, deviating (sub)cultures. This is usually permitted as long as the minorities overtly conform to a number of central aspects of the dominant culture. However, if the deviating group is seen as threatening the core of the dominant culture or as trying to overthrow the dominant culture, reactions will follow. The occasion for learning in the culture metaphor is a culture shock or confrontation, a dilemma or clash of values that in that context and time seems insoluble. A culture or an organization-as-culture can be said to learn if the process of dealing with such a dilemma is conscious and chosen. Basically, there are three options open to a culture to react when deviation becomes substantial and seems to threaten a valued way of life (Katz, 1985):

1. Incorporation. Whether incorporation is an option depends on how central the values are that are being threatened. If people do not feel strongly about these, there may be some initial opposition, but eventually the deviance becomes incorporated in the mainstream.

---

[6] Since acculturation is mainly conditioning and single-loop learning, we will not go into this phenomenon extensively here.

An example of this might be the way in which permissable or acceptable forms of dress have diverged in modern cities during the past few decades (behavioural codes). However, when more central values are at stake, the end result of incorporation can still be variety, as in the variety of religious groups and affiliations present in the Western world. In that case a core of central values has also developed, a core which is shared, despite the undeniably different communities and diverging beliefs, and which contains something akin to "respect for differences". It also means that the process by which the incorporation is finally achieved, evolves through different stages, during which both expulsion and dispensation play a role.

2. Exclusion. Exclusion is another option. Although the dress example given above is valid in the street, there are definitely areas in society where the dress code is more narrowly specified and more strictly adhered to. A fashionable restaurant will exclude people who are not, by its definition, suitably dressed. A stock exchange and a mosque will do the same, even though their particular codes may be at odds with each other. In a similar fashion, when people get to know each other more intimately, they may find that their core religious values are so divergent that it is nearly impossible to continue their relationship. Exclusion can take the form of actually expelling people from the society or the organization. Exclusion can also be partial, as when certain groups are not admitted to the circles of power, or forbidden to serve in the army. Partial exclusion is less rigid and absolute, but it also allows the "threat" to continue. Sooner or later, the debate over values and practices will start to spread again, and solutions will need to be found.

3. Dispensation. Dispensation codes are used to work out to what extent, among who, and under what circumstances certain kinds of deviations will be acceptable. They form a way of dealing with deviation which avoids exclusion and leaves open the option of allowing deviation to become an innovation in a more or less controlled fashion. This process involves debate at some level of authority. The authority is in communication with a set of (absolute) core values in the background. A system of checks and balances is set in motion. First of all, it needs to be decided whether the threatening issue involves the whole community or only a part of the community, next what the issue or topic is, what qualifications or delimitations can be brought to bear (since the dispensation code aims to encapsulate the deviation and keep it within manageable limits) and finally, what purpose is served, i.e. what justifications are valid on this issue. The greater the perceived threat to the core culture, the greater the need for encapsulation. Consequently, the more it will be necessary to move through all these checks and balances before it can be determined who may deviate and under what circumstances they may do so. In this way, dispensation codes allow variation, change and development over time while maintaining control.

As Katz (1985) points out, the process of dispensation is not a simple choice of clear-cut alternatives: "Assessment of the consequences may result in the decision to give one of the alternatives a try. Oscillating between alternatives may be as much a part of systems with built-in dilemmas, as are clear-cut choices. The labeling and re-labeling of the same phenomena (a particular form of deviance, for instance) may reflect different degrees of genuine transformation" (p. 355) She points to the example of a group which was expelled by the Catholic Church in 1184, the Waldensians. This group challenged the wealth and privileges of the Catholic Church, claiming that Christ had lived in poverty and asceticism, and that his followers should do the same. The Waldensians were excluded and burned at the stake, as was usual at that time. Thirty years later, a similar group, the Franciscans, was recognized and incorporated into the church.

Another case in point is the way homosexuality has been viewed in some Western societies: labelling proceeded from "eternally damned" to "sinful and reprehensible", to "a sickness or disease", to "protest and provocation", to "a specific sexual preference" and finally to just another form relationships can take. Note that in the course of relabelling there is a movement through dispensation to incorporation.

To summarize: in the culture metaphor, organizational learning is occasioned by a confrontation, culture clash, or a seemingly "insoluble" dilemma of values. This confrontation can take place between the individual and the organization, between a group or team and the corporation as a whole, or between groups or divisions within the firm. As the existing culture is more challenged, the reactions will be stronger and more extreme.[7] At different levels, both formally and informally, there will be a process of exclusion, dispensation and finally incorporation, in which both the deviants and the main system will undergo change. The end result does not need to be one unified set of values, codes and practices. It can take the form of a "theme with variations"—by virtue of some shared core values, divergence on other values and practices becomes acceptable.

Stress in the culture metaphore can be generated by the restrictiveness of the "mother culture", leaving too small a breathing space for comfort, or from the experience of being ignored or expelled. It can ensue from the confrontations, when basic assumptions are called into question by the reformers, and when the one former "truth", or "reality" is replaced by different options, each vying for credibility. It can be the result of the incorporation of strange and new or contradicting beliefs, leaving individuals suspended and seemingly without guidance. And finally, stress in the culture metaphore results from the feeling that "one's cheese has been moved", without consultation (Johnson, 1998). The trusty souls in the rear are brought up short when they realize that what once gained them acclaim and credits no longer works.

21.3.2 The Brain Metaphor

The brain metaphor offers a completely different perspective. In this metaphor the learning process takes three distinct shapes: that of cybernetics, where learning is connected to the use of specific *negative* feedback in order to continually adjust one's course; that of single-loop learning, i.e.being able to detect and correct error in relation to a given set of operating norms; and thirdly, the process of double-loop learning, or learning to learn. Essential here is that the operating norms are called into question, and consequently can be changed. We will deal with cybernetics under the heading of "flux and transformation". Here we limit the discussion to single- and double-loop learning.

According to Morgan (1986), "Many organizations have become proficient at single-loop learning, developing the ability to scan the environment, to set objectives and to monitor the general performance of the system in relation to these objectives. These skills are often institutionalized in the form of information systems designed to keep the organization on

---

[7] If only one person is in this position and there is no ground for supposing that there could be movement towards the values or practices the person represents, the dilemma could fail to become manifest, since the person can just leave the organization and seek a culture with a better "fit". However, if the person represents a substantial group or a movement in society, in due course the dilemma will return.

Table 21.1 Single- and double-loop learning

Single-loop learning
  Ability to detect and correct error, in relation to a given set of operating norms
Double-loop learning
  Step 1: sensing, scanning and monitoring the environment
  Step 2: comparison of this information against operating norms
  Step 3: questioning whether operating norms are appropriate
  Step 4: initiating appropriate action

course. Advances in computing have done much to foster this kind of single-loop control. For instance, budget systems monitor expenditure, sales, profits and other indicators of financial performance" (p. 89). These systems typically maintain single-loop learning. In contrast, double-loop learning could come about in this same situation as follows: a newcomer arrives in the organization and starts to question the way in which the indicators of financial performance are defined and put into practice. He points out that the direction the firm is moving in, and the aspirations the firm has, call for other indicators than the ones typically used at this point. His intervention is the occasion for an ongoing debate among various groups in the firm. In the course of this debate, information regarding the environment is gathered, this information is compared to the prevailing system, and in due course the budgeting and accounting systems are adjusted to the direction in which the firm wants to move. The whole exercise is cause for reflection: how come we needed a newcomer to draw our attention to these system flaws? How can we avoid this situation arising in future? How can we build learning into the system itself?

Proficiency at double-loop learning proves hard in practice. The calling into question of existing norms, practices and procedures can only come about in an environment where regular discussion and debate are approved and where innovation is encouraged. Many actual environments lack the qualities needed for double-loop learning.

Enhancing and Obstructing Organizations-as-Brains

Effectiveness, defined as the achievement of the organization's espoused purposes and norms, is a good criterion for single-loop learning. For double-loop learning, however, it is incomplete and inappropriate. Processes of organizational enquiry that meet high standards of both single-loop and double-loop learning require, in Argyris' terms, organizational deuterolearning. This means that organization's members reflect on and inquire into their organizational learning system and its effect on organizational inquiry. The learning process is threatened by defensive communication, "undiscussables",[8] compartmentalization, and a climate that leads employees to deny or hide legitimate errors.

The learning process is enhanced by encouraging the analysis and solution of complex problems by exploring different viewpoints, by using the "scenario method"[9] rather than simple extrapolation, or by alternatively confronting different perspectives (e.g. "left" and "right" brain) with each other.

---

[8] This issue is described in Chapter 27.
[9] In the "scenario method", a method for the development of strategy and vision, instead of extrapolating current trends (a linear prediction), the future is explored under the presupposition of unexpected nonlinear changes in important areas.

Stress is a definite by-product of the defensive communication in the long run, but defensive communication is itself a reaction to stress. One could say that in situations where the need for double-loop or deuterolearning threatens to become manifest, people sometimes react by repressing this "threatening" awareness, and covering up the circumstances that could facilitate their becoming conscious. In order to avoid the possible stress of confronting the need for change in their learning system, people can go to great lengths, using "coping" strategies that in themselves build stressful systems. The way out of this dilemma is to provide enough safety for the members of the organization to feel comfortable contemplating their long-term coping strategies and possible alternatives. Only then can the alternatives be explored and chosen.

21.3.3   Organizations as Flux and Transformation

In the metaphor of flux and transformation, both processes are understood to be implicate and fundamental, underlying the explicate processes. The implicate process is creative: like a hologram, everything is enfolded in everything else. The explicate process follows from it in a coherent process of transformation, the "logics of change" (Morgan, 1986). If the image holds true, organizations can best be understood by decoding these logics, or searching for the basic dynamics that generate and maintain organizations and their environments.

One option is to explore the unconscious as an implicate source of organizational life. Although this is a fascinating topic, it is beyond the scope of this chapter.[10] Another option is the analysis of organizations as cultural phenomena, the patterns of meaning and symbolic action (see Section 21.3.1).

A third option is to understand organizations as closed systems that produce and reproduce themselves, the notion of autopoiesis. Change is internally generated, usually on the basis of random variation. For the learning organization this metaphor seems to offer little scope—until we realize that autopoiesis can mean that organizations interact with *projections* of themselves, which they call "the environment". As Morgan states, "The charts of the environment that decorate the walls of the meeting room are really mirrors, projections of the organizations' own interests and concerns"(Morgan, 1986, p. 241).

In this view, the central notion is an organization's identity: by projecting itself onto the environment, the organization sets in motion an (inter)action by which it actually produces itself. The process can lead to egocentrism, where organizations fail to notice that their identities are actually destroying their chances of future existence—examples are the typewriter or watchmaker firms which failed to understand that a redefinition of self was in order in view of computer technology: they ended by becoming obsolete and extinct. Autopoiesis in these instances seems to be more of a barrier to learning than an opportunity for organizational learning. However, there are still possibilities, as we shall see at the end of this section.

In contrast to the egocentrism described, organizations can realize their interdependence with others. Cybernetics shows how systems of positive feedback depend on stabilizing loops; lacking these loops, this can lead to exponential change that becomes uncontrollable. Survival is contingent upon a system of relations and interconnections that need to be

---

[10] The realm of the unconscious is linked to organizations in the works of some psychoanalytical thinkers such as Melanie Klein and W.R. Bion. The role played by "splitting" and projective identification is significant in these theories.

managed and reshaped in order to create and maintain patterns of change and stability. In this context, learning relies heavily on the (re)definition of relations, recognizing mutuality, searching for long-term common goals, and establishing feedback loops.

While the cybernetics model is an integrative model, the model of dialectic change is one of contradiction and crisis. Different interest groups or functionaries can play roles that play out the drama of opposites, thereby using a crisis to project a situation that is shaped by broader forces underlying the contradiction. But there are also less mundane forms, derived from the dialectic model, but manifesting the inherently paradoxical nature of organizational processes. For instance, the paradox between formal procedures of control on the one hand, and creativity or innovation on the other, shows formal control mechanisms to be both functional and dysfunctional. Such paradoxes create tension that stimulates reframing. The process of doing organizational work, of building units, assigning tasks and evaluating people, requires distinctions to be made. Labels are assigned that define, identify and evaluate. The labels lead to dualities, contradictions and ultimately to a sense of paradox. The discomfort arising from such paradoxes creates a felt need for change, leading people to challenge existing frameworks.

In this model organizational learning requires the recognition of paradox, the management of polarities, and ultimately the reframing or the construction of new paradigms.

Different disciplines advocate different ways of doing this: in the economic models, optimizing or satisficing strategies are recommended. Psychological models advocate sequencing or tolerating multiple realities. Everyday behaviour shows most people block out one alternative in favour of the other, thereby creating a "comfortable" one-dimensional reality. Obviously, the learning effect of the paradox is dependent on strategies used in everyday life.

Both the cybernetic model and the dialectic model demand quite a lot of the people and organizations using them. To profit from a learning situation conforming to these metaphors, the participants need to be fairly sophisticated in their own world views, and comfortable living with different realities and truths. If this is not the case, the stress caused by these models will be counterproductive, and will actually inhibit learning rather than facilitate it.

Enhancing and Obstructing Organizations-as-Flux-and-Transformation

Most of the hampering conditions for learning listed earlier are operative within the flux-and-transformation metaphor as well. They will not be enumerated again here. What is more interesting is the question of how to make use of these potential forces in organizations in order to enhance a learning process. One of the most interesting answers to this problem has been put forward by Nonaka & Takeuchi (1995). Their vision, which is illustrated with many examples from real-world organizations, rests first of all on a holistic concept of knowledge, and secondly on a cycle consisting of the forces of externalization, combination, socialization and internalization. The continuous search for new processes of knowledge creation is fuelled by the organizational knowledge base, but equally by the knowledge bases lying dormant within each individual (and not always inside the realm of everyday conscious process). To unlock the latter, chaos and fluctuation are amplified, dialogue is stimulated and the use of analogy and metaphor is encouraged. By the ensuing processes of externalization and socialization, the knowledge creation becomes shared and development and utilization can take shape.

21.4   CONDITIONS FOR LEARNING

21.4.1   Constraints on Individual Learning

Individually, constraints on learning are set by (i) intelligence, (ii) practice, norms and situational factors, and (iii) the relation towards self and others. We will deal with each of these factors consecutively.

Intelligence, though mentioned first, is by no means the most important constraint. Obviously, some people are more gifted than others, but only a minority of people re-alize their full potential in a way that is recognizable to themselves and others. Jaques (1986) studied the careers of people in the top earning brackets of military and industrial or-ganizations. He found that these people were occupied with long-range time spans, and that their cognitive capacities went on improving way past the normal retirement age. In con-trast, people in occupations encompassing relatively short time spans stopped developing intellectually at a quite early age, and started deteriorating in middle and old age.

This finding was taken as evidence that really bright people just go on developing; but the same outcome can be, at least in part, be taken as the result of working conditions and challenges in the work situation.

Top positions usually offer a number of stimulating conditions: concerns that are deemed fleeting or of little importance are kept away from the leaders and dealt with by others. Pains are taken to structure arguments, select and present relevant information, and generally dress up problems before putting them to the higher echelon. Inevitably, they are confronted with different interests and viewpoints, and need to weigh the one against the other. Importance is attached by many to their opinions and decisions. In other words, the situational and relational context is one that is designed to make the most of the capabilities available in the people fulfilling the function at that time—and therefore most probably conducive to their continued development.

Obviously, situational factors such as institutional practice and norms regulating be-haviour can work the other way as well—constraining development, leading to boredom and actually even becoming counterproductive to the very goals that people are supposed to be striving for. Examples of these situations are given throughout this chapter, so we will not go into this here.

Finally, the relation between self and others is extremely important as a condition for individual learning. A primitive view of the relation between self and others sets important limits for learning. People who believe that it is all-important to guard their own interests, because everyone else is doing the same, perceive the world in simple, stereotypical terms: good or bad, true or untrue. They are rarely self-critical; negative outcomes are blamed on "others". Their main preoccupation is with domination and control, since they have trouble conceiving of other ways of dealing with the outside world. This primitive world view limits the possibility of trust. Instead of sharing knowledge, knowledge is guarded jealously. If other people use it, they have not been inspired but have "stolen" it. The primitive world view not only limits the sharing of knowledge, but also impedes the confrontation of different perspectives or viewpoints—ultimately, there is only one truth, only one way of thinking and of doing that is "right". This leads to closure and compartmentalization in the individual mind. Since the primitive stage is linked to notions of "good and bad", the view has consequences at the group and organizational level. From this viewpoint, one can only deal with people who think and feel the same—the others are part of the outside world and therefore bad by definition.

The primitive stage is found in individuals and in some groups, but can at times spread to whole communities, especially when leaders systematically install and feed distrust.

Examples of the primitive world view on a national scale can be found in Germany in the 1930s, when Hitler had risen to power. The formal or "state" view of the world was the primitive world view. In this pattern, the mass dismissals of intellectuals, the burning of books and the anti-intellectual climate were predictable steps. Discussion, confrontation and the existence of different viewpoints could not be tolerated. Another example of the primitive world view can be found in Talibaan society, where a similar pattern is imposed: information is banned, no television, no books, no learning (other than indoctrination). The pretext in the Hitler society was the doctrine of ethnic hatred; in the Talibaan it is a specific interpretation of religious doctrine. What the two situations have in common is the primitive world view, the mechanisms accompanying this view, and the resulting dynamics: a narrowing of scope that ultimately can only lead to escalating conflict.

In contrast, a sophisticated relation between self and others is conducive to learning. In a sophisticated world view, the person feels a bond with humankind and realizes our interdependence as human beings and as living creatures worldwide.

There is an understanding that different values and truths have their place in the world, an acceptance of alternatives without one necessarily being the "only truth". There is a continued exploration of the world and of new insights, a facility to integrate various viewpoints into a shared vision, delight in ambiguity and paradox, and a general concern with sharing and sense-making.

The sophisticated world view offers a wide scope for learning. Intermediary stages in the way people experience their relations with others have their own specific limitations for learning (see Meyer, 1994, for a further discussion). However, in the course of their lifetime, many people develop from a primitive world view to a more sophisticated one. These shifts to a more sophisticated view are not studied systematically at this point, nor are they taken explicitly into account when people apply for a position in business or government. Implicitly, they probably do play a role in the career development of individuals. Moreover, they should be taken into account when learning is at stake. To benefit from a learning opportunity, there should be a "fit" between the person's world view, and that which is being offered to him or her as a learning experinece. The disparity should not be too great in the case of a more sophisticated view being presented, or the person will not be able to make the connection. However, a more primitive world view should also be avoided since it holds no challenge or appeal for the person. Lack of fit will lead only to stress, but not to insight or understanding.

21.4.2 The Organizational Context

Not all organizations have equal chances of becoming learning organizations. One of the important aspects relevant for learning is the organization's vitality or its stage in the organizational life cycle.

Financial institutions tend to classify organizations according to output criteria. The portfolio analysis classifies firms according to two variables: market share and growth:

- Starters: small market share, large growth
- Rising stars: large market share, large growth
- Cash cows: large market share, small growth
- Lame dogs: small market share, small growth

Usually, financial experts will advise closing a "lame dog" and advise against long-term investments in cash cows.

However, financial data rarely depicts the actual situation of an organization. Usually, there is at the least a time lag. For instance, the "cash cow" situation has been operative for quite some time before the financial results reflect the status quo. This obviously makes the stock market such an interesting playing field, but can hamper efforts to bring about organizational changes, at least, if one should go by the financial data alone. Organization experts[11] have therefore developed a system by which they can gain insight into a firm's vitality at an earlier stage. The four stages recognized are the following:

- Phase 1: Expansion. Characterized by enormous energy and multidirectional approach to market.
- Phase 2: Growth. Growth is enhanced by concrete choices and by choosing a specific direction in which to grow.
- Phase 3: Consolidation. Strategies are concentrated on the safekeeping of past gains and perfection of proceedings.
- Phase 4: Decline. Runs of "bad luck", decline of results, panic reactions.

Organizational climate, defined as the interplay of habits, attitudes, values and orientations of members towards each other and their products, offers a better indication of vitality, since these signs are more direct than financial indicators. There are considerable differences in norms between the various stages in the life cycle. What is considered normal in one phase, can be strange or undesirable in another phase. For instance, the jealous guarding of one's own position is quite accepted in phase 4 organizations, whereas organizations in phase 1 would find this incomprehensible.

In the expansion phase, firms are still fighting for their existence. The climate is open, speed is essential, members are keen to seek out risks and opportunities. The firm is geared to action, official positions and structure lag behind the actual situation. In this stage, learning is important, and usually the conditions for learning are good. There is an open climate. Members confront each other over issues of importance. People are aware of their responsibility.

In the growth phase, there is less room for improvisation than in phase 1. The organization is striving for more planning, more thought-out moves and strategies. Members try to perceive risks, calculate possible effects and reduce or avoid them. Decision making is quick and clear-cut. New markets are still being developed. Expertise is "bought" when it is considered necessary.

In the consolidation phase, the organization has proved its existence is justified. Risk-taking is avoided. On the contrary, the good name of the company must be held up, and efforts concentrate on giving the customers value for money, among other things by way of greater precision and care in organizational processes. In this stage, firms are especially prone to the defensive routines described by Argyris. People behave towards each other in

---

[11] I wish to thank the Galan Group Management Consultants for this material. An article is in preparation.

a friendly fashion and avoid confrontations. Improvement and change can only come about after lengthy discussion and consideration.

Finally, in the fourth phase, the decline of the organization manifests itself in external results. Members seek assurance from approved methods, acquired rights, due procedure. Process becomes inflexible. Decision making is slow—there is always some opposition somewhere. Leadership is usually staid and experienced, and policies are defensive. In the last stages of the decline, panic reactions can occur—sudden complete changes in leadership or production, seemingly uncalled for actions, are common ocurrences at this stage.

From the above, it will be clear that the phase in the organizational life cycle sets limits on the possible development of a learning organization. Especially in phases 3 and 4, what can be learned and the extent to which a learning process can be adopted are severely limited. In phase 4 the organization is completely dependent on outside influence, if learning is to take place. Moreover in a phase 4 organization the stress levels are invariably high, leading quickly to disruption if anything beyond the current routines is introduced. In phase 3 the climate is resistant to innovation, so a learning process will be bent into the perfecting of that which is already known. In phase 1 people are set on learning, but they are also in a great hurry, and gaining a toehold in the market takes priority over all else. In the struggle for survival, they can easily overreach themselves, or lack overview on account of the constant chaos. The best climate for the learning process is provided by phase 2, where growth is coupled with the wish to systematize what is learned on the way.

Finally, the larger and more complex an organization is, the more opportunity there is for individuals and groups to hide out in organizational pockets, where the results of their actions are hard to trace back to them, and where the possibility that they will be held directly accountable for outcomes is extremely remote or even non-existent. Some people seek out these situations, since they afford them a pastime and a set of "colleagues", in addition to a salary, status and a predictable future, without the risks they would run as entrepreneurs or employees in direct view and in more challenging environments.

21.4.3 Management and Team Learning

Specific obstructions to group learning processes are commonly found in organizations. They originate in the hierarchical and horizontal divisions common in large and bureaucratic organizations. Discretionary power is fragmented, and employees are discouraged from considering matters beyond the confines of their own or their department's jurisdiction. Many structures in firms are specifically designed to keep people in their places, and to discourage them from transcending boundaries, even in their own minds. In addition, organizational climate stresses the importance of doing well. From a short-term perspective, this often means that people pretend to know what they don't really know, or pretend all is well when actually things are going wrong. This obviously prevents learning on central issues, although it does teach people how to cover up.

A set of conditions which can enhance or limit the development of a learning organization consists of the way management and teams deal with situations designed to move the organization forward. Senge (1990) points to various learning "disabilities" common in organizations. These disabilities are in line with the obstacles pointed out by Argyris and Schon, in the sense that people protect themselves from appearing uncertain or ignorant, and other people go along in this protection. However, Senge argues that present-day managers need to undergo a personal transformation, becoming more open to their fellow people and equipped with an integrated and coherent understanding of the world around them. It is important to note that Senge describes the transformation as a mental leap that is both cognitive and emotional. Learning is hampered by fears, frustrations, prejudice, existing positions in the hierarchy, and vested interests. Part of the conditions necessary for learning are created by "unlearning" the previous organizational niceties and distinctions, and by clearing the way for vision and creative abilities. Various practical tools are offered to safeguard the learning situation in practice.

21.5 CONCLUSION

In conclusion, we can state that organizational learning is an ideal that up to this time has not often been effected in practice. Part of organizational learning must necessarily consist of "unlearning", since what is advocated as learning carries the seeds of bureaucratization and indoctrination. Two things seem important on the basis of what has been put forward here. First, external influences are insufficient safeguards. They need to be complemented by a different attitude from within. This attitude must make better use of the implicit and unconscious mental processes, of feelings, paradoxes, and of the power of imagination, to counterbalance linear thinking.

Second, not only the products of learning need to be scrutinized periodically, but the processes of learning as well. Striving for unity of insights needs to be counterbalanced by making better use of conflicts, confrontations and cultural shocks and exploring the meanings given them by different parties. Though initially painful, in the long run paying attention to disharmony provides the best safeguards for negative autopoiesis.

The role played by stress in organizational learning involves a dynamic interplay of forces. Too great a restrictivenes of the mother organization can lead to stress, both for those trying to adjust to a cramped conceptual and developmental space, and for those being ignored, harassed for deviance, or actually expelled.

When mismatch occurs, and when confrontation threatens or takes place, these events are stressful in and of themselves. However, depending on the way they are handled, the air can be cleared for creative new solutions, in which the stress can be viewed as an impulse, a challenge, ultimately leading to rewarding experiences for both the individuals and the organization. Alternatively, of course, if handled badly, the same stressful events can lead to a cover-up, the construction of "undiscussables", more stress, health problems and even violence. Essential for the handling is that confrontations can be made explicit and interpreted as opportunities for learning (instead of taking the position that the view, person or group that is "different" should be eliminated). This calls for managers and responsible workers with tolerance and sophisticated world views.

REFERENCES

Argyris, C. & Schön, D.A. (1996) *Organizational Learning II: Theory, Method and Practice*. Reading, MA: Addison-Wesley.
Csikszentmihalyi, M. (1990) *Flow: The Psychology of Optimal Experience*. New York: Harper & Row.

Csikszentmihalyi, M. (1997) *Creativity*. New York: Harper Perennial.

Giddens, A. (1982) *Profiles and Critiques in Social Theory*. London and Basingstoke: The MacMillan Press.

Jaques, E. (1986) The development of intellectual capability: a discussion of stratified systems theory. *Journal of Applied Behavioral Science, 22(4), 361–83.*

Johnson, S. (1998) *Who Moved My Cheese?* London: Vermilion.

Katz, R. (1985) Societal codes for responding to dissent. In W.G. Bennis, K.D. Benne, and R. Chin, (eds) *The Planning of Change.* New York: Holt, Rinehart & Winston, pp. 354–68.

Kuhn, T.S. (1962, 1970) *The Structure of Scientific Revolutions.* Chicago, IL: University of Chicago Press.

Meyer, J. (1994) *De Psychologie van Organisatieverandering (The Psychology of Organizational Change).* Utrecht: Elsevier.

Morgan, G. (1986) *Images of Organization.* London: Sage.

Nonaka, I. & Takeuchi, H. (1995) *The Knowledge-Creating Company.* Oxford: Oxford University Press.

Quinn, R.E. & Cameron, K.S. (eds) (1988) *Paradox and Transformation.* Cambridge, MA: Ballinger.

Senge, P. (1990) *The Fifth Discipline.* New York: Doubleday.

Watzlawick, P., Beavin, J.H. & Jackson, D.D. (1986) *Pragmatics of Human Communication.* London: Faber & Faber.

CHAPTER 22

Management Development, Well-Being and Health in the Twenty-First Century

J. Lee Whittington
University of Dallas, USA
Paul B. Paulus and **James Campbell Quick**
University of Texas at Arlington, USA

22.1 INTRODUCTION

Stress and challenge in European, Japanese and American work organizations are increasing due to the dramatic globalization of business activity starting at the end of the 1980s and the direct, head-to-head competition emerging among the core industries in these economies (Friedman, 1999; Thurow, 1993). This competitive environment and attendant economic pressures make managing organizations in the United States, and other countries, during the twenty-first century especially challenging (Whetten & Cameron, 1998). Global competition among the United States, Europe and Japan is expected to continue, even increase. Lawler (2000) identifies four major changes that will contribute to this increasingly complex environment: a boundaryless economy, worldwide labor markets, instantly linked information, and agile new organizations. With the American Management Association's projected shortfall in executives through the mid-twenty-first century, increasing amounts of competitive pressure can be expected to shift to the management ranks in organizations. Hence, the creation of healthy work environments that flourish in these challenging, stressful times is a priority. Whetten & Cameron (1998) are hopeful and optimistic that management has, or can acquire, the knowledge base to meet the challenge effectively. They concluded that, "Good people management" was more important than all other factors in predicting profitability (Whetten & Cameron, 1998). This position is also supported by Pfeffer (1998), who argues that people may be the only sustainable source of competitive advantage. Pfeffer points out that historic sources of competitive advantage have shifted over time and even become less important. Yet, the one competitive advantage that remains and becomes even more important in the current business environment is an organization's employees and how they work. A similar argument is made by Lawler (2000), who argues for a "new logic"

The Handbook of Work and Health Psychology. Edited by M.J. Schabracq, J.A.M. Winnubst and C.L. Cooper.
© 2003 John Wiley & Sons, Ltd.

organization that recognizes people as the organization's primary asset. Thus management development and employee well-being have become a strategic imperative.

This chapter focuses on management development and the design of healthy work environments. The chapter has six major sections. Section 22.2 examines the characteristics of new logic organizations as healthy, vital, and active workplaces. Section 22.3 addresses managing teams for productivity and well-being. Section 22.4 discusses the framework of preventive stress management, its relationship to health psychology, and management's role in creating healthy work environments. Section 22.5 considers career development as an essential aspect of overall management development. Section 22.6 is a brief and important one, addressing how to implement management development through education and training. The sixth and final section, Section 22.7, discusses the manager's whole-life model as a way of placing work in a larger life context.

22.2   THE NEW LOGIC ORGANIZATION

The complexity of the current environment requires a paradigm shift in the way organizations are structured and managed. Traditional models of strategy and organization are no longer sufficient. Pfeffer (1998) argues that in this new competitive environment the only sustainable source of competitive advantage is people. He advocates that organizations should develop strategies and structures that emphasize seven characteristics: (i) employment security, (ii) selective hiring of new personnel, (iii) self-managed teams and decentralized decision making as the basic principles of organizational design, (iv) comparatively high compensation that is contingent upon organizational performance, (v) extensive training, (vi) reduced status distinctions and barriers, and (vii) extensive sharing of financial and performance information throughout the organization.

The development and implementation of Pfeffer's keys to organizational effectiveness require a new mindset. According to Lawler (2000, p. 17) a new form of managing and organizing must be created that addresses three vital issues: how will individuals know what to do, how will they be trained and developed, and what will motivate them to do it? To address this need, Lawler advocates a "new logic" organization built around six principles:

1. Organization can be the ultimate competitive advantage. This principle suggests that management systems, processes and structures are the critical elements in creating a competitive advantage that allows organizations to perform in ways that competitors cannot.
2. Employee involvement is the most effective source of control. Involvement creates intrinsic controls because the employees have a sense of ownership and they focus their energy and creativity on the improvement of organizational processes.
3. When employees are involved in their work it is possible for all employees to add significant value to the organization.
4. Lateral processes are the key to achieving organizational effectiveness.
5. Team-based work designs are necessary and the various organizational subsystems, such as reward and performance evaluations, must be aligned to support this structure. Lawler suggests that this team-based approach to organizing should be centered around products and customers rather the traditional functions of the organization.

6. Finally, Lawler calls for transformational leadership that impacts the organization's effectiveness by setting direction, defining the agenda, adjusting strategy to address the changing business environment, and serving as role models for leadership throughout the organization.

RadioShack is an organization that recognizes the strategic implications of the new logic and the importance of people in creating and sustaining its competitive advantage. RadioShack CEO Len Roberts clearly understands this link. He has repeatedly told stakeholders that "before a store can be a great place to shop, it must first be a great place to work." He has stated a bold goal of RadioShack (1999) becoming the best company to work for in America. To achieve this goal, Roberts created a committee of employees from a cross-section of the organization to identify practices that would enhance employee well-being while making RadioShack a great place to work. The list developed by the employees was published. Among the practices identified by the employees were enhanced group insurance, improved vacation and personal leave policies, and provision of resources for personal and family needs, development of a mentor program and the creation of a culture of positive motivation. These principles were to be guided by a focus on the RadioShack values of teamwork, pride, trust and integrity. Regular updates on the company's progress implementing the practices is provided each month in the company news magazine. The approach taken by RadioShack exemplifies the characteristics of Lawler's new logic organization and Pfeffer's emphasis on people as the primary source of sustainable competitive advantage.

22.2.1 Managers Who Are Learners

The new logic organization also requires a change in the way we think about organizational development. Traditionally, management and career development focused on knowledge acquisition and the mastery of various skills: technical, communication, managerial, team-building, and organizational. Given the permanent whitewater of contemporary organizational reality, the critical element in managerial development may no longer be the acquisition of new skill sets: the self-reliant capacity to learn may be more critical for managers and their careers. This assumes that learning is possible. However, Isabella & Forbes (1994) found that only 10% of managers have a "learning mindset." This minority who are learners may be characterized as follows:

1. They have experienced numerous events that caused them to dramatically rethink their basic assumptions.
2. They possess high cognitive complexity as demonstrated by agility of thought. This is evident in their ability to see solutions not readily apparent to others, to adapt easily to new situations, and to see patterns and connections between seemingly unconnected variables.
3. They focus on learning from a wide variety of sources.
4. They communicate readily in metaphors and analogies, and conduct discussions in a nonlinear manner.

To this point, we have discussed the responsibility of managers to develop their individual learning capacities, yet an equally important responsibility rests on the organization's leaders to create a culture that encourages and supports this mindset. This requires the creation of a learning culture that is characterized by clear and consistent openness to experience, encouragement of responsible risk taking, and willingness to acknowledge failures and learn from them.

Learning organizations are healthy organizations and learning managers have specific characteristics. McGill and associates (McGill & Slocum, 1993; McGill et al., 1992) call for the creation of a learning organization. Learning organizations are characterized by generative learning, also called double-loop learning by Argyris (1993), as opposed to the adaptive learning that characterizes most organizations. Generative learning emphasizes continuous experimentation and feedback in an ongoing examination of the very way in which organizations go about defining and solving problems.

Managers in the learning organization demonstrate the following five characteristics.

- Openness: this includes the suspension of the manager's need for control and the development of cultural/functional humility.
- Systemic thinking: this refers to the ability to see the connection between issues, events, and data points.
- Creativity: this dimension involves personal flexibility and willingness to take reasonable business risks.
- Self-efficacy: managers possessing this characteristic are actively self-aware and proactive problem solvers.
- Empathy: managers in the learning organization are concerned for human nature and capable of repairing strained relationships. Thus, learning is linked to larger purposes beyond day-to-day problem solving.

The description of the empathy dimension of the learning organization is similar to Lundin & Lundin's (1994) notion of healing managers. They suggest that organizations need to build trust by directly confronting feelings and emotions in the workplace. Healing managers help others grow emotionally and intellectually by evoking the spirit and values of an organization committed to creating a caring, humane and compassionate work environment. Healing managers forge the emotional pathway to healthy relationships.

22.2.2 The Manager and the Organization

We call for learning and development at two interdependent levels: the individual manager and the organization. The development of this dual learning capacity can have beneficial effects on health and well-being, not by reducing uncertainty, but by equipping managers to respond to change and uncertainty in new ways. Once the learning mindset has been adopted, critical events and uncertainty present additional opportunities for growth and development. The ultimate goal of the learning organization is the development of self-reliant managers who are able to accept long-term responsibility for self-development and to experience several metamorphoses during the careers (Nelson et al., 1995; Waterman et al., 1994).

22.3 MANAGING TEAMS FOR PRODUCTIVITY AND WELL-BEING

Given the emphasis placed on self-managed teams, decentralized decision making and lateral processes in the "new logic" organizations by Pfeffer (1998) and Lawler (2000), it is important to examine the role of teams in organizations and the effect that teams have on management development and employee well-being. Managers may find it difficult to create healthy, productive work environments free of distress. However, as team leaders and as managers of teams, they have an opportunity to use teams for enhancing health at work. Cooperative teamwork is presumed to increase productivity and morale (Tjosvold, 1991). Teams vary greatly in their make-up, organization, and degree of independence. While it is difficult to develop broad generalizations that apply to all teams, there appear to be some general, widely applicable principles with which managers should be familiar. We will highlight these in relation to a variety of issues.

22.3.1 Team Management and Performance

Occupational health psychology (OHP) is concerned with performance and productivity as well as with health and well-being. Although much of the philosophy of teams suggests that collaborative efforts are associated with productivity, research has shown that this is not inevitably true. Groups are renowned for their flawed decision making, unproductive members or loafers, and conformity to conventionality (Paulus, 1989). Teams, when left to their own devices, may drift into unproductive patterns as much as individuals in other types of organizational structures (Hackman, 1990; Paulus, 2000). For example, groups may set fairly unchallenging goals for themselves to ensure success (Larey & Paulus, 1995). Teams need extensive training to learn how to work together most effectively (Swezey & Salas, 1992), and they need effective leadership to be successful (Hogan et al., 1994).

Charisma is one leadership characteristic related to team performance (Bass, 1985). The vision of such leaders is important to team building and motivation to perform beyond expectations (House, 1977). Teams vary in their response to leaders' use of participative or task-oriented styles. Teams that perform various realistic or concrete tasks (e.g. engineers, accountants, athletic teams) usually function best with authoritative or task-oriented leadership (Hogan et al., 1988). Teams involved primarily in enterprising or social activities (e.g. management teams, teachers) usually react more positively to participative leadership (Foels et al., 2000).

There are a number of straightforward guidelines for effective leadership of teams (Hackman & Walton, 1986; Swezey & Salas, 1992). In most cases, it is important for group members to have a clearly defined and respected leader. Such leaders should keep the group oriented toward its task and recognize the importance of both task and team skills. The leader should be a good communicator who encourages communication among group members. It may require a certain amount of training to develop the appropriate leadership and communication skills for teamwork. Finally, the organization needs to provide the rewards, resources, and information required for teams to function effectively (Locke et al., 2001). Not all teams have a clearly defined hierarchy or leadership structure (e.g. self-managing teams; Pearce & Ravlin, 1987). If these teams are to function effectively, it is necessary to have a clearly defined structure for group interaction. For example, specific procedures for enhancing collaboration and appropriate productivity norms are important for their success (Cohen & Bailey, 1997; Gammage et al., 2001; Gladstein, 1984; Swezey & Salas, 1992; Turner & Horvitz, 2001).

The reward structure is also a critical factor in team performance and morale. Teams expect that rewards will be related to their effectiveness. Group-based feedback and rewards are indeed associated with effective team performance (Fandt et al., 1993; Shea & Guzzo, 1987). However, this does not mean that team members no longer care about individually based compensation systems. Effective teamwork in individualistic cultures may involve a degree of individual accountability (Gammage et al., 2001) and the use of compensation systems that reflect differences in individual contributions (Locke et al., 2001). This process may involve within-team assessment. To minimize friction within the team, final compensation decisions should be made by outsiders.

22.3.2 Diversity and Conflict in Teams

Regardless of how skilled, knowledgeable and self-reliant a person becomes, he or she never becomes self-sufficient. Therefore, one important reason for developing teamwork is the need to effectively integrate different skills and knowledge bases. This is reflected in the use of cross-functional teams, in which members of different organizational units work together to better coordinate activities (Sashkin & Sashkin, 1994). Knowledge work, as in research and development teams, can also benefit greatly from diversity (Paulus et al., 2001; West, in press). However, such benefits are not inevitable. Individuals from diverse backgrounds (training, culture) may have difficulties working together and communicating effectively (Ancona, 1990; Kirchmeyer, 1993). Groups that are based on common characteristics (e.g. gender) and interests are likely to be more cohesive. High levels of cohesiveness can increase commitment to the group and productivity (Mullen & Copper, 1994). There is also a tendency in groups to focus on common bits of information, and this may inhibit the exchange of the diverse knowledge contained in the group (Stasser, 1999). Effective leadership is required to achieve a full exchange of knowledge and ideas. Training in group dynamics, problem solving, and effective teamwork may also be useful.

Friction can occur between group members and between teams because of conflicts of interest. Conflicts of interest within and/or among teams can develop because of competition over limited resources, such as money or personnel (Van de Vliert & Janssen, 2001). Conflicts frequently occur when reward structures are competition-based. It is important for team and organizational leaders to keep members focused on the common goals and emphasize reward structures that promote cooperation (West, 2002). In a cooperative atmosphere individuals may share tasks and information, as well as social support. This sharing process is important to the team-building process and its maintenance.

22.3.3 Stress and Well-Being in Teams

Members of teams and organizations experience a range of stressors as part of their work lives. Performance demands, interpersonal conflicts, and competition are a few examples. Although a certain amount of tension, pressure, and accountability is needed for optimal performance, overly high levels of these variables can have detrimental effects on performance and well-being (Seta et al., 2000; Turner & Horvitz, 2001). Teams should theoretically have fairly low stress levels. A cooperative and supportive social atmosphere in teams should minimize interpersonal conflicts and provide a socially supportive network for dealing with stressors outside the workplace. Unfortunately, teams can also be sources of stress. If teams are not appropriately structured, there may be role ambiguity or role conflict. Individuals may not be sure about the scope of their tasks and responsibilities. This may sometimes be a deliberate strategy to give teams creative freedom. However, not all individuals are equally comfortable with such wide latitude in their jobs. If performance appraisal requires members to rate one another, interpersonal conflicts and discomfort can arise. Teamwork involves close collaboration with others rather than independent work. Such close interactions provide increased opportunities for conflict or friction about ways in which the tasks should be distributed or managed. Teams may also require individuals to play multiple roles, some of which may be outside their perceived area of competence. This stretching process may be accompanied by concerns about failure or embarrassment. Finally, teamwork may increase rather than decrease the work demands on the individual. Some team members may not carry their full load. In cooperative endeavors, there may be a tendency for some individuals to loaf when they are not individually accountable. Others may take a free ride on the efforts of highly productive and motivated workers. Unfortunately, the lack of effort or capability on the part of some team members may put extra pressure on other team members to maintain the team's level of performance. Interestingly, when organizations experience stress, they may become more authoritarian in structure, and decision-making becomes more centralized, which is antithetical to a team-based philosophy (Driskell & Salas, 1991; Staw et al., 1981). At first, teams may also deal with failure by increasing their reliance on existing practices or routines (Gersick & Hackman, 1990). However, they should discover that these are typically counterproductive. They may then actually become more egalitarian and open to input from others (Ziller & Behringer, 1960). Of course, if stress persists, groups may drift back to a more authoritarian structure as a last resort (Janis, 1982).

How can these team-related stresses be reduced? The approach required is similar to that required to produce effective performance in groups. There needs to be a clear structure for group interaction and performance that reduces job ambiguity (Turner & Horvitz, 2001). Some degree of individual accountability needs to be maintained to minimize loafing or free-riding (Gammage et al., 2001). Individuals also need training to develop the type of skills necessary to work in a collaborative environment (Stevens & Campion, 1994; Swezey & Salas, 1992). Some people prefer working collaboratively, while others prefer working independently (Larey, 1994). It is likely that the independent types will experience some degree of frustration and stress when they are forced to work in collaborative efforts. It may be important to allow individuals some degree of choice about the extent to which they will be involved in collaborative activities. Of course, most teamwork involves a combination of individual and collaborative work. This allows each individual to obtain a personally comfortable level of social interaction in the workplace.

22.3.4 How to Get the Most out of Teams and Groups

It is quite evident that teams and groups do not inevitably excel on their own. Many forces may lower performance in groups (Paulus, 1989). Successful groups need effective leadership, an appropriate reward structure, a minimal level of stress, and an interpersonally supportive atmosphere. In general, it appears that teams seem to thrive best under the following conditions: participative management, cohesiveness, group training, feedback, goals and performance rewards, and appropriate diversity of skills and knowledge (Cohen & Bailey, 1997; Seta et al., 2000; Sundstrom et al., 1990). However, it should also be recognized that not all activities benefit equally from group or team-based efforts. Moreover, some types of individuals may function more effectively in groups than others (Barrick et al., 1998). To improve worker productivity and well-being, it is important to match the right activities and individuals to the teams, to train teams and individuals to work collaboratively, and to provide the appropriate leadership and organizational support (Hackman & Walton, 1986; West, in press).

22.3.5 Managing Creative Teams

One of the key functions of many teams is to develop creative solutions to problems. Knowledge teams are often seeking new ideas or perspectives on the basis of shared knowledge. Product development teams often use brainstorming techniques to facilitate the generation of unique and useful products (Sutton & Hargadon, 1996). Although there are many practitioners who strongly endorse the creative power of groups (e.g. Kayser, 1994), there is only limited empirical evidence for the creative genius of teams (Dunbar, 1997; Paulus, 2000). That does not mean that teams cannot be creative, only that teams may have difficulty overcoming some of the problems inherent in group interactions such as loafing, distraction, response inhibition, and premature consensus. Recent evidence suggests that several techniques may be helpful in managing creative teams. First it is important to structure the interaction so that a full exchange of ideas occurs. This can take the form of written or computer exchanges (Dugosh et al., 2000; Paulus & Yang, 2000) or the use of facilitators who carefully manage the group process (Oxley et al., 1996). It is also important to insure that group members pay careful attention to the ideas exchanged and that they have some period of time to integrate these ideas with their own knowledge bases (an incubation session; Dugosh et al., 2000). Finally, it is important to have some organized evaluation and decision-making process so that groups can carefully evaluate all of the ideas in coming to a decision about which ideas to implement (Paulus, 1998).

22.4 PREVENTIVE STRESS MANAGEMENT AND HEALTH PSYCHOLOGY

Work related psychological disorders and distress have been among the 10 leading occupational health risks in the United States for a decade (Sauter et al., 1990). There are a variety of contributing factors for such health risks, including the corporate warfare manifested in mergers, acquisitions, downsizing and bankruptcies, which has come with increasing competition (Nelson et al., 1989; Thurow, 1993). One has to go back to the Great Depression in America to find a time when as many businesses were failing as today (Whetten & Cameron, 1998). Based on the translation of the epidemiological and public health notions of prevention into a stress-process framework, *preventive stress management* was developed as an organizational philosophy for leading and managing organizations to enhance health while averting distress in the workplace (Quick et al., 1997). Two of the guiding principles of preventive stress management are especially relevant to managers interested in creating healthy work environments.

1. Principle 1: individual and organizational health are interdependent.
2. Principle 2: leaders have a responsibility for individual and organizational health.

Principle 1 calls for managers to enhance their own health and well-being because they make important contributions to the health and well-being of the organization as a whole as well as being important role models for their employees. Organizations cannot maintain vitality and productivity when the individuals throughout them are distressed and in varying degrees dysfunctional. Hence, management has a responsibility for individual and organizational health (Principle 2). As managers develop their own health, they should do so considering the personal, family, spiritual, and community arenas of their lives, because parenting, community involvement, and recreation have positive benefits for their functioning in the work area (Kirchmeyer, 1992).

Within the preventive stress management model, Quick et al. (1990) found that chief executives who managed stress in a healthy manner varied substantially in the prevention methods each found personally most effective. However, all were found to be self-reliant in the way they formed and maintained a social support network of professional and personal (e.g. family, spiritual, and community) relationships (Quick et al., 1987). Furthermore, a study of the US Navy's top 140 major weapon system managers found that such social support constituted an effective prevention method for reducing burnout associated with perceived environmental uncertainty (Bodensteiner et al., 1989).

22.4.1 Occupational Health Psychology

Whereas preventive stress management has a dual focus on enhancing health and averting distress in the workplace, occupational health psychology (OHP) focuses on the design and construction of healthy work environments (Murphy & Cooper, 2000; Quick, 1999a, b; Quick & Tetrick, 2003). OHP is concerned with both the physical and the psychosocial, interpersonal design features of the work environment in order to manage the health risks that these design features may present. OHP is, therefore, a science of design aimed at creating opportunities for employees to grow, develop, and strive to maximize their intellectual and physical potential free from unreasonable and/or unnecessary psychological risks.

22.4.2 Design Dimensions

OHP has three design dimensions: the work environment, the person, and the work environment–family system interface. First, the work environment dimension devotes attention to psychosocial aspects of work. The work environment design dimension addresses the issues of work design, organizational culture, corporate policies and procedures related to personal actions, families, and due process. Control, uncertainty and conflict are parameters of particular interest within this design dimension (Landy et al., 1994). Second, the person dimension requires attention to cognitive, moral, and human development, as well as to skills and abilities required for the demands of a competitive or stressful work environment (Whetten & Cameron, 1998). Third, the work–family interface dimension addresses

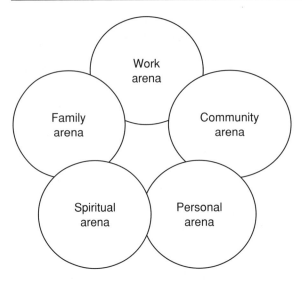

Figure 22.1   The manager's whole-life model: five arenas of life

the manager's non-work life arenas shown in Figure 22.1. While the family is of particular concern in this regard (Piotrkowski, 1979; Quick et al., 1994), the community, spiritual, and personal arenas are important as well (Seta et al., 2000).

22.4.3   Goodness of Fit

The person–environment fit theory of stress concerns the interaction between person and environment dimensions, thus offering a point of departure for understanding the flexible fit dynamics required in OHP (Edwards & Cooper, 1990). The three design elements of OHP operate interdependently, not independently. Goodness of fit is an important element in a design process. Hence, blaming distressed victims or workplaces for health problems is of little value when design modifications in one or the other design dimensions may solve the problem. Principles 1 and 2 of preventive stress management imply a shared responsibility for health at work, and imply joint problem solving to enhance healthy human potential in organizations. The notion of goodness of fit between the person and the work environment suggests the potential for no-fault problems and the need to mold each. The work environment, the person, and the family all must have degrees of flexibility. Hence, the need for a flexible fit among the three design dimensions. Quick et al., (2001) recently used dynamic effect spirals in proposing an isomorphic theory of stress that extends person–environment fit theory and the goodness of fit concept. An isomorphic theory refers to a dimension-specific extension of person–environment fit theory and focuses attention on corresponding characteristics in the person and the environment. The isomorphic theory proposed by Quick et al. (2001) brings attention to the dimensions of control, uncertainty, and interpersonal relationships. Further, the theory suggests that through mutual, dynamic accommodations along each dimension, goodness-of-fit and healthy levels of stress can be achieved.

22.4.4 Health Management: Johnson & Johnson Health Care Systems Inc.

Johnson & Johnson Health Care Systems Inc. advances physical and psychological health in the workplace. The company grew out of the Johnson & Johnson "Live for Life Program" comprehensive health promotion program (Nathan, 1984). Many workplace health promotion programs emphasize exercise and physical fitness as central, if not the primary, components of the program. The Johnson & Johnson approach has a more comprehensive program, which begins with a public health approach to health risk assessment and diagnosis followed by behavioral and lifestyle re-engineering. There is no explicit component targeting workplace redesign or re-engineering. Rather, the emphasis is on secondary and tertiary prevention through person-change strategies, such as physical fitness training and cognitive restructuring for stressful situations. In addition to the health risk assessment services that the company offers, Johnson & Johnson Health Care Systems has an array of educational, health, and fitness services and products for managers to address preventive stress management, nutrition, and cholesterol management, weight control, smoking cessation, and blood pressure management.

Fielding (1984) found that the evaluation of health promotion programs focused on return on investment from a cost–benefit standpoint or a cost-effectiveness perspective. His review of four corporate health promotion/disease prevention programs concluded that: (i) there was no single successful model, and (ii) seven important keys for success were long-term commitment, top management support, employee involvement, professional leadership, clearly defined objectives, careful planning, and family involvement. One evaluation of the Johnson & Johnson Health Management "Live for Life" program by Bly et al. (1986) used two health promotion groups ($N = 5192$ and 3259) and one control group ($N = 2955$). The two groups in the Live for Life program had (i) lower mean inpatient health care cost increases; (ii) lower rates of increase in hospital days; and (iii) no difference in outpatient and other health care costs.

22.4.5 Managers as Healing Agents and Organizational Heroes

Frost & Robinson (1999) suggest that organizational pain and suffering, in the form of sadness, anger, and emotional turmoil are endemic to organizational life for a variety of reasons. Further, organizational pain management may contribute to the organization's bottom line financial health and it may be managers in the form of organizational heroes who shoulder much of the organizational pain and become toxin handlers. However, by engaging in handling the emotional toxins of organizational life, these managers also expose themselves to significant health risks, psychologically and physically. Their role as toxin handlers, however, does provide a healing function at work. In Edgar Schein's conceptual framework, this may be one way of performing organizational therapy (Quick & Gavin, 2000).

In addition to being a referent leader for others in the work environment, managers must play the role of triage agent at work. That is, managers must have resources, whether through an employee assistance program (EAP) or a psychology department, to which people in need may be referred. The array of resources to consider includes medical, psychological, spiritual and other counseling services. A manager is expected to be knowledgeable enough to determine when someone needs help and then to refer the person to the proper professional. When in doubt, the manager must have available through an EAP a more sophisticated triage resource person who can screen the individual at risk into a professional's hands. Finally, a manager can help improve health at work by being sensitive to employee problems in other life areas, such as family or personal arenas, which intrude on or affect the work arena.

22.5 CAREER DEVELOPMENT

To meet the challenge of competition and chaos in the world of work, Waterman et al. (1994) call for a career-resilient, self-reliant workforce. Self-reliant managers and workers stand ready to reinvent themselves developmentally in order to keep pace with change. Self-reliance is a flexible pattern of behavior for developing and maintaining healthy relationships (Quick et al., 1990). Self-reliance operates in all of life's arenas, and management development is one aspect of overall life development. The manager's whole-life model shown in Figure 22.1 includes five major life arenas. The size and relative importance of each arena varies by individual manager. Special attention has been focused on the potential for conflict and the desirability of balance in the allocation of investment in the work and family arenas (Lobel, 1991). For example, problems in the work arena may spill over into the family arena, or the reverse may also occur, which can be problematic (Kabanoff, 1980; Quick et al., 1994). Therefore, as we focus on management development in the work arena, sensitivity to the interdependence of a manager's five life arenas is important. Management development is an ongoing process of learning, growing, and changing to enhance one's skills and/or knowledge. In the United States alone there are more than five million managers, and management development is provided to qualify managers for their jobs and/or to upgrade their positions (Pace et al., 1991). Management development is one way to design and build healthy, vital work environments. Management development may be undertaken by an individual manager or by the organization, or it may be a shared responsibility. Career development enhances management development while encouraging individual and organizational health. This process constitutes an important part of the individual–organization exchange relationship. Individuals look to the organization to provide a series of meaningful, satisfying work experiences and organizations expect high levels of performance and commitment from individuals to whom they provide opportunities. Career development consists of the actions individuals take, alone or with the aid of others, to manage their careers in specific ways (Quick et al., 1997).

Successful career development efforts can encourage the health of both managers and organizations, although a demanding career may also have adverse effects on a manager's family investment (Kirchmeyer, 1992). For individuals, career development serves several functions. It serves to increase self-efficacy by building in opportunities for growth and success. It decreases some career management uncertainty while giving the manager a sense of control. In addition, sound career choices can serve to decrease strain. For the organization, inattention to career development can have dysfunctional consequences. Poor performance, low commitment, low job satisfaction, and high turnover rates can result from the frustration that employees experience in conjunction with poorly managed careers. Career development can best be considered a joint responsibility for individuals and organizations.

22.5.1   Key Components of Career Development

There are two key components of effective career development (Greenhaus, 1987). One component is a process of self-analysis that provides information about individual strengths, weaknesses, interests, and abilities. The other key component is environmental exploration, which includes an analysis of opportunities available to the individual. By combining the self-assessment and the environmental exploration, an individual prepares a personal strategic SWOT analysis in much the same way organizations do.

Self-Analysis

In order to set meaningful career goals, individuals must develop an accurate self-assessment in terms of their values, interests, abilities, and preferences. The process of self-analysis can be formal or informal. It can be accomplished through careful introspection or with the help of assessments by others. Various standardized inventories are available to assist individuals with self-analysis (Roe & Lunneborg, 1990).

Opportunity-Analysis

Identifying the range of organizational roles available for an individual is the second key aspect of career development. This activity has become increasingly challenging in today's organizations because of the flattening of organizations, downsizing, and the elimination of many middle management jobs. Career paths in organizations are no longer feasible because of the increasing pace of change (Dalton, 1989). Nevertheless, individuals must develop information about the role requirements of particular jobs that they envision filling.

22.5.2   A Strategic Career Plan

Good self-analysis and opportunity analysis lead a manager to form a strategic career plan, which should be placed in the context of an overall balanced life. The concept of a career as a series of upward moves may no longer be realistic in light of the radical organizational changes afoot (Thurow, 1993; Waterman et al., 1994). Careers may need to be reconceptualized as a series of lateral moves with attendant breadth in skill acquisition, a perspective very consistent with a developmental view for management. Organizations should not relinquish their roles in opportunity analysis in the face of such challenges. Instead, they should be as honest and forthright as possible with individuals about their futures. Self-analysis and opportunity analysis are reciprocally related and are both essential to forming a strategic career plan. Extensively relying on one process without sufficient attention to the other will produce incomplete career development.

22.5.3   Alternative Sources of Career Development Support

Career development support may come in the form of self-help, counselor assistance, organizational programs, and career planning courses (Gray et al., 1990). Organizations can take some initiatives and can provide opportunities for managers to undertake others.

Self-Help

Individuals can engage in career development pursuits on their own. Self-exploration should be a part of such activities, and individuals should assess their values, interests, skills, work preferences, strengths, and weaknesses. There are many techniques for enhancing self-awareness, including written self-interviews, career graphs, daily activity diaries, and interest inventories (Kotter et al., 1978). By learning as much as possible about themselves, individuals can begin to develop meaningful career goals and strategies for achieving the goals. In addition to self-exploration, individuals can conduct library research on careers of interest or contact organizations of interest and ask for published materials. Another alternative is the informational interview, which has the advantage of learning the perspectives of others who have insights about potential career strategies. While self-help avenues of career development have the advantage of low cost, they require significant investments of the individual's time.

Counselor Assistance

A second career development source is engaging the assistance of a career counselor or consultant. While universities provide such services at relatively low cost to students, counselors in private practice provide these services for substantially higher fees. Most counselors take a comprehensive approach to career development, combining individual assessment with opportunity analyses. A typical approach uses both standardized instruments that focus on job interests, career maturity, and abilities, along with in-depth interviews. The advantages of using counselors or consultants include the interactive feedback provided to the individual and the expertise provided by the counselor. Two potential disadvantages of this approach are its cost and the danger of the employee forming an unhealthy dependency reliance on the counselor.

Organizational Programs

Many organizations have their own programs for career development that integrate individual career planning with human resource planning. By creating career paths that encourage individual growth and development, organizations ensure a supply of future talent to meet their staffing needs. Career development programs in organizations may include newcomer orientation, job rotation, goal setting, mentoring, assessment center evaluations, and management training. These efforts all work to strengthen the individual–organizational relationship.

Career Planning Courses

Universities or professional associations often offer career-planning courses that individuals can take. One advantage of such courses is the information exchange between individuals and their fellow students and instructors. This exchange provides several points of independent feedback, and provides opportunities for considerable interaction. Typical courses include readings, lectures, standardized tests, cases, individual and group experiential activities, and guest speakers.

In summary, there are several sources of career development support, and a variety can be used to achieve maximum benefits.

22.5.4   Value Added to the Workplace

Career development encourages individual health by providing individuals with opportunities to learn new skills, acquire more knowledge, and work toward achieving their full potential. By providing and developing goals and direction, it reduces the uncertainty and related anxiety and frustration that individuals can experience without a guiding force behind their careers.

For organizations, the value of career development is that it helps identify training needs, staffing opportunities, and undiscovered potential talent in the workforce. It forces an organization to look ahead in terms of its human resource needs, and to proactively develop individuals who can meet those needs. Career development also serves an important communicative function within organizations. It conveys a message to employees that management believes individual well-being and organizational well-being are linked, and that investing in the long-term developmental activities of employees ultimately pays off in organizational health.

22.6   HOW TO IMPLEMENT MANAGEMENT DEVELOPMENT

The primary method for implementing management development is through management education and training, which is why a learning mindset and learning organization culture are so important. For example, at Chaparral Steel Company, all sectors of the company are engaged in educational activities. While many employees participate in technical skill development through the Apprenticeship Program developed in collaboration with the US Department of Labor (Quick & Gray, 1989/90), senior executives engage in management education, which focuses on communication and managerial skill development (Forward et al., 1991). Management development programs are most effective when education and training curricula are developed appropriate to each managerial level. Therefore, while lower levels of management may well require emphasis on technical education with some managerial skill development, increasingly higher levels of management require greater emphasis on communication and managerial skills, with less attention to the technical (Bracey et al., 1986).

22.7   THE MANAGER'S WHOLE-LIFE MODEL: FIVE ARENAS OF LIFE

The language of the "healing manager" and the empathy called for in learning organizations join a growing trend to recognize managers and employees as whole beings, not mere factors of production. The concept of well-being extends beyond the organization, and the non-work arenas of life may well affect occupational well-being. Borrowing from Sherman & Hendricks (1989), our view of well-being transcends the work arena and includes the four non-work arenas of life shown in Figure 22.1. This whole-life model emphasizes each of life's five arenas. Well-being is a function of balance of time, commitment, and the investment of emotional energy in these five areas of life. Managers who define themselves in terms of these five arenas have greater self-complexity (Linville, 1985). Linville's (1987) self-complexity buffering hypothesis suggests that individuals with high levels of self-complexity are buffered from distress and strain when a stressful life event occurs in one life arena. According to Linville, when an individual's self-worth is based on their total self-concept, stressful events in one life arena are not as devastating. Individuals whose self-worth is dominated by only one role or arena are more likely to be experience higher levels of distress when a stressful event occurs in that arena. While Linville's (1985) notion of self-complexity argues for the relative independence of the areas in life, we have argued for recognition of the interdependence.

The personal arena includes a person's emotional and innermost life; that is, the private world of the self (MacDonald, 1985). This private world can be viewed as our essence, and the ordering of this arena in life provides an anchoring stability around which the other life arenas may be ordered. This arena includes personal health, exercise, stress management and leisure time activities. Relationships with mentors and protégés would properly fall in the personal arena.

The family arena emphasizes a manager's responsibilities to spouse and children, yet also includes obligations to siblings and to parents. Planning and budgeting for household management requirements, spending significant time with children, and continuously cultivating one's spousal relationship are all activities associated with the family arena. Family demands appear to be related more strongly to psychological distress for women than men because women may take more responsibility in the family arena than do men (Baruch et al., 1987). The reverse appears to occur for men, with work demands related more strongly to psychological distress (Seta et al., 2000).

The spiritual arena includes the cultivation of a relationship with God, as enhanced by personal efforts in prayer, meditation, and study, as well as involvement in a community of like believers. Internalized, intrinsic and individually active religion has been associated with less illness and better physical health (McIntosh & Spilka, 1990). The community arena suggests the need to be involved in the community, with the intent to serve others. A manager's spiritual and secular communities may or may not overlap. Community suggests the need for healthy interpersonal attachments for the purpose of social support. Secure interpersonal attachments may exist in the work, family, and community arenas, while a secure transcendent attachment to God exists within the spiritual arena (Quick et al., 1995).

The manager's whole-life model suggests that one must perform in all five of life's arenas. This imagery suggests the interdependence, not complete independence, of the five arenas. This advocates a whole-life model of well-being and balanced investment in the five arenas that may buffer a manager from distressing events in life (Linville, 1987).

The manager's whole-life model implies a broader perspective for management development in contrast to a narrower perspective. Rather than emphasizing career and work development to the exclusion of a manager's family, personal, spiritual, and community life, the model places career and work in the context of overall life development. The underlying dynamic for the model is a cooperative, win–win strategy as opposed to a competitive, win–lose strategy.

ACKNOWLEDGEMENTS

The authors would like to thank Edwin A. Gerloff, Bruce D. Evans, and Giovanna Romero for their helpful comments on earlier drafts of the original chapter and its revision. The authors would also like to thank Tim S. Larey and Debra L. Nelson for their contributions as co-authors in the first edition of this chapter. We would also like to thank Jodi Grubstein for her administrative support of this effort.

REFERENCES

Ancona, D.G. (1990) Top-management teams: preparing for the revolution. In J.S. Carroll (ed.) *Applied Social Psychology and Organizational Settings.* Lawrence Erlbaum, Hillsdale, NJ, pp. 99–128.

Argyris, C. (1993) Education for leading-learning. *Organizational Dynamics,* **21**(3), 5–17.

Barrick, M.R., Stewart, G.L., Neubert, M.J. & Mount, M.K. (1998). Relating member ability and personality to work-team processes and team effectiveness. *Journal of Applied Psychology,* **83**, 377–398.

Baruch, G.K., Biener, L. & Barnett, R.C. (1987) Women and gender in research on work and family stress. *American Psychologist,* **42**, 130–6.

Bass, B.M. (1985) *Leadership and Performance Beyond Expectations.* Free Press, New York.

Bly, J.L., Jones, R.C. & Richardson, J.E. (1986) Impact of worksite health promotion on health care costs and utilization. *Journal of the American Medical Association,* **256**, 3235–40.

Bodensteiner, W.D., Gerloff, E.A. & Quick, J.C. (1989) Uncertainty and stress in an R&D project environment. *R&D Management,* **19**, 309–323.

Bracey, H., Sanford, A. & Quick, J.C. (1986) *Basic Management: An Experience-Based Approach.* BPI, Piano, TX.

Cohen, S.G. & Bailey, D.E. (1997). What makes teams work: group effectiveness research from the shop floor to the executive suite. *Journal of Management,* **23**, 239–90.

Dalton, G.W. (1989) Developmental views of careers in organizations. In M.B. Arthur, D.T. Hall and B.S. Lawrence (eds) *Handbook of Career Theory.* Cambridge University Press, New York, pp. 89–109.

Driskell, J.E. & Salas, E. (1991) Group decision making under stress. *Journal of Applied Psychology,* **76**, 473–8.

Dunbar, K. (1997). How scientists really reason: scientific reasoning in real-world laboratories. In R.J. Sternberg & J.E. Davidson (eds) *The Nature of Insight.* MIT Press, Cambridge, MA, pp. 365–95.

Dugosh, K.L, Paulus, P.B., Roland, E.J., & Yang, H.-C. (2000) Cognitive stimulation in brainstorming. *Journal of Personality and Social Psychology,* **79**, 722–35.

Edwards, J.R. & Cooper, C.L. (1990) The person–environment fit approach to stress: recurring problems and some suggested solutions. *Journal of Organizational Behaviour,* **11**, 293–307.

Fandt, P.M., Cady, S.H. & Sparks, M.R. (1993) The impact of reward interdependency on the syner-gogy model of cooperative performance: designing an effective team environment. *Small Group Research,* **24**, 101–15.

Fielding, J.E. (1984) Health promotion and disease prevention at the worksite. *Annual Review of Public Health,* **5**, 237–65.

Foels, R., Driskel, J.E., Mullen, B. & Salas, E. (2000). The effects of democratic leadership on group member satisfaction: an integration. *Small Group Research,* **31**, 676–701.

Forward, G.E., Beach, D.E., Gray, D.A. & Quick, J.C. (1991) Mentofacturing: a vision for American industrial excellence. *Academy of Management Executive,* **5** (3), 32–44.

Friedman, T.L. (1999) *The Lexus and the Olive Tree: Understanding Globalization.* Farrar, Straus, Giroux, New York.

Frost, P. & Robinson, S. (1999) The toxic handler. *Harvard Business Review,* **77**, 97–106.

Gammage, K.L., Carron, A.V. & Estabrooks, P.A. (2001) Team cohesion and individual productivity: the influence of norm for productivity and the identifiability of individual effort. *Small Group Research*, **32**, 3–18.

Gersick, C.J. & Hackman, J.R. (1990) Habitual routines in task-performing groups. *Organizational Behavior and Human Decision Processes*, **47**, 65–97.

Gladstein, C.J.G. (1984) Groups in context: a model of task group effectiveness. *Administrative Science Quarterly*, **29**, 499–517.

Gray, D.A., Gault, F.M., Meyers, H.H. & Walther, J.E. (1990) Career planning. In J.C. Quick, R.E. Hess, J. Hermalin & J.D. Quick (eds) *Career Stress in Changing Times*. Haworth Press, New York, pp. 43–59.

Greenhaus, J.H. (1987) *Career Management*. CBS College Publishing, New York.

Hackman, J.R. (1990) *Groups that Work (and Those that Don't)*. Jossey-Bass, San Francisco, CA.

Hackman, J.R. & Walton, R.E. (1986) Leading groups in organizations. In P.S. Goodman (ed.) *Designing Effective Work Groups*. Jossey-Bass, San Francisco, CA, pp. 72–119.

Hogan, R., Raza, S. & Driskell, J.E. (1988) Personality, team performance, and organizational context. In P. Whitney and R. Ochsman (eds) *Psychology and Productivity*. Plenum Press, New York, pp. 93–103.

Hogan, R., Curphy, G.J. & Hogan, J. (1994) What we know about leadership: effectiveness and personality. *American Psychologist*, **49**, 493–503.

House, R.J. (1977) A 1976 theory of charismatic leadership. In J.G. Hunt & L.L. Larson (eds) *Leadership: The Cutting Edge*. Southern Illinois University Press, Carbondale, IL, pp. 189–207.

Isabella, L. & Forbes, T. (1994) The interpretational side of careers: how key events shape executive careers, paper presented at the Academy of Management national meeting, Dallas, Texas.

Janis, I.L. (1982) *Groupthink*, 2nd edn. Houghton-Mifflin, Boston, MA.

Kabanoff, B. (1980) Work and nonwork: a review of models, methods, and findings. *Psychological Bulletin*, **88**, 60–77.

Kayser, T. A. (1994). *Building Team Power: How to Unleash the Collaborative Genius of Work Teams*. Irwin, New York.

Kirchmeyer, C. (1992) Perceptions of nonwork-to-work spillover: challenging the common view of conflict-ridden domain relationships. *Basic and Applied Social Psychology*, **13**, 231–49.

Kirchmeyer, C. (1993) Multicultural task groups: an account of the low contribution level of minorities. *Small Group Research*, **24**, 127–48.

Kotter, J.P., Faux, V.A. & McArthur, C.C. (1978) *Self-Assessment and Career Development*. Prentice Hall, Englewood Cliffs, NJ.

Landy, F., Quick, J.C. & Kasl, S. (1994) Work, stress and well-being. *International Journal of Stress Management*. **1**, 33–73.

Larey, T.S. (1994) Convergent and divergent thinking. group composition. and creativity in brainstorming groups, Doctoral dissertation, University of Texas at Arlington.

Larey, T.S. & Paulus, P.B. (1995) Social comparison and goal setting in brainstorming groups. *Journal of Applied Social Psychology*, **25**, 1579–96.

Lawler, E.A. (2000) *From the Ground Up: Six Principles for Building the New Logic Corporation*. Jossey-Bass, San Francisco, CA.

Linville, P.A. (1985) Self-complexity and affective extreme: don't put all your eggs in one cognitive basket. *Social Cognition*, **3**, 94–120.

Linville, P.A. (1987) Self-complexity as a cognitive buffer against stress-related illness and depression. *Journal of Personality and Social Psychology*, **52**, 663–76.

Lobel, S.A. (1991) Allocation of investment in work and family roles: alternative theories and implications for research. *Academy of Management Review*, **16**(3), 507–21.

Locke, E.A., Tirnauer, D., Roberson, Q., Goldman, B., Latham, M.E. & Weldon, E. (2001) The importance of the individual in an age of groupism. In M.E. Turner (ed.) *Groups at Work: Theory and Research*. Lawrence Erlbaum, Mahwah, NJ, pp. 501–28.

Lundin, W. & Lundin, K. (1994) *The Healing Manager*. Berret-Kohler, New York.

MacDonald, G. (1985) *Ordering Your Private World*. Oliver Nelson, Nashville, TN.

McGill, M.E. & Slocum, J.W. (1993) Unlearning the organization. *Organizational Dynamics*, **22**, 67–79.

McGill, M.E., Slocum, J.W. & Lei, D. (1992) Management practices in learning organizations. *Organizational Dynamics*, **21**, 5–17.

McIntosh, D. & Spilka, B. (1990). Religion and physical health: the role of personal faith and control beliefs. *Social Science of Religion*, **2**, 167–94.

Mullen, B. & Copper, C. (1994) The relation between group cohesiveness and performance: an integration. *Psychological Bulletin*, **15**, 210–27.

Murphy. L.R. & Cooper, C.L. (2000) *Healthy and Productive Work: An International Perspective.* Taylor & Francis, London.

Nathan, P. (1984) Johnson & Johnson's Live for Life: a comprehensive positive lifestyle change program. In J.D. Matarazzo, S.M. Weiss, J.A. Herd, N.E. Miller & S.M. Weiss (eds) *Behavioral Health: A Handbook of Health Enhancement and Disease Prevention.* John Wiley & Sons, New York, pp. 1064–70.

Nelson, D.L., Quick, J.C. & Quick, J.D. (1989) Corporate warfare: preventing combat stress and battle fatigue. *Organizational Dynamics*, **18**, 65–79.

Nelson, D.L., Quick, J.C., Eakin, M.E. & Matuszek, P.A.C. (1995) Beyond organizational entry and newcomer socialization: building a self-reliant workforce. *International Journal of Stress Management*, **2**, 1–14.

Oxley, N.L., Dzindolet, M.T. & Paulus, P.B. (1996) The effects of facilitators on the performance of brainstorming groups. *Journal of Social Behavior and Personality*, **11**, 633–46.

Pace, R.W., Smith, P.C. & Mills, G.E. (1991) *Human Resource Development: The Field.* Prentice Hall, Englewood Cliffs, NJ.

Paulus, P.B. (1989) *The Psychology of Group Influence.* Lawrence Erlbaum, Hillsdale, NJ.

Paulus, P.B. (1998) Developing consensus about groupthink after all these years. *Organizational Behavior and Human Decision Processes*, **73**, 362–74.

Paulus, P.B. (2000) Groups, teams, and creativity: the creative potential of idea-generating groups. *Applied Psychology: An International Journal*, **49**, 237–62.

Paulus, P.B. & Yang, H.-C. (2000) Idea generation in groups: a basis for creativity in organizations. *Organizational Behavior and Human Decision Processes*, **82**, 76–87.

Paulus, P.B., Larey, T.S. & Dzindolet, M.T. (2001) Creativity in groups and teams. In M.E. Turner (ed.) *Groups at Work: Theory and Research.* Lawrence Erlbaum, Mahwah, NJ, pp. 319–38.

Pearce, J.A. & Ravlin, E.C. (1987) The design and activation of self-regulating work groups. *Human Relations*, **40**, 751–82.

Pfeffer, J. (1998) *The Human Equation: Building Profits by Putting People First.* Harvard Business School Press, Boston, MA.

Piotrkowski, C.A. (1979) *Work and the Family System.* Free Press, New York.

Quick, J.C. (1999a) Occupational health psychology: historical roots and future directions. *Health Psychology*, **18**(1), 82–8.

Quick, J.C. (1999b) Occupational health psychology: the convergence of health and clinical psychology with public health and preventive medicine in an organizational context. *Professional Psychology: Research and Practice*, **30**(2), 123–8.

Quick, J.C. & Gavin, J.H. (2000) The next frontier: Edgar Schein on organizational therapy. *Academy of Management Executive*, **14**, 31–44.

Quick, J.C. & Gray, D.A. (1989/90) Chaparral Steel Company: Bring "world class manufacturing" to steel. *National Productivity Review*, **9**(1), 51–8.

Quick, J.C. & Tetrick, L. (2003) *Handbook of Occupational Health Psychology.* American Psychological Association, Washington, DC.

Quick, J.C., Nelson, D.L. & Quick, J.D. (1987) Successful executives: how independent? *Academy of Management Executive*, **1**(2), 139–45.

Quick, J.C. Nelson, D.L. & Quick, J.D. (1990) *Stress and Challenge at the Top: The Paradox of the Successful Executive.* John Wiley & Sons, Chichester.

Quick, J.C., Joplin, J.R., Gray, D.A. & Cooley, C.E. (1994) Occupational life cycle and the family. In L.L. Abate (ed.) *Handbook of Developmental Family Psychology and Psychopathology.* John Wiley & Sons, New York, pp. 157–75.

Quick, J.D., Nelson, D.L., Matuszek, P.A.C, Whittington, J.L. & Quick, J.C. (1995) Social support, secure attachments and health. In C.L. Cooper (ed.) *The Handbook of Stress, Medicine, and Health.* CRC Press, Boca Raton, FL, pp. 269–87.

Quick, J.C., Quick, J.D., Nelson, D.L. & Hurrell, J.J., Jr (1997) *Preventive Stress Management in Organizations.* American Psychological Association, Washington DC.

Quick, J.C., Nelson, D.L., Quick, J.D. & Orman, D.K. (2001) An isomorphic theory of stress: the dynamics of person–environment fit. *Stress and Health,* **17**, 147–57.

RadioShack Intercom (1999) "Think best", January.

Roe, A. & Lunneborg, P. (1990) Personality development and career choice. In D. Brown & L. Brooks (eds) *Career Choice and Development,* 2nd edn. Jossey-Bass, San Francisco, CA, pp. 68–101.

Sashkin, M. & Sashkin, M.G. (1994) *The New Teamwork: Developing and Using Cross-Function Teams.* AMA Membership Publications Division, New York.

Sauter, S.L., Murphy, L.R. & Hurrell, L.L. (1990) Prevention of work related psychological distress: a national strategy proposed by the National Institute for Occupational Safety and Health. *American Psychologist,* **45**, 1145–58.

Seta, C.E., Paulus, P.B. & Baron, R.A. (2000) *Effective Human Relations: A Guide to People at Work.* Allyn & Bacon, Needham Heights, NJ.

Shea, Q.P. & Guzzo, R.A. (1987) Group effectiveness: what really matters? *Sloan Management Review,* **28**, 25–31.

Sherman, D. & Hendricks, W. (1989) *How to Balance Competing Time Demands.* NavPress, Colorado Springs, CO.

Stasser. G. (1999) The uncertain role of unshared information in collective choice. In L. Thompson, J. Levine & D. Messick (eds) *Shared Knowledge in Organizations.* Lawrence Erlbaum, Mahwah, NJ, pp. 49–69.

Staw, B.M., Sandelands, L.E. & Dutton, J.E. (1981) Threat-rigidity effects in organizational behavior: a multilevel analysis. *Administrative Science Quarterly,* **26**, 501–24.

Stevens, M.J. & Campion, M.A. (1994) The knowledge, skill, and ability requirements for teamwork: implications for human resource management. *Journal of Management,* **20**, 503–30.

Sundstrom, E., De Meuse, K.P. & Futrell, D. (1990) Work teams: applications and effectiveness. *American Psychologist,* **45**, 120–33.

Sutton, R. I. & Hargadon, A. (1996). Brainstorming in context: effectiveness in a product design firm. *Administrative Science Quarterly,* **41**, 685–718.

Swezey, R.W. & Salas, E. (eds) (1992) *Teams: Their Training and Performance.* Ablex, Norwood, NJ.

Thurow, L. (1993) *Head to Head: The Coming Economic Battle among Japan, Europe and America.* Warner Books, New York.

Tjosvold, D. (1991) *Team Organization: An Enduring Competitive Advantage.* John Wiley & Sons, New York.

Turner, M.E. & Horvitz, T. (2001) The dilemma of threat: group effectiveness and ineffectiveness under adversity. In M.E. Turner (ed.) *Groups at Work: Theory and Research.* Lawrence Erlbaum, Mahwah, NJ, pp. 445–70.

Van de Vliert, E. & Janssen, O. (2001) Description, explanation, and prescription of intragroup conflict behaviors. In M.E. Turner (ed.) *Groups at Work: Theory and Research.* Lawrence Erlbaum, Mahwah, NJ, pp. 267–98.

Waterman, R.H., Waterman, J.A. & Collard, B.A. (1994) Toward a career-resilient workforce. *Harvard Business Review,* **72**(4), 87–95.

West, M.A. (2002) Sparkling fountains or stagnant ponds: an integrative model of creativity and innovation implementation in work groups. *Applied Psychology: An International Review,* **51**.

Whetten, D.A. & Cameron, K.S. (1998) *Developing Management Skills,* 3rd edn. HarperCollins, New York.

Ziller, R.C. & Behringer, R.D. (1960) Assimilation of the knowledgeable newcomer under conditions of group success and failure. *Journal of Abnormal and Social Psychology,* **60**, 288–92.

CHAPTER 23

Conflict at Work and Individual Well-Being

Carsten K.W. De Dreu, Dirk van Dierendonck and
Marjolein De Best-Waldhober
University of Amsterdam, The Netherlands

Individual well-being has been among the core concepts of industrial and organizational psychology since its inception. It is widely recognized that reduced well-being, stress, psychosomatic complaints and burnout are associated with reduced task performance, increased absenteeism and undesirable high levels of turnover, frequent and severe accidents at work, and increased apathy and reduced commitment. Organizational psychologists have, accordingly, examined a wide variety of individual and organizational variables that influence stress and psychosomatic complaints, and increase the likelihood of burnout. Among the variables identified are factors intrinsic to the job such as the amount of control and the physical and ergonomic work conditions, opportunities for career development, organizational culture and structural features of the organization such as the tendency towards bureaucratization, and work–home interfaces (for reviews see Arnold et al., 1998; Danna & Griffin, 1999; Murphy, 1984; Schaufeli & Enzmann, 1998).

One group of variables that has been connected consistently with individual well-being is the social context in organizations. It is assumed that other people at work such as one's colleagues, superiors or subordinates can dramatically affect the way we feel about our work and about ourselves (Van Dierendonck et al., 2001). The social setting in which we work provides support but also constitutes a major source of stress. Poor relationships characterized by low trust, low supportiveness and low interest in the problems that confront an organizational member reduce individual well-being and contribute substantially to stress, the development of psychosomatic complaints and feelings of burnout.

Within this social domain surprisingly little is known about the interplay between conflict at work and reduced individual well-being, including psychosomatic complaints, stress and burnout,[1] and those few studies that have included interpersonal conflict as part of job

---

[1] This is not to ignore research on well-being as a function of role ambiguity and role conflict. Role conflict exists when an individual is torn by contradictory job demands or by doing things that he or she does not really want to do. Seen as such, role conflict is an instance of within-person conflict (about equally positive or equally negative decision alternatives) and not an interpersonal or social conflict (about one's own versus another person's goals, views and values). Role conflict may be an antecedent or consequence of interpersonal conflict, but they are not to be equated.

The Handbook of Work and Health Psychology. Edited by M.J. Schabracq, J.A.M. Winnubst and C.L. Cooper.
© 2003 John Wiley & Sons, Ltd.

stressor surveys can be criticized on methodological or conceptual grounds. This state of affairs is troublesome because, as we will elaborate upon below, organizations are inherently competitive and conflict-ridden (Pondy, 1992) and in the near future this situation is likely to become more rather than less intense. In this chapter we review the relationships between conflict at work and indicators of individual well-being such as stress, psychosomatic complaints and burnout. We begin with an introduction of the concept of conflict at work and briefly discuss some leading theoretical models that provide the basis for further discussion. We then turn to published and unpublished research about the relationships between conflict at work and individual well-being, noting, in passing, gaps in our knowledge that need future research. We end with a summary of the main conclusions, some avenues for future research and a brief discussion of possible interventions.

23.1   CONFLICT AT WORK

Based on 25 years of consulting and research experience, Pondy (1992) has concluded that organizations are inherently competitive and conflict-ridden. Thomas (1992) reports that managers spend an average of 20% of their time managing conflicts between themselves and others. De Dreu (1999) replicated this finding in a random sample of over 100 Dutch personnel officers ($M = 18\%$), and also found this percentage to be independent of tenure, hierarchical position, gender and income. This situation is likely to become more rather than less apparent in the near future of work organizations. Tendencies to replace bureaucratic rules and regulations with self-managed teams and empowered employees imply that individuals need to negotiate on a daily basis their duties, rights and responsibilities. The growing diversity of the work force (Williams & O'Reilly, 1998) comes together with heterogeneous value and belief systems that bear the potential for misunderstanding and disrespect. And increased specialization in terms of educational and professional background, together with an increased complexity of internal and external relations, increases both information dependency among key players within organizations and the need to co-ordinate and work together. Such increased interdependency is just one step away from misunderstanding, disagreement, annoyance and irritation.

That organizations are competitive and conflict-ridden, and likely to become more so in the near future, is of great concern to scientists and practitioners alike. Many of us tend to react negatively to conflict and perceive it as bad, costly and detrimental to individual and organizational effectiveness. Such is illustrated in the sheer number of academic and practitioner-oriented writings that have appeared in recent years, bearing such titles as *Barriers to Dispute Resolution* (Arrow et al., 1995), *Controlling the Cost of Conflict* (Slaikeu & Hasson, 1998) and *Difficult Conversations* (Stone et al., 1999). It is also illustrated in the responses of a random sample of 118 personnel managers from large Dutch profit and not-for profit organizations when asked about their beliefs about conflict at work. As shown in Figure 23.1, the vast majority (72%) see vice in conflict (e.g. "conflict at work is bad") and only a minority of 34% see both vice and virtue (e.g. "conflict at work can be productive").

Growing evidence indeed suggests that conflict and conflict management substantially influence individual, group and organizational effectiveness, and has illustrated the vice of conflict at work. For instance, conflict has been linked to increased turnover and absenteeism,

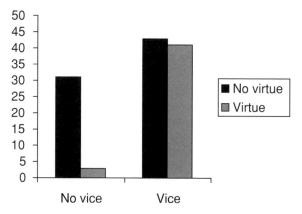

Figure 23.1   The numbers of personnel managers seeing vice and/or virtue in conflict at work ($N = 118$)

to reduced coordination and collaboration, and to lower efficiency and waste of (costly) time and energy (for a review, see De Dreu et al., 1999). In contrast to what the majority view appears to be, however, conflict at work does not have exclusively negative consequences; under specific circumstances it appears to be functional and to contribute to individual and organizational effectiveness (Amason, 1996; De Dreu & Van de Vliert, 1997; Jehn, 1995). We return to this issue later when we discuss the distinction between task conflict and relationship conflict. First, however, we introduce the concept of conflict in more detail.

23.1.1   Conflict in Organizations: A Process Model

In everyday speech conflict is seen as a fight, a struggle, or the clashing of opposed principles (e.g. *Concise Oxford Dictionary*). The problems with this definition are that it confounds conflict issues (what the conflict is about), feelings and cognitions (within-person experiences) and conflict management (between-person experiences) and that it remains mute about conflict outcomes. In organizations people often avoid conflict, and those who instigate conflict may be unaware of doing so (Kolb & Bartunek, 1992; O'Connor et al., 1993). These situations are not recognized as such as long as we define conflict as struggle and fight. For analytical purposes, we need to approach conflict such that conflict issues are separated from within-person and between-person experiences (Pondy, 1967; Schmidt & Kogan, 1972).

In this chapter, conflict is seen as a process (see Figure 23.2) that begins when an individual or group perceives differences between itself and another individual or group about interests, beliefs or values that matter to them (De Dreu et al., 1999; Kelley & Thibaut, 1969; Levine & Thompson, 1996; Rapoport, 1960). How individuals respond to perceived differences depends on their concerns for their own outcomes and for the opposing party's outcomes. According to dual concern theory (Carnevale & Pruitt, 1992; Pruitt & Rubin, 1986; Rubin et al., 1994; see also Blake & Mouton, 1964; Thomas, 1992), conflict management is a function of high or low concern for self combined with high or low concern for

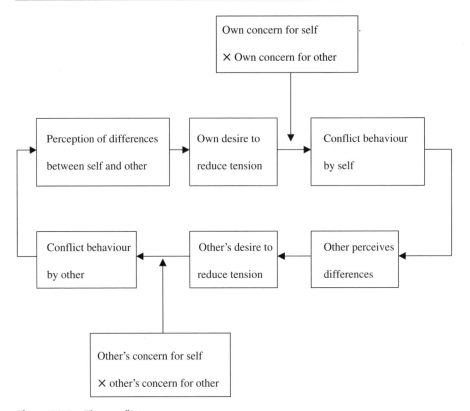

Figure 23.2   The conflict process

other.[2] As displayed in Figure 23.3, high concern for self and low concern for other results in a preference for *forcing* focused on imposing one's will on the other side. Forcing involves threats and bluffs, persuasive arguments, and positional commitments. Low concern for self and high concern for other results in a preference for *yielding*, which is oriented towards accepting and incorporating the other's will. It involves unilateral concessions, unconditional promises and offering help. Low concern for self and other results in a preference for *avoiding*, which involves reducing the importance of the issues, and attempts to suppress thinking about the issues. High concern for self and other produces a preference for *problem solving*, which is oriented towards an agreement that satisfies both own and other's aspirations as much as possible. It involves an exchange of information about priorities and preferences, showing insights, and making tradeoffs between important and unimportant issues. Finally, intermediate concern for self paired to intermediate concern for other results in a preference for *compromising*. A scale-development study by De Dreu et al. (2001) provided empirical support for this conclusion. Their study aimed at examining the psychometric qualities of the Dutch Test for Conflict Handling to measure the five conflict strategies discussed above

---

[2] The labels for these two dimensions vary. Concern for self is sometimes labelled "resistance to concession making" (Carnevale & Pruitt, 1992), "concern for the task" (Blake & Mouton, 1964) or "assertiveness" (Thomas, 1992). Sometimes, concern for other is labelled "concern for people" (Blake & Mouton, 1964) or "cooperativeness" (Thomas, 1992). For more detailed discussion of these concepts we refer the reader to De Dreu et al. (2000) and Van de Vliert (1997).

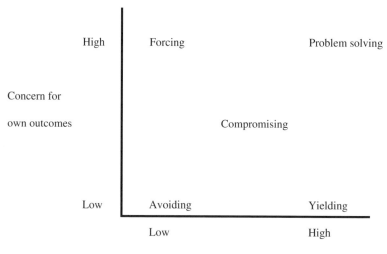

Figure 23.3 Dual concern model

in organizations. The scale is presented in the Appendix. Psychometric analyses showed the 20-item scale to have good to excellent qualities, and multidimensional scaling showed that the pattern of intercorrelations between the five subscales fitted a two-dimensional space that closely resembled Figure 23.3.

23.1.2 Conflict Management: Person, Situation or Culture?

An important question is whether concerns and concomitant conflict management styles are stable over time, and whether they reside in the individual or the situation. In dual concern theory conflict management is seen as the product of concern for self and concern for other. Concern for self and concern for other are, in turn, predicted by one's personality and the situation (De Dreu et al., 2000; Pruitt & Rubin, 1986; Van de Vliert, 1997). A good example is that stable individual differences in social value orientation correlate with concern for other: conflict parties with a prosocial orientation have higher concern for other than conflict parties with an individualistic or competitive value orientation (De Dreu & Boles, 1998; McClintock, 1977). Likewise, evidence suggests stable individual differences in collectivist versus individualistic values predict concern for other (Carnevale & Probst, 1997). At the same time, instructions by constituents, incentive structures (Deutsch, 1973), the expectation of cooperative future interaction (Ben-Yoav & Pruitt, 1984), and positive mood inductions (Carnevale & Isen, 1986) all increase the concern for other.

The fact that conflict management is the product of both personality and the situation does not necessarily suggest that within a particular work setting conflict management is highly unstable. Work settings tend to remain relatively stable over time. Employees interact with the same co-workers, incentive structures do not change overnight and employees do the same kind of work for longer periods of time and thus face the same (interpersonal) problems on a recurring basis. In addition, individuals within the same unit, team or department tend to influence one another (Salancik & Pfeffer, 1977), thus creating their own social environment with, most likely, rather stable preferences for dealing with conflict. The consequence is that an individual's actual and preferred conflict management strategies are likely to be relatively stable over time. We cannot know, however, whether this is due to stable individual differences, to the fact that the situation is relatively impervious to change, or both. Consistent with dual concern theory (Pruitt & Rubin, 1986), however, we expect that the individual's conflict management strategies at work are relatively stable over time due to both stable individual differences *and* the relatively stable situations in which people work.

There is another reason why, within a particular work setting, conflict management is relatively stable over time. Although concerns and concomitant preferences for conflict management reside within the individual through behavioural interaction, there is a tendency to converge, within the dyad or group, towards a collective frame of reference and concomitant conflict management style. In general, people have a strong tendency to reciprocate each other (e.g. Gouldner, 1960; Putnam & Jones, 1982) and this holds for behaviours as well as for cognitive and emotional perspectives on the situation (De Dreu et al., 1994; Pinkley & Northcraft, 1994). In conflict, behaviour tends to be reciprocated, including procedural statements, integrative behaviours, distributive behaviours, conflict avoidance, and affect statements (Putnam, 1983; Donohue, 1981). In a study of reciprocation and complementary conflict behaviour, Weingart et al. (1990) observed that negotiators mostly engage in reciprocation, regardless of whether their opponent's behaviour is competitive or cooperative. In all, it appears safe to conclude that the initial actions taken by oneself in a conflict set the stage for subsequent reactions by one's conflict opponent—if one begins with forcing the conflict tends to escalate more compared to a situation in which one avoids or pursues problem solving.

An interesting implication of the notion that concerns and conflict management strategies are relatively stable within a particular work setting and that conflict management tends to be reciprocated and reinforced during conflict interaction is that work groups and teams develop what may be called a *conflict culture*. That is, we hypothesize that units within organizations, and even entire organizations, develop, over time, a relatively stable set of orientations toward and strategies to manage conflict within that unit. It is this conflict culture that has long-term consequences for both the individual employee and the work unit's effectiveness.

23.1.3   Conflict at Work: Vice or Virtue?

Up to this point we have noted in passing some of the negative consequences of conflict and discussed conflict in general. We may have, inadvertently, given rise to the idea that all conflicts are the same and detrimental. This is not the case. First of all, it has been argued that some conflict in organizations is better than no conflict at all, and that there exists a curvilinear relationship between individual and group effectiveness and the level of conflict between individuals or within that group (e.g. De Dreu, 1997; Robbins, 1974; Walton, 1969). For instance, research on groupthink (Janis, 1972) and devil's advocacy (Schwenk, 1990) has shown that extreme concurrence-seeking in groups may lead to ineffective decision making, sometimes with disastrous consequences. Such biased and defective group decision making is mitigated when dissent and conflict is fostered rather than suppressed

(Turner & Pratkanis, 1997). Likewise, research on minority dissent in groups has shown that majority members confronted with a deviant minority become more creative in their thinking (Nemeth, 1986), generate more correct problem solutions (Butera & Mugny, 1995) and develop and implement more innovations (De Dreu & West, 2001).

For conflict to be productive rather than dysfunctional, it appears that not only the level of conflict matters but also what the conflict is about. When the conflict is about simple and routine tasks, it hurts rather than helps effectiveness. But when the task is more complex and ambiguous, conflict may be functional. In the past decade researchers have distinguished between two broad classes of conflict that seem to have rather different consequences for individual and group performance (Amason, 1996; Amason & Schweiger, 1997; De Dreu, 1997; Jehn, 1994, 1995, 1997; Turner & Pratkanis, 1997). When conflict is *task-related* members of a team or work unit disagree with one another about the way their work is done, about the goals they seek to achieve, about what the best strategy is to achieve their goals, and so on. When conflict is *relationship-oriented* members of a team or work unit disagree with one another about proper norms and values, and interpersonal style, and engage in personality clashes.[3] Teams with task-related conflict and low levels of relationship conflict tend to have satisfied team members, perform effectively, make high quality decisions and are innovative (Amason, 1996; Jehn, 1995, 1997; for reviews, see De Dreu & Van de Vliert, 1997). Teams with high levels of relationship conflict tend to have dissatisfied members, perform not effectively, reach decisions of poor quality, and are not innovative (Amason, 1996; Jehn, 1995, 1997). A review of the research literature by De Dreu and Van Vianen (2001) showed, for example, that relationship conflict is strongly and consistently associated with low satisfaction in team members. In a meta-analysis of 19 studies, they found average correlations between relationship conflict and team effectiveness of $r = -0.27$, $p < 0.01$, and an average correlation between relationship conflict and member satisfaction of $r = -0.48$, $p < 0.001$.

Finally, for conflict to be productive rather than dysfunctional, the ways in which participants approach the conflict and manage their differences is critical, for without a constructive approach task-related disagreements are likely to escalate into heated personality clashes. An impressive programme of research by Tjosvold (1997, 1998) indicates that when individuals in conflict perceive their own and their conflict opponent's goals as cooperative and compatible, they are more likely to engage in "constructive controversy" and debate in an open-minded way about their opposing views, beliefs and opinions. When, in contrast, individuals in conflict perceive their own and their conflict opponent's goals as competitive and incompatible, they are unlikely to engage in constructive controversy and try to "beat" their opponent. Constructive controversy has been shown, like task-related conflict, to result in stronger interpersonal relations, better and richer understanding of the issues under debate, and more effective employees and work teams. Consistent with dual concern

---

[3] Relationship conflict may be conceived of as an escalated phase of what started as a task-related conflict that was managed through forcing, including the use of personal attacks, rather than through problem solving. However, task conflict may be the result of relationship conflict, for instance when personality clashes lead participants to attack one another's task-related behaviours, opinions and beliefs. Research suggests that although task-related and relationship conflict may be related, this is less so when there is high interpersonal trust and more so when there is low interpersonal trust (Simons & Peterson, 2000). High levels of interpersonal trust may prevent task-related conflict from turning into relationship conflict. In addition, research suggests that effective teams with relationship conflict manage these conflicts through avoiding and ignoring the issues. Ineffective teams with relationship conflict, in contrast, tend to manage these conflicts in a more active way, through forcing or problem solving (De Dreu & Van Vianen, 2001; Jehn, 1997; Murnigham & Conlon, 1991). Avoiding and ignoring personality differences and relationship conflict may prevent the conflict from translating into, and affecting, task-related conflict and task performance.

theory, this research has shown that individuals are more likely to see own and other's goals as compatible and cooperatively linked when they share a future, when a collectivist rather than individualistic orientation is valued, and when participation in decision making is high rather than low. In other words, task conflict is more likely when individuals and teams have cooperative goals and trust each other, and relationship conflict is more likely when they have incompatible and competitive goals.

23.2 INDIVIDUAL WELL-BEING: A NEGLECTED CONSEQUENCE OF CONFLICT

The fact that different conflict management strategies and different types of conflict are associated with different outcomes, including team effectiveness and satisfaction, poses the question of whether, to what extent, and when conflict influences individual well-being, including mental and physical complaints. Several studies address this issue, but before we discuss these in more detail we first define the general concept of individual well-being and discuss the relevant background literatures briefly.

23.2.1 Individual Well-Being

Individual well-being in this context comprises an individual's evaluation of his or her work environment. The experiences at work may affect an individual in several ways, ranging from depression and despair to elation and work satisfaction. Although frameworks and definitions of well-being exist (e.g. Diener, 1984; Warr, 1987), a generally accepted conceptualization of well-being is lacking. In studies that explore the impact of conflicts on individual well-being, the emphasis lies on negative outcomes, that is stress, psychosomatic complaints and burnout.

Stress

If one were to ask different individuals for a definition of stress, one would get very different answers. Stress is an ambiguous word that is used as an overarching rubric encompassing, among other things, the adaptation of individuals to their environment, and feelings of distress resulting in various physiological, behavioural and psychological consequences (Quick et al., 1997). In the stress literature we usually differentiate between the stressor, the stress response and distress. Within organizations, stressors are another name for the demands at the workplace. These demands bring about the stress response: a generalized, patterned, unconscious mobilization of the body's natural energy. We may feel an elevated heart rate, increased respiration, a dry mouth and an increased alertness. This mobilization is a normal and healthy way to help us deal with the challenges of daily living. The stress response becomes detrimental for an individual's well-being if the demands tax or exceed his or her adaptive resources. The resulting distress refers to the unhealthy and damaging outcomes of the stress response. Distress can manifest itself in various ways, including behavioural consequences (e.g. absenteeism, accident proneness, drug abuse), psychological consequences (e.g. depression, psychosomatic complaints, burnout) and medical consequences (e.g. heart disease) (Quick et al., 1997).

Psychosomatic Complaints

Most of us have been plagued one time or another by headaches, tense muscles, racing heart and other bodily sensations. These so-called psychosomatic complaints have a warning function that can be compared to pain and fear. They are signals that the body is dealing, or trying to deal, with environmental demands (Pennebaker, 1982). Physical reactions are often the first signs that we are suffering from distress. The complaints may vary between gastrointestinal symptoms (e.g. nausea, stomach cramps), respiratory symptoms (e.g. pressure on chest, unable to breath deeply enough), cardiac symptoms (e.g. rapid heart rate, pounding of heart), dizziness and fainting, headaches, and tingling sensations in the limbs. Such signals warn us that we are running the risk of becoming overworked and that it is time to change our behaviour (Gaillard, 1996). If we neglect psychosomatic complaints for a longer period, or bring only makeshift measures into action, these complaints may become chronic.

Burnout

Burnout can be considered as a long-term stress reaction that is caused by the prolonged exposure to job stress. The term "burnout" is a metaphor that refers to the draining of energy—that is, more energy is lost than replenished, comparable to a car battery which will drain if not enough energy is generated from the dynamo (Schaufeli & Enzmann, 1998). Burnout is nowadays defined as a syndrome consisting of three dimensions: exhaustion, cynicism and ineffectiveness (or reduced personal accomplishment) (Maslach & Leiter, 1997). *Exhaustion* refers to mental and physical exhaustion, a feeling of being overextended. One feels drained, used up and unable to unwind and recover. *Cynicism* refers to a cold and distant attitude toward work and the people on the job. Cynicism results from defensive coping with the demands of the job (Van Dierendonck et al., 2001), an inadequate attempt to protect oneself from stressful organizational circumstances and disappointments. *Ineffectiveness* is the third burnout dimension, which refers to doubt in one's ability to make a difference, signifying an increasing perception of incompetence at work.

23.2.2 Conflict and Well-Being: Initial Theory and Research Findings

Why would conflict at work influence health and individual well-being? Conflict in itself is emotional and elicits anger, disgust and fear. Being in conflict threatens one's self-esteem and requires cognitive resources to cope with the situation. Negative emotions, threatened self-esteem and heightened cognitive effort impact the physiological system in a multitude of ways: adrenalin levels go up, heartbeat accelerates, and muscle tension increases (McEwen, 1998; Quick et al., 1997). In addition, interaction with conflict opponents may come hand in hand with verbal, and sometimes physical, violence, resulting in soar throats, bloody noses and twisted arms. Quite obviously, in the short run conflict and conflict interaction have more negative than positive consequences for health and well-being. In the long run, however, matters may be more complicated. On the negative side, research suggests that continuously high levels of stress hormones deplete the physiological system (McEwen, 1998) and result in psychosomatic complaints, including persistent headaches, upset stomach, and the like (Pennebaker, 1982). In addition, enduring conflict at work may deteriorate the work climate and increase rumination, alcohol intake, and trouble sleeping, which in turn affect the physical and psychological well-being of the individuals involved (Cooper & Marshall, 1976; Danna & Griffin, 1999). In other words, the occurrence of conflict at work results in a decline in psysical and psychological functioning, which, in the long run, leads to psychosomatic complaints, feelings of burnout and, perhaps, depression.

Initial Research Findings

Several studies by Spector and colleagues address the relationship between conflict at work and individual well-being. In these studies, conflict at work is measured using the Inter-personal Conflict at Work Scale, and individual well-being is measured using a Physical Symptoms Inventory. The Interpersonal Conflict at Work Scale contains four items including, "How often do you get into arguments with others at work?" and "How often do other people do nasty things to you at work?". The Physical Symptoms Inventory contains ten items, including questions about the subject's experience of the following symptoms during the past 30 days: upset stomach or nausea, trouble sleeping, chest pain and headache. Spector & Jex (1998) summarized the findings of 13 samples involving over 3000 employees through meta-analytical techniques. Their results showed an average correlation between conflict at work and physical health complaints of $r = 0.26$. A somewhat lower, but significant, relationship was found in a more recent study involving 110 employed graduate students of the University of South Florida. In this study, Spector et al. (2000) measured conflict at work, anxiety, frustration and physical complaints. Analyses revealed positive and moderate correlations between conflict at work and anxiety ($r = 0.35$) and frustration ($r = 0.38$), and a small but significant correlation between conflict at work and physical complaints.

Using a different set of measurement scales, Rahim (1983) conducted a study with 57 employees of a manufacturing plant in Kentucky. His results showed a positive and moderate correlation between conflict at work and stress ($r = 0.45$), and burnout ($r = 0.39$). Beehr et al. (1997) examined members of families who owned small family firms, and found interpersonal conflict at work to be related to psychological strain ($r = 0.46$). Shirom & Mayer (1993) examined over 1000 Israeli high-school teachers, and included measures of stress and conflict at work (teacher–principal conflicts). Their results revealed a positive and moderate correlation between conflict and somatic complaints ($r = 0.32$), and a positive but small correlation between conflict and burnout ($r = 0.20$). Several other studies reported moderately positive correlations between conflict at work and the exhaustion dimension of burnout, among nurses ($r = 0.48$; Leiter, 1991), traffic agents ($r = 0.24$; Brondolo et al., 1998), sports officials (beta $= 0.21$; Taylor et al., 1990), baseball umpires ($r = 0.54$; Rainey, 1999), health care workers ($r = 0.30$; Richardsen et al., 1992) and general practitioners (Van Dierendonck et al., 1994).

Indications that not all conflicts are created equal can be found in a study by Hillhouse (1997), who examined the effects of the work environment on stress among 260 nurses. Their results suggest that intra-professional conflict (i.e. with other nurses) is less stressful than interprofessional conflict (i.e. with physicians). In a study among 319 adolescents between 16 and 19 years old, Frone (2000) showed that conflicts with co-workers were related to personally relevant psychological outcomes (depression, self-esteem and somatic symptoms), whereas conflicts with supervisors were related to organizationally relevant outcomes (job satisfaction, organizational commitment and turnover intentions).

The detrimental effects of conflict at work may even go beyond well-being, as is shown by a prospective study among 15 530 Finnish employees (Appelberg et al., 1996; Romanov et al., 1996). In this 6-year follow-up study the impact of interpersonal conflict at work was investigated on work disability and psychiatric morbidity. Interpersonal conflict at work predicted work disability among those women who also reported simultaneous marital conflicts. Cross-sectional analysis indicated that recent interpersonal conflict was associated with an increased risk of physician-diagnosed psychiatric morbidity.

These studies together support the idea that conflict at work is related to individual well-being and health complaints. What is unclear from these studies is whether different types of conflict have different relationships with individual well-being; that is, whether task-related conflict has less severe consequences for individual health than relationship conflict. In addition, it is unclear from these studies whether different ways of managing conflict at work relate differently to individual well-being and health complaints. The extent to which conflict at work affects physical and psychological functioning depends, first of all, on the intensity and type of conflict. It seems reasonable to expect a linear relationship between the level of conflict and the decline in indicators of health and well-being. Also, it seems reasonable to expect task-related conflict and constructive controversy to be less strongly related to indicators of health and well-being than relationship conflict. Moreover, it seems reasonable to expect different relationships between conflict management practices and health indicators. A passive approach to conflict, exemplified by avoiding and yielding, is likely to be negatively related to health because the conflict either lingers on (and thus stress continues to exist) or is settled at one's own expense with its negative consequences for self-esteem and self-efficacy. Alternatively, it has been argued that a more active approach exemplified by cooperative problem solving results, if successful, in improved interpersonal relations, stronger feelings of self-worth and self-efficacy, and reduced tension in the future (De Dreu et al., 2001; Rubin et al., 1994). As such, cooperative problem solving in conflict at work may even be positively related to indicators of health and well-being. Below we summarize the results of some recent studies that address these possibilities.

The Study by Friedman and Colleagues

Friedman et al. (2000) were the first to examine individual well-being as a function of conflict type and conflict management at work. Their study involved 82 staff members from a local hospital who filled out a series of questionnaires measuring conflict types and conflict management along with a general measure of work-related stress. We summarize the relevant correlations from their study in Table 23.1. As can be seen, stress is positively related to task conflict, and positively and more strongly related to relationship conflict. Furthermore, stress is positively related to avoiding and negatively related to problem solving. This pattern of correlation is consistent with our theorizing about the role of conflict types and conflict management in individual well-being, and provided the basis for some subsequent studies we conducted in the Netherlands.

Table 23.1 Conflict, conflict, management and deteriorated individual well-being among professionals

	Conflict type		Conflict management			
	Task	Relationship	Yielding	Solving	Avoiding	Forcing
Friedman et al. (2000)						
(N = 82) Stress	0.39**	0.48**	0.18	−0.25*	0.32**	0.18
Study 1 (N = 110)						
Physical symptoms	−0.03	n.a.	n.a.	n.a.	n.a.	n.a.
Study 2 (N = 43)						
Physical symptoms	−0.19	0.30**	0.64***	−0.23	0.34**	−0.05
Study 3 (N = 298)						
Fatigue	0.18**	0.25**	0.17*	−0.11*	0.16**	0.10*
Tension	0.24**	0.30**	0.17*	−0.18**	0.16**	0.20**

Note: $*p < 0.10$, $**p < 0.05$, $***$ $p < 0.01$ (two-tailed).

Study 1: Conflict and Well-Being in Self-Managed Teams

In a first study we examined the relationship between conflict in teams using the task-conflict scale developed by Jehn (1994), perceived team effectiveness using a measure designed by Hackman (1983) and individual well-being using a Dutch version of the Physical Symptoms Inventory described above. Respondents ($N = 110$) participated in teams in various organizations and were accessed via our contacts with several consulting firms engaged in team-building practices. Respondents filled out questionnaires and when doing so were asked to reflect upon the past three months. All relevant constructs were measured reliably. Results showed a positive but non-significant correlation between team conflict and perceived effectiveness ($r = 0.12$), and a non-significant correlation between team conflict and individual well-being ($r = -0.03$; see Table 23.1). These results are inconsistent with those reported by Spector and colleagues, but not with our theoretical argument that task conflict does not necessarily deteriorate effectiveness and individual well-being. This position was examined in more detail in Study 2.

Study 2: Conflict and Well-Being Among Professionals

The association between type of conflict (task or relationship), conflict management (yielding, problem solving, avoiding and forcing) and individual well-being was examined in a cross-sectional study involving 43 professionals from a variety of organizational backgrounds such as finance and accounting, consulting, and project management. Respondents participated in a seminar on organizational conflict and received, prior to the seminar, a short questionnaire. All participants responded and were included in the data set. Task and relationship conflict was measured with a Dutch version of the questionnaire developed by Jehn (1994). Task conflict was measured with items like "in my unit we disagree about how to proceed with our tasks". Relationship conflict was measured with items like "in my unit there are personality clashes". Conflict management was measured with the Dutch Test for

Conflict Handling (De Dreu et al., 2001; see Appendix). Performance was measured with a Dutch version of Hackman's team effectiveness measures (e.g. "in my unit we approach the task in an effective way"), and individual well-being was measured with a Dutch version of the Physical Symptoms Inventory described above. All scales were measured reliably.

Consistent with past research, task and relationship conflict were positively correlated, $r = 0.35$, $p < 0.01$ (see also Simons & Peterson, 2000), and relationship conflict was negatively related to performance ($r = -0.10$, non-significant) while task conflict was positively related to performance ($r = 0.30$, $p < 0.05$). More importantly, the association between conflict and individual well-being is quite different depending on the type of conflict—it is negative and significant where relationship conflict is concerned, but positive and non-significant where task conflict is concerned (see Table 23.1). In other words, and consistent with our theorizing, conflict is negatively related to individual well-being when conflict at work is about (inter)personal issues. This qualifies the conclusions derived from the work by Spector and colleagues. Finally, from Table 23.1 it can be seen that conflict management is related to individual well-being, such that yielding and avoiding are negative and significant predictors of deteriorated well-being, while problem solving is a positive (albeit non-significant) predictor of deteriorated well-being.

Study 3: Conflict and Well-Being in a Manufacturing Organization

In Study 3, the same constructs were measured as in Study 2. The respondents in Study 3 were employees of a company specializing in the development and construction of food processing systems. On the initiative of both management and labour unions, a project with regard to work stress was started. The DUTCH was included in the instrument as well as measures to assess stress-related concepts such as fatigue and tension (based on Evers, Cooper & Frese, 2000). All employees (including employees from the general management and financial and sales departments, as well as employees in production or technical positions) were asked to participate. Out of 364 employees 308 returned the questionnaire (response rate of 85%). A research assistant invited employees to participate in the study, and an accompanying covering letter from the firm's CEO emphasized the importance of participating as well as its voluntary and anonymous character. The covering letter further explained the purpose of the study, which was to get a better understanding of the way employees work together, experience their work environment (e.g. technical equipment, internal communications) to be able to improve the situation where necessary. The research assistant administered the questionnaires in small groups (it was sent to the home address of employees who were not able to attend these group sessions). The questionnaires were filled in anonymously and collected by the research assistant.

Results showed that task and relationship conflict were moderately correlated ($r = 0.43$, $p < 0.001$). From Table 23.1 it can be seen that conflict is positively related to health complaints but these relationships are (somewhat) stronger for relationship conflict than for task conflict. Also, and consistent with Study 2, yielding and avoiding are positively related to health complaints, while problem solving is negatively related to health complaints. Forcing is positively related to health complaints, which is inconsistent with the non-significant correlation found in Study 2.

Summary of the Research Findings

The results of these four studies reveal, together, a rather consistent picture. First, task-related conflict is less negatively related to deteriorating individual well-being than relationship conflict and this is consistent with past research showing that task conflict can be functional and productive in groups and organizations. This finding also qualifies the earlier work by Spector and others in that it specifies that the kind of conflict matters when it comes to health and individual well-being—task-related conflict appears less of a job stressor than relationship conflict. Second, the results of the four studies together suggest that a passive and obliging way of dealing with conflict has more negative consequences for health and individual well-being than a more proactive and problem solving approach to conflict. This is consistent with the hypothesis that problem solving in conflict strengthens interpersonal relationships, and increases self-esteem, feelings of self-efficacy and satisfaction (De Dreu et al., 2001; Rubin et al., 1994)

Before concluding this section, a word of caution is needed. The work by Spector and others as well as the research summarized in Table 23.1 is, without exception, cross-sectional and based on self-report. Although valid scales were used and results are consistent across studies, we cannot exclude the possibility that deteriorating health and reduced well-being cause relationship rather than task-related conflicts, and lead individuals into a passive and obliging rather than active, problem-solving style of conflict management. Research using experimental or longitudinal designs is needed to increase our confidence that conflict and conflict management affect health and well-being rather than vice versa. For now, we can conclude that conflict at work, and conflict management, go hand in hand with deteriorating health and reduced individual well-being.

23.3 CONCLUSIONS, AVENUES FOR FUTURE RESEARCH AND POSSIBILITIES FOR INTERVENTION

In this chapter we have argued that organizations are inherently competitive and conflict-ridden (Pondy, 1992) and that this is likely to be more pronounced in the near future as organizations become more diverse and heterogeneous, employees more autonomous, and self-management and individual responsibility replace traditional values and focus on the collective. We have also argued that conflict may be task oriented when parties perceive their goals to be cooperative and compatible, but is likely to develop into relationship conflict when parties perceive their goals to be competitive and incompatible (cf. De Dreu et al., 1999; Tjosvold, 1998). When conflict is task oriented and parties engage in constructive controversy, the conflict is more likely to be functional and increase effectiveness than when conflict is relationship oriented and parties fail to debate incompatibilities in an open-minded way (Amason, 1996; De Dreu & Van de Vliert, 1997; Jehn, 1995).

23.3.1 Main Conclusions

The most critical contribution this chapter sought to make was to link contemporary insights in conflict and conflict management at work to individual well-being, stress, psychosomatic complaints and burnout. Research by Spector and colleagues revealed that interpersonal conflict is negatively related to individual well-being, and contributes to stress and psycho-somatic complaints. We have argued, however, that the relationship between conflict and individual well-being may be somewhat more complex. A review of recent published and unpublished research showed that relationship conflict has stronger negative implications for individual well-being than task conflict, and that yielding and avoiding in conflict situations has stronger negative implications for well-being than problem solving and forcing. The main conclusion we derive from this review is that conflict at work is detrimental to individual well-being but especially when conflict is concerned with relationships and dealt with in a passive, obliging manner. When conflict is task related and dealt with in a cooperative, active way its consequences for individual well-being appear less severe.

Our conclusions about the consequences for conflict and conflict management at work suggest a series of interventions in organizations that mitigate the negative consequences of conflict while maintaining or stimulating its positive, healthy side. Conflict is not bad, as many practitioners seem to believe (see Figure 23.1). Organizations are inherently competitive and conflict-ridden, and to some extent conflict can be functional and healthy. What organizations and their leaders need to do is to induce procedures and manage relationship such that relationship conflict is prevented and employees engage in task-related debates which they approach in an active and cooperative way. The research programme by Tjosvold and colleagues offers some important and interesting cues as to what organizations and its leaders should do and avoid in order to promote functional conflict and to mitigate dysfunctional conflict, with its strong negative consequences for health and individual well-being. To foster functional conflict organizational members should emphasize cooperative goals and learn to engage in constructive controversy. Management increases the likelihood that employees will perceive goal compatibility when it emphasizes shared goals, common tasks, complementary roles, and the need for coordination, and focuses on shared rewards. Management reduces the likelihood that employees will perceive goal compatibility when it focuses on win–lose rewards and attitudes, when it rewards employees for "getting it their way", and when it fails to deal with resource scarcity in procedurally and distributively fair ways (for reviews see De Dreu et al., 1999; Tjosvold, 1991, 1997, 1998).

23.3.2 Avenues for Future Research

In the past four decades we have developed a rich and thorough understanding of conflict at work on the one hand, and individual well-being and health issues in organizations on the other. Unfortunately, little cross-fertilization has taken place and only a handful of studies have addressed the important interface between conflict and health at work. This pioneering research is far from perfect and leaves a multitude of issues unresolved. First, research has examined individual well-being and health as a function of conflict from a variety of perspectives, and we need to increase homogeneity in the key indicators of health and well-being. That is, we gain cumulative insights especially when we define a relatively narrow set of key indicators that can be measured in a reliable and valid way. Past research has examined general stress, feelings of burnout, psychosomatic complaints, fatigue, and so on. In a sense, some of these health indicators are related only in time, such that chronic stress and fatigue may result in psychosomatic complaints and feelings of burnout more than vice versa. It would be both interesting and important to separate these issues and study over longer periods of time the relationships between conflict and conflict management on the one hand, and health indicators on the other. Our analysis suggests a sequence that begins with conflict at work and results, if not resolved successfully, in stress and chronic fatigue that subsequently feeds into psychosomatic complaints and feelings of burnout.

At this point we cannot and should not exclude an entirely different perspective on the relationship between conflict at work and reduced well-being and deteriorating health. The correlational evidence available thus far lends itself to a multitude of interpretations, and renders conclusions about causality virtually impossible. An interesting possibility is that conflict is not so much a precursor to deteriorating health and well-being, but rather one of its consequences. Imagine an employee who suffers from bad health, for whatever job-related or external reasons. This employee is likely not to be the most pleasant person around and not to be the most effective co-worker one can imagine. Because bad health and reduced individual well-being may negatively affect social relationships and productivity at work, it may appear related to conflict at work and a passive and obliging approach to such conflicts simply because of reduced productivity and effectiveness. In other words, we cannot exclude the possibility that reduced individual well-being causes, directly or indirectly, conflicts at work and renders some conflict management styles more likely than others.

Before closing, we wish to address a third possible explanation for the initial research findings reported in Table 23.1. It cannot be excluded that the associations between conflict (management) at work and health indicators is not reflecting a causal sequence in one way or the other, but merely reflecting two different consequences of a third variable. It may be that those employees with high levels of negative (positive) affectivity develop more (less) conflict at work and, independently, have lower (higher) well-being and more (fewer) health complaints. Likewise, it may be that interpersonal or group relations in organizations characterized by high levels of perceived goal compatibility have fewer and less intense conflicts and, independently, more healthy and happier members.

Future research is needed to test the validity of each of the above models, using longitudinal and experimental designs. Before such research evidence becomes available, scientists and practitioners should be cautious in jumping to conclusions about the precise meaning of the relationship between conflict (management) at work and indicators of well-being and health. In this chapter we have shown that causal relationships are likely from a theoretical perspective, that they are potentially important for organizations, and that empirically relationships between conflict (management) and health exist. Moreover, we have argued that some conflicts, and some ways of managing conflict, are more or less (dys)functional to individual and organizational effectiveness, and relate in more or less negative ways to individual well-being and health. We reject some practitioners' tendency to view all conflict as equal and as equally bad, and challenge scientists to pursue solid research at the crossroad of two critical aspects of organizational life.

REFERENCES

Amason, A.C. (1996). Distinguishing the effects of functional and dysfunctional conflict on strategic decision making: resolving a paradox for top management groups. *Academy of Management Journal*, **39**, 123–48.

Amason, A.C. & Schweiger, D. (1997). The effect of conflict on strategic decision making effectiveness and organizational performance. In C.K.W. De Dreu & E. Van de Vliert (eds) *Using Conflict in Organizations*. London: Sage, pp. 101–15.

Appelberg, K., Romanov, K., Heikkilä, K., Honkasalo, M. & Koskenvuo, M. (1996). Interpersonal conflict as predictor of work disability: a follow-up study of 15,348 Finnish employees. *Journal of Psychosomatic Research*, **40**, 157–67.

Arnold, J., Cooper, C.L. & Robertson, I.T. (1998). *Work Psychology: Understanding Human Behaviour in the Workplace*, 3rd edn. London: Prentice Hall.

Arrow, K., Mnookin, R.H., Ross, L., Tversky, A., & Wilson, R. (1995). *Barriers to Dispute Resolution*. New York: Norton.

Beehr, T.A., Drexler, J.A. & Faulkner, S. (1997). Working in small family businesses: empirical comparisons to non-family businesses. *Journal of Organizational Behaviour*, **18**, 297–312.

Ben-Yoav, O. & Pruitt, D. (1984). Resistance to yielding and the expectation of cooperative future interaction in negotiation. *Journal of Experimental Social Psychology*, **34**, 323–35.

Blake, R. & Mouton, J.S. (1964). *The Managerial Grid*. Houston, TX: Gulf.

Butera, F. & Mugny, G. (1995). Conflict between incompetencies and influence of a low-expertise source in hypothesis testing. *European Journal of Social Psychology*, **25**, 457–62.

Brondolo, E., Masha, R. Stores, J., Stockhammer, T., Tunick, W., Melhado, E., Karlin, W.A., Schwartz, J., Harburg, E. & Contrada, R.J. (1998). Anger-related traits and response to interpersonal conflict among New York City traffic agents. *Journal of Applied Social Psychology*, **28**, 2089–118.

Carnevale, P.J. & Isen, A. (1986). The influence of positive affect and visual access on the discovery of integrative solutions in bilateral negotiation. *Organizational Behavior and Human Decision Processes*, **37**, 1–13.

Carnevale, P.J. & Probst, T. (1997). Good news about competitive people. In C.K.W. De Dreu & E. Van de Vliert (eds) *Using Conflict in Organizations*. London: Sage, pp. 129–46.

Carnevale, P.J.D. & Pruitt, D.G. (1992). Negotiation and mediation. *Annual Review of Psychology*, **43**, 531–82.

Cooper, C.L. & Marshall, J. (1976). Occupational sources of stress: a review of the literature relating to coronary heart disease and mental ill health. *Journal of Occupational Psychology*, **49**, 11–28.

Danna, K. & Griffin, R.W. (1999). Health and well-being in the workplace: a review and synthesis of the literature. *Journal of Management*, **25**, 357–84.

De Dreu, C.K.W. (1997). Productive conflict: the importance of conflict issue and conflict management. In C.K.W. De Dreu & E. Van de Vliert (eds) *Using Conflict in Organizations*. London: Sage, pp. 9–22.

De Dreu, C.K.W. (1999). Conflicten in organisaties: Wat hebben we eraan en wat moeten we ermee? [Conflicts in organizations: what use do they have and what should we do with them?]. *Gedrag en Organisatie*, **12**, 189–204.

De Dreu, C.K.W. & Boles, T. (1998). Share and share alike or winner take all. The influence of social value orientation on use and recall of heuristics in negotiation. *Organizational Behavior and Human Decision Processes*, **76**, 253–67.

De Dreu, C.K.W. & Van de Vliert, E. (eds) (1997). *Using Conflict in Organizations*. London: Sage.

De Dreu, C.K.W. & Van Vianen, A.E.M. (2001). Responses to relationship conflict and team effectiveness. *Journal of Organizational Behavior*, **22**, 1–20.

De Dreu, C.K.W. & West, M.A. (2001). Minority dissent and team innovation: the importance of participation in decision making. *Journal of Applied Psychology*, **86**, 1191–1201.

De Dreu, C.K.W., Carnevale, P.J.D., Emans, B.J.M. & Van de Vliert, E. (1994). Effects of gain–loss frames in negotiation: loss aversion, mismatching, and frame adoption. *Organizational Behavior and Human Decision Processes*, **60**, 90–107.

De Dreu, C.K.W., Harinck, F. & Van Vianen, A.E.M. (1999). Conflict and performance in groups and organizations. In C.L. Cooper & I.T. Robertson (eds) *International Review of Industrial and Organizational Psychology*, vol. 14. Chichester: John Wiley & Sons, pp. 376–405.

De Dreu, C.K.W., Weingart, L.R. & Kwon, S. (2000). Influence of social motives in integrative negotiation: a meta-analytic review and test of two theories. *Journal of Personality and Social Psychology*, **78**, 889–905.

De Dreu, C.K.W. Evers., A., Beersma, B., Kluwer, E.S. & Nauta, A. (2001). Toward a theory-based measure of conflict management in the work place. *Journal of Organizational Behavior*, **22**, 645–668.

Deutsch, M. (1973). *The Resolution of Conflict: Constructive and Destructive Processes*. New Haven, CT: Yale University Press.

Diener, E. (1984). Subjective well-being. *Psychological Bulletin*, **95**, 542–75.

Donohue, W.A. (1981). Analyzing negotiation tactics: development of a negotiation interact system. *Human Communication Research*, **7**, 273–87.

Druckman, D. (1994). Determinants of compromising behaviour in negotiation. *Journal of Conflict Resolution*, **38**, 507–56.

Evers, A., Frese, M. & Cooper, C.L. (2000). Revisions and further developments of the Occupational Stress Indicator: LISREL results from four Dutch studies. *Journal of Occupational and Organizational Psychology*, **73**, 221–40.

Friedman, R.A., Tidd, S.T., Currall, S.C. & Tsai, J.C. (2000). What goes around comes around: the impact of personal conflict style on work group conflict and stress. *International Journal of Conflict Management*, **11**, 32–55.

Frone, M.R. (2000). Interpersonal conflict at work and psychological outcomes: testing a model among young workers. *Journal of Occupational Health Psychology*, **5**, 246–55.

Gaillard, A.W.K. (1996). *Stress, productiviteit en gezondheid*. [*Stress, Productivity and Health.*] Amsterdam: Uitgeverij Nieuwezijds.

Gouldner, A.W. (1960). The norm of reciprocity: a preliminary statement. *American Sociological Review*, **25**, 161–78.

Hackman, R. (1983). The design of effective work groups. In J.W. Lorsch (ed.) *Handbook of Organizational Behaviour*. Englewood Cliffs, NJ: Prentice Hall, pp. 315–42.

Hillhouse, J.J. (1997). Investigating stress effect patterns in hospital staff nurses: results of a cluster analysis. *Social Science and Medicine*, **45**, 1781–8.

Janis, I.L. (1972). *Victims of Groupthink: A Psychological Study of Foreign-Policy Decisions and Fiascos*. Boston, MA: Houghton Mifflin.

Jehn, K. (1994). Enhancing effectiveness: an investigation of advantages and disadvantages of value-based intragroup conflict. *International Journal of Conflict Management*, **5**, 223–38.

Jehn, K. (1995). A multimethod examination of the benefits and detriments of intragroup conflict. *Administrative Science Quarterly*, **40**, 256–82.

Jehn, K. (1997). Affective and cognitive conflict in work groups: increasing performance through value-based intragroup conflict. In C.K.W. De Dreu & E. Van de Vliert (eds) *Using Conflict in Organizations*. London: Sage, pp. 87–100.

Kelley, H.H. & Thibaut, J. (1969). Group problem solving. In G. Lindzey & E. Aronson (eds) *The Handbook of Social Psychology*, 2nd edn, vol. 4. Reading, MA: Addison-Wesley.

Kolb, D.M. & Bartunek, J.M. (eds) (1992). *Hidden Conflict in Organizations: Uncovering Behind-the-Scenes Disputes*. London: Sage.

Leiter, M.P. (1991). Coping patterns as predictors of burnout: the function of control and escapist coping patterns. *Journal of Organizational Behaviour*, **12**, 123–44.

Levine, J.M. & Thompson, L.L. (1996). Conflict in groups. In E.T. Higgins & A.W. Kruglanski (eds) *Social Psychology: Handbook of Basic Principles* New York: Guilford, pp. 745–76.

Maslach, C. & Leiter, M.P. (1997). *The Truth about Burnout. How Organizations Cause Personal Stress and What to Do about It*. San Francisco, CA: Jossey-Bass.

McClintock, C. (1977). Social motives in settings of outcome interdependence. In D. Druckman (ed.) *Negotiations: Social Psychological Perspective*. Beverly Hills, CA: Sage, pp. 49–77.

McEwen, B.S. (1998). Protective and damaging effects of stress mediators. *Seminars in Medicine of the Beth Israel Deaconess Medical Center*, **338**, 171–9.

Murnighan, J.K. & Conlon, D.E. (1991). The dynamics of intense work groups: a study of British string quartets. *Administrative Science Quarterly*, **36**, 165–86.

Murphy, L.R. (1984). Occupational stress management: a review and appraisal. *Journal of Occupational Psychology*, **57**, 1–15.

Nemeth, C. (1986). Differential contributions of majority and minority influence processes. *Psychological Review*, **93**, 10–20.

O'Connor, K.M., Gruenfeld, D.H., & McGrath, J.E. (1993). The experience and effects of conflict in continuing work groups. *Small Group Research*, **24**, 362–82.

Pennebaker, J.W. (1982). *The Psychology of Physical Symptoms*. New York: Springer-Verlag.

Pinkley, R. & Northcraft, G. (1994). Conflict frames of reference: implications for dispute processes and outcomes. *Academy of Management Journal*, **37**, 193–205.

Pondy, L. (1967). Organizational conflict: concepts and models. *Administrative Science Quarterly*, **17**, 296–320.

Pondy, L. (1992). Reflections on organizational conflict. *Journal of Organizational Behavior*, **13**, 257–61.

Pruitt, D.G. (1998). Social conflict. In D. Gilbert, S.T. Fiske & G. Lindzey (eds) *Handbook of Social Psychology*, 4th edn, vol. 2. New York: McGraw-Hill, pp. 89–150.

Pruitt, D.G. & Carnevale, P.J. (1993). *Negotiation in Social Conflict*. Pacific Grove, CA: Brooks/Cole.

Pruitt, D.G. & Rubin, J. (1986). *Social Conflict: Escalation, Stalemate and Settlement*. New York: Random House.

Putnam, L.L. (1983). Small group work climates: a lag sequential analysis of group interaction. *Small Group Behavior*, **14**, 465–94.

Putnam, L.L. & Jones, T.S. (1982). Reciprocity in negotiations: an analysis of bargaining interaction. *Communication Monographs*, **49**, 171–91.

Putnam, L.L. & Wilson, C.E. (1982). Communicative strategies in organizational conflicts: reliability and validity of a measurement scale. In M. Burgoon (ed.) *Communication Yearbook*, vol. 6. Beverly Hills, CA: Sage, pp. 629–52.

Quick, J.C., Quick, J.D., Nelson, D.L. & Hurrel, J.J. (1997). *Preventive Stress Management in Organizations*. Washington, DC: American Psychological Association.

Rahim, A. (1983). Measurement of organizational conflict. *Journal of General Psychology*, **109**, 188–99.

Rapoport, A. (1960). *Fights, Games, and Debates*. Ann Arbor, MI: University of Michigan Press.

Richardsen, A.M., Burke, R.J. & Leiter, M.P. (1992). Occupational demands, psychological burnout and anxiety among hospital personnel in Norway. *Anxiety, Stress, and Coping*, **5**, 55–68.

Robbins, S.P. (1974). *Managing Organizational Conflict: A Nontraditional Approach*. Englewood Cliffs, NJ: Prentice Hall.

Romanov, K., Appelberg, K., Honkasalo, M. & Koskenvuo, M. (1996). Recent interpersonal conflict at work and psychiatric morbidity: a prospective study of 15,530 employees aged 24–64. *Journal of Psychosomatic Research*, **40**, 169–76.

Rubin, J.Z., Pruitt, D.G. & Kim, S.H. (1994). *Social Conflict: Escalation, Stalemate, and Settlement*. New York: McGraw-Hill.

Salancik, G.R. & Pfeffer, J. (1977). An examination of need satisfaction models of job satisfaction. *Administrative Science Quarterly*, **22**, 427–56.

Schaufeli, W.B. & Enzmann, D. (1998). *The Burnout Companion to Study and Practice: A Critical Analysis*. London: Taylor & Francis.

Schmidt, S.M. & Kogan, T.A. (1972). Conflict: toward conceptual clarity. *Administrative Science Quarterly*, **17**, 359–70.

Schwenk, C.R. (1990). Effects of devil's advocacy and dialectical inquiry on decision making: a meta-analysis. *Organizational Behavior and Human Decision Processes*, **47**, 161–76.

Shirom, A. & Mayer, A. (1993). Stress and strain among union lay officials and rank-and-file members. *Journal of Organizational Behavior*, **14**, 401–13.

Simons, T.L. & Peterson, R.S. (2000). Task conflict and relationship conflict in top management teams: the pivotal role of intragroup trust. *Journal of Applied Psychology*, **85**, 102–11.

Slaikeu, K.A. & Hasson, R.H. (1998). *Controlling the Cost of Conflict*. San Fransisco, CA: Jossey-Bass.

Spector, P.E. & Jex, S.M. (1998). Development of four self-report measures of job stressors and strain: interpersonal conflict at work scale, organizational constraints scale, quantitative workload inventory, and physical symptoms inventory. *Journal of Occupational Health Psychology*, **3**, 356–67.

Spector, P.E., Dwyer, D.J. & Jex, S.M. (1988). Relation of job stressors to affective, health and performance outcomes: a comparison of multiple data sources. *Journal of Applied Psychology*, **73**, 11–19.

Spector, P.E., Chen, P.Y. & O'Connell, B.J. (2000). A longitudinal study of relations between job stressors and job strains while controlling for prior negative affectivity and strains. *Journal of Applied Psychology*, **85**, 211–18.

Stone, D., Patton, B. & Heen, S. (1999). *Difficult Conversations*. New York: Viking.

Rainey, D.W. (1999). Stress, burnout and intention to terminate among umpires. *Journal of Sport Behavior*, **18**, 312–23.

Taylor, A., Daniel, J.V., Leith, L. & Burke, R.J. (1990). Perceived stress, psychological burnout and paths to turnover intentions among sport officials. *Applied Sport Psychology*, **2**, 84–97.

Thomas, K.W. (1992). Conflict and negotiation processes in organizations. In M.D. Dunnette & L.M. Hough (eds) *Handbook of Industrial and Organizational Psychology*, 2nd edn. Palo Alto, CA: Consulting Psychologists Press, pp. 651–717.

Tjosvold, D. (1991). *The Conflict-Positive Organization*. Reading, MA: Addison-Wesley.

Tjosvold, D. (1997). Conflict within interdependence: its value for productivity and individuality. In C.K.W. De Dreu & E. Van de Vliert (eds) *Using Conflict in Organizations* Thousand Oaks, CA: Sage, pp. 23–37.

Tjosvold, D. (1998). Cooperative and competitive goal approach to conflict: accomplishments and challenges. *Applied Psychology: An International Review*, **47**, 285–342.

Turner, M.E. & Pratkanis, A.R. (1994). Social identity maintenance prescriptions for preventing groupthink: reducing identity protection and enhancing intellectual conflict. *International Journal of Conflict Management*, **5**, 254–70.

Turner, M.E. & Pratkanis, A. (1997). Mitigating groupthink by stimulating constructive conflict. In C.K.W. De Dreu & E. Van de Vliert (eds) *Using Conflict in Organizations*. London: Sage, pp. 53–71.

Van de Vliert, E. (1997). *Complex Interpersonal Conflict Behaviour*. London: Psychology Press.

Van de Vliert, E. & Kabanoff, B. (1990). Toward theory-based measures of conflict management. *Academy of Management Journal*, **33**, 199–209.

Van Dierendonck, D., Schaufeli, W.B. & Sixma, H. (1994). Burnout among general practitioners: a perspective from equity theory. *Journal of Social and Clinical Psychology*, **13**, 86–100.

Van Dierendonck, D., Schaufeli, W.B. & Buunk, B.P. (2001). Toward a process model of burnout. Results from a secondary analysis. *European Journal of Work and Organizational Psychology*, **10**, 41–52.

Wall, J. & Callister, R. (1995). Conflict and its management. *Journal of Management*, **21**, 515–58.

Walton, R.E. (1969). *Interpersonal Peacemaking: Confrontations and Third Party Consultation*. Reading, MA: Addison-Wesley.

Warr, P. (1987). *Work, Unemployment, and Mental Health*. Oxford: Clarendon Press.

Weick, K.E. (1979). *The Social Psychology of Organizing*. New York: Random House.

Weingart, L.R., Thompson, L.L., Bazerman, M.H. & Carroll, J.S. (1990). Tactical behaviour and negotiation outcomes. *International Journal of Conflict Management*, **1**, 7–31.

Williams, K.Y. & O'Reilly, C.A., III (1998). Demography and diversity in organizations: a review of 40 years of research. *Research in Organizational Behavior*, **20**, 77–140.

APPENDIX

The DUTCH Test for Conflict Handling

When I have a conflict at work, I do the following:

Yielding
1. I give in to the wishes of the other party.
2. I concur with the other party.
3. I try to accommodate the other party.
4. I adapt to the other party's goals and interests.

Compromising
5. I try to realize a middle-of-the-road solution.
6. I emphasize that we have to find a compromise solution.
7. I insist we both give in a little.
8. I strive whenever possible towards a fifty–fifty compromise.

Forcing
9. I push my own point of view.
10. I search for gains.
11. I fight for a good outcome for myself.
12. I do everything to win.

Problem solving
13. I examine issues until I find a solution that really satisfies me and the other party.
14. I stand for my own and other's goals and interests.
15. I examine ideas from both sides to find a mutually optimal solution.
16. I work out a solution that serves my own as well as other's interests as well as possible.

Avoiding
17. I avoid a confrontation about our differences.
18. I avoid differences of opinion as much as possible.
19. I try to make differences loom less severe.
20. I try to avoid a confrontation with the other.

Note. Items could be answered on a five-point scale (1 = very unlikely, to 5 = very likely). Items are translated from Dutch and were presented in a random order.

CHAPTER 24

Creating Shared Commitment for Results: How to Talk about Accountability

Kathleen D. Ryan
The Orion Partnership, Issaquah Washington, USA

We live in a time when productivity, profitability, and speed surface as primary measures of organizational success. Organizational leaders want to accomplish as much as possible, with an efficient use of resources. Within this context, the concept of accountability has taken on new prominence. In its neutral and theoretical state, *accountability* is frequently cited as another word for *responsibility*. People who hold certain jobs are considered accountable, or answerable, for certain results. They are asked to account for their time, their accomplishments, and their use of resources. When it comes time to evaluate an individual's performance, an important consideration is the degree to which he or she has demonstrated accountability for the desired outcomes. It is through the realization of individual and group accountabilities that organizations are able to execute their plans and accomplish their goals.

24.1   THE DILEMMA OF ACCOUNTABILITY

Accountability, as described above, is a straightforward workplace dynamic, a neutral organizing principle. Enter human beings: workers in all types of jobs, whose behavior is shaped by values and emotions along with intellect and logic. Exit the neutral view of accountability: people operating within fast-paced dynamics are judged by others on how they *seem* to meet expectations, on whether or not they "deliver the goods." Even in settings where participation, information sharing, and teamwork are emphasized, *accountability* can take on a harsh, judgmental tone. Frustrations at the inevitable barriers that block success inspire some to look for individuals or groups to blame, "to hold accountable." Out of a desire for the organization to be successful, some become inclined to complain that problems would be solved, if only *he* or *she* or *they* "would take accountability."

This pattern in the workplace reflects trends in the larger culture, where concerns about accountability are directed toward education, government, and religion—as well as toward

---

The Handbook of Work and Health Psychology. Edited by M.J. Schabracq, J.A.M. Winnubst and C.L. Cooper.
© 2003 John Wiley & Sons, Ltd.

organizations. A recent search of the internet revealed, for example, over 500 000 web sites where issues of accountability were referenced. There were demands for education and government to be more responsive and responsible to constituents. A lack of accountability also framed accusations by those who disagreed with decision makers or outcomes. When it comes to religion, there is a strong call for leaders and members to routinely act according to the values of one's faith. For organizations, the focus is on results, shareholder return, and service or product liability. When institutions or their representatives do not appear to live up to one's expectations, a common response is to charge that they are not being accountable.

Whether voiced as reasonably framed newspaper editorials, vitriolic diatribes on talk-radio, or bad-mouthing "them" over a beer, people in organizations are influenced by this frequent tone of criticism and judgment. Instead of a simple description of the expectations related to a job, *accountability* for an employee can take on a connotation of blame, triggering reactions of cynicism or fear. People believe that when someone is labeled as "not accountable," some will question that person's integrity. When managers and organizational leaders call for greater employee accountability, the more cynical interpret this as off-loading of responsibility or a set-up for future blame. Often employees worry that they might be held accountable for:

• situations they do not control or cannot influence;
• results when they do not have the knowledge, tools, or resources needed to be successful;
• tasks, assignments, or outcomes of which they are unaware.

And so what begins as a useful word to call out basic expectations about job responsibilities ends up—for some—as a tangle of worries about performance, credibility, and fair treatment. When left undiscussed (Ryan & Oestreich, 1998, pp. 279–83) these concerns can spawn a variety of unhealthy and unnecessary stresses which diminish an employee's affective connection to an organization and may block eventual achievement. When voiced from an employee's experience, these strains sound like:

• "I can't believe he's asking me to do this—on top of everything else!"
• "They want me to make sure this project comes in on time and within budget, but are not willing to give me the authority to do what I need to do to get it done. They still make all the key decisions."
• "I had no choice in the matter. I was told that I had to take it on—even though I don't really have the background that is needed."
• "I don't really believe this is the right way to go. But if I want to stay on this team, I have to play along."

24.1.1 The Purpose of this Chapter

At the core of these patterns is the notion of individualized accountability. In many situations when a manager assigns additional responsibility, it is as though the employee is cut loose, like a boat leaving the dock. He or she is expected to follow through to achieve the results by relying on his or her individual abilities and the available resources. Once the accountability has been handed off, the manager monitors and provides oversight, remaining at a distance and focused on other matters.

My purpose in writing this chapter is to offer a practical alternative to this approach. This model, which I will refer to as Shared Accountability, is characterized by two distinctive elements:

- Managers and employees actively share a sense of responsibility for the results assigned to the employee.
- Effective conversations between the manager and employee take place throughout the life of the assignment.

My primary audience for these suggestions consists of managers—anyone who has supervisory responsibility, who depends on others to get a job done, and needs to talk with them about doing so. I will highlight workplace dynamics that influence the experience of accountability and suggest methods of communicating that will enhance the chances of both individual and organizational success. In doing so, I have two larger goals, both of which link to the subject of workplace health and psychology:

- To suggest ways for managers to get the results they want from employees and simultaneously build a work environment where employees feel respected and valued.
- To reframe the way the concept of *accountability* is actually experienced in the workplace, shifting it from a negative blame-oriented dynamic to one where the individuals involved have a high sense of contribution and personal meaning in their work.

Within this context, my suggestions should serve to support many of the points made in previous chapters about the importance of job-fit, stress, resistance to change, orientation to work, burnout, interpersonal conflict, and coaching. What follows can be applied to any level of the organization—from team leaders to executive vice-presidents. "Manager" will refer to the person who asks someone else, the "employee," to take on a new or revised assignment. The "employee" can be anyone, in any function at any level, other than the most senior executive.

24.1.2   When to Use this Approach

Talking about work is a fundamental process within organizations. Thus, Shared Accountability is applicable to a wide range of workplace situations. However, the primary focus for this chapter is within the manager–employee relationship, when the manager needs to ask the employee to do things beyond his or her routine assignments. This is a rigorous approach and can represent a substantial investment of time and energy. As such, it is not practical for all instances when a manager desires an employee to be more accountable. Shared Accountability has its greatest pay-off when one or more of these factors are present:

- An important change is involved, specifically people need to do different things or do the same things in new ways. For example, a group of city building inspectors are required to adopt an attitude of "customer service" rather than "policing" when it comes to interacting with building contractors and developers.
- An aspect of a person's job is given heightened priority for the organization or for the manager. For example, a major customer of a manufacturing company rejects a shipment due to quality defects. The manager of the production units makes high-priority

assignments to two individuals—one for addressing the customer's dissatisfaction and the second for improving the manufacturing process.

- The project or responsibility is critical to the organization's mission. For example, a vice-president in an insurance company is asked to lead a three-year effort that will transform the business systems technology, and thus the way in which the company will conduct its business in the future.
- A manager does not have full confidence in the person receiving such an assignment and recognizes that to be successful, the employee will need to be more consciously prepared, supported, and coached. For example, a director takes a risk by promoting a supervisor into a management role; the director believes the supervisor has the potential to be successful in the new role, even though he or she has not been fully successful in his or her current job.

24.1.3 Why Managers Pay Attention to Accountability

A manager's job is to engage people in ways so that results are achieved. Responsibilities tied to such positions include setting targets, establishing plans to reach those goals, creating a structure of jobs through which people will accomplish what the plan sets forth, delegating responsibility, monitoring performance against plans, and planning and organizing to solve the problems that come up (Kotter, 1990, p. 104). By doing all of this, managers have an interdependent relationship with employees: managers cannot do the amount of work that needs to be done to achieve results by themselves—therefore they engage others in the process. Managers find themselves squarely in the middle of issues related to organizational performance. They are the ones who:

- are held accountable, by their managers, for specific organizational results;
- translate visions and organizational strategies into messages that help supervisors and employees know where they fit, have the capability to do what needs to be done, and maintain the motivation necessary to follow-through on the critical commitments that will accomplish the organization's goals;
- are responsible for making sure employees have the resources they need to get the work done;
- work through the frustrations and inefficiencies of various systems in order to overcome the day-to-day barriers that get in the way of quality performance;
- have direct influence on the work environment of people who make a difference to overall performance—front-line employees.

Thus the issue of accountability—of taking responsibility for the action that leads to the identified desired results—rests firmly on managers' shoulders. To accomplish it all, managers delegate portions of this responsibility to others through the structure of defined jobs, plans, and specific assignments.

24.1.4 Underlying Principles of Shared Accountability

When the circumstances warrant special attention, significant benefit is gained when a manager secures a personal commitment from the employee to be accountable for the desired results. Commitment is the key. For the employee, it represents a level of interest, energy, and meaning that goes beyond what is normally present when he or she agrees to do a certain assigned task. Once the commitment is gained, open, two-way, and ongoing conversations increase the likelihood that the desired results will be achieved. Such conversations also help build a healthy work environment, where employees feel respected and find meaning in what they are asked to do. The ongoing dialogue is built upon principles of trust, interdependence, and the belief that, with sufficient knowledge and the right kind of support, most employees can be successful at taking on new challenges. Four phases of conversation are involved; they are described in detail in the second half of this chapter.

- clarifying expectations
- making commitments
- checking-in on progress
- wrapping-up.

A handful of underlying principles shape this approach. They include the following.

1. Interdependence. In each phase, due to their interdependence, the manager and the employee actively share the responsibility to deliver the desired results. Each has his or her own part to play. One cannot succeed without the other. Without the commitment of both, the desired results are much less likely to be achieved.

2. The power of commitment. Given the multitude of priorities that shape many employees' work lives, establishing a sense of personal commitment is a critical step toward insuring that newly requested results are achieved. Personal commitment inspires an employee to devote the extra energy or attention that is needed to assure the delivery of desired results—especially within complex, challenging, or ambiguous assignments. Commitment is increased when:

- an employee can exert influence on or make choices about either the outcomes or methods involved in an assignment;
- the employee's manager follows through on his or her commitments to secure resources and address larger systems issues that may block the employee's success;
- the manager maintains ongoing communication with the employee about the progress of the work.

3. Creating true commitment. The word *commitment* is often linked to a sense of personal obligation or a promise to do something. For some, giving one's "word" to follow through is as significant as signing a legal contract. When an employee makes a personal commitment to do something, there is usually a high level of motivation, interest, or significance in following through. Such commitment is far more than a head-nod or an undiscussed, assumed acceptance of a new assignment. Shared Accountability relies on a process that asks both managers and employees to consciously accept and articulate their mutual commitments to each other and the task at hand. Through open sharing of information, discussion of priorities, and mutual problem solving, employees are much more likely to be willing to personally accept—and perhaps even embrace—new accountabilities. Without this two-way dialogue, a manager should not assume that enough has been done to assure successful completion of important or complex assignments.

4. Open conversations. In organizations characterized by high-trust relationships, employees are much more likely to push back if they disagree with the direction or results related to an assignment. In reality, these circumstances are rare. Even in settings where

participation and teamwork are valued, very few employees feel free to directly refuse or challenge an assignment requested by a manager. This is especially so when the assignment has been called out as a high priority or critical to the mission of the organization. Even though the manager is giving the assignment and the employee feels obliged to accept it, managers can initiate ongoing conversations that will lead to the type of commitment described above. Dialogue, based upon respect for the employee's energy and capability and grounded in the notion of interdependence, is the key. These exchanges make it possible to:

- identify and understand employee concerns related to delivering the outcomes;
- make plans or adjustments in the assignment so that the employee and the manager can successfully do their individual parts to achieve the desired results;
- negotiate adjustments in plans and resources as the need arises;
- identify lessons learned and build trust.

24.1.5   The Dynamics of an Assignment: Trust is a Critical Factor

Imbedded within this type of delegation of new accountability, for both the manager and the employee, is the issue of trust. At its essence, one person's trust of another is shaped by his or her perceptions of the other around three interrelated factors: competence, follow-through, and motivation (Reina & Reina, 1999, p. 64; Shaw, 1997, pp. 17–18):

- Competence focuses on the presence or lack of the knowledge, skills, or experience necessary to accomplish any task.
- Follow-through pertains to the delivery of results and whether or not the expectations are met—not at all, partially, or completely.
- Motivation is the least tangible of the three and reflects subjective values or beliefs and the way they influence relationships at work. Motivation is tied to the positive or negative intent that shapes behavior and the degree to which someone makes any assignment a priority.

While separate, these three intertwine. Competence and motivation both contribute to a person's ability to follow-through. Past experiences with another person's follow-through shape current perceptions of his or her competence or motivation. A person's motivation can inspire someone to gain necessary skills or pay particular attention to the details that lead to delivering results on time and to specification.

These tangled elements play themselves out on a daily basis. For example, when assigning a new level of accountability, a manager consciously or unconsciously considers these questions:

- Competence: does the employee have the skills, knowledge, and relationships necessary to successfully do the required work?
- Follow-through: will the employee deliver the identified outcomes?
- Motivation: do I have an experience or know something that causes me to have concerns about the employee's ability or willingness to follow-through?

The employee has his or her version of the same questions:

- Competence: do I have the skills, knowledge, and relationships necessary to be successful?

- Motivation and follow-through: will I have the resources, information, and support I need from my manager and other parts of the organization in order to do what is asked of me?
- Motivation and competence: will my manager back me up if I need to challenge current practice or powerful players in the organization?
- Motivation: what levels of influence will I have about the results I am expected to deliver or the way in which that work gets done?

Within the delegation of new responsibilities, risk is present for both the manager and the employee—even though when trust is greater, the perceived risk is less. For both there is the potential loss of or damage to their credibility, their relationships, or their security (Ryan & Oestreich, 1998, pp. 279–83). The risk is quite similar for each, with the internal message going something like this: "If things do not go well, there could be negative impact for the organization and for me personally. People could lose confidence in me, my reputation could be tarnished, my future in the company could be threatened." In the face of this shared risk, both the manager and the employee take a leap of faith by trusting each other and themselves—believing that between them, the inevitable challenges will be successfully met. Even when full trust is not present, acting as if it were—through principles of respect, open communication, and collaboration—becomes a practical strategy for moving ahead. By behaving according the to principles of trust—through conversation—trust has a chance to grow.

24.2 CONVERSATIONS ABOUT ACCOUNTABILITY

Written documentation and email messages can be useful tools to help any assignment move from inception to the achievement of outcomes, but they cannot supplant the need for a manager and an employee to talk—face to face and in some depth—about the work needing to be done. This interaction shapes the nature of the relationship that any employee has with his or her direct supervisor. The issues discussed and the way in which those conversations take place have direct ties to four critical measures of organizational success: productivity, profitability, customer satisfaction, and employee retention. If retention can be viewed as an indicator of a healthy and satisfying workplace, primary factors include: clarity of expectation, availability of necessary resources, opportunity to do one's best work, being cared about as a person, and having a chance to influence the way things happen (Buckingham & Coffman, 1999, pp. 32–3).

The process of Shared Accountability creates opportunities for these aspects of the manager–employee relationship to flourish. The strength of the interpersonal communication skills possessed by both the manager and the employee will strongly influence the success of those interactions. Following here is a description of the terrain covered in these multiple conversations.

24.2.1 Conversation 1: Clarifying Expectations

A variety of critical elements are included in this first conversation. Developing and using a checklist based upon these factors is useful. There are three primary objectives for this first discussion:

- The employee understands the details of the expectations and the factors that will influence the work that is requested.
- The manager understands the employee's view of the request and the elements that may need to be negotiated or rearranged in order for the employee to feel positive about making the commitment.
- Trust is built.

Expectations are Defined at the Front End: Results, Timeline, Specifications, Preferences for Methods

In order to deliver the desired results, employees need to understand what is expected of them. To do so, they need specific guidance about the end product or service, the time frames, and descriptions of any additional characteristics for the product or service. If the manager has a preference for the way in which the employee is to do the job, that should be made clear as well.

The Reasons, Benefits, and Challenges are Discussed and Understood

In order for any piece of work to have meaning beyond collecting a paycheck, employees need to understand its context and the benefits. This step enables a conversation about such issues as: Why is this work important for the organization? How does it fit with our overall mission or goals? What benefits will come to the employee or the workgroup for following through? Here, the manager has an opportunity to highlight any challenges he or she has identified in advance. Asking the employee for his or her sense of the difficulty builds a sense of joint ownership and, in some cases, may help to reshape the assignment. Conversations around such questions ground the assignment in reality and identify potential barriers that may need to be addressed.

The Priority is Clarified and Discussed in Light of Existing Responsibilities

Given their charge to get things done, managers frequently ask employees to take on new work—without thinking about the way the additional tasks will impact other responsibilities. Employees can be reluctant to push back at their manager's request. They do not want to seem uncooperative or unable to do what is requested. They do not want to be perceived as being critical of their manager's judgment for making the assignment—even though they might worry about their ability to "pull everything off." To open up these potential concerns, a manager could say something like, "I realize that your current responsibilities take all but ten per cent of your time. I know that this project will add at least an additional 40 hours a month. We need to talk about what to do so that you can be successful— and not be working double-time." By doing so, the manager demonstrates sensitivity to the employee's circumstance and a realistic view that the addition of new work requires tradeoffs. Not everything can be a priority—even when there are many important things to do. Conversations like this help an employee feel respected and prevent worries that he or she is being set up for burnout or failure.

Information or Assumptions are Clarified

The manager who delegates accountability has information about the circumstances surrounding an assignment. There can be background reports, past studies, or a summary of other attempts to accomplish a similar goal. Additionally, there can be a set of assumptions—theories, values, or opinions that have shaped the assignment and its priority. When a manager shares such relevant information, the employee gains a more complete understanding of what will be involved in accepting the new accountabilities. To not do so can result in wasted time, rework, and frustration once under way. This is particularly so if the employee spends time and energy discovering or addressing issues about which the manager was already informed.

24.2.2   Conversation 2: Making Commitments

Sometimes it is possible to talk about the delegated accountability and the necessary commitments in the same conversation—sometimes not. The factors that influence this include the level of trust between the manager and the employee, the nature of the assignment being discussed, and the amount of time available for the discussion. It is useful, however, to think of these as separate discussions in an ongoing series of interactions. If the assignment is complex and the employee voices concerns or hesitations, allowing time for reflection can be useful. When the manager and employee do come back together, the objective is to determine the agreements the manager and employee will make to assure that the work moves ahead successfully.

Support Needed for Success is Identified and Secured

Each of the elements explored in Section 24.2.1 can help to identify the resources and assistance required for success. The focus for this discussion is centered around the employee's perspective. The manager begins by saying something like, "What do we need to put in place in order for you to be successful?" As the employee responds, the manager's primary job is to listen carefully and then, with the employee, sort the answers to the question into one of two categories: resources to secure or actions for the manager or others to take. Once the needed resources or actions are listed, both people need to think critically about each item. Questions such as the following help to move the conversation from "what might be nice to have" to "what is essential for success." These include:

- Why is this resource or action necessary? How will its presence or absence impact success?
- Can we realistically provide the resource or take the action in the timeframe required? Do others need to be involved? If we cannot, how do the concerns get addressed?
- What room is there for negotiation?

Commitments to Doing and Supporting the Assignment are Made

The manager opens this phase of the interaction by paraphrasing the understandings reached about needed resources and supportive action. He or she then continues by offering commitments: "In order to make sure we succeed at this, here's what I will do: . . . " It is important for the manager to clearly acknowledge what cannot be done so that the employee has realistic expectations about the manager's support. Once these points are stated and understood by the employee, it is time to ask for the employee's commitment. In marketing terms, this is "asking for the sale." The manager could say something like: "Given all that we have talked about and the commitments on my part, are you ready to take on this assignment?" Once made, it is useful to record the commitments and the basic elements of the assignment for reference in future discussions.

Rarely will the employee refuse; however, hesitation may be expressed either verbally or non-verbally. If so, careful listening may lead to the identification of additional barriers or concerns that need to be explored and addressed. In the unusual situation where the employee declines the assignment, it is important not to conclude that the unwillingness to accept the assignment as a sign of disloyalty or insubordination. Again, listening is the key to gain insight into the employee's perspective and work situation. This twist in the conversation may lead to a discussion of the employee's fit with a particular role or within the organization. This type of direct discussion should be viewed as positive because it can prompt more honest communication about other issues that are significant to the employee and to the manager as well.

Agreements about Ongoing Communication and Problem Solving are Established

Employees accept accountability delegated in this manner because they understand the assignment, have commitments for support that increase the likelihood of success, and feel valued by the process that has led to their commitment. One final assurance needs to be put in place, however. These are the agreements about how the manager and employee will communicate with one another about problems which arise and progress that is made over the life of the project. Specifics to talk about and record include:

- What information should be exchanged, with whom, and how.
- Face to face meetings: their purpose, time, place, and frequency.
- How to raise concerns, worries, or negative feedback.
- How to solve problems, identify lessons learned, and recognize accomplishments; how to communicate these points to enhance learning in other parts of the organization.
- What to do when delivery dates and other deadlines are in doubt or become impossible.
- What to do when conflicts about task-related issues or interpersonal style arise.

24.2.3   Conversation 3: Checking-In

Checking-in conversations happen throughout the life of an assignment. Typically they happen in both formal and informal ways according to the working agreements drafted by the manager and the employee. These conversations focus on actions that will assure eventual success; they are characterized by a positive spirit, openness, joint commitment, and mutual support. Classic questions, asked by either party include: "How is it going?" "What's the latest development on ... ?" "How are you doing with ... ?" "What can I do to help?" The essential point to remember about checking-in conversations is that they are *not* conversations where the manager "checks-up on" the employee. Checking-in conversations are based upon and build trust. Checking-up-on discussions reinforce the hierarchical positions of a "boss" and a "worker" and reflect mistrust of the employee's capability or intentions. Typically, they carry a tone of judgmental oversight and an implication of possible repercussions for inadequate performance. From a manager's point of view, the objectives of checking-in are:

- Reporting on action taken to support the work.
- Interceding in a timely way or working with the employee to solve problems if things are not going well.
- Sending a message that says I care, I'm paying attention, your work is an important priority for me.

A variety of interrelated issues shape these discussions, in which the manager is wise to adopt the role of a skilled and successful athletic coach:

- Encouraging the employee's confidence.
- Offering practical feedback.
- Advising on strategy and technique as appropriate.
- Facilitating the employee's self-awareness and sensitivity to environmental circumstances and dynamics.
- Being sensitive to the way personal issues can impact the achievement of results.

Feedback is Sought and Offered on a Regular Basis

After the updates which follow the question, "How is it going?," it is time for the manager to ask the employee for feedback. For example: "Are you seeing any impact since I followed-through on ... ?" or, "At yesterday's meeting, what did you think about the way the decision turned out? Do you have any suggestions for how I might have done it differently?" or, "Are you getting the support you need from me so that you can be more effective with ... ?" Once the employee responds, the manager listens carefully and paraphrases the key points. With this approach, the manager demonstrates the openness and genuine curiosity that ideally will come to characterize the employee's own requests for feedback. After the conversation, if the manager makes changes based on the employee's feedback, the employee will recognize the value of such exchanges when it comes to influencing another's behavior or making adjustments in plans.

If the employee seems hesitant to ask for feedback, it might be because of old habits about "not wanting to look bad in front of the boss." The manager can encourage this exchange by offering specific positive feedback on some aspect of the employee's performance. A question such as "How are you feeling about your efforts to ... ?", followed by careful listening and paraphrasing, can also help the reluctant employee to open up. In the event that the manager has concerns, those should be raised directly with a respectful tone of voice. For example, "There were two things that concerned me in your last report. I'd like to talk with you about them to make sure I understood what you wanted to convey. Is this a good time to do so?" In exchanges such as these, it is important not to confuse respectful, direct communication with manipulation or avoidance. Respectful and direct interaction deals with potentially difficult issues honestly, openly, and concretely—and in a way that does not discredit the employee's value or motivations. It is quite the opposite of indirect methods designed to drop hints in hopes that the employee will "get the message"—without ever having to talk directly about a difficult issue.

Problems, Barriers, and Mistakes are Identified in a Timely Manner

A manager's efforts to work from the principles of Shared Accountability begin to pay off at this point. Mission-critical, complex projects are more likely to succeed when employees identify problems, barriers and mistakes—sooner rather than later. Without this ability, the natural and inevitable challenges have a compounding effect: the negative affects of faulty decisions, ineffective systems, damaged relationships, poor customer service or product reliability, and lowered morale can build one upon another to create huge barriers to success. The ideal situation is when the employee and the manager have the type of relationship where they can easily hold honest conversations about problems that arise. If that is not the case, managers can set the tone for this type of interaction by relying on the principles described earlier. The purpose of the problem-focused discussion is early identification, resolution, damage control, and prevention of additional negative consequences that will affect the desired results. Throughout, managers are wise to:

- Stay focused on the issues, seeking solutions rather than laying blame.
- Employ listening skills to identify core elements needing to be addressed.
- Keep note of systems, culture, or other leadership issues that require attention and follow through as appropriate.
- Remember that resources and strategies may need to be realigned depending on the problems that come up.
- Directly—and respectfully—raise concerns that might pertain to the employee's performance or intentions, providing feedback to the employee on the impact of behavior and seeking to understand reasons for behaving in those ways.
- Keep track of agreements about follow-up action and return to those in subsequent check-in conversations

Effort and Progress are Acknowledged and Appreciated

In many organizations, recognition and appreciation are frequently neglected or glossed over. Busy leaders, once seeing that certain milestones have been accomplished, shift their attention to the next set of challenges. Slowing down to acknowledge both the effort and progress made throughout the course of an ongoing accountability has significant benefits: employees who have accepted additional responsibilities feel supported and appreciated; specific effective behaviors or strategies are reinforced; relationships are strengthened. As with all other suggestions about communication, sincerity on the part of the manager is critical. Additionally, the most powerful acknowledgement comes when the manager is specific and concrete in describing the impact of the employee's effort or actual achievement. Saying something like, "When you made the link between this initiative and our customer satisfaction data, several people shifted their opinions" is far more useful to an employee than, "You did a great job at yesterday's meeting."

24.2.4   Conversation 4: Wrapping-Up

The final phase in these ongoing conversations includes more acknowledgments. However, in this case, they are focused on the purpose and objectives of the overall assignment, rather than on the various steps leading up to the final outcomes. Wrapping-up enables the manager and the employee to reach closure, in a conscious way, on the effort they have mutually undertaken. The primary focus is on the employee's performance and the results that were achieved—not on elements of the work systems or culture. The manager's fulfillment of his or her commitments is a secondary aspect of the conversation. If careful attention has been paid to checking-in, there should be no surprises in this discussion—either for the employee or the manager.

Successful Performance is Acknowledged and Rewarded

Shared Accountability is designed to produce success. The careful attention to establishing expectations, securing commitments, and checking in should lead to the desired results— or something very close to them. If this is so, the wrapping-up conversation is all about appreciation and learning. A set of questions guide the discussion between the manager and employee:

- When it comes to expectations and outcomes, where did we start? How have we ended up?
- What factors made the difference in our success?
- What have we learned along the way? About the work, the organization, and how we have worked together?
- If we were to do this all over again, would we make any changes? What are they and why are they worth trying?
- Are there any lessons or suggestions that we want to pass on to others in the organization? How do we do that?

Organizations vary in their approach to rewarding high performance. However, three factors seem pertinent: the acknowledgement should be meaningful to the employee, fit the culture of the organization, and correspond to the significance of the accountability fulfilled. The range of possibilities is huge, including cash awards, promotions, salary increases, title changes, time off, additional paid vacation time, additional training or development opportunities, special mentoring, written commendations, plaques or trophies, lunch, write-ups in employee newsletters, or a simple and heartfelt thank-you. Regardless of the options, in wrapping-up, the manager's job includes directly and formally acknowledging the contribution made by the employee and a description of the award attached. Managers might also consider commenting on or engaging the employee in a discussion about the way trust has been affected by the work accomplished. This can be particularly meaningful in cases where the manager delegated accountability to someone in whom he or she was not fully confident.

Continued Poor or Non-Performance is Addressed

One of the most challenging aspects of managing in respectful, people-oriented ways is dealing with poor performance. Nonetheless, within the process of Shared Accountability, checking-in provides many opportunities for the manager to address concerns about the employee's work. It is possible that the discussion and action taken in those conversations might not produce the needed corrections. If the employee continues to *not* meet expectations along the way, in spite of all of the support provided, the wrapping-up phase will require the manager to directly address the employee's performance. Problematic systems or other issues—besides the employee's behavior—should have been addressed previously in the checking-in conversations. Appropriate consequences must be delivered in these circumstances—otherwise the entire process of Shared Accountability will be meaningless. Careful preparation is essential and may include consultation with the organization's human resource department and the manager's direct supervisor.

Points the manager will want to make include:

- The employee is not being blamed for flaws in the system; consequences come because of poor performance of the employee and his or her failure to respond to guidance for corrections discussed during the check-in conversations.
- The nature of the consequence.
- The specific reason it is being administered, with a description of the negative impact created by the poor performance.
- The implications of the consequence for the employee.

As with the rewards for excellent performance, the consequence should be meaningful to the employee, fit the culture of the organization, and correspond to the significance of the degree to which the accountability was not fulfilled. There is also a comparable range of possibilities for poor performance. Options include an expression of extreme disappointment on the part of the manager, a letter of reprimand, loss of opportunity for future special assignments, assignment to retraining or remedial work, reduction of current scope of work, loss of pay, demotion, or being fired.

Unlike all of the other Shared Accountability interactions, the conversation where a manager confronts an employee about poor performance and metes out consequences tends to be more of a one-way communication. Nonetheless, the manager is wise to apply the same principles that have guided all other interactions:

- Be clear, direct, and matter-of-fact.
- Deal with behavior not the intent of the employee—unless some type of manipulation has been uncovered and is the offending behavior.
- Do not convey a blaming tone.
- Invite employee reactions, listening carefully.
- Describe actions the employee might take to recover from or make amends for the poor performance.

24.3 THE FUTURE OF ACCOUNTABILITY

The neutral principle of accountability, individuals being responsible for delivering a set of described and assigned results, is the core of any employment contract. It is the means by which any collection of individuals produces and brings its product or service to market. And thus accountability strikes to the heart of what any of us experience in the workplace. Unfortunately, the pace and swirl of change, competition, and shrinking resources have caused spread-too-thin managers to neglect many of the fundamental elements of effective leadership. Shared Accountability attempts to pull many of these together, to be directed back toward the heart of workplace dynamics—what goes on between a manager and an employee.

In his introduction to *Leadership is an Art*, Max DePree outlines his purpose: "The book is about the art of leadership: liberating people to do what is required of them in the most effective and humane way possible" (DePree, 1989, p. 1). Among the collection of elegant principles that have guided decades of success of his company, Herman Miller, is the idea that employees have a right to be accountable. He suggests that we all "need to have the opportunity to contribute to the group's goals. We need the opportunity to share in the ownership of the group's problems and also the inherent risk. We need to have our contributions measured according to previously understood and accepted standards of performance, and this transaction needs to take place in an adult-to-adult relationship. At the heart of being accountable is the matter of caring" (DePree, 1989, p. 41).

DePree links required work, employee contribution and ownership, risk, measurement, adult communication, and caring. Each of these easily finds its way into situations where managers and employees share accountability, where managers initiate conversations that clarify expectations, call out commitments, check-in on progress and barriers, and acknowledge success or poor performance. Each contributes to a workplace where the desired results are achieved while at the same time employees at all levels feel respected and valued and have a high sense of contribution and meaning in their work. These elements combine in ways to produce practical, effective outcomes for organizations and a healthy and satisfying workplace for the people involved.

REFERENCES

Buckingham, M. & Coffman, C. (1999) *First Break All the Rules: What the World's Greatest Managers Do Differently*, New York: Simon & Schuster.

DePree, M. (1989) *Leadership Is an Art*. New York: Dell.

Kotter, J. (1990) What leaders really do. *Harvard Business Review*, **68**(3), 103–11.

Reina, D. & Reina, M. (1999) *Trust and Betrayal in the Workplace: Building Effective Relationships in Your Organization*. San Francisco, CA: Berrett-Koehler.

Ryan, K. & Oestreich, D. (1998) *Driving Fear Out of the Workplace: Creating the High-Trust, High-Performance Organization*, San Francisco, CA: Jossey-Bass.

Shaw, R. (1997) *Trust in the Balance: Building Successful Organizations on Results, Integrity, and Concern*, San Francisco, CA: Jossey-Bass, 1997.

CHAPTER 25

Stress Management at Work: Secondary Prevention of Stress

Lawrence R. Murphy

National Institute for Occupational Safety and Health, Ohio, USA

25.1 INTRODUCTION

In the first edition of this handbook, the chapter on stress management provided detailed descriptions of various stress management techniques, reviewed the scientific literature on effectiveness for each technique, identified gaps in research and offered ideas for future research needs (Murphy, 1996b). This chapter follows the same general outline, but with two exceptions. First, the descriptions of each technique are abbreviated in favor of presenting more detail on key elements of successful stress management interventions. Second, the literature on stress management is assimilated with research on job- and organizational-level stress interventions in an effort to bring these two fields into closer proximity. Only when the latter is done will the field make substantial advances in reducing stress at work, and practitioners will be enabled to design effective, comprehensive stress management interventions.

The nature and complexity of occupational stress have been addressed in numerous research articles and books (Caplan et al., 1975; Cooper & Marshall, 1976; Ivancevich & Ganster, 1987; Murphy & Schoenborn, 1989; Quick & Quick, 1984). This literature indicates that stress is a common problem in work settings, and can lead to physical and psychological ill health; that stress is often determined by personal appraisals of work environment situations (one person's meat is another person's poison); and that stress is costing companies substantial amounts of money in the terms of health care costs, productivity losses, and worker compensation claims (Cooper, 1987; DeCarlo, 1987; Sauter et al., 1990). Increasingly, more and more companies are exploring ways to deal with occupational stress.

There are three distinct approaches to the problem of occupational stress, each addressing different aspects of the problem. The most common approach is to provide treatment services to troubled workers, usually in the form of employee assistance programs. This is a reactive approach, in as much as the health problems already exist, and the main efforts are focused on treatment of the health outcomes. This approach typically does not involve efforts to

The Handbook of Work and Health Psychology. Edited by M.J. Schabracq, J.A.M. Winnubst and C.L. Cooper.
© 2003 John Wiley & Sons, Ltd.

identify and reduce job/organizational factors that create stress. In medical terminology, this is *tertiary prevention*.

In contrast, *primary prevention* seeks to identify and reduce the sources of stress, which can be work or non-work factors. This approach can be reactive (that is, dealing with an existing stress problem) or proactive (preventing stressful work conditions from becoming a problem), but deals directly with the source(s) of stress at work, not just the outcomes of exposure to stressors. Evaluations of this type of intervention are relatively rare in the published literature (see Murphy, 1988; Ivancevich et al., 1990). However, a recent review of such interventions in health care settings identified a critical mass of studies that provide guidance on how to design successful interventions (Murphy, 1999).

Intermediate between primary and tertiary approaches is *secondary prevention*, which aims to reduce the severity of stress symptoms before they lead to more serious health consequences. Commonly called *stress management*, these programs are individual-oriented, and usually seek to educate workers about the nature of stress, and to teach workers specific techniques for reducing physiological and psychological symptoms of stress, and fostering a state of relaxation. The most common types of stress management strategies are progressive muscle relaxation, biofeedback, meditation, and cognitive-behavioral skills training.

This chapter focuses primarily on stress management methods as narrowly defined above, and does not review job and organizational interventions for preventing or reducing stress, nor does it review interventions involving individual counseling, physical fitness, or conflict intervention. As noted earlier, however, there is a section that attempts to assimilate research on stress management with research on job- and organizational-level interventions.

25.2   DESCRIPTION OF STRESS MANAGEMENT INTERVENTIONS

With the exception of meditation, the stress management interventions (SMI) described in this chapter were borrowed from the field of clinical psychology, where they had demonstrated success in the treatment of anxiety and psychosomatic disorders (Pomerleau & Brady, 1979). Stress management techniques can be classified in various ways, but the problem-focused versus emotion-focused dichotomy proposed by Lazarus and colleagues (Cohen & Lazarus, 1979; Folkman & Lazarus, 1980) for stress coping strategies is most common. *Problem-focused coping* involves actions to reduce or eliminate the source(s) of stress, such as problem-solving techniques or environmental changes. *Emotion-focused coping*, on the other hand, involves attempts to reduce or eliminate the symptoms of stress, such as relaxation training or biofeedback. Problem- and emotion-focused coping can be further subdivided into somatic and cognitive methods of coping. Somatic methods seek to reduce arousal levels during stress (lower blood pressure, muscle activity, etc.), while cognitive methods seek to alter the thinking patterns and stress appraisal processes.

Because nearly all SMIs include some type of relaxation exercise, however brief, the issue of relaxation-induced anxiety (RIA) needs to be mentioned. Heide & Borkovec (1984) describe RIA as feelings of anxiety and discomfort, and occurring primarily among a small percentage of clinical patients suffering from chronic anxiety, and pervasive, generalized anxiety. Heide & Borkovec (1984) offered several possible reasons for RIA, which include fear of losing control as patients become more deeply relaxed, and becoming frightened of the sensations which accompany relaxation (that is, warmth or tingling in the hands and fingers). There have been no reports of RIA in worksite stress management interventions, perhaps because the training is offered to all employees, most of whom do not have exceptionally high levels of anxiety. Indeed, workers with very high levels of anxiety require supervised, medical treatment, not brief stress management training.

In the remainder of this chapter, each stress management technique is described in detail, followed by a review of the evidence for the effectiveness of each technique in helping workers manage stress.

25.2.1 Progressive Muscle Relaxation

Progressive muscle relaxation (PMR) involves focusing one's attention on muscle activity levels, learning to identify even small amounts of tension in a muscle group, and practising releasing tension from the muscles (Jacobson, 1938). PMR training aims to foster awareness and heightened control over muscle activity. The underlying theory of PMR is that since relaxation and muscle tension are incompatible states, reducing muscle tension levels indirectly reduces autonomic activity and, consequently, anxiety and stress levels. PMR is usually accomplished by a series of alternating tensing and relaxing exercises; first, creating tension in a muscle group (for example, clenching one's fist), studying the feelings of tenseness, then allowing the muscles to relax, and noticing the difference between the tense and relaxed states. By systematically moving through the major muscle groups of the body, individuals become proficient at recognizing tension in a muscle group and relieving that tension (Bernstein & Borkovec, 1973).

The original progressive relaxation exercises were quite long, involving all of the muscle groups of the body (Jacobson, 1938), and could involve 50 or more sessions. However, the exercises have been shortened for use with other clinical therapies. For example, Wolpe (1958) abbreviated the exercises to 10 sessions for use in systematic desensitization therapy. Likewise, other variations of PMR, such as differential relaxation and cue-controlled relaxation, have been offered (Bernstein & Borkovec, 1973). In any case, as proficiency at the exercises increases, the exercises can be abbreviated in length and scope to the point where a state of muscle relaxation can be self-induced in a matter of minutes.

The state of deep muscle relaxation produced by PMR is usually associated with a variety of sensations that are unfamiliar to most participants. For example, in one of my studies (Murphy, 1984), a highway maintenance worker complained of a tingling sensation in his fingertips, and feelings of heaviness in his arms and legs after training. He was relieved to find out that those sensations were simply the by-products of deep muscle relaxation (Bernstein & Borkovec, 1973). This example underscores the fact that people have much more familiarity with the physiological sensations accompanying stress than sensations associated with relaxation.

PMR would be classified as a somatic stress management strategy, since it focuses exclusively on the reduction of muscle tension levels, and the resulting state of deep muscle relaxation. It is emotion-focused because the training helps individuals to reduce the symptoms of stress, but not the sources of stress (the stressors).

25.2.2 Biofeedback

Biofeedback is based on a fundamental principle of learning: people learn best when they are provided with feedback on their performance, that is, "knowledge of results." In biofeedback training, an individual is provided with continuous information or feedback about the status of a physiological function and, over time, learns to control the activity of that function. Thus, the electrical activity produced when muscles contract or tense can be recorded and transformed into a tone, whose pitch rises as muscle activity increases, and falls as muscle activity decreases. Using the feedback tone as an indicator of muscle tension level, individuals learn how to reduce muscle activity levels, and create a state of relaxation. Biofeedback techniques have been used to teach individuals to exert voluntary control of a wide range of biological functions, including heart rate, blood pressure, blood flow, stomach contractions, and muscle tension (Birk, 1973). Research has demonstrated that biofeedback is especially helpful for people suffering from muscle contraction headaches (Blanchard & Andrasik, 1985, although the use of biofeedback as a generalized relaxation technique has been questioned (Alexander, 1975). Although some of the early research in biofeedback involved feedback of brain waves (alpha rhythms) to achieve relaxation, all of the research in work settings used either feedback of muscle activity levels or blood pressure. Like PMR, biofeedback is a somatic stress management method, and would be classified as emotion-focused coping.

How individuals are able to reduce arousal levels during biofeedback is less well defined. Often, it is recommended that participants visualize a relaxing scene during biofeedback, like lying on a beach, or strolling through woods, and noticing the effects of this imagery on the biofeedback signal. The best advice is to let participants select their own strategy, by letting their mind wander, and noticing which thoughts tend to be associated with lower physiological activity levels. An example will illustrate why it is better to let participants develop their own biofeedback strategy. In a study conducted by the author, one of the nurses in the biofeedback group did remarkably well at lowering her forehead muscle tension levels. When asked how she did it, she replied that she was planning the remainder of her workday on the hospital unit. Her job was to assign staff on the unit to accomplish various tasks, and once she had made the staffing decisions for the day, she could sit back and relax during the session. She had devised a problem-focused strategy, applied the strategy successfully, and reduced her physiological activation levels.

25.2.3   Meditation

Numerous forms of meditation have been developed, the most widely known of which is Transcendental Meditation (TM). TM was developed as a component of yoga by the Maharishi Mahesh Yogi. TM involves sitting upright in a comfortable position with eyes closed, in a quiet place, and mentally repeating a secret mantra (a word or sound), while maintaining a passive mental attitude. The meditation should be performed twice per day.

Two secular versions of meditation, one developed by Herbert Benson (1976), and the other by Patricia Carrington (1978), have been the most widely used forms of meditation in work settings. In Benson's modification of TM, one finds a quiet place and sits comfortably for 20 minutes twice a day. While maintaining a passive attitude toward intruding thoughts, the word "one" is repeated with each exhalation. The choice of the word "one" instead of a mantra reflects Benson's attempt to produce a secular version of meditation. However, Benson recommends that people of faith use whatever they feel is appropriate as a mental focus. For example, Christians might choose to meditate on the first verse of Psalm 23 ("The Lord is my Shepherd"), followers of Judaism might use the word *shalom*, and the nonreligious can use the word *one*, or *relax* as a mental focus (Benson, 1993).

In any case, Benson argues that such meditation invokes a "relaxation response," which is the opposite of the stress response. With practice, individuals learn to invoke the relaxation response whenever they wish. Indeed, Benson has published impressive data showing that the relaxation response can be learned quickly, and is associated with significant decreases in physiological and psychological symptoms of stress, and increases in feelings of relaxation (Benson, 1976, 1993).

The other secular method, clinically standardized meditation (CSM), was developed by Carrington (1978), and is similar to Benson's method, except that the "mental repetition of a sound is not systematically linked with each breath, is allowed to proceed at its own pace, and is intended to be taught by a qualified instructor" (Carrington, 1978). Also, CSM uses a "mantra," and in this sense is more similar to TM than is Benson's technique. CSM has been associated with significant reductions in physiological activity levels (for example, blood pressure) and psychological symptoms of stress, such as anxiety and somatic complaints (Carrington, 1978; Carrington et al., 1980).

Like biofeedback, but unlike progressive relaxation, meditation methods focus more on mental processes (mental quieting), than physical or somatic relaxation, although the latter usually accompanies the mental quieting achieved during meditation (Benson, 1976). Meditation would be considered emotion-focused coping, in that the technique does not aim to alter the sources of stress.

25.2.4 Cognitive-Behavioral Skills Training

Cognitive-behavioral skills (COG-BEH) refer to an assortment of techniques designed to help participants modify their appraisal processes which determine the stressfulness of situations, and to develop behavioral skills for managing stressors. Cognitive methods help people *restructure* their thinking patterns, and are often referred to as cognitive restructuring techniques. One such technique is called rational-emotive therapy (RET), and was developed by Albert Ellis (1977). RET focuses on identifying the specific stages of a person's thought processes, forces patients to realize the irrationality of some thought patterns, and teaches them to interrupt the thought process with more rational thoughts. Ellis (1977) defined the therapeutic procedure as involving an A-B-C-D-E paradigm: **A**ctivating experience (the original disturbing experience), **B**eliefs (which enter one's mind in response to **A**), **C**onsequences (emotional and behavioral consequences of **B**), **D**isputing of irrational beliefs that occur during therapy, and the **E**ffect of the therapy (a restructured belief system).

Another type of cognitive skills training was developed by Meichenbaum (1977) called *stress inoculation*. This training involved three stages: education (learning about how the person has responded to past stressful experiences), rehearsal (learning various coping skills techniques, such as problem-solving, relaxation, and cognitive coping), and application (the person practices the skills under simulated conditions guided by the therapist). Unlike RET, stress inoculation training is not restricted to cognitive elements, but additionally can include skills like muscle relaxation and desensitization (Meichenbaum, 1977).

Cognitive therapies have important elements in common: (i) examination of thinking patterns to modify irrational thoughts (for example, "everybody must like me all the time," "everything I do must be perfect," etc.); (ii) substitution of positive "self-talk" for the more common negative "self-talk"; and (iii) development of flexible problem-solving skills (Meichenbaum, 1977).

Finally, cognitive-behavioral strategies deal with a fundamental symptom of stress: disordered thinking. To understand the impact of stress on thinking patterns, one must appreciate that the wide array of physiological and biochemical changes which occur under stress prepare the body for "fight or flight." The "fight or flight" response is characterized by a syndrome of bodily changes, including increased respiration, discharge of adrenalin from the adrenal cortex, elevated blood pressure, and redirection of blood flow to the large muscle groups, and away from the brain and the gastrointestinal system (Cannon, 1929). Under stress, people are prepared for efficient action and inefficient thinking, and this increases the likelihood of well-worn, reflexive thoughts and behaviors, not new, innovative thoughts and behaviors. This state of affairs argues for increased attention to cognitive factors in stress management training.

Unlike all of the stress management methods described up to this point, COG-BEH is an example of problem-focused coping. The method analyzes thinking patterns that may cause stress, and teaches participants how to address the problem directly. Like biofeedback and meditation, COG-BEH is primarily a cognitive, rather than somatic, stress management method.

25.3   STRESS MANAGEMENT AS APPLIED IN WORK SETTINGS

In clinical settings, stress management techniques are taught to patients over an extended period of time (at least 12 weeks) during individualized, weekly sessions in a clinician's office. In work settings, significant modifications have been made to the usual approach. For example, stress management is usually offered as a prevention activity designed to educate workers about the nature and sources of stress, and to provide basic relaxation skills that are useful in everyday life. Programs typically contain a series of brief, daily training sessions (one hour or less), and range from one-day seminars to programs lasting many weeks. These modifications to the usual treatment protocol are warranted because the programs are not designed for treatment of severely troubled workers or those with manifest clinical problems.

The fact that most SMIs considered to be in work settings were offered to all workers, not just those under high levels of stress and/or who display a high frequency of stress symptoms, has implications for evaluations of the effectiveness of SMIs. In contrast to clinical treatment settings where individuals might have high blood pressure, high anxiety, or debilitating muscle tension problems, most participants in worksite stress management studies enter the training with subclinical levels of stress symptoms. To demonstrate a decrease in anxiety from "normal" levels is more difficult than finding a decrease from very high levels to the normal range. This logic is used in many SMI studies where the observed reductions in physiological or psychological measures did not reach statistical significance.

25.4   EFFECTIVENESS OF STRESS INTERVENTIONS

The primary sources for information presented in this section are reviews of the stress intervention literature by Bunce (1997), Murphy (1996a), and Van der Klink et al. (2001). Table 25.1 provides a comparison of the findings of these major reviews. The three reviews

Table 25.1 Comparison of the findings from three recent reviews of the stress management intervention literature

Type of stress management training	Murphy (1996a) Traditional literature review of all published studies ($N = 64$ studies)	van der Klink et al. (2001) Meta-analysis of published studies having at least a quasi-experimental design ($N = 48$ studies)	Bunce (1997) Review of studies that directly compared two or more training techniques ($N = 10$)
Multi-component training (combination of two or more training techniques)	Rated the most effective type of training across the various outcome measures (psychological, somatic complaints, and physiological measures)	Rated the second most effective technique overall and most effective for improving physiological symptoms (e.g. muscle tension levels)	Rated better than either arousal reduction or miscellaneous training techniques (three studies)
Cognitive-behavioral skills training	Rated most effective for improving psychological symptoms (e.g. anxiety) and second most effective technique overall	Rated the most effective type of training across the various outcome measures (psychological, somatic complaints, etc.)	Did not produce significantly better outcomes than other training techniques (three studies)
Arousal reduction (includes muscle relaxation)	Rated very effective for improving physiological symptoms (e.g. muscle tension levels)	Rated very effective for improving physiological symptoms (e.g. muscle tension levels)	Did not produce significantly better outcomes than other training techniques (four studies)

provide different perspectives on this field of research based on their criteria for selection of studies in each review. For instance, Murphy (1996a) reviewed all published studies ($n = 64$), even though some of them did not utilize randomized controls or comparison groups. Van der Klink et al. (2001), on the other hand, included only those studies which utilized an experimental or quasi-experimental design ($n = 48$) and the authors conducted a meta-analyses of the studies and presented effect sizes for each type of intervention. Finally, Bunce (1997) included only those studies that directly compared two or more stress interventions ($n = 10$), so the results from this review provide strong evidence of relative effectiveness of various interventions. As one moves from left to right across the columns of Table 25.1, the summary findings deal with an increasingly small but in some ways more rigorous sample of studies.

The training techniques in Table 25.1 are listed in the first column and the reviews are shown in the first row, across the top of the table. Cells in the table describe the summary results. Thus, for multi-component training programs (listed in the second row), Murphy (1996a) concludes that they are the most effective stress intervention, Van der Klink et al. (2001) conclude that they are the second most effective intervention, and Bunce (1997) finds that such interventions fare better than others in studies which included direct comparisons.

Most studies in the literature used a combination of stress intervention techniques, and these multi-component studies produced consistent and significant results across the various health-outcome measures. As shown in Table 25.1, all three reviews rate multi-component techniques as highly effective for reducing psychological and physiological symptoms of stress. Conceptually, the combination of two particular techniques, cognitive-behavioral skills plus muscle relaxation, creates a dual focus on cognitive and somatic aspects of stress, and additionally involves the development of specific coping techniques. This particular blend of training techniques is not only the most common but also the most effective type of stress intervention.

Cognitive-behavioral skills training was the single intervention technique used most frequently in stress intervention studies, and produced consistent effects on psychological outcomes, especially anxiety. This is not surprising given that training focuses on understanding and altering the cognitive aspects of stress (i.e. thinking patterns) and on acquiring stress coping skills. All three reviews rated cognitive techniques as effective although Bunce (1997) did not find any special superiority of these techniques over arousal reduction approaches. Bunce (1997) did report that both cognitive and other interventions were better than control or comparison groups.

Finally, arousal reduction strategies (e.g. muscle relaxation) were rated by Murphy (1996a) and Van der Klink et al. (2001) as particularly effective in reducing physiological outcomes, perhaps because of their focus on somatic aspects of stress. However, when compared directly to other techniques, arousal reduction does not seem to be superior (Bunce, 1997).

On balance, it seems that stress interventions that involve a combination of training techniques produce more consistent results across the various health-outcome measures than any of the individual techniques. The reason for the superiority might be that the combination of muscle relaxation and cognitive-behavioral skills training provides workers with a balance of somatic and cognitive skills, and this combination may be more effective across more types of outcome measures than either technique alone. For example, muscle relaxation alone was effective for physiological outcomes and cognitive-behavioral skills training was effective for psychological, so the combination of the two should increase the overall range of effective results. Another reason for the effectiveness of combination training is that because more than one skill is taught, there may be fewer participants who fail to learn the stress-management skills. In the empirical studies that reported the success rates of participants, it was common to find that about one-third of participants failed to learn a particular stress-management technique (see Murphy, 1984).

Among the individual techniques, cognitive-behavioral skills training was judged as most effective by Van der Klink et al. (2001) and second only to multi-component training by Murphy (1996). Cognitive techniques seemed especially effective for reducing psychological outcomes like anxiety and depression.

25.5 STRESS REDUCTION VERSUS STRESS MANAGEMENT

In most articles and books on stress interventions at work (including the present one), stress reduction (primary prevention) and stress management (secondary prevention) are addressed separately. This has occurred in part because of the wide philosophical differences underlying primary and secondary prevention of stress, but also because there has been so little integration of findings from these two classes of intervention techniques in review articles. This state of affairs has prevented, or at least retarded, reasonable discussions of how stress interventions might incorporate elements of both primary and secondary techniques. Consequently, research that evaluates comprehensive stress interventions, ones that combine primary and secondary stress prevention, is virtually non-existent.

In this section, the theoretical underpinnings of primary and secondary stress interventions are examined, studies of primary and secondary stress interventions are compared, and ideas for the advancement of this field are offered.

Primary prevention of stress at work, through job redesign or organizational change interventions, was the subject of two recent literature reviews (Parkes & Sparkes, 1998; Van der Klink et al., 2001). A similar conclusion was reached in both reviews: organizational interventions do not lead to significant reductions in worker symptoms of stress. This is an important though disturbing conclusion because of the "broadly shared vision that there is a hierarchy of interventions in which primary prevention should prevail over interventions that focus on individuals" (Van der Klink et al., 2001).

The belief that the preferred way to reduce stress at work is to change those aspects of the job or the organization that create stress for workers is fundamental to job stress research because it follows from our most salient theories. For instance, the demand–control theory of Karasek (1979) suggests that the main cause of worker stress or strain is having an excess of job demands over worker decision latitude. To reduce worker stress, one needs to either reduce job demands or improve the amount of decision latitude in the job. In a similar fashion, the person–environment fit theory (Caplan, et al., 1975) proposes that job stress stems from a lack of fit between job and worker, so efforts to reduce stress at work should focus on improving this fit, usually by altering aspects of the job such as quantitative workload, autonomy, and so on.

In no case do the prominent job stress theories explicitly recommend adding a worker-focused element to primary stress prevention interventions. As Van der Klink et al. (2001) point out, organizational change interventions by their very nature often require workers to cope with intervention-induced changes which might create stress. Workers may need training and assistance to help them adapt and adjust to new work routines and interpersonal relationships, beyond the need to cope with change *per se*. Since a fundamental tenet of stress is that change of any type is stressful, then interventions that focus on job redesign might increase worker stress in the short term. This would argue for longer evaluation periods to accurately assess benefits. Second, the change may decrease stress for some workers (the ones who see the change as positive) but increase stress for other workers (those who see the change as negative). This suggests the need for evaluation protocols that include subgroup analyses or which attempt to identify workers who were positively and negatively affected by the interventions. In the same way, organizational change may decrease stress for one group of workers but increase stress for other worker groups. Along these lines, Payne et al. (1999) demonstrated that psychological strain moderated the relationship between work characteristics and work attitudes (i.e. job satisfaction). That is, the relationship was lower for high-stress than low-stress workers. The authors suggested that stress interventions first should help workers deal with their high strain (through individual-oriented strategies) before attempting to change the stresses in the work environment.

This is not to say that companies should not attempt organizational change interventions. The mixed findings from the research literature may simply reflect the fact that organizational interventions are far more complex to design and evaluate than stress management programs. For example, it is almost impossible to perform a true experiment in a work setting, with random assignment of workers to conditions and control of extraneous factors. Organizations are dynamic entities and concurrent (and uncontrollable) changes often occur alongside the planned interventions. During post-intervention evaluation, it is difficult to untangle the respective role of the planned intervention and other changes that may have taken place.

Not all of the news is bad with respect to organizational stress interventions. Kompier et al. (1998) reviewed 10 Dutch studies of primary stress prevention that involved attention to either work redesign, sickness absence management, or training to improve coping capacity. Many of the studies demonstrated improvements in sickness absence and benefits of the intervention outweighed its costs. The authors concluded that successful interventions have five key ingredients: (i) clear identification of the aims, tasks, planning, and responsibilities; (ii) a diagnosis or risk analysis to identify the major problem areas; (iii) combination of worker and work-directed measures; (iv) a participative approach with worker and middle management involvement and commitment; and (v) top management support.

Murphy (1999) reviewed studies of organizational interventions in health care settings and identified a handful that reported positive effects. Although not all of these were scientifically rigorous, the results were sufficiently positive to warrant attention from researchers and practitioners. For instance, participatory job redesign in a 50-bed surgical unit (Abts et al., 1994) led to improvements in both employee and patient satisfaction. Likewise, a thorough redesign of the patient care delivery system, whose impetus was to resolve role conflicts, led to reduced stress, better cooperation among nurses from different shifts, and higher job satisfaction. Finally, comprehensive restructuring of work at a large US medical center led to increased feedback, task significance, meaningfulness of work, internal motivation and job satisfaction (Parsons & Murdaugh, 1994).

It is noteworthy that Murphy (1999) concluded that three elements are necessary for organizational interventions to be successful—worker involvement, management commitment, and a supportive organizational culture—which are similar to the ingredients listed by Kompier et al. (1998). If these elements are missing, even the best designed intervention can fail. Future studies should incorporate these elements into the design of organizational stress interventions, and evaluate them as moderators of program effectiveness.

25.6 STRESS PREVENTION: AN AGENDA FOR FUTURE RESEARCH

Action to reduce stress at work is usually prompted by an organizational crisis, such as high sickness absence or employee turnover. Consequently, actions tend to be driven by a desire to reduce costs (i.e. problem-driven, negative motives) rather than the desire to maximize potential and improve competitive edge (i.e. gains-driven, positive motives). The danger of this type of approach is that once sickness absence or labor turnover rates stabilize at an acceptable level, interventions may lose their impetus and be considered no longer necessary. Organizations need to consider stress prevention not only as a means of cost reduction or containment, but also as a means of maintaining and improving organizational health and increasing productivity.

Future research in stress management would benefit from better grounding in theory and should begin with an explicit conceptual model. There are a number of such models in the literature, and many of them have similar features. One of the oldest, though least utilized, models was offered by Stoner & Fry (1983). Other stress intervention models have been proposed by Heaney & van Ryn (1990), Israel et al. (1996), Ivancevich et al. (1990), Newman & Beehr (1979) and Cox et al. (2000). National groups also have offered conceptual frameworks and guidance for stress interventions (COMCARE Australia, 1997a, b; Health and Safety Executive, 1998 a, b; Healthcare Canada, 2001; Health Education Board for Scotland, 2000; National Institute for Occupational Safety and Health, 1999). Clearly there is no lack of conceptual models and specific advice to guide stress interventions; they just are not being used very often (or at least authors are not explicit about their use).

A proactive approach would involve efforts to improve the overall health of both the worker and the organization, and has recently been described as a "healthy work organization approach" (Murphy, 2000; Sauter et al., 1996). The basic premise is that it is possible to improve worker well-being and organizational effectiveness. Research on healthy work organizations takes place at the intersection of worker well-being and organizational effectiveness, and seeks to identify those job and organizational factors which predict both health and performance outcomes.

The notion that worker well-being and organizational effectiveness can be improved simultaneously is not novel; it has been discussed in one form or another in the organizational behavior, health promotion, and job stress literatures for many years. For example, Pfeiffer (1987) suggested expanding traditional health promotion programs to include attention to work group and organizational-level factors. The model offered by Pfeiffer (1987) was well articulated and specific, and listed three key components: individual health, team health, and organizational health. Individual health is affected by heredity, the environment, lifestyle, and the medical care system. Team health focuses on the execution of assigned work, quality of services provided, nature of the work environment, and health and satisfaction of team members. Poor team health occurs when a team is forced to work short-handed, or when the team discourages individual participation in decision making. Organizational health is a function of the interrelationship of the psychosocial work environment (i.e. the accepted or prescribed culture and norms), the quality of its products and services, the administrative systems that regulate day-to-day performance (e.g. policies, procedures, and program), and the employees themselves. Organizational health requires coordination of occupational health and safety, human resources, health promotion, medical services, and training/development functions.

Another example comes from the organizational behavior literature. In his book *The Healthy Company*, Rosen (1991) developed a values-based organizing system for managing and developing human assets. This system consists of thirteen dimensions, closely intertwined and mutually reinforcing, which would maximize individual and organizational health and performance.

Finally, the National Institute for Occupational Safety and Health (NIOSH) is developing a model of healthy work organizations based on analyses of employee survey data from a large manufacturing company (Sauter et al., 1996). Questionnaire data on management practices, organizational culture/climate, core values, job satisfaction, work stress, and organizational effectiveness from over 15 000 workers from 1993 to 1997 were analyzed to identify those factors which were related to both worker well-being and organizational effectiveness. Key characteristics associated with organizational health were: workers rewarded for performance, open, two-way communication, worker growth and development (training), trust and mutual respect, strong commitment to core values among top management, and strategic planning to keep the organization competitive and adaptive.

The examples offered above suggest that organizational culture is an important ingredient of successful change programs. This has been noted by well-known writers in the business literature, including Peters & Waterman (1982), Blanchard & O'Connor (1997), and Collins & Porras (1994). Each of these authors emphasized the pivotal role of culture and commitment to core values as key to an organization's success in the marketplace. Similar recommendations for improving the effectiveness of stress interventions can be found in the writings of job stress researchers from the UK (Cooper & Williams, 1994), Finland (Lindstrom, 1994), Sweden (Aronsson, 1996), The Netherlands (Kompier & Cooper, 1999), and Australia (Hart & Wearing, 2000).

Far less research has been published on how organizations can change their culture to foster desired change. However, a few thoughts can be offered. First, the organization's culture cannot be changed directly through edicts or policies but these are necessary to begin the process. The culture changes as the organization aligns its actions and decisions to comply with its stated policies and goals. For example, if an organization decides that it would like to create a culture for innovation, it should set goals, establish policies and procedures, and initiate actions that reflect its commitment to innovation. This might mean defining innovation, explaining why the organization thinks it is important, and disseminating this information to workers at all levels, providing training for all workers and supervisors on innovation, with examples of innovative ideas used in other companies (i.e. benchmarking), and adding innovation to employee job descriptions as a basic element of all jobs. The same logic applies to commitment to core values. Commitment to core values is judged by the actions and decisions of upper and middle management, so care needs to be taken to insure that the organization's actions are in line with the values. Such decisions could include everything from placement and selection, to job training, to decisions about the processes to be used for restructuring and reorganizing. For example, if dignity is a core value, and involves treating all workers with dignity and respect, then it should permeate management actions and decisions. It should be evident in things like employee performance appraisal, hiring, firing and placement, how management handles restructuring and reorganization, performance reward systems, and supervisor support for workers. A recent article (Taft et al., 1999) offered a concise description of the specific steps involved in embedding the core values into everyday work life in a hospital setting.

Another example comes from the retail sales industry. In a remarkable turnaround led by CEO Arthur Martinez, Sears undertook a complete revamping of the way it did business. Sears involved 80 000 employees in a process that involved first identifying six core values, and then formulating a statistical model that linked core values to employee satisfaction, which in turn, was related to increased customer satisfaction and greater profit (Rucci et al., 1998). The statistical model revealed that a five-point improvement in employee attitudes led to a 1.3 point improvement in customer satisfaction, which led to a 0.5% improvement in revenue growth. Clearly, companies that integrate the values at work so that they permeate every aspect of work could see tangible benefits on a variety of performance and financial indicators. Additional examples of how companies try to "live out" their core values can be found in Harmon (1996) and in Anderson (1997).

The web is fast becoming an excellent source for information on what companies are doing to foster healthy organizational cultures. Many companies have web pages showing a mission statement, core values and strategic objectives, as well as information on current health and safety programs. Industry-specific web sites also offer good information on successful companies. Builder Online (*www.builder.hw.net/monthly/1999/mar/covstry/index.htx*) published a list of eight great home building companies to work for which contained interviews with management and employees at each company and examples of why each company is so successful.

Finally, *Fortune* magazine annually publishes its list of the 100 Best Companies to Work For (*www.pathfinder.com/fortune/bestcompanies/index2.html*) with links to each company's home page. The 100 best companies are selected based on several types of information, one of which is a 32-page survey that measures company philosophies, policies, programs, and practices influencing the management of people in organizations. Ten primary subject categories are measured, including Recruiting/Hiring/Orientation, Development and Learning, Rewards and Recognition, Health and Well-Being, Financial Security, Organizational Culture, and Unique People Practices. Visiting the web sites of these 100 companies and examining their policies, programs, and practices should provide sufficient ideas for organizations that are interested in creating successful organizational cultures.

The overlap of the subject categories used to select the 100 Best Companies To Work For with the list of healthy work organization characteristics presented earlier should not be lost on the reader.

REFERENCES

Abts, D., Hofer, M. & Leafgreen, P.K. (1994). Redefining care delivery: a modular system. *Nursing Management*, **25**, 40–6.

Alexander, A.B. (1975). An experimental test of the assumptions relating to the use of electromyographic biofeedback as a general relaxation technique. *Psychophysiology*, **12**, 656–62.

Anderson, C. (1997). Values-based management. *Academy of Management Executive*, **11**, 25–46.

Aronsson, G. (1996). Psychosocial issues at work: current situation and trends in Sweden. In *Proceedings of Occupational Health and Safety in Progress: Northern-Baltic-Karelian Regional Symposium*. Lappeenranta, Finland: Finnish Institute of Occupational Health.

Benson, H. (1976). *The Relaxation Response*. William Morrow & Co., New York.

Benson, H. (1993). The relaxation response. In D. Goldman & J. Gurin (eds) *Mind/Body Medicine*. Consumer Reports Books, Yonkers, NY.

Bernstein, D.A. & Borkovec, T.D. (1973). *Progressive Relaxation Training: A Manual for the Helping Professions*. Research Press Company, Champaign, IL.

Birk, L. (1973). *Biofeedback: Behavioral Medicine*. Grune & Stratton, New York.

Blanchard, E.B. & Andrasik, F. (1985). *Management of Chronic Headaches: A Psychological Approach*. Pergamon, New York.

Blanchard, K.H. & O'Connor, M.J. (1997). *Managing by Values*. Berrett-Koehler, San Francisco, CA. Publishers, Inc.

Bunce, D. (1997). What factors are associated with the outcome of individual-focused worksite stress management interventions? *Journal of Occupational and Organizational Psychology*, **70**, 1–17.

Cannon, W.B. (1929). *Bodily Changes in Pain, Hunger, Fear, and Rage*. C.T. Branford Boston, MA.

Caplan, R.D., Cobb, S., French, J.R.P., Jr, Harrison, R.V. & Pinneau, S.R. (1975). *Job Demands and Worker Health*. DHHS (NIOSH) publication no. 75-160, US Government Printing Office, Washington, DC.

Carrington. P. (1978). *Clinically Standardized Meditation (CSM)*, Instructors Kit. Pace Educational Systems, Kendall Park, NJ.

Carrington, P., Collings, G.H., Benson, H., Robinson, H., Wood, L.W., Lehrer, P.M., Woolfolk, R.L. & Cole, J.W. (1980). The use of meditation-relaxation techniques for the management of stress in a working population. *Journal of Occupational Medicine*, **22**, 221–31.

Cohen, F. & Lazarus, R.S. (1979). Coping with the stresses of illness. In G.C. Stone, F. Cohen, & N.E. Adler (eds) *Health Psychology—A Handbook*. Jossey-Bass, San Francisco, CA.

Collins, J. & Porras, J. (1994). *Built To Last: Successful Habits of Visionary Companies*. Harper-Business, New York.

COMCARE Australia (1997a). The Management of Occupational Stress in Common-wealth Agencies—A Joint ANAO/Comcare Better Practice Guide for Senior Managers. http://www.comcare.gov.au/publications/betterpract/fs-cover.html

COMCARE Australia (1997b). The Management of Occupational Stress in Common-wealth Agencies—Implementing an Occupational Stress Prevention Program. http://www.comcare.gov.au/publications/implementosp/fs-cover.htm

Cooper, C.L. (ed.) (1987). Stress management interventions at work. *Journal of Managerial Psychology*, **2**, 1–30.

Cooper, C.L. & Marshall, J. (1976). Occupational sources of stress: a review of the literature relating to coronary heart disease and mental ill health. *Journal of Occupational Psychology*, **49**, 11–28.

Cooper, C.L. & Murphy, L.R. (2000). Developing healthy corporate cultures by reducing stressors at work. In L.R. Murphy & C.L. Cooper (eds) *Healthy and Productive Work: An International Perspective*. Taylor & Francis, London.

Cooper, C.L. & Williams, S. (1994). *Creating Healthy Work Organizations*. John Wiley & Sons, Chichester.

Cox, T., Griffiths, A. & Rial-Gonzalez, E. (2000). Research on work-related stress. European Agency for Health and Safety at Work. http://agency.osha.eu.int/publications/reports/stress/full.php3

DeCarlo, D.T. (1987). New legal rights related to emotional stress in the workplace. *Journal of Business and Psychology*, **1**, 313–25.

Ellis, A. (1977). The basic clinical theory of rational-emotive therapy. In A. Ellis & R. Grieger (eds) *Handbook of Rational-Emotive Therapy*. Springer-Verlag, New York.

Folkman, S. & Lazarus, R.S. (1980). An analysis of coping in a middle-aged community sample. *Journal of Health and Social Behavior*, **21**, 219–39.

Harmon, F.G. (1996). *Playing for Keeps: How the World's Most Aggressive Companies Use Core Values to Manage, Energize, and Organize their People and Promote Advance and Achieve their Corporate Missions*. John Wiley & Sons, New York.

Hart, P.M. & Wearing, A.J. (2000). Using employee opinion surveys to identify control mechanisms in organisations. In A. Flammer, W.J. Perrig & Grob, A. (eds). *Control of Human Behaviour, Mental Processes and Consciousness*. Mahwah, NJ: Lawrence Erlbaum.

Heide, F.J. & Borkovec, T.D. (1984). Relaxation-induced anxiety: mechanisms and theoretical implications. *Behavior Research and Therapy*, **22**, 1–12.

Healthcare Canada (2001). Best advice on stress risk management in the workplace. http://www.hc-sc.gc.ca/hppb/ahi/workplace/pdf/stress_risk_management_2.pdf

Health and Safety Executive (1998a). *Work-Related Stress: A Short Guide.* HSE Books, Sudbury. http://www.hse.gov.uk/pubns/indg281.pdf

Health and Safety Executive (1998b). *Managing Occupational Stress in the Education Sector.* HSC Education Services Advisory Committee. HSE Books, Sudbury.

Health Education Board for Scotland (2000). *Stress in the Workplace: A Simple Guide.* http://www.hebs.scot.nhs.uk/services/pubs/pdf/SimpleGuide_Stress.pdf

Healthy Companies (1994). *Work Environment Survey.* Final report to the National Institute for Occupational Safety and Health. Healthy Companies, Inc., Washington, DC.

Heaney, C.A. & van Ryn, M. (1990). Broadening the scope of worksite stress programs: a guiding framework. *American Journal of Health Promotion*, **4**, 413–20.

Israel, B.A., Baker, E.A., Goldenhar, L.M., Heaney, C.A. & Schurman, S.J. (1996). Occupational stress, safety, and health: conceptual framework and principles for effective prevention interventions. *Journal of Occupational Health Psychology*, **1**, 261–86.

Ivancevich, J.M. & Ganster, D.C. (eds) (1987). *Job Stress: From Theory to Suggestion.* Haworth Press. New York.

Ivancevich, J.M., Matteson, M.T., Freedman, S.M. & Phillips, J.S. (1990). Worksite stress management interventions. *American Psychologist*, **45**, 252–61.

Jacobson, E. (1938). *Progressive Relaxation.* University of Chicago Press, Chicago, IL.

Karasek, R.A. (1979). Job demands, job decision latitude, and mental strain. *Journal of Occupational Behavior*, **24**, 285–307.

Kompier, M.A.J. & Cooper, C.L. (1999). *Preventing Stress, Improving Productivity: European Case Studies in the Workplace.* Routledge, London.

Kompier, M.A.J. & Levi, L. (1994). *Stress at Work: Causes, Effects, and Prevention.* European Foundation for the Improvement of Living and Working Conditions, Dublin.

Kompier, M.A.J., Geurts, S.A.E, Gründemann, R.W.M., Vink, P. & Smulders, P.G.W. (1998). Cases in stress prevention: the success of a participative and stepwise approach. *Stress Medicine*, **14**, 155–68.

Lindstrom, K. (1994). Psychosocial criteria for good work organization. *Scandinavian Journal of Work Environment and Health*, **20**, 123–33.

Meichenbaum, D. (1977). *Cognitive Behavior Modification.* Plenum Press, New York.

Murphy, L.R. (1984). Occupational stress management: a review and appraisal. *Journal of Occupational Psychology*, **57**, 1–15.

Murphy, L.R. (1988). Workplace interventions for stress reduction and prevention. In C.L. Cooper & R. Payne (eds) *Causes, Coping, and Consequences of Stress at Work.* John Wiley & Sons, Chichester.

Murphy, L.R. (1996a). Stress management in work settings: a critical review of the research literature. *American Journal of Health Promotion*, **11**, 112–35.

Murphy, L.R. (1996b). Stress management techniques. In C.L. Cooper, M. Schabraq & J.A.M. Winnubst. *Handbook of Work and Health Psychology.* John Wiley & Sons, Chichester, pp. 427–41.

Murphy, L.R. (1999). Organizational interventions to reduce stress in health care professionals. In Payne, R. & Firth-Cozens, J. (eds) *Stress in Health Professionals*, 2nd edn. John Wiley & Sons, Chichester.

Murphy, L.R. (2000). Models of healthy work organizations. In L.R. Murphy & C.L. Cooper (eds) *Healthy and Productive Work: An International Perspective.* Taylor & Francis, London.

Murphy, L.R. & Schoenborn, T.F. (eds) (1989). *Stress Management in Work Settings.* Praeger, New York.

National Institute for Occupational Safety and Health (1999). Stress at work. http://www.cdc.gov/niosh/pdfs/stress.pdf

Neale, M.S., Singer, J.A., Schwartz, G.A. & Schwartz, J. (1989). Conflicting perspectives on stress reduction in occupational settings: a systems approach to their resolution. In L.R. Murphy & T.F. Schoenborn (eds) *Stress Management in Work Settings.* Praeger, New York.

Newman, J.D. & Beehr, T. (1979). Personal and organizational strategies for handling job stress: a review of research and opinion. *Personnel Psychology*, **32**, 1–43.

Parkes, K. & Sparkes, T.J. (1998). *Organizational Interventions to Reduce Work Stress. Are they Effective? A Review of the Literature*. Health and Safety Executive, RR193/98. HSE Books, Sudbury.

Parsons, M.L. & Murdaugh, C.L. (1994). *Patient-Centered Care: A Model for Restructuring*. Aspen, Gaithersburg, MD.

Payne, R., Wall, T., Borrill, C. & Carter, A. (1999). Stress as a moderator of the relationship between work characteristics and work attitudes. *Journal of Occupational Health Psychology*, **4**, 3–14.

Peters, T. & Waterman, R.H., Jr (1982). *In Search of Excellence: Lessons from America's Best-Run Companies*. Warner Books, New York.

Pfeiffer, G.J. (1987). Corporate health can improve if firms take organizational approach. *Occupational Health and Safety*, October, 96–9.

Pomerleau, D.F. & Brady, J.P. (1979). *Behavioral Medicine, Theory and Practice*. Williams & Wilkins, Baltimore, MD.

Quick, J.C. & Quick, J.D. (1984). *Organizational Stress and Preventive Management*. McGraw-Hill, New York.

Rosen, R.H. (1991). *The Healthy Company. Eight Strategies to Develop People, Productivity, and Profits*. Jeremy P. Tarcher, Los Angeles, CA.

Rucci, A., Kirn, S. & Quinn, R. (1998). The employee–customer–profit chain at Sears. *Harvard Business Review*, Jan.-Feb., 82–97.

Sauter, S.L., Murphy, L.R. & Hurrell, J.J., Jr (1990). A national strategy for the prevention of work-related psychological disorders. *American Psychologist*, **45**, 1146–58.

Sauter, S.L., Lim, S.Y. & Murphy, L.R. (1996). Organizational health: A new paradigm for occupational stress research at NIOSH. *Japanese Journal of Occupational Mental Health*, **4**, 248–54.

Stoner, C.R. & Fry, F.L. (1983). Developing a corporate policy for managing stress. *Personnel*, May/June 66–76.

Taft, S., Hawn, K., Barber, J. & Bidwell, J. (1999). Fulcrum for the future: the creation of a values-driven culture. *Health Care Management Review*, **24**, 17–32.

Van der Klink, J.J.L., Blonk, R.W.B., Schene, A.H. & van Dijk, F.J.H. (2001).The benefits of interventions for work-related stress. *American Journal of Public Health*, **91**, 270–6.

Wolpe, J. (1958). *Psychotherapy by Reciprocal Inhibition*. Stanford University Press, Stanford, CT.

CHAPTER 26

A FIT Approach to Work Stress and Health

Ben (C) Fletcher

University of Hertfordshire, Hatfield, UK

26.1 INTRODUCTION

Research on work stress and health has not yet succeeded in integrating the theoretical with the practical (see Chapter 6). The concerns of science and of theory have not really sat comfortably with the demands of practitioners, nor have they made significant inroads into reducing the massive human and financial costs of stress and work. I suspect this is because work stress research and theory has lost sight of the whole person to a significant degree. Companies have tried to change cultures and redesigned jobs with limited benefits for people and organisations (Briner & Reynolds, 1999). Some commentators have even suggested that work-level interventions to reduce stress may have the opposite effect due to the stress of the change process itself, and that individual-level interventions may be necessary before organisational-level ones can have any effect (Payne et al., 1999). This chapter discusses these issues and introduces a concept called "FITness" that may help to bring more practical action levers to work stress and health issues.

First, the chapter raises some questions about the ways in which current research in occupational stress is conducted, and the assumptions it makes. It is proposed that an alternative approach may prove more useful from a practical perspective, if not a scientific one. In particular, it is proposed that the emphasis in stress research needs to shift away from the work environment and so-called "objective" stressors even more towards personal perceptions than recent models of stress have recommended. Moreover, organisational interventions to reduce stress at work will, it is suggested, only work to the degree that the interventions transform the individual perceptions of people towards themselves and their work. They must do this through changes to the underlying cognitive architecture of the person, and not by altering context-specific reports. It is contended that most organisational stress initiatives and job redesigns do not achieve this, long term. Stress interventions, should, therefore, be focused at the person level (and the FITness of individuals) and not at the job factor, job design or organisational level.

The Handbook of Work and Health Psychology. Edited by M.J. Schabracq, J.A.M. Winnubst and C.L. Cooper.
© 2003 John Wiley & Sons, Ltd.

26.1.1 Preliminary Remarks

I have marvelled at the intelligence, perspicacity, methodological thoroughness, statistical competence and considerable labour of my peers researching the important area of occupational stress and health. However, I have always had the "feeling" something was missing, even with research which is acknowledged to be at the cutting edge, as well as with the work-a-day writings that abound. I used to think this was because of the lack of conceptual clarity in the models of work stress and the "definitional problems" that were often referred to in reviews.

Older models of work stress were either "environmental" stimulus-based models which searched for work factors that "caused" strain, or focused on the response outcomes—be they biological or psychological—or they were an interaction of the two perspectives (Cox, 1978; Jones & Bright, 2001). Mixed models also took account of individual differences, and many other moderators and mediators, in an attempt to refine our understanding. In 1980 Roy Payne and I (Fletcher & Payne, 1980), for example, distinguished between "primary" and "secondary" stressors. Primary stressors were the "true" causes of strain, and secondary stressors were only apparently associated or correlated with strain because individuals had reached a strain threshold: in short the stressed person perceived the world differently because they were stressed. This early idea was tested on a group of schoolteachers with some support (Payne & Fletcher, 1983) and a more sophisticated "catastrophe" model of stress proposed (Fletcher, 1991). More recent papers have made some of the points we raised in a much more elegant way (e.g. Payne et al., 1999).

A related discussion about the significance of negative affectivity (NA) is now receiving considerable attention (Jones & Bright, 2001). NA relates to a general predisposition of some people to feel bad generally in a way that contaminates many self- and environmental evaluations. This topic has raised issues about how such matters should be dealt with statistically and theoretically in work stress research. These issues are of crucial importance because they question the whole notion of what might constitute causes of work stress as well as how such things should be investigated. For example, from a practical perspective, the influence of negative affectivity and secondary stressors would imply that the cleanest way of searching for real environmental causes of job strain might be to study only those people who are not stressed. This would appear odd to many. Spector et al. (2000), for example, suggest that even if NA has a substantial biasing role, statistically partialling out NA removes the effects of the variables one wants to know about!

I wish to reflect on some basic assumptions made in stress research. First, however, some statements of belief. I *believe* work stress is a major issue from many angles: the person who suffers directly, as well as by its transmission to others; the organisation whose productiveness is affected; the legal systems that are beginning to tackle the burden of proof in compensation cases; as well as society that has to cope in the broadest sense. I also *believe* work stress compromises basic cognitive processing. For example, stress probably results in a greater intolerance of ambiguity (which may be at the root of a raft of practical outcomes, from making appropriate decisions in an uncertain business world, to prejudices and discrimination). I *believe* that work factors affect a person's basic cognitive architecture—the fundamental building blocks of perception and categorisation at the core of thinking and behaving—and thus probably cause much physical illness and shortened life expectancy, as well as affecting the life expectancy and cause of death of those indirectly exposed to the work stressors. These beliefs are based on research findings as much as on hunch (see, for example, Fletcher, 1988, 1991; Fletcher & Jones, 1993; Jones & Fletcher, 1996).

26.1.2 Work and Basic Cognitive Processes

If basic cognitive processing is affected by the work we do, this would be immensely important from a practical viewpoint because it would suggest that we as individuals might be *fundamentally* altered by our work. If these cognitive processes were core ones, they would be basic to our perceptions, and to all our decisions, actions and interactions. The fact that our health and life expectancy might be affected by our work, via these cognitive processes, would be a small part of their action. If this were so, any measures that were dependent upon those "basic processes" would be "contaminated" by them. If we do not take adequate account of such contaminating factors in stress research (which I suggest current research does not) then we will not be able to find out about real work influences. The influence of our core cognitive processes is likely to be much wider than their affective influences. They are likely to include aspects that determine core characteristics of our personal identity and the way we think. Stress research—and practical interventions— have to account for such core person-level factors. The FIT approach outlined below does this.

It does appear that work can have quite subtle and powerful effects on the way we think and behave. At one level this is not surprising: as we have already suggested, people who are stressed at work have a very different way of looking at their organisation, their work and their worlds in the widest sense. In a sample of 350 managers, it has been found that those with higher strain levels (i.e. the most stressed) showed significantly fewer associations between and within their work factors and outcomes, as measured by the Work-FIT Profiler (Fletcher, 1999), than those in the normal range (Dietman & Stead, 1999). The stressed or anxious workers seemed unable to perceive the aspects of their work environment that might assist them in coping with the demands. Moreover, the level of Awareness (a FIT variable discussed below) of stressed workers was also lower. Individuals who are not under stress—those who score low on anxiety and other strain scales—however, may see their world in a more positive manner and understand the importance of balancing the demands made upon them and the support they receive in their working environment. Other research supports the view that strain levels moderate the relationship between work characteristics and work attitudinal outcomes (e.g. Payne et al., 1999).

We have also investigated whether people who are stressed at work appear to have a constrained or restricted cognitive architecture. These cognitive constraints can be very powerful, subtle, yet unconscious. In three studies of public sector employees, medical general practitioners and commercial managers, those staff members working more hours were not only more anxious and depressed, but were also significantly more likely to be "abnormal categorisers". We used a simple categorisation task in which individuals had to rate everyday exemplars in terms of how typical they are as examples of their semantic category (e.g. a duck as a bird). Abnormal categorisers are individuals whose ratings of items is outside the normal range, in the sense that they do not see the less typical exemplars as members of the category (Stead et al., 1996, 1997). We also observed that those who were more stressed scored much higher on a measure of everyday cognitive failures (such as forgetting shopping or bumping into things). In a sense it is remarkable that the number of working hours should appear to be related to such core functions. However, in another sense it supports the idea that work is a "way of death", as well as a "way of life" to re-centre a well-known phrase.

These very preliminary studies of what I call "cognitive architecture" are important. They begin to show how broad the influence of work may be, and also why it may be impossible (conceptually as well as practically) to dissect stressors from strains unless the person-level cognitions can be accounted for in some way. The fact that work stressors appear to be transmitted to those who are not directly exposed to the work environment may also be very important. If the work of one marital partner can influence the conjoint (and very specific) causes of death of both partners, this suggests such basic cognitive processes may be fundamental in many ways, including health (Fletcher & Jones, 1993, 1996; Jones & Fletcher, 1993, 1996).

26.2   THE ASSUMPTION OF EFFECT AND SCIchange

26.2.1   What Can be Inferred from a Correlation in Stress Research?

One of the basic building blocks of stress research is the correlation or association between two variables. Many experimental and between-group studies of work stress do not use derivations of such power statistics, but the points made below are equally applicable conceptually to this research also.

There are many specific issues that could be raised about the use of correlational and regression statistics. Many effect sizes are small, cause cannot be strongly implicated, there are problems of common methods variance, there are many confounding issues, statistical control implications, chance correlations in large matrices, clinical significance being relatively orthogonal of correlation size, and so on. These are issues that come as part and parcel of the approach. If the researcher is aware of them, they can be tackled systematically and appropriately. Longitudinal research, "objective" measures, and techniques such as structural equation modelling have been deployed to address such issues (e.g. De Jonge et al., 2001).

I share a concern about these matters but believe the problems may lie somewhat deeper. Is the correlation (and its statistical and non-statistical allies) any kind of sensible building block *in occupational stress research* at all? What **can** any correlation do? This is an old chestnut I wish to revisit.

The correlation coefficient provides a way of showing the magnitude and direction of a relationship between two variables. In stress research, however, we cannot be sure that we are measuring anything sensible when we do this because the correlation is completely contaminated by what I call the *assumption of effect*. This is the assumption that *in stress research* one is measuring (or can measure) an objective or real environmental (E) property which is independent of the person (P). I want to contend that—in most work stress research, at least—there is a failure to partial out real environmental aspects that are independent of the whole psychology of the individual. There is an illusion that true environmental aspects are isolated. The apparition is due to the aggregation of the differences between people that are not related to the environmental factors being investigated. Moreover, when there is an apparently real E/P partialling the results are of no practical use in stress terms at all because all the fundamental core of the issue has been lost.

I wish to make a formal distinction between E-properties and P-properties. An E-property is an objective aspect of the world that can be measured, or can be implied from measures, that is independent of the perceptions of it. The term "independent" here may be considered as a relative term, since nothing is independent of perception. However, I am using the term in a formal sense and in the sense of being independent of perception in all *practical* senses. An example of an E-property is temperature: however different people perceive the temperature of their workplace, it can be measured by a thermometer. P-properties, on the other hand, are perceptions of the environmental properties, but reflect aspects of the person and how they perceive the world, rather than how it is in an E-sense. I would suggest that the P-properties refer to the *inter*personal variations in the cognitive architectures of individuals and not to short-term or *intra*-personal variations. Jobs may differ in terms of E-properties, or they may not. The differences in the perceptions of those jobs (and any part of them and their consequences) may also differ, or they may not, irrespective of the E-properties.

I am concerned that most research in occupational stress and health, even of the most sophisticated kind, is based on the *assumption of effect*. I think we labour under an *E-property mirage*. That is, we take it as axiomatic that our methods are teasing out E-properties, however contaminated we think these are with P-properties. I doubt this. I believe we view the contamination as incidental, or at worst, methodologically controllable. I doubt this too. I also believe that the most fruitful approach to be taken in stress research is to take an approach that is not affected by such an assumption and I will propose one example of that later. As an aside, however, it is also important to note that the degree to which the assumption of effect operates (or is likely to) in any research situation is directly related to the uselessness of the correlational techniques—however sophisticated—which are deployed to remove the problem. One cannot reasonably use correlational techniques (including partialling) if the correlation does not get at what it was assumed to.

Most of the variables in work stress research, especially psychological stressors, are prone to the assumption of effect. I distinguish between three levels of the assumption of effect:

- The objective level. This is the assumption that the E-property is a stressor, independent of the way it is perceived by the worker. This might be assumed in cases of physical stressors, such as environmental and ergonomic aspects. A high temperature, or a poorly ergonomically designed workstation is never good, even if some people do not seem to mind or be affected by it. It used to be assumed that other categories of psychological stressors had this status. For example, work demands were (and still are in some quarters) considered synonymous with stress, although we know now that this is not a sensible conceptualisation of work stress (see Chapter 6). Some studies of work stress do measure psychological stressors "objectively" by using techniques such as independent observers/raters or peer assessment of job stressors. One can question what is actually being measured by such techniques since the label of potential stressor has to be proven by its effect in the job incumbent. It may measure some aspect of E, but not necessarily in a way that is at all relevant to work stress. The relationship between the so-called objective and subjective work characteristics is not always strong (e.g. Spector & Jex, 1991; Spector et al., 2000).

- The subjective level. This is the assumption that the E-properties of the stressors, as revealed in the P-property scores obtained, are actually stressful or have negative effects. One demonstration that this may be an unreasonable assumption is shown by Payne & Morrison (1999). They considered the affective meaning of 30 job demands by getting respondents to rate both their frequency and their level of dissatisfaction with the demands. They found that for only 16 of the work stressors was there any reasonable relationship between frequency and level of dissatisfaction. Furthermore, these two measures combined was a better predictor of GHQ strain levels than the demand frequency score alone.
- The person level. This is the most important level in terms of the thrust of this chapter. The assumption of effect at this level is that the variations between different people's perceptions of the world can be used as a lever to tease out specific E-properties (because the organisation can then intervene to change them to reduce the stress effects). It is my contention that this is not so, and that the variation between people's perceptions is often erroneously taken as evidence of an E-property. In my view, many factors that are considered as E-properties are no more that P-properties masquerading as E-properties.

The assumption of effect is not simply the issue of the poor validity of self-report measures under a different guise. Consider an example (thanks to Briner, 2001, personal communication). If we have two identical work environments, two identical jobs and two apparently similar people, most stress researchers would agree that there will be a considerable variation—easily discernible at the practical level by any third party—between what will happen and what can be observed. There will be large physical differences in how each arranges their office and how messy they are; they will interact differently with others, which will have its own consequences; they will probably see their jobs differently and be quite differently affected by them. Their jobs are the "same" (in an E-sense) only at a shallow level, because they make them different as soon as they interact in them. The dynamic effects are multi-layered and are person-dependent and probably quite difficult to predict from a research point of view. I would also contend that this is almost always true, irrespective of the type of job, the E-properties (e.g. job decision latitude), or the situation in which it is performed: essentially, people make the difference, not the jobs.

Let us take the case a step further with another example that is closer to real work stress research. Suppose the correlation coefficient between a measure of job control or autonomy and a strain measure (say, a clinical measure of free-floating anxiety, or perhaps some cardiovascular-relevant morbidity) is +0.5, accounting for 25% of the attributable variance between the variables. Subject to various safeguards which can be controlled for and are increasingly well documented (see Chapter 6), this suggests that the lack of job control may be an important work stressor. This is especially useful given that it seems to be a variable that can be quite easily manipulated from a practical point of view in the flow of work within a company (although Jones & Fletcher question this in Chapter 6).

To what do the assessments of job control relate if not to the E-property, the degree of autonomy? I want to maintain that the correlation is often (practically) *wholly* a function of the P-properties. The attribution of E-properties is often not justified at all. Figure 26.1 attempts to illustrate this with the data from 7 people out of an n-sized sample. In Figure 26.1a—which is a simple stressor–strain model—there is a distinction drawn between the person (P) and the environment (E), however fuzzy in reality, and that is shown by the vertical line which differentiates the one from the other. The different levels of a (E)

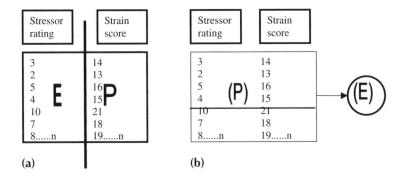

Figure 26.1 Assumption of effect: example

stressor are perfectly positively correlated with the individual's strain scores (P), suggesting that E is of significance for P. To reduce the strain scores one might reduce the levels of the stressors. In Figure 26.1b, however, the same correlation exists, but there is no clear E/P distinction that is relevant to understanding the correlation—that is why the letters are parenthesised. The stressor and strain scores are correlated in this example because they are obtained from the same people (or perhaps, from independent others who share similar perceptions, values and evaluative frameworks). The correlation is a result of person-level differences, not environmental differences at all, because the different people (for whatever reason) see things differently. The horizontal line might represent a threshold level above which practical steps are necessary to act to reduce clinical or operationally dysfunctional strain levels. The practical reductions of strain levels do not reside in the E at all, nor just in tackling the P strains, but rather in changing the factor that connects them both—the person or individual level. It requires changes in the cognitive architecture of individuals.

The assumption of effect is suggesting more than simply that people have different perceptions of the same world. Nor is the assumption of effect a different version of the NA model, or the "primary/secondary stressors" model discussed above. The crucial distinction here does not rely on stressed people seeing the world differently, or the possible bias that NA may have on how job stressors are evaluated. Rather, it is the individual (not the individual difference, or the personality, or perceptual differences, etc.) that is placed at the most basic possible level of analysis and of effect. People are different in the way they construct their worlds and are consequentially affected by these worlds—from perceptions, evaluations and decisions, to responses and "outcomes" (such as strain, performance, job satisfaction and life expectancy). The proposal is that it is the individual's core cognitive architecture that is responsible for all these aspects, and that it makes no logical or empirical or practical sense to build models of stress that do not take account of this "whole person" dimension. Most stress research violates this principle.

The debate over the role of NA in stress research is relevant here. In an excellent paper, Spector et al. (2000) presented various alternative mechanisms that could explain why NA might affect job stressors and job strains (although they also suggest that the evidence for an NA bias effect is weak). NA might be considered an individual-level phenomenon and, therefore, satisfy my earlier demands. None of the alternative mechanisms outlined by Spector et al., however, take account of the individual/person level in the way I am suggesting is necessary. For example, a high-NA person could be said to perceive the world more negatively (the "perceptual mechanism"), which itself increases strain levels (or, alternatively, people with low levels of NA are more inclined to deceive themselves and distort the world to seem more positive than it is, according to Judge et al., 2000). This view separates cause (stressor) and effect (strain) mechanisms *within* the individual. In the individual conceptualisation I am proposing, this is an artificial separation which does not have practical or sensible force, since causes and effects are not isolated at the individual level: individuals feel the constellation of factors. Some of the other mechanisms offered by Spector et al. to explain NA do not suffer from this problem (for example, that high-NA people cause negative things to happen to them). However, what all the explanations are trying to do is to encompass the effects of NA to the degree than such "distortions" might exist. An individual-level focus in stress research needs to take account of a much broader envelope of person-level measures that might determine how people perceive, interact, are affected by and respond to, their situation in a more holistic way. NA might be one determinant of overall "cognitive architecture". It would be my guess, however, that it is a strain measure and is, therefore, more likely to be an outcome of the architecture, and not itself a concept of much practical value.

It is the case that there are E-property differences between jobs. Jobs do differ in the degree to which they allow workers autonomy and control (see Chapter 6). There is more to job differences than P-properties and related perceptual or affective matters. The degree of control of the assembly line worker is a good deal less than that of the plant manager or the directors of the company. Four things are relevant here with respect to the assumption of effect. First, to have any substance, the stressor construct (the E-property) must itself describe the degree to which the presumed E-property effects are independent of broader factors, such as job level, job variety, and factors that make up the (job-defined) social class differences and the like. The perception of job control for the director, for example, is likely to be affected by many aspects of his or her job, as well as by the factors that affect his or her perception of it (such as strain levels, personality etc.). If this is not clearly shown—if these other non-job or broader variables are not clearly distinguished from the E-property—the perception of the target variable (in this case job control or autonomy) should not be presumed to be independent, or to include any job-specific E-property at all. I have previously argued, for example, that Karasek's job demand-discretion model is a social class explanation masquerading as an occupational job factor one (Payne & Fletcher, 1983). Second, it would also be necessary to remove the variance due to P-effects by partialling out the same-job variance. If these first two things are done, however, all that will be left (if anything) will be the E-property. E-properties, however, only have the potential to be stressors, depending on how they are perceived by the job incumbent. This does not help the stress researcher in any real sense. E-properties cannot be labelled as stressors without independent evidence that they have such effects. Third, anyone who has done practical research in the workplace will know that when people make their assessments of their own jobs they do not do so in any "objective" sense, but in the context of their (limited) experience. Ratings are often anchored in a P-property sense, not an E-property way. That is the only explanation for job incumbents rating some low-skill jobs as high in job significance, or high in variety and so on (see also the debate about job analysis in Harvey & Wilson, 2000; Morgeson & Campion, 2000; Sanchez & Levine, 2000). Fourth, I would guess that the between-person variations in E-property ratings are much greater than the P-property ratings. This makes E-properties even more difficult to investigate, if they exist.

Many researchers may disagree, but for me the assumption of effect means that it is virtually nonsensical to do stress research that does not have P-properties as its basic focus. Moreover, the P-properties investigated must have some claim to considering a meaningful aspect of the "whole person" and not just their perception of a small aspect of themselves or their environment. This suggests that the study of individual or personal differences, not job property differences, would be a more fruitful direction for stress research. Moreover, this is likely to be true at both the theoretical and practical level. If one wants to max-imise the pragmatic benefits of research it should have action lever consequences at the person-level, not at the job-factor or job level. This is because manipulations of the objec-tive work environment are only going to be effective to the degree that P-, not E-, properties are affected. It is no surprise, then, that some commentators have been very critical of the ability of stress researchers to effect any real changes in strain levels through inter-ventions that have manipulated job (E-) factors and have not focused on individual-level change (e.g. Briner, 1997, 2001, Briner & Reynolds, 1999; Payne et al., 1999). On the other hand, individual-level interventions that do change the way people perceive and behave (e.g. cognitive behavioural training) can be very effective in changing self-esteem, at-tributions, motivation for work, life satisfaction, job seeking success and mental health (Proundfoot et al., 1997). They can also dramatically lower subsequent morbidity and mor-tality rates (Eysenck & Grossarth-Maticek, 1991).

Of course, practitioners, consultants, job analysts and even managers, cannot believe that the organisational interventions that cost considerable money make little difference in the long term. The workers whose jobs are changed also sometimes report positive perceptions, albeit only in the short term (e.g. Wall et al., 1986). Why do organisational interventions and job redesigns not have the sustained power to improve things for workers? I suggest they do not provide any persisting benefits unless the individual is fundamentally transformed to some degree by the intervention. I do not mean that they see some aspects of their work differently, but that a core self-concept needs to be affected. By this I mean the way the individual perceives the world, decides and behaves accordingly—their cognitive architecture. I propose that most organisational initiatives (re-engineering, Kaizen, total quality management, job redesign, Investors in People, culture change etc.) do not work at all in the way assumed, and fail in the long term (Stacey et al., 2001) precisely because they fail to change the individuals within the working systems. It simply makes more sense to focus directly on individual change and transformation—albeit it in the collective context of the organisation or the team where the individuals can support each other—rather than making it a hoped-for consequence of an organisational change.

It is not just a greater individual-level perspective that is required in stress research. It is also necessary to do the research within a framework that encompasses a broad spectrum of factors that might be related to decisions and behaviours. That is, the individual level needs to measure the individual and not just a minor component of them. A specific focus on just a small part of them (e.g. job satisfaction or strain) or the way they perceive things (e.g. job characteristics) will not work because they will not provide E-P distinctions to be made with any validity.

The FIT approach below attempts to focus more on the individual envelope and the core self-concept (or at least a meaningful aspect of the person that is potentially changeable).

It also tries to do so in a parsimonious manner. FIT tries to measure things that, if changed, might make the person see things fundamentally differently, to empower them at their core, and to change the way they think and do things. However, the FIT approach suggests that traditional personality traits are unlikely to be useful factors to consider in this context, even though they are "individual level". On the contrary, personality traits can be considered the gaolers or resistors of change and appropriate behaviour. They also play a central role in person–environment misfit (Fletcher & Stead, 2000a, discuss this in greater detail). In general, personality traits change very little with time except to become more and more fixed with age, and "the child is the man" (e.g. Caspi, 2000; Roberts & DelVecchio, 2000). Personality research and theory offers little guidance to assist individual change and development.

26.2.2   Stress Research and SCIchange

The FIT framework is based on a positive view that people can change and do not need to be the prisoners of their own personalities, their habits, or their own illusions of intention (Ouellette & Wood, 1998). It is not Panglossian or a universal curative; it is a different and no less rigorous or scientific perspective. I have called the science necessary to investigate many practical change issues "SCIchange", to signify that its emphasis is on the analysis of circumstances that are most conducive to improving or changing a state of affairs. SCIchange presents slightly different criteria for doing science and evaluating it. The methodological approach is also different to the traditional scientific methods. In traditional science the emphasis is on understanding the theoretical mechanisms which underlie a phenomenon or explain an aspect of the world. Models, tests and an emphasis on falsification and refinement do this where such issues as methodology, experimental design, robustness, detachment, simulation and control are the watchwords and determinants of quality. SCIchange does not emphasise such aspects—they are secondary to the change and influence in any situation. The emphasis is on the context that will effect most change in the object of the study (this might be in terms of health, scores on a psychological or medical test, changes in performance, reductions in negative things like strain, smoking, or whatever). In the FIT context it might be improved well-being, health and organisational performance. Table 26.1 shows the difference in emphasis between traditional approaches to science and the SCIchange framework.

SCIchange is not an appropriate framework for all scientific studies because for some areas of 'pure' science it may be necessary to learn about the actual mechanisms underlying the object of investigation. This may be an essential aspect of some branches of medicine, but for work stress and health research a SCIchange, as opposed to a traditional scientific approach, would be more useful. It is, I believe, time for stress research to be judged by its ability to effect real improvements in people, their self-reports and health. This should change the type of research that is done, as well as the thrust of the theories. The criteria of SCIchange, not traditional science, should be applied to work stress research. It is interesting to note that in some basic areas of occupational theory such as job analysis, consequential outcomes—rather than the illusory search for accuracy—are increasingly seen as important (e.g. Sanchez & Levine, 2000).

Table 26.1 The differences between traditional science and SCIchange

Traditional science	SCIchange
Success criteria/progress	
Understanding of mechanisms	Observing effects
Enhancing theory	Enhancing change
Stability and consistency	Degree of change
Control of circumstances	Innovations in situations
Refinement of theory	Practical benefits
Robustness of theory	Beneficial outcomes
Precisely defining conditions	Seeing an effect
Single "winning" theory	Success in effects
Characteristics of the approach	
Narrow methods/hard science	Soft expansive science
Systematic stasis	Systematic change
Theoretical considerations	Factors that effect change
Single factors	Multidimensional
Clarity	Ambiguity
Certainty of attribution	Doubt about "causes"
Defence of position/theory	Openness about alternatives
Single method approach	Multi-method approach
Deconstruction/simplification	Complication
Experiment and step-by-step	Experiment and hunch
Factors isolated separately	Multiple factors involved
Casual view of world	Constellational view
Observe	Do/action
Detachment	Involvement
Amoral	Moral dimension
Laboratory	Real settings
Analogy, theory and models	Reality frameworks
Gradual simplification	Gradual elaboration
Primacy of independent variable (i.e. the conditions)	Primacy of independent variables (i.e. the benefit)

Source: Adapted from Fletcher & Stead (2000a).

26.3   AN ALTERNATIVE APPROACH: FITNESS AT WORK

I am suggesting that we need to take a core P-property approach in work stress research. What does this really imply for the nature of the research? Various approaches are possible. One approach might be to concentrate on case studies and to chart and document how the experiences of work change over time in the same and different situations—perhaps delving much more into the overt and covert interpretations of reactions and events and interpretations that we make. Another might be to take a much more inclusive strategy in traditional stress research and measure many more dimensions—using ever more powerful statistics to dissect the subjective from the objective, and the cause from the effect. Another might be to adapt and invent more powerful methods to monitor and measure people denuded of their normal psychological overlays and defences—perhaps techniques that get at reflexive responses at unexpected times; for example, the use of interrogative devices that require people to respond at random times in the day or night. Or, perhaps, better observational techniques could be deployed in workplace situations that do not normally come under the microscope (e.g. very sensitive areas, catastrophes, issues at the moral edge). There are many other possible research strategies, each with its obvious weaknesses and less obvious weaknesses put forward as strengths by ardent but prejudiced supporters.

My own preference is to take greater account of the individual by incorporating personal measures that might provide a handle on aspects that may play a fundamental role in determining perceptions, decisions and actions. Some traits have been extensively studied in stress research such as hardiness, Type A behaviour, reactive personalities, growth need strength, self-efficacy and locus of control. These individual differences may well act as buffers or vulnerability factors altering the impact of stressors on strains. I do not, however, advocate the use of traditional measures of individual difference such as "personality" for four reasons. First, I would guess that most traits are relatively enduring and fixed, as we discussed earlier. Second, personality traits are, by definition, measures of the inflexibility of the person across different circumstances, and as such do not tap personal potential at all. Potential is important from a practical perspective if improvement is a goal. Third, it would be my guess that such concepts do not account for enough of the individual context or whole person. Finally, they provide no clue to how to change and improve. This has obvious consequences for practical matters such as work stress research. These are some of the reasons I have developed the "anti-personality" or "oxymoronic personality" concept I have called "FIT".

A really FIT person is adaptable (psychologically and behaviourally) and would not be stressed to any degree by any work environment. This is not a personality issue, but a flexibility issue. It is also a highly practical matter. None of us of are completely FIT, however. It is only for this reason that people can benefit from work that is well designed, supportive and done in a context or work organisational culture that is "hygienic" psychologically speaking. This is a very different way of looking at the role of work stressors and the relationship they may have to strain indicators.

FIT is an acronym for a "Framework for Internal Transformation", or for "Flexible, Innovative, Trainable", which can be considered analogous to, or the psychological equivalent of, physical fitness. FIT is concerned with both decisions and behaviours: about perceptions and actions. FITness is measured using *The FIT Profiler*™ (Fletcher & Stead, 1999). This measures people's "Comfort Zone" in terms of their "Behavioural Flexibility" and five core cognitive "Constancies" that, in the FIT person, would drive appropriate behaviour. *The FIT Profiler*™ has been subjected to normal psychometric evaluation. It has been used in a wide range of smaller and multinational organisations to improve such areas as selection and assessment, organisational training and development, personal development, and the assessment of the financial value of the intangible assets of a company. It has also been used in higher education to facilitate student performance and study strategies.

The FIT Profiler™ measures Behavioural Flexibility by allowing individuals to indicate the possible *range* of their behaviour in various circumstances across 15 scales:

Unassertive	Assertive
Trusting of others	Cautious of others
Calm/relaxed	Energetic/driven
Reactive	Proactive
Definite	Flexible

Risky	Cautious
Behave as expected	Behave as wish
Spontaneous	Systematic
Single-minded	Open-minded
Introverted	Extroverted
Conventional	Unconventional
Individually-centred	Group-centred
Predictable	Unpredictable
Gentle	Firm
Lively	Not lively

The FIT Profiler[TM] allows people to rate their behaviours on either a single point on the scale, or any *range* of points that they consider applies to them. The summation of the range of behaviours provides a score of what is called *Behavioural Flexibility*. A FIT person would comfortably display the entire range of behaviours on each dimension if the circumstances required them, and would have a relatively large repertoire of behaviours. However, having a wide repertoire of behaviours is not itself sufficient to ensure their appropriate deployment. *The FIT Profiler*[TM], therefore, also measures the level of five psychological "building blocks" (called "Constancies") which, according to FIT theory, are responsible for performance, behaviour and individual integration. The level of these Constancies should not vary with situations but should play a central role in determining behaviour and decision making.

The FIT Constancies are:

- *Awareness*: the degree to which an individual monitors and attends to their internal and external worlds.
- *Fearlessness*: acting without fear or trepidation, or essentially facing the unknown with the same bravado as the known.
- *Self-responsibility*: the degree to which an individual accepts personal accountability for their world irrespective of the impact of factors outside themselves.
- *Morality and ethics:* differentiating right from wrong and doing what is right.
- *Balance*: making sure each aspect of life receives due care and attention. The important parts should have a sufficient level of effort put into them and the person receive sufficient satisfaction from them.

Scores on the five Constancies are combined together to produce a measure of *FIT Integrity*. *Overall FITness* is a multiplicative combination of FIT Integrity and Behavioural Flexibility scores.

Fletcher & Stead (2000a) proposed that FITness has important implications in the context of work stress research. In the FIT framework, strain is likely to be the result of unFITness in both direct and indirect ways. According to the FIT framework, for example, a situation that requires an appropriate behavioural response outside the person's normal repertoire is more likely to cause strain and discomfort. Low levels of any or all of the Constancies should also be associated with strain. For example, a lack of Balance may lead to an unhealthy over-focus on work. Low Fearlessness may substantively alter the situations a person will face. Low Self-responsibility may fundamentally alter attributions and how an individual sees their role and influence. Low Awareness will reduce the richness of information the individual has on which to base decisions and actions. According to FIT, there are no negative outcomes associated with high levels on the Constancies, unless there are large variations between the scores on each (see Fletcher & Stead, 2000a). FITness generally is likely to affect self-esteem, commitment, job and life satisfaction, work performance, strain levels etc. It is also likely to affect self, work, and life attitudes in many ways. FITness levels will also relate to the way a person perceives themselves and their environment (including work). In short, FITness levels are hypothesised to have major direct and indirect, bias and substantive, cognitive and behavioural, perceptual and response, effective and affective, individual and social, self, non-work and work influences: FITness affects things fundamentally.

In the context of FIT theory, the FITter people are, and the more of them in the particular group being studied, the less likely it is that traditional approaches in stress research will reveal any useful or meaningful links and explanations. The FITter people will be aware of the important environmental dimensions, but will not be as affected negatively by them. It is not that the FIT person does not notice or experience the stressors (on the contrary, they would be more aware of them), but it is the way that they deal with them that sets them apart. The environment is potentially stressful for the FIT and the unFIT alike. However, unFIT people find themselves engulfed by the world and by their own ineffective strategies learned from their past, and will succumb to strain. This results from their perception of high constraints and from their negative evaluations (both conscious and unconscious). FIT people, on the other hand, base their behaviour and decisions on the Constancies, and they will have a wide repertoire of behaviours to cope appropriately with different situations. This means they will not, therefore, be affected in a negative way by a less than optimal environment because they have taken responsibility for the state of affairs, are aware of the various options and alternatives, and have a properly evaluated personal position (i.e. their FIT *Integrity* is high). The traditional stress research findings are only applicable to the unFIT, and the models derived from them—they are only useful in this negative way. In terms of FIT theory, chronic effects of stress occur because unFIT people fail many times to deal with a recurrent situation. The unFIT fail to learn from this past and to change their decisions and behaviours.

Stress management techniques, and any organisational and job redesigns, will only be of potential short-term benefit to the unFIT unless they positively change their evaluation of their situation in FIT-related ways. There are three reasons for this. First, changes to the work environment are only hypothesised to have effects via the person: unless the individuals are changed or transformed in some way, there will be no benefit. Second, FIT-related transformations do not take place just from making the work environment a more psychologically hygienic one to work in (i.e. one that is less dangerous or cleaner in an E-property sense). There may be some benefits from organisational-level initiatives, but these will not be positive—rather they may remove potential negative effects. Third, stress management techniques that do not have a FIT-related benefit (albeit by design or accident) will simply result in the person changing the focus of their P-property dissatisfaction from one area to another (and probably back again later).

These are strong claims. They do not, however, mean that the design of work, and the context in which it is done, is not at all important to worker health or contentment. There are two reasons for this. First, according to the FIT approach, I suggest that the job and the context in which it is done should be psychologically "clean" or "hygienic". By "clean" I want to imply that work should attempt to provide a safe psychological environment for the incumbent, although it is unlikely that the hygiene levels will play much of a role (if any) in determining

Table 26.2 Anxiety and depression associated with overall FITness and FIT Integrity (n = 356)

Overall FITness
    r = −.31 general anxiety (a)
    r = −.23 depression (d)
FIT Integrity (overall): r = −.64a, −.51d
Individual constancies:

Awareness	−.45a, −.25d,
Self-responsibility	−.54a, −.44d
Balance	−.46a, −.40d
Morality/ethics	−.23a, −.19d
Fearlessness	−.62a, −.53d

the positive aspects of worker perception and performance (*á la* Herzberg). Job design has an important but limited contribution in this area. Second, we know that people are not very FIT (most people score between 100 and 200 on a 1000-point scale) and their perceptions of their work and its context are going to be unduly influenced by these poor self-perceptions.

To date, the research from my own team and others lends strong support to the approach. It seems that FITness does measure fundamental aspects of people and how they behave, decide and are affected by their worlds, including work. I will provide some illustrative examples to show the range of ways in which FITness may play an overall role in self and work evaluations.

Overall FITness (a score based on a combination of *Behavioural Flexibility* and *FIT Integrity*) is strongly related to strain levels. In all studies done to date, on managerial samples, public sector workers, students, job applicants etc. the FITter people are, the less anxious and depressed they are. For example, in one study of 356 managers, we compared free-floating anxiety and depression scores with various FIT variables. In all cases there was a marked correlation between the FIT variable and these measures of stress or strain (Fletcher & Stead, 2000b). These results are shown in Table 26.2 (in all cases the correlations are significant to at least the p < 0.001 level).

Of course, the correlational caution discussed needs to be applied here too, although the findings appear to be very robust in all the FIT studies done (with many different groups) and persist when other aspects are statistically controlled. In the same study we also observed that there were correlations between strain levels and 12 of the 15 "personality" dimensions of the Behavioural Flexibility scale: the more dominant a trait (i.e. the smaller the range of scores on the scale and the more towards one pole these are), the greater the strain (anxiety/depression). Thus, inflexibility has its emotional as well as behavioural consequences, as predicted.

Individual FITness, though, has a very broad set of consequences that seem to touch many cognitive, affective, interpersonal and behavioural outcomes. Moreover, these effects extend far beyond the workplace in a way suggesting many aspects of life are affected by FITness levels. Previous researchers have, of course, considered the way in which one area of life spills over into another (see, for example, Fletcher, 1983, 1991). These effects can be quite subtle, as suggested by Karasek in an early paper (1978), in which he showed that job characteristics were linked with leisure-time pursuits and even political activity.

Stets (1985) also shows how men and women react to low job autonomy by controlling their spouses, independently of some obvious factors. I suggest that individual FITness, however, is a dominant "contextual bias" that determines many aspects of perception, decision and behaviour: it is not that one area affects another—they are related because both are reflections of FITness.

Our most recent research shows, for example, that FITness is not only related to cognitive decision making, but also to the way one lives one's life. Hanson & Fletcher (unpublished work) report a study of people's personal projects, such as dieting, exercising, drinking less, and getting on at work. FITness was strongly linked with these. For example, the Overall FIT scores of those in the sample who were at the time engaging in at least one personal project were over one-third higher (148 versus 110). Moreover, FITness was related to various lifestyle factors. For example, the Overall FIT scores were related to fatness (body mass index, BMI) levels, the lowest BMI group having a mean of 196, medium BMI a mean of 160 and the high BMI group of 119. Of the FIT variables, Behavioural Flexibility seems to play the most important role. Using Lisrel on the data to explore structural models, the influence of FITness also appears central and much more marked than other psychological variables.

I have suggested that FITness may be relevant in cognitive decision making. There is empirical support for this. In a prospective study by Stead & Fletcher (1998) 150 higher education business students completed *The FIT Profiler*™ (as well as other tests, including a questionnaire which assessed their learning styles). At the end of the year their examination performance was assessed in relation to these measures. The results were very clear-cut. Both Overall FITness and FIT Integrity were predictive of their academic performance. For example, the 10% of students with the highest Overall FITness scores obtained the equivalent of a whole class of degree better. On average their unseen examination marks were 8–10% higher than other students (despite the fact that the mean FIT levels of the students was only 131, suggesting considerable capacity for improvement in all).

Why is FITness of beneficial use in learning? We have suggested that aspects of FIT Integrity are likely to encourage deeper and more strategic approaches to learning and decision making as opposed to surface-level learning. For example, the FITter the learner, the more the learning environment should be approached with greater awareness, both internally and externally, the more they will take responsibility for outcomes, and the lower their fear and apprehension might be. The research has confirmed a relationship between FITness and strategy: on the basis of Entwistle's ASSIST measures, we found that people with higher FIT scores use significantly more strategic, more supportive, less surface, and deeper learning styles. It also appears that individual FITness facilitates group-based performance in problem-solving situations, primarily because of the enhanced Behavioural Flexibility levels (Lee et al., 2000).

If FITness is associated with positive cognitive and behavioural outcomes, one might also expect FIT people to do better in job selection interviews, even when, on the quality of their Curriculum Vitae, everything else appears equal. In one such study (see Fletcher & Stead, 2000b), we employed *The FIT Profiler*™ in a large company recruiting for new staff. *The FIT Profiler*™ results were not known to selectors until they had made their selection decisions. The "successful" candidates obtained much higher FIT scores than the unsuccessful ones: 236 versus 156 in Overall FITness, 74 versus 69 in FIT Integrity, and 43 versus 32 in Behavioural Flexibility.

In the context of work stress research, we would predict that a FITter person (i.e. one whose FIT scores are higher) is more likely to be healthy and less likely to suffer strain.

The research we have done so far, using psychological morbidity measures, supports this. I believe that this is partially because the FITter workers will not perceive their work environment as damaging or problematic as those who are less FIT: they will not be negatively affected by work stressors because, for them, they have no affective outcome (Payne & Morrison, 1999). In addition, it does appear that—independent of the "objective" work situation—FITter individuals perceive their job demands as being lower anyway, as well as providing them with greater support (intrinsic to the job, such as autonomy and feedback, as well as interpersonal support). Moreover, those who have higher levels of strain seem to have an imbalance in their FIT Awareness: they show a higher level of Awareness to the *external* world and a higher sensitivity to their environment that is not balanced by a high level of *internal* Awareness. This may make them more susceptible to negative outcomes (Dietman & Stead, 1999). Deitman (2001) also suggests that higher organisational commitment is related to higher levels of FITness levels too.

26.3.1 Practical Implications

One major practical advantage of the FITness framework is that it places the possibility of change and improvement at its very core. Individuals whose scores are low in FITness terms can endeavour to change them. There are now a series of "FIT EXERcises", allied to the principal components in the FIT framework, as well as more formal training courses, that endeavour to increase the FITness levels of individuals at all levels of the workforce (see www.fitcorporation.com). These EXERcises are based on the notion that trying new behaviours (or deploying existing ones in a new context), allied to the structured contemplation of thoughts and actions, can also act as a lever for deeper psychological changes.

I have suggested that some key areas of occupational and organisational psychology need refocusing because the consequences for current practices are wrong-headed, and some are even potentially damaging for individuals and organisations (Fletcher, 2002). It is my contention that the discipline has not contributed a great deal to reducing the massive human and financial costs of stress and work. I suspect this is because work stress research and theory has lost sight of the person to a significant degree. It is also, to my mind, not surprising that despite the knowledge that people make the difference in business, human resource practitioners have been unable to convince chief executives that they can make effective use of releasing this human potential. This people-power paradox exists because the discipline has not delivered on promises (Fletcher, 2001). The massive industry in selection and testing also, I believe, generally pedals a very negative perspective that has massive costs for both individuals and organisations. For example, I would contend that psychometric tests based on personality traits or concepts 100% guarantee that the selected individuals will behave inappropriately in future business contexts (because a personality trait is based on the invariance of behaviour). Selection and assessment should be based on criteria that can be integrated with company training and yet provide the person with new and empowering horizons. It is a moot point, too, whether or not psychology as a discipline should move away from theoretical approaches that may no longer hold at least a major (theoretical) practical advantage.

I have offered the FIT framework as an alternative tool that has increasing empirical support. The major conceptual points made here, however, do not rely on the FIT framework.

At a very practical level, the FIT framework has been adopted in an array of organisational settings to develop people and improve their overall situation. We have taken the approach that if a work setting can be made safe and psychologically hygienic, then the major advantages of any intervention will be derived from improving the FITness levels of the individuals. The advantages to be had from changing the nature of the work itself, or the cultural context of the organisation, will be severely limited and far outstripped in their power by transformations of FITness in the individuals. We have seen that in terms of individual FITness levels there is massive potential. On the average, people are only utilising about 15% of their FIT potential—that is, the mean score obtained overall is around 150 out of 1000. Improvements are likely to have personal and work benefits. FITter individuals are, apparently, protected to some degree against psychological and physical illness, they have more information on which to base decisions, greater freedom and fewer constraints, better performance, more efficient strategy management, greater flexibility, and enhanced cognitive flexibility and learning ability. Changing the nature of work itself, on the other hand, probably has restricted benefits that are likely to be short lived. Organisations should endeavour to make themselves "FIT Corporations™" by developing the FITness of their employees, and by selecting FIT individuals, rather than spending money on structures and processes. They would then reduce stress, improve health, and be more profitable in all likelihood. At the organisational level, a FIT organisation will be self-developmental, transforming as opposed to static, inherently strong and stable, information rich and successful.

REFERENCES

Briner, R. B.(1997) Improving stress assessment: toward an evidence-based approach to organisational stress interventions. *Journal of Psychosomatic Research*, **43**(1), 61–71.

Briner, R. B. (2001) Evidence-based occupational psychology. Paper presented to the British Psychological Society Centenary Conference, April 2000.

Briner, R. B. & Reynolds, S. (1999) The costs, benefits, and limitations of organisational level stress interventions. *Journal of Organisational Behaviour*, **20**, 647–64.

Caspi, A (2000) The child is the father of the man: personality continuities from childhood to adulthood. *Journal of Personality and Social Psychology*, **78** (1), 158–72.

Cox, T. (1978) *Stress*, Baltimore, MD: University Park Press.

De Jonge, J., Dormann, C., Janssen, P. P. M., Dollard, M. F., Landerweerd, J. A. & Nijhuis, J. N. (2001) Testing reciprocal relationships between job characteristics and psyhological well-being: a cross-lagged structural equation model. *Journal of Occupational and Organisational Psychology*, **74**, 29–46

Dietmann, A. M. (2001). An exploratory study into the relationship between (Inner) FITness, stress and organisational commitment. Paper given at the 59th Annual Conference of the International Council of Psychologists, Winchester, UK, July 2001.

Dietman, J. & Stead R. (1999) Managerial stress: organisational cultures, convergence/divergence and the FIT corporation. International Council of Psychologists Annual Convention, Salem, MA, August. University of Hertfordshire Business School working paper UHBS 2000:5.

Eysenck H. J. & Grossarth-Maticek, R. (1991) Creative novation therapy as a prophylactic treatment for cancer and coronary heart disease. Part II—effects of treatment. *Behaviour Research and Therapy*, **29**, 17–31.

Fletcher, B. (C) (1983) Marital relationships as a cause of death: an analysis of occupational mortality and the hidden consequences of marriage—some UK data. *Human Relations*, **36**(2), 123–34.

Fletcher, B. (C) (1988) Occupation, marriage and disease-specific mortality concordance *Social Science and Medicine*, **27**(6), 615–22.

Fletcher, B. (C) (1991) *Work, Stress, Disease and Life Expectancy*. Chichester: John Wiley & Sons.

Fletcher, B. (C) (1999) *The Work–FIT Profiler^TM*. St Albans: The FIT Corporation.

Fletcher, B. (C) (2001) The people–power paradox. *Financial Times Mastering Management Online*, issue 6, September.

Fletcher, B. (C) (2002) Where occupational and organisational psychology is going wrong: the FIT-IQ™ Solution. British Psychological Society Annual Occupational Conference, 2–5 January, Blackpool.

Fletcher B. (C) & Jones, F. (1993) Disease concordances amongst marital partners: not "way of life" or mortality data artifact. *Social Science and Medicine*, **12**(3), 1525–33.

Fletcher B. (C) & Jones, F. (1996) Occupational psychological factors in multiple sclerosis. *Neuroepidemiology*, **15**, 222–8.

Fletcher, B. (C) & Payne. R. L. (1980) Stress at work: a review and theoretical framework, Part 2. *Personnel Review*, **9**(20), 4–8

Fletcher B. (C) & Stead R. (1999) *The FIT Profiler^{TM}*. St Albans: The FIT Corporation.

Fletcher B. (C) & Stead R. (2000a) *(Inner) FITness and The FIT Corporation: Living in the Present Tense*. London: International Thomson.

Fletcher, B. (C) & Stead, R. (2000b) Intuition and FITness in a personal and organisational context. *Drishti:Insight: Journal of ARTDO International*, **1**(1), 9–16.

Harvey, R. J. & Wilson, M. A. (2000) Yes, Virginia, there is an objective reality in job analysis. *Journal of Organizational Behavior*, **21**, 829–54.

Jones, F. & Bright, J. (2001) *Stress: Myth, Theory and Research*. Englewood Cliffs, NJ: Prentice Hall.

Jones, F. & Fletcher, B. (C) (1993) An empirical study of occupational stress transmission in working couples. *Human Relations*, **46** (7), 881–903.

Jones F. & Fletcher, B. (C) (1996) Taking home work: a study of daily fluctuations in work stressors, effects on moods and impacts on marital partners. *Journal of Occupational and Organizational Psychology*, **69**, 89–106.

Judge, T. A., Erez, A. & Thoresen, C. J. (2000) Why negative affectivity (and self-deception) should be included in job stress research: bathing the baby with the bath water. *Journal of Organizational Behavior*, **21**, 101–111.

Karasek, R. (1978*)* Job socialisation, a longitudinal study of work, political andleisure activity in Sweden. IX World Congress of Sociology (RC30), 15 August Swedish Institute for Social Research, Stockholm University.

Lee, J., Fletcher, B. (C), Tan C. P. & Lai M. L. (2000) FIT Thinking in Business and IT Higher Education: A Force for Change? NZARE International Conference, 30 November–4 Decemeber, Waikato University, Hamilton, New Zealand.

Morgeson, F. P. & Campion, M. A. (2000) Accuracy of job analysis: toward an inference-based model. *Journal of Organizational Behavior*, **21**, 819–27.

Ouellette, J. A. & Wood, W (1998) Habit and intention in everyday life: the multiple processes by which past behaviour predicts future behaviour. *Psychological Bulletin*, **124**(1), 54–74.

Payne R. L. & Fletcher B. (C) (1983) Job demands, supports and constraints as predictors of psychological strain among schoolteachers. *Journal of Vocational Behaviour*, **22**, 136–47.

Payne, R. L. & Morrison, D (1999) The importance of knowing the affective meaning of job demands revisited. *Work and Stress*, **13**(3), 280–8.

Payne, R.L., Wall, T., Borrill, C. & Carter, A (1999) Strain as a moderator of the relationship between work characteristics and work attitudes. *Journal of Occupational Health Psychology*, **4***(1)*, 3–14.

Proundfoot, J, Guest, D., Carson, J, Dunn, G. & Gray, J (1997) Effect of cognitive-behavioural training on job-finding among long-term unemployed people. *Lancet*, **350**, 96–101.

Roberts, B. W. & DelVecchio, W (2000) The rank-order consistency of personality traits from childhood to old age: a quantitative review of longitudinal studies. *Psychological Bulletin*, **126**(1), 3–25.

Sanchez, J. I. & Levine, E. L. (2000) Accuracy or consequential validity: which is the better standard for job analysis data? *Journal of Organizational Behavior*, **21**, 809–18.

Spector, P. E. & Jex, S. M. (1991) Relations of job characteristics from multiple data sources with employee affect, absence, turnover intentions, and health. *Journal of Applied Psychology*, **76**, 46–53.

Spector, P. E., Zapf, D., Chen, P. Y. & Frese, M (2000) Why negative affectivity should not be controlled in stress research: don't throw the baby out with the bath water. *Journal of Organizational Behavior*, **21**, 75–95.

Stacey, R., Griffith, D. & Shaw, P (2001) *Complexity and Management: Fad or Radical Challenge to Systems Thinking?* London: Routledge.

Stead, R. & Fletcher, B. (C) (1998) *FIT for Learning: The Learning Personality*. 3rd Annual Learning Styles Conference, Sunderland, 29–30 June.

Stead, R, Fletcher, B. (C) & Jones, F. (1996) Relationships between workload, cognitive decision making and psychological well-being. British Psychological Society: Occupational Division, Eastborne, January.

Stead, R, Fletcher, B. (C) & Jones, F. (1997) Workaholism, and Working Smart: hours of work, job factors, managerial performance and decision making. British Academy of Management, London, September.

Stets, J. E. (1985) Job autonomy and control over one's spouse: a compensatory process. *Journal of Health and Social Behaviour*, **36**, 244–58.

Wall, T. D., Kemp, N. J., Jackson, P. R. & Clegg, C. W. (1986) Outcomes of autonomous workgroups: a long term field experiment. *Academy of Management Journal*, **29**, 280–304.

CHAPTER 27

Coaching and Counselling in Organizational Psychology

Joan L. Meyer

University of Amsterdam, The Netherlands

27.1 INTRODUCTION

Coaching and counselling are both forms of expertise offered to individuals in work situations. In *coaching*, executives or entrepreneurs seek a second opinion, devil's advocate or sounding board. The subject matter is their personal effectiveness in a broad sense, and so their strategies, policies and interventions are scrutinized. In *counselling*, the focus is on coping strategies, career development, relations, competencies and well-being at work. Curative interventions can be indicated by definite complaints,[1] whereas preventive interventions are more general and directed at the future.

In practice, the person in his or her work context is central. Both coaching and counselling can include catharsis, redefining situations, behavioural training and change, learning, coping and prevention. As far as the counsellor or coach is concerned, boundaries can be fluid, though limiting conditions vary.

Clients use a different perspective: an individual seeks counselling because the organization has become a source of stress, whereas in coaching the client defines problems in terms of choices and options. The client for counselling tends to define his or her role as reactive, whereas the client for coaching claims a proactive stance. In counselling the client feels relatively powerless *vis-à-vis* the organization and perceives the relation with the change agent as one of receiving help. The client for coaching tends to feel more powerful towards the organization, and perceives the relation with the change agent as one of purchasing additional know-how.

Whatever the starting position, the relationship with the consultant evolves in interaction with the client's dealings with the organization(s). Depending on developments, interpretations can be redefined, and emphasis can shift from stress reduction and coping to the exploration and defining of choices, and to the building of desired future states.

---

[1] It should be made clear from the beginning what will be part of the coaching relation and what will be the policy if other professionals need to be consulted, for instance if therapy is indicated.

The Handbook of Work and Health Psychology. Edited by M.J. Schabracq, J.A.M. Winnubst and C.L. Cooper.
© 2003 John Wiley & Sons, Ltd.

27.2 THEORETICAL CONTEXT

27.2.1 Dynamics of Problem Solving in Organizations

Organizations can be conceived as dynamic systems involved in processes of individual and collective problem solving. Some of these problems are seen as inherent in the normal functioning of the organization. Other problems are taken as signals that something is amiss. Two dimensions are important for this framework in organizations. The first is the responsibility taken for problems; the second is the responsibility taken for solutions (Brickman et al., 1985). Together, these dimensions define four models of helping and coping, each with their own consequences for the pattern of relationships that ensues (Figure 27.1).

- In the *moral model*, responsibility on both dimensions is high. This model does not completely rule out the influence of external circumstances or preclude receiving help, but it does underline the basic responsibility of the individual for both problems and solutions.
- In the *compensation model*, the individual is not held accountable for problems. Problems can be the result of social, economic or technological developments outside the individual's range of influence. However, in order to work out solutions, the individual needs to stop deploring these circumstances and start taking responsibility for improvement.
- In the *enlightment model*, the basic assumption is that the individual is to blame for problems, but is unable to take responsibility for solutions. A leader, doctrine or other "higher" agency is needed to find a way out.
- In the *medical model*, the individual is not held responsible for problems or solutions. Problems are blamed on others and solutions are expected from others. In the medical model the person is defined as weak and helples; in consequence, he or she is expected to act in a docile way and take the "medicine" prescribed.

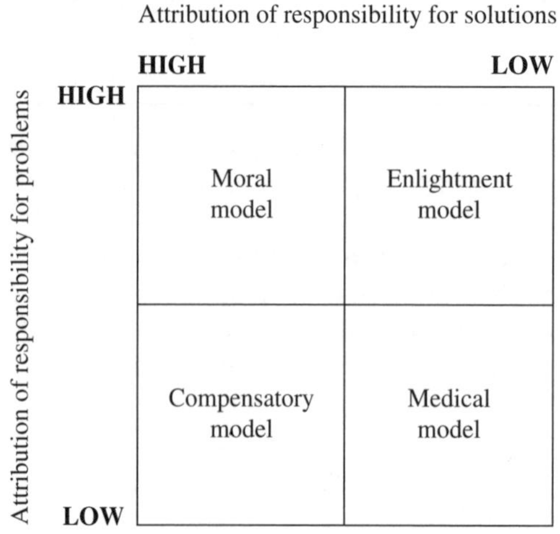

Attribution of responsibility for solutions

	HIGH	**LOW**
HIGH	Moral model	Enlightment model
LOW	Compensatory model	Medical model

Attribution of responsibility for problems

Figure 27.1 Four models of helping and coping

Psychological Context

In regular organizational functioning, these dimensions and models can be used to describe and understand the psychological context in which people do their work. For instance, someone who occupies a low position on both dimensions (assigns himself or herself to the *medical mode*), does not feel very responsible for either problems or solutions in the organization. Other people cause the problems, other people (the mysterious "they") must see to it that problems are solved. The person feels that he or she has little power in the organization, or is justified in not becoming too involved in the organization's concerns. In the long term, this psychological state can lead to dependency, discontent and revolt or to "letting go internally": although the person may still be present in the organization, he or she is only going through the motions of fulfilling their obligations. Another risk, if this position is adopted for a longer time, is that energy gets turned away from creating desired changes, and goes instead into the legitimizing of inaction.

We can contrast the previous position with the situation in which a person feels highly responsible for both problems and solutions (assigns himself or herself to the *moral mode*). People who tend towards this position quite often develop into valued leaders or employees in key positions, but also run fairly high risks regarding stress and burnout. Because they feel responsible, others in the organization find it relatively easy to burden them with extra assignments, which they find hard to refuse or defuse. In the long run, people in this position run the risk of the "Atlas syndrome": feeling disillusioned because they have been burdened with the world's troubles while others are having an easy time. Taking blame for what one really could not have prevented can also lead to depression, a feeling of being trapped or other destructive consequences. For instance, think of the situation where people tell a patient with a terrible disease that "deep down" he must have had a desire for this to happen. People who assign themselves to the *enlightment mode* usually have high guilt feelings. They blame themselves for problems, but at the same time they feel relatively powerless to find solutions. For the individual this is an uncomfortable position. The search for the right leader or agent who can show the way can lead to new disillusions. Long-term dependency and intensified self-blame are the risks in this position. These pose a threat to effective functioning.

Finally, people who take the *compensation position* recognize the various external sources which generate problems. At the same time they take responsibility for working at solutions. This psychological state allows people to tackle complicated social and organizational problems and sustain long-term efforts for change. There is a slight risk of carrying the position to extremes, i.e. creating insider–outsider patterns where all the problems are blamed on others while the self or insider group takes credit for "progress". However, this risk applies only to extreme situations.

Reactions

It is important to realize that the pattern of influence in *interaction* moves diagonally across the model. In other words, in a relation between A and B, if A occupies a particular position in the model, B is pushed to react in the mode diagonally opposed to A's position. So, for instance, if a leader takes the psychological position that is described as the moral mode followers are pushed to react according to the medical mode. To a certain extent, desired behaviour can be elicited by choosing the corresponding mode (diagonally opposite) in the model.

Organizational Structure

A second way in which the model can be applied is for the diagnosis of organizational structure. What is the pattern of formally assigned responsibilities to individuals and groups?

Is this pattern the optimal choice[2] in regard to the relationships and interpretations it will generate? What will be the long-term effects for morale, motivation and initiative in the organization if this pattern is left unchanged?

Next, one can determine whether the parties concerned actually have the means (such as discretionary power, resources, personnel, know-how) to fulfil the responsibilities assigned to them. Many tensions in organizations spring from paradoxical or double-bind situations, where people are held accountable (or made to feel responsible) for results which they can only marginally affect.

For instance, it is well recognized that responsibility tends to be unevenly distributed in organizations, with high concentrations at the top. Top-level executives and management are usually held accountable for both problems and solutions regarding the whole firm. But the problem of global market failure, for instance, can hardly be laid at the door of the top management of a single firm. Organization members will indeed rarely blame management in such cases, but they will look to them for solutions and expect them to take responsibility and "do the best they can", given the crisis situation.

In the face of discrepancies between accountability and actual influence, the area of (potential) effectivenes needs to be defined, at the individual, team and organizational levels. Situational givens need to be recognized, or new venues for influence found. The result of such an operation is not just separating ideology from fact, or better organizational results or less guilty and stressed–out employees. By pinpointing the exact locations of influence and non-influence, the firm gains accurate leverage where it is possible and necessary.

Balancing Responsibility

Analysis of various situations and relations can be helpful in arriving at a better balance between groups and concerns in an organization. For instance, analysis might reveal that a leader held subordinates responsible for problems, while taking all responsibility for solutions on himself. In this way, he is putting himself in the position of "rescuer" while reducing his staff to "helpless followers" (enlightment model). Subordinates might feel that the only way they can clear themselves from blame is by following their leader unquestioningly. At first, this may appear gratifying to the leader, but the precedent is set for a future where leadership is expected to provide all solutions and is deprived of much-needed critical feedback.

---

[2] The formal responsibilities are usually assigned from the need to get certain tasks done or goals achieved. They seldom get scrutinized from the viewpoint of relationships generated. However, since they do influence these relations, long-term effects will ensue and can be quite different from what was intended.

Research brings to light another imbalance sometimes found in organizations where leaders and top management, although formally accountable for problems and solutions, feel that rules and social norms are for the others (they are "above" the law) and actually behave irresponsibly or violate general codes of conduct. These effects are attributed to the "metamorphic aspects of power" (Kipnis, 1976; Mitchell, 1994), the phenomenon that people in power positions tend to believe in their own superiority and to devalue subordinates. Such attitudes can become permanent strategies for the individuals concerned, and cause much harm to people and relations both in the firms and outside.

To summarize, the simple two-dimensional model presented here can be used in a number of ways:

1. To understand and describe the psychological context in which the individual at work is functioning.
2. To chart the system of formally assigned responsibilities, or the structure of a group or organization. The structure can be analysed according to the correspondence of responsibilities and means, leading to greater leverage and effectiveness.
3. To check whether individuals and groups actually *feel* responsible for the problems or solutions formally assigned to them.
4. The model can also be used to analyse the extent to which individuals and groups hold *each other* accountable for problems and solutions, and so point up discrepancies in expectations, or between expectations and formal positions.
5. Finally, the model can of course be applied to the relation between the client and the consultant in coaching or counselling. To what extent is the client held responsible for the problems described? To what extent is the client stimulated to take responsibility for solutions? Which interpretational mould offers the best perspective for the coaching relation and the client's future development in a work context? It is important for the coach to keep in mind that there are no absolutes in "good" or "evil" involved in these models. Which model is an appropriate choice depends on the psychological situation of the client at the time of intervention.[3] A coach or consultant needs to take into account how a person interprets his own situation—refusing to do this can mean losing the client altogether, since he will feel he is not being taken seriously or that he is "misunderstood". The same goes for organizational change operations. If they are to be effective, they need to take account of the psychological "reality" adopted by their clients and tailor their approach to fit their actual current interpretation. Once they have entered into a relation with the client, of course, they can start to plot the desired and desirable development with the client.

To summarize, positions in organizations differ according to the responsibility assigned for problems and for solutions. Individuals differ in the ways in which they interpret their own and other people's functioning in terms of these dimensions. In the course of time, people can change or adapt their interpretations, for instance as a result of specific events, role transitions or critical events. The coach or counsellor can assist in analysing positions and interpretations, and help find limiting elements. As the client starts to realize how these limiting elements influence both actual options and concrete behaviour, the motivation to find more promising ways of interpreting the situation and to explore new alternatives can take hold.

---

[3] For instance, the success of organizations such as Alcoholics Anonymous or WeightWatchers is that they take account of the interpretations favoured by their (prospective) clients and incorporate them into their operations.

27.3   THE ROLE OF ORGANIZATIONAL CULTURE

The topic of culture has been covered from a broad range of disciplines and perspectives. However, the most influential theorist on organizational culture is Schein (1985), who in his turn, based much of his work on Parsons. Schein holds a broad view of organizational culture, encompassing multiple phenomena. These phenomena range from fairly superficial, highly visible aspects of culture to the more central and harder to determine characteristics. Visible signs of organizational culture such as behavioural codes and style of presentation form the outer layer of culture. More centrally, we find the organizational "folklore" (who were/are the heroes, who were/are the villains, which major feats are important in its history), followed by explicit norms and values.

The core of culture is formed by the "taken-for-granted assumptions" which give meaning and guide action. These basic assumptions deal with the dual problem of adapting to the environment and at the same time preserving internal integration. Together, they provide the organization's unique answer to the question of organizational identity and continuity. Basic assumptions are usually heavily influenced by the organization's founding entrepreneurs. The rules of the game they set store by are incorporated into its basic code, and faithfully observed by second- and third-generation personnel. Through behavioural "modelling", culture is perpetuated. As in the general culture, organizational culture in due course comes to involve a person's emotions, feelings and habits. Because of this, culture change is a painful and intrusive process.

27.4   ORGANIZATIONAL CULTURE AND STRESS

On the one hand, the coach needs to be able to empathize with the socially constructed reality of a client's organization. On the other hand, the coach needs to be able to take a critical view of this same culture. There are a number of ways in which a culture can become stressful to members of an organization. Five of these are discussed here:

- The content of the culture can be stress-inducing in and of itself.
- Inconsistencies and internal discrepancies can lead to stress.
- The temporal lag between developments in the organization and its environment, and the culture can be stressful.
- There can be friction between the individual's values and the culture.
- Leaders can influence culture in unintended ways.

27.4.1   The Content of the Organization's Culture

The basic assumptions of an organization sometimes carry the seeds of stress in them. For example, if an organization is committed to a strategy of concealing mistakes and covering up errors, this strategy can become a taken-for-granted way of dealing with issues at work. Trying to maintain a positive image for customers can lead to this behaviour. The storefront of perfection creates stresses and strains in the backroom. People strive to maintain "faultless" images. Newcomers quickly learn to avoid asking for advice or admitting to mistakes. The result of this pattern is that large areas of behaviour become undiscussable, thus creating new strains. Since the opportunity to correct errors and to learn from failures is minimalized, it is only a matter of time before the organization starts to dysfunction, thereby contributing to more stress for everyone concerned.

A similar example would be an organization where there is a culture of repression and control, combined with a bureaucratic way of thinking. By laying a heavy emphasis on accounting for past procedure, members of such an organization become caught up in a culture of legitimization. In the struggle for "clean bills of health" the actual goals and results move out of focus. As in the previous example, in due course, errors and failures will add their momentum to the stress that has already built up over time.

In the coaching situation it is important to provide a "safe" climate, in which the client can take a new look at the culture where he or she is trying to function. Questions can be raised and alternatives explored.

27.4.2 Discrepancies and Inconsistencies in the Culture

Every organizational culture has its inconsistencies. In a changing world, new problems must be confronted and new ways of dealing with them need to be worked out. Implicit, value-laden systems are tied to feelings and habitual behaviour. They do not change in the same way or at the same pace as rational and cognitive systems. The fact that people are usually not conscious of their basic assumptions makes it hard to evaluate them in a rational way.[4]

As a multi-layered phenomenon, inconsistencies are inherent in culture. There are inconsistencies between the conscious ideals ("espoused theory"; see Argyris & Schön, 1985), and the shared norms to which we pay lip service, the ancient "dos and don'ts" programmed into our system, and the way we actually behave. Paradoxes abound: work should be creative and predictable, co-workers should compete and cooperate, decision making should be swift, democratic and clear-cut, and so forth.

In the coaching relation, such paradoxes can be located and exposed. The question of which function they fulfil in the greater scheme of things can be explored. The dynamics created by the tension of conflicting ideals can be understood and put to work, opening up new possibilities, first of all for the client himself, and secondly for his staff, workers, clients and relations.

27.4.3 Failure of the Culture to Keep Pace with Organizational Developments

Culture is the binding element and plays an important role in the organization's survival. Culture is not invariable, but change does not automatically follow structural changes or new developments. Upholding the same core values can demand quite different measures in the course of the organization's life cycle.

For instance, a group of pioneers who know each other and work together on the basis of mutual trust and commitment can be successful and evolve into a much larger organization. In the larger organization, more formalized systems of selection, organization and control will be needed due to the larger scale of operations. Accordingly, new ways of communicating and interacting will need to be learned. What has been taken for granted in the past

---

[4] Since these are taken for granted, people do not realize how their behaviour is influenced by them.

now leads to friction and misunderstanding. To preserve the valued trust and commitment, new behaviour needs ultimately to become habitual and taken for granted.

Other major changes in organizational development, such as the transition from a functional to a more organic structure, or a decentralization process towards smaller, cost-effective business units, or privatization, can also mean that the original culture becomes in part counterproductive. When management recognizes the problem but lacks (or fails to supplement) expertise as to how cultural change processes are set in motion, this can lead to treating personnel as "disposables". A large number of employees are laid off and culture change is sought through the selection of new personnel who will (hopefully) fit the new model. For the remaining employees this strategy can be extremely threatening and may disrupt feelings of trust and loyalty towards the firm. Although it is hard to specify the exact cost of such choices, executives tend to agree that the chopping block is "penny-wise, pound-foolish", when all is taken into account.

In the coaching relation the existing organizational culture is placed in the perspective of desired developments. How does the client see his own desirable future in ten years time? And how does the client see the organization's desirable future over the same period? What is the ideal scenario, and how realistic is it? In this way a yardstick is provided to evaluate the way in which the culture is developing. If desired, expert guidance can be sought from specialists in culture change.

27.4.4 Friction Between Organizational Culture and Individual Values

Most organizations try to make sure that new personnel will fit in with the desired or existing culture. To this end, they tailor selection procedures and advertising campaigns, and make use of internal training procedures. In spite of these efforts people can and do obtain jobs in firms where the culture diverges from their personal value systems.

Discrepancies can arise through diverging views on how best to realize the organization's goals, and take the form of a conflict about means. Or people project *assumed* characteristics on an individual as a result of some external characteristic (for instance, a homosexual *"can't possibly* belong in the rugged old boy's culture") leading to conflicts about discrimination. Dealing with this type of conflict can take different forms, depending on the power position and the resources the person is able to mobilize. If conditions are favourable, and a person has a strong reason to remain with the firm, the coach can help him to change the culture. On the other hand, a new career move may be a simpler solution.

27.4.5 Unintended Influence by Leaders

Although there are still some CEOs who are firm believers in structure, most people in top management are aware that culture is a major influence on organizational functioning, from which success or failure may depend. Therefore, many leaders use sanctions to reward or discourage certain attitudes, interpretations and behaviour. In this way, they hope to achieve the kind of culture most conducive to their vision of the future. However, the effect leaders have is only partly the result of their conscious efforts. Being a leader entails high visibility for subordinates. Employees listen to what their superiors say, and watch what they do and make others do.

They also hear what is left unsaid and notice what is left undone. The conclusions they draw from this total pattern are not always the conclusions their superiors would have them draw. Let us take an example: a chairperson strives to make a committee meeting go forward, paying attention to both content and process. However, his energetic behaviour in taking the lead seems to communicate to others his sense of responsibility for and control over the issues discussed. They react by leaving *more* responsibility to him. Though the meeting seems efficient and effective, some central issues remain undiscussed and creative content is a great deal less than it could have been.

Often, ideals start out by being explicitly formulated and discussed. Over time, they evolve into shared values, become part of the culture. Finally, they get taken for granted. In the course of time values tend not to come under scrutiny anymore. However, this can mean that counterproductive effects are not recognized.

For instance, the explicit norms that work should be done accurately, and that due procedure should be followed, can lead over time to processes of bureaucratization where obsolete procedures are followed meticulously to the detriment of all else. Or the espoused value of client-centred behaviour can threaten integration, leading to unintended divergence between teams, and between teams and the organization as a whole (Van Oosterhout, 1990).

Unintended influence by leaders can be explored in the coaching situation. Many clients are leaders, and it is important to check their awareness of these processes. Most people are very aware of the ways in which they are being influenced, but much slower to realize their own impact on others. Role-playing offers the opportunity to bring non-verbal and symbolic behaviours into view and explore whether they enhance what the client is trying to communicate.

27.4.6 Being Nice: Defensive Routines and Paradoxical Communication

A special instance of unintended influence is that of paradoxical communication. The forms discussed here are especially likely to crop up in firms where people try to keep interpersonal relations as pleasant as possible. Paradoxically, these people are creating unpleasantness by trying to avoid it—the aim of their actions is to circumvent painful communications. On an organizational level paradoxical communications evolve into defensive strategies or routines. They have the following characteristics:

1. They are learned through socialization processes in the organization itself.
2. The strategies serve to avoid threatening situations or to save face.
3. Defensive routines are supported by the organizational culture.
4. Defensive routines remain in place despite the turnover of individual personnel.

As a result of defensive routines, the causes of threat or loss of face cannot be dealt with. The threatening condition is obscured from view by the defensive behaviour. The underlying problems cannot be solved. The defensive routines seem to offer protection from threat, but actually serve to maintain it.

Paradoxical communication can be recognized in mixed messages delivered by superiors, for instance: "I have complete confidence in your judgement, but be sure to report to..." (followed by an instruction of control).

The defensive strategy consists of delivering an inconsistent message, either verbally or through inconsistencies between the content and relational level. In this way, the sender pretends that no inconsistency exists. Both the inconsistency in the message and the ignoring of the inconsistency are undiscussable (Argyris, 1991; Argyris & Schön, 1996).

In the coaching situation, the existence of defensive routines in an organization can come to light. A manager wanting to break the pattern of defensive routines in his organization will need help from external advisers. Defensive routines have sprung into being because people felt safer avoiding certain issues. A process of consciousness raising, reframing, training and change, with or without conflict mediation, will be needed to effect real change in this situation.[5]

27.5   COACHING KEY FIGURES IN ORGANIZATIONS

Management coaching of key figures takes place in a one-to-one situation, but is ultimately directed at behaviour in the organization, such as communication, human resource management, functional changes etc. The focus can even be on external relations of the organization. For instance: what should the long-range policy look like? Which agents or firms should be part of the external network? What kind of relations should be formed? What future aims are desirable? Critical transitions in the life cycle of the organization (transition from "entrepreneurial" to growth and consolidation, major market shifts, mergers, acquisitions or joint ventures) can be the occasion for top management to seek guidance or a sounding board.

The whole gamut of problems that form the area of organizational change and the expertise of change agents can also be the subject matter in individual coaching, provided one accepts that the scope of influence is limited. However, there is another crucial difference. The change agent operates in the actual organization and has at his disposal explicit information from many sources. He is able to take direct action and implement change. The coach, on the other hand, deals only with one key figure and "sees" the situation through this person's eyes. Any action taken in the organization is taken by the client, not by the coach. For the coach it is hard to perform crosschecks,[6] although of course the fact that the client is under intensive (joint) scrutiny, means that person's bias will usually show up during the coaching. There are a number of reasons why key figures in an organization prefer coaching either as an alternative or in addition to change agents or consultants. These will be treated in the next Section.

27.5.1   Occasions for Coaching

A manager or key figure in an organization can decide to consult an expert on a one-to-one basis for a number of reasons. First, the position of the manager can be the reason to choose this option rather than calling in a firm of consultants. Specifically, top managers who have only recently started working in a firm or position, or who have been given an assignment to

---

[5] Such extensive change efforts are beyond the scope of coaching and counselling.
[6] This goes for both the diagnosis as the change process and implementation.

effect certain changes, tend to choose coaches rather than change agents. Their main concern is to have a sounding board or sparring partner, with whom they can explore alternatives, and take a critical look at their planned policies and spontaneous judgements.

Second, lack of consensus between a key manager and his surroundings can be the occasion for coaching. To find out how views or values came to clash and to determine the meaning of these differences, the support of a coach outside the organization can be essential.

A third occasion is if the key figure discovers that change operations seem repeatedly to flounder and lead to nothing. This could be the case in an organizational culture rife with defensive routines and undicussables. Here deeper analysis is needed to uncover the underlying resistance to change. For the client, what is at issue is the situation in the organization, and at the same time a personal choice, whether to remain and try to effect change, or decide to move elsewhere.

A fourth indication for coaching is where the organization is still in the aftermath of major change operations, mergers, privatization or other upheavals. In such times, the main issue for the firm is to find a new stable equilibrium. For the key manager, it is important not to rock the boat. Coaching is less obtrusive and therefore preferred.

Fifth, the position of the leader is lonely. On the one hand, leaders are held responsible for processes and outcomes, both good and bad. On the other hand, subordinates streamline information towards their superiors in order to make a good impression or to reap desired benefits. Subordinates expect leaders to react adequately, to alleviate their doubts and insecurities, to take decisions and to show them the way. They also expect leaders to maintain "face". In the relation between superior and subordinate there is very little room for the leader's own doubts and insecurities. Moreover, venting these too freely might lead others inside or outside the firm to exploit that information. So, the confidentiality of the coaching situation has its advantages. A trustworthy coach can deal with questions that demand time, thorough analysis, and organizational, strategic or psychological expertise.

Finally, a coach can be chosen for more personal reasons. In the course of their active lives, people meet with many problematic situations. Not all of these are solely due to situations at work. Each individual has his or her unique experiences, and has been programmed by parents and parent figures in a different way. Situations at work can evoke ancient patterns that the person thought he had left behind long ago. Especially for leadership, such personal factors are important to recognize and deal with, since a leader's behaviour can influence the lives of many people. Counterproductive forces can be recognized and dealt with in the coaching situation, leaving the key figure free to deal with real-world issues in an effective, unbiased way.

27.6 THE MAIN APPROACH IN COACHING AND COUNSELLING

The core of the method of coaching and counselling described here is built on the concept of empowerment. This approach can be traced to political views of power (Hardy, 1989; Lukes, 1974) and generative theory-building (Gergen, 1982) in social science, and to rational emotive therapy and neurolinguistic programming in psychotherapy. In individual counselling these approaches have proved effective. In regard to organizational functioning, the evidence is less clear-cut (Geuzinge, 1995; Meyer, 1994). The ideal of the empowered organization is to utilize resources optimally, and to effect more choices and better outcomes through better processes. However, research supporting these claims is scarce (Thomas et al., 1993; Veenkamp, 1995).

In the approach described here, empowerment is a perspective from which the client's interpretations are analysed. Together, coach and client review the concepts, images and relations which make up the client's everyday working life. The question is to what extent these are "generative", in the sense that promising new avenues are opened up for feeling, thinking and acting. To broaden the range of influence for the client, "inevitables", para-doxical elements and bias in his interpretations are tracked down. "Inevitables" often take the form of the *quasi-choice*, as in "Your money or your life".

Clients unintentionally formulate "alternatives" that are unacceptable and that function as threats. The result is that they feel cornered, have their back to the wall, and cannot seem to get out of the deadlock. The narrowing of vision described here is dangerous to both the clients and their environment. When a person is convinced that there is only one (undesirable) way in which a situation can evolve, he more often than not through his own behaviour contributes to the bringing about of that situation ("self-fulfilling prophecy").

In the process of tracking down and exposing "inevitables", it slowly becomes clear how many blind alleys and mazes have unintentionally been created or have just come into being in the conceptual world that has formed. When coaching takes hold, clients get actively involved in this process. For client and coach it becomes like a game to explore the alternative interpretations, and find among them building blocks for the new desirable future. The broadening of the range of options can take many different forms:

- One method we have already seen is the separation of responsibility for problems from the responsibility for solutions.
- A second way we have described is by locating and pointing out the "inevitables" due to organizational culture, which block effective functioning.
- A third way in which interpretations can be opened up is by tracing their origins. This method is especially useful when dealing with personal doctrine and dogmas which hamper the client's functioning and cramp his personal or business style. Many times one finds that the doctrines were useful at their point of origin, but have outlived their usefulness due to new developments, a broader range of application for which they are not suited (briefly, what made good sense in the nursery does not necessarily do the same in the boardroom) or the fact that the client, having lived a full life, now has much more sophisticated strategies at his disposal with which to tackle similar problems.

Since the client is usually the only source of information in coaching and counselling, special attention is paid to non-verbal behaviour. Body language, intonation, but also the images used by the client, the special ways in which seemingly mundane statements are formulated—all are important sources of information both regarding the problems involved and the client's progress towards solutions.

The fourth element in this approach is the systematic analysis of situations and events from a meta-level of communication (Meyer & Schabracq, 1990; Watzlawick et al., 1970). In business-as-usual, there is little time to deploy this viewpoint, but the coaching situation offers a unique opportunity to develop this perspective. Improvements and changes in strategy, policy or facilities of organizations are good focal points since they are especially prone to become the source of unintentional slights and friction. People are so concentrated on the content of their assignments that they either forget to communicate to certain groups and individuals, or fail to realize how their lack of communication impacts others. As in everyday life, one cannot *not* communicate. For instance the financial manager may think that he is taking a decision which is only about rewards and compensations. He may have no intention whatsoever of stirring up interpersonal relations in the firm. However, when he changes rewards and compensations, in one and the same gesture he is telling people what he thinks of their importance to the firm, to each other and to the future. If he deals with this aspect *unintentionally*, (social) accidents are bound to happen.

To take another example, imagine that a redistribution of offices and furniture is taking place in a firm. Imagine endless meetings between a small group, deciding on the new layout and furnishing. And imagine what will happen if the new plans become action while many people have not been told when, how or where they are going to be moved.[7] Such Kafkaesque situations happen all too often in business life.

In coaching, such situations are explored by letting people "sit in the chair" of others impacted by their policy or decisions. Through role-playing and the active use of imagination, people learn to anticipate communication problems and to handle multiple perspectives and viewpoints, and to do so *before* toes have been trodden on or relationships have been damaged.

The fifth element in this approach is the use of metaphor. By skilful use of metaphor the coach can achieve a fairly exact definition of feelings and experience. Metaphor serves to focus the client on the emotional undertones of incidents and situations. No matter that there is no exact fit between the descriptions and the described—sometimes the very exaggeration of a well-chosen metaphor can trigger the client into awareness. Coach and client together bandy about the various metaphors in order to arrive at an interpretation of what incident x actually means to the client—with the client in the role of the expert.[8] In the course of the coaching relation, a special language is developed in which various elements are described in the personal "short-hand" developed in the relation and involving metaphor.

As regards process, change is sought through the cycle: analysis, awareness, reflection, exploration and choice.

Interventions can take the well-known forms of accepting, catalysis and, confrontation (although the emphasis is on catalytic interventions). Confrontation is used sparingly and reserved for situations in which it is absolutely necessary, since it is intrusive to the relation between coach and client. Moreover, interventions are usually more effective if the client discovers his or her own answers, instead of being given the coach's version of the world to replace his own.

27.7 FINAL CONSIDERATIONS

The main goal in coaching and counselling is defined as "Optimal and effective functioning of the individual in the organization", where the functioning of the individual is taken to include the individual's range of influence. In other words, depending on the individual's position, many people in or around the organization can have an interest in the succesful implementation of coaching. On the one hand, this is good news, since it is easier to free

---

[7] In the ideal situation leaders would enquire after people's wishes and needs, before making and implementing plans.
[8] The person is the ultimate expert on his or her own feelings.

funds for coaching. On the other hand, it places a heavy responsibility on the shoulders of the coach—not only does he or she have a responsibility towards the client, but also towards the organizational environment of the client in so far as this is impacted. Because of this aspect, it is essential that a coach is an expert in the field of organizational change. Viewpoints put forward by the client need to be reviewed from a position of expertise not only in the coaching process *per se*, but also from theoretical knowledge and practical know-how on organizations and change. Particular attention needs to be paid to processes of power and the dynamics of power struggle—these add their own flavour to relations at work and can be hard to grasp for the individuals involved.[9]

For analyses and interventions in coaching executives and key figures, and for counselling, the primary aim is the effective functioning of the individual in the organization. A number of conditions needs to be kept in mind to ensure sound process and quality.

First, a good consultant is aware of his or her limitations. The method described here constitutes an interface of psychological counselling on the one hand, and organizational change and development on the other. Expertise in these fields enables the consultant to recognize obstructions to effectiveness on a general level and to show or open up possible directions and avenues for change. Sometimes it is advisable to point the client to specialists in the respective areas. The consultant thus needs to have an overview of consultant firms and to be familiar with their methods. The method of coaching described here is not a form of therapy. Should the need for therapy become clear in the coaching situation, the client can be referred.

The second condition is absolute confidentiality. To meet this condition, it is not sufficient that the consultant be independent of the organization employing the client. After all, higher level managers and key figures operate within larger networks in the political and economic environment of the organization. Moreover, they have access to classified information and their actions have far-reaching consequences. The consultant for coaching must ensure the independence of his or her position and guard against the merest suspicion of interest linkage.[10] If there is a possibility of overlapping networks the client must be referred to another consultant.

For coaching and counselling the primary aim is development of the client in his or her work situation, with the secondary aim of ultimate effects in and for the organization. This approach fits in with contemporary aims of management to move from a traditional paradigm of control/order/prescription to a more action-oriented paradigm designed for acknowledging and empowering people (Evered & Selman, 1989). At the same time, coaching of leaders puts to use the classic strategy advocated by Ignatius Loyola, of influencing the "head" in order to change the entire body.

REFERENCES

Argyris, C. & Schön, D. (1985) Evaluating theories of action. In W.G. Bennis, K.D. Benne & R. Chin (eds) *The Planning of Change*. Holt, Rinehart & Winston, New York.

Argyris, C. & Schön, D. (1996) *Organizational Learning II: Theory, Method, Practice*. Reading, Massachusetts: Addison-Wesley.

---

[9] Many people in organizations tend to take power relations at face, i.e. formal, value.

[10] Obviously, this means that the phenomenon of socalled "coaching leaders", where managers claim to be their subordinate's coach, is not a possibility in the method described here.

Argyris, C. (1991) Crafting a theory of practice: the case of organizational paradoxes. In R.E. Quinn & K.S. Cameron (eds) *Paradox and Transformation.* Ballinger, Cambridge.

Berger, P.L. & Luckmann, T. (1996) *The Social Construction of Reality.* Doubleday, New York.

Brickman, P., Rabinowits, B.C., Karuza, J., Jr, Cohn, E. & Kidder, L. (19985) Models of helping and coping. In W.G. Bennis, K.D. Benne & R. Chin (eds). *The Planning of Change.* Holt, Rinehart & Winston, New York.

Evered, R.D. and Selman, J.C. (1989) Coaching and the art of management. *Organizational Dynamics,* **18** (2), 16–32.

Gergen, K.J. (1982) *Toward Transformation in Social Knowledge.* Springer-Verlag, New York.

Geuzinge, C. (1995) Empowerment, doctoral thesis, University of Amsterdam.

Hardy, C. (1989) *The Contribution of Political Science to Organizational Behaviour.* In Lorsch, J.W. (ed.) *Handbook of Organizational Behaviour.* Prentice Hall, Englewood Cliffs, NJ.

Kipnis, D. (1976) *The Powerholders.* University of Chicago Press, Chicago, IL.

Lukes, S. (1974) *Power: A Radical View.* Macmillan, London.

Meyer, J. (1994) The power to change, paper presented at the 23rd Annual Conference of the International Association for Applied Psychologists, Madrid.

Meyer, J. & Schabracq, MJ (1990) *Alledaagse macht [Everyday Power].* Swets & Zeitlinger, Amsterdam.

Mitchell, T. (1994) Power and accountability, paper presented at the 23rd Annual Conference of the International Association for Applied Psychologists, Madrid.

Schabracq, M. J. (1991). *De inrichting van de werkelijkheid [The Structure of Reality].* Boom, Meppel.

Schein, E.H. (1985) *Organizational Culture and Leadership.* Jossey-Bass, San Francisco, CA.

Thomas, J.B., Clark, S.M. & Gioia, D.A. (1993) Strategic sense-making and organizational performance: linkage among scanning, interpretation, action and outcomes. *Academy of Management Journal,* **38**, 230–70.

Van Oosterhout, N. (1990) *Cultuurverandering bij het NOB [Culture Change in the National Broadcasting Corporation],* doctoral thesis, University of Amsterdam.

Veenkamp, I. (1995) *De kerntakendiskussie bij gemeenten [Discussion of core functions in municipal government],* KPMG Management Consultants, The Hague.

Watzlawick, P., Beavin, J.H. & Jackson, D.D. (1970) *Pragmatics of Human Communication.* Faber & Faber, London.

What an Organisation Can Do about its Employees' Well-Being and Health: An Overview

Marc J. Schabracq

University of Amsterdam, The Netherlands

28.1 INTRODUCTION

This chapter is primarily practically oriented. It does not go into empirical studies, nor into extensive theoretical matters. It just gives an overview of what organisations themselves do and can do to promote the health and well-being of their employees, with as little interference from external consultants as possible. The perspective here is an organisational one, not one of the individual employee.

The approach adopts the following elements and guidelines:

- The organisation appoints people of sufficient influence and importance to look after its employees. These people are responsible for the employees' experienced health, well-being and satisfaction in their departments. To this end, they have to know the employees involved, as well as their possibilities and limitations. It also implies that they have to spend sufficient attention, time and money on the employees in their care, All this can be part of the normal task package of the line managers. However, when this is not feasible, special so-called co-managers can be appointed.
- If special co-managers are appointed, all of them together can form a project team that occupies itself with the employees' well-being and health, as well as with the implementation of necessary changes in general (Schabracq, 2001).
- Learning about potential problems, and solutions, of experienced health and well-being is a matter of questioning employees about it. In bigger organisations, this may imply doing periodical audits about these issues (Schabracq et al., 2001).
- Frequent problems with health and well-being can be used as an indication of more systemic causes, which may have other undesired effects, and severe consequences for the organisation (see also Chapter 2).

The Handbook of Work and Health Psychology. Edited by M.J. Schabracq, J.A.M. Winnubst and C.L. Cooper.
© 2003 John Wiley & Sons, Ltd.

- Often—and certainly in times of scarcity of personnel—turnover is a better indicator of employees' well-being and health than sick leave and work disability figures.
- Preventing problems with well-being and health is to be preferred over curing, while it is also better to strive for positive outcomes than to counteract negative outcomes (Ofman, 1995). It is obviously better to spend money and effort to maximise effectiveness, pleasure and development than to counteract all kinds of unnecessary problems.
- Interventions should be tailored, as much as possible, to individual employees' needs and desires.
- To realise the previous guideline, it is essential to ask these employees to give their input about the status quo, its causes and options for improvement, and to make as much use of these ideas as possible. Workshops can be a good medium for this.
- In solving organisational problems, one should concentrate on solving the problem that forms the main constraint first (Goldratt, 1990).
- Real leadership is one of the most important means to prevent problems with well-being and health.
- The relevant existing human resource management (HRM) interventions should be used more consistently for all age groups.
- The way organisations deal with well-being and stress will become a critical strategic factor in global competition (Schabracq & Cooper, 2000).

Section 28.2 pays attention to the place of this approach within HRM. Section 28.3 is about leadership; that is, the role that management may play in preventing problems in the area of well-being and health. Section 28.4 sketches the approach itself. Section 28.5 gives short descriptions of HRM interventions that can be of help here. Sections 28.6 and 28.7 discuss, respectively, the positive outcomes of such an approach and some of its inherent problems. Lastly, Section 28.8 introduces the concept of co-management, which can help to solve some of the problems.

28.2   WELL-BEING AND HEALTH WITHIN HRM

Essentially, taking care of employees' well-being and health is a logical element of consistent HRM. Isn't the main objective of HRM simultaneous development of the goals of the organisation and its employees in such a way that both parties profit optimally? Within the frame of reference of HRM, good employees—the human capital!—are considered to be the main asset of the organisation. From this point of view, it is only logical to take care of and develop this human capital as well as possible. It is self-evident that exposing these employees needlessly to stress and other threats to their health and well-being would be a foolish form of destruction of capital.

Within the HRM body of thought, investment in the organisation's own employees is the usual approach. In order to safeguard employee well-being and health and to prevent them encountering needless problems in this respect, HRM disposes of an appropriate arsenal of techniques and methods. The main difference from more traditional forms of HRM consists of applying this arsenal with more attention, precision and consistency than usual. Though this costs time, attention and money (Doeglas & Schabracq, 1992), the outcome may be that the organisation becomes more effective, is troubled less by stress phenomena and probably lives longer (De Geus, 1997).

28.3 LEADERSHIP

Employees' well-being and health depend to an important extent on the degree to which their managers behave as real leaders. Essentially, this implies that they should follow normal moral standards such as decency, fairness, justice, honesty, respect and mindfulness. Still, some training or coaching in leadership may be needed. One reason is that it is not always self-evident to everybody that these standards contribute significantly to employees' well-being. Another is that it is not always easy to pay sufficient attention to these standards. Essentially, guarding the emotional climate is one of the most important managerial tasks.

There are many ways in which a leader can make a difference in preventing or counteracting unnecessary stress—and which can all be part of some leadership programme. Though most, if not all, of these issues may appear self-evident, flaws in this respect are among the most prominent causes of problems of well-being and health. A real leader should engage, for example, in the following activities:

- Paying sufficient attention to the department and being actively involved with its interpersonal sides. For one thing, this implies also that the manager should not treat the department exclusively as a useful "leg-up" to a next job. This also means that he or she stays long enough in the same job.
- Respecting your employees and overcoming your own prejudices and stereotypes towards them (Kaye & Jordan-Evans, 1999).
- Paying attention to, acknowledging and rewarding good performance and not exclusively focusing on correcting substandard performance (Kaye & Jordan-Evans, 1999).
- Focusing on realising the right conditions to allow the employees to perform well: the principle of subsidiarity (Handy, 1994).
- Trying to act fairly and making that clear; that is, not acting out of self-interest, favouritism or nepotism.
- Gathering enough knowledge about the department's or team's past (from different sources!) and the problems that occurred in it (Ryan & Oestreich, 1988).
- Recognising employees' stress symptoms as such, looking for systemic causes in the organisation and their work, and doing something about them (Schabracq & Cooper, 2001).
- Really putting problems on the agenda and discussing these in a constructive, problem-solving way in works progress meetings and in individual talks with the people with whom one has these difficulties (Ryan & Oestreich, 1988).
- Informing employees as early as possible in face-to-face interactions, about approaching radical changes (for example a merger, a reorganisation, a change in their jobs, replacement and lay-off).
- Discussing things periodically during works progress meetings, especially in times of change. To prevent needless worrying and rumours, it is useful to explicitly ask about rumours during these meetings and to comment on these as openly as possible.
- Protecting employees from external threats and, if needed, giving them emotional support.
- Coaching. This implies helping with setting goals, planning, pointing out pitfalls and giving advice if necessary (Schabracq, 1998a).
- Regularly interviewing employees about their individual functioning, professional development and career, and, if needed, offering training, further coaching or mentoring.
- Being reserved about implementing changes (no changes for the sheer purpose of change in itself).

- Implementing changes in such a way that they evoke the least negative emotions.
- Bringing bad news in such a way that it evokes the least negative emotions.
- Being focused on recognising and overcoming difficulties at the level of tasks and jobs, such as over- and underload (Schabracq et al., 2001).
- Being focused on recognising and overcoming interpersonal problems such as stereotyping, conflict, isolation, bullying and scapegoating (Adams, 1992).
- Keeping in touch with ill employees, preparing for their return to the department or team, and investing extra time and attention in them after their return.
- Giving extra time and attention to employees who have experienced a traumatic event. Here, it is especially important to let them talk about what they have gone through and to find out whether referral to a specialist is necessary (see Chapter 18).

In order to develop some of the above-mentioned skills, it may help to attend a good leadership course, which pays attention to such issues. A good alternative may be to have some professional coaching by an external expert (Schabracq, 1998a). A coach may help to set goals and may act as a listening ear, sparring partner, devil's advocate, individual trainer, psychotherapist, organisational consultant and adviser. At all times, however, the manager remains entirely responsible for his or her own decisions and interventions. The coach is just an independent discussion partner from outside the organisation. Seeking a coach is not a sign of weakness, but a matter of wanting to perform optimally and develop oneself.

Though all of the above-mentioned issues matter in creating appropriate working conditions without unnecessary risks, it is especially important for managers to get some extra training in social skills and stress prevention.

Social skills programmes for managers should focus on increasing their sensitivity as well as their authenticity. Keywords are leadership and team-building. To create the proper conditions for optimal performance, motivation and learning possibilities, as well as to bring about an atmosphere of good social support, managers need to master the following skills:

- Listening skills, such as empathising, "reading" non-verbal behaviour, interviewing, delaying immediate responses, responding appropriately to violent emotions, recognising and acknowledging individual differences, and moral sensitivity.
- Other coaching skills, such as internal congruence (being undivided; see Laborde, 1987), showing approval and disapproval, positive re-labelling, helping to make choices (generating "win–win" solutions), goal-setting, and delegating,
- Other social skills to lead groups, such as making use of individual differences in order to accomplish synergy, negotiating and conflict management, and appropriately leading workshops and other meetings.

All this is a matter of instruction, discussion and, primarily, much exercise and role-playing, with each other or with actors, while the trainees serve as observers also.

Training in stress prevention focuses on the following outcomes:

- Being able to notice stress risks and reactions of employees earlier and better.
- Acquiring a conceptual framework to talk about stress, overcoming the taboo on talking about stress at work and talking more easily about it with one's employees.
- Knowing about stress effects and their costs.

- Some knowledge about interventions and knowing what not to do.
- Implementing some interventions in one's own department.
- Dealing with crises and traumatic events.
- Knowledge about options of referral.
- Dealing with one's own stress sources and reactions, and being a role model in this respect.

A stress audit in the organisation or department is a good occasion for such a programme. Here, too, it is important to practise, in role-playing and in real life, and to get and give feedback.

All in all, accomplishing all these leadership tasks is far from simple and it is quite justified to ask whether all this can be realised by one person, who is also responsible for the bottom line of the department.

28.4   THE GENERAL APPROACH

Problems with employees' well-being and health are a good occasion to talk with them to find out what is going on and what can be done about it. The employees' suggestions are crucial here. After all, they are the experts on their own well-being and have the greatest interest in improving things. Inviting them several times explicitly to comment and making them responsible—"It is your work!"—as well as actually doing something about it, or—even better—letting them do something about it, is a logical and effective method. Beforehand, it should be made clear that not all suggestions can be realised. This approach is especially appropriate to find out about potential bugs in a recently implemented change: "Initially, all kinds of things will go wrong and it is your task to monitor what exactly goes wrong and devise better solutions". Apart from informal individual talks and interviews, meetings about work progress are an appropriate context for this.

In bigger organisations, it makes sense to audit employees' well-being, experienced health and work satisfaction periodically with the help of a questionnaire. Here too, the idea behind this is to explore possible problems and solutions in this area. Departments and teams that show problems then can be scrutinised in more detail by interviewing key informants about what is going on (see Chapter 8).

If needed, a workshop can be organised, led by the person responsible for the audit. A workshop is a meeting of an existing group to solve a certain problem. It is led by one or two facilitators. Usually, it takes place somewhere outside the organisation and takes from half a day to two days. Interviews with key participants precede most workshops. The objective of a workshop is to reach agreements and to record these in writing. As such, they lead to a division of tasks, each with a definite time path. Participants can put themselves forward for tasks and roles that appeal to them. In this way, the participants make use of their mutual differences and complement each other. As a result, synergy may occur.

In a workshop, the objective of the session is pointed out first. This objective can be used as a criterion of the relevance of separate contributions in order to guard the workshop's progress. Also, it is made clear beforehand that—for several reasons, among which are financial ones—not all solutions can be accepted. The next step consists of coming to a common, shared definition of the problems and their importance and causes. If there is agreement on these issues, the group tries to find solutions, which they then can try to improve during several rounds. This may involve some brainstorming techniques, as well as other exercises and games, such as role-playing.

In this approach, it is essential that employees raise matters themselves. Also, they have to think for themselves, make their own choices and devise their own solutions. It is also important that employees take responsibility for their own destiny in matters of their own development and future, especially during radical organisational change. Sometimes, it is necessary to provide employees with some extra tools. A self-management programme can be of help here (see Section 28.5.6).

Of course, the group members cannot solve all problems by themselves, but they can solve some and they can point out directions to solve other ones. Here, the whole arsenal of HRM methods and techniques can be deployed.

28.5   HRM INTERVENTIONS

Taking employees' health and well-being as our objective, career and job policies can be used to attain a better person–job fit and to realise further personal and professional development (see also Chapters 20 and 22). In all organisations where personnel is an important factor, these policies can be appropriate. Such a policy should be applied as much as possible in an individualised way, in order to make the best of everybody's individual talents, motives and career stage. This applies also to job redesign. Here, we take a brief look at the following interventions.

- selection
- career policy
- job rotation and and replacement
- secondment, projects and sabbaticals
- outplacement and lay-off
- training and coaching
- job redesign.

28.5.1   Selection

The organisation can use the selection procedure to create an optimal point of departure for new employees with respect to health and well-being. Something similar applies to assessment procedures for employees who are already working for the organisation. In both cases, this may involve interviews, psychometric tests and forms of self-assessment, such as writing an autobiography. Usually, selection and assessment are about determining skills, abilities and potential for further development. From the perspective of health and well-being, though, there are more options.

An important point is mapping training needs, as well as personal interest and preferences, in order to find out how employees can develop further. Also, it is important to get an idea of their attitude to work, colleagues and the organisation: what they want; what they allow and oblige themselves to do. This also applies to determining whether somebody fits in the organisation, even when there is no intention at all to develop a pure culture of clones in this respect.

Another part of the procedure is establishing how people deal with change and stress, as well as assessing their specific vulnerabilities in this respect. In addition to interviewing them about critical events, this can be done by designing specific assessment situations, in which candidates are observed while they are exposed to relevant stress sources.

All this implies that, during the selection procedure, real contact with the candidates is necessary and that this cannot be a matter of just taking a set of paper and pencil tests. Though an external selection agency can play a role, it does not make sense to outsource the whole procedure. Selection is simply too important to the organisational identity and competition position: preferably, the organisation has its own experts, who can play a decisive part in this procedure.

28.5.2 Career Policy

In order to enable employees to develop in a way that is optimally attuned both to their own needs, talents and values, as well as to the organisational ones, the organisation tries to meet individual training needs and develop individual talents in a way that benefits the organisation as well. The organisational interest in this respect lies in retaining good personnel, optimising their motivation and output, and developing them professionally in such a way that they can take over the organisational key positions in the near future. This implies enabling employees to prepare and make their next career steps in time. Coaching, mentoring—that is, a form of coaching by a more experienced, often older colleague— and training (we return to training under a separate heading later on) can be very useful here.

It means also that, from time to time, the parties involved have a closer look at the employee's present options, skills and further training needs. This may consist of period-ical interviews about issues such as individual progress, problems, expectations, options, well-being, training needs, career issues, etc. A proper insight of the employee into the organisational mission and vision and the policies stemming from these are crucial as well. Only then, is it possible to really shape one's own career in a proactive way.

28.5.3 Job Rotation and Replacement

Job rotation, changing jobs from time to time as a structural element of personnel policy, can contribute to professional development. As such, it is a normal part of management trainee programmes. Moreover, it may help to prevent the problems stemming from doing the same job for too long. An additional advantage is that, if needed, people can be employed in a more flexible way as their competence is broader. The outcomes are highest when the different jobs somehow are related: changing merely to change often makes no sense and usually is not motivating. Also, for some transitions, on-the-job training or a specific training course may be necessary.

Replacement, changing jobs on a more incidental basis, for instance to a job with a different work pace and job demands, sometimes helps to attain a better person–job fit, for instance when a job has become too heavy or does not offer sufficient challenges any more. Another reason can be that somebody is not so popular in a department and wants to start with a clean slate elsewhere.

28.5.4 Secondment, Special Projects and Sabbaticals

Seen from the perspective of career policy, job change can also be of a more temporary nature.

The first option is seconding employees in other organisations temporarily. These other organisations may be clients or suppliers, though research institutes or universities are likely candidates also. In the non-profit realm, this may take the form of exchange programmes between related organisations to learn from each other. Secondment can greatly contribute to the professional development of the employee involved, but the organisation may profit also. The employee can act as a kind of consultant or "liaison officer" and pass information and wishes between both organisations, to the profit of both sides. For example, somebody from a supply firm can help a client organisation in developing new products. Also, the same person can help the supplier to develop new contributions or new applications of existing products within the products of the client firm.

Another option is becoming a member of a temporary project team to develop and realise a certain goal that is important to the organisation. Within such a project, participating employees can develop and broaden their specific skills and knowledge by learning from each other and the process. Also, they can extend their social network. Some organisations are even based almost completely on working in projects (which, for that matter, may not be the best way to prevent stress).

A last option here is a sabbatical; that is, allowing an employee to take several months or a year for the purposes of personal reorientation, additional education or training. This option is becoming increasingly popular.

My own research indicates that, at least in a professional organisation such as a university, these interventions on a temporary basis are among the most powerful interventions for the good with respect to motivation and job satisfaction (Meyer & Schabracq, 2000).

28.5.5 Outplacement and Lay-Off

For different reasons, organisations and individual employees sometimes have to go their different ways. In that case, it is often—especially in the case of long-term employment—wise to invest in employees' employability by offering specific training programmes or investing in a different way in their professional future, and helping them to find a good job elsewhere. When lay-off is inevitable, the organisation, generally speaking, should act so that those directly involved experience the least possible pain and disadvantage. This is not only a matter of simple decency to these employees. It also gives an important signal to the personnel that remain employed. A considerate approach can prevent the latter group experiencing feelings of guilt, loss of faith in the organisation and demotivation, the so-called survivors' syndrome.

28.5.6 Training and Coaching

In order to promote employees' health and well-being, different kinds of coaching and training programmes for individual employees can be helpful. Here, too, the outcomes are determined by the degree to which the programme is tailored to the individual employees' wishes and needs. So participation always has to be based on agreement with or a request from the individual employees involved.

Training may be purely directed at the job content, including ergonomic training programmes, or even may consist of a form of general education to equip somebody better for a new career move. However, it also may be about social skills and personal growth. In principle, all these kinds of education should be open to employees of all age categories, including the oldest category. We look briefly at the following programmes:

- Training in personal effectiveness or assertiveness
- Training in time-management
- Training in self-management and employability
- Training in stress management.

Training in Personal Effectiveness or Assertiveness

Training programmes in personal effectiveness or assertiveness focus on dealing in a better way with questions and demands of clients, superiors or colleagues. Learning goals may be:

- saying "no" to clients, superiors or colleagues (or avoiding saying "yes indeed" to new exciting projects for which no time is available);
- sticking to one's own priorities and limits;
- counteracting task disturbances;
- explaining one's own dilemmas and impossibilities;
- dealing with stereotyping;
- dealing with scapegoating, bullying and harassment;
- dealing better with one's own anger and preventing unnecessary conflicts.

Time Management

Time management programmes focus on formulating clear and realistic goals and setting priorities (important/unimportant; urgent/not urgent), as well as on phasing, grouping and shielding tasks. This enables one to dedicate oneself to what really matters, to delegate better and not to spend time on irrelevant activities. This is primarily a matter of becoming aware of what is important and what is not. In addition, trainees learn about causes of unnecessary time loss and may practise all kinds of methods to minimise these. The latter vary from fixed procedures for routine activities and referral, to less time-consuming ways of handling visitors, mail, telephone, email etc. All this can help to push back all kinds of task disturbances and stress.

Self-Management and Employability

Courses in self-management and employability focus on developing new options for employees of different age groups to become more effective, motivated and creative in their jobs, career and further life. This should lead to more effective steering of one's own life and career. In such training programmes, trainees determine their basic themes, motives and talents. They then set goals for their different life realms and learn how to make and execute plans to realise these goals. An additional outcome of such a programme may consist of being able to cope with change more adaptively: the trainees teach themselves to deal with changes in a "standardised" way. This gives them more influence on the way change takes place, while it decreases their resistance and stress. It also enables them to influence the result of the change, in a way that they like best.

Stress Management

Stress management training programmes focus on coping with stress and stress prevention (for example Schabracq & Cooper, 2001). The outcomes are partially similar to those of training programmes for managers. In addition, such programmes may aim at the following outcomes:

- taking pauses for regular recuperation, reflection and planning;
- a healthier lifestyle;
- keeping a stress diary to get more insight into one's own stress sources and reactions;
- tracing one's own suppositions underlying one's stress reactions;
- some knowledge about time management and planning;
- some skill in personal effectiveness and thought-stopping;
- some knowledge of and skill in one or more of the many ways to bring about mental quiet, such as breathing techniques, relaxation exercises, guided fantasies, running etc.);
- applications of "mental quiet", such as:
  - relaxation, refreshing, or centring;
  - asking oneself questions ("focusing");
  - motivating oneself, as well as setting goals for oneself;
- methods to prepare difficult tasks.

28.5.7 Job Redesign

Another important issue is to design and redesign jobs in such a way that they become attuned to what the individual employees are able and willing to do. To prevent stress, these jobs have to enable employees to remain motivated, work effectively, develop themselves and not become isolated. There are different principles and methods of job redesign to improve all jobs in an organisation along standardised principles. Though these principles may be of importance as general guidelines (see Chapter 20), it is nevertheless preferable to tailor job redesign to the needs of the individuals involved. This is, again, a matter of good communication. Examples of directions for job redesign are making jobs more diverse (in order to prevent fatigue or physical wear-and-tear) or complete, allowing more autonomy in job performance, and providing more opportunities for social interaction.

28.6 OUTCOMES

To the degree that the approach sketched above is successful, it may have all kinds of positive outcomes for the organisation. These outcomes can even reinforce each other. This is successively about improvements in the following areas:

- The primary outcome consists of a reduction of stress complaints and a higher level of well-being and health.
- Another effect is that employees are thoroughly socialised by the organisation. In the longer run, they identify themselves with it, so that being a member of the organisation becomes more and more a part of their own identity. This implies, among other things, that employees are going to see the organisation's interest as their own. As such, this can reflect itself in increased work motivation and commitment.
- Working with more pleasure, motivation and commitment implies, among other things, that people want to do a good job and are willing to do something extra. This makes them more effective and productive, while the quality of what they do and make tends to improve also. This means making fewer errors, resulting in lower costs for quality control and repair, while the expenses associated with such errors have increased considerably. In addition, employees tend to make more effective use of all kinds of chances and opportunities that may be important to the organisation's survival. These self-steering abilities become more and more important because of the greater prominence of flexible production and meeting all kinds of deadlines.
- People who are motivated to do their work well are, generally speaking, also more attentive and creative. In this way, they learn more too. As a result, they are bound to develop better individual mastery and collective effectiveness.
- Another effect may be that employees are less likely to become angry. They are less prone to act callously towards each other and generally interact in a better way. This prevents conflicts and disturbed relationships between employees and between departments, which in its turn contributes to a better working climate and smoother collaboration in the organisation.
- A similar effect may be that the organisational members are able to build and maintain better relationships with clients, suppliers, sister organisations and government. As a result the communication with these parties may improve.
- An organisation with a good working climate, few stress complaints and high work satisfaction is an attractive employer. This decreases the risk that good employees, in whom the organisation has invested heavily, leave for another company. Certainly in times of scarcity of well-trained personnel, turnover is an important issue. It is also often a better indicator of organisational health than sick leave.
- A good working climate and few stress complaints among employees are of influence on the corporate image. All this indicates that the organisation takes its corporate values about well-being and health seriously. Corporate image and values have become increasingly important, both with respect to clients and relationships with the government, as well as to hiring new personnel. An additional point is that young, well-educated employees more and more make a point of working for a company that has more to offer in this area.
- The policies outlined above make and keep employees broadly employable, also at an older age. This prevents the dangers of staying too long in one job and the build-up of unbridgeable arrears in training and education (see Chapter 16).

- In the longer run, this approach leads to a group of well-informed and knowledgeable potential managers who can take up key positions in the organisation. In this way, the organisation is not dependent on scarce and expensive outsiders, who moreover have no special bind with the organisation and who have to be fully introduced to the specific expertise and culture of the organisation.
- A final outcome is that the organisation gradually acquires its own core competencies and corporate style, precisely tailored to its own niche of clients and products. Essentially, this is a feature of a "learning organisation" (Mintzberg et al., 1998; see also Chapter 21). Such competencies usually cannot be copied easily by the competition. As such, they may represent an important factor for the organisation's survival.

All in all, the effects mentioned above positively influence the corporate results. This leads to shareholder satisfaction and a satisfied management that reinforces the employees to go on in this way, and so on. This gives rise to a positive spiral, which Reichheld (1996) calls the "loyalty effect", a phenomenon characteristic of successful companies. Similar arguments are described in Rosenbluth & Peters (1992) and De Geus (1997). Essentially, the same kind of reasoning applies to the body of thought behind "organisational health" and the "healthy organisation". Though this may all sound overly optimistic, such a positive spiral is a well-documented phenomenon, even though many of us may work in organisations where such a spiral is not very prominent.

28.7 PROBLEMS

The success of the approach described above is heavily dependent on the time, information and attention that the organisation gives to its employees. The main problem here is that in most organisations, the line manager is essentially responsible for all those tasks described above. However, much of this often gets stuck in paper rules, good intentions and lip service. Most managers are simply too busy with technical problems or external matters to occupy themselves deeply with their employees. Moreover, their heart often is not primarily in "people tasks". They are not selected for these matters; it usually is not the reason why they ever aspired to their present job and—most importantly—it has not been an important criterion for the way their job performance was evaluated. For some of them, a training programme might help, but it is not very likely that most of them will alter their way of working afterward. Their "own" tasks will still absorb them too much.

If things are like this, somebody else should take up this task. However, as noted before, this preferably must be somebody of some influence. As it is, this would mean a major shift in the organisation, including its division of power. Apart from the fact that, for this, commitment by the top management is necessary, creating such a job will probably evoke intense reactions and resistance, not least from some of the managers involved.

For several reasons, it would not be easy for most present HR officers to take up such tasks either. As it is, they usually are staff members, who are not used to taking responsibility for the everyday affairs of a department. Apart from the fact that this would demand another attitude from the HR officer, this might lead to a power struggle with the department manager, which the HR officer is not likely to win. Moreover, HR officers usually know little of the actual work and are also too far removed from actual employees to know them well personally. All this means that in a bigger organisation these tasks preferably are not to be left to the central HR department either.

28.8 CO-MANAGEMENT: A POSSIBLE APPROACH

28.8.1 What is Co-management?

In order to solve the problems with making managers or HR officers responsible for the employees' well-being and health, it is a logical step to design a new job to take care of this, the one of co-manager. Generally speaking, the co-manager works at two levels: in the individual departments as well as in a team of other co-managers, at a level above the individual departments.

First, co-managers are responsible for the performance, collaboration, well-being and professional development of the employees of one or more departments. This demands close collaboration with the original managers. The specific power relation between manager and co-manager can vary. In some organisations, the co-manager holds the higher position. This is for instance the case in the Research and Development Department of the Visual Displays Division of one of the big electronic multinationals. However, in most cases the original manager is leading, while the co-manager acts as a kind of minister of internal affairs. Examples are to be found in armies, hospitals, a merchant bank, a chemical industry and a law firm. Lastly, co-managers can even be seconded by a specialised agency on a temporary basis to get things organised in client organisations.

Second, the co-managers of the different departments form a special team that concerns itself with the same issues from a higher level, be it divisional or corporate. The team members act as each other's sounding board and together approach relevant issues at a more strategic level. In this context, they can devise audits about well-being, bottlenecks and possible solutions. Next, they can centrally initiate and guide improvement projects. Though they may initially need some supervision of an external expert, they will gradually develop themselves into a team of specialists in this respect, with an important advisory role towards their top management as well.

Another important co-management task is shaping and guiding the implementation of radical changes in organisations. This task in particular makes co-management important at a strategic level. The ability to deal with change adaptively threatens to become a major constraint in the survival and further development of many organisations (see Chapters 3 and 29). This is about the way in which organisations can prevent such changes generating so much stress that an orderly course of affairs becomes impossible. That is why the ability to prevent and counteract such stress becomes an increasingly important strategic factor in the global competition. Moreover, dealing with change in this way may contribute to the kind of unique expertise, which the competition cannot copy. This also indicates why co-managers preferably should be organisational employees, and not external consultants. Their role is simply too strategically important and too central to the organisational objectives.

28.8.2 Advantages and Pitfalls

All in all, the idea of co-management is also a logical consequence of the body of thought of HRM. As such, it may contribute to all the positive consequences mentioned in

Section 28.6. This in itself can be sufficient reason to implement it. However, there may be some additional positive effects. Apart from the fact that co-management can help an organisation to deal better with change and a turbulent environment, it enables line managers to spend more time on their original core tasks. Also, it opens up for managers the option of more "normal" working times and, possibly, even of a part-time job. This would also make a management career much more attractive to many women. Moreover, co-management allows the organisation to make better use of good HR officers, while it also contributes to organisational policies for management development, employability and senior employees.

The most obvious pitfalls of co-management are issues such as power struggles, conflicts and people being played against each other. This is often a matter of sliding back into "old" familiar ways of functioning, personal as well as organisational ones. Solutions usually lie in better communication, with or without the help of an external facilitator and, of course, the success of it all is heavily dependent on a careful implementation.

28.8.3   Implementing Co-management

Successfully implementing co-management implies a serious form of cultural change, with all accompanying shifts in responsibility and power. As such, implementation will always involve a kind of jolt in the organisation. A good implementation implies that all parties should get the necessary information, time and attention to familiarise themselves with it and develop forms of adaptation. In the implementation stage, the following steps have to be taken, preferably guided by some external expert:

- Establishing to what degree it is realistic to implement co-management in the organisation. This concerns the compatibility of the approach with the existing culture, the available means and time, and the presence of sufficient good candidate co-managers.
- Getting sufficient support and commitment from the top management to implement co-management. To this end, it is necessary that the highest level gets a clear picture of the nature and implications of co-management, both for the whole organisation and their own functioning as a role model. One or more workshops about the subject by an expert can be useful in this respect.
- Appointing responsibility for the implementation to one of the highest level managers, preferably a volunteer with a positive attitude to the project.
- Making a plan and time path for the implementation.
- Communication of the intended implementation to the line managers, and subsequently to the rest of the organisation.
- Selection of the co-managers. Of course, the line managers in question are involved in the procedure. As inside candidates have the great advantage of knowing the organisation, co-managers preferably are recruited from the pool of existing managers, HR officers and other professionals. The focus here is on volunteers who have the right feel for such matters. However, sometimes it is appropriate to choose one or two "fresh" outsiders who have some experience in this area and can act as protagonists. For two reasons, it usually makes sense to include some older employees. First, they know the organisation and its specific culture very well. Second, some of them have developed the cognitive skills that I elsewhere have described under the denominator of wisdom (Schabracq, 1998b; see also Chapter 17), which essentially consist of dealing with as well as giving form and meaning

to the radical changes that life forces upon us. Apart from motivation and affinity with the job, good social skills, good general intelligence and experience with functioning at a higher organisational level are important selection criteria. Some expertise in the department's business is useful, but not necessary *per se*. The main guideline here is that they should be able to act as good sparring partners for the line managers.

- Training the selected candidates. First, they go through a short educational programme. This deals with the nature of the job and issues such as stress, stress management and organisational diagnosis and change. Also, it involves training in social skills needed for coaching, advising, leading workshops, recognising and discussing stress reactions, and conflict management. Subsequently, they mainly learn by practice on the job, and by regular group supervision sessions.
- Introduction of the co-managers into the own departments, by individual talks with the line manger and all employees involved, followed by a workshop with the departments in question to clarify mutual role expectations.
- A short course of joint coaching of manager and co-manager.
- Intervision at regular time intervals about occurring problems.
- Conducting specific improvement projects and accompanying occurring change projects.
- Evaluation.

28.9   CONCLUSION

This chapter described an organisational approach for optimising its employees' well-being and health. It demands organisational changes, but for most organisations this does not imply a total break. The approach is primarily about a more consistent HRM policy, and willingness to follow up the implications. Of course, this implies expenses. However, when we take the positive outcomes for the organisation and the potential costs of ill-conducted organisational changes into account, this is probably money well spent.

REFERENCES

Adams, A. (1992) *Bullying at Work: How to Confront and Overcome it*. London: Virago Press.

Doeglas, J.D.A. & Schabracq, M.J. (1992) Transitiemanagement [Transition Management]. *Gedrag en Organisatie [Behaviour and Organisation]*, **5**, 448–66.

Geus, A. de (1997) *The Living Company*. New York: Longview.

Goldratt, E. (1990) *What is this Thing Called Theory of Constraints and how should it be Implemented?* Croton on Hudson, NY: North River Press.

Handy, C. (1994) *The Age of Paradox*. Boston, MA: Harvard Business School Press.

Kaye, B. & Jordan-Evans, S. (1999) *Love 'em or Lose 'em: Getting Good People to Stay*. San Francisco, CA: Berrett-Koehler.

Laborde, G.Z. (1987) *Influencing with Integrity*. Palo Alto, CA: Syntony.

Meyer, J. & Schabracq, M.J. (2000). *Ouder wetenschappelijk personeel: situatie, beleving en scenario's. [Older Scientific Personnel: Situation, Experience and Scenarios]*. Amsterdam: University of Amsterdam.

Mintzberg, H., Ahlstrand, B. & Lampel, J. (1998) *Strategy Safari*. London: Prentice Hall.

Ofman, D.D. (1995) *Bezieling en kwaliteit in organisaties [Inspiration and Quality in Organisations]*. Cothen: Servire.

Reichheld, F.F. (1996) *The Loyalty Effect*. Boston, MA: Harvard Business School Press.

Rosenbluth, H.F. & Peters, D.M. (1992) *The Customer Comes Second*. New York: Quill/Morrow.

Ryan, K.D. & Oestreich, D.K. (1988) *Driving Fear out of the Workplace*. San Francisco, CA: Jossey-Bass.

Schabracq, M.J. (1998a) *Management Coaching*. Deventer: Kluwer Bedrijfsinformatie.

Schabracq, M.J. (1998b) *Medewerkers van boven de veertig* [*Employees over Forty*]. Deventer: Kluwer Bedrijfsinformatie.

Schabracq, M.J. (2001). De HRM-functionaris [The HRM officer]. In *Praktijkboek gezond werken* [*Manual of Healthy Working*]. Maarsen: Elsevier, I 2.2-1-12.

Schabracq, M.J. & Cooper, C.L. (2000) The changing nature of work and stress. *Journal of Management Psychology*, **15**, 227–41.

Schabracq, M.J. & Cooper C.L. (2001). *Stress als keuze. Werkboek persoonlijk stressmanagement* [*Stress as a Choice. Workbook for Personal Stress Mangement*]. Schiedam: Scriptum.

Schabracq, M.J., Maassen van den Brink, H., Groot, W., Janssen, P. & Houkes, I. (2000) *De prijs van stress* [*The Price of Stress*]. Amsterdam: Elsevier.

Schabracq, M.J., Cooper, C.L., Travers, C. & Maanen, D. van (2001) *Occupational Health Psychology: The Challenge of Workplace Stress*. Leicester: British Psychological Association.

CHAPTER 29

Epilogue

Marc J. Schabracq
University of Amsterdam, The Netherlands
Cary L. Cooper
Umist, Manchester, UK
and
Jacques A.M. Winnubst
Utrecht University, The Netherlands

During recent decades, we have been confronted by an unprecedented acceleration in the rate of change. Maybe the most salient side of this is the technological development we are witnessing. An avalanche of new technological possibilities, products and production processes is being poured out over us, which deeply affects our everyday life, including our work life. This development is boosted by the growing globalisation of the economy, resulting in quickly escalating worldwide competition. Though this may lead to severe damage to all parties involved, as well as depletion of natural resources used in production, there has been—up to now—no glimmer of forthcoming de-escalation.

So, survival of the fittest or—as Morgan (1986) suggests—"the best fitting" ("the one most apt in adapting to a certain environmental niche") still appears to be the name of the game. Only the game is no longer about strong or clever specific adaptations to certain more or less stable environmental demands. What counts now is the pace at which players (individual entrepreneurs, organisations, branches of business, nations) are able to adapt cleverly to a continuously changing environment, which demands a highly flexible approach. So the development of persons and organisations at least has to match the environmental changes.

However, as we have seen in Chapters 2 and 3, the essence of individual as well as cultural adaptation and survival consists of the ability to create stability by consistent repetition. Being continuously forced to change this stability may give rise to serious stress reactions. This leaves us in a difficult situation: our obviously limited ability to adapt to change has become a crucial bottleneck when it comes to further organisational and personal survival and development.

Put differently, the ability to change without experiencing stress is becoming one of the most important strategic factors in global competition. So, work and health psychology, as a science of well-being and health in work and organisations, is—at least in our opinion—a discipline that has become strategically important when it comes to the survival

The Handbook of Work and Health Psychology. Edited by M.J. Schabracq, J.A.M. Winnubst and C.L. Cooper.
© 2003 John Wiley & Sons, Ltd.

of organisations and maybe even national economies. Essentially, we are talking here about what work and health psychology can contribute to the organisational ability to prevent changes from generating so much stress that good management of organisational affairs becomes impossible.

To give an idea of the great diversity of changes individual employees are and will be facing, we first list some ways in which organisations are trying to adapt to their changing environment.

- All kinds of new technologies, which demand different skills and additional training, and, in some cases, lead to impoverished jobs.
- Focusing on adding maximal value to the raw materials, which implies working with more complicated and expensive means of production, demanding additional training and responsibility.
- Minimising labour costs, which often leads to higher individual task load.
- Longer or permanent daily production times in order to use the means of production optimally, which means working odd hours.
- Qualitative flexibility of labour, i.e. deploying employees to do different tasks, resulting in more complex and internally changing jobs, which demand additional training.
- Quantitative flexibility of labour, i.e. deploying employees only when and for as long as needed, resulting in less individual autonomy, planning possibilities and interpersonal relationships.
- A kind of "neo-Taylorisation" in some jobs such as those of cashiers and employees in call centres.
- Being more client-oriented, resulting in being more dependent on the whims of individual clients.
- Flexible production lines that manufacture different products, also in small quantities, leading to much more complicated jobs with more responsibility.
- More coordination or integration of marketing, production, and research and development, implying making more errors, quicker changes and more difficult communication.
- Reducing the number of hierarchical levels and pushing responsibility down to the lowest level possible, for example by installing autonomous task groups or quality circles, demanding more knowledge of organisation and production objectives, more complicated communication, more responsibility and an "intrapreneurial" attitude at the lowest organisational levels.
- Just-in-time management and other kinds of logistically driven forms of organising, which means continuous high work pressure, no means to deal with unforeseen events and less autonomy in pacing one's own work.
- Outsourcing all kinds of staff and service departments, demanding an entrepreneurial attitude and leading to more job insecurity and a more turbulent environment in the outsourced entities, as well as a lack of knowledge in the original organisation.
- New forms of organising, such as in matrix, project and network organisations, which greatly add to the complexity of jobs and communication processes.
- Strategic alliances with other companies, leading to communication problems, often of an intercultural nature.
- Mergers or acquisitions, to accomplish scale advantages or vertical integration, at a national or international level of scale, leading to great internal upheaval, job insecurity, and communicational and intercultural problems.

- Becoming a learning organisation, resulting in much more complicated forms of communication and permanent change.
- All (other) kinds of HRM interventions, such as mentioned in Chapter 28, leading to all kinds of reorientation and learning processes.

Though this list is far from exhaustive, it makes clear that an increasing number of people, now and in the future, are having to deal to an increasing degree with very diverse forms of change that affect their effectiveness, motivation, creativity and social relationships. For instance, it has become unclear to many of us for whom we actually work: for ourselves, for the organisation that pays us, or the organisations where we work? And who is responsible for what we do?

All in all, this leads to very complex and diverse situations in organisations. In such a context, top-down standard approaches to solve all problems cannot be successful. Management simply cannot think for everybody involved. Here too, this implies that solutions, as much as possible, should be devised at the work site with a maximal input from the employees involved. Only when people at all levels are allowed to use their own imagination and creativity is it possible to deal successfully with such diverse forms of change.

If management cannot be the architect of all change, what can it do? Chapters 3 and 28 gave some suggestions. Here, there follow some more. Essentially, managers—or co-managers for that matter (see Chapter 28)—should limit themselves to creating the right conditions for their employees to work out solutions, at different levels (individual, dyadic, team and department) and facilitating any promising attempt in a desired direction. Another point is that managers should be cautious about instigating change on their own.

First, managers have to create a rewarding atmosphere of mutual respect, where good performance is acknowledged, people can be confident, errors and failure are learning points, and laughter is not frowned upon. The most important point here is that employees can feel completely free and welcome to come up with ideas, suggestions and criticism, also when this implies criticism about the manager.

Also, managers have to be very quick to notice stress reactions and other signs of diminished well-being. These can be used as an occasion for a talk with the employee in question, to determine whether there is an underlying problem that has to be addressed. In general, managers should focus on mapping all kinds of problems, constraints, inconsistencies and unusual events. The next step consists of encouraging reflection about these phenomena, involving all employees concerned. This is a matter of asking questions, challenging, listening, paraphrasing and commenting. This is about the status quo, causes, new ways to go and the problems that lie ahead. The focus here is on legitimising new points of view, creating room for experiments and recording and actually institutionalising changes, also when it is only about partial solutions. Other points of attention are supporting protagonists, organising sufficient means, generating further political support, turning around resistance, and taking away hindrances and constraints.

This is also about supporting employees by allowing them to develop themselves by following special training programmes on an in-company basis, that is with existing groups that normally work together. Here we can think about courses on subjects such as coping with change, self-management, development of creativity, enhancement of intuition, personal effectiveness, stress management, and all kinds of social skills varying from group decision making, to learning how to operate in new groups and project groups, and dealing with intercultural issues. One of the outcomes of such training programmes may be that individual employees as well as teams learn to change in standardised ways, in the sense that they learn to use flexibly applicable scenarios of more or less standardised steps to deal with radical change.

Another issue is institutionalising change and reflection about change in such a way that it is optimally integrated in the unchanging cycles of daily, weekly and yearly everyday life. In a sense, this is about ritualising change, giving it its own familiar behavioural and mental forms. It may also involve the use of symbolic means to mark certain transitions and important points in time and space. Ideally, all this results in a stable background that does not demand extra attention, against which the project at hand stands out as a clear *Gestalt*. Institutionalising change also involves creating standard opportunities for reflection, discussion and planning. This can be realised both at an individual level—for example a quarter of an hour at the start of each working day—and team level, such as weekly meetings. Issues can be: Where do we stand? Are we on track? What is the main focus now? Other standard points are monitoring everything that goes wrong or not completely right, as well as devising ways to do them better, smarter and more pleasantly. In this way, dealing with change may become an organisational core competency.

It is only logical that a manager sometimes feels lonely facing all those tasks. However, he or she can always consult colleagues, also from other companies, to get information, advice and support. Managers more or less can institutionalise this by organising regular intervision sessions, in which they can discuss difficult cases. Reading relevant books or articles, as well as attending congresses and training programmes about these matters may also help. Moreover, managers can always seek assistance. They can take a coach, or they can delegate tasks to somebody else. If the option of co-management is still not realised, this then may be the logical way to go.

In Chapter 17, wisdom was described as a set of abilities and skills that enable one to let go a previous station of life gracefully and to design and shape a new one along the lines of one's basic motives and life themes. Acquiring wisdom was introduced there as a developmental task of middle age, though it was also noted that this task is not fully accomplished by everybody. It is easy to see that wisdom is an important quality when it comes to organisational change. So, elderly employees who have realised this developmental task successfully can be an important asset for any organisation facing radical changes. Important qualities here are patience, experience, the ability to read the game, reflexivity and relativisation, as well as being very cautious in instigating unneeded changes.

One last point is that change and its undesired effects confront all competing parties alike. This implies that we do not have to be perfect in this respect. We only have to do somewhat better than the competition. Following the guidelines described above may then represent a promising approach.

REFERENCE

Morgan, G. (1986) *Images of organization*. Beverley Hills, CA: Sage.

Index

Page numbers ending with t refer to tables